Beach, Hebb, Morgan, and Nissen   The Neuropsychology of Lashley
Berkowitz   Aggression: A Social Psychological Analysis
Berlyne   Conflict, Arousal, and Curiosity
Blum   Psychoanalytic Theories of Personality
Brown   The Motivation of Behavior
Brown and Ghiselli   Scientific Method in Psychology
Butcher   MMPI: Research Developments and Clinical Applications
Campbell, Dunnette, Lawler, and Weick   Managerial Behavior, Performance, and Effectiveness
Cofer   Verbal Learning and Verbal Behavior
Cofer and Musgrave   Verbal Behavior and Learning: Problems and Processes
Crafts, Schneirla, Robinson, and Gilbert   Recent Experiments in Psychology
Crites   Vocational Psychology
D'Amato   Experimental Psychology: Methodology, Psychophysics, and Learning
Davitz   The Communication of Emotional Meaning
Deese and Hulse   The Psychology of Learning
Dollard and Miller   Personality and Psychotherapy
Edgington   Statistical Inference: The Distribution-free Approach
Ellis   Handbook of Mental Deficiency
Ferguson   Statistical Analysis in Psychology and Education
Forgus   Perception: The Basic Process in Cognitive Development
Franks   Behavior Therapy: Appraisal and Status
Ghiselli   Theory of Psychological Measurement
Ghiselli and Brown   Personnel and Industrial Psychology
Gilmer   Industrial and Organizational Psychology
Gray   Psychology Applied to Human Affairs
Guilford   The Nature of Human Intelligence
Guilford   Psychometric Methods
Guilford and Fruchter   Fundamental Statistics in Psychology and Education
Guilford and Hoepfner   The Analysis of Intelligence
Guion   Personnel Testing
Haire   Psychology in Management
Hirsch   Behavior-genetic Analysis
Hirsch   The Measurement of Hearing
Hurlock   Adolescent Development
Hurlock   Child Development
Hurlock   Developmental Psychology
Jackson and Messick   Problems in Human Assessment
Krech, Crutchfield, and Ballachey   Individual in Society

Lakin Interpersonal Encounter: Theory and Practice in Sensitivity Training
Lawler Pay and Organizational Effectiveness: A Psychological View
Lazarus, A. Behavior Therapy and Beyond
Lazarus, R. Adjustment and Personality
Lewin A Dynamic Theory of Personality
Lewin Principles of Topological Psychology
Maher Principles of Psychopathology
Marascuilo Statistical Methods for Behavioral Science Research
Marx and Hillix Systems and Theories in Psychology
Miller Language and Communication
Morgan Physiological Psychology
Mulaik The Foundations of Factor Analysis
Nunnally Psychometric Theory
Overall and Klett Applied Multivariate Analysis
Robinson and Robinson The Mentally Retarded Child
Rosenthal Genetic Theory and Abnormal Behavior
Scherer and Wertheimer A Psycholinguistic Experiment on Foreign Language Teaching
Shaw Group Dynamics: The Psychology of Small Group Behavior
Shaw and Costanzo Theories of Social Psychology
Shaw and Wright Scales for the Measurement of Attitudes
Sidowski Experimental Methods and Instrumentation in Psychology
Siegel Nonparametric Statistics for the Behavioral Sciences
Spencer and Kass Perspectives in Child Psychology
Stagner Psychology of Personality
Townsend Introduction to Experimental Methods for Psychology and the Social Sciences
Vinacke The Psychology of Thinking
Wallen Clinical Psychology: The Study of Persons
Warren and Akert The Frontal Granular Cortex and Behavior
Waters, Rethlingshafer, and Caldwell Principles of Comparative Psychology
Winer Statistical Principles in Experimental Design
Zubek and Solberg Human Development

SECOND EDITION

SYSTEMS AND THEORIES IN PSYCHOLOGY

MELVIN H. MARX
Professor of Psychology
University of Missouri

WILLIAM A. HILLIX
Professor of Psychology
San Diego State College

McGRAW-HILL BOOK COMPANY

New York   St. Louis   San Francisco   Düsseldorf   Johannesburg
Kuala Lumpur   London   Mexico   Montreal   New Delhi
Panama   Rio de Janeiro   Singapore   Sydney   Toronto

Library of Congress Cataloging in Publication Data

Marx, Melvin Herman.
    Systems and theories in psychology.

    (McGraw-Hill series in psychology)
    Includes bibliographies.
    1. Psychology. I. Hillix, William Allen, 1927-
joint author. II. Title.
BF38.M38 1973   150'.1'9   72-2482
ISBN 0-07-040669-3

SYSTEMS AND THEORIES IN PSYCHOLOGY

1234567890DODO798765432

This book was set in Press Roman by Creative Book Services,
division of McGregor & Werner, Inc.
The editors were Walter Maytham and David Dunham;
the designer was Nicholas Krenitsky;
and the production supervisor was Thomas J. Lo Pinto.
The printer and binder was R. R. Donnelley & Sons Company.

Acknowledgments

The authors wish to thank the following copyright owners, authors, and publishers for permission to reprint excerpts from copyrighted material:

THE AMERICAN ASSOCIATION FOR THE ADVANCEMENT OF SCIENCE
Boring, E. G. When is human behavior predetermined? *Scientific Monthly*, 1957, **84**, 189-196.
Smith, C. S. Matter versus materials: A historical view. *Science*, 1968, **162**, 637-644.

THE AMERICAN JOURNAL OF PSYCHOLOGY
Murray, E. Peripheral and central factors in memory: Images of visual form and color. *American Journal of Psychology*, 1906, **7**, 227-247.

THE AMERICAN PSYCHOLOGICAL ASSOCIATION
Coan, R. W. Dimensions of psychological theory. *American Psychologist*, 1968, **23**, 715-722.
Guthrie, E. R. Psychological facts and psychological theory. *Psychological Bulletin*, 1946, **43**, 1-20.

AMERICAN SCIENTIST
Skinner, B. F. The experimental analysis of behavior. *American Scientist*, 1957, **45**, 343-371.

ANNUAL REVIEWS, INC.
Adelson, J. Personality. *Annual Review of Psychology*, 1969, **20**, 217-252.
Ford, D. H. & Urban, H. B. Psychotherapy. *Annual Review of Psychology*, 1967, **18**, 333-372.

APPLETON CENTURY CROFTS, EDUCATIONAL DIVISION, MEREDITH CORPORATION
Boring, E. G. *The physical dimensions of consciousness*. New York: Appleton-Century-Crofts, 1933.
Boring, E. G. *A history of experimental psychology*. New York: Appleton-Century-Crofts, 1950.
Boring, E. G., & Lindzey, G. (Eds.) *A history of psychology in autobiography*. New York: Appleton-Century-Crofts, 1967.
Estes, W. K., Koch, S., MacCorquodale, K., Meehl, P. E., Mueller, C. G., Jr., Schoenfeld, W. N., & Verplanck, W. S. *Modern learning theory*. New York: Appleton-Century-Crofts, 1954.
Heidbreder, E. *Seven psychologies*. New York: Appleton-Century-Crofts, 1933.
Thorndike, E. L. *Selected writings from a connectionist's psychology*. New York: Appleton-Century-Crofts, 1949.
Turner, M. *Philosophy and the science of behavior*. New York: Appleton-Century-Crofts, 1967.

BASIC BOOKS, INC.

Jones, E. *The life and work of Sigmund Freud.* Vol. 3. New York: Basic Books, 1957.

Nagel, E. The nature and aim of science. In S. Morgenhesser (Ed.), *Philosophy of science today.* New York: Basic Books, 1967.

BOLLINGEN FOUNDATION

Jung, C. G. *Symbols of transformation.* New York: Random House, 1956.

BUREAU OF PUBLICATIONS, TEACHERS COLLEGE, COLUMBIA UNIVERSITY

Thorndike, E. L. *Educational psychology.* Vol. 2. *The psychology of learning.* New York: Teachers College, 1913.

CLARK UNIVERSITY PRESS

Murchison, C. (Ed.) *A history of psychology in autobiography.* Vol. 3. Worcester, Mass.: Clark University Press, 1936.

Watson, J. B. What the nursery has to say about instincts. In C. Murchison (Ed.), *Psychologies of 1925.* Worcester, Mass.: Clark University Press, 1926.

Watson, J. B. Recent experiments on how we lose and change our emotional equipment. In C. Murchison (Ed.), *Psychologies of 1925.* Worcester, Mass.: Clark University Press, 1926.

E. P. DUTTON & CO., INC.

Evans, R. I. *B. F. Skinner: The man and his ideas.* New York: Dutton, 1968.

HARVARD UNIVERSITY PRESS

Bridgman, P. W. *The way things are.* Cambridge, Mass.: Harvard University Press, 1959.

HOLT, RINEHART AND WINSTON, INC.

James, W. *The principles of psychology.* New York: Holt, 1890.

HOUGHTON MIFFLIN COMPANY

Platt, J. R. *The excitement of science.* Boston: Houghton Mifflin, 1962.

J. B. LIPPINCOTT COMPANY

Watson, R. I. *The great psychologists from Aristotle to Freud.* (Rev. ed.) Philadelphia: Lippincott, 1968.

THE MACMILLAN COMPANY

Bridgman, P. W. *The logic of modern physics.* New York: Macmillan, 1927.

Horwitz, L. Theory construction and validation in psychoanalysis. In M. H. Marx (Ed.), *Theories in contemporary psychology.* New York: Macmillan, 1963.

Wundt, W. *Principles of physiological psychology.* New York: Macmillan, 1904.

McGRAW-HILL BOOK COMPANY

Prentice, W. C. H. The systematic psychology of Wolfgang Köhler. In S. Koch (Ed.), *Psychology: A study of a science.* Vol. 1. *Sensory, perceptual, and physiological formulations.* New York: McGraw-Hill, 1958.

Tolman, E. C. Principles of purposive behavior. In S. Koch (Ed.), *Psychology: A study of a science.* Vol. 2. *General systematic formulations, learning and special processes.* New York: McGraw-Hill, 1959, pp. 92-157.

Wooldridge, D. E. *Mechanical man: The physical basis of intelligent life.* New York: McGraw-Hill, 1968.

W. W. NORTON & COMPANY, INC.

Watson, J. B. *Behaviorism.* New York: Norton, 1925. Rev. ed., 1930.

Watson, J. B., & McDougall, W. *The battle of behaviorism.* New York: Norton, 1929.

PHILOSOPHICAL LIBRARY, INC.

Bridgman, P. W. *The nature of some of our physical concepts.* New York: Philosophical Library, 1952.

THE PHILOSOPHICAL REVIEW
Titchener, E. B. The postulates of a structural psychology. *Philosophical Review*, 1898, **7**, 449-465.

PSYCHOLOGY TODAY
Hall, M. H. An interview with "Mr. Behaviorist" B. F. Skinner. *Psychology Today*, 1967, **1**, 21-23, 68-71.

ROCKEFELLER UNIVERSITY PRESS
Weiss, A. P. 1 + 1 ≠ 2 (one plus one does not equal two). In G. C. Quarton, T. Melnechuk, & F. O. Schmitt (Eds.), *The neurosciences*. New York: Rockefeller University Press, 1967.

THE RONALD PRESS
Woodworth, R. S., & Sheehan, M. R. *Contemporary schools of psychology*. New York: Ronald Press, 1964.

SIMON & SCHUSTER, INC.
Russell, B. *A history of Western philosophy*. New York: Simon & Schuster, 1945.

SPRINGER-VERLAG OHG
Harrower, M. R. Organization in higher mental processes. *Psychologische Forschung*, 1932, **17**, 56-120.

STANFORD UNIVERSITY PRESS
Barker, R. G. *Ecological psychology*. Stanford, Calif.: Stanford University Press, 1968.

THE UNIVERSITY OF CHICAGO PRESS
Kuhn, T. S. *The structure of scientific revolutions*. Chicago: University of Chicago Press, 1962.
Lashley, K. S. *Brain mechanisms and intelligence*. Chicago: University of Chicago Press, 1929.

VINTAGE BOOKS, RANDOM HOUSE, INC.
Beveridge, W. I. B. *The art of scientific investigation*. New York: Vintage Books, 1957.

JOHN WILEY & SONS, INC.
Hall, C. S., & Lindzey, G. *Theories of personality*. New York: Wiley, 1957.

The authors also wish to thank the following authors and publishers for permission to reproduce figures and quotations from their publications:

THE AMERICAN JOURNAL OF PSYCHOLOGY
Orbison, W. O. Shape as a function of the vector field. *American Journal of Psychology*, 1939, **52**, 31-45.

THE AMERICAN PSYCHOLOGICAL ASSOCIATION
Brunswik, E. Representative design and probabilistic theory in a functional psychology. *Psychological Review*, 1955, **62**, 193-217.
Coan, R. W. Dimensions of psychological theory. *American Psychologist*, 1968, **23**, 715-722.
McGeoch, J. A. The formal criteria of a systematic psychology. *Psychological Review*, 1933, **40**, 1-12.

INSTITUTE OF ELECTRICAL AND ELECTRONIC ENGINEERING
Peterson, W. W., Birdsall, T. G., & Fox, W. C. The theory of signal detectability. *Transactions of Professional Group on Information Theory, Institute of Radio Engineers*, 1954, PGIT-4, 171-212.

McGRAW-HILL BOOK COMPANY

Lewin, K. *Principles of topological psychology*. (Tr. by F. Heider & G. Heider.) New York: McGraw-Hill, 1936.

THE NEW YORK ACADEMY OF SCIENCES

Tanner, W. P., Jr. Physiological implications of psychophysical data. *Annals of the New York Academy of Science*, 1961, **89**, 752-765.

UNIVERSITY OF CALIFORNIA PRESS

Tolman, E. C., & Honzik, C. H. *Insight in rats*. Berkeley: University of California Press, 1932.

THE UNIVERSITY OF CHICAGO PRESS

Brunswik, E. The conceptual framework of psychology. *International Encyclopedia of Unified Science*, 1952, **1**, 1-102.

W. P. VAN STOCKUM

Brunswik, E. The conceptual focus of some psychological systems. *Journal of Unified Science*, 1939, **8**, 36-49.

JOHN WILEY & SONS, INC.

Hall, C. S., & Lindzey, G. *Theories of personality*. (2d ed.) New York: Wiley, 1970.

Contents

Preface

The format and underlying rationale of the second edition of this book have not been changed. The following discussion describes major changes in content that have been made in the three parts of the book. The present edition endeavors to make use of the remarkably improved, methodologically sophisticated approaches now being applied to the study of the history and systems of psychology. The book remains a collaborative venture, with each of the authors making additions to, and revisions of, the writing of the other.

Our primary purpose in writing the book has been to provide a single source containing the basic information about systematic and theoretical psychology which any student of psychology should have. The book is directed mainly at the senior undergraduate major and the beginning graduate student. We hope that it will serve a coordinating function in helping the advanced student to integrate some of the diverse materials and approaches to which he has been exposed in his various courses.

In accordance with this general objective, our treatment is extensive rather than intensive. The book gives surveys rather than exhaustive accounts of any one topic. No text of this scope can practicably do more, since each of the three parts of the book deals with a topic that could be the subject of several volumes. The student who goes on in scientific psychology can further his knowledge of systematic and theoretical problems by taking more specialized courses in history, experimental and theoretical methodology, and theory within particular subject-matter areas. If he does not go on or does not touch further on the scientific concerns of psychology, the book should give him a broad overview and general understanding of fundamental systematic and theoretical problems.

Part 1 is designed to give the student a basis for a critical analysis of the systems and theories that follow. Our experience in teaching this kind of material indicates that this is a necessary task, even at the senior and beginning graduate levels. It is true that much of the material is contained in some introductory courses, in courses in philosophy of science, or in some other course that the student may have had. It is also true that students state frequently and strongly that they already know this material. The fact is, however, that we have found the typical senior student who takes the first course in systematic psychology to be badly in need of further exposure to these concepts. Part 1 therefore endeavors to fill in gaps in students' experience and lay the groundwork for their understanding of the relationship of basic scientific and systematic matters to psychology.

In presenting this elementary philosophy of science, we do not intend to give the impression that formal study of how science is made is necessary for the making of science. In fact, we talk more about the criticism of "finished" science as it may exist at a given time than about the construction of science. But we do feel that a little philosophy of science helps the student to avoid some of the more obvious errors that might be made by the scientifically unsophisticated and, further, that it is essential to the critical evaluation of systems and theories.

In Part 1 we have been able to take account of recent work by Coan and Watson, as well as the earlier work of Kuhn and some of our own work. The reader will recognize that the task of criticism is continuous and that one must always stop somewhat short of the very last word.

Part 2 deals in abbreviated form with standard material usually covered in a textbook on systematic psychology. Although historical material is presented, we have tried to emphasize the portions of each system that have some present significance. Our choice of six systems was based on our estimate of the relative importance of the several systems usually treated. Structuralism, functionalism, and associationism were chosen because of their importance in the historical development of modern psychology. Behaviorism, Gestalt psychology, and psychoanalysis were chosen because of their historical importance and their continuing importance in contemporary developments in psychology.

Part 2 has been changed relatively little, since the classical systems and their basic tenets are dormant. We have noted the passing of some very significant men (e.g., Wolfgang Köhler) and have added a few facts unearthed or clarified since 1962, when our first edition was completed. The advent of the new *Journal of the History of the Behavioral Sciences* has been helpful in this respect.

Part 3 deals with contemporary developments, particularly as they relate to the historical systems of psychology. Our purpose has been to provide a broad view of the contemporary theoretical scene, such as would not easily be obtained from more specialized treatments. We have added discussions of more recent and contemporary developments. The bridge between the past and the present is not easily understood unless one is well acquainted with present trends. We have therefore attempted to outline some of the more important trends, particularly within general and experimental psychology, since 1962.

An Appendix is included, consisting of summaries by experts of the vigorous trends in non-American systematic developments. We should like to commend and thank our Appendix authors for their admirable jobs of updating, and in one case creating, their materials on non-American systematic developments. We feel that the Appendix remains one of the more valuable features of the book, giving it a coverage and scope that no *ganz amerikanisch* authors could provide alone.

One underlying theme of the book is that interest in psychology has shifted from the orthodox general systems of twenty or thirty years ago to the more limited theories described in Part 3. The reader may view Part 1 as a presentation of the reasons why it was necessary that the shift occur. A desire to portray the shift and give the explanation for it has been a part of our motivation for writing the book. Another reason has been that in the process of teaching a course in systematic psychology, we felt the need for a single text that would be adequate to the task of presenting a background and a foreground to the development of systems, as well as the systems themselves.

In writing a book, authors present their own biases toward the subject matter. Our biases are experimental, and we accordingly have written an experimentally oriented book. We have been only incidentally concerned with psychology as a therapy, an art, or an applied science. Thus, for example, we have not portrayed the recent developments in existentialism or humanism in more than a rather sketchy fashion because we simply did not see how to fit this material into systematic psychology as we have understood it. Our biases within experimental psychology are those of methodological behaviorism, S-R variety (broadly conceived). However, we have tried to compensate for these biases sufficiently to enable us to present other points of view in a fair manner.

The brief reading suggestions at the end of each chapter are designed to provide an easy referral to selected sources for further examination of the systematic and theoretical issues examined in this book. No attempt has been made to be in any sense comprehensive or exhaustive. Rather, a limited sampling of relevant materials is given, with emphasis more on books, both older (classic) and recent, than on journal papers, although the latter are cited where they are especially valuable. Although certain of the sources are also cited (and in some cases discussed) in the text, they are supplemented by a number of additional annotated references.

Supplementary source books are now in preparation. The first is an instructor's manual, which teachers will find helpful in their utilization of the text. The second is a book of readings keyed to this text but also designed to be independently usable. It is expected that this book, which will be directly relevant to students' needs, will also prove useful to teachers as a reference source for supplementary assignments.

We wish to express our appreciation to the many publishers who have given permission to reproduce excerpts from their work, as indicated specifically in the Acknowledgments. We should also like to express our general appreciation to our colleagues at the University of Missouri and elsewhere for their direct and indirect contributions to the book, and to our many students whose detailed criticisms of the various drafts of the book were extremely valuable.

MELVIN H. MARX
WILLIAM A. HILLIX

PART ONE

PSYCHOLOGY AS SCIENCE

Psychology is not always and exclusively scientific. Nevertheless, much of it is scientific, and it becomes more so as it develops. The status of psychology and of systems and theories within psychology cannot be evaluated without a clear understanding of what science involves. Accordingly, our first chapter examines the nature of science. The second chapter examines the position of psychology within the domain of science, partially from the point of view of the present subject matter dealt with by psychologists. The third chapter is concerned with the nature of psychological systems and theories. Criteria for evaluating them are discussed there. Although it is impossible to arrive at final conclusions concerning the nature of science, the status of psychology, or the desiderata for psychological systems and theories, this review of the problems involved should enable the reader to approach the study of systems and theories with more sophistication.

1   The Nature of Science

IDENTIFICATION OF SCIENCE

Science is a many-sided social enterprise that defies complete description. The finished product is a body of *knowledge* which has been acquired through the use of scientific *methods* applied with a scientific *attitude*. Each of these three aspects of science is complex and changes with time. As science ages, our conceptions of it change; moreover, just as the final answers about nature continue to elude us, a final conception of science eludes us. Nevertheless, it is possible to say some things about the positive characteristics of science, after which we shall turn to an examination of several incomplete criteria for distinguishing between scientific activities and other activities.

Science as a Linguistic Activity

It is often said that science seeks *facts*. Almost equally often, we hear that science involves the development of *theory*. The usual connotations of these words include a high degree of certainty for facts, and a low degree for theories. Thus the two quests of science appear, at first, contradictory. The paradox seems deepened by another connotation of fact versus theory; to many, *fact* connotes solidity and reality, while *theory* connotes something less substantial, something merely verbal.

The late Edwin Guthrie was one psychologist who said clearly and forcefully that *both* facts and theories are verbal. We know that some things originally accepted as facts are later rejected; thus it seems that facts cannot be equated with concrete events. Events cannot at one time be "true" and later become "false," although statements about them may be accepted at one time and not at another. Here is some of what Guthrie had to say on the subject (1946, p. 1):

Objects and events are not facts; they are merely objects and events. They are not facts until they are described by persons. And it is in the nature of that description that the quintessence of fact lies. Only when an event has been given a very specific kind of description does it become a fact.

When we say, "Let's get down to the facts," what we are saying is much more than that we should look at or listen to or smell or touch real objects, or that we should all observe an event. What we are really proposing is that we all try to find certain statements on which we can all agree. Facts are the basis of human cooperation.

This view of facts robs them of much of the solidity and immutability that they are often felt to have. Neither cows nor falling bodies are facts; only the statements made about them are facts. Since facts are verbal, the manner in which they are stated is arbitrary. The statements which we call facts we usually also call "true"; thus truth, as we use the word, will have the same element of arbitrariness and relativity that facts have. What is true for one set of people may not be true for some other set. Further, for any one set of people facts change, and the truth changes as we rephrase our statements about the universe and as our knowledge increases. We cannot insist that scratches on paper or vocally produced pressure patterns in the air are true; the scratches and the pressure patterns are stimuli which either are or are not useful in directing the behavior of people and which either do or do not produce the response "true" under appropriate conditions in people listening to or reading the statement. If the patterns of stimulation play their complex roles well in the learning situations in which they acquire meaning and in the situations where they direct behavior, then the patterns tend to persevere and to be called true. If they do not, they will eventually be replaced by other truths, other facts. Even the statements that continue to be called true because they make precisely correct predictions are liable to eventual replacement by superior truths that make the same predictions more simply and thus allow man to code "truth" more economically.

It is therefore the business of science to make statements, even when it is dealing with facts. The more factual statements made by scientists tend to be those which "follow directly" from observations. The more theoretical statements are not so directly related to observation, although the theoretical statement may be so universally accepted that it, too, is called a "fact."

The critical reader should not allow himself to be too easily seduced by the glib statement that, in the case of facts, the verbal statement follows directly from observation. Let us examine some of what is involved in relating empirical events to symbolic formulations of those events.

Nearly every human being undergoes a long course of training in the use of his native language. After this training, he regards certain kinds of statements as "grammatical" and "meaningful," and he is able to "describe" events with these grammatical and useful statements. Without the training, he could not do so. Thus we must stipulate that we are dealing with a trained human being before we can possibly maintain that any statement follows directly from an observation, and twenty years of training, more or less, would seem to be enough to introduce a lot of direction of its own.

The human being receives a similar course of training in observing. He comes to regard some aspects of objects and events as significant, and others as insignificant. Different cultures give their members different courses of study in observation; striking examples for citizens of the United States are the many kinds of snow that the Eskimo can distinguish and the ability of the Pygmy to follow the trail of an animal. Unfortunately, the scientist is not likely to be struck by his own remarkable sensitivity to certain aspects of events or by his equally remarkable insensitivity in some cases. It is difficult to evaluate our own peculiarities unless we can compare our behavior with that of others.

"Well," one might conclude, "then what we need to do is to become sensitive to all aspects accurately and completely." Nothing could be farther from the truth. Imagine, if you will, an all-seeing eye which photographed in living color, and recorded in stereophonic sound, *everything* that happened. Imagine further that predictions are made by searching the records until a sequence with the same beginning as the sequence we are now examining is found. For one thing, we would probably never find a recorded sequence which is a perfect match for the one we are now interested in. For another, how would you like to look for it? It would obviously be impossible. The task of science is to *avoid* this kind of literal approach.

How is this procedure to be avoided? First, by choosing very selectively the aspects of events which are to be treated by science, and second, by formulating the "principles" or "laws" governing events so creatively, simply, clearly, and economically that we can predict and control unique sequences of events *without* recourse to the approach that "what has happened before will happen again." Science is irrevocably in the business of creating new relationships between the world of symbols and the world of reality. Its business demands the utmost in patience and ingenuity. We now turn to some of the characteristics of science which grow out of the "fact" that its quest is for an effective working relationship between symbol and reality through the intervention of man.

Some Defining Criteria for Science

There are several legitimate ways to try to know and understand the world. The scientific way is thus but one among many. What is it that distinguishes science from other types of enterprise? Science has many characteristics, and each of these has been selected at some time as *unique* to science. However, we cannot expect to distinguish science from other human activities on the basis of a single property, any more than we would expect to be able to distinguish all dogs from all cats because they possess a black nose or a wagging tail. One characteristic of science, the use of control in observation, is most nearly unique; however, the other features of science are also usually descriptive of it and thus merit some consideration before we turn to a discussion of the principle of control. It is the combination of its characteristics that distinguishes science, not any characteristic taken alone.

Purpose. The general purpose of science is to provide an objective, factual, empirical account of the world. It is thus contrasted with the artistic, literary, and religious ways of thinking. However, many laymen have aims similar to those of scientists: the police detective, for example, may wish to render an equally objective, factual account. Pratt (1939) has pointed out the difficulty of making an objective-subjective distinction that would allow us to set off science from nonscience on these grounds. The generality of the scientist's knowledge may be stressed in order to contrast it with these more limited and specific endeavors, but then it cannot on these grounds alone be separated from an artistic or religious account.

Subject Matter. It is commonly said that science deals with a different subject matter from that which is the concern of nonscience. This is only partially true. Scientists tend to work with subject matter which is somewhere near the transition zone between knowledge and ignorance. Moreover, at some stage in the development of knowledge in a given area, it may be that only scientists are working with that subject matter. For example, there may have been a time when only psychologists or physiologists were interested in the changes in breathing rate or blood pressure that accompany emotion. Today the same subject matter interests the police officer. Conversely, the so-called psi phenomena (extrasensory perception) at one time interested chiefly nonscientists; today, these alleged phenomena have been the object of considerable scientific investigation. These examples demonstrate the fact that scientists and nonscientists often study the same subject matter.

Conclusions. The conclusions of science have been said to be more final, more correct, or more accurate than the conclusions reached by other disciplines. Poets, among others, may sometimes be indignant about this (Newman, 1957), but the claim is seldom made by working scientists themselves. They recognize the tentative nature of their own statements and look upon scientific methods as simply the methods that they themselves prefer to use in the quest for knowledge. A study of early theories about heat, light, nerve impulses, or matter itself is calculated to make scientists humble rather than dogmatic. Heat is no longer thought of as a subtle fluid, nor is the nerve impulse thought to travel at the speed of light, although both these beliefs were once reputable scientific theories and held by some as "facts." The scientist can look forward only to a continuous process of revision of present facts. One psychologist with a philosophical bent puts it nicely (Turner, 1967): "Each new advance emits a spark of certainty, and then the certainty is gone" (p. 7). Since the scientist's conclusions are not correct or accurate in any ultimate sense, one cannot claim that scientific conclusions are necessarily superior to conclusions reached by other means. However, any scientific conclusion is based on a careful evaluation of the available evidence. Any well-established scientific theory, even though it is subject to revision, will typically lead to approximately correct predictions.

Prediction and Control. Science is sometimes said to be distinguished by its concern with the prediction and control of events. However, many groups share an interest in prediction and control. The baseball pitcher is concerned with the control of the behavior of a spheroid of a certain standard size and density, and the batter is most interested in predicting the behavior of that same ball. These interests are shared by the physicist. The mother, as well as the psychologist, attempts to predict and control the behavior of children. Thus this kind of control does not distinguish science from nonscience. The shared interest in control is probably the chief reason for the high level of public support of science. The layman perceives science as the source of control over sickness, war, hunger, and eventually perhaps mortality. Much of psychology's support springs from the oft-nurtured belief that psychologists now do, or soon will, contribute to man's well-being. We would be foolish to deny this possibility, but we do wish to emphasize that this interest in control over the world is very far from unique to science.

In the present context control means "influence"; one needs to be quite sure to distinguish this meaning from the more common scientific or technical meaning of control as a method of eliminating extraneous sources of variation in observations.

Theory versus Applications. Science is not necessarily concerned with theory, as opposed to applications. A scientist may work exclusively with either, or with both. Physicists were among those assigned to the Manhattan project during World War II. Their goal was very applied: the development of the atomic bomb. The vision of this goal was made possible by many men whose curiosity about the universe had led them to formulate theories purely for their own satisfaction. Other sciences, like physics, could be used to illustrate the fact that scientists may have either pure or applied interests without jeopardizing their status as scientists. The relationship between theory and applications, or between pure and applied science, constitutes a very complex problem, various facets of which will be discussed at other places in the text.

Terminology. The terminology of the scientist is not necessarily more unique or more precise in meaning than the language of others. Scientists sometimes use esoteric new words, and they sometimes give new meanings to old words. Scientific language may then seem mere jargon to the layman. Yet science may at times use almost exactly the language of the layman. The language of mathematics is exemplary for its precision and sometimes its uniqueness; yet mathematics is not an empirical science and therefore is not a science in the restricted sense in which we shall use the word. Engineers may also use a language as unique and precise as that of their scientific counterparts, physicists and chemists. We cannot distinguish science from nonscience on the basis of the words that are used, although we shall see that science does use special methods for clarifying the meanings of words.

Exactitude. Exactitude and precision, especially in measurement, are often said to distinguish the scientist. Again, exactitude and precision are not the property solely of scientists. Equally precise and quantified measurements may be used by the engineer or the inventor.

We should, however, distinguish between the *use* of measurements and the *construction* of measurement scales and procedures. The person who sets up a new means of measuring is engaging in an activity which is at the very heart of science; he is establishing a new relationship between symbol and reality, and he is enriching the store of things that can be said about the measured reality. The man who more sharply or more clearly defines a phenomenon in nonmathematical language engages in the same general type of activity. Thus, the terminology used and the exactitude with which quantities can be expressed are results of a critical part of the scientific process, even though they are not unique features of science. We shall return to this issue later in this chapter, and again near the end of the book.

Although no one of the features we have discussed necessarily distinguishes science from nonscience, the notion that they do does not occur by chance; these features generally do *describe* science, though they do not *distinguish* it. Science does strive for rigor in terminology, for the ability to predict and control, for more quantification, for better theory, and for an objective account of the world.

However, we believe that the most adequate single distinction between science and nonscience is a feature of scientific methodology. It is this feature—the *principle of control*—that is most nearly unique to science among all human enterprises.

CONTROL IN OBSERVATIONS

The Need for Control

Control is a method used by the scientist in an attempt to identify the "reasons" for, or "causes" of, what he observes, or, to put it another way, to identify the sources of variation in his observations. An experiment is a carefully controlled situation in which there are one or more conditions whose influence the investigator wishes to determine. These conditions, or factors, are generally called *independent variables*. The conditions which are directly measured or otherwise observed are called *dependent variables* (in psychology, these are typically responses of one kind or another). Now, in order to obtain unambiguous results—that is, changes in the dependent variables that can be attributed with reasonable confidence to the independent variables—the scientist needs to eliminate—control—all other potentially effective conditions. These other conditions are called *controlled variables*.

It is easy to show that the principle of control can be used outside science. For example, a farmer with both hounds and chickens might find that at least one of his four dogs is sucking eggs. If it were impractical to keep his dogs locked away from the chicken house permanently, he would want to find the culprit so that it could be sold to a friend who has no chickens, or to an enemy who does. The experiment could be run in just two nights by locking up one pair of hounds the first night and observing whether eggs were broken; if so, one additional dog would be locked up the second night, and the results observed. If none were broken, the two dogs originally released would be locked up with one of the others, and the results observed. Whatever the outcome, the guilty dog would be isolated. A careful farmer would, of course, check negative results by giving the guilty party a positive opportunity to demonstrate his presumed skill, and he would check positive results by making sure that *only* one dog was an egg sucker.

In science, the potential culprits are variables rather than dogs. Control is again the method for isolating their effects. Nagel indicates agreement with our evaluation of the importance of control and provides us with another example of its necessity in the following statement (1967, p. 11):

A detailed account of the logic of testing hypotheses cannot be given here, but brief mention must be made of the notion of a *controlled inquiry*—perhaps the most important single element in that logic. A simple example must suffice to indicate what characterizes such inquiries. The belief, widely held at one time, that cold salt water baths were beneficial to patients suffering from high fevers seems to have been based on repeated observations of subsequent improvement in the condition of patients subjected to this treatment. However, irrespective of whether or not the belief is sound—in point of fact, it is not—the evidence on which it was based is insufficient to establish its validity. It apparently did not occur to those who accepted the belief on that evidence to ask whether patients not given such treatment might show a similar improvement. In short, the belief was not the product of a controlled inquiry—that is, the course of the disease in patients receiving the treatment was not compared with its course in a control group who did not receive it, so that there was no rational basis for deciding whether the treatment made any difference.

Nagel's example is an especially instructive one for psychologists. Saltwater baths, like bloodletting and other horrible examples, were a treatment applied to human beings, organisms with a great capacity for self-healing. Thus the well-being of the human being is a function of time, or (more precisely) of influences which act over time, and a control for such influences is absolutely necessary if any conclusions are to be drawn. The analogy with psychology is clear: Mental well-being, like physical well-being, is a function of variables which act over time, and patients sometimes recover if left to their own devices. Also, as in medicine, our humanistic tendencies often prevent us from refusing presumably beneficial treatments (like saltwater baths or bloodletting?) to those who ask for them.

The exercise of control over observations is therefore an essential process in science; the use of experimentation rather than naturalistic observation is preferred because it makes better control possible. If control is not used, the sources of variation cannot be discovered with certainty because the uncontrolled variables will always remain potential alternative explanations. This is *not* an argument against naturalistic observation. Willems and Raush (1969) have presented a convincing argument, complete with examples, for the use of naturalistic observation in psychological research. We argue only that the laboratory provides the best-controlled situation and must not be denied its critical role.

Much of the elaborate paraphernalia of the scientist is directed at this one objective of control of observations. The scientist's apparatus and the setting in which he works are designed to *eliminate* extraneous variations, so as to increase his confidence that his results are attributable to the particular variable or set of variables he is studying.

Statistics and Control

Statistical procedures play a related role in increasing the confidence with which statements can be made. In that sense, statistical procedures provide another means of control. Statistical techniques cannot eliminate the variability in the observations; when the statistical work (in the narrow sense) begins, the experiment has ended, and the data already reflect the extraneous variation which crept in despite the control provided by the setting and the apparatus. However, the statistical procedures allow the scientist to decide whether it is reasonable to assume that the extraneous sources of variation could account for his results. If they could not, the implication is that the changes in the dependent variable are related to the independent variable he manipulated. Thus both the experimental procedures and the statistical procedures are but means for choosing between alternative explanations of the observed results.

The fact that elaborate equipment and experimental procedures are sometimes used leads some people to think of controls *only* in terms of such complexities. This is a faulty conception of the principle of control. The following discussion is intended to demonstrate that there is a fundamental continuity in the principle of control through a variety of observational techniques.

Methods and Techniques

Let us start by distinguishing between method and technique, as these terms are used with reference to scientific methodology. By *method* we mean the fundamental processes by which science proceeds; the key aspect of scientific method is control. By *technique* we mean the particular manner in which the general method is implemented; there are many techniques, often differing from one subject-matter field to another and often appearing highly complex, specialized, and demanding.

In psychology, there are some excellent techniques for controlling variables; they are quite simple in principle. Hereditary variables can be controlled by using identical twins and assigning one twin of each pair to the control group and the other twin to the experimental group. All environmental conditions within the experiment would be made identical for the two groups—except for the independent variable. Random variations in outcome would be attributable to preexperimental variations in environment; that is, one twin would not have been subjected to exactly the same environment as the other. Systematic effects would be related either to differences between pairs of twins or to the effects of the independent variable.

Lesser degrees of control could be obtained through other techniques; for example, littermates could be used, or animals of about the same age from the same genetic pool. It is clear from these examples that many techniques of varying degrees of effectiveness can be used for implementing the general "method of control."

When it is sometimes asserted, then, that psychology requires different methods in its scientific progress, we would revise the wording to say that psychology requires different techniques in its application of the basic scientific method. It would be foolish for us to assert that scientific method is now fixed for all time, almost as foolish as it would be to assert that scientific laws are fixed for all time. From our present perspective, however, the broad, basic methods of science appear to have been surprisingly stable for the past 350 years or so. This stability in method can be contrasted to the rapid changes in technique; for example, techniques of visual observation have progressed, during roughly the same period, from the magnifying glass to the electron and field ion microscopes.

The failure to make the distinction between method and technique accounts for much of the experimental-clinical schism that is sometimes observed within psychology. Clinical and counseling psychologists are prone to regard experimental psychologists as of a different breed on the grounds that they use a different kind of method; the clinician may justify his own techniques by insisting that science permits of many methods and that psychology does not need to ape the older sciences, especially physics, in its methodology. Experimental psychologists, on the other hand, very often prefer to dissociate themselves from the clinicians and the counselors on the assumption that the latter do not use scientific methodology. The heart of this prejudice is their belief that controlled observations are not adequately utilized by clinicians and counselors. While this may be true in many individual cases, we hope to show that it need not be the case. However, it is easy to see that misunderstandings may arise because of a failure to make the distinction between method and technique.

The Activity Continuum

The process of controlling observations can be understood better if we recognize that control may be achieved either through active or through passive methods. The experiment is often said to be the ideal method for achieving control. The experimenter can control and manipulate variables within the context of the experiment; for example, he might equate the temperature in the experimental chamber and the number of reinforcements between groups, while varying the amount of reinforcement. Yet we have already seen that the experimenter may have to be somewhat more passive in order to control other kinds of variation; for example, he may have to wait until human twins occur in order to control for genetic factors. Precise control over the preexperimental environment of the subjects in the experiment is usually not possible. Variation in the preexperimental environment is simply allowed to occur and is assessed statistically because there is usually no alternative.

Many of the refinements of apparatus used in psychological experimentation are directed toward the objective of increased control. In some situations, however, neither apparatus nor experimentation is appropriate. Even on this relatively passive end of the continuum, away from experimentation, a kind of control can be exercised. The astute counselor, for example, entertains hypotheses which he attempts to check during the course of an interview. These hypotheses may be about a particular client or about more general relationships. If the latter, a series of clients would have to be checked (see Hunt, 1951). We are more concerned here with the case in which the counselor wishes to state general relationships, since general laws are of more direct scientific importance. Such general lawfulness ("nomothetic" in character) presumably underlies the individual relationships ("idiographic") with which the clinician is typically concerned.

Once the counselor or clinician attempts to check evidence selectively on various factors or conditions, he must begin to apply some degree of control. Suppose that he is looking for certain kinds of consequents (symptoms, say) as related to antecedent factors (such as infant experiences or home conditions). In checking these possible relationships, he will sooner or later have to take into account other conditions in which he is not now interested (e.g., sex, age, or educational level). Controls are needed at this point. He may be forced to eliminate certain clients from consideration because they are not sufficiently similar in educational level, for example. When he does this, he is attempting to eliminate the effects of some variable while checking the influence of others. He is doing so without benefit of formal experimental design or active manipulation of variables; even so, what he is doing is applying the essence of the principle of control in what may be the only way possible in his situation. This is true whether his primary interest is scientific (nomothetic) or clinical (idiographic).

There are enormous difficulties facing the scientist who attempts to utilize the principle of control in this passive way. He may be tempted to regard the observations on which he bases his hypotheses as *tests* of the same hypotheses. The experimenter who actively controls his observation should find it easier to separate his hypotheses from their sources, and therefore to give the hypotheses the necessary independent testing. The more passive situation also encourages reliance on memory of past events; this is even more serious to the extent that it allows subjective selection and distortion of observations, rather than the more objective recording of all of a particular type of measure, formally determined in advance of the experiment. But the fact remains that it is possible to use the kind of thinking characteristic of the use of the principle of control even in situations which make active control impractical. This passive control can increase the scientific usefulness of otherwise uncontrolled observations. If this were not true, Charles Darwin could not have demonstrated, to the satisfaction of his fellow scientists, the principle of evolution.

THE ROLE OF ANALYSIS

Examples of Analysis

A considerable amount of confusion has developed about another basic tool in the kit of science—analysis.

Let us illustrate its role in controlled observations by an example from the history of psychology. In 1938 Norman Maier won the annual award given by the American Association for the Advancement of Science. His contribution consisted of a paper (Maier, 1938) accompanied by an impressive motion picture in which he described his research on "neurotic" behavior in the rat. Maier had been able to produce very striking abnormal symptoms in rats by presenting them with an insoluble discrimination problem. His achievement seemed to be the culmination of several years of strenuous effort by psychologists to develop a technique for producing neurosis in the rat so that neurosis could be experimentally investigated with this handy subject.

Maier interpreted the abnormal behavior observed as a reaction to conflict. As the features of his experimental procedure were studied and isolated—analyzed—some psychologists became interested in the role of a factor whose importance in the situation Maier had not emphasized. This was the use of an air blast to force the animal off the testing platform in the jumping-stand apparatus. For Maier this factor had no significance beyond that of forcing the animal to jump; he had found it to be effective for this purpose and so used it instead of some other technique. Not very long after Maier's report, however, C. T. Morgan and Morgan (1939) reported that they could duplicate Maier's results without producing any apparent conflict at all. Their rats, when simply exposed to the same type of sound that Maier had used to make his rats leave the jumping stand, showed the same convulsive and comatose behavior that Maier's rats had shown! It appeared that the elaborate discrimination training and the presumed conflict resulting when the problem became insoluble, was not necessary. The term *audiogenic seizure* then became popular as a label for the convulsive behavior, in view of its apparently auditory basis. It appears that—just as in the case of the saltwater baths—a necessary control had not been run.

Without entering into the ensuing controversy over whether some other kind of conflict is or is not an essential factor, we can point to the present example as an interesting and important illustration of the necessity for the combination of analytic thinking and control as a basis for interpretations. Many other examples will be apparent to the reader of the psychological literature.

It is impossible for us to see how science can proceed without some analysis. The process of control implies that some variables have been analyzed that need controlling; different potentially relevant factors are isolated, controlled, and studied in relation to selected effects. The complexity of most everyday life situations is so great that scientifically useful relationships can be determined only through the twin processes of conceptual analysis and controlled observation.

Analysis and Synthesis

Our emphasis on analysis should not be construed as any rejection of synthesis. Once relevant variables have been isolated through analysis, there must be synthetic laws which tell us how the variables combine in producing the final effect. Synthetic thinking has tended to be preferred by clinically oriented psychologists; the synthesis of a number of variables is necessary in multivariable situations if interpretation and explanation must be attempted. Analysis may be rejected because its critic is concerned primarily with the world "as is," rather than with the "irreality" that comes from scientific analysis, abstraction, and control. Although analysis may not afford complete and practical answers, we feel that a rejection of analysis is fundamentally unscientific. Until an analytic procedure has isolated separate variables out of a complex situation, synthesis has nothing to work with. Antianalytic attitudes will probably tend to disappear as the nature of the whole scientific process becomes better understood.

The importance of analysis and control follows from the kinds of materials with which science works. We can understand science fully only if we understand these materials. We noted that finished science, considered as a body of knowledge, consists of statements. These statements are regarded differently from the way we regard other items in our experienced world. Control, analysis, and synthesis play their roles in setting up the relationships which the scientist either discovers or invents—those between the empirical and the symbolic worlds. Analysis provides us with terms which can be used in experimental hypotheses. The use of control helps us to check our hypotheses in reliable and unambiguous experiments and observations. Synthesis is used to combine variables so that our knowledge can apply to complex situations which have not been directly observed before. Synthesis tells us—if it is used correctly—how variables combine to bring about an effect. We turn next to a consideration of one of the basic factors determining correctness of scientific procedure—the principle of operationism, which is concerned with the problem of effective communication.

OPERATIONISM

History

The work of the physicist Percy Bridgman (1927) stands as a milestone in pointing clearly and in abundant detail to a precaution that should be taken if scientific concepts are to be reduced in ambiguity. Bridgman analyzed the historical habits of thought and expression in physics preceding Einstein; he wondered why Einstein's theories, indicating a need for a drastic revision of the concepts of length, space, and time, had come as such a shock to physicists. He wished to avoid a repetition of this shock. In his analysis, he discovered that the Newtonian meanings of time, length, and space contained elements of meaning which were not justified by the results of physical experimentation. To Newton, time was a kind of absolute scale, independent of any process that might be required to find out what "time" is. Bridgman said of Newton's definition (1927): "Now there is no assurance whatever that there exists in nature anything with properties like those assumed in the definition" (p. 4). When Einstein examined some of Newton's concepts, he was led to reformulate them completely. One essential feature of Einstein's relativistic theory is its fundamental dependence upon the *operations* required for measuring time and position; for example, how does one establish that two events occurring at widely separated places occur "at the same time"? Obviously, a message must be sent from one place to the other. Meanwhile, the places may have shifted their absolute or relative positions. Working out these problems led Einstein to his relativity theory.

Bridgman proposed to place more stringent requirements upon the definition of physical concepts so that no such revolution as the one brought about by relativity theory need again take place in physics (1927, p. 5):

The new attitude toward a concept is entirely different. We may illustrate by considering the concept of length: what do we mean by the length of an object? We evidently know what we mean by length if we can tell what the length of any and every object is, and for the physicist nothing more is required. To find the length of an object, we have to perform certain physical operations. The concept of length is therefore fixed when the operations by which length is measured are fixed: that is, the concept of length involves as much as and nothing more than a set of operations; *the concept is synonymous with the corresponding set of operations.*

The last sentence of this quotation should make it clear why Bridgman's point of view has been labeled *operationism* and why his kind of definition is called *operational definition*. His aim was to clarify the meaning of all concepts and to remove all connotations of terms which might not be meaningful. In other words, the aim was to make sure that concepts have a clear reference, a meaning in terms of operations for the listener or reader as well as for their inventor or user.

There is continuing discussion and criticism of the operational point of view within science; Benjamin (1955) has thoroughly examined operationism from the point of view of a philosopher of science. It is probably fair to say that operationism is incomplete, is beset with philosophical difficulties, and, if taken literally, cannot provide an altogether consistent program for scientific advance. Nevertheless, operationism as a loosely interpreted methodological prescription is still viable and still needed in psychology to prune away the scientifically meaningless speculation that continues to make our scientific grove look more like a forest than a garden.

Operationism was early taken into psychology, and its acceptance was early opposed. Stevens (1939) pointed out that operationism should not be regarded as a religion or a panacea; it is simply a formal statement of the methods that have always been used within science when it is necessary to clarify the meanings of words or other symbols. Misfortune sometimes lurks in the wings for those who let their verbal concepts assume too much of an independent identity. Concepts do not have their own reality, and the operationists' warning helps the scientist keep the origin of the concept in mind.

There was at first much disagreement on the grounds that many concepts have proved to be highly useful despite the lack of directly observable operations or events to which they correspond. Bridgman has been clear that paper-and-pencil operations and verbal concepts are admissible even though they do not *immediately* correspond to physical operations, but he insists that they must be eventually reducible to operations that actually can be performed, or else they can have no meaning for science. In a book that followed his earlier one by twenty-five years (Bridgman, 1952), he reaffirmed the usefulness of such abstract concepts. Most scientists would probably agree that science must follow roughly the operational prescription at some stage of the game if science is to provide communicable knowledge. Experience has shown that when a term is being defined, disagreement usually stops when we point to what we have done in defining the word and say, "This is what I mean by [the term at issue]." We *must* in some way ensure that our statements inspire others to a predictable kind of response, for that is part of the business of science. Operational definition is a way of doing this.

Physicists like Einstein and Bridgman were concerned with the change in a concept which might have to occur because of the new operational requirements of a new context; for example, the technique of placing measuring rods end to end in order to determine length must be abandoned if length is to be measured on an astronomical scale. The question arises: In what sense are the two concepts of length the same? In psychology, one operational definition of anxiety may involve the verbal responses to verbal questions by human subjects. Another may depend upon their galvanic skin responses. A third definition of anxiety may be based on the amount of urination and defecation by rats in an open-field situation. Are the three definitions concerned with the "same thing"? If so, what are the operations which allow us to relate the three operationally distinct definitions? This type of question is not easily answered, but it requires an answer. It serves the useful purpose of keeping us close to our data.

OPERATIONISM RELATED TO CONTROL

We can now return to the discussion of control from another point of view. It is clearly necessary to specify the context within which operations are performed if the meanings of concepts based on operations performed within the contexts are to be free of all ambiguity. Only then can the operations be repeated exactly. Part of the specification of the situation must be a description of the values and relationships of the variables within the situation; that is, we must control variables through the use of the principle of control if we are to use operational definitions. Without adequate control, we cannot be sure that our operations can be reliably repeated.

The scientist wishes to make statements about the relationships between events. He may wish to make a statement in the form "A is related to C." In order to do so, he must be certain that some other factor is not responsible for the supposed relationship. In an example previously cited, Maier wished to assert that conflict was responsible for the behavior observed in his experimental animals. The Morgans, however, showed that another factor—high-frequency sound—was related to the behavior in the absence of the original type of conflict. This threw Maier's original statement into question. In general, then, positive scientific statements can be made only when alternative assertions are eliminated through control of variables. It is clear that control is a most pervasive characteristic of the scientific process. Historically, the need for control of all variables within a situation was recognized long before Bridgman stated his views of operationism. Nevertheless, we see that one way of regarding control is as a prerequisite for adequate operational definition of more complex relational concepts.

SCIENTIFIC HYPOTHESES

The foregoing discussion may make science sound like a cut-and-dried body of statements. Finished science may indeed be highly formalized, and the interpretation of the statements of science at a given time may require more perseverance than imagination. Yet the creation of science requires imagination and ingenuity of the highest order, as well as hard work. The thrill of scientific discovery is as satisfying as anything derived from any vocation. The devotion of many scientists to their work is a testimonial to this statement. The use of operational definitions and the control of variables are prerequisites of good scientific workmanship, but the employment of these techniques does not guarantee that the scientist will make a great contribution.

The scientist must work on significant problems and formulate effective hypotheses if he is to do important work. He must formulate a problem so that it can be attacked by scientific techniques. This implies that any questions must be expressed so that they can be answered empirically. The questions formulated initially are not a part of science, but arise from prescientific considerations. Later questions may be suggested by the outcomes of previous experiments or may arise from a study of some theoretical framework which is itself related to experimental results.

The first requirement for a scientific hypothesis is that it be testable, and the first requirement for a scientific question is that it be answerable. Perhaps this boils down to saying that the terms of the hypothesis or question must be operationally defined, the operations performed as required by the question, and the results observed. If an experiment is performed for the purpose of testing some hypothesis, the hypothesis must be sufficiently clear in implication so that the results of the experiment are predicted in advance; one outcome must be specified from among the various alternatives. We shall later see examples in psychology of theories about behavior which purport to explain behavior after it occurs, although they cannot predict in advance which behavior will occur. Upon closer examination, these so-called theories turn out to be capable of explaining whatever behavior occurs. In short, no conceivable outcome could *disconfirm* the theory. One requirement for scientific hypotheses is that they be stated with sufficient precision so that they *can be disconfirmed*. Hypotheses that cannot be disproved are too general to be scientifically useful; science strives for, among other things, the ability to predict events given the preceding set of circumstances. If a hypothesis is so general that it cannot be disconfirmed, it is also so general that it cannot effectively predict; it therefore fails an important test for scientific hypotheses. For example, if someone tells us that the reason events proceed as they do is that this is the best of all possible worlds, we are in no better position than before to predict the events of tomorrow. This type of statement is not disconfirmable and is therefore scientifically useless.

There is a type of hypothesis for which the requirement that it be directly testable or disconfirmable does not hold. These are the hypotheses that are analogous to mathematical postulates. Their function is not to specify directly an empirical outcome, but to serve as a starting point for the derivation of other statements that do specify an empirical outcome. Such statements have operational meaning only in terms of their derivations. Examples of these are less common in psychology than in some more advanced sciences, but some mathematical learning theories seem to contain postulational statements; Estes' (1950) statements about stimulus pools and the organism's sampling from them are of this type. Hull's (1952) statement about afferent stimulus interaction is also postulational as far as his system is concerned, although the "postulated" relationship was derived from observed experimental results. Some people regard Freud's statements about the unconscious as the same type of statement, although here the case is less clear. Such postulates are always subject to revision in the light of new experimental results, despite their lack of direct experimental reference, and they must be interpretable at some stage in empirical terms. They must *lead* to predictions.

Margenau and Bergamini (1967) cite an exciting sample of scientific work which exhibits clearly the nature of an advanced science which uses abstract mathematical postulates and works through to eventual empirical observation. They call the story "The Pursuit of Omega Minus." In its broadest outlines, the story goes like this. Murray Gell-Mann and Yuval Ne'eman, two outstanding physicists, independently applied a type of nineteenth-century mathematics to describe the properties and behavior of atomic particles. Each particle required eight numbers for the specification of its eight quantum values: previous experimentation, when analyzed, indicated the need for the eight properties. Gell-Mann called the deductive system the "eightfold way," after Buddha's eight ancient prescriptions for the good life. The system classified a welter of subatomic particles into a limited number of classes and suggested that there ought to be a particle of a certain specified mass, never yet observed, which they named "Omega Minus."

The theory predicted that an Omega Minus particle should be produced roughly once in 50,000 photographs. The properties deduced for the as-yet-unseen particle allowed Gell-Mann and Ne'eman to predict what should be observed experimentally; that is, experimental physicists could expect to see a particular kind of track in the bubble chamber used to detect particles.

Nicholas Samios was the experimental physicist at Brookhaven who directed the successful search for Omega Minus. After 97,025 tries, an Omega Minus particle was produced, and manifested itself as a tiny scratchlike mark on the photograph; these marks appeared "meaningless to the layman but beautifully legible to the technicians, who read meaning in the tiniest scratch." The experimental hypothesis had been verified.

Several points can be extracted from this sample. First, the work was heavily dependent on past experiments and theories. Second, an unusual symbolic system had been developed for quite another purpose, at another time, and this system was a critical part of the scientific effort. Third, very special conditions had to be set up in order to make the required observations (the Brookhaven atom smasher was used). Fourth, the terms of the theory had, at least superficially, an indirect and tenuous relationship to the final observation; yet the observation was an absolutely critical—and in this case, dramatic—part of the scientific process. Fifth, the theory specified *exactly* what observations were to be made. Theories are directed by observation, and in turn they direct the scientist in making further observations. Sixth, the importance of the observation was enormously enhanced by its relationship to a complex and sophisticated theory. What, in itself, is the importance of a minor, inch-long scratch on a photographic plate?

Finally, we would like to note that Gell-Mann endowed his system with a poetic name borrowed from a religious philosopher. Perhaps the beauty of his borrowed mathematics, together with the use to which he was able to adapt it, inspired him with something like the number mysticism of Pythagoras. Certainly the scientist confronted by the multitudinous harmonies and symmetries of nature can be pardoned if his feelings in scientific creation are difficult to distinguish from the feelings of the artist or the mystic. The role of beauty and elegance in scientific theories has been strongly championed. We can afford a healthy respect for the logical and mathematical systems we use as tools—provided an empirical and operational approach makes it a cautious respect.

Scientific hypotheses and theories should have other characteristics beyond testability or, for that matter, beauty. For one thing, we would like them to be as simple as possible. The principle of parsimony (sometimes called *Occam's razor*) is the traditional statement that unnecessary complication should be avoided. Lloyd Morgan's canon is an adaptation of this principle to psychological problems. Morgan held that behavior should never be explained in terms of a faculty found high in the phylogenetic scale if some faculty found lower in the scale is adequate. Morgan stated his canon as an antidote to the tendency to attribute human characteristics to animals whenever the animals showed apparently intelligent behavior (that is, Morgan objected to what is commonly called *anthropomorphizing*).

The desire for simplicity should not be construed to mean that a simpler hypothesis should be held to in the face of contrary evidence or when it is found to be inadequate. If this were the case, physicists would still be clinging tenaciously to their older, simpler view of the atom as a single, unbreakable particle. They do not, because evidence has been amassed to show that such a simple model is inadequate. Models and theories *must* be consistent with all the known evidence. The scientist's acquiescence in the face of evidence is expressed in the adage "save the phenomena." Another version is "the subject is always right" (Skinner, 1959). When phenomena became available which contradicted the model of the atom as an unbreakable particle, a three-particle model which saved the then known phenomena was proposed. It, in turn, had to be replaced by a more complex view. When complexity is required, simplicity is abandoned. But search parties are immediately sent out to hunt for it again. When complex theories are required in order to "explain" phenomena, the advance of theory is likely to take the form of simplification. For example, the Ptolemaic theory was replaced by the apparently simpler Copernican theory; the latter was made possible by taking a new point of view.

The foregoing discussion makes it clear that hypotheses and theories are never final. If evidence accords with their predictions, confidence in their validity grows. If confidence in a hypothesis is great, it may become part of a theory. By theory we shall, in the ideal case, mean what Bergmann (1957) means: "A theory is a group of laws deductively connected" (p. 1). In this sense, a scientific law is an honored hypothesis, one that has been widely accepted and whose implications have been observed to hold without fail. Our psychological theories, unfortunately, do not always consist of laws; in psychology, the hypotheses found in theories are often without much honor, and they may have a deductive connection only in the loosest sense.

Though hypotheses and even laws may finally be replaced, that does not mean that the old statement was useless; it was required to have predictive value within the range and era of its usefulness. There is no one who would argue that Newton's laws were or are useless, even though they have been replaced as *complete* physical accounts. Even now, Newton's statements are used for many applications because they are effective within their limitations and range of applicability.

As another example, we could predict the passage of heat from one body to another if we conceived of heat as a subtle fluid, just as we do now that it is conceived of as related to molecular movement. Heat is no longer conceived of as a fluid, not because one could not predict temperature changes, but because this view of heat does not fit into the overall theoretical account of the nature of matter.

THE ROLE OF PARADIGMS

Kuhn (1962) emphasizes a very important element that has thus far been left out of our discussion of science. Normal science, he says, progresses by working within the framework of a "paradigm." A paradigm does include laws and theories, which we have suggested are important parts of science. But Kuhn thinks of paradigms as being somewhat more concrete and inclusive (1962, p. 10):

matters and that, fundamentally, they have to learn their science in the laboratory (broadly defined) rather than through the study of philosophy of science or logic. The scientist cannot allow philosophy to make him too skeptical. Science seems to demand an intermediate degree of skepticism for its successful prosecution. Too much skepticism may keep one from taking those first positive steps along a path which cannot always be clearly seen ahead of time—steps which are, however, necessary for real scientific advance; too little skepticism subjects one to the serious risk of accepting grossly inadequate hypotheses as though they have been confirmed. Perhaps most of the skepticism should be concentrated on the scientific level, with some things taken for granted.

The thing the scientist most often takes for granted is himself, and he thereby avoids many of the most troublesome philosophical puzzles. He may succeed in escaping the trap of solipsism and ignoring the mind-body problem. Bridgman (1959, p. 128) puts it this way:

The scientist, as he functions in the laboratory, is usually not conscious of himself nor is he explicitly present in the report which he makes of his findings. In fact, one of the ostensible ideals of such a science as physics or chemistry is to report the facts in such an impersonal way that any other scientist could put himself into a position to make a similar report. The physicist or chemist takes himself for granted—he accepts the findings of his senses at their face value and is not bothered by such questions as the nature of knowledge or by a self-doubt which would continually question his own sanity. Here is a feature which in common usage pretty much distinguishes all "science," namely, science as such appears not to raise the issue of self-doubt. This applies not only to the so-called physical sciences, but also to biology or the life sciences, and to the mental sciences, at least so far as mental science is typified by experimental psychology in the laboratory.

SUMMARY AND CONCLUSIONS

We set out in this chapter to examine the nature of science. Disagreements about what science is alert us to the fact that science is not yet defined in a way with which everyone agrees. We believe, however, that the characteristics we have suggested would win general acceptance. Science does involve establishing relationships, in a prescribed way, between events and language. The "empirical method" is used. Operational definitions, analysis, the principle of control, and hypothesis testing are all part of scientific procedure. The purpose of science is to establish new empirical-symbolic definitions which are "correct" in the sense that they lead to prediction and control. Though the conclusions reached by science should not be regarded as final, they are guaranteed at least a limited utility by the use of the procedures outlined above. Ideally, the conclusions are expressed in well-defined, exact, and quantitative terminology. All the methods of science may be applied in different ways or to different degrees; we have paid particular attention to differences in the mode of application of the principle of control. It is doubtful, despite fairly frequent espousals of a very descriptive orientation, whether interest in the development of theory is ever absent.

Probably every endeavor has to take some things for granted. The scientist is often unconcerned with many philosophical issues, and the value of studying such issues is moot. The scientific attitude tends not to be highly philosophical. It may sometimes resemble the poet's in its respect for human creativity and for the orderliness of our world. The scientist's open acceptance of the world as it is contrasts vividly with the sharp-eyed criticality he brings to his evaluation of the scientific constructions of man.

Only extremely simple definitions can be couched in terms of single characteristics. Science, having many characteristics, cannot be easily defined. We shall examine a scheme for constructing precise multiple-characteristic definitions in Chapter 3. Our examination of the characteristics of science, together with our later examination of the nature of definition, will make it possible for both authors and readers to consider a common set of properties and to share a common attitude toward a definition when we wish to evaluate the scientific status of systems of psychology.

Further Readings

Valentine and Wickens (1949), in their classic *Experimental foundations of general psychology*, provide examples of the importance of the principle of control. The relevance and interest of the examples have not decreased with age. Sidman's *Tactics of scientific research* (1960) presents a positivistic view of experimental practice which has both aroused controversy and become extremely popular. Pratt's *Logic of modern psychology* (1939), while no longer contemporary, offers a readable logical analysis of behavioral methodology. Nagel's *Methodology and philosophy of science* (1962) is good, but may be too much for less advanced students to tackle as a reading; more manageable introductions to some of the philosophical problems may be found in Caws's *Philosophy of science* (1965, Ch. 35) and in Benjamin's *Science, technology, and human values* (1965). Bridgman's *Logic of modern physics* (1927) is the classic on operationism. Some of Bridgman's later views are given in *The way things are* (1959). Benjamin analyzes the operational viewpoint from a philosopher's point of view in *Operationism* (1955). Skinner's *Verbal behavior* (1957b) is very thought-provoking in the context of this chapter because it examines the empirical-symbolic relationship and describes how Skinner thinks it comes about. Chomsky's review (1959) of Skinner's book points out basic disagreements between Chomsky, writing as a linguist, and Skinner; these disagreements have started a controversy which is still raging. Two philosophical texts oriented toward problems in the study of behavior treat nearly every philosophical issue which will be touched on in the present book: Turner's *Philosophy and the science of behavior* (1967) and Taylor's *Explanation of behavior* (1965). Taylor, though a philosopher, focuses on problems arising directly from psychology. Turner, though a psychologist, starts with philosophy and wins his way back to psychology. Turner's easy style often makes wrestling with hard intellectual problems more a game than a chore, and his book is worth reading for the gems contained in the notes alone. Finally, *The physicist's conception of nature* (Heisenberg, 1958), written by one of science's all-time great troublemakers, qualifies as a dessert for the present list, in that it gives a concise survey of the history of science and of several very basic problems, all in under 200 pages.

2 Psychology's Place in Science

Psychology has been short on both history and historians. As time passes, so will the shortages. There are several signs indicating that the history of psychology is emerging into robust health. The *Journal of the History of the Behavioral Sciences* started publication in 1964 and continues to provide an outlet within psychology for articles on our history. The International Society for the History of the Behavioral and Social Sciences, established in 1969, holds annual meetings. It is called Cheiron after the wisest of the mythological centaurs. Division 26 of the American Psychological Association is the Division for the History of Psychology; it first met as a formal division in 1966. There is now an archive for the history of psychology at the University of Akron. Finally, the first American Ph.D. awarded on the basis of a dissertation on the history of psychology was awarded to Dr. Barbara Ross of the University of New Hampshire under the guidance of Dr. R. I. Watson, editor of the *Journal of the History of the Behavioral Sciences*. Thus nearly all the marks of professional maturity have come to the history of psychology only since 1964.

There are also some encouraging signs that professional historians, rather than professional psychologists, are beginning to pay attention to the history of psychology. For example, Sokal (1971) has written on one of America's leading early psychologists, James McKeen Cattell.

Even before the history of psychology showed these signs of maturity, psychologists were fascinated by their own past. Solso (1971) studied the lists of books recommended by graduate departments of psychology in the United States and found that Boring's *A history of experimental psychology* was among the exclusive group of books most recommended in 1953, and has remained there since. There seems to be no doubt that psychologists, like other scientists, regard the study of their history as an extremely important subject. We now turn to a very brief sketch of a little of that history and to some of the lessons that seem to derive from this overview.

The schools of psychology can be better understood with these lessons clearly in mind. Accordingly, this chapter sketches several ideas relevant to the understanding of psychology's emergence and its position in science. First, we discuss the growth of some general philosophical ideas which seem critical to the emergence of science. Then some more specific problems which contributed to the emergence of psychology as a separate science are outlined. Third, the initial subject matter of psychology is compared with its contemporary subject matter. We next turn our attention to psychology's place in the corporate organizational chart of science. Three topics help in this assessment: psychology as a part of the hierarchy of science, pure versus applied science, and special problems related to the subject matter of psychology.

THE GROWTH OF SCIENTIFIC IDEAS

Table 2-1 presents, for ready reference, a summary of the contributions of some of the men who helped to develop the scientific ideas that finally led to a science of psychology. Their birth and death dates are approximate both because the historical record may be incomplete and because calendar changes often make interpretation of existing records difficult.

Many historians have noted the apparently stepwise progress of the sciences, beginning with those farthest from man and moving toward those closest to him and his immediate affairs, and the consequent late development of the science of psychology. Astronomy and physics were the first sciences to develop. Archimedes, in the third century B.C., was in some ways a sophisticated physicist. In the early seventeenth century, Kepler's mathematical description of the motions of the planets around the sun was already the culmination of a long line of astronomical discoveries. The body of man was investigated long before there was a science for the "mind" of man. Harvey, in 1628, described the circulation of the blood, about 250 years before Ebbinghaus did his pioneer work on memory.

Two reasons have been suggested for this long-time neglect of the behavior of man. One is the sanctity of the human being as maintained by human institutions. The other is the complexity of the human being as proclaimed by those who have tried to study him. We might add that it is often easiest to be objective about the things that concern us least.

The foregoing statements, of course, are ruthlessly selected to make the general point. We know that philosophers and laymen have long wrestled with explanations of the human being, but there was not a formal *science* of behavior, as there were other sciences. Some of the contributions of these men will be discussed in more detail in the text to follow, but it will be helpful if the reader has an overall view of them before examining certain key concepts.

Explanation: External and Internal

There was a time in the history of man when events were typically explained in terms of forces outside the scope of observable natural events. For example, Norse

TABLE 2-1   Summary of Major Contributions to the Development of Psychology

Philosophy		
Man	Approximate Birth and Death Dates	Contribution
Thales	Sixth century B.C.	Naturalistic explanation; universe composed of water.
Socrates	c. 470-299 B.C.	Idealistic philosopher; essentially antiscientific.
Democritus	c. 460-370 B.C.	Universe composed of atoms; reductionistic account of complex phenomena.
Plato	427-347 B.C.	Rationalistic, dualistic approach.
Aristotle	384-322 B.C.	Rationalistic and observational methods; classification systems for biology; laws of associative memory.
Roger Bacon	c. 1214-1294	Emphasis on free empirical observation.
Francis Bacon	1561-1626	*Novum organum*: gave philosophical support to empirical science.
Descartes	1596-1650	Dualistic interactionism; action of body mechanistic.
Leibniz	1646-1716	Activity as basic; degrees of consciousness; co-inventor of calculus.
La Mettrie	1709-1751	Mechanistic explanation applied to man's behavior.
Kant	1724-1804	Importance of native abilities in ordering the data of experience.

Physics and Astronomy		
Man	Approximate Birth and Death Dates	Contribution
Archimedes	c. 387-212 B.C.	First well-known experimental physicist.
Ptolemy	Second century	Alexandrian astronomer; his view of earth as center of universe held for centuries.
Copernicus	1473-1543	Polish astronomer who placed sun at center of solar system; changed man's view of his own importance.
Galileo	1564-1642	Reestablished observation as final court of appeal; made astronomical and physical discoveries.
Kepler	1571-1630	Mathematical description of planetary orbits.
Newton	1642-1727	Co-inventor of calculus; set pattern of physics for 200 years.
Bessel	1784-1846	Astronomer at Königsberg; worked out personal equations and thus posed a problem for psychology.

Biological Science		
Man	Approximate Birth and Death Dates	Contribution
Hippocrates	c. 460-380 B.C.	"Father of medicine"; an excellent observer; naturalistic view of man.

TABLE 2-1 (continued)

Man	Approximate Birth and Death Dates	Contribution
Herophilus and Erasistratus	Third century B.C.	First inference of distinction between sensory and motor nerves.
Galen	Second century	Famous physician and anatomist; performed animal experiments.
Vesalius	1514-1564	First thorough treatise on human anatomy.
Harvey	1578-1657	Demonstrated the circulation of the blood.
Van Leeuwenhoek	1632-1723	First effective microscope; discovery or identification of protozoa, bacteria, and human sperm.
Linnaeus	1707-1778	Binomial system of biological classification.
Darwin	1809-1882	*The origin of species*: primary publication on organic evolution.

Emergence of Modern Physiology		
Man	Approximate Birth and Death Dates	Contribution
J. Mueller	1801-1858	Comprehensive *Handbuch der Physiologie des Menchen*: doctrine of "specific energies of nerves."
Bernard	1813-1878	Concept of the internal environment.
Helmholtz	1821-1894	Eminent physiologist; first experimental measurement of speed of nerve impulse; theories of hearing and seeing.

Emergence of Psychology		
Man	Approximate Birth and Death Dates	Contribution
Weber	1795-1878	Pioneer physiologist; formulated law: $dR/R = C$; really a psychological law.
Fechner	1801-1887	*Elemente der Psychophysik*: believed by some to mark beginnings of experimental psychology; modified Weber's law into Weber-Fechner form: $S = C \log R$.
Galton	1822-1911	Work in eugenics, statistics, individual differences; set many problems for psychology.
Wundt	1832-1920	Founder of first psychological laboratory, at University of Leipzig.

mythology explained storms by saying that the warrior of the gods was angry, and Homer explained victory in war in terms of the favoritism of the Greek gods. From the scientific point of view, there are two very basic things wrong with these explanations: (1) they refer the explanation to unobservables, and (2) the events used as explanations do not fit within the same context as the events to be explained; there is thus no apparent logical connection between the alleged causes and their consequences. Such explanations are therefore called *external*, as opposed to *internal*.

It is not always easy to tell whether a particular explanation is internal. The extremes are easy: theological explanations of natural events are clearly external, and accepted scientific accounts are usually internal. Paradoxically, some of the most sophisticated scientific explanations are the most difficult ones to classify. These sophisticated explanations often depend on postulated but initially unobserved entities like genes, stimulus elements, or Omega Minus particles. Most scientists accept explanations couched in terms of such concepts as internal because they or their effects are potentially observable, are "observed" indirectly, or have implications for observations at another level. Questions arise, however, if it is not clear that the concept is formulated so that it is potentially observable, if the supposed indirect observation can be accounted for in other ways, or if the implications from the deductive system containing the concept are not clear.

Although there are still people who explain disasters in terms of "the wrath of God," scientific explanation does not have recourse to such descriptions. Thales, a Greek philosopher of the sixth century B.C., is sometimes given credit for initiating attempts to explain natural events in terms of other natural events; he explained the nature of matter in terms of a single basic *natural* element, water. Democritus soon after explained matter in terms of basic particles called *atoms*, and modern man still holds to a similar conception. Whether these men really deserve credit for the swing toward internal explanation, however, is not important; the important thing is that science as we know it depends on the use of explanations which refer to observables within the same natural framework as the observables to be explained.

The Greek culture that developed this idea eventually disappeared. The idealistic skepticism of Socrates and Plato, ingenious as it was, may have contributed to its disappearance. The ensuing Middle Ages showed little concern for internal types of explanations or for scientific problems; perhaps the attitude was that great interest in natural events was bad for the soul. Such science as there was during the medieval period was largely in the East. It remained for the Renaissance, beginning (by the most common convention) with Galileo and his contemporaries, to renew European interest in natural science. An example of the external thinking that was predominant in the Middle Ages is the typical treatment of convulsions by flogging; such action was thought to drive out of the body the demons or evil spirits that were considered to be responsible for convulsive behavior. Today, of course, such treatment is not used because convulsive behavior is generally viewed as determined by organic conditions within the body (an internal explanation). Convulsive electroshock is used in the treatment of psychosis with explanations of its effectiveness which are probably less satisfying than if we still believed in evil spirits; however, it may be significant that we are *seeking* an internal explanation.

In denigrating external explanations, we are not assuming that the implications of the explanation *necessarily* lead to ineffective treatments. People are frequently "right for the wrong reasons." For example, recent work in behavior modification would lead us to believe that flogging, systematically administered every time the "evil spirit" was seen at work, might eliminate the undesirable behavior in some cases. R. I. Watson (1963) gives an example which shows that a more nearly correct conclusion may follow from a kind of evidence which we would find altogether unacceptable today, while an inferior conclusion about the same issue derives from an attempt at "internal" explanation. Watson says of Aristotle's views (1963, p. 52):

In identifying life with the *psyche* and this, in turn, with the heart, he also rejects the Platonic doctrine of the brain as the organ of the soul. He used as one argument for doing so the fact that he found the brain to be insensible to direct stimulation. It is ironical that Plato was right for the wrong reasons. Plato assigned reason to the brain on the basis of several irrelevant reasons typical of which is the fact that the brain was the part of man nearest the heavens. Aristotle, on the other hand, was wrong for the "right," *i.e.*, naturalistic reasons.

If some right decisions follow from the wrong theories, the theories have a greater life expectancy than if all decisions turn out badly. Phrenologists recommended practicing algebra for those who had an inadequate bump in the area responsible, according to their system, for algebraic proficiency. If this "treatment" both followed from the theory and produced algebraic ability, the theory could be regarded as "confirmed"; as a matter of fact, it did take phrenology a long time to disappear.

Such examples bring home the fact that observations cannot logically confirm theories; they can only disconfirm them. In scientific practice, theories are seldom rejected because of a single disconfirmation. They can almost always be saved by finding a flaw in the observation or in the relationship between the observation and the theory. Even if these modes of rescue fail, most theories are complex enough so that a change in a part will bring the theory into line with the observation, and the bulk of the theory can be saved. On the confirming side, too, the dictates of pure logic are not followed. If an observation occurs as a theory says it should, confidence in the usefulness of the theory increases, despite the illogic of the increase in confidence. Certainly the illogic is not without reason; the theory, after all, *has* been demonstrated to be "right" with respect to the observation.

Reliance on Observation

Parallel with the use of internal explanation was an increasing reliance on observation. Most of the earlier Greek thinkers relied more on rationalistic methods than is the case in the modern era. For example, Euclid early developed a deductive geometry, and Pythagoras and his followers had a mystic belief in the efficacy of numbers. Socrates and Plato lent support to a rationalistic approach, Socrates with his logical questioning procedure and Plato with his emphasis on the importance of the ideal world, which he somehow regarded as above and beyond the real world.

Both tended to suspect the evidence of the senses as the source of truth and thus helped to turn the tide against what is now regarded as an essential feature of scientific method—a primary reliance on observation.

Aristotle was one early thinker who used observational as well as rational methods. He was an advocate of logic and reasonableness, but not a respecter of authority. His own authority, however, was accepted during the Middle Ages at the expense of observational methods. Galileo was important in renewing the scientific attitude toward observation and authority. He relied, for example, upon *observation* of the time of fall of bodies of unequal weight, rather than upon the authoritative statement that heavy bodies fall faster than light ones. Francis Bacon, in his *Novum organum* of 1620, made one of the most famous appeals for empiricism. He felt that science should work strictly by induction, piling observation upon observation until general facts emerge from specific facts.

The English empiricists who came after Bacon tried to follow his approach to its logical conclusion. Locke denied the innate ideas attributed to man by thinkers like Socrates and Descartes. Berkeley denied that we could be sure of the existence of the external world, since we have only experience to go on. Though he returned the external world to us only slightly used, with the help of the assumption of the existence of God, his skeptical position was more convincing than his retreat, and has been more influential. Finally, Hume applied empiricistic thinking to the notion of causality and maintained that all we really know is that some events are invariably contiguous in space and time. Our notion of causality is based on this observation. (But see Chapter 4 for a fuller discussion.)

Kant reacted to the empiricists, particularly Hume, and proposed a compromise type of theory in which experience remains the teacher, but needs a student with a certain native endowment. Kant's specific statements about what is known prior to experience have been rejected, but his general point that the attainment of knowledge requires certain prior abilities is still accepted.

Despite the contrast between the extremes of empiricism and rationalism, there is no such thing as a *purely* rationalistic or *purely* empiricistic approach, nor is there a clear-cut line of demarcation between the two approaches. Francis Bacon, in his "discarding" of the rationalistic approach, had to use rationalistic methods in his arguments. The most empirically minded, "hardheaded" scientists eventually make general statements based on their observations—and hence depend for their application on the use of the rationalistic method. On the other hand, the rationalistic philosopher very probably takes the plausible assumptions with which he begins from some kind of empirical observations. The scientific usefulness of his rationalistically derived conclusions depends on their consonance with observations. Though there is no pure approach and no clear method of classifying the techniques of particular individuals as more rationalistic or more empirical, we believe it is reasonable to say that science has tended to emphasize the empirical more than the rational. The final arbiter of truth for a scientist is not what rationally *ought to be* but what observationally *is*.

Simplification

Thales and Democritus tried to simplify the apparent complexity of nature by appealing to simpler elements and to assumptions which allowed them to derive the observed complexity from the assumed simplicity. Their attempts were also *reductionistic*, since they reduced complexity by explanations depending on the existence of phenomena at a different, "lower" level; for example, Democritus supposed man to be built of particles much like those which compose other forms of matter. Physiological psychologists make similar reductionistic statements when behavioral data are explained in terms of physiological events, which again are at another level of observation. It does not follow that a reductionistic account will also necessarily be a simple account, or even the simplest available at a given level of explanation. Science seeks and accepts not only simple hypotheses but also the simplest overall theory which adequately explains all the observations made.

Reductionistic explanations offer at least a potential economy of concepts, since a single concept can serve at more than one level of explanation. These economies may serve as the basis for choice between otherwise equivalent theories. Turner says (1967, pp. 178-179):

When we turn to the idea of a hierarchy of explanation, we especially realize that there is a guidance implicit within scientific invention. One seeks not only an explanation of a particular set of events but also a theoretical construction that itself is derivable from within some still more basic science. Chemical explanations, for example, were conceived in terms wholly unique to the phenomenology of chemistry itself. But the advantages and the guidance of atomic constructions are now all too apparent. Geneticists could have continued to think in terms of the gross characteristics of genotypes, but the molecular model of biochemistry offered explanations of the duplicative powers of the genes. And psychology can continue to build hypothetico-deductive models in learning theory, knowing (perhaps unconsciously) that issues of alternative theories will be resolved by developments in neuropsychology.

In his later book (1971), Turner continues to favor reductionism but discusses the issues in much greater detail. For example, he considers various alternative routes that might be taken in a reductionistic program: linguistic reduction, mechanical reduction (through computer simulation), and neurological reduction.

Placement of Man in Nature

The Greeks seem to have regarded man as having no special status apart from the rest of nature. Many of the Greek philosophers would probably have agreed that the behavior of man is lawful and predictable, just like the behavior of inanimate nature. The Middle Ages, however, took a different view of man. He was regarded as a creature with a soul, possessed of a free will which set him apart from ordinary natural laws, subject only to his own willfulness and perhaps to the rule of God. Such a creature, being free-willed, could not be an object of scientific investigation.

Even the body of man was regarded as sacrosanct, and dissection was dangerous for the dissector. These strictures against observation hindered the development of anatomy and medicine for centuries, and misconceptions that are today considered incredible persisted for over a thousand years. A science of man could not flourish in such an atmosphere.

Today concern for the rights of the living has superseded concern for the rights of the dead. However, if the reader is tempted to believe that performance of research is no longer an issue, he should familiarize himself with the current, continuing, and often acrimonious controversy surrounding the treatment of animal and human subjects. Wolfensberger (1967), for example, discusses the use of human subjects. Related battles have raged around psychological testing. The entire issue of the *American Psychologist* for November, 1965, was devoted to an examination of the testing issue. The basic conflict involved is between the right of the human individual to privacy and the need of others—scientists and government agencies particularly—to get information about him. We do not wish to prejudge such issues; ethical matters are not yet decidable by scientific methods, so we shall limit ourselves to pointing out that problems in the ethics of science may always be with us.

Descartes started a trend which again favored psychological, or at least human, research. A predictable system is a researchable system. Descartes regarded the body of a man as a machine which will move and behave in predictable ways if we know what the "inputs" are. He salvaged free will for man by possessing him of a soul which was free and which decided the actions of the body. Such a view made at least dead (soulless) bodies accessible to scientific investigation; animals, since Descartes regarded them as soulless, were also accessible.

The idea that man might be an object of scientific study was furthered by La Mettrie. He was convinced, apparently largely by the deterioration of his own thought processes during a fever, that man was *altogether* a machine, dependent in mind as in body upon physical events. He espoused this view, despite strong opposition, until his death.

The man-machine analogy to which Descartes and La Mettrie contributed is a good example of the kind of partial analogy which starts persistent controversy. It is clear that man is not identical to any existing machine either in his construction or in his mode of operation. Descartes and La Mettrie, both brilliant thinkers, cannot seriously be considered stupid enough to have overlooked this glaring fact. Neither can other mechanistic thinkers. All of them are supporting a limited likeness between man and machine. Machines are constructed and fairly well understood by man, and their behavior can be predicted. Man, although neither constructed nor understood by himself, seems also to be a creature of his construction and should in principle be predictable like machines. Critics of the "mechanistic" position attack the complete, unintended analogy of the mechanist as often as the partial analogy he intends.

There was still much resistance to viewing man within a deterministic, natural framework when Charles Darwin advanced his theory of organic evolution. Evolution itself was not a new idea, but Darwin buttressed the evolutionary theory with so much evidence that it took the scientific community by storm. Evolution restored the continuity between man and other animals which Descartes had denied when he attributed a soul to man alone. It also contradicted the Biblical account of creation. The theologically based opposition aroused a heated controversy which persisted into the twentieth century and was heard around the world. Today there is little questioning of the correctness of the general outlines of evolutionary theory. Evolution is a fact for the scientific community, if not for all the lay community. Its acceptance has made the science of psychology more acceptable by making it more plausible than ever to view the behavior of man as lawful. It has also made the study of animals an important part of that science; the assumed continuity between animals and men supports the belief that knowledge gained in the study of animals will have significance for the behavior of men.

PSYCHOLOGY'S LEGACY OF PROBLEMS

Finally, then, the behavior of man came to be regarded as lawful, and a science of psychology was possible. But the basic scientific and philosophical assumptions prerequisite for the development of a science were not all that psychology found in its legacy when it began as a formal science. Psychology also inherited certain problems that developed within science and philosophy before it won its independence. Problems, as well as necessary assumptions, must exist before a new science will arise. Some of the problems passed on to psychology were phrased in such a way that their scientific resolution through experiment was impossible, but they nevertheless stimulated research as attempts were made to find those elusive answers. We shall consider four problem areas: the mind-body problem, the physiology of perception, the reaction-time problem, and questions related to individual differences.

The Mind-Body Problem

The ghostly apparitions of dreams may first have convinced man that there was more to him than met the physical eye. The writing of Plato shows that the thinking of his time divided man into two components. Descartes's dualistic views did not differ greatly from Plato's. Both systems fit into the Christian theology; some unobservable component is necessary if the immortality of man is logically to be maintained, since the observable portions of man are mortal. Even today, the thinking of the layman separates man into two components.

If man has both a mind and a body, then the question naturally arises: "What is the relationship between the two parts?" A long tradition of thought made the question inevitable. Before psychology ever had a formal beginning as a science, a German physicist, Theodor Fechner, started work on the problem. It was his intention to write equations that described the functional relationships between the psychic and the physical realms. The result which he believed he found is the

TABLE 2-2 Major Philosophical Solutions to the Mind-Body Problem (An early important exponent of each position is identified in parentheses, with the approximate date of his contributions.)

Dualism*	
Cartesian interactionism (Descartes, 1641)	Two separate and interacting processes assumed.
Psychophysical parallelism (Spinoza, 1665)	Two separate, independent, but perfectly correlated processes assumed.
Occasionalism (Malebranche, 1675)	Two separate and independent processes assumed; correlated by the intervention of God.
Monism†	
Materialism (Democritus, 400 B.C.)	A single underlying physical reality assumed.
Subjective idealism (Berkeley, 1710)	A single underlying mental or spiritual reality assumed.
Phenomenalism (Hume, 1740)	There are neither minds nor bodies as far as can be known; only ideas resulting from sense impressions exist.
Compromises	
Double-aspect view (Russell, 1915)	Two processes assumed to be a function of one underlying reality.
Epiphenomenalism (Hobbes, 1658)	Mind assumed to be a noncausal by-product of body.

*Any point of view implying a basic difference between mind and body and therefore a relationship to be explained.

†Any point of view ignoring either mind or body or subsuming both under the same rubric.

Weber-Fechner law, so named because E. H. Weber had already expressed much the same psychophysical relationship in a simpler, more primitive form. Boring (1950, p. 483) has questioned whether Fechner really intended to take a dualistic position, but certainly his problem was stated in dualistic terms. For example, in his *Elemente der Psychophysik* (1860), Fechner said he was concerned with "the exact science of the functional relations or relations of dependency between body and mind." In order to demonstrate these functional relations, it is necessary to measure mind and body separately and therefore to have two separate things to measure. Fechner thought he was measuring two different things. On the one side he had the stimulus, which acted on the body. On the other side he had the sensation, which he thought of as a mental event. Fechner wished to demonstrate the identity of the two kinds of events, but it was difficult to reunite the two aspects that had been separated by assumption. He wanted to demonstrate empirically an identity that philosophers, using rationalistic methods, had been alternately proving and disproving for hundreds of years.

The major mind-body positions that have been taken by philosophers are classified and summarized in Table 2-2. The reader should familiarize himself with the general outline presented here, for the "solutions" reappear in the following chapters. There is no scientific method for deciding among them. Early psychologists, as we shall see, nevertheless felt it necessary to take some stand on the mind-body problem. Then, for several decades it became fashionable to reject the problem altogether as meaningless. Today, whether it is meaningless or meaningful, soluble or insoluble, it seems to be coming back to the front as a topic of psychological conversation. We shall return to the problem in more detail later.

The Psychology of Perception

Other scientists, notably physiologists, were interested in another relationship, that between physiological processes and perception. Hermann Ludwig Ferdinand von Helmholtz is the most famous of those interested in this relationship; he modified Thomas Young's color theory and developed his own theory of hearing. Helmholtz, along with the English empiricists, believed that all knowledge depends upon sense experience. If this is our assumption, then the problem of sense physiology is also the problem of epistemology—the problem of the origins, nature, and limitations of knowledge. Physiological findings in this area of study have philosophical implications. Helmholtz tried to refute Kant's statement that there is innate knowledge. Kant had believed that the axioms of geometry are known independently from any experience of them. Helmholtz asked whether we would have developed the same geometry if we had inhabited the inside surface of a hollow sphere. He discussed non-Euclidean geometries in a spirit which is surprisingly modern.

If the views of Helmholtz and Kant are viewed only in broad outline, however, the two differ less than they may have thought. Although Kant is categorized with nativists and Helmholtz with empiricists, Kant did admit the role of experience. Helmholtz recognized the need for some basic mental faculties to exist in order that the mind be able to develop the concept of space out of the raw materials of experience. There is, of course, a considerable difference in emphasis. The empiricist, by virtue of his philosophy, wants to observe and thus wants observable things to be as important as possible. The nativist tends to be a rationalist, and it is convenient for rationalists if the uncertain stuff of experience can be assigned as small a role as possible.

The Reaction-time Problem

The new science of psychology took over a second problem with epistemological implications. F. W. Bessel, the astronomer, noticed an account of the firing of an assistant at Greenwich Observatory. The assistant's readings did not agree with the readings of the head astronomer, and it is easy to guess whose readings were assumed to be wrong. Bessel recognized the possibility that the error might have been due to a difference in the time required for the two observers to react to information presented to different senses, rather than being the result of carelessness. He checked his hunch by comparing the times at which he recorded star transits with the times at which other astronomers under the same conditions recorded the transits. There were discrepancies in nearly all cases. Bessel then tried to write personal equations, or correction terms, which would reduce all the readings to a common basis. However, it was obvious that there could be no absolute standard of correctness where the human observer was concerned. Our knowledge was once again shown to depend upon observers and their methods of observing and recording. If the determination of the time at which a star crosses a line is subject to error. then it seems logical that more complex judgments and observations must be even more subject to error. It was not the philosophical point, however. which was important; it was the fact that the theoretical problems of epistemology were shown to be real, practical problems that stimulated Bessel and others after him to action.

Donders, a physiologist, further developed the problem, and Wundt took over the subtractive procedure from Donders. The subtractive procedure was supposed to reveal the time for psychological functions; the time for a high-level function was the total time for the activity, minus the time for some lower-level activity which was a part of the total. Wundt and many other early psychologists believed that by making the reaction required successively more difficult, the time for sensing, perceiving, apperceiving, discriminating, and the like could be found by subtracting the time for the next simpler reaction from that for the just more complicated reaction. Few psychologists would still hold this view; for example, it is not clear that perceiving involves sensing plus perceiving. The whole nature of the process being timed may change as the task is progressively complicated. The subtractive assumption is invalid.

Individual Differences

Two fields of study that have remained extremely important up to the present day are individual differences and statistics, which was initially taken over and developed by psychology as a method for studying these differences. Much of the American acceptance of psychology may be attributed to the effectiveness of aptitude testing, which is part of the study of individual differences.

Sir Francis Galton pioneered in the development of both statistics and the study of individual differences. He developed the technique of correlation in connection with his inheritance studies. He was led to it by the observation that children typically *regress* toward the mean relative to their parents in such characteristics as height and intelligence; that is, children of extremely tall or short, or bright or stupid, parents *tend* to be closer to the norm in these characteristics than their parents. Correlation is symbolized by r, for regression, and Galton is remembered for his early perception of the importance of statistics.

The major factor underlying the development of these interests was the Darwinian theory of evolution. Galton, who was Darwin's cousin, was himself interested in a practical problem—the improvement of the race through eugenics. In order to practice genetic manipulation, he needed to know how traits were inherited. This type of practical concern was in the direct line of conceptual descent that led from evolution to American functionalism. Stress on the organism's adjustment to the environment as a determining condition of survival or nonsurvival became a primary concern of psychology. The intellectual ferment produced by the theory of evolution raised questions that led directly to Galton's interest in individual differences, mental testing, and the statistical evaluation of differences and to the flourishing school of functionalism in the United States.

The theory of evolution also had implications for man's view of the philosophical controversy between rationalism and empiricism. Previously, most rationalists had had to buttress their positions by postulating some kind of farfetched preestablished harmony between the constitution of the world and man's ideas about it. How could it happen that man possesses correct innate ideas about the world in which he lives? It is not scientifically convincing to suggest that God gives ideas to man. From the evolutionary point of view, however, it could be suggested that the rational (physiological?) side of man has been *pushed into harmony with the world* by the pressures of evolution. We can, according to this argument, count on the outcomes of rational analysis because man, through evolution, has come to think the right things about the world. Men who were mistaken about the world presumably took the wrong course of action and died. Those who were "rational" survived. Evolution solidifies the effects of the world on man into a kind of physiological rationalism.

PSYCHOLOGY'S INITIAL SUBJECT MATTER

We now turn from our discussion of prepsychological scientific developments to a discussion of psychology's beginnings. The prepsychological problems that we have discussed were all taken over as experimental problems, but the systematic framework imposed on psychology by Wilhelm Wundt at the University of Leipzig in Germany was not exactly what one would expect.

It seems natural that psychology should be experimental, physiological, and interested in problems of sensation and perception. Since it came out of philosophy, one would also expect it to be interested in epistemological problems. Physiology actually played a very small direct role. Although Wundt called his psychology an experimental physiological psychology, there was almost no physiological experimentation; R. I. Watson (1963, p. 249; 1971, pp. 275-276) does note that pulse and breathing rates were monitored in studies of feeling. The minimization of physiology is doubly surprising because Wundt was himself a physiologist. However, psychology needed primarily the name of physiology. Physiology had prestige, which the young science of psychology wanted. Accordingly, physiology was often invoked to illustrate the scientific respectability of psychology in general and of specific theories in particular.

Physics and mathematics have served similar functions and controversies have raged about whether the alleged dependence of psychology on older disciplines is good or bad. In the case of physiology, at least, much progress has been made. Psychologists today are much more prone to practice physiology and much less prone merely to invoke it. It is interesting that, despite his training, Wundt refused to tie his infant science to the tail of physiology 100 years too soon.

Wundt was able to justify avoiding physiological experimentation because of his philosophical position on the mind-body problem. He believed that the mind and body run parallel courses but that one cannot say that bodily events *cause* mental events; external events simply give rise to certain bodily processes and, at the same time, to parallel mental processes (cf. Table 2-3). He thought the primary task of psychology was to discover the elements of conscious processes, the manner of their connection, and the laws determining their connection. Since mind and body are parallel, the simplest way to do this, in Wundt's opinion, was to make a *direct* study of the mental events through the method of introspection. Psychology might later turn to the question of just what bodily processes accompany given mental processes, but that problem was secondary. This aspect of Wundt's thought has a modern parallel. Skinner, among others, has insisted that the *direct* study of *behavior* is more likely to be profitable than the attempt to relate it to physiological processes.

Wundt thus brought a kind of problem of dualism to psychology. He also brought a strong belief in the experimental method. His research was laboratory inspection, not armchair introspection. He intended to rule metaphysical speculation out of psychology. He was constantly looking for experimental ways to attack mental processes. Wundt's experimentalism implied that he had accepted the necessary ideas which developed within science and which had to be accepted before a *science* of psychology could become a reality: the necessity for internal explanation, the reliance on observation, and the placement of man within the realm of the scientifically knowable. His search for the elements of consciousness also showed his attempt at simplification, or his reductionism, if one prefers.

The Leipzig laboratory, officially founded in 1879, also took over many of the specific problems that were waiting for a psychology. The reaction-time problem has already been mentioned. Problems in sensation and perception were taken over from Helmholtz, Fechner, and others.

There was less at Leipzig to remind one of psychology's predecessors on the other side of the channel. Only through a brash American student, James McKeen Cattell, did the Leipzig laboratory turn out any work on Galton's problem of individual differences. Wundt, with prophetic accuracy, called Cattell's interest *ganz amerikanisch* (typically American). It has indeed turned out to be America's armies, schools, and industries that have placed the greatest emphasis on testing individuals for most efficient placement.

It would be interesting to trace the beginning of psychology further than this passing glance allows, but our present purpose is simply to place the field of psychology in some kind of perspective relative to its history and role in modern science. Therefore, we now turn to an examination of the subject matter of psychology as it appears from a modern viewpoint. This will give us a basis for comparing what we know to be the subject matter of our field with the more limited views of the proper subject matter of psychology usually adhered to by the members of various of psychology's older schools. We shall also see later how the emergence of each new school tended to add breadth to the prior conceptions of the subject matter of psychology.

MODERN PSYCHOLOGY'S SUBJECT MATTER

There is no way to define the subject matter of psychology so that the definition will please all psychologists. Any definition turns out to be either too exclusive to be useful or too general to be meaningful. Yet it is possible to sketch in some approximate lines of demarcation.

First, there is practically universal agreement that psychology studies the behavior of organisms. There are those who hotly contend that psychology also studies experience; they are opposed by methodological behaviorists, who believe that experience is *used* by the psychologist in his study, but has no special status as a subject matter for psychology. We choose to skirt this issue here, and shall take it up in more detail in connection with the chapter on behaviorism. Meanwhile, we shall consider some possible limitations on the type of behavior studied by psychologists.

Many definitions of psychology stipulate that the behavior to be studied must be emitted by an intact organism or that it must be studied in terms of large, molar units. With this latter restriction, the swinging of a bat would be considered an appropriate unit for psychological study, while the flexion of the left arm would not. Others might exclude the smaller, molecular units on the grounds that there is no purposefulness in such responses, although this criticism is now less frequently heard. In fact, neither the restriction to intact organisms nor the restriction to molar units seems justified in terms of what psychologists are now studying. Although it is true that most studies are concerned with large units of behavior, some theorists (e.g., Guthrie, 1952) believe that the most effective conceptualization and experimentation will be in terms of more elementary units of behavior, such as flexions of individual muscles. Some recent studies have used the contraction of individual *motor units* as the dependent variable. No one denies that the men who do these studies are psychologists. Therefore, it seems meaningless to deny that what they are studying is psychology. We agree with Bergmann and Spence (1944) that the choice of units of study is a matter of convenience.

Similarly, we see no reason to stipulate that psychology, by definition, can study only intact organisms. That stipulation would exclude from psychology much interesting experimentation, for example, that on brain-damaged monkeys (e.g., Harlow, Davis, Settlage, and Meyer, 1952). The line between intact and nonintact organisms would have to be carefully drawn; recent work on the effects of electrical and chemical stimulation of tiny areas of the brain (N. E. Miller, 1958a; Olds, 1955) would have to be brought before the court for a ruling on whether the damage done was sufficient to disqualify the organism from intactness. There is no point in such quibbling. Let the man who calls himself a psychologist study whatever he pleases. We can best discover what psychology is by seeing what he studies.

Science (and psychology as a part of it) studies relationships. What, then, does psychology study in relation to responses? The answer seems to be: "Nearly everything that *can* be related." Stimulus-response (S-R) psychology has today become so popular that it obscures the fact that many of the relationships studied by psychologists are relationships between responses made at two different times; for example, the responses made on an intelligence test, or the resulting "IQ," may be related to other response-determined numbers assigned in a scholastic or industrial situation. This is an important part of psychology. Certainly we do not deny that stimulus-response relationships are important. Historically, these became an object of study very early. Bessel became interested in the time relationships between stimuli and responses and initiated the reaction-time experiment. Helmholtz, with his interest in the relationship between the stimulating situation and the contents of perception, was actually studying a functional relationship between stimulus and verbal response. Thus it hardly seems necessary to reiterate the importance of such laws relating stimulus and response.

There are, in addition, many experiments relating behavior to antecedents which are neither stimuli nor responses. These antecedents may usually be characterized as *state variables* (see Skinner, 1938); for example, we may change the state of an organism by injecting certain drugs, by extirpating part of the brain, by administering electroshock, or by starving the organism. We might study individual differences in behavior; this would mean a study of the effects of different initial conditions of unknown nature and origin upon behavior. We might, of course, enlarge the conception of stimulus to include all these instances of antecedents, but this would simply make "stimulus" equivalent to "any antecedent condition that we do not call a response." We may as well preserve the orthodox general definition of a stimulus as a physical energy impinging upon a receptor and note that the above-mentioned state variables do not exclusively affect receptors.

A rough initial definition of psychology then might be: "Psychology is the science which studies the relationships between antecedent events or conditions and the behavior of organisms." This is admittedly a broad definition, but psychology has become a broad field. Even this definition excludes much work actually being done, unless our definition of "behavior" encompasses nearly anything, including changes in brain size or composition, for example. A narrower definition might more cleanly excise psychology from the rest of the body of science, but we feel that it should not be so excised. Even as the physiologists initially found themselves studying psychological problems, so the psychologist finds himself studying physiology in order to understand psychology better. Some of the first psychological studies were psychophysical. Modern psychologists still find themselves making physical measurements in describing stimuli, and so some overlap with physics remains. Certainly the overlaps on the other end of the scale, with sociology and

Many apparently applied scientists have made major contributions to basic knowledge. For example, Pasteur's primary interest was in the production of vaccines, but he was also instrumental in, and is today possibly best known for, the development of the germ theory of disease. On the other hand, many apparently pure scientists have discovered facts and produced theories which have then been more or less directly applied to practical problems. The most recent and spectacular example of this is the contribution of the host of mathematical physicists whose work in one way or another was utilized in the development of atomic energy. This example of collaboration between the scientific and the engineering professions is characteristic of many less striking cases and illustrates the fact that the ultimate utility of new knowledge cannot readily be predicted in advance (Bronk, 1954).

SPECIAL PROBLEMS RELATED TO THE SUBJECT MATTER OF PSYCHOLOGY

Controls

We have emphasized the fact that control is essential to the development of science. Only through appropriate measures can we be sure that hypothesized relationships between variables really hold. Fundamentally, psychology is no different from any other science in its need for control. It *is* different in its ability to impose the necessary controls, especially when the object of our curiosity is human behavior. For example, we may wonder whether form perception in the human being is highly dependent on early experience with the visual world. In order to investigate this problem, we might like a supply of human infants who can be deprived of all visual stimulation for varying periods of their early life. Where is our supply of such infants? Our value system does not condone treatment of this kind. We may wonder whether social isolation in childhood is really conducive to the development of schizophrenia; here we have the same problem of unavailability of subjects. We may wish to study the effects of mating individuals with certain characteristics on the behavior patterns of the offspring, but who will engage in this carefully controlled mating? Examples could be multiplied indefinitely. There are quite obviously limits to the manipulations we can perform with human subjects. It is true that if we wait long enough, the events we desire may happen by chance, or we can piece together isolated cases that represent something of the kind of treatment we need. But the progress of science is slowed when it must wait for the desired events to occur.

Psychology and astronomy are in similar positions in this regard; the astronomer has had to wait, for example, until Mars comes close to Earth before he can make the most useful observations of that planet. With the availability of interplanetary vehicles, the astronomer may be somewhat better off. With the increasing concern for the protection of the rights of subjects, the psychologist may be somewhat worse off!

It is largely this kind of limitation which has turned many psychologists to the study of animals. The limitations of control with animals are much less severe, so the psychologist need not wait for the chance occurrence of the situation he wishes to observe.

Psychology, like physics, has a problem with its observations. In physics, the Heisenberg principle sets clear, mathematically stated limits on the accuracy with which elementary particles can be observed. In psychology, the problems of observation cannot be so clearly formulated, but they nevertheless are quite serious in practice. The recent work of Rosenthal (1966, 1968a, 1968b) is currently the best known among the investigations of the effects of the experimenter on the outcome of the experiment. Obvious types of effects involve the conscious or unconscious attempt to influence the outcome so that it will conform better to the experimenter's hypothesis and the recording of results in such a way that they will bear out this hypothesis. Less obvious examples of biasing by experimenters would include acting differently toward male and female subjects (Rosenthal, 1968a). Some types of errors in experimentation could be avoided by having the experiment conducted by computer. Others can be avoided by the usual "double-blind" procedures, in which persons conducting the experiment do not know which condition any subject is in until the data are obtained and recorded. Still others— like smiling more at female subjects if the experimenter is male—must be specifically guarded against even in double-blind procedures, if a human experimenter is involved. These problems arise because people, like particles, are extremely sensitive to the effects of observation. Even lower animals clearly reveal this property at the overt behavioral level; every rat-runner who has used a clear plastic operant chamber has noticed the rat observing the experimenter for long periods of time, seemingly preferring this exploratory activity to what the hungry animal is "supposed" to be doing—pressing the bar for food. The rat's sensitivity to the experimenter's preconceptions has also been documented (Rosenthal & Lawson, 1964).

Quantification

Mathematics is a specialized language. It is closely related to logic: Both are abstract, both are somewhat remote from the language of everyday life, and both have a grammar which is restricted and precise. These characteristics have made specialized symbolic systems useful for the well-established sciences, especially physics and chemistry. However, mathematics and logic are *only* symbolic systems, and no magic inheres in either. Empirically they are abstract systems which are thus testable only when given some observational content. From this viewpoint, the scientific usefulness of such systems depends on their ability to produce empirical predictions. These predictions must then hold within the empirical events to which the mathematics or logic has been coordinated through more or less precise definitions.

Different types of mathematics are useful for different problems even within physics. For example, the complex number system is useful for problems in electric circuitry, and non-Euclidean geometry is useful for relativity theory. We saw in the previous chapter that the "eightfold way" required still another type. An inappropriate type of mathematics would lead only to confusion in any given case. The only way one can discover whether a given mathematics or logic or geometry is useful for testing a given empirical system is to try to set up definitions relating the symbolic system to the empirical system. These rules are rules for measurement. It may not be possible even to finish the definitional step. If it is, one can then see whether the predictions made on the basis of the permissible deductions within the symbolic system lead to empirical sense or empirical nonsense.

Psychology has not yet been as successful as the older sciences in its attempt to apply mathematical treatment to its problems. However, there are many recent books on mathematical developments in psychology, and the *Journal of Mathematical Psychology* is devoted exclusively to such developments. These developments indicate that strong efforts are being put forth and substantial progress is being made in this direction.

Before we can use mathematics, we must establish the required relations between the empirical object of study and the mathematics we wish to use. We call this process *quantification* when we are using the ordinary mathematics of real numbers. A more general word for the establishment of the required relationship to the elements of any mathematical system is *scaling*. Stevens (1951), among others, has discussed the different types of scaling. Psychology has usually had to be content with coordinating its subject matter to weaker kinds of systems than the mathematics of real numbers; the bulk of our subject matter is treated only with the language of the everyday world, and probabilities are assessed with statistics that may or may not be appropriate.

Does the subject matter of psychology lend itself to traditional measurement and traditional mathematics, or are some different symbolic systems necessary? It is too early in the history of our science to know the answers to these questions. On the one hand, Weitzenhoffer (1951) has suggested that psychologists persist in their attempts to measure in the traditional fashion, and Reese (1943) has recommended that we go ahead and use mathematics as though we were justified in doing so, being always careful to remember just what our measurements mean and assigning them no meaning beyond the operations performed. On the other hand, Stevens (1955) has stated that the weakness of psychology's measuring operations invalidates many of the statistical tests performed. Nevertheless, Burke (1963) has argued that our statistics are appropriate in many cases, despite the weakness of our measurements, and some studies (Box, 1953) do indicate that statistical tests are approximately correct in many cases, despite violations of the assumptions on which they are based (that is, the tests are "robust").

Stevens (1968), who has been an advocate of limiting statistical operations according to the measurement operations which produced the numbers, has extended and clarified the dialogue. He points out, as we have, that science is in the business of relating empirical structures to symbolic structures. Statistics can indeed proceed with its manipulations regardless of the character of the measurements which produced its numbers. The critical question is, however, what the effect of this will be on the whole "schemapiric" endeavor—that is, on the whole attempt to map empirical domains with symbolic domains. Burke has been arguing for maximum freedom for the statistician, and Stevens for maximum caution. In his 1968 article, Stevens argues for calculation rather than debate in order to find out how likely it is that an inappropriate statistic will lead to a deviant conclusion. (Burke would add that, paradoxically, there are cases in which an inappropriate statistic is less likely to lead to a deviant conclusion than is an appropriate statistic.) At any rate, Stevens seems willing to submit questions about measurement and its relationship to statistics to the judgment of time, and so are we.

In view of this rather confused state of affairs, we cannot say for sure that quantification is unusually difficult for psychology or even more difficult than for the other sciences; at the present stage, it *seems* more difficult. Certainly psychologists need to become more sophisticated in handling mathematics, measurement, and logic. Then they can use or develop appropriate systems, appropriate coordinations of existing systems to psychological problems, or both. Psychologists must concern themselves with the use of deductive systems before psychology will be a finished science. We cannot say whether enough empirical data are available to make extensive attempts of this kind profitable at present.

Some have argued against the desirability of quantification. These critics say that attempts at quantification tend to interfere with the meaningfulness of the phenomena in question. Others argue that the attempt to quantify is an instance of the tail wagging the dog, of the method unnecessarily restricting the problem. These critics hold that quantification can succeed only if the problem dealt with is so restricted as to lose all significance. None of these arguments can be positively refuted, but the usefulness of quantification in the other sciences argues against their ready acceptance. Quantification is a tool and is not an end in itself, and we believe that most psychologists recognize that fact clearly.

Quantification and mathematical treatment have at least two advantages: The statements are precise and clear, and the richness of deductive possibilities is greatly increased. The reasons for increased clarity are the explicit statement of rules for deduction within mathematical systems and the necessity, before measurement can occur, for rules of correspondence between events and the numerical symbols used. "Richness of deductive possibilities" can be illustrated by an example using psychoanalytic language. Suppose it is said that all neurosis is caused by the symbolic expression of intrapsychic conflicts. The implication of (deduction from?) this statement seems to be limited to the expectation that wherever we find neurosis, we shall also find the symbolic expression of intrapsychic conflicts. We would probably ask many other questions, answers to which are not supplied by the nonquantitative form of the statement. How much neurosis will we find for how much intrapsychic conflict? Are the measurement operations for neurosis different from those for intrapsychic conflicts? (If not, the statement is circular as well as limited.) What is the mathematical statement of the quantitative relationship between the two studies? (For example, if neurosis is symbolized by N and intrapsychic conflict by C, it could be that $N = C$, $N = \frac{1}{2}C^2$, or $N = \frac{1}{4}C^3$ + a constant.) If we have measurement operations and the functional relationship, for example, $N = \frac{1}{2}C^2$, we can make an infinite number of precise predictions, either from values of N to values of C or from values of C to values of N, depending upon which we measure first. Such deductive possibilities are certainly "rich."

Deutsch, Platt, and Senghass (1971) have concluded that two-thirds of all the major advances in social science between 1900 and 1965 involved a quantitative component. Psychology, which was among the sciences considered, was a leader in contributions. If these authors have evaluated the situation correctly, there can be no doubt that quantification has been profitable *already* in psychology, and one cannot reasonably expect anything other than ever-increasing profit from the endeavor as psychologists increasingly equip themselves to engage in it.

Subjectivism

Psychology involves the study of living organisms, often people. It seems to be more difficult to achieve the unbiased scientific attitude toward this subject matter than toward any other. The medical student studying anatomy doubtless has certain qualms when he pulls his first cadaver out of the formaldehyde, and part of this qualm doubtless comes from the realization that the object of his investigation and dissection bears a marked similarity to himself. Psychology has had some difficulties on the same score; as the analysts would say, there have been resistances to the acceptance of certain ideas, among them the basic one that man's behavior can be studied scientifically—especially if the man is oneself.

Beyond this, the psychologist himself has difficulty in achieving objectivity toward his field. Since psychologists are people, they have a tendency to anthropomorphize. The objects of psychological study seem especially receptive objects for the projection of our own ideas, even though sober evidence may be lacking. The call of common sense, too, is particularly strident when we feel that we understand humankind simply by virtue of being human. Yet the facts may be exactly otherwise; we might achieve undreamed-of insights were we but Martians studying man in the cool light of an earth day.

Complexity

There are certain senses in which the subject matter of psychology seems to be more complex than that of many sciences. From a reductionistic point of view, for example, one would have to understand much of chemistry in order to understand the nature of nerve transmission, which people think one would have to understand before one could understand behavior completely. However, the biologist might argue that his field is equally complex on this score, and the sociologist might argue that his field is even more complex, since an understanding of individuals would presumably be necessary before one could understand social behavior.

Another, and perhaps more fundamental, way in which complexity can be defined is in terms of the number of interacting variables that are effective in the determination of some consequence. Certainly behavior appears to be influenced by a large number of such variables. But the same thing can be said of many other sciences, and how many important variables operate in behavior determination remains to be discovered.

The degree of complexity a subject matter is judged to have may depend upon the stage of development of the science that deals with that subject matter. At the beginning, the subject matter may look simple. As some facts are gathered, however, problems develop, and the field begins to look complex. The development of special instrumentation may reveal new complexities even as it solves old puzzles; for example, the microscope literally brought to light a bewildering array of microscopic life, at the same time that it made diseases comprehensible. In physiological psychology, equipment to record bioelectrical potentials has played a similar role. As theories are developed, they play a similar role in relation to complexity. At first, the theory seems to solve problems, though it suggests additional observations for its own evaluation. The initially reduced complexity seems always to return as soon as some disconfirmatory observations are made. The degree of manifest complexity may fluctuate, in this way returning to the high side after having seemed to be lower for a while. At present, psychology seems to be in the process of immersing itself in a complex welter of facts, and this may account for its apparent complexity.

Thus, the common argument that the subject matter of psychology is more complex than that of the other sciences does not rest on perfectly firm ground. Nonetheless, psychologists agree that the subject matter is sufficiently complex for them, in many instances downright confusing. Perhaps another 100 years of study will give a better indication of relative complexity. In our present state of ignorance, the argument that many of psychology's difficulties can be explained in this way is appealing.

Our general thesis throughout has been that the criteria that apply to science in general also apply to psychology. The discussion of problems that seem to be accentuated because of the nature of the subject matter is not to be construed as meaning that psychology is in these respects apart from science. It follows that psychology shares the general problems and will find its special solutions as the other sciences have done. Perhaps the only problem which cannot be circumvented is that science can advance only through work, and work takes time.

Psychology has not existed long enough to solve its problems. The weaknesses that we shall see in its systems and theories exist partially for that reason.

SUMMARY AND CONCLUSIONS

Several scientific ideas had to develop within science before psychology could emerge. Prominent among these were the following propositions: that explanation of an event should be sought within the same system as the one within which the event occurred, that observation is the arbiter of scientific truth, and that man is a part of the natural order. It follows that man's behavior can be studied scientifically to determine the laws governing that behavior.

Certain problems were willed to psychology because of its immediate prehistory within science and philosophy. Among them were relating the mental and physical aspects of man, explaining the physiology of perception and the contents of perception, determining the basis for description of the personal equation, and analyzing individual differences and heredity. The effects of these problems upon experimental psychology as it was conceived by its founder, Wilhelm Wundt, have been examined.

The subject matter of modern psychology has been defined broadly. The intensification of certain scientific problems as a result of the nature of the subject matter has been pointed out: the difficulty of controlling conditions is enhanced, the problem of quantification is rendered more difficult, the subject matter disposes the psychologist toward subjectivism, and the subject matter is complex. These problems are not unique to psychology, but they seem to be exaggerated there.

Further Readings

For the general historical background of psychology, the student can consult Boring's *History of experimental psychology* (1950) or Murphy's *Historical introduction to modern psychology* (1949). The five volumes of autobiographical material edited by Murchison (1930-1936), by Boring et al. (1952), and by Boring and Lindzey (1967) are extremely valuable in providing insight into some of the personal factors, ordinarily out of sight or in the background, in the careers of many historically important men in the field. *A source book in the history of psychology* (1965) provides selected classics ranging from Aristotle to McDougall for the student who likes his history firsthand. For a general orientation to the history of science, the following classic works may be recommended: Conant's *On understanding science: A historical approach* (1947) and *Harvard case histories in experimental science* (1957); Butterfield's *Origins of modern science: 1300-1800* (1957); and Sarton's *Guide to the history of science* (1952). A variety of works in the philosophy of science are available for the reader who wants to delve into this area. Particularly relevant to the mind-body issue is *Concepts, theories, and the mind-body problem*, edited by Feigl, Scriven, and Maxwell (1958) and published as Volume 2 in the *Minnesota studies in the philosophy of science*. Volume 1 in that series, edited by Feigl and Scriven (1956) and entitled *The foundations of science and the concepts of psychology and psychoanalysis*, also contains many informative papers. Feigl and Maxwell's *Current issues in the philosophy of science* (1961) contains papers and rebuttals read at symposia in the 1959 meetings of the American Association for the Advancement of Science. Several books of readings in this field are available, for example, Danto and Morgenbesser's *Philosophy of science: A reader* (1960); P. P. Wiener's *Readings in philosophy of science* (1953), Feigl and Sellars' *Readings in philosophical analysis* (1949); and Feigl and Brodbeck's *Readings in the philosophy of science* (1953). The best introduction to the problems of mathematics, measurement, and their relationship to statistics can probably be gained by reading Stevens's chapter entitled "Mathematics, measurement, and psychophysics," in his *Handbook of experimental psychology* (1951); Burke's "Measurement scales and statistical models," which appears in Marx's *Theories in contemporary psychology* (1963), should be read to round out the picture.

3 Systems and Theories

Our intent in this chapter is to set the stage for a critical evaluation of systems and theories. Terms will be defined, the nature of systems and theories will be outlined, and some requirements will be proposed. Though many of the issues raised will be controversial, we hope to provide a background that will make the controversies meaningful.

DEFINITIONS OF BASIC TERMS

Definition

Webster's Third New International Dictionary gives the following as one meaning of the word *define*: to "determine with precision or exhibit clearly the boundaries of . . . to make distinct in outline or features." This definition of *define* is in perfect agreement with a geometric representation of the classification process given by Sebestyen (1962). Since it seems that this kind of classification procedure is a formalization of the usual less formal, more intuitive approach to definition, we shall describe a simple version of what classification is. We think that substantial gains to understanding may come from this formal approach.

Simple Geometric Representation. Sebestyen's procedure starts with a simple geometric representation. Membership in a class is determined by noting whether a particular event to be classified falls within a geometric region. If there are only two "characteristics" or "measures" of objects considered, the geometric representation can be in two dimensions, and the defining regions can be areas in two-dimensional space, one dimension for each characteristic under consideration. Figure 3-1 is an abstract representation of a classification space with two regions outlined, one for each of two classes. Each class is centered on a point which represents the class best. Note that the "best," or "prototypical," example of a member of class 2 has a value of 2 on characteristic 1 and a value of 2.5 on characteristic 2. Anything which falls within the range of 1 to 3 on characteristic 1

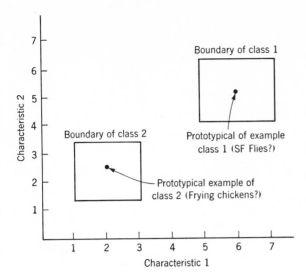

Fig. 3-1 A classification scheme which formalizes the properties of definitions.

and within the range of 1.5 to 2.5 on characteristic 2 is "defined" to be within class 2. Class 1 is defined within the same "classification space," but differs in definition.

If characteristic 1 were number of legs and characteristic 2 were number of pounds, then class 2 would include frying chickens. Baby monkeys might also fit. The reader may think of other interesting examples. Class 1 is more difficult to populate. Science-fiction flies come to mind; 5- or 6-pound six-leggers are (we think fortunately) rare among terrestrial creatures.

In setting up a definition, the definer is free to use whatever characteristics he chooses. This type of formalization is not limited to two characteristics; an indefinite number of characteristics can be accommodated. The two-dimensional geometric representation can handle only two characteristics; for three characteristics, three-dimensional space can be used. The class definition will be represented by a volume within the three-dimensional space. If the representation of the element in question, within the character space, falls within the volume, it is a member of the class. If more than three characteristics are used, the situation must be represented algebraically rather than geometrically.

Algebraic Representation. The algebraic representation of the specific example already given would be as follows. The relevant characteristics are number of legs and weight in pounds, in that order. The prototypical example of class 1 would be written (6,5); the prototypical example of class 2 would be written (2, 2.5). The class definition for class 1 would be $(5 < C_1 < 7; 4 < C_2 < 6)$. This means simply that any object for which characteristic 1 is between 5 and 7 and for which characteristic 2 is between 4 and 6 is within class 1. Definitions which depend on

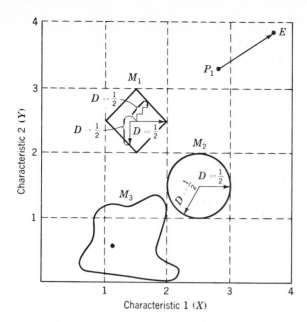

Fig. 3-2 Illustrations of classes defined by distance measures.

any number of characteristics can be handled in approximately this way, simply by increasing the number of characteristics for which a prototypical number and limits are stated.

A more economical method for stating class limits, which may be used in many cases, involves establishing a boundary on each class by stating a "distance" from the prototypical element within which an element to be classified may be considered a member of the class. Figure 3-2 illustrates the relevant concepts. In the upper right-hand corner are two points connected by a line; the line is the distance between the two points P_1 and E. P_1 represents the prototypical value for some class. E represents an element whose distance from the prototypical point is to be determined. We ordinarily think of distance as being defined in the Euclidean way implied by drawing the straight line. The Euclidean definition of the distance between two points in a two-dimensional space is the square root of the sum of the squares of differences between the coordinates, that is, $D_E = \sqrt{(X_1 - X_2)^2 + (Y_1 - Y_2)^2}$. Here the coordinates of the first point are X_1, Y_1, and the coordinates of the second point are X_2, Y_2. The class labeled M_2 is a class defined by using the Euclidean distance measure; all points lying within the circle of points one-half unit away from the prototypical point are defined to be within the class.

The class labeled M_1 is defined by using a different definition of distance. The distance is defined as the sum of the absolute differences, on each individual dimension, between the prototypical point and any point under examination; in this case, $D_{CB} = |X_1 - X_2| + |Y_1 - Y_2|$. This distance has been called the *city-block distance* because it is like the distance one has to go if one must travel on city streets, rather than being able to "cut across." If someone lives one block north of you and one block west of you, he is two blocks away in practice, and this is exactly what the city-block definition of distance would tell us. The straight-line (Euclidean) distance would be the square root of 2, a little over 1.4 units.

Either definition of distance is easily extended to any number of dimensions; one simply has to work with an additional *difference* for each additional *dimension*. If, for example, one lived in one of the vertical cities that we may inhabit in the future, it would become habitual to compute city-block distances in three dimensions, summing the north-south, east-west, *and* vertical distances from point to point. In describing things other than physical position, it may be helpful to use more than three dimensions, with the general procedure for determining distance remaining exactly the same.

Any definition of distance determines its own characteristic set of points that are equidistant from a given point. The Euclidean distance definition makes the points that lie on a circle with the given point as center equidistant from that center; thus all points within a circle of a given radius from a prototypical point would belong to a class, according to a Euclidean definition. Points equidistant from a prototypical point lie on a diamond, however, according to a city-block definition of distance! This is illustrated for the case of class M_1 in Figure 3-2.

Arbitrary Features of Definitions. Careful thought about this method of formalizing definition, or class membership, reveals that definitions are arbitrary in several respects. First, there is freedom to choose whatever defining characteristics one wishes to include. Second, there is freedom to choose any available method for establishing boundaries to classes. One could, for example, draw a freehand figure around the prototypical point, as illustrated by M_3 in Figure 3-2. Even if a distance measure is used, there is freedom to define distance in any of several ways. We have not discussed more complex ways to define distance, but several are available (and it should be clear that some dimensions can be weighted more heavily than others by multiplying "more important" dimensions by some constant). Third, the boundaries on the class can be made very exclusive (by including only those elements which are very close to the prototypical point) or very inclusive (by including elements a greater distance away). Definitions can be changed by changing any of the above properties. It is often the case that an event to be classified falls within the limits of more than one class. One then might want to construct a "cleaner" definitional scheme for that context.

Illustrations of Definitional Problems. Whittaker (1969) furnishes an interesting example of such an attempt at definitional and classificatory sharpening. Most of us have asked the question "Animal, vegetable, or mineral?" so many times that the classification of living things into plants and animals seems almost a fact of nature rather than a classification scheme imposed by man.

Whittaker, however, finds the definitions of plants and animals inadequate to determine clearly the class membership of some living things. The prevailing definitional scheme is also inadequate to reflect what is known or suspected about the evolutionary relationships between families. He considers a four-category classification system, but prefers a five-way system, which he believes better corrects the above deficiencies. Whittaker (1969) makes his definitional bases quite explicit: "A five-way kingdom system is proposed here, based both on levels of organization and on types of organization as evolved in relation to three principal means of nutrition —photosynthesis, absorption, and ingestion" (p. 158). Whittaker also explicitly recognizes the fact that definitions are not, despite superficial appearances, completely arbitrary. He states (1969): "Revised broad classifications deserve wide consideration, for they may better express major relationships in the living world and more effectively classify the phyla than the two-kingdom system" (p. 158).

Willems and Raush (1969, p. 47) provide an example which is of more direct relevance to psychology and which happens to use the same kind of definitional formalization we are proposing here. A "space" is established for describing research activities. The two dimensions which establish the space are the degree of manipulation of antecedent conditions by the experimenter and the degree of imposition of units on the subject matter by the investigator. It is suggested that research low on both dimensions is prototypical of naturalistic research and that research high on both dimensions is experimental research. Once the space is established, it becomes obvious that research may also be intermediate on either or both dimensions, or it may be low on one dimension and high on the other. This fact provides an illustration of the gains that sometimes follow the systematic, formal specification of what we are "really" doing; in the present case, new possibilities are nearly forced to our attention by the formal framework.

Summary. Let us summarize our discussion of definition: (1) A geometric description of classification—which is intimately related to definition—is general and precise and therefore has advantages over a purely verbal description of definition. (2) Both the dimensions of description and the borderlines of the classes defined within these dimensions can be chosen arbitrarily, but some definitions will turn out to be better than others because they make better theory possible, provide for cleaner distinctions between classes, or direct attention to more useful facets of the things defined. (3) Definitions are flexible, not permanent; those which play a role in useful laws will last longer than those which do not. (4) There is therefore an intimate but often overlooked relationship between definition and theory. Definitions are very important and deserve more emphasis than they usually receive.

Terms: Primitive and Defined

Within theories and systems, two kinds of terms will occur: *defined terms*, which are completely expressible within the framework of a given system, and *primitive terms*, which are not (see Achinstein, 1968, pp. 68-69). A primitive term may be connected (by semantic rules) to something which is more familiar and which is external to the theory. That is, it may be defined by pointing to some observable operation, event, or object. In some cases, primitive terms are left undefined.

Hull's system (Hilgard & Bower, 1966) is one of the better-known attempts at axiomatization in psychology. One of his postulates states that the relationship between habit strength ($_sH_r$) and number of trials (N) is

$$_sH_r = 100(1 - 10^{-iN})$$

$_sH_r$, then, is defined in terms of N. From the context of the preceding discussion, it can be seen that habit strength, as a term in Hull's system, takes its definition from number of trials, which is also a part of the system (i is a constant defined by Hull). However, number of trials is defined on the basis of a reading on a counter, a tally on a worksheet, or a quantity determined by some other appropriate measuring device, which is *not* part of the Hullian system. N, then, is a primitive term.

Many theories are not as structurally explicit as Hull's, making it difficult to ascertain which theoretical terms are primitive and which are defined. Psychoanalytic theory is an example of this; Freud did not clarify the relationships between many of his terms, so that those which are expressible completely within his system are not always distinguishable from those which are not.

There is no logical hindrance to defining any term of a theory by relating it to terms or events outside the theory. If a term is defined externally, we may wish to distinguish between the meaning of the term as defined externally and its meaning as defined internally. In the case of variables, the externally defined variable might be called an *experimental variable*, and the theoretically defined variable might be called a *theoretical variable*. If a theory is "correct," the value determined through the theoretical definition will be the same as the value determined by making empirical observations. The primitive term, having no theoretical definition, can have at most an external definition. It may simply be left undefined. Scientists prefer theories with the fewest possible undefined terms, but a theory may be acceptable provided every term makes at least indirect contact with empirical observations.

Constructs

A construct is a special kind of concept. It is less simple than a concept like "man" or "house" or "boat." These are named correctly because they, as objects, share with other members of the class the properties which give them membership (see our discussion of definition). Some concepts may be more complex than the examples above, and constructs are always more complex. Constructs represent relationships between objects or events. Common psychological constructs such as "anxiety," "fear," and "habit" are in this respect similar to more general constructs like "patriotism," "school spirit," and "justice." Thus, responses alone are insufficient to define the concept of fear or habit; some reference to the stimulus situation as well as to the response situation must be given. In defining habit, we must know the probability that a certain response will occur to a given stimulus situation, not just that a response has occurred. Constructs, therefore, are a subclass of concepts, including some of the more complex concepts. English and English say (1958): "As compared with concept, a construct is a planfully designed model, with full awareness of the relationships between the data and the model" (p. 116). However, these authors point out that the distinction between the two terms seems to be a matter of degree.

Constructs are useful in summarizing relationships succinctly, and they may also be helpful in generalizing from some sets of observed relationships to other, as yet unobserved sets. However, many difficulties in psychology stem from a failure to define constructs unambiguously. The development of simpler and more empirically meaningful constructs is an important objective of contemporary psychology. This is the area in which the simple, basic proposition of the operationist—that we should make clear the empirical referents of our complex terms—has the most to offer.

MacCorquodale and Meehl (1948) made a much-cited distinction between two "kinds" of constructs: hypothetical constructs and intervening variables. Constructs vary along several dimensions, but the MacCorquodale and Meehl distinction emphasized one important dimension more than the others. Their emphasis was on the degree to which a construct is operationally clear in meaning. The intervening variable, as they used the term, is a construct with a clear, limited, operational meaning. The hypothetical construct has "excess meaning" in the sense that it has meanings beyond those justified by its operational definition. An example of such excess meaning would be the assumption that some particular physiological changes underlie the behavioral changes that occur as habit strength increases. Another kind of excess meaning would be the kind brought to a construct by its role in a deductive system (theory or model).

Although MacCorquodale and Meehl were arguing for intervening variables and against hypothetical constructs, it seems to us that both kinds of constructs are important. One cannot give a blanket endorsement of either type, or a blanket condemnation of either type. The initial negative attitude toward hypothetical constructs probably came about because some horrible examples of this type had no clear operational meaning, no clear place in a formal theory, no physiological meaning, and hence no useful role to play in science. However, constructs with sound operational meaning, a clear theoretical definition, and potential physiological meaning would seem to be ideal—more interesting than concepts whose meaning is exhausted by the observations already made. If we limited ourselves to constructs of this latter type, we would need to establish a new construct for every new set of operations. Scientists do not, because they could not, proceed in this way. Such "exhausted" constructs have never been used, and we discuss them only as a hypothetical pure case. We are *not* against the clear identification of the source and operational meaning of constructs. We do, however, believe that constructs are fruitful only when they are embedded in a larger theoretical context.

Postulates

This term has two major usages. First, it is used to refer to a fundamental assumption which is not to be directly or intentionally tested. The assumption may be essential to the pursuit of science, for example, the assumption that the world is consistently orderly and that the order is discoverable by man. The assumption may be of more restricted importance, as in the case of the early behavioristic assumption that all behavior can be analyzed into stimulus-response relationships. As is true of this example, most such postulates are informal, natural-language statements. It is generally held that such assumptions, which are often on a philosophical level, should be as few, simple, and carefully set forth as possible.

The second type of postulate is a theoretical proposition which is intended to be more directly tested by means of empirical work. A set of these propositions, in the case of a deductive theory, could be used within a given logical framework to yield further propositions implied by the original set. The further propositions (theorems) derived will depend upon the rules for deduction as well as upon the original statements. Within mathematics or logic, theorems are "true" or "valid" by definition, given the original statements and the rules for deduction. Asking whether a theorem which follows from the postulates and rules for deduction is true is exactly like asking whether a chess move that follows from the rules is true. The answer is "yes" to both in the sense that the theorem and the move followed from the rules. Both the theorem and the move might be silly, useless, or false as descriptions of some empirical state of affairs.

Within science, theorems must at some stage make statements about empirical observations if they are to have any scientific utility. The postulates of a system are thus tested indirectly by observing the concurrence or lack of it between theorems and observations. The best example of an extensive and highly formalized set of postulates within psychology is afforded by the work of Hull (1943, 1951, 1952; Hull, Hovland, Ross, Hall, Perkins, & Fitch, 1940), which is described in Chapter 10. His system suffered from logical weaknesses not shared by more recent, less extensive efforts; examples of these latter systems will also be touched on in Chapters 10 and 13.

Hypotheses

Experimental. The hypothesis is a guess about the explanation of some natural phenomenon. Its elaboration may take many forms. One important dimension along which hypotheses vary is their degree of specificity. The most specific hypotheses apply to a particular situation. The best example is the experimental hypothesis, which is the particular prediction that is made about the outcome of an experiment. Such particular hypotheses may come from a more general theoretical framework or from more general hypotheses.

Public versus Private. In one form or another, the hypothesis plays a central role in the advance of science. Two different types of hypotheses, with quite different roles, should be carefully distinguished. These are what we shall call *public* and *private* hypotheses. Public hypotheses are those which have been formally explicated and publicly advanced, usually in published form. Private hypotheses are those which have been entertained by some investigator or thinker, but have not been publicly expressed.

Although it is the public, or formally explicated, hypothesis that receives most of our attention, a little reflection quickly reveals the more pervasive nature of the private hypothesis. For every public hypothesis there are uncounted numbers of private hypotheses. In scientific thinking these undergo almost constant revision, and the point at which they are made public varies with the investigator and as a result of many situational factors. Charles Darwin, for example, worked on his private hypotheses about the theory of evolution for more than twenty years before the appearance of a competitive manuscript containing the same basic idea stimulated him to make his hypotheses public. Had Wallace's manuscript not come into his hands, there is no way of knowing how long the eccentric Darwin might have held his hypotheses to himself. The unpublished hypothesis is in the somewhat peculiar position of being critical to scientific progress, but worthless in itself. For science to move ahead, it is, indeed, eventually a matter of "publish or perish," when hypotheses are being considered.

We may think of the mass of all scientific hypotheses as being like an iceberg. It is only the top one-tenth (or much less) of the total thought that is open to the criticism and empirical attack of the scientific public. Publication of a hypothesis invites such attack, and it is only through such attack that effective scientific evaluation can be made. Unfortunately, psychologists do not always recognize that it is necessary to publicize their hypotheses in this way. Public formalization of a hypothesis for empirical attack does not require the investigator to stop thinking and revising his hypotheses, but it is a necessary step if the product of his thinking is to be tested by others.

Conscious versus Unconscious. Another distinction can be made between conscious and unconscious hypotheses. Sidman (1960) argues that many significant experiments are done to satisfy simple wonderment, as it might be expressed in "I wonder what would happen if . . . ." The implication is that hypotheses need not precede experimentation. Others might argue that an unconscious hypothesis is being tested and that the hypothesis can be inferred from the behavior of the investigator. We cannot settle this disagreement and shall state only that it seems safe to say that some investigators believe strongly in formulating hypotheses, and others do not.

The source of hypotheses—and why some persons are so much better than others at producing them—is a fascinating problem. Little progress has been made to date toward its solution. About all we can say is that as a person becomes more and more thoroughly immersed in his subject matter, he tends to develop more and better ideas. More specific rules of thumb for developing effective scientific ideas await future investigations.

Laws

A scientific law is generally held to be a well-established empirical relationship; for example, under certain conditions, water freezes at 32°F. Laws constitute the anchorage points for theories, and sometimes the backbone of the theory itself. Laws are generalizations of an empirical sort that have the greatest degree of factualness. The science of physics has developed a large number of lawful relationships. Many observers believe that psychology must develop a larger number of such laws before it can develop effective theory.

The term *law* is also used to refer to an especially well-established theoretical proposition. The proposition becomes well established because it successfully plays its part in the derivation of predictions which are empirically tested. It is often hard to draw the line between the two kinds of usage of the word *law*. The step from the concrete observation to its verbal statement always involves some degree of abstraction. There is thus no purely empirical law in the strictest sense of the word. On the other hand, the most abstract proposition may rest on some kind of informal observation of nature by the proponent of the proposition. In spite of the difficulty of making this distinction, we should recognize the dimensions of abstractness and of generality when speaking of scientific laws.

THE NATURE OF SYSTEMS

Characteristics of Systems

Part 2 of this book consists of descriptions and discussions of psychological systems; in this section we are discussing some of the general characteristics of systems. Psychological systems are closely related to those of philosophy. One important similarity is that both philosophers and psychological systematists tend to give great scope to their systems; a system is thus a set of very general statements. McGeoch (1933) writes about systems as they might ideally be. His definition of a system makes them sound highly desirable: "By the term 'psychological system' is implied a coherent and inclusive, yet flexible, organization and interpretation of the facts and special theories of the subject" (p. 2).

This definition makes it clear that a system is a large order. It is inclusive and organizes theories, which themselves possess generality. The definition leaves a good deal of room for ambiguity; words like *coherent, flexible, organization,* and *interpretation* come from the lay language and are not themselves clearly defined. These words seem to be as much an attempt to sell systems as to define what they are.

According to McGeoch, we cannot have systems until we have facts and theories, since systems are organizations of these prior elements. We have few real theories in psychology, in the strict sense of the term; most psychological theories are better viewed as programs or as informal or preliminary theories. One can thus question whether psychology has ever had a system in McGeoch's sense of that word. But certainly there have been plenty of systems of some kind.

Edna Heidbreder, one of McGeoch's contemporaries and fellow psychologists, said (1933): "Psychology, especially in the United States, has risked everything on being science; and science on principle refrains from speculation that is not permeated and stabilized by fact. Yet there is not enough fact in the whole science of psychology to make a single solid system" (p. 3). We shall see that her statement is still true today.

Functions of Systems

What, then, was the function of the systems that did exist? If they did not have the facts that Heidbreder said science requires or the predictive power implied by McGeoch's definition, what power did they have? Heidbreder (1933, p. 9) felt that they had a sort of comforting power; in the absence of real knowledge, they served in its place. We would put it in a somewhat different way. A theory, or a *finished* system of the kind McGeoch described, would tell a scientist or a layman what to expect as a result of any given manipulation of the subject matter of psychology; it would provide for the prediction, and perhaps for the manipulation, of the events within the scope of the system. According to this usage, a system would be a supertheory. Unfortunately, there is a time in the development of any science when the information for such prediction and manipulation is simply not available. The chief problem then is to *direct the scientist in his study of the subject matter* so that his efforts will be most efficiently used to further knowledge. When this is the state of affairs, a system for directing his efforts tends to appear. Thus, one aspect of the philosophy of science is an attempt to describe the scientific process as it is and ought to be and thereby to direct scientists in general in what they should do. A system of psychology does the same thing partially, except that it is concerned with psychologists rather than with scientists in general. Such systems contain statements about what the subject matter in question is or ought to be. They tell the psychologist what problems ought to be studied, by providing a purpose for the scientists. They tell him how he ought to go about studying the suggested problems. These directive statements, however, are not couched in a form which makes their functions obvious. They are not directed to the scientist in the form of orders, and yet his behavior is influenced by them.

We can make this last point by rephrasing some of the key contentions of some of psychology's systems in a form which makes their influence more obvious:

Structuralism. As psychologists you ought to study the contents of consciousness through the method of introspection.

Behaviorism. You ought to study stimulus-response connections through strictly objective methods.

Gestalt psychology. You can arrive at useful formulations only through the consideration of large units of both stimulus and response; you should study configurations or fields.

Functionalism. Prime concerns of psychology should be the study of the function of behavior in adapting to the environment and the formulation of mathematical functions relating behavior to antecedent variables.

Associationism. The psychologist should study the principles of association of ideas (or of words or stimulus-response connections), analyzing complex events into simpler ones.

Psychoanalysis. The core of psychology is motivation, much of which is unconscious and must be studied through its manifestations in dreams, errors, symptoms, or free association.

There is a continuing interplay between the systematic philosophical prescriptions of a particular school and its empirical findings. Gestalt psychology, for example, became a formal school after particular findings had been interpreted in a unique way by its founders. The empirical, theoretical, and systematic statements tend to be stirred together, and the amalgam then is the system. We tend to use the words *school* and *system* almost interchangeably, but the word *school* implies people, and the word *system* implies their findings and beliefs (see the Glossary).

A word which applies roughly to the directive or superordinate aspects of a system is *metatheory.* A metatheory in general is a set of methodological considerations used in constructing or evaluating a theory; it is, so to speak, a theory about theory. A metatheory differs from a psychological system in being more highly formalized. A loose, informal metatheory can usually be sifted out of a school or system, but there will be a large remainder of empirical and philosophical statements.

Proposed Prescriptions for Psychology

R. I. Watson (1967) has taken a position similar to the one outlined above. He proposes a set of prescriptive, directive dimensions which he thinks are critical for systematic psychology. A system of psychology can be described by checking its position on each of the eighteen dimensions listed by Watson. The eighteen dimensions then constitute an eighteen-dimensional space like the definitional spaces discussed earlier in this chapter. The list of dimensions given below is taken from Watson (1967, pp. 436-437):

THE PRESCRIPTIONS OF PSYCHOLOGY ARRANGED IN CONTRASTING PAIRS

Conscious mentalism-Unconscious mentalism (emphasis on awareness of mental structure or activity—unawareness).

Contentual objectivism-Contentual subjectivism (psychological data viewed as behavior of individual—as mental structure or activity of individual).

Determinism-Indeterminism (human events completely explicable in terms of antecedents—not completely so explicable).

Empiricism-Rationalism (major, it not exclusive source of knowledge is experience—is reason).

Functionalism-Structuralism (psychological categories are activities—are contents).

Inductivism-Deductivism (investigations begun with facts or observations—with assumed established truths).

Mechanism-Vitalism (activities of living beings completely explicable by physiochemical constituents—not so explicable).

Methodological objectivism-Methodological subjectivism (use of methods open to verification by another competent observer—not so open).

Molecularism-Molarism (psychological data most aptly described in terms of relatively small units—relatively large units).

Monism-Dualism (fundamental principle or entity in universe is of one kind—is of two kinds, mind and matter).

Naturalism-Supernaturalism (nature requires for its operation and explanation only principles found within it—requires transcendent guidance as well).

Nomotheticism-Idiographicism (emphasis upon discovering general laws—upon explaining particular events or individuals).

Peripheralism-Centralism (stress upon psychological events taking place at periphery of body—within the body).

Purism-Utilitarianism (seeking of knowledge for its own sake—for its usefulness in other activities).

Quantitativism-Qualitativism (stress upon knowledge which is countable or measurable—upon that which is different in kind or essence).

Rationalism-Irrationalism (emphasis upon data supposed to follow dictates of good sense and intellect—intrusion or domination of emotive and conative factors upon intellectual processes).

Staticism-Developmentalism (emphasis upon cross-sectional view—upon changes with time).

Staticism-Dynamicism (emphasis upon enduring aspects—upon change and factors making for change).

Any list like Watson's is bound to have some component of arbitrariness, and the dimensions are not necessarily independent of one another. Nevertheless, this list represents a thoughtful analysis by one student of psychological systems, and it should help to direct the attention of other students to some of the important issues. As with any dimensions, it is of interest to know whether the values of psychological systems on these dimensions can be judged reliably by persons presumed to be somewhat familiar with the systems and with the dimensions.

In order to make a rough assessment of the reliability of judgment of values on these dimensions, twenty-three graduate students in a course in advanced systematic psychology were asked to rate the six systems treated in this book on each of Watson's eighteen dimensions. A five-point scale was used for the ratings. The number 1 represented the extreme left-hand position on a dimension, while 5 indicated the extreme right. For example, if psychoanalysis were rated on the staticism-dynamicism dimension as being *extremely* dynamic, it would be assigned a 5. The students also chose and ranked the three dimensions thought to be most heavily emphasized by each school. Most students might be expected to choose

TABLE 3-1   Standard Deviations of Twenty-three Student Judgments of Six Psychological Systems on Each of Watson's Eighteen Prescriptive Dimensions

Watson's Dimensions	Systems					
	Associa-tionism	Struc-turalism	Func-tionalism	Behav-iorism	Gestalt theory	Psycho-analysis
Mentalism: conscious versus unconscious	0.84	0.62	0.70	1.29	1.10	0.95
Content: objective versus subjective	1.05	1.11	0.72	1.12	0.75	1.27
Determinism-indeterminism	0.86	0.85	1.08	0.94	1.00	1.22
Empiricism-rationalism	0.88	0.99	0.83	0.80	0.87	1.07
Functionalism-struc-turalism	1.12	1.06	0.83	0.94	0.93	0.71
Inductivism-deductivism	0.63	1.23	0.85	0.16	0.79	1.25
Mechanism-vitalism	1.05	1.18	0.57	1.19	0.66	1.26
Methods: objectivism versus subjectivism	1.25	1.23	0.94	0.91	1.17	1.13
Molecularism-molarism	0.57	1.25	0.94	1.17	1.11	1.10
Monism-dualism	0.68	1.01	1.01	0.68	0.54	0.77
Naturalism-supernatu-ralism	0.74	1.08	0.70	0.13	1.01	1.26
Nomotheticism-idiograph-icism	1.05	1.25	0.87	1.15	1.18	1.45
Peripheralism-centralism	1.03	0.94	0.79	0.39	0.73	0.52
Purism-utilitarianism	0.87	1.16	0.63	0.37	0.41	0.52
Quantitativism-qualitativism	1.03	0.58	0.82	0.95	0.83	0.55
Rationalism-irrationalism	1.00	0.81	0.90	1.00	0.93	1.61
Staticism-developmentalism	1.04	1.17	1.10	0.99	1.24	1.35
Staticism-dynamicism	1.01	0.80	0.72	1.10	1.25	1.19

methodological objectivism-methodological subjectivism as one of the dimensions most heavily emphasized by the behavioristic school.

Although the instructions for rating did not require it, most of the students used only whole numbers—1, 2, 3, 4, or 5. If students knew absolutely nothing about the positions of the systems on the dimensions and assigned the numbers with equal probability, the standard deviation of the numbers so assigned would be 1.414. If the standard deviation of the numbers actually assigned is less than this, it means that the students responded on the basis of some information they had about the dimensions. Table 3-1 shows that the standard deviation of the judgments of the twenty-three students was nearly always below what would be expected on the basis of random assignment of the values, although there were some exceptions.

TABLE 3-2 Mean Judgments by Twenty-three Students and the Authors of the Positions of Six Psychological Systems on Each of Watson's Eighteen Prescriptive Dimensions

Watson's Dimensions	Associationism		Structuralism		Functionalism		Behaviorism		Gestalt Theory		Psychoanalysis	
	Students	Authors	Students	Authors	Students	Authors	Students	Authors	Students	Authors	Students	Authors
Mentalism: conscious versus unconscious	2.9	2.2	1.2	1.2	2.4	2.5	3.3	4.4	2.7	2.3	4.4	4.8
Content: objective versus subjective	2.3	3.2	4.1	4.9	2.3	2.1	1.6	1.1	3.8	3.8	4.1	4.2
Determinism-indeterminism	2.0	1.3	2.8	2.2	2.9	2.2	1.4	1.1	3.0	2.2	1.9	1.1
Empiricism-rationalism	1.8	1.1	1.7	1.7	2.6	2.2	1.4	1.3	3.0	3.2	2.8	3.6
Functionalism-structuralism	2.6	2.4	4.5	4.8	1.4	1.1	1.9	1.5	3.5	3.7	3.7	3.1
Inductivism-deductivism	2.3	1.5	2.6	3.2	1.9	1.9	1.7	1.7	3.4	4.1	3.4	4.3
Mechanism-vitalism	2.5	1.4	2.9	2.0	2.8	3.0	1.4	1.1	2.8	2.9	3.4	2.3
Methods: objectivism versus subjectivism	1.5	1.9	3.0	5.0	2.4	2.0	1.7	1.1	3.8	3.7	4.2	4.6
Molecularism-molarism	1.9	1.2	1.7	1.6	3.3	3.2	1.9	1.3	4.6	4.8	4.2	3.3
Monism-dualism	2.7	3.3	3.6	4.6	2.6	4.1	1.1	1.1	3.6	4.1	3.5	4.2
Naturalism-supernaturalism	1.5	2.3	2.1	1.6	1.8	1.4	1.1	1.1	2.2	2.4	2.4	1.9
Nomotheticism-idiographicism	2.4	1.3	2.6	1.2	3.2	2.9	2.3	1.0	2.6	4.1	3.3	3.1
Peripheralism-centralism	1.8	2.5	3.6	4.4	2.7	2.2	1.2	1.1	3.9	4.7	4.4	4.6
Purism-utilitarianism	3.6	1.6	1.4	1.1	4.2	4.9	3.5	3.2	2.6	2.2	4.1	4.6
Quantitativism-qualitativism	1.8	1.9	3.4	3.2	2.6	2.1	1.2	1.6	4.1	4.7	4.7	4.6
Rationalism-irrationalism	2.2	1.9	2.0	2.0	2.4	3.1	3.0	4.0	4.0	2.8	3.0	4.8
Staticism-developmentalism	3.2	3.3	2.7	1.3	3.2	4.1	3.0	2.8	3.9	2.3	2.7	3.6
Staticism-dynamicism	3.1	2.6	1.9	1.4	3.7	4.6	3.7	2.6	3.0	4.2	3.6	4.6

It is interesting to examine the adequacy of these dimensions as a definitional scheme, at least in a crude way. The students' mean ratings were taken as defining the "prototypical points" for each of the six psychological systems. Then two "experts" (the authors) also rated the six systems. Each of them used a 4-inch line for each dimension as a rating aid and indicated the position of each system on each dimension on one of the lines. The extreme left was labeled 1, and the extreme right was labeled 5. The number assigned a system was then determined by measuring its position on the line with a ruler. The students' and the authors' mean ratings are shown in Table 3-2.

The authors' ratings were averaged for each dimension for each system. Then the city-block distances of the eighteen authors' means from the eighteen students' means were determined for each system. The sum of the differences gave the city-block distance (see page 60).

The distance of our own structuralism from structuralism, functionalism, associationism, behaviorism, Gestalt psychology, and psychoanalysis, as rated by the "mean student," was computed. It was closest to the students' prototypical point for structuralism and hence would have been correctly identified as a set of ratings for structuralism, had its identity been unknown. Table 3-3 shows all the intersystem distances. In five out of six cases, the classification based on this definitional system was correct. In the sixth case—Gestalt psychology—the system misclassified it as psychoanalysis. It thus appears that the system based on Watson's criteria is a promising definitional scheme for systems of psychology, and we shall refer the student back to the positions of various systems of psychology on these conceptual dimensions as each system is discussed. Relating one system to another on these dimensions should help the student to obtain an integrated picture of all systems.

Empirically Derived Characteristics of Systems

Watson's dimensions, though based on a careful study of history and philosophy, were conceived by a single individual. Coan (1968) found a systematic procedure for tapping the judgments of a *group* of experts in the history of psychology. He

TABLE 3-3   City-block Distances between Authors' Mean Rating of Each System and Students' Mean Rating of Each System

		Students					
		Associa- tionism	Struc- turalism	Func- tionalism	Behav- iorism	Gestalt theory	Psycho- analysis
	Associationism	12.4	16.3	17.9	15.5	23.8	27.9
A	Structuralism	25.5	12.3	29.4	32.8	23.3	24.6
u t	Functionalism	12.7	24.0	8.8	16.4	21.1	22.6
h o	Behaviorism	15.6	30.3	22.7	8.3	32.0	32.9
r s	Gestalt theory	24.9	18.6	21.2	32.2	10.4	10.2
	Psychoanalysis	27.8	26.3	22.7	31.5	16.2	11.9

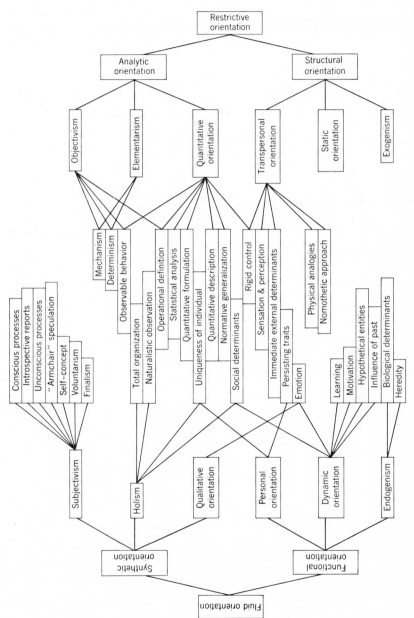

Fig. 3-3 A bipolar hierarchy of theoretical variables. (The variables shown in the middle are relatively specific, while those on the left and right sides represent more general and mutually opposing trends.) (From Coan, 1968, p. 720.)

73

asked 232 correspondents to rate 54 carefully selected famous psychologists as to their emphasis on 34 characteristics, such as nomothetic emphasis. All rating was done on a five-point scale ranging from positive emphasis on the characteristic to rejection of the characteristic. What this study uncovered, then, was the opinions of 232 expert judges as to whether and to what degree 54 psychologists had emphasized 34 variables in their theorizing and/or experimentation.

Coan derived six specific factors from the judgments. Factor 1 is labeled *subjectivistic* versus *objectivistic*. According to Coan's findings, subjectivistic theorists would be exemplified by McDougall, Piaget, and Jung, while the latter type include Estes, Hull, and Watson. Factor 2 is labeled *holistic* versus *elementaristic*. Holistic theorists are Goldstein, Köhler, and Koffka. Elementaristic theorists are Spence, Titchener, and Ebbinghaus. Coan calls factor 3 *transpersonal* versus *personal*, and factors 4 to 6 he labels *quantitative* versus *qualitative, dynamic* versus *static*, and *synthetic* versus *analytic*, respectively.

Coan finds that these specific factors are themselves interrelated, with subjectivism, holism, and a qualitative trend tending to go together to make up a synthetic trend opposed to an analytic trend composed of the objectivistic, elementaristic, and quantitative trends. A second general factor at this level is the structural orientation (transpersonal, static, exogenistic) versus the functional orientation (personal, dynamic, endogenistic). Finally, the analytic and structural orientations relate to a general restrictive orientation, with the synthetic and functional orientations relating to a general fluid orientation.

Coan's system thus provides an interesting additional way to organize the views of particular systematists and theorists. There is a surprising and comforting amount of overlap between the issues raised by Watson's prescriptions and Coan's factors, despite the great differences in detail.

PARADIGMS

The reader should now be better equipped to relate psychological systems to Kuhn's paradigms (see Chapter 1). Kuhn thinks of paradigms as *accepted* examples of scientific practice, including all its elements: law, theory, application, and instrumentation. The paradigm must stimulate research by defining the problems of a field and by being revolutionary enough to attract individuals away from other fields of, or approaches to, scientific inquiry.

R. I. Watson (1967), cited above, dubbed psychology a prescriptive science because he wanted to distinguish it from the more advanced sciences, which more clearly have paradigms. Psychology has never been "of one mind" enough for Watson to feel that any one approach can claim paradigmatic status. The reader will recognize that an argument about whether psychology has any paradigms would be an argument about definition; the settlement of such an argument must be arbitrary. Certainly if we drop the "universality of agreement" dimension from our definitional space, we might think of several candidates for psychological paradigms: the classical conditioning paradigm, operant conditioning, verbal learning, and others. All have the kind of guiding function Kuhn attributes to paradigms.

Contemporary Skinnerian psychology—what might be called the *operant conditioning paradigm*—seems an especially strong candidate. It has fairly wide acceptance and includes law, application, instrumentation, and a kind of theory. It has been revolutionary enough to attrack many strong adherents and stimulate research. "Normal science," of the everyday puzzle-solving type emphasized by Kuhn, is busily working out unfinished business within the confines of this paradigm.

Krantz (1972) found some evidence that operant psychologists form a school. The *Journal of the Experimental Analysis of Behavior*, for example, cites itself quite often; this high rate of self-citation is some evidence, admittedly rather weak, of isolation from other aspects of psychology. After evaluating this and other evidence, Krantz answers with a qualified "yes" the question whether operant psychology is a school. Most students of operant techniques, however, do not see themselves as members of schools. This is probably true of nearly any psychologist, past or present; we all tend to see ourselves as psychologists and dislike admitting that we have been too much influenced by any single point of view.

Psychology thus might or might not be said to have paradigms, depending on how one wishes to restrict the definition. Whether it has or not, Watson (1971) finds his prescriptive approach to the study of the history of psychology very useful. Through it, he believes one can avoid both excessive emphasis on the exclusively antiquarian view of the past and, at the same time, avoid excessive distortion of the past because it is viewed too much in terms of present conceptualizations. Fuchs and Kawash (1972) have used Watson's prescriptions as a starting point for a factor analytic approach similar to Coan's and have used the factors to describe five schools of psychology. The systematic approach to the study of the history of psychology is well on its way.

CRITERIA FOR SYSTEMS

We will now turn the calendar back about forty years to find out how systems were seen by psychologists when systematic issues were still extremely prominent. It will be clear that the questions asked were less systematic and detailed and that there was no attempt at quantitative treatment. However, the level of analysis was close to the same level of sophistication as the systems being analyzed. McGeoch (1933) presented six criteria which he felt should be met by a system of psychology. Table 3-4 is adapted from McGeoch's criteria.

The criteria are consistent with our contention that the systems of psychology have served chiefly to direct the behavior of psychologists in their pursuit of scientific knowledge about psychology. Why should McGeoch require a system to provide a definition of the field? Because the definition functions to tell psychologists what to study. The postulates McGeoch is talking about also have at times a

TABLE 3-4   McGeoch's Criteria for a System

I	The system must contain a definition of the field of psychology
II	The system must make its postulates explicit
	A Postulates should be as few as possible
	B The postulates should be necessary
	C The postulates should contain little of the finished system
III	The nature of the data to be studied must be specified
	A Objective-subjective
	B Qualitative-quantitative
	C Units of description
	D Provide genetic starting point
IV	A mind-body position must be taken
V	The organization of the data, its principles of connection, must be accounted for
VI	Principles of selection must be given

SOURCE: Adapted from McGeoch, 1933.

directive function. McGeoch's postulates are not the type from which theorems in the formal sense are derived; they are the underlying assumptions that direct or justify the behavior of the man who accepts them. The nature of the data to be studied must be specified with sufficient clarity to direct scientific investigation. Requirements IV to VI specify problems that McGeoch felt must be dealt with. To meet the last two requirements—accounting for the organization of the data and giving the principles of selection—the system would have to consist of at least some empirical information, unless the principles were based completely on rational guesses.

Modern psychologists, unlike McGeoch, are likely to be casual about the definition of psychology. They recognize that boundaries of fields are always shifting and that new disciplines arise along the boundaries as fields become more specialized. Certainly few psychologists would refuse to study a promising new problem simply because it didn't look like "psychology."

McGeoch's requirements for postulates, if applied to *formal* postulates, are certainly reasonable. However, they may not be so important if intended to apply to the informal assumptions or hypotheses which were developed—and may be discarded—in connection with the development of the formal postulates.

Psychology today uses all kinds of data. A given psychologist uses whatever data are helpful in attacking a problem. While we like to feel that our data are objective, the distinction between objective and subjective is difficult to make. We require that our data be such that they can be gathered again by any investigator who wishes to check the validity of our results. Beyond this, we can say little. Units of description are chosen for the sake of convenience, and if the data cannot be quantitative, qualitative data are used.

It is clear that McGeoch made an arbitrary choice of the mind-body problem as one on which a system had to take a stand; he might have chosen the nativism-empiricism question or any one of a number of others. Although

McGeoch's criteria are somewhat incomplete and unrealistic, they do include the kinds of factors that actually were considered important when systematic issues were of great interest, and their level of sophistication is similar to the level of sophistication reflected in the systems themselves.

McGeoch himself said of the mind-body position (1933): "The problem need not, of course, be stated in traditional metaphysical fashion. . . . The point is that the problem is there and must be treated (or avoided) somehow if an adequate system is to be constructed" (p. 8). He thus lef: open the alternative of avoiding the problem. Many psychologists today choose this alternative and would argue that the problem is *not* there until someone poses it and that it is not a useful problem to pose, at least at present. We shall discuss these issues at greater length when we consider the attack of the behaviorists on consciousness.

The last two requirements are still legitimate. They require for their fulfillment the statement of relevant variables and the statement of the functional relationships between them. Much of science is concerned with such statements.

These criteria provide a sample of what psychologists of over three decades ago felt a system should be. The requirements are stated without great attention to detail. No attempt is made to apply them to a particular theory or system. The desired characteristics are generality and scope of attempted coverage rather than predictive power.

THE NATURE OF THEORY

Pure versus Practical

Often the word *theory* is used in contrast to *practice* or *application*. This usage is correct in that it implies that theories involve some use of abstraction. It is not correct if it is taken to imply that theories are impractical, or not applied. Theories, observations, and applications usually arise in intimate interactions. Rarely does the investigator find a handy mathematical or logical system and then go looking for data that it might fit. Theories and areas of investigation grow after applications are demonstrated; who would doubt that the military applications are partly responsible for the billions that have been spent on particle physics in the last twenty-five years?

Degrees of Confirmation

Some authors use the word *theory* to refer to a hypothesis that has received a considerable amount of empirical support. When *theory* is used in this sense, the term *law* is used for the most thoroughly tested and verified propositions (Warren, 1934, p. 128).

In its more general scientific usages, the word *theory* refers to some proposition from which a large number of empirical observations can be deduced. For example, Bergmann (1957) defined a theory as a "group of laws deductively connected" (p. 31). If he limits the components of theory to laws, then he must be using a broad definition of the word *law*. Theories can certainly be built from postulates which are not well demonstrated empirically or which are incapable of empirical demonstration, or even from analogies whose parts are known not to correspond to the phenomena covered by the theory. An example of the latter would be the hydraulic analogy with electric currents. We are quite sure that there is no water in the wires, and yet predictions can be made from such an analogy if the appropriate mathematics is used.

Bergmann's requirement for any theory, then, is that the key components be "deductively connected." This means simply that there must be a method of arriving at new statements from the original statements; there must be appropriate operations which result in deductive statements.

An Abstract Theory

Since there is considerable emphasis on deduction in any theory, let us construct and examine an extremely simple postulate set, using a rule for deduction to derive theorems.

POSTULATES

1 *"*-"
2 " ' "-+

RULE FOR DEDUCTION

1 If a symbol or symbols appear in any postulate on opposite sides of the symbol -, all symbols on one side of the - may be substituted for all symbols on the other side of the -, wherever they appear in any postulate or theorem.

What theorems can we derive in this simple system? Starting with postulate 2, we might replace ", wherever it appears, with its equivalent from postulate 1. We then have *"*'*"*-+ (theorem 1).

We can operate on theorem 1 in one direction to produce theorem 2—+-+— and in the other direction to produce theorem 3—*"*'*"*-*"*'*"*. (We could as easily have derived theorem 2 from postulate 2.)

The student who has a strong stomach and a high threshold for boredom may proceed to discover a few additional theorems, like "-". Others will already be wondering what the point of this construction is, especially in view of the meaningless and abstract nature of the "statements" made. The system was made intentionally abstract so that the student could look at our "theory" as a kind of game, free of the distractions that empirical interpretation brings, and see in stark outline the nature of such abstract games.

The theory can be given empirical interpretation by letting * stand for one apple, " for two apples, and + for four apples. The operation plus, as usually understood for apples, can be indicated by ', and equals by -. We can now interpret our theory as being about apples, making wise statements like "One apple plus one apple plus one apple plus one apple equals four apples" (theorem 1). If our operations on empirical apples are described by a statement that agrees with this interpretation of our abstract theorem, we have a successful theory about apple combinations. Our little exercise, which started life as a rudimentary abstract system, would become a rudimentary scientific theory, since it would then say something about apples. It has all the necessary elements of a scientific theory: abstract formal statements, rules for manipulating these abstract statements, and a "dictionary" which relates the terms of the statements to empirical observations.

Motivation for Theory Construction

The abstract portions of a theory may be developed because the theorist has either of two motives: He may wish to deal with the empirical world more effectively and want an abstract system to help him do so, or he may just be playing a mathematical game and develop the system as a matter of curiosity. Euclid's geometry was probably based, ultimately, on problems of surveying. Many modern mathematicians deal with symbols at a very abstract level and do not much care about any possible correspondence between the mathematical system and an empirical system. There are therefore many extant mathematical systems available for new scientific applications if the scientist has the necessary sophistication to find them and to set up appropriate relationships between his subject matter and the mathematical system. Kurt Lewin (1936), for example, took advantage of a relatively new mathematics (topology) in developing his psychological theory, and he even developed a new mathematics (hodology) to deal with his conceptualization of directionality (vectors) in behavior. Estes (1959) used standard mathematics in developing his mathematical model of learning.

Dimensions of Theories

Scientific theories may differ in many ways. They yield deductions about different *subject matters*. They differ greatly in *generality*; Hull's theory (1952) dealt with all simple mammalian behavior, while Estes' theory (1950), as he originally proposed it, dealt only with the probability of a certain type of response. Theories differ in *precision* of statement; some make predictions that are at best qualitative, while at the other end of the scale are the very precise quantitative statements. Even within the same degree of quantitativeness of prediction, theories may differ as to the degree of *rigor* of the predictions; sometimes the argument, though involving quantitative statements, is loose and relatively informal, and in other cases the processes of derivation and prediction may be better formalized and more rigorous logically. Theories differ in the *origins* of their component statements, or postulates; some theories are combinations of empirically based statements, which are verifiable or potentially verifiable, and other theories are composed of statements arrived at rationally rather than empirically. No theory, whatever its qualities, is ever final, even though all the predictive statements made from it have been verified perfectly. There always remains the possibility that any given theory will be replaced by another theory which is simpler, more general, or more consistent with other relevant theories.

On the other hand, theories are seldom discarded simply because they are too specific or even because some of the predictions made from them are wrong. Rather, they are discarded when they are replaced by something better. A theory will generally be modified and used as long as it is the only thing available within some problem area.

Models

A model is a particular subclass of theory, as we have defined theory. Some authors separate them completely, and others treat them as synonyms, but we prefer to make models a subclass of theories, since both function in the derivation of theorems and in making predictions. Boring summed up the difference between the two succinctly (1957, p. 191):

Today we hear less about theories and more about models. What is the difference? The theory claims to be true, even though we all know that assurance about the validity of these claims varies greatly from theory to theory and from time to time for the same theory. The theory is an *as*, whereas the model is an *as-if*. The theory is indicative; the model, subjunctive. The model is a pattern to be abandoned easily at the demand of progress.

By an *as*, Boring means that the theorist expects to observe, or has observed, empirical referents for the terms of his theory. The postulates of the theory are, or can become, empirical laws. The postulates of a model are not expected to become laws. The model builder knows that his postulates are purely abstract and cannot be coordinated with the empirical observations at the postulate level. We might draw an example from psychoanalysis. Freud's thinking with regard to the id, ego, and superego was probably *as-if* thinking; these elements functioned in a model. Yet labeling the functions or aspects of personality in this way (drawing diagrams of them, etc.) led many to believe that these words represented actual, observable entities; that is, these people believed that Freud had a theory, not a model.

A mathematical model, then, would be a "computational device." The mathematical function clearly does not reflect reality. A physical model is computational in a nonmathematical sense; that is, it behaves analogously to the thing modeled, and like the mathematical model, it serves as a basis for making predictions. A man is *not* a machine, nor is an atom a collection of billiard balls; yet machines and billiards may be useful analogies (models), and they can "be abandoned easily at the demand of progress."

The model may be differentiated from the metatheory in terms of its closer relationship to the structure of the empirical measures and the observations. That is, the metatheory provides general guidelines for the kind of theory to be developed; the model provides more specific guidelines for the empirical research and thus for the laws that are developed.

CRITERIA FOR THEORIES

Estes, Koch, MacCorquodale, Meehl, Mueller, Schoenfeld, and Verplanck (1954) presented an outline for the criticism of learning theories. In comparing this outline with McGeoch's criteria, several contrasts strike us. The questions asked in the outline are specific and logically sophisticated. They concern the ability of the theory to make predictions. There are no questions or requirements which *demand* any directive statements regarding the behavior of the investigator. There is one question about generality ("range of data for which interpretation or explanation in terms of the theory has been claimed"), but there is no implication that the range must be great. The authors' first concern seems to be with the *language* of the theory. This implies a growing recognition that much of science is verbal behavior. The outline deals with theories rather than with the more inclusive systems and thus would not be expected to parallel McGeoch's discussion exactly; however, this dealing with smaller problems is itself a significant trend in psychology. Initially, all sciences tend to present "big," general problems. These problems usually are not amenable to experimental attack until they are broken down into smaller problems and perhaps rephrased completely.

Some attitudes of Estes et al. toward the evaluation of theory are given in a quotation from their discussion of the outline (1954, pp. xiv, xv):

We believe wide agreement would obtain among current writers in the logic of science that an adequate review of any scientific theory must include essentially the same features. . . . Scientific theories are evaluated not on some absolute scale of "theoryness," but with respect to what we expect them to do. Some of the functions of a useful theory are: (1) clarifying the description of the world possible in ordinary language, (2) summarizing existing knowledge, (3) mediating applications of our knowledge to new situations, (4) leading to fruitful lines of experimental inquiry.

Table 3-5 presents the outline in full. The student should study every point very carefully. As we write, more than fifteen years after this outline was prepared, we still find the questions useful. The issues raised are still issues, and our hopes for theory are now as they were then.

TRENDS IN SYSTEMS AND THEORIES

Increasing Explicitness

We can now look back on what has been said and see what has happened and is happening to systems and theories. First, they are growing more limited and more explicit.

Theorists are no longer content with superficial statements that have no real predictive value; even the most sophisticated-appearing theory is subjected to careful examination and may at times be found lacking. For example, Cotton

TABLE 3-5   Outline for Reviews of Theories

I	Structure of the Theory

    A   Delineation of empirical area
        1   Data language
            Is the data language explicit and theoretically neutral?
            How does the theorist relate his empirical variables to the data language?
        2   Dependent and independent variables
            How does the selection of variables compare with those of other learning theories?
            What influence does the choice of variables exert upon the form of the theory?
    B   Theoretical concepts
        1   Primitive terms
            Are primitive terms of the theory reducible to physical or object language?
            Is the usage of primitive terms fixed by implicit or explicit definitions?
        2   Principal constructs
            Do these serve only a summarizing function or are they related by definition or by hypothesis to terms of other disciplines (e.g., physiology)?
        3   Relations assumed among constructs
            How are the major theoretical variables interrelated in the foundation assumptions of the theory?
            How are such interrelations constructed from the observation base of the theory?
        4   Relations assumed or derived between constructs and experimentally defined variables

II	Methodological Characteristics

    A   Standing of the theory on principal methodological "dimensions"
        1   Explicit axiomatization
        2   Quantitativeness
        3   Consistency and independence of principal theoretical assumptions
        4   Use of physical or mathematical models
    B   Techniques of derivation
        Are the empirical consequences of the theory developed by informal arguments or formal derivations?

III	Empirical Content and Adequacy

    A   Range of data for which interpretation or explanation in terms of the theory has been claimed
    B   Specificity of prediction demonstrated
    C   Obvious failures to handle facts in the area III-A
    D   Tours-de-force
        Has it been possible to predict new experimental phenomena?
        Have any predictions of this sort been confirmed?
        Does the theory account for facts not predictable from competing theories in the same area?
    E   Sensitivity to empirical evidence
    F   Programmaticity
    G   Special virtues or limitations. Techniques which may prove useful outside the context of the specific theory

SOURCE: Estes et al., 1954, pp. xiii, xiv.

(1955) has shown that Hull's learning theory really is not adequate for making some predictions that it purports to be able to make. Psychologists are no longer content with comfortable generalities that allow labels to be tacked on to results after they occur; they want theories or systems to say what is *going* to happen and to say it clearly and exactly. They want theorists and systematists to show exactly how they know and how they predict. It follows from these demands that any contemporary system that fulfills them must be a miniature system, covering only a very small range of behavior, perhaps only for a single kind of organism in a single simple situation. We still have too few facts to build full-scale systems.

Laboratory and Field

The demand for increased rigor and precision has led to a growing concern for measurement and for mathematical statements. The same demands have led to two trends that at first glance seem opposed: a trend toward the laboratory and ever more carefully controlled experimentation and a trend toward a greater amount of naturalistic observation. The trend toward better-controlled experimentation is intended to ensure that the statements made are correct; inadequacies in past experiments, and hesitancy to accept results because of lack of control, have led to the laboratory. The trend toward naturalism arises partly out of a similar concern; the "naturalist" recognizes that it is as illegitimate to generalize when the base situation failed to include all relevant *variables* as when the base situation did not include all the relevant *controls*. It seems to us that both trends are desirable and are occurring because of increased sophistication on the part of psychologists. However, some psychologists of the less tough-minded variety have objected to the increasing abstraction and artificiality which often characterize the laboratory experiment. Skinner is one of many who have defended the position of the laboratory worker (1957a, p. 370):

Have we been guilty of an undue simplification of conditions in order to obtain this level of rigor? Have we really "proved" that there is comparable order outside the laboratory? It is difficult to be sure of the answers to such questions. Suppose we are observing the rate at which a man sips his breakfast coffee. . . . It is unlikely that we shall record a smooth curve. But although our behavioral curve will not be pretty, *neither will the cooling curve for the coffee in the cup*. In extrapolating our results to the world at large, we can do no more than the physical and biological sciences in general. Because of experiments performed under laboratory conditions, no one doubts that the cooling of the coffee in the cup is an orderly process, even though the actual curve would be difficult to explain. Similarly when we have investigated behavior under the advantageous conditions of the laboratory, we can accept its basic orderliness in the world at large even though we cannot there wholly demonstrate law.

There are two other divergent contemporary tendencies, which are related to a demand for more rigor. On the one hand, there is a greater tendency to regard theoretical statements as *as-if*s, that is, a tendency to use models rather than theories. If the psychologist is ignorant of what physiological events correlate with his behavioral observations, rigor dictates that he should not couch his theory in physiological terms. Many psychologists simply ignore physiology on these grounds and point out that the predictive value of a model does not depend on any assumptions about the existence of components of the model. On the other hand, there are many psychologists today who feel that ignorance of physiology is deplorable. However, they generally *do not* "physiologize"; that is, they do not talk about physiological explanations in the complete absence of physiological knowledge. Physiologizing in this sense is, we hope, disappearing from psychology.

Despite all the changes, parts of the old systems still persist in the "foundation assumptions" that we saw mentioned by some of our leading modern theorists (see Table 3-5). R. I. Watson (1967) sees these attitudes as very important, as does Koch (1959). These orientative attitudes are still defended and attacked, and the struggle still generates friction, heat, and, we may hope, experimentation. Psychology's systems may be dead, but the remnants are still with us. It is a fascinating business to study their modern rearrangements and modifications. If systems are regarded chiefly as specializations of the general philosophy of science for application to a particular discipline, then some kind of system will always be found in every science.

SUMMARY AND CONCLUSIONS

A working idea of what a system is, and should be, is necessary for our later evaluation of systems. The origins of systems were largely philosophical. They may be loosely defined as organizations of facts and theories. Yet psychology's sytems have not really been exemplifications of our definition; they have been less statements about the subject matter of psychology than statements about the way that subject matter ought to be approached. They have had some usefulness in motivating people to perform experiments and to be cautious and critical; they have hindered by turning attention too much to big questions that at present are answerable only on the basis of rational guesses. There is a growing tendency to replace the traditional system with a more limited type of theory, to use models as well as theories, and to demand far more precision, logical development, and explicitness of the more limited type of statement. Yet the basic orientative attitudes of the old systems live on in modern psychology.

Further Readings

The introduction to Estes et al., *Modern learning theory* (1954), is still modern despite its age. Historical perspective on how the issues have changed (or remained the same) can be gained by reading McGeoch's (1933) paper, "The formal criteria of a systematic psychology," or Heidbreder's old but very readable *Seven psychol-*

ogies (1933). Popper's *Logic of scientific discovery* (1959), P. Frank's *Modern science and its philosophy* (1949), and Bergmann's *Philosophy of science* (1957) deserve mention. *The language of psychology*, by Mandler and Kessen (1959), and *Theories in contemporary psychology*, by Marx (1963), both treat important issues, though they, like the seven volumes in the series edited by Koch, are too much for casual reading in connection with a single chapter! Lichtenstein's article "Psychological systems: Their nature and function" (1967) gives a good overview of the area it claims to treat. However, the best set of reasonable readings might well consist of Kuhn's *Structure of scientific revolutions* (1970), available in a 210-page paperback; R. I. Watson's (1967) article "Psychology: A prescriptive science"; Coan's (1968) article "Dimensions of psychological theory"; and Lakatos' (1970) "Falsification and the methodology of scientific research programmes." This combination will give the devoted reader an excellent picture of what science is about, how it relates to its history, what prescriptions have concerned psychologists, and the combinations of them accepted by representative psychologists (as seen by representative students of psychologists). Two historically oriented recent works that should be consulted by the interested student are Neel's *Theories of psychology: A handbook* (1970) and Krantz's *Schools of psychology: A symposium* (1970).

MAJOR FIGURES IN THE FORMATION AND DEVELOPMENT OF SIX PSYCHOLOGICAL SYSTEMS

	1870	1880	1890	1900	1910	1920	1930	1940	1950	1960
STRUCTURALISM		Wundt	Titchener							
FUNCTIONALISM		James		Dewey	Angell	Carr Woodworth	McGeoch	Melton	Underwood	
ASSOCIATIONISM		Ebbinghaus		Pavlov	Bekhterev	Thorndike	Guthrie		Estes	
BEHAVIORISM				Meyer	Watson Weiss	Hunter Tolman	Skinner Hull	Miller Spence		
GESTALT THEORY		von Ehrenfels			Wertheimer Koffka	Köhler				
		Mach								
PSYCHOANALYSIS		Breuer Freud		Adler Jung	Rank Jones Ferenczi	Horney	Sullivan	Fromm		

PART TWO

SYSTEMS OF PSYCHOLOGY

We turn now to consideration of the major systematic developments in the recent history of psychology. Our plan of procedure is to present a minimal account of the historical antecedents of each of the systems treated, in order to indicate their ties with the past. In each case the founding of the system, its major structural characteristics with regard to content and methodology, and its development and fate are treated. The six criteria listed by McGeoch (1933) are utilized as a framework for the exposition of each system in order to facilitate comparisons, and the dimensions of Coan (1968) and R. I. Watson (1967) are used as a basis for systematic description. The table at the left shows the major figures associated with the origin and development of each of the six systems treated. These names are placed on a common time line to indicate temporal relationships.

TABLE 4-1   Important Men in Associational Psychology

Antecedent Influences	Associationists		
	Founder	Developers	Contemporary Representatives
Aristotle (384-322 B.C.)	David Hartley (1705-1757)	Thomas Brown (1778-1820)	William K. Estes (1919-)
		James Mill (1773-1836)	
Thomas Hobbes (1588-1679)		John S. Mill (1806-1873)	
John Locke (1632-1704)		Alexander Bain (1818-1903)	
George Berkeley (1685-1753)		Hermann Ebbinghaus (1850-1909)	
David Hume (1711-1776)		Ivan P. Pavlov (1849-1936)	
		Valdimir M. Bekhterev (1857-1927)	
		Edward L. Thorndike—Columbia (1874-1949)	
		Edwin R. Guthrie—Washington (1886-1959)	

4 Associationism

Associationism is more a principle than a school of psychology. The principle of association derives from epistemological questions within philosophy. The epistemological question, "How do we know?" is answered by empiricist philosophers, "Through the senses." Immediately the next question arises: "Then where do the complex ideas come from, since they are not directly sensed?" The answer to this second question gives the first principle of association: "Complex ideas come from the association of simpler ones."

Since associationism thus has its roots in philosophy, its history extends back into antiquity. Its influence extends into the present, since it is still an active force underlying much of psychology. In one form or another associationistic ideas have been taken over by all the schools. For this reason, we treat associationism first. Although structuralism is usually regarded as the first formal school of psychology, it was preceded by a long historical development within the associationistic tradition. The founders of structuralism were greatly influenced by that tradition. Table 4-1 lists the names of the most important men in associationistic psychology.

The British empiricists probably constitute the closest approach to a "school" of associationism. It was their attempt to explain mental activity which led to the statement of the several factors important in forming associations. In our description of the development of British empiricism, we shall attempt to show the continuity of thinking in which empiricism and associationism were fused. Although these philosophers were concerned more with epistemological than with psychological problems, they definitely anticipated later psychological developments in their attempt to apply something more than purely philosophical efforts to these problems.

Historically, associationistic concepts have served as substitutes for more detailed learning theories. Three men stand out as contributors to this aspect of the associationistic movement. Hermann Ebbinghaus caused a profound shift in the associationistic way of working. Prior to his studies on the learning of nonsense syllables, the tendency had been to begin with the associations already formed and attempt to infer backward to the process of formation of the associations. Ebbing haus began at the other end, with the study of the formation of the associations; it was thus possible for him to control the conditions under which the associations were formed and to make the study of learning scientific. I. P. Pavlov, the great Russian physiologist, has primary responsibility for shifting the kind of association studied to S-R connections rather than ideas. His prior research on the conditioned reflex thus helped to objectify psychology. E. L. Thorndike developed the most complete account yet rendered of psychological phenomena along associationistic lines; we shall therefore treat his system as the most appropriate representative of associationism.

It is difficult to single out modern associationistic systematists, since they do not belong to any cohesive school. A man is considered an associationist to the extent that he uses associationistic principles; but associationistic principles pervade recent and contemporary psychology, so we must select "associationists" according to their tendency to use *only* or *primarily* associationistic principles.

BRITISH EMPIRICISM

The British empiricists used the same principles of association that had been suggested centuries before by Aristotle. He had suggested that items which are similar or opposite or contiguous tend to be associated with one another. The last principle, contiguity, comes closest to winning universal acceptance: If two things are experienced closely in time, they are likely to be associated. Similarity and contrast are accepted by some and rejected by others. The only principle of association added to Aristotle's list by the British empiricists was the principle of causality suggested by Berkeley and treated at length by Hume.

Table 4-2 summarizes the principles of association accepted by the most important figures within the associationistic movement.

TABLE 4-2   Principles of Associationism

Author	Date	Contiguity	Similarity	Contrast	Causality
			Principles		
Aristotle	ca. 330 B.C.	X	X	X	
Thomas Hobbes	1651	X			
John Locke	1700	X	X		
George Berkeley	1733	X	X		
David Hume	1739	X	X		X
David Hartley	1749	X			
James Mill	1829	X			
John Stuart Mill	1843	X	X		
Alexander Bain	1855	X	X		
Herbert Spencer	1855	X	X		

Thomas Hobbes (1588-1679) was a political philosopher who helped to found British empiricism. He saw reason as the dominant guiding factor in man's behavior; however, he took a strongly deterministic, mechanical view. Mental content was accounted for by recourse to sensual data only, eliminating the need for innate ideas. The lawful succession of ideas was held to be responsible for all thought and action. Hobbes accounted for this succession in terms of association by contiguity: If an idea had been followed by another previously, it would again tend to lead to the contiguous idea.

John Locke (1632-1704) is usually regarded as the originator of British empiricism, although Hobbes preceded him. Locke's early life was concerned mainly with political activities, as Hobbes's had been, and he was relatively late in maturing as a philosopher. Only the last fourteen years of his life were spent in philosophy.

After twenty years of thinking on the problem, Locke published his famous work, *Essay concerning human understanding*, in 1690 at the age of fifty-seven. In this work his main concern was the problem of the validity of knowledge. Locke said that all knowledge comes from experience, either through the senses or through reflection on sensory data. This extreme empiricism with no innate knowledge allowed represented a return to the Aristotelian notion of the *tabula rasa* (blank tablet, symbolic of the infant "mind," on which sensory experience is presumed to write) and an attack on Descartes's belief in innate ideas.

Locke's ideas on association were also similar to Aristotle's. He added a chapter entitled "Of the association of ideas" to the fourth edition of the *Essay*, in which he pointed out that ideas are combined in experience according to principles very much like those of similarity and contiguity. However, his emphasis on association was not great, and he certainly did not stress it as a universal principle underlying the connection of ideas. He believed that ideas are ordinarily connected by "natural" connections, and he clearly implied that associationistic principles are useful primarily for the explanation of abnormal connections. Locke thus began a sequence of views on association. Berkeley made association more inclusive in scope; Hume characterized it as a "gentle force"; and James Mill made it into an inexorable principle of connection. Within the tradition of associationism man's mind started out free except for a little accidental determination, with Locke, and ended up completely determined with Mill.

Locke also started a trend with his special theory of primary and secondary qualities, which were said to be the basis for sensory "ideas." According to this dichotomy, primary properties are those which inhere in bodies. They offer the main avenue between the mind and the external world. Properties such as solidity, figure, motion, and number are representative of this category. Secondary properties, such as colors, sounds, and tastes, were not supposed to belong to objects, but were instead considered functions of the mind itself. This distinction was soon destroyed by Berkeley (see below), but reappeared as the problem of distinguishing between psychology and physics. As we shall see later, Wundt made the distinction by saying that physics studies *mediate* experience and psychology studies *imme-*

diate experience. Titchener, two centuries after Locke, said that physics studies experience as *independent of* the experiencing organism, while psychology studies experience as *dependent on* the experiencing organism.

George Berkeley (1785-1753) was Locke's immediate intellectual successor. A one-time bishop of Cloyne, he was also a philosopher and educationalist. In contrast to Locke's late publication, Berkeley published his two important works at the age of about twenty-five: *New theory of vision* (1709) and *Principles of human knowledge* (1710).

Philosophically, Berkeley was a subjective idealist. For him mind was the ultimate reality. This position is represented by the famous Latin phrase *esse est percipi* (to be is to be perceived). For Berkeley the main problem was not the relation of mind to matter (Descartes) or how matter generates mind (Locke), but how mind generates matter. This kind of position leads, to follow it to its logical conclusion, to a solipsism (belief that there is only one mind, one's own, in which all else, including other minds, exists only as ideas).

Berkeley was an active and ingenious psychological thinker. He used tactual and kinesthetic sensations to break down the distinction Locke had made between primary and secondary qualities. Berkeley pointed out that the alleged primary qualities are really also functions of perception. This argument is congruent with his philosophical idealism. He believed that visual depth perception depends upon experience. He stressed tactual and kinesthetic sensations and their association with ocular movements in looking at near and far objects; the complex association then became "depth." This was a specific psychological attempt to answer his general philosophical question of how mind generates matter. It shows Berkeley inverting the materialistic practice of taking the external world for granted and asking how we come to know about it. Berkeley regarded the data of consciousness as beyond doubt, and the problem was to account for complex ideas, like those of space and external objects.

In line with his theological background, Berkeley attempted to explain the stability, independence, and order of external objects by bringing in the all-perceiving mind of God. His metaphysical position is humorously presented in the following limerick (quoted in Russell, 1945, p. 648, and attributed to Ronald Knox):

> *There was a young man who said, God*
> *Must think it exceedingly odd*
> *If he finds that this tree*
> *Continues to be*
> *When there's no one about in the Quad.*

Reply:

> *Dear Sir:*
> *Your astonishment's odd:*
> *I am always about in the Quad.*

And that's why the tree
Will continue to be,
Since observed by
       Yours faithfully,
         God.

David Hume (1711-1776), like Berkeley, was brilliantly precocious. His *Treatise on human nature*, on which most of his reputation was based, appeared in three volumes when Hume was twenty-eight and twenty-nine. He made a distinction between more vivid impressions (what we would call *sensations* or *perceptions*) and less vivid ideas (what we would call *images* or *recollections*). This distinction was later revived by the structuralists when they began the introspective analysis of mind, an analytic process which grew easily out of the associationistic tradition.

Hume also applied his analytic tendencies to one of the three principles of association he "discovered," the principle of cause and effect. He found that this principle was closely related to the principle of contiguity and that indeed cause and effect came into being as an idea only if the cause had been contiguous with the effect. In addition, the cause had *invariably* to be followed by the effect. Superficially, it seems that Hume reduced cause and effect to contiguity via his analysis, but the case is not so simple. N. K. Smith (1949), who made a thorough study of Hume's position, concludes that Hume definitely believed that the principle of cause and effect retained its independence despite its close relationship to temporal and spatial contiguity. However, cause and effect were not to be found existing in the things observed, but only in the mind of the observer. Cause and effect might seem to be a complex idea, one which might have been reduced to simpler ideas had Hume been so inclined. This view, too, is mistaken. Turner (1967) says of Hume's position: "We find, then, that *causation, resemblance*, and *contiguity* are the relations by which we associate ideas. As such, these relations have no existential significance; they represent activities of the imagination, and not ideas reducible in any way to impressions" (p. 34). One must conclude that Hume retained three distinct principles of association.

Finally, Hume's skeptical and antimetaphysical biases have been enormously influential. His famous paragraph from *An enquiry concerning human understanding* reads (1902, p. 165):

When we run over libraries, persuaded of these principles, what havoc must we make? If we take in our hand any volume; of divinity or school metaphysics, for instance; let us ask, *Does it contain any abstract reasoning concerning quantity or number?* No. *Does it contain any experimental reasoning concerning matter of fact and existence?* No. Commit it then to the flames; for it can contain nothing but sophistry and illusion.

This viewpoint is the forerunner of modern positivism and operationism. Psychology from its formal beginnings has had the problem of freeing itself from philosophy, and Hume is one of its heroes.

ASSOCIATIONISM AS A SYSTEMATIC DOCTRINE

Associationism as a system growing out of empiricism was "founded" in the eighteenth century by a scholarly physician, David Hartley (1705-1757). He took Locke's chapter title, "The association of ideas," and made it his thesis. Hartley developed his psychology around associations, thus making associationism a formal doctrine with a name.

In contrast with the earlier politically active philosophers, Hartley led a relatively unexciting, orderly, and leisurely life. His single major publication was *Observations on man* (1749). He was much influenced by Newton and Locke. His theorizing was somewhat similar to earlier, less elaborated speculation by Hobbes on motion as an explanatory concept in brain activity; Hartley postulated vibratory actions within the nervous system which corresponded to ideas and images. More intense vibrations were sensations, and less intense vibrations ideas. He thus gave a physiological interpretation to Hume's distinction between impression and idea. Since vibrations take a little while to die out, sensations persist after removal of the stimulus; this was offered against the then-current view of flow of animal spirits in tubular nerves. Contiguity was stressed as the principle of association, and associationistic principles were used to explain visual depth perception, following Berkeley. Such principles were also said to explain diverse other phenomena, such as emotional pleasure and pain and the meaning of words.

Following Hartley, the next important development in associationism occurred in Scotland. Thomas Brown (1778-1820) rephrased Hartley's principles as principles of suggestion in order to get around the orthodox Scottish school's objection to associationism and its analytic tendencies; however, there was no real difference in the substance of what Brown was saying and what the British empiricists had been saying about the basic principles of mental activity.

Brown is notable because of his emphasis on secondary principles of association. He was concerned with the problem of selection, in a train of associations, of the single association that actually occurred when there were several that might occur. In this sense, he was interested in the problem of improving prediction. He presented several factors that might account for the selection of the particular association: the number of times it had been associated with the preceding mental content, how recently the association had previously occurred, the vividness of the original association, its duration, and the number of ideas now present which had connections with the following idea and thus added to its associative strength. Analogs to several of Brown's principles appear in much more recent learning theories. Concepts like number of trials, recency, stimulus-intensity dynamism, and stimulus summation are obvious parallels to Brown's secondary principles.

James Mill (1773-1836) presented one of the most extreme associationistic positions. His *Analysis of the phenomena of the human mind* (1829), published after seven years of summer-vacation writing, presents Mill's "mental mechanics." He held that the law of association could account for the most complex mental experience. The idea of "every thing," for example, presumably contains all lesser ideas and is simply their sum. Simple ideas were supposed to coalesce to form more complex ones, which might through long usage become so consolidated that they appeared as a single idea. Once the complex idea appeared thus, it might in turn coalesce with other ideas to form even more complex ideas. Mill's position was the ultimate in simplicity, if not in accuracy, because of his use of simple addition and a single principle of association—contiguity.

John Stuart Mill (1806-1873) transformed the mental mechanics of his father into a kind of "mental chemistry." According to his more sophisticated notion, ideas lose their original identity in fusion into more complex ideas by association. He accepted his father's notion of coalescence of ideas in association, but believed that very rapid combinations result in a loss of some parts. As Mill put it (1956, p. 558):

The laws of the phenomena of the mind are sometimes analogous to mechanical, but sometimes also to chemical laws. When many impressions or ideas are operating in the mind together, there sometimes takes place a process of a similar kind to chemical combination. When impressions have been so often experienced in con-junction, that each of them calls up readily and instantaneously the ideas of the whole group, those ideas sometimes melt and coalesce into one another, and appear not several ideas but one; in the same manner as when the seven prismatic colors are presented to the eye in rapid succession, the sensation produced is that of white. But in this last case it is correct to say that the seven colors when they rapidly follow one another *generate* white; so it appears to me that the Complex Idea, formed by the blending together of several simpler ones, should, when it really appears simple, (that is, when the separate elements are not consciously distinguish-able in it) be said to *result from*, or be *generated by*, the simple ideas, not to *consist* of them. . . . These are cases of mental chemistry: in which it is possible to say that the simple ideas generate, rather than that they compose, the complex ones.

The younger Mill also treated the problem of how mind creates matter, the problem posed by Berkeley. Mill was willing to admit the power of expectation to the mind of man. From this it followed that one might come to expect certain sensations to be possible, given other sensations which arose from a particular "object." Mill named this set of expectations *permanent possibilities of sensation* and thought that these possibilities adequately explained man's belief in the material world. We shall see the same general problem reappear later as the problem of meaning in Titchener's psychology.

Alexander Bain (1818-1903) was nominally a logician (at Aberdeen, Scot-land), but represents the closest approach we have met to a formal psychologist. Bain was largely a self-made college student and had difficulty in securing Scottish university professorships, finally moving into London circles with John Stuart Mill. He published a comprehensive and systematic two-volume psychology with a strong associationistic basis, *The senses and the intellect* (1855) and *The emotions and the will* (1859). Although at first slow to sell, these books were ultimately very successful, requiring several revisions and remaining the standard psychological text in Britain for almost fifty years. They may be considered a kind of physiological psychology, since they emphasize sensory phenomena. In 1876 Bain founded the first psychological journal, *Mind*. He supported it financially until 1892.

Bain had a well-developed set of laws of association. There were two principles of the formation of associations: contiguity and similarity. In addition, there was a kind of summation effect, whereby "associations that are individually too weak to operate the revival of a past idea, may succeed by acting together" (1886, p. 544). And there was a principle of creativity, whereby "by means of Association, the mind has the power to form *new* combinations or aggregates, *different* from any that have been presented to it in the course of experience" (1886, p. 570). Bain thus accepted Brown's secondary principle that associative strength is increased by several ideas working together and J. S. Mill's notion of the generation of complex ideas.

British associationism left a legacy of the utmost significance to the newly developing experimental science of psychology. A major part of this significance lay in the methodological point of view which associationism developed and refined. The stimulus-response type of thinking and experimenting grow more or less directly out of it. This is so much part and parcel of our basic mode of thinking— even for those of us who are most critical of some aspects of modern associationism—that we tend to take it for granted, along with the rest of our cultural heritage.

A somewhat less important part of the heritage of associationism was the content of associationistic theorizing. By and large this contribution consisted of the various laws concerning the formation of associations. Much of the historical content of associationism was more or less directly absorbed into the assumptions and biases of the early psychologists; for example, we have noted the resemblance between one aspect of Titchener's systematic formulation and the earlier notions of Locke and Hume.

We now turn to the kind of associationism that emerged during the last decades of the nineteenth century. Association of ideas was gradually replaced, in psychology, by association of stimuli and responses. The shift was related to the transition of psychology, so long a part of philosophy, into an empirical and natural science in its own right.

THE ASSOCIATION OF STIMULUS AND RESPONSE

Ebbinghaus's Invention of the Nonsense Syllable

Hermann Ebbinghaus (1850-1909) was an extremely capable German experimentalist who published (1885) the first systematic laboratory investigation of memory. He is to be credited as the first psychologist to make a thoroughly empirical study of association, or learning, although his major interest was in memory. He was concerned with controlling the kind of learning whose retention he wanted to investigate and so devised the nonsense syllable in an effort to minimize prior associations (prior, that is, to his laboratory study). The nonsense syllable consisted simply of two consonants separated by a vowel (e.g., WOY, XAM, CIR). Ebbinghaus thought he would be able to obtain more reliable memory curves if his learned materials were more homogeneous than ordinary words, whose associations with other words from prior learning would vary widely. The measure of Ebbinghaus's success is the fact that the negatively accelerated recall curve which he reported for the human subject, with number of syllables retained plotted as a function of time, has not been radically revised over the succeeding decades. Seldom do empirical curves retain their form despite the onslaught of new apparatus and more refined methods.

Ebbinghaus's contribution was particularly important since he was able to show that orderly results could be obtained by means of carefully controlled objective data even in so complex and variable a function as human learning and memory. This first laboratory application of strict associationistic principles in the field of learning was a milestone in the history of scientific psychology.

Pavlov's Discovery of the Conditioned Reflex

Ivan P. Pavlov (1849-1936) was a distinguished Russian physiologist, from 1890 to his death in 1936 director of the physiological laboratory at the Institute for Experimental Medicine. In 1904, he was awarded a Nobel prize for his investigations of glandular and neural factors in digestion. Somewhat earlier, however, he had made an accidental discovery which was destined to change entirely the direction of his scientific career and to have a profound and lasting effect upon the development of psychological science.

Pavlov had developed an apparatus which made it possible to hold and measure the amount of saliva secreted by a dog under various conditions of feeding. In essence, this consisted of a calibrated glass tube inserted through a fistula in the animal's cheek. Pavlov went to some lengths to ensure a very high degree of control over environmental stimuli in the laboratory stituation; the animal was harnessed in the apparatus within a relatively isolated experimental chamber, with recording devices outside. Pavlov's discovery consisted of his noting the persistent occurrence of *anticipatory* salivary flow. That is, the stimuli previously associated with the feeding of the animal (e.g., the approach of the attendant or the sight of the food dish) came to initiate salivation in animals as their training proceeded.

Extended thinking about the implications of such signals in the adaptive behavior of the animal eventually led Pavlov to a program of active research designed primarily to lead to new insights concerning the physiology of the brain. The term *conditioned reflex* was used, taking account of the acquired nature of the stimulus-response relationship. Pavlov's continuing interest in cortical functions is indicated in his choice of other terms to refer to processes he investigated, for example, *irradiation*, implying a presumed excitatory brain function, for the phenomena that are more commonly now called *generalization*. His entire research program was devoted to an exhaustive analysis of the factors involved in conditioning, on the assumption that by investigation of this relatively simple kind of reflexive learning he would be able to penetrate some of the mysteries of the so-called higher mental processes.

It is somewhat ironic that Pavlov's great influence has been in psychology, a discipline toward which he never seemed to feel too kindly (cf. 1932), rather than in the area of brain physiology, with which he was concerned primarily. This irony has not been perpetrated because of any perversity on the part of either physiologists or psychologists. The reason Pavlov was more honored by psychologists is simply that he was doing psychological work and developing constructs that, though they sounded physiological, were based on behavioral observations. Irradiation, for example, may sound like something that occurs in the cortex, but it was known only through the observation of what we would now call *stimulus generalization*. Kimble (1967) has given a very clear exposition of this facet of Pavlov's thought.

The details of his work are beyond the scope of our present endeavor (see Pavlov, 1927, 1928, 1941, 1955 for some of his own reports, in translation), but should be familiar, at least in skeleton form, to every student of psychology. His research represents completion of the shift of the concept of association from its historical application to ideas, to the relations between entirely objective and highly quantifiable glandular secretions and muscular movements, with which the behaviorist was soon to become concerned. Once discovered by Watson, Pavlov's research provided a most useful grist for the behaviorist mill, as we shall later see in Chapter 7. However, the significance of his work for psychology is indicated by the fact that it has outlived the early period of Watsonian behaviorism and continues to stimulate the much more sophisticated theories of the neobehaviorists.

Bekhterev and Motor Conditioning

The third major figure in the shift of associationism away from ideas and toward overt behavior is Vladimir M. Bekhterev (1857-1927). His most significant contribution was the motor conditioned response. Pavlov's research had been almost entirely with glandular secretions, whose direct influence on overt behavior seemed somewhat restricted. Bekhterev, a Russian contemporary and rival of Pavlov, extended the conditioning principle to involve the striped musculature. His major research paradigm involved the application of shock to the paw of a dog or the hand of a man following the presentation of a conditioned stimulus, such as a buzzer (1913).

Bekhterev had studied psychology under Wundt and was much more concerned than Pavlov with developing a kind of behavior system and relating his research to other behavior problems. His *reflexology* became the dominant theme in Russian psychology. Although American psychologists have preferred his motor conditioning technique to the salivary conditioning of Pavlov, they have found the latter's comprehensive experimentation and conceptualization more stimulating. Consequently, Bekhterev played a less important role than Pavlov in the further development of associationism as a laboratory technique.

THORNDIKE'S CONNECTIONISM

The systematic stimulus-response psychology of Edward Lee Thorndike (1874-1949) represents the closest approach to a purely associationistic system since James Mill. Thorndike began his psychological career with the laboratory study of learning in various animal species, but soon shifted his interests to human learning and many aspects of educational and social psychology. Although he did not initiate a school in the same sense that Titchener or Watson did, his mode of thinking was thoroughly associationistic throughout all his investigations in many diverse fields. Thorndike's connectionism offers, therefore, a wide-ranging application of associationism to psychological problems.

Thorndike studied under James at Harvard and under Cattell at Columbia. He began his investigations of animal learning at Harvard, where he trained chicks to run through improvised mazes (formed by placing books on end). He carried on this kind of research at Columbia, then working with cats and dogs in the puzzle box, which he devised, and took his doctorate there in 1898. His dissertation was entitled *Animal intelligence: An experimental study of the associative processes in animals*. It was subsequently republished (1911) together with new material on associative learning in chicks, fish, and monkeys.

Thorndike reveals a typically associationistic attitude in his description of his own career, a description that is deterministic, environmentalistic, and passive in its view of the organism (Thorndike, 1936, pp. 265-266):

The motive for my first investigations of animal intelligence was chiefly to satisfy requirements for courses and degrees. Any other topic would probably have served me as well. . . . I have recorded my beginning as a psychologist in detail because it illustrates what is perhaps the most general fact about my entire career as a psychologist later, namely, its responsiveness to outer pressure or opportunity rather than to inner needs. . . . Obviously I have not "carried out my career," as the biographers say. Rather it has been a conglomerate, amassed under the pressure of varied opportunities and demands.

Thorndike was appointed an instructor in psychology at Teachers College, Columbia University, in 1899. He stayed there for the remainder of his career. He retired in 1939 after four decades, but continued his activities for another decade until his death. Shortly after his original appointment he shifted his interests, at the suggestion of Cattell, to problems of human learning and education. It was in these areas that he spent most of his succeeding years.

Thorndike's fully developed system of connectionism is nowhere presented in a single, comprehensive account. This is understandable: Thorndike did not think of himself as a systematist or of his thinking and writing as contributing to a school. However, some of his later papers and chapters from books are collected in *Selected writings from a connectionist's psychology* (1949), which probably offers the best single source of his work. Our analysis of his system in terms of McGeoch's criteria (Chapter 3) is based primarily on this collection.

Definition of Psychology

Thorndike's opinion on definitions is suggested by his statement (1949) that "Excellent work can surely be done by men with widely different notions of what psychology is and should be, the best work of all perhaps being done by men such as Galton, who gave little or no thought to what it is or should be" (p. 9). His own definition of psychology is implicit in his writing. Thorndike was a functionalist in his emphasis on utilitarian aspects of psychology. More particularly, however, psychology was for him first and foremost the study of stimulus-response connections, or bonds. But Thorndike's conception of such associations went far beyond the simple connections between discrete, molecular, and highly localized events sometimes assumed to be characteristic of his thinking by his critics. The following excerpt indicates the scope of his interpretation of connections and indirectly gives us a picture of what Thorndike considered to be the subject matter of psychology (1949, p. 81):

Connections lead from states of affairs within the brain as well as from external situations. They often occur in long series wherein the response to one situation becomes the situation producing the next response and so on. They may be from parts or elements or features of a situation as well as from the situation as a whole. They may be largely determined by events preceding their immediate stimuli or by more or less of the accompanying attitude, even conceivably by his entire makeup and equipment. They lead to responses of readiness and unreadiness, awareness, attention, interest, welcoming and rejecting, emphasizing and restraining, differentiating and relating, directing and coordinating. The things connected may be subtle relations or elusive attitudes and intentions.

Postulates

Although explicit statements of postulates are not available in Thorndike's writing, some implicit assumptions are clearly made. The most fundamental one is probably that behavior can be analyzed into associations of the kind described by him in the quotation given above. Another is that behavioral processes are quantifiable. He is responsible for the much-cited proposition to the effect that if something exists, it must exist in some amount, and that if it exists in some amount, then it can be measured. An interesting incidental indication of the extent to which Thorndike was prone to practice his preaching on this topic is his estimate, given in his autobiographical sketch (1949), that he had "probably spent well over 20,000 hours in reading and studying scientific books and journals" (p. 7).

Mind-Body Position

Thorndike was too much the matter-of-fact utilitarian to be concerned with this problem, and he adopted no formal mind-body position. He stated (1949): "Under no circumstances, probably, could I have been able or willing to make philosophy my business" (p. 2). His common use of the words *mind* and *mental* therefore has no implication for a mind-body view, but indicates merely that Thorndike was relaxed about the use of ordinary language.

Nature of the Data

Thorndike's data are predominantly objective and very often, as has been noted, quantified. One incidental example of his use of quantified estimates has been mentioned. His research on the "goodness" of cities offers an illustration of the way in which he used quantification and objective data professionally. His own succinct summary of this research follows (1949, pp. 10, 11):

It seemed to me probable that sociology would profit by studying the differences of communities in the same way that psychology studies the differences of individuals. Therefore I collected nearly 300 items of fact concerning each of 310 cities, studied their variations and intercorrelations, computed for each city three scores for the general goodness of life for good people for each city (G), for the personal qualities of its residents (P), and for their per capita income (I), and studied the causes of the differences among cities in G.

Principles of Connection

Thorndike's best-known and most controversial contribution to psychological theory is his *law of effect*. In his early research with animals in puzzle boxes, he had been impressed with the gradual learning of the correct response and the gradual elimination of the incorrect one. Although this kind of learning has come to be called *trial and error*, actually Thorndike recognized the primary role of *accidental success* in the fixation of responses. *Exercise*, or frequency of occurrence, was accorded some strengthening powers, but not as much as occurred with the addition of success. He published the following formal statement (1905, p. 203):

Any act which in a given situation produces satisfaction becomes associated with that situation, so that when the situation recurs the act is more likely than before to recur also. Conversely, any act which in a given situation produces discomfort becomes disassociated from the situation, so that when the situation recurs the act is less likely than before to recur.

After extensive research on human learning (1931, 1932), Thorndike decided that the role of punishment or dissatisfaction was not at all comparable, on the negative side, to the positive action of reward. He therefore revised his law of effect to give the predominant role to reward; punishment, he said, serves mainly to make the organism try something else rather than directly to dissociate the response from the situation.

Thorndike suggested a cerebral function, the so-called confirming reaction (1933b), as the physiological basis of reinforcement, but this suggestion was not closely connected with his strictly behavioral research program. It was typical of

Thorndike that he was not timid about making physiological suggestions, but the suggestions were not taken particularly seriously, nor were they critical for either his experimentation or his theorizing.

Nevertheless, one should not overlook Boring's insightful comment on the easy compatibility between the neuron theory which emerged in the last half of the nineteenth century and the associationistic theory which preceded and followed it. Boring says in part (1950, pp. 69-70):

The scheme of mind for which the associationists stood is a mental arrangement that much resembles this physical arrangement of the brain. For the associationists, mind is composed of an infinitude of separate ideas, just as the brain is constituted of an infinitude of cells. But these ideas are bound together into more complex ideas or into higher mental processes by a huge number of associations, just as the nerve cells are connected by fibers. . . . The important point is that the new picture of the brain, arrived at unpsychologically by discoveries in histological technique, nevertheless bore a close resemblance to the new picture of the mind that associationism yielded.

The relevance of Boring's comments in the particular case of Thorndike's connectionism is obvious.

In 1933, Thorndike reported an extension of his theory of reinforcement. He had discovered (1933a) what he called an "independent experimental proof of the strengthening after-effect" (p. 2). This was the so-called spread of effect. It appeared that *nonrewarded* stimulus-response connections close to the rewarded connection acquired a strengthening from reinforcement. The closer the nonrewarded connection was to the rewarded one, the greater the strengthening. The observed strengthening was greater than the strengthening that would be produced by exercise alone.

Although the empirical data in support of this phenomenon have been amply verified, Thorndike's interpretation has not been generally accepted (cf. Marx, 1956). Alternative explanations in terms of guessing sequences or other types of bias were not eliminated. If an automatic strengthening effect, not dependent on cognitive (rational) factors, is eventually demonstrated, Thorndike's general reinforcement theory will look more attractive. Some published research has suggested that Thorndike's basic explanation may yet prove acceptable (Marx, 1957a, 1957b; Postman, 1961).

Principles of Selection

Stimulus-response associations account for the selection of behavior as well as for its acquisition. Thorndike's recognition of the problem of selection in behavior is clearly given in the following excerpt from his *Psychology of learning* (1913, pp. 111-112):

All man's learning, and indeed all his behavior, *is selective*. Man does not, in any useful sense of the words, ever absorb, or re-present, or mirror, or copy, a situation uniformly. He never acts like a *tabula rasa* on which external situations write each its entire contribution, or a sensitive plate which duplicates indiscriminately whatever it is exposed to, or a galvanometer which is deflected equally by each and every item of electrical force. Even when he seems most subservient to the external situation—most compelled to take all that it offers and to do all that it suggests—it appears that his sense organs have shut off important features of the situation from influencing him in any way comparable to that open to certain others, and that his original or acquired tendencies to neglect and attend have allotted only trivial power to some and greatly magnified that of others.

He interpreted problems of selective behavior, such as creativity in thinking (*learning by influence*), in terms of the same set of principles he applied to all learning, as indicated in this statement from the same source (1913, pp. 112-113):

A closer examination of selective thinking will show that no principles beyond the laws of readiness, exercise, and effect are needed to explain it; that it is only an extreme case of what goes on in associative learning as described under the "piecemeal" activity of situations; and that attributing certain features of learning to mysterious faculties of abstraction or reasoning gives no real help toward understanding or controlling them.

It is true that man's behavior in meeting novel problems goes beyond, or even against, the habits represented by bonds leading from gross total situations and customarily abstracted elements thereof. One of the two reasons therefor, however, is simply that the finer, subtle, preferential bonds with subtler and less often abstracted elements go beyond, and at times against, the grosser and more usual ones. One set is as much due to exercise and effect as the other. The other reason is that in meeting novel problems the mental set or attitude is likely to be one which rejects one after another response as their unfitness to satisfy a certain desideratum appears. What remains as the apparent course of thought includes only a few of the many bonds which did operate, but which, for the most part, were unsatisfying to the ruling attitude or adjustment.

CRITICISMS OF CONNECTIONISM

Elementarism

The essence of an associationistic position is that it is elementaristic. It was through their empiricism, elementalism, and analytic attitude that the British empiricists furthered psychology's progress as a science. It was through his acceptance of these attitudes, as manifested in his specificity, matter-of-factness, and attention to detail, that Thorndike made his most important contributions. Yet such views are open to attack, especially by those who want psychology to concern itself immediately with the "big picture."

Thorndike's theory of transfer of training (Thorndike & Woodworth, 1901) is the epitome of his elementarism. The theory was that improved efficiency at one task, acquired as a result of training, would transfer to another task only insofar as the two tasks had "identical elements." The more identical elements, the greater the transfer of efficiency from one task to another. This is a simple and specific view, one that is open to experimental attack through the manipulation of the number of elements that are similar. It has therefore certainly been of some value. However, in some situations it has appeared that some principle was learned which transferred perfectly to other tasks whose individual elements were quite different; therefore, the theory requires at least some qualifications before it can be accepted as a complete theory of transfer. Gates (1942), in his carefully documented defense of connectionism, has pointed out that Thorndike's elements were never intended to mean only the narrowest S-R connections; rather, they meant such things as factors, features, aspects, or relations and thus could mean such things as principles. "Identical," too, might be modified slightly to allow for degrees of similarity and to allow the theory more flexibility.

Trial and Error

Thorndike has been attacked for his emphasis on the randomness of learning, as implied in his characterization of learning as a trial-and-error process. Köhler (1947) and other Gestaltists have been especially active critics of all aspects of Thorndike's connectionism. The Gestaltists have suggested that learning in puzzle boxes and mazes necessarily appears to be random, stupid, and undirected because the animal cannot get an overview of the whole situation. The animal appears stupid because he is in a stupid situation, not because he is really lacking in insight.

Thorndike's supporters might offer several defenses to such criticism. First, the behavior of the animal in the puzzle box is by no means altogether random or stupid; much of the early behavior is directed at the exit, rather than at the device arbitrarily selected by the experimenter to release the animal. Such behavior is not stupid; it is intelligent in terms of the animal's past experience. Second, there may be a considerable amount of trial-and-error behavior which is not observed or recorded in the more open, less controlled situations which allow the animal an overview of the problem. It may be that Thorndike's situation was designed to reveal more clearly the nature of the basic learning process. Third, and last, there is plenty of evidence from outside the puzzle box to show that learning can be slow, random, blind, and continuous rather than fast, intelligent, and sudden. The psychological clinic or the counseling situation provides many cases which seem to exemplify connectionistic rather than Gestalt learning processes; criticisms of Thorndike's description should be tempered by this consideration.

Exercise

The sufficiency of frequency of occurrence, or the exercise principle per se, was seriously and tellingly questioned by the Gestalt critics. Here so strong a case was made that Thorndike revised his learning theory to add a new principle, *belongingness* (1935). The evidence against exercise came partly from experiments which showed that contiguous terms are not necessarily associated in ordinary learning situations. For example, suppose that a subject has learned a set of paired associates such as A-1, B-2, C-3, D-4. These have been presented in the order indicated. He responds perfectly with response terms 1, 2, etc., to stimulus terms A, B, etc. Now, however, if he is given one of the response terms—such as 1 or 2—as a stimulus, he does not readily respond with the learned stimulus term that actually followed—in this case B and C. But B followed 1 and C followed 2 just as closely in time as 1 followed A and 2 followed B. A similar situation holds for successive sentences, such as "John is tired" and "Jim is hurt." Here the connections John-tired and Jim-hurt are more readily formed and remembered than the connection tired-Jim, even though the purely physical relationship of these two terms is more nearly contiguous. Obviously something beyond mere contiguity in these cases is required for an effective association, and belongingness is the concept Thorndike used. He held that it is an important modifying condition of the strength of associations but is not essential to the formation of associations.

Thorndike's own research (1932, p. 184) gave further evidence against the sufficiency of the old law of exercise. Subjects attempting to draw lines of a certain specified length while blindfolded did not show improvement even with many repeated trials. Thorndike's general conclusion was that exercise is a framework within which other conditions, such as effect, can operate.

Law of Effect

This oldest of Thorndike's contributions has been attacked by behaviorists as well as by Gestalt critics. First, some behaviorists objected to what they felt was a mentalistic and subjective concept; they interpreted effect to mean pleasurable sensations or something similar. However, Thorndike met this challenge (1913, p. 2) by pointing out that by a satisfying state of affairs he meant simply a state of affairs which the animal did nothing to avoid, often doing things which maintained or renewed it; by an annoying state of affairs he meant one which the animal often did something to end. Thorndike was not proposing a hedonism; he meant effect, not affect.

Once it became clear that Thorndike was defining terms in a behavioral manner, he was subjected to the accusation that his law was circular. Critics said that acquisition of response would have to be measured in order to determine whether or not the state of affairs was satisfying, and acquisition was just what the law of effect was intended to explain. If justified, this charge would show that Thorndike was saying, "If an animal will learn when his behavior is followed by a given state of affairs, he will learn when his behavior is followed by this state of affairs." This criticism is not fully justified, for the operations that Thorndike specified for satisfaction and annoyance may be different operations from those which constitute a test of new learning. Once satisfiers and annoyers have been determined in some standard situation, they can be used in other situations to test their efficacy as reinforcers. Such tests will be tests of the law of effect. The question, then, becomes one of how generally a given effect will reinforce behavior. Meehl (1950), among others, has directed considerable attention to this point.

Another criticism has been that Thorndike assumed that the satisfier or annoyer had to act backward upon a connection which had already occurred in order to strengthen it. However, it is just as easy to assume that the action is upon the persisting traces that are still active from the occurrence of the stimulus and response that preceded the satisfaction or annoyance. Neobehavioristic Hullian theory (Hull, 1952) has a specific postulate about stimulus traces which assumes that the action of a reinforcer depends upon its temporal relationship to the stimulus traces. This is simply a more sophisticated statement of Thorndike's position. There is no necessary retroaction implied by Thorndike's law of effect.

A last criticism has been of the automaticity of the strengthening which was supposed to occur. Thorndike believed that learning could occur independently of any consciousness about what was being learned or why it was being learned (Thorndike & Rock, 1934). He was particularly gratified by the discovery of the spread-of-effect phenomenon (1933a), since even the most ardent of his critics would not attempt to explain the strengthening of errors as an intelligent or purposive process. The extent to which Thorndike was correct in his emphasis on automaticity cannot yet be determined, so we cannot say whether or not the criticisms of his position were justified; there is currently a considerable body of empirical evidence for both sides. It is interesting, however, that something very much like Thorndike's hypothesized "OK," or confirmatory, reaction is suggested by the intracranial self-stimulation technique (N. E. Miller, 1958a; Olds, 1955); electrical stimulation of certain brain areas apparently has an automatic reinforcing effect on preceding responses.

Mechanistic Determinism

Our final example is related to the last criticism. It concerns the widespread feeling that mechanistic science, such as that represented by Thorndikian connectionism, destroys human values. Thorndike had a characteristic answer to this kind of objection. Here is the way that he posed the problem (1949, pp. 346-347):

We must consider one final objection to using the methods of science in the world of values. Science, according to a very popular view, deals with a fatalistic world in which men, their wants and ideals, are all parts of a reel which unwinds year by year, minor whirls in a fixed dance of atoms. Values can have no place in such a world, and efforts to attain them by science must fail.

The truth of the matter, which is rather subtle, may best be realized by considering what I have elsewhere called the paradox of science, which is that scientists discover "causal" sequences and describe the world as one where the same cause will always produce the same effect, in order to change that world into a form nearer their heart's desire. Man makes the world a better home for man and himself a more successful dweller in it by discovering its regular unchangeable modes of action. He can determine the fate of the world and his own best, not by prayers or threats, but by treating it and himself by the method of science as phenomena, determined, as far as he can see, by their past history.

And here, in a nutshell, is his solution (1949, p. 362):

Thus, at last, man may become ruler of himself as well as of the rest of nature. For strange as it may sound man is free only in a world whose every event he can understand and foresee. Only so can he guide it. We are captains of our own souls only in so far as they act in perfect law so that we can understand and foresee every response which we will make to every situation. Only so can we control our own selves. It is only because our intellects and morals—the mind and spirit of man—are a part of nature, that we can be in any significant sense responsible for them, proud of their progress, or trustful of their future.

THE CONTRIBUTIONS OF THORNDIKE

Thorndike's fifty years of professional activity at Teachers College were among the most productive that have ever been recorded for a single man. Quantitatively, he accumulated a bibliography which at his death in 1949 had reached the amazing total of 507 items (Lorge, 1949). Many of these were long books and monographs, and many of them were stuffed full of quantitative data. Thorndike worked and published in a remarkably wide range of fields: he initiated the systematic laboratory investigation of animal learning; produced the first formalized associationistic learning theory; proceeded to an exhaustive analysis of human learning, as a result of which he revised his learning theory; became an active leader in the area of mental testing and educational practices; pioneered in the application of quantitative measures to certain sociopsychological problems; and contributed to the development of new techniques in the field of lexicography. All this within the span of a single lifetime!

Thorndike brought to all these fields the same direct and factual kind of approach that was so generally characteristic of his thinking. He was able to cut through to what he saw as the heart of a problem with a minimum of the verbiage and double-talk found in many writers. Whatever one may think of some of his ideas and whatever their eventual fate, we cannot fail to admire the freshness and perseverance of attack that he brought to the discipline.

Systematically, Thorndike's influence has declined, first as the more brash behaviorism took over in the 1920's, and more recently as the more sophisticated versions of neobehaviorism have emerged. But his work remains a bulwark of associationism, especially in the fields of animal and human learning and of educational psychology. Hilgard (1956) has given over his first chapter to Thorndikian connectionism, while recognizing the decline within psychology of interest in the system. He quotes Tolman on the importance of Thorndike as a standard; Tolman's judgment was (1938, p. 11):

The psychology of animal learning—not to mention that of child learning—has been and still is primarily a matter of agreeing or disagreeing with Thorndike, or trying in minor ways to improve upon him. Gestalt psychologists, conditioned-reflex psychologists, sign-gestalt psychologists—all of us here in America seem to have taken Thorndike, overtly or covertly, as a starting point.

Three decades later the picture has changed, as new kinds of learning theories and models have appeared. But Thorndike's systematic significance remains secure. Hilgard and Bower (1966) continue to give Thorndike an important place in their book. If James Mill represented the culmination of a crude associationism of ideas, Thorndike represented the climax of a gross associationism of S-R relations. If Titchener gave introspectionism a thorough trial, Thorndike gave simple S-R associationism an equally thorough trial. His work is a major and lasting contribution.

CONTEMPORARY ROLE OF ASSOCIATIONISM

Interpreted most broadly, associationism is practically synonymous with an orthodox interpretation of science: it is a belief that the primary job of science is to relate phenomena, to look for functional relationships. This is a methodological characteristic it shares with functionalism. The two systematic movements have been closely connected in this country, as we have suggested throughout the discussion. Thorndike could well have been considered, along with Hall and Cattell, as a pioneer functionalist. But there is a justification for considering associationism separately. For one thing, it is a special kind of functionalism. And certainly one can be a systematic functionalist without being an associationist (James and Dewey are examples); contrariwise, one can be a systematic associationist without accepting anything but the shared methodological characteristic from functionalism (as is true of many neobehaviorists). The functionalist puts greater emphasis on adaptation in general than the associationist; in addition, functionalists study this adaptation on a scale of evolutionary time, while associationists tend to limit themselves to the life of the individual organism.

Moreover, most associationists have a more restricted view than the functionalists, attempting to explain behavior with a more limited set of variables. Older associationists attempted to explain complex thought and behavior as *nothing but* the association of ideas. Thorndike was also a "nothing-butter": Behavior was explicable on the basis of nothing but stimulus-response connections, inherited or acquired. Present-day association theorists tend to be more cautious in their objectives and accept a more restricted domain—a miniature system—for their theory.

Today associationism as a methodological tool, if not as a systematic position, has been fairly well incorporated into the body of psychology; association of variables is generally recognized as a fundamental task of science. However, exactly what is to be associated remains one of the critical problems for psychology. Thorndike's answer emphasized the wide range of possible stimulus and response factors, although his own work was not a convincing demonstration, important as it was in a limited way. Whether S-R associationism can be effectively applied to a broad range of behavioral problems will need to be determined by the more refined varieties of associationism currently being developed.

There are four interrelated lines of such development. First, systematic research on the conditioned reflex as a primary learning phenomenon continues. Most of this is occurring in Russia, where the reflexology emphasis stimulated by Pavlov and Bekhterev has remained a strong force (see Appendix B and Razran, 1961), but at least one modification of this interest has occurred in the United States. This is the research of Gregory Razran (1949), who made an interesting adaptation of Pavlov's salivary conditioning procedure to human subjects. Razran used cotton dental plugs, inserted into the subject's mouth, to gather the saliva; he has been concerned with problems of verbal conditioning.

Second, the neobehavioristic stimulus-response theory of Hull and his many followers and collaborators represents a very important continuing influence. Here again the interest has been mainly in the field of learning, animal as well as human, where in addition to Hull himself, Kenneth Spence (1956, 1960) has been one of the foremost users of strict associationism (see Chapter 10). A more flexible kind of S-R associationism is evident in the work of Neal Miller and John Dollard (Dollard & Miller, 1950; N. E. Miller & Dollard, 1941), where the basic S-R concepts have been extended into the fields of social and abnormal behavior (see Chapter 12).

A third line is represented by the early associationistic theory of Guthrie (1935, 1952) and the more recent mathematizing of this kind of thinking in Estes' statistical association theory of learning (Estes, 1950). Here associationism is presented in perhaps its boldest form, since the single principle of contiguity between stimulus and response is utilized as the fundamental law of learning. Within learning theory, Guthrie has long been, almost single-handedly, an articulate supporter of a single contiguity position wherein learning is seen as fundamentally a matter of associations and nothing else; Estes' mathematical theorizing has given rigorous quantitative expression to this basic associationistic principle. In later writing (1959, pp. 402-405), Estes has indicated some acceptance of reinforcement as a descriptive concept if not an explanatory principle. These issues are elaborated in Chapters 10 and 13.

Finally, there are some versions of associationism which are somewhat less orthodox than the preceding but which have enjoyed vigorous success. Two important examples are the learning theories of Tolman and Skinner. Tolman's purposive behaviorism (1932) is a cognitive type of learning theory that postulates association between stimuli—a sign-Gestalt or sign-significant theory (see Chapter 11). Skinner (1938) has been concerned with the stimulus as well as the response aspects of the relationship that he called generically the *reflex*, but most of his interest has centered on *operant*, or emitted, behavior, and he has been content to assume internal eliciting forces for such behavior without speculating on or investigating them. The important association for him is between the response and the reinforcement (see Chapter 10).

Now that we have examined the origins of associationism and have discussed one theorist who exemplified it in its finished American form, it is appropriate to see whether we can describe it in terms of the dimensional systems provided by Coan and Watson (see Chapter 3). The authors will undertake a rough rating of associationism on Coan's dimensions, after which the student should attempt a rating on Watson's eighteen prescriptive dimensions before looking at the mean ratings of other students.

Referring to Figure 3-3, one recalls that the general factor proposed by Coan opposes a restrictive to a fluid orientation. Since we have already argued that a "nothing-but" orientation is characteristic of associationists, we must put associationism close to the restrictive extreme. The case for the analytic-synthetic orientation is almost equally clear; associationism is by nature analytic. The structural-functional dimension is less clear, although associationists in general tend toward a structural approach. A James Mill or a Wundt (as we shall see later) is more clearly structural in approach than a Thorndike. The first-order factors associated with the structural-functional distinction seem clearer; the associationist does tend to take a transpersonal orientation which is static and *definitely* emphasizes exogenous factors. The last three first-order factors are even clearer; Thorndike, for example, was the very epitome of an objectivist who took an elementarist, quantitative approach.

It would be a valuable exercise for the student to assign values for associationism on Watson's eighteen dimensions as described in Chapter 3 and to select the three most important dimensions. The method used by the authors (pp. 69-72) is recommended as a technique for assigning the values. The student could then see whether he rates associationism more like associationism than any of the other five systems by computing the city-block distances between his values and those assigned by the authors (Table 3-2).

The consensus in the class of twenty-three graduate students, as measured by frequency of choice of a dimension as one of the three most important, was that associationism emphasizes empiricism-rationalism most heavily (choosing empiricism), determinism-indeterminism next (choosing determinism), and quantitativism-qualitativism third (choosing quantitativism).

The largest disagreement between the authors and the graduate students occurred on the purism-utilitarianism dimension, with the students' ratings toward the utilitarianism end of the scale and the authors' mean nearer the purism end. Possibly this difference can be explained by the lack of consistency among the theorists of the associationistic school. Pavlov represents a fairly puristic outlook, while Thorndike was more utilitarian. The observed discrepancy could have occurred because the authors were thinking more of Pavlov, while the students were thinking of Thorndike. Such variations between individual theorists are a source of difficulty whenever schools are being described.

SUMMARY AND CONCLUSIONS

In this chapter we have traced associationism from its origins and development in British empiricism, where the important tradition of association of ideas was elaborated, through its modification more recently to an association of behavior, and to its emergence in the work of Thorndike as a full-fledged association of stimulus and response. We have treated Thorndike's connectionism as the best representative of associationism, although it was not developed by him as a comprehensive system. We have tried to indicate the kinds of answers that can be given to some of the major criticisms of Thorndikian connectionism and have presented our evaluation of the significance of Thorndike's work. We have indicated the role of associationism in contemporary psychology, pointing out that in a broad methodological sense, association of variables is the primary task of all science. Finally, we have sketched the major lines of current development of the basic associationistic principle.

It is clear that the associationistic principle must be accorded a key role in psychology, whatever the ultimate fate of the various systems and theories which build upon it as a necessary and sufficient principle. Some kind of associationism is certainly necessary, in a methodological if not a systematic or theoretical sense; whether it is also sufficient as a learning theory is much more doubtful, but still remains to be seen. In any case, it is remarkable that so ancient and simple a notion should persist so long, let alone be accorded an increasingly significant role in contemporary behavior theory. Its long viability attests to its vitality, especially when one considers that empirical tests have been applied since the work of Ebbinghaus and Pavlov. It will be most interesting to observe the fate of associationism under the increased empirical and theoretical attack which it is now sustaining, as in the rapidly expanding research utilizing mathematical models.

Further Readings

Historical treatments of the important British empiricists and associationists are found in Boring's *History of experimental psychology* (1950) and Murphy's *Historical introduction to modern psychology* (1949). Herrnstein and Boring provide, in *A source book in the history of psychology* (1965), beautifully introduced, organized, and selected readings from the British empiricists and related theorists in the early part of the twentieth century. Turner's *Philosophy and the science of behavior* (1967) gives a sophisticated and admiring analysis of these same philosophers and demonstrates their immediate contemporary significance. Pavlov's *Conditioned reflexes* (1927) is still perhaps the best introduction to the classic Russian contribution, although a number of more recent presentations of his work have appeared. Recent surveys of the Russian post-Pavlovian developments are available in Razran (1961), Mintz (1958, 1959), and Brozek (1962), as well as in the latter's chapter in the Appendix to the present volume. Kimble's revision of Hilgard and Marquis's *Conditioning and learning* (1961) offers a fairly up-to-date American treatment of the vast conditioning literature. Thorndike's connectionism is most readily available in the single volume *Selected writings from a connectionist's psychology* (1949). The modern associationism long promulgated by Guthrie is summarized in his *Psychology of learning* (1952). Estes' development of statistical association theory is documented in Chapter 13.

TABLE 5-1   Important Men in Structuralism

Antecedent Influences	Structuralists	
	Pioneers and Founders	Developers of Related Positions
Franz Brentano (1838-1917)	Wilhelm Wundt—Leipzig (1832-1920)	Carl Stumpf—Berlin (1848-1936)
Gustav Fechner (1801-1887)	Edward B. Titchener—Cornell (1867-1927)	G. E. Müller—Göttingen (1850-1934)
H. L. F. von Helmholtz (1821-1894)		Oswald Külpe—Würzburg (1862-1915)
		J. P. Nafe—Washington University (St. Louis) (1888-1970)
		Edward G. Boring—Harvard (1886-1968)

5 Structuralism

The highly developed introspective psychology that goes under the name *structuralism* or *existentialism* is represented in its finished American form by the work of E. B. Titchener. In 1898, Titchener so sharpened and dramatized the structural-functional distinction, made almost casually by James in 1884, that he effectively named both systems (see R. I. Watson, 1968, pp. 397-399). He pointed out the analogy between the type of psychology he favored and the study of structure in biology. Titchener's system was a refinement of the psychology of his mentor, Wilhelm Wundt, founder of the Leipzig laboratory. During the early years of psychology, in Germany, structural psychology was *the* psychology. Its purpose was the introspective analysis of the human mind; psychology was to be a kind of chemistry of consciousness. The primary task of the psychologist was to discover the nature of the elementary conscious experiences and, later, their relationships to one another. Introspection by a highly trained person was thought to be the necessary tool.

Table 5-1, on the left, lists the most important men in structuralism.

The major significance of structuralism has been threefold. First, it gave psychology a strong scientific impetus, getting the name *psychology* attached for the first time to a scientific type of endeavor with formal academic recognition and clearly separated from the two main parental fields, physiology and philosophy. Second, it provided a thorough test of the classic introspective method as the only method for a complete psychology. Third, it provided a strong orthodoxy against which the functional, behavioristic, and Gestalt forces could organize their resistance. The newer schools arose from a progressive reformulation and final discarding of the basic structural problems. This fact alone makes the analytic introspective psychology of Wundt and Titchener a necessary subject for contemporary study.

The Psychology of Wundt

It is customary, at least in America, to cite Titchener as the founder of structural psychology. Certainly he named it, developed it, and buttressed it against functional and behavioristic trends. However, Titchener's system was basically the same as that of Wilhelm Wundt (1832-1920), under whom Titchener had studied. Wundt himself was a self-conscious systematizer and the "father" of the new experimental psychology. He established the first formal laboratory for psychology at the University of Leipzig in 1879. We shall, however, follow American tradition and treat Wundt as a forerunner of the structuralist school, meanwhile recognizing that he was far more than a mere antecedent.

Wundt himself had antecedents, some of whom were discussed in Chapter 2. Another antecedent which was partly oppositional in its views was the phenomenological tradition found in German philosophy and psychology at that time. Turner (1967, p. 60) defines phenomenology as a philosophy which regards the entities of experience as possessing an irreducible integrity of their own. Kant, in his *Critique of pure reason*, developed a part of the phenomenological viewpoint. He believed that whatever is known is phenomenon and that knowing requires an appearance in consciousness. Knowledge was thus restricted by Kant to appearances. This influence is still felt in modern phenomenology, for example, in this statement by Lauer (1965): "If we are to know what anything is—and this the phenomenologist will do—we must examine the consciousness we have of it; if this does not give us an answer, nothing will" (p. 7).

In 1856, Lazarus and Steinthal first distinguished between phenomenology and psychology (see Capretta, 1967). They asserted that the former is concerned with a description of the phenomena of mental life, while the latter seeks to establish causal explanations of these phenomena. Thus when Wundt appeared on the scene, distinctions were already being made, distinctions that helped free psychology from the shackles of a particular descriptive methodology applied to mental events.

Wundt's philosophy was neither materialistic nor spiritualistic. He opposed the latter type of view because he thought it erred in trying to establish a science of mental experience in terms of speculations about a "thinking substance." He opposed materialism because he did not think a science of mind could be developed through physical investigations of the brain. Wundt felt that the study of mind must be a science of experience (agreeing on this point with the phenomenologists).

Wundt, however, believed that psychology must be experimental. Schultz (1969) quotes Boring as saying: "The application of the experimental method to the problem of mind is the great outstanding event in the history of the study of the mind, an event to which no other is comparable." We owe Wundt a great debt for establishing psychology as an experimental science. Here is some of what he has to say on the subject (1894, p. 10):

It is experiment, then, that has been the source of the decided advance in natural science, and brought about such revolutions in our scientific views. Let us now apply experiment to the science of mind. We must remember that in every department of investigation the experimental method takes on an especial form, according to the nature of the facts investigated. In psychology we find that only those mental phenomena which are directly accessible to physical influences can be made the subject matter of experiment. We cannot experiment upon mind itself, but only upon its outworks, the organs of sense and movement which are functionally related to mental processes.

The subject matter of psychology was to be *immediate experience*, as contrasted to *mediate experience*. By mediate experience Wundt meant experience used as a means of knowledge about something other than the experience itself. This is the usual way in which we use experience in acquiring knowledge about the world. We say, "The *leaf* is green"; the quotation implies that our primary interest is in the leaf, not in the fact that we are experiencing green. Immediate experience for Wundt was experience per se, and the task of psychology was the study of this immediate experience in itself. This distinction looks backward at Locke's distinction between primary and secondary qualities and forward toward Titchener's distinction between the subject matters of psychology and physics. If we attempt to describe the experience we have in connection with a toothache, we are concerned with immediate experience. The physicist studies experience only as mediate, but the psychologist, if he is a Wundtian, studies immediate experience. The study of experience was to be accomplished by *introspection*, by self-observation (*Selbstbeobachtung* was Wundt's word). Introspection was the *controlled* observation of the contents of consciousness under experimental conditions. Nonexperimental introspection was useless for scientific purposes. Wundt clarifed his position in the preface to his *Principles of physiological psychology* (1904, p. 45):

All accurate observation implies that the object of observation (in this case the psychical process) can be held fast by the attention, and any changes that it undergoes attentively followed. And this fixation by the attention implies, in its turn, that the observed object is independent of the observer. Now it is obvious that the required independence does not obtain in any attempt at a direct self-observation, undertaken without the help of experiment. The endeavor to observe oneself must inevitably introduce changes into the course of mental events—changes which could not have occurred without it, and whose usual consequence is that the very process which was to have been observed disappears from consciousness. In the first place, it (the experimental method) creates external conditions that look towards the production of a determinate mental process at a given moment. In the second place, it makes the observer so far master of the general situation, that the state of consciousness accompanying this process remains approximately unchanged.

Wundt thought that mind and body were parallel, but not directly interacting systems. Thus the mind did not depend on the body and could be studied directly with profit. Psychology was formally called *physiological psychology*, but the explanation of the mind through the study of physiology could, at the very least, come later. Wundt did not think that introspection yielded the only psychological knowledge, however (1904, p. 5):

We may add that, fortunately for the science, there are other sources of objective psychological knowledge, which become accessible at the very point where the experimental method fails us. . . . In this way, experimental psychology and ethnic psychology form the principal departments of scientific psychology at large. They are supplemented by child and animal psychology, which in conjunction with ethnic psychology attempt to resolve the problems of psychogenesis. Workers in both these fields may, of course, avail themselves within certain limits of the advantages of the experimental method. But the results of experiment are here matters of objective observation only, and the experimental method accordingly loses the peculiar significance which it possesses as an instrument of introspection.

Wundt at least formally recognized methods and areas of psychology other than the particular brand in which he was most interested. Moreover, he did not simply talk about such topics as ethnic psychology; he published ten volumes of his *Völkerpsychologie* (1900-1909) between 1900 and his death in 1920. He did largely "simply talk" about child and animal psychology. The translation of his work *Human and animal psychology* (1894) devotes only 26 of its 454 pages to animal psychology. Wundt's publications and those of his students indicate that he felt these aspects of psychology were of much lesser importance.

Although there are some unevennesses in Wundt's treatment of psychology, there is a much greater unevenness in the modern psychologist's picture of Wundt's psychology. We probably stereotype or parody the position of almost every historical figure, but Wundt and Titchener receive particularly unjust treatment. Anderson (1971) submitted a list of Wundt's statements to a group of graduate students and asked the students to match the quotations to the names of a group of outstanding figures in the history of psychology, one of whom was Wundt. In no case was a quotation attributed to Wundt most often, although they all came from him. It seemed clear that many of the statements were too modern or too experimentally or behaviorally oriented to have come from Wundt!

Wundt conceived of the problem of experimental psychology as threefold: to analyze conscious processes into elements, to discover how these elements are connected, and to determine the laws of connection. Wundt's attitude toward the thing analyzed, toward consciousness, left some room for ambiguity. He explicitly talked about mental *process*, not mental *contents* (1894): "As a matter of fact, ideas, like all other mental experiences, are not *objects*, but *processes, occurrences.*" (p. 236).

Yet the view of psychology as the science that searches for the elements of process was a difficult one. The result of the lack of clarity was that Wundt was accused of a static elementism—of regarding the contents of consciousness as though they were stationary, structural elements. The name *existentialism* was affixed to the school because it seemed that the elements of consciousness were regarded as existing just as physical objects exist. The experimental work at Leipzig sometimes seemed to justify the critics in their accusations, in spite of the systematic opposition of Wundt to such a view of his psychology. Nevertheless, Boring's (1950) description of the naming of structural psychology is a beautiful summary of the general treatment accorded structural psychology in the United States: "The enemies of this orthodox psychology name it, but always in accordance with what they most dislike in it" (p. 431).

Other European Psychologists

Although Wundt was clearly the most important systematizer and organizer in the early, formative days of psychology, he was by no means the only psychologist in the European tradition who influenced Titchener. Many followed Wundt's lead more or less closely, but others sprang from a different lineage. None of them, however, disagreed with Wundt about the central importance of introspection as *the* methodology to be used in psychology. As Boring (1953) has pointed out in his account of the history of introspection, none of these early psychologists thought of themselves especially as *introspectionists*; they were simply *psychologists*, regarding the importance of introspection as absolutely axiomatic. The only arguments were about the details of the method.

Franz Brentano (1838-1917) was perhaps the most influential of the non-Wundtians because of the diverse effects he had within psychology. He was originally trained for the priesthood, but took a doctoral degree in philosophy and taught this subject on university appointments first at Würzburg and later at Vienna. He resigned his priesthood because he could not accept the doctrine of infallibility of the Pope. He was known as a great Aristotelian, and he influenced Gestalt psychology and psychoanalysis, in addition to providing a contemporary competitor to Wundt and Titchener.

Brentano's name is associated with *act psychology*. Its major tenet is that psychology should study mental acts or processes rather than mental contents. He believed that mental acts always refer to objects; for example, if we regard hearing as the mental act, it always refers to something heard. In this case, the truly mental event is the hearing, which is an act and not a content. If we see a color, again it is the seeing which is mental, not the thing seen. His *Psychologie* (1874) was the most important of his psychological publications. Brentano was basically a philosopher rather than a scientist and an empiricist rather than an experimentalist. He influenced structural psychology by his opposition rather than by any positive contributions, and he also had a strong influence on phenomenology.

Carl Stumpf (1848-1936) was Wundt's major direct competitor. In 1894, he was awarded the outstanding professorship in German psychology at the University of Berlin, when Wundt, as dean of German psychologists, had seemed the logical choice. It has been rumored that the opposition of Helmholtz prevented Wundt from getting the appointment.

Stumpf was strongly influenced by Brentano. This influence may have been the cause of his accepting a less rigorous type of introspection than that considered acceptable by Wundt. Their difference of opinion is illustrated by the fact that they carried on an acrimonious argument in a series of publications. The problem concerned tones, and the issue was whether one should accept the results of highly trained introspectors (Wundt) or of trained and expert musicians (Stumpf). Stumpf refused to accept the results obtained in Wundt's laboratory. The disagreement was what one would expect between a man who took a more phenomenological view and one (Wundt) who insisted on a more analytic type of introspection. It was one of Stumpf's students, Husserl, who is usually credited with starting phenomenology as a formal doctrine. Husserl, however, had earlier studied with Brentano, and that association plus his study with Stumpf may have helped to nurture his phenomenological views. He would not have received that nurturance with Wundt or Titchener!

Stumpf's laboratory at Berlin never rivaled Wundt's in scope or intensity of research, but there was a number of research projects. Stumpf's special field of research was audition, and his true love was music. Also, there were several men who were destined to be of great importance in the development of psychology—notably the three founders of Gestalt psychology, Wertheimer, Köhler, and Koffka; Kurt Lewin, an important field theorist; and Max Meyer, who was an early behaviorist. Stumpf, like Brentano, was of greater significance for his differences from Titchener than for his similarities to him, although he accepted without question the use of introspection.

The most capable and productive experimental psychologist of the time was G. E. Müller (1850-1934). He spent some forty years directing the laboratory at Göttingen. His major work was in the fields of memory, psychophysical methodology, and vision. With Pilzecker, he developed the interference theory of forgetting, and they called the phenomenon wherein new learning interferes with old retroactive inhibition. Müller also refined Fechner's techniques in psychophysics and extended Hering's theory of color vision.

More than Wundt or Stumpf, Müller succeeded in cutting free from philosophy and metaphysics, which had been his own early interests. In this respect he was similar to Titchener, who also struggled to free himself of the encumbrance of too much concern for philosophy.

Oswald Külpe (1862-1915) was trained in the Leipzig laboratory by Wundt and for a shorter time in the Göttingen laboratory by Müller. While at Leipzig, Külpe became a friend of Titchener, but the two men were later to have fundamental disagreements; Külpe was not to be a carrier of the Wundtian orthodoxy, and Titchener essentially was.

The first part of Külpe's psychological career was spent in more or less classic research efforts. He published a textbook (1895), which was quickly translated by Titchener and in which he attempted to report only the experimental facts obtained by careful experimental introspection. Very soon thereafter he went to Würzburg, where he directed a series of ingenious and provocative introspective experiments on thought. Classic introspection was found to be incomplete; the continuity in thinking appeared to elude the orthodox introspective analysis. The

Würzburg interpretation of the results was that there are *impalpable awarenesses* which do not appear in consciousness as contents usually do and which should be regarded as functions. They were to be included, however, as genuine conscious data. The points of view of both Brentano and Wundt were accepted by Külpe when he accepted both contents and functions (acts) as conscious experience.

Külpe had a more direct relationship to Titchener in that he made the distinction between psychology and physics on a different basis from the one Wundt used; to Külpe, and later to Titchener, psychology was distinguished by its concern with the dependence of experience upon the experiencing organism. Both men apparently borrowed this distinction from the philosophers Mach and Avenarius, although its relation to Locke's distinction is also clear.

TITCHENER'S STRUCTURALISM

Edward Bradford Titchener (1867-1927) was exposed to Wundt's conception of psychology as a student at Leipzig. Although he was an Englishman by birth, he was a German by virtue of two years of training with Wundt, and he remained a German for the thirty-five years he lived in the United States, where he came in 1892 to take over the laboratory at Cornell. Titchener's continuing Germanness of personality has become a legend: his autocratic personality, the formality of his lectures in academic robes, and even his bearded, Germanic appearance. Every lecture was a dramatic production, with the staging carefully prepared by assistants. It was gravely discussed afterward by staff members and graduate assistants, who were expected to attend.

Titchener's intellectual Germanness is quite as remarkable as this legendary Germanness of personality, although it may not be as much emphasized. There were other non-German students whose exposure to Wundt was more protracted than Titchener's but whose deviations from the line of orthodoxy laid down by Wundt were marked; a number of these students came from America and returned to America. Perhaps the English culture from which Titchener came provided better nurture for a German psychology than the practical-minded American spirit did. Wundt did owe a great debt to the English empiricists, and no doubt Titchener in England had already been influenced by these predecessors of Wundt. It is even possible that much of the perceived Germanness of his personal demeanor may have been in the eyes of the beholders—the provincial Americans—who may not have distinguished between a truly German personality and a generally European one. At any rate, psychology for Titchener was very much like psychology for Wundt.

A major theme throughout Titchener's work is the unity of science. It seemed self-evident to him that all sciences were erected from the same foundation—the world of human experience. When this world was observed in different ways, different sciences evolved. For example, Titchener believed that just as physics evolved when man began to view the world as being a vast machine, so did psychology evolve when he looked at it as a mind, a set of experiences subject to psychological laws. To illustrate this idea of scientific unity further, at various junctures he drew analogies between the then-nascent science of psychology and the more established sciences of biology (1898) and of physics and chemistry (1910).

Titchener (1910) felt that the hallmark of scientific method was observation, which in his view subsumed experimentation. He saw an experiment as an observation that could be repeated, isolated, and varied, thereby ensuring clearness and accuracy. He then distinguished between the physical science type of observation (looking at) and psychological observation or introspection (looking within).

States of consciousness were the proper objects of this psychological study. Titchener launched structural psychology in the United States in his paper, "The postulates of a structural psychology," partly as follows (1898, pp. 449-450; see also Dennis, 1948, p. 366):

Biology, defined in its widest sense as the science of life and of living things, falls into three parts, or may be approached from any one of three points of view. We may inquire into the structure of an organism, without regard to function—by analysis determining its component parts, and by synthesis exhibiting the mode of its formation from the parts. . . .

We find a parallel to morphology in a very large portion of "experimental" psychology. The primary aim of the experimental psychologist has been to analyze the structure of the mind; to ravel out the elemental processes from the tangle of consciousness, or (if we may change the metaphor) to isolate the constituents in the given conscious formation. His task is a vivisection, but a vivisection which shall yield structural, not functional results. He tries to discover, first of all, what is there and in what quantity, not what it is there for.

It is difficult to tell, from this quotation, just what Titchener thought about mind and consciousness. He changes metaphor, self-consciously, in midsentence. From the context it seems that the bulk of his writing and thinking fits the second metaphor, although he speaks of consciousness as composed of processes rather than elements in his most rigorous, self-conscious writing. Yet by analogy he lends reality status to consciousness, since the word *structure* and the biological attitude toward morphology lend such reality status.

It is not even safe to assume that the founder of America's brand of structuralism rejected functionalism. On this subject, R. I. Watson (1968, p. 393) makes the following flat statement:

Description of Titchener's system of psychology is sometimes oversimplified. He was a structuralist, critics said, meaning that the static elements of experience were his concern, as contrasted with functional study of the process of experience which had been espoused by James and others. This is simply not true. There is no doubt he utilized functional material; and the findings of psychophysics, which formed one major segment in his system, are readily viewed as depending upon the functions of discrimination and estimation. Unequivocally, he accepted the existence of a functional aspect of psychology.

Still, a stubborn critic might argue that Titchener *regretted* the existence of functionalism, though he *recognized* it.

Consciousness was defined by Titchener as the sum total of a person's experiences as they are at any given time. Mind was regarded as the sum total of a person's experiences considered as dependent on the person, summed from birth to death. Thus (1899, p. 12):

"Mind" is understood to mean simply the sum total of mental processes experienced by the individual during his lifetime. Ideas, feelings, impulses, etc., are mental processes; the whole number of ideas, feelings, impulses, etc., experienced by me during my life constitutes my "mind."

Titchener also listed three problems for psychology that were very similar to Wundt's (1899, p. 15):

The aim of the psychologist is three-fold. He seeks (1) to analyze concrete (actual) mental experience into its simplest components, (2) to discover how these elements combine, what are the laws which govern their combination, and (3) to bring them into connection with their physiological (bodily) conditions.

Titchener modified Wundt's distinction between psychology and physics much as Külpe did. He could not agree with Wundt that physics studied mediate experience and psychology immediate experience; he thought that all experience must be regarded as immediate. The distinction, rather, was in the *attitude* to be taken toward the study of the ever-immediate experience. The physicist studied the experience as independent of the experiencing person, while the psychologist studied the experience as it *depended* on the experiencing person.

One might object that the astronomers after Bessel were quite concerned with the dependence of experience upon the nature of the experiencing observer and that the physicists would also be prepared to evince concern. The reply to such an objection might be that the physicists' concern with the role of the observer was evinced only so that observations could again be made completely reliable and independent of the observer and thus illustrated their basic attitude rather than an exception to it.

Titchener's concept of *stimulus error* was related to the distinction between psychology and physics. By stimulus error, Titchener meant the error of paying attention to, and reporting on, the known properties of the stimulus rather than the sensory experience itself. This is probably the most important and the most obvious error made by untrained introspectors. Titchener pointed out that this tendency to describe the conscious state in terms of the stimulus rather than of the experience per se is beneficial and necessary in everyday life. All of us, therefore, grow up with strong habits of this kind, since responses to the objective character of the stimulus are ordinarily the effective ones. But such strong habits must be unlearned if one is to become an adequate psychological observer, and the only way to do this is through a new and intensive learning effort. Thus the trained introspector is one who learns to ignore the objects and events as such and to concentrate instead on the pure conscious experience.

The use of a reduction screen in visual research offers a good illustration of this situation. If the experimenter permits the subject to see the stimulus object and also the illumination impinging upon it, the subject reports that a piece of white paper is white even if it is very dimly illuminated—and is actually reflecting less light energy to the eye than, say, a piece of coal under bright illumination. The common judgment of untrained subjects is that the paper is brighter than the coal. This stimulus error can be eliminated by means of a reduction screen, which permits the subject to see only a small part of the stimulus object through a kind of peephole. Such a device prevents the subject from seeing either the nature of the object or the amount of illumination, and now his judgment follows the "true" character of the isolated sensory experience: a piece of white paper dimly illuminated is called dark gray, and a piece of black coal brightly illuminated is called light gray. These latter judgments are more in accord with the physical energies of the stimuli, although they are less accurate descriptions of the reflectivities of the coal and the paper. Neither type of sensory description need be viewed as more true in any ultimate sense. The structuralists wanted the description that correlated most closely with the momentary stimulation. Titchener felt that a kind of functional reduction screen needed to be built into each psychological introspector through extensive practice. Physicists and all other scientists make the stimulus error as a matter of course. They wish to report on observations in such a way that their reports agree with the objective character of the stimulus, regardless of any momentary effects that may presently be determining their perception of the stimulus. Only the introspective psychologists want to know the pure character of the present experience.

Titchener thought psychology ought to study experience as it seems to exist when we try to detach it from learning; that is, we should refuse to attribute meaning to it and thus avoid committing the stimulus error. These meanings become attached to stimuli through learning, and our reactions to the stimuli so directly incorporate the related experiences that the "percept" is no longer a product of the stimulus only.

Titchener exorcised child psychology and animal psychology from the main body, which we saw that Wundt did not do. Titchener did not deny that the study of the behavior of children and animals would yield valuable information; he denied rather that the information would be *psychological* information.

Wundt's hardheaded experimentalism was expressed in perhaps more exaggerated form by Titchener. He held not only that psychology must be experimental but also that it must be *pure*. Applied science seemed to Titchener a contradiction. The scientist, as Titchener saw him, must keep himself free of considerations about the practical worth of what he is doing. He accordingly never accepted the work by Cattell and others on individual differences as making any important contribution to psychology. He decried the notion that the function of psychology is to find ways of ministering to sick minds. He was caustic about the possibility of becoming a psychologist through the process of untrained, morbid self-examination.

Titchener at first accepted Wundt's psychophysical parallelism as his practical solution to the mind-body problem, but philosophy really did not interest him. He accepted it because it allowed him to pursue the study of psychology with the methodology in which he believed. Titchener, like Wundt, boasted about the new freedom of psychology from philosophical speculation. Thus we see in these two practitioners of a fledgling science the full-blown scientific tendency to take philosophy for granted, to view it as irrelevant, and to carry Hume's philosophical antimetaphysical attitude into laboratory practice.

The new freedom from philosophy, they felt, flowed partly from their use of the experimental method. The psychological experiment should be a controlled introspection, with states of consciousness held constant by the external conditions, and the factors within the situation varied one at a time in different experiments. The experimenter need only set up apparatus, devise and explain the problem, and record the trained introspector's comments.

THE METHODOLOGY OF STRUCTURALISM

The technique of investigation for Titchener, as for Wundt, was introspection; but, as indicated above, Titchener's introspection was an even more highly formalized and practiced procedure than Wundt's *Selbstbeobachtung* had been. Introspection, according to Titchener, could be carried on scientifically only by exceptionally well-trained observers.

One instance of his feelings about naive observers is given in a discussion of phenomenology (1912b, p. 489):

In the present connection, I mean, by a phenomenological account of mind, an account which purports to take mental phenomena at their face value, which records them as they are "given" in everyday experience; the account furnished by a naive, common-sense, non-scientific observer, who has not yet adopted the special attitude of the psychologist. . . . It is more than doubtful whether, in strictness, such an account can be obtained.

It is clear that Titchener did not favor the use of untrained observers, nor did he at this time favor phenomenology as science.

It is difficult for untrained observers to say just what it is that the trained observers learned to do. Introspection changed to some extent as the years passed. Apparently Titchener thought introspection was becoming more refined and more generally applicable with the passage of time. He commented (1912a): "Our graduate students—far better trained, it is true, than we were in our generation—sit down cheerfully to introspective tasks such as we had not dreamed of" (p. 427).

Still—although we are told that the graduate students were getting better at something—it is hard for an outsider to be sure what that something was. Introspection has been said to be the direct observation of consciousness, of mental processes. However, Titchener said (1912b): "The course that an observer follows will vary in detail with the nature of the consciousness observed, with the purpose of the experiment, with the instruction given by the experimenter. Introspection is thus a generic term, and covers an indefinitely large group of specific methodological procedures" (p. 485).

Even Titchener seems not to have had an easy time finding a satisfactory definition of introspection and to have fallen back on a specification of the experimental conditions, a commendably operational procedure. But are there then no commonalities among the different applications of the term? Surely there is a self-consciousness about introspection, an awareness of observing? Not according to Titchener (1912a): "*In his attention to the phenomena under observation*, the observer in psychology, no less than the observer in physics, *completely forgets to give subjective attention to the state of observing*" (p. 443). Titchener, and Wundt before him, recognized that self-consciousness might interfere with the phenomena under observation and thus invalidate the results (see the criticisms of introspection given later in this chapter).

If Titchener's description of introspection is accurate and complete, we would seem to have little to question. The psychologist's report would be just like the physicist's report of the same thing. But Titchener was speaking of a *trained* introspector. What happens to the observer as he undergoes training? We note that he gives verbal reports from the beginning; we do not deny that we may get interesting results in physics by accepting the reports of other experimenters who describe the things they have seen, and other investigators do not question the fact that we have seen certain things. We accept the words of another's report with only the reservation that he must be able to tell exactly what he means, by pointing to an instance if necessary.

The observer learning to introspect, however, is in a different kind of circumstance. Certain classes of words, which we may call "meaning words," are not accepted. A structural psychologist is not interested scientifically in the statement, "I see a table," for table is a meaning word, based on preknowledge about the aggregation of visual and tactual sensations by which we identify the table. The structural psychologist believes that he is interested in this aggregate as a meaningless aggregate; he does not want the aggregate summarized in a meaning word, for he is interested in the direct contents of experience, not in the inferences made on the basis of the contents. So when the observer says *table*, he is cautioned against the stimulus error, and eventually he excludes this type of word from his professional vocabulary. What words are left then? Are only such words left as have no external referents, but referents only in experience? Again it is a difficult question. Wundt and Titchener alike emphasized that the external conditions must be carefully controlled so that the contents of consciousness can be precisely determined and so that more than one observer may experience the same thing and therefore cross-check the results of the experiment. We can then say that a workable vocabulary should be possible, based on the commonalities in experience under the carefully controlled conditions. After all, how else do we agree on a convention for the meaning of the word *table*? A reasonable inference is that we check that part of our experience which consistently occurs in conjunction with the use of the word *table* by others. Therefore, it seems possible to create a language, or language usage, of the type the structuralists required. However, it must be easier to correlate words with objects than with experiences, since we have more useful object languages within science than we have experience languages. It may be too difficult a task for the introspector to isolate that aspect of his manifold experience to which a particular word should apply. Certainly two introspectors cannot reach agreement on the relevant aspect by pointing to it, as one can do in the case of objects. Fingers will not fit in the remoter reaches of the world of experience. The findings of introspection could not always be agreed upon, even with very careful control of conditions. Had it been possible to secure sufficient scientific agreement on introspective statements of findings, the structural school might still be a vital force today.

That it was not possible we shall see later. Meanwhile, we may attempt to delineate introspection by discussing those features of it which a nonintrospective psychologist of today can understand. Introspection may be more, but it involves at least this: a generic term for several types of observation carried out in psychology. Different investigators, for example, at Cornell and Würzburg, tended to use somewhat different subvarieties. The Cornell variety of observation was carried out under laboratory conditions, with the stimulating situation, including instructions, carefully determined by the investigator. Only those subjects were used who had been carefully trained by the investigator or by another investigator who was versed in the method. The training included, among other things, at least the admonition to observe the contents of experience and report on them. It also included punishment when the observer used words that we may designate meaning words or thing words as we ordinarily conceive of these classes of words. The use of words that were considered descriptive of conscious states was no doubt rewarded.

In order to give the reader something of the flavor of the introspective method, as developed by Titchener, we reproduce below part of a representative account of an introspective experiment. In it the subjects, observers (*O*s) C. and P., were instructed to report their memory images; the stimuli used were geometric shapes of various colors. E. Murray's account (1906, pp. 230-231) follows:

> 1 *Introspections.* Manner of appearance of image. As a rule, the memory image appears spontaneously at the beginning of the recording period, or in the preceding after image period. Thereafter it returns at irregular intervals, which usually grow longer toward the end of the minute. On a few occasions, C. reports, the image was apparently evoked by chance twitches of the eyeball or eyelid, by inspiration, or, automatically, by rhythmic pressure of the key. Occasionally, also, the observer reports a faint anxiety at the momentary failure of the image, and a temptation to summon it by movement of the eyes (*O*. C.), by steady fixation, or by recall of detail after detail (*O*. P).
>
> 2 *Localization of image.* The memory image usually appears in the same direction and at the same distance as did the original. P. distinguishes it from the sensory after image by its position outwards on the screen (the after

image appearing "on the eyelids"), and remarks that "Its appearance is often accompanied by the feeling of turning toward it." Occasionally it seems to be situated "in the head," but in this case its distinctness is materially lessened.

That this localization is correlated with the presence of motor elements, actual or ideated, has abundant evidence. Thus C., noting that the memory image usually appears as an object with spacial relations, states that in this case "the feeling of accommodation" is present, with "tendency to move the eyes and locate the image directly in space." The less real this feeling (of accommodation and convergence), the less distinct the image. Thus, toward the end of the recording period (C. sometimes reports), the images become less vividly "visual," are accompanied by almost no tendency to fixation, and are localized, not in any definite portion of the visual field, but vague, "in the head,"—a type of image described by C. as "more subjective," or "more purely memorial."

It seems probable that P. also refers to the muscular sensations attending fixation in her less concretely phrased account of the semispontaneous recall of images. "I seem to turn my attention toward the place where I expect the image to appear. If I hold my attention on this place, several more images are likely to follow." And again, "my attention vacillates about the place on the board where the image is expected, then settles down, and below unfolds the image, sometimes indistinctly, but as the attention turns more decidedly toward it growing in vividness."

> 3 *Incompleteness of image.* Images are rarely complete. The lower right hand portion is most often missing, and the upper left hand portion the most distinct,—a condition possibly correlated with the characteristic grouping of matter on the printed or written page, and the acquired habit of attending primarily to the upper left hand word. In cases *where the outline is complete, it is often doubtful whether* there are not gaps in the main body of the figure. Whether complete or incomplete in relation to the original, the image is usually reported as flashing in and out as a whole, without growth or alteration.

After this examination of the problems in defining introspection, one may have less tendency to laugh at the futile definitional efforts of those who are still vitally concerned with introspection. Natsoulas (1970) shrugs off the problem this way: "Here 'introspection' is a relatively neutral term for the process(es) whereby one arrives on the spot at introspective awarenesses" (p. 90).

EMPIRICAL PROPOSITIONS

In science, not only do observations determine theory, but theory also determines observations. The empirical propositions of structuralism seem today to be mixed with theoretical presuppositions, but to the structuralists their propositions seemed to be based directly on observation.

The three basic elements of consciousness that came down all the way from the English empiricist philosophers seemed to be verified by the introspective observations of Wundt and later of Titchener. These three elements were *sensations, images,* and *feelings.* The elements were thought to be basic and incapable of further analytic reduction.

Images were the elements of ideas, and sensations were the elements of perception. Images were supposed to differ from sensations by being less vivid, less clear, less intense, and sometimes less prolonged. Both images and sensations had certain basic attributes. For Wundt, these were two: intensity and quality. Titchener expanded the list to four: *intensity, quality, attensity,* and *protensity.*

Quality had its usual meaning of a difference in kind; attensity was synonymous with clearness, except that it was understood to mean a type of clearness which varies with attention rather than with the objective characteristics of the stimuli; intensity had its usual meaning of strength; and protensity was a word for the duration in time of the sensation of image. Some sensory modalities produced sensations with the additional attribute of *extensity* in space.

Titchener saw that it was not easy to distinguish image from sensation, but held that there was at least a difference of a quantitative sort; for example, there would be a point along the attensity dimension at which image turned into sensation. An experiment by Perky (1910) at Cornell illustrated the difficulty of deciding what was image and what was sensation. Subjects told to "project" a banana on a blank screen did not report the appearance of a dim picture of a banana actually flashed on the screen, but attributed the sensation to unusually clear imagery on their part at that time; other subjects told to observe the actual banana failed to report when it was turned off, apparently maintaining a sort of equivalent of the dim sensation via their own imagery. We should note that Perky was distinguishing between image and sensation on the basis of the presence or absence of an objective stimulus; this is not a distinction on the basis of conscious contents and seems inconsistent from the point of view of a structuralist. However, Perky's experiment cast doubt on the sensation-image distinction, and as a result there was a tendency to speak more about the attributes of sensations and less about images. Boring (1950, p. 201) cites a later experiment by Schaub (1911) as providing even stronger evidence that images might be more intense than sensations, but he says that Titchener believed Perky's conclusions.

The Würzburg school got into heated controversy with Titchener on the subject of "imageless thought," which they claimed to have "discovered." The admission of such an entity would have necessitated a revision of Titchener's view that images are the elements of thoughts. Accordingly, he rejected the views of Külpe, Binet, and Woodworth on imageless thought and felt that their results might have been caused by faulty introspection. In any event, he did not find clear evidence for the existence in consciousness of this new upstart element, this imageless thought. His subjects, in fact, failed to confirm Woodworth's experimental findings. Titchener's verdict was that the so-called "thought" element was probably an unanalyzed complex of kinesthetic sensations and images, which were always difficult to find in consciousness. The "will" element was also excluded. An *act of will* was simply a complex of images forming ideas in advance of action.

Titchener was able to bring *attention* into his system in a simple way by equating it with clearness of sensation. He found in some subjects only a two-part breakdown of clearness, into central and clear versus peripheral and unclear; in other subjects, there was a multistep progression from clear to unclear.

Titchener rejected Wundt's tridimensional theory of feeling. Of the three dimensions—pleasant-unpleasant, strained-relaxed, and excited-calm—he retained only the first. He reduced the other two to sensations and images, especially kinesthetic. They were therefore not to be regarded as special characteristics of feeling; in fact, they were not feeling at all.

Nafe (1927), one of Titchener's students, later reduced even the remaining attribute of feeling to sensations: pleasantness was regarded as a "bright pressure" localized in the trunk at a higher level than the "dull pressure" of unpleasantness. He suggested that vascular changes might be responsible for these sensations. If Nafe's point of view were accepted, even affect would be reduced to sensation.

So far, we have examined the empirical propositions which had direct systematic relevance for Titchener. In addition, there are more directly empirical propositions (statements of experimental results), which were generally accepted by the structuralists; some of these are asystematic and acceptable to any psychologist regardless of systematic beliefs. For example, Titchener's first "empirical" chapter in *An outline of psychology* (1899) is entitled "The quality of sensation." In it are examined the qualities of visual, auditory, olfactory, gustatory, and other sensations. Each examination of these qualities is based on a relevant experiment or demonstration. The data may be of interest in the modern area of "sensation and perception." An argument could be made that such directly experimental results constitute the basic contribution of every psychological system.

STRUCTURALISM AS A SYSTEM

Definition of Psychology

The structural definition of psychology was "the analytic study of the generalized adult normal human mind through introspection." This summarizes our previous discussion; "generalized" adds the feeling of Titchener and of Wundt before him that psychology is not basically concerned with individual differences, and "normal" excludes the mentally disturbed and defective.

Basic Postulates

The postulates of structural psychology were not formal postulates, but statements designed to guide the behavior of the scientist. The underlying assumptions of structuralism are not explicated in easily available form, but must be combed out of the statements of the structuralists and sometimes must be garnered by inference from their proponents' behavior. It is impossible to make any adequate, logical statement about the number, sufficiency, or adequacy of the structuralistic postulates.

The best that can be done is to make a few possibly defensible statements about the assumptions of the school. Certainly both Wundt and Titchener accepted the two basic methods of science: control and analysis. They put extreme emphasis on experimentation and excluded other methods as unscientific. Neither could affirm too strongly that psychology had won its fledgling wings and was independent of metaphysics. Knowledge was empirical, not a priori. Mind and consciousness were clearly assumed to be useful concepts and the proper province for psychological study. Introspection was assumed to be a valid method for that study and to be a method which required extended training for efficient performance. Consistency and law were assumed to hold for the realm of consciousness, and mind and body were supposed to be parallel systems.

Nature of the Data

To summarize the previous discussion: Titchener believed that the primary data of psychology must be obtained by means of introspection and under strict experimental conditions. Titchener no doubt believed that the data were as objective as any data could be. Were a controversy to arise today about the objectivity of Titchener's data, we would be objective about making the objective-subjective distinction; the data would be referred to a computer for reliability analysis. The intuitive analog of such an analysis condemned introspective data to the subjective category; it is not certain whether this particular judgment was adequately justified.

Mind-Body Position

Titchener's postulate regarding a mind-body position has already been discussed. However, lest we too easily accept the view that Titchener simply accepted Wundt's psychophysical parallelism, we should note another Titchenerian theme (1899): "The metaphysics to which Science points us is rather a metaphysics in which both matter and spirit disappear, to make way for the unitary conception of *experience*" (p. 366). Here, Titchener sounds as though he accepts a monism of experience, or the view that mind and body are two aspects of experience. His view is similar to that of Mach, of whom Titchener was fond and who emphasized experience as the basis of all science. Titchener later elaborated his position. He pointed out that the commonsense conception of mind leads to dead-end questions. He says (1910, p. 14):

Where, for instance, on that view, does the body end and the mind begin? Do the senses belong to mind or to body? Is the mind always active and the body always passive? Do body and mind ever act independently of each other? Questions such as these arise at once; but it is a hard matter to answer them. Parallelism has no logical pitfalls of this kind.

Principles of Connection

The problem of connection was a secondary one for Titchener; until the detailed nature of the elements to be connected was worked out, there was no point in trying to connect them. His view of connection was similar to his view of function; he recognized the necessity for working out functions eventually, but felt that the study of structure must come first.

To the extent that he concerned himself with connections, he explained them by association. Titchener reworded the principle of association by contiguity as his main law (1910, pp. 378-379):

Let us try, however, to get a descriptive formula for the facts which the doctrine of association aims to explain. We then find this: that, whenever a sensory or imaginal process occurs in consciousness, there are likely to appear with it (of course, in imaginal terms) all those sensory and imaginal processes which occurred together with it in any earlier conscious present. . . . Now the law of contiguity can, with a little forcing, be translated into our own general law of association.

His law of association furnished him with a principle of successive connection; that is, item A tends to elicit item B immediately afterward. There remained the problem of connection of the elements within the cross section which is consciousness. This was to be solved by the presentation of the laws of synthesis. This task seems never to have been completed. From his discussion, it is clear that Titchener recognized the difficulty of synthesis, that the elements did not simply sum to the unitary experience which was there in the first place (1899, p. 17):

If the conscious elements were "things," the task of reconstruction of an experience would not be difficult. We should put the simple bits of mind together, as the bits of wood are put together in a child's puzzle-map or kindergarten cube. But the conscious elements are "processes"; they do not fit together, side by side and angle to angle; they flow together, mix together, overlapping, reinforcing, modifying or arresting one another, in obedience to certain psychological laws.

Titchener was never able to give these laws, for his first task of analysis was never finished.

A further kind of connection for Titchener to explain was the problem of meaning: How does meaning become connected with sensation? He regarded the problem as outside psychology, but developed an explanation, his famous *context theory*, anyway. The meaning of a sensation for Titchener's theory was simply the context in which it occurred in consciousness. A simple sensation does not have meaning; it gets meaning only from the other sensations or images accompanying it. The context of the sensation, and hence its meaning, is a result of past experience with the sensation; it is the result of associations between past sensations or images. What we call *meaning* is simply the totality of sensation accompanying the meaningful sensation (1910, pp. 367-369):

No sensation means; a sensation simply goes on in various ways, intensively, clearly, spatially, and so forth. All perceptions mean. . . . For us, therefore, meaning may be mainly a matter of sensations of the special senses, or of images, or of kinesthetic or other organic sensations, as the nature of the situation demands. Of all its possible forms, however, two appear to be of especial importance: kinesthesis and verbal images. . . . But is meaning always conscious meaning? Surely not; meaning may be carried in purely physiological terms.

Principles of Selection

The basic problem of explaining why certain stimuli are selected in consciousness was handled by the use of the concept of attention, which was reduced to sensory clearness. Titchener initially believed there were two degrees of clearness, but one of his students at Cornell, L. R. Geissler (1909), found that subjects could rate up to ten gradations along a numerical scale. Wirth, at Leipzig, produced similar findings (see Titchener, 1908).

According to Titchener, there are three general stages of attention: (1) native, involuntary primary attention, where native factors like the intensity and quality of the sensory experience determine attention along with involuntary attentive set or perhaps novelty; (2) voluntary secondary attention after the novelty wears off—this stage is difficult to get through in terms of attempting to maintain attention at a high level of clarity; and (3) derived primary, or habitual, attention, which is the ultimate objective; the attention is again involuntary, this time because of its history of learned development rather than because of native, unlearned factors.

As stages, these three conditions were obviously intended to be viewed as continuous and not as clearly separable. An example of this continuity in stages is the development of interest in reading a certain kind of subject matter, such as that in a psychology text. Originally, attention will be held by factors like novelty and certain expectations generated by presuppositions concerning the subject matter. As reading progresses, however, negative or inhibitory factors may develop as a result of the student's encountering new and unfamiliar terminology, difficult expositions, and the like, and also, perhaps, as a result of disappointment of some of the expectations. The second stage will thus appear, and the student will find it difficult to keep attending clearly, to reading assignments, for example. Fixation at this stage of attention is a serious problem in education and might be used to account for much academic difficulty as well as for many students' complaints. If this troublesome stage can be survived, according to Titchener's account, the third stage will emerge. Then familiarity with the material will suffice to maintain a certain level of attention. Reaching this stage of derived involuntary attention in a variety of subject matters is an important objective of education.

CRITICISMS OF STRUCTURALISM

Such was the system called *structuralism*. It made many positive contributions to the science of psychology: It freed it from metaphysics, gave it a careful experimental method and a nucleus to organize around, and contributed experimental facts. Yet perhaps its greatest contribution to psychology was the criticism it elicited.

Introspection

The severest attack on structuralism was on its very heart, the introspective method. Many of these criticisms were recognized as problems by Wundt and Titchener, and they took steps to make sure that the criticism would not remain valid. The following are key problems that were considered.

Introspection must really always be retrospection, since it takes time to report on a state of consciousness. Forgetting is rapid, especially immediately after having an experience, so that some of the experience will perhaps be inadvertently lost. It is also possible that the necessity for retrospection will lead to embellishment or error, especially if the introspector has a vested interest in a theory that will be affected by the experimental results.

This objection was answered partly by having only well-trained observers work within time intervals short enough to reduce forgetting and partly by postulating a *primary memory image*, a kind of mental echo which preserves the experience for the introspector until he can report it. If the report is made within the limits of this immediate memory, before conscious attention has changed, then little of value will be lost.

A second difficulty recognized by structuralists and critics alike is that the act of introspecting may change the experience drastically. The classic example is an introspection regarding anger; if the state is attended to, it tends quickly to disintegrate and may even disappear completely. Thus the measuring technique interferes with experience, as it does with electrons for the physicist. A somewhat analogous situation concerns the role of the cultural anthropologist who wishes to observe in detail the habits and customs of some other culture. His very presence in the household serves to contaminate the behavior of his subjects. The undesirable effects of such an intrusion can be minimized if the observer comes to live in the household and is eventually accepted; the behavior of his subjects will then become progressively more normal and unaffected by his intrusion. But this process, like that of training oneself to accept the act of introspecting into the mental household, can be accomplished only by long and arduous effort. In the case of the mental household, the state of affairs may be affected by the training process. Wundt postulated an independence of the thing observed with experience, but Titchener apparently did not claim as strong a position; he did feel that the experienced observer becomes unconscious of the act of observation with practice.

A third difficulty is that psychologists relying on the introspective method at different laboratories were not getting comparable results; rather, scientists in one laboratory asserted things that contradicted the results of scientists elsewhere (Boring, 1953). In our discussion previously, we said that it does not seem to be *in principle* impossible to agree on a language describing experience as it is observed by the introspector; this would be possible, however, only because of the control over external elicitors of sensation. It does seem to have been *empirically* impossible to devise a useful, agreed-on introspective language. Titchener continued to maintain that agreement could be reached eventually, but to no avail; the tide of criticism rose ever higher, until structuralism was engulfed.

A fourth argument was perhaps the most decisive. There was growing concern for data which seemed properly to belong to psychology but which were not accessible to introspection. Titchener himself recognized unconscious meanings. The Würzburg school was pressing for the existence of imageless thoughts as elements; today we might say that the status of thought was not clear, that thought seemed to go on independently of the elements that introspective analysis had so far revealed. The animal psychologists were getting interesting results without using introspection; the psychoanalysts had clearly demonstrated the importance of *unconscious* influences in maladjustment. The rising tide that had been pitching over the wall of orthodoxy eventually tore it down, and introspection was no longer the exclusively accepted psychological method.

Other Objections

There were other criticisms besides those which pertained to method. The narrowness of structural psychology was attacked. Titchener was an outstanding compartmentalizer, and he seemed to prefer putting an area of investigation into a nonpsychological category to claiming it as a new province for psychology. This was not a definitional exclusion; Titchener's catalogue of psychology seemed to include an adequate shopping list of areas. It was a behavioral exclusion. Titchener's personal interests did not include animal psychology and child psychology, nor did he encourage his students to do research in these areas. When Watson started publishing his behavioral studies, Titchener disclaimed knowing what they were, but he did know what they were not: they were *not* psychology. Even physiological psychology as it is now conceived was a subsidiary problem to be attacked later. This conception of the limits of psychology was too narrow to withstand the explosive pressure of the empirical interests manifested by a growing band of psychologists.

Structuralism was castigated for its artificiality and its emphasis on analysis. These shortcomings were most vigorously attacked by the Gestaltists, who deplored the loss they felt must be engendered by analysis. They pointed to the primacy of the whole as whole, a whole that they felt could never be recovered by any synthesis of elements. For them, the primary method was phenomenological observation, not the analytic introspection of Titchener.

A last criticism was based on the pragmatic American attitude, with its emphasis on the importance of overt behavior. What difference did the elements of experience make in initiating action? The functionalists perhaps were the first to ask this type of question. Beginning with James, the question was: "What is the function of consciousness in adjustment?" The behaviorists were more extreme, pointing to the fact that the law of conservation of energy must hold in physical systems and that consciousness must therefore be irrelevant to predicting and explaining the behavior of organisms considered as physical systems. These matters are examined at greater length in our discussion of behaviorism (Chapter 7).

THE FATE OF STRUCTURALISM

Structuralism, like any other system, was sensitive to criticism and empirical results. It started with an ambiguous view of its subject matter, consciousness, a view which at least failed to deny vehemently enough that consciousness could be thought of as an existent real. This led to an alternative name, existentialism, for the school. The search for the elements of this consciousness finally led to the conclusion that there was but one established element, sensation. In Titchener's posthumous publication, *Systematic psychology: Prolegomena* (1929), he concluded that introspective psychology deals exclusively with sensory materials. Its problem by this time was reconceived as an examination of the dimensions of sensation.

In this reformulation of its problem, structural psychology may be said at the same time to have solved its original problem and to have arrived exactly nowhere. The problem of searching for elements had been eliminated; there seemed to be no laws of combination of elements to look for, since there was but one element to work with. This logical cul-de-sac was brilliantly foreshadowed by James in chapter 9 of his *Principles of psychology* (1890, p. 224):

It is astonishing what havoc is wrought in psychology by admitting at the outset apparently innocent suppositions, that nevertheless contain a flaw. The bad consequences develop themselves later on, and are irremediable, being woven through the whole texture of the work. The notion that sensations, being the simplest things, are the first things to take up in psychology is one of these suppositions. The only thing which psychology has a right to postulate at the outset is the fact of thinking itself, and that must first be taken up and analyzed. If sensations then prove to be amongst the elements of the thinking, we shall be no worse off as respects them than if we had taken them for granted at the start.

Time was running out for structural psychology as it ran out for Titchener. He had withdrawn progressively from psychology as the years passed. His early burst of productivity in this country produced about nine papers a year for seven years, but it diminished thereafter. He withdrew early from the American Psychological Assocation and formed his own group. His relationships with other psychologists were mixed. He went through a fierce period in his relationship to Thorndike after ripping apart the latter's book (Joncich, 1968). Paradoxically, he was an admirer of Watson, though Watson and Thorndike would not seem to have differed significantly in either brashness or iconoclasm. Moreover, it was Watson's highly successful promulgation of the behavioristic doctrine that served to attract increasing numbers of psychologists and thereby hasten the demise of structuralism. Perhaps the battles were too much, and the old warrior gradually withdrew even from his students and his field and turned to his hobby of numismatics.

E. G. Boring's book, *The physical dimensions of consciousness* (1933), was in effect the death throe of structuralism. As a prominent student of Titchener and in some ways his most likely successor, Boring in 1933 was actually concerned chiefly with correlating conscious and physiological processes; this was Titchener's third problem. Boring seems still to have been trying to salvage whatever he could of the structuralist systematic position (1933, p. vii):

The doctrine of conscious dimensions, which I believe without proof to be essentially Titchener's way of meeting the challenge of Gestalt psychology and the anti-atomists, seems to me very important and the correct approach to the adequate description of mind. However, I am not willing to stress the doctrine as much as some of its friends would like, because I believe that categories of description, whether they be the psychological dimensions of quality and intensity or the physical dimensions of space, mass and time, are scientifically arbitrary and temporary, matters of the convenience or economy of description. One does not attempt to discover conscious elements, attributes, or dimensions; one makes them up and uses them as phenomenological exigencies require.

At this point, Boring was trying to wed structuralism and the increasing scientific and logical sophistication of his vantage point in time. He recognized the arbitrariness of scientific concepts and the importance of verbal convention even in the communication of introspective results. Yet the influence of Titchener was still strong, and Boring was fighting to salvage consciousness as a fit subject of scientific investigation.

Four years later, he had apparently given up the struggle. He examined the definition of consciousness and the role of private experience. He concluded that private experience could not be scientifically useful until it became public; therefore, it was defined out of science. After arriving at "an awareness of an awareness" as the closest approximation to a definition of consciousness, he had this to say about the word (1937, p. 458):

Having understood, tough-minded rigorous thinkers will, I think, want to drop the term *consciousness* altogether. A scientific psychology is scarcely yet ready to give importance to so ill defined a physiological event as an awareness of an awareness. This concept might never have come to the fore had not people tried to interpret others in terms of their own "private" minds—that egocentric Copernican distortion which properly leads to desolate solipsism.

Thus Boring furnished first the capstone, then the tombstone, of structuralism. Structuralism today is dead. Its positive contributions have been absorbed back into the body of its mother science. Other bits of it are still showing aboveground in psychology, but these are few and insignificant indeed. It died of a narrow dogmatism, a disease which no school of psychology can long survive. Structuralism lacked the support of practical application and of connections to other areas of psychology; its demise was mourned by few.

The foregoing comments on the fate of the structural system must not be interpreted to mean that all use of introspection as a methodological tool is also past. It is not. If by introspection we mean the use of experience and the use of verbal reports based on this experience, then "introspection" is simply coextensive with science and will presumably always be used. However, the kind of introspection used is not the structuralistic kind, and reports are in the language of behavior rather than in the language of the structuralists. The various contemporary forms of introspection have been summarized by Boring (1953).

Meanwhile, the phenomenological tradition, which furnished part of the matrix from which structuralism sprang, denying its origin as it rose, lives on. Husserl had posited the individual's potential for grasping the "essence" or "central core" of reality, which he thought lies in consciousness. Sartre carries through Husserl's ideas of essences and concludes that phenomena are not appearances of objects, but rather are the beings which objects leave in appearing to consciousness. He regards consciousness as the opposite of objectivity (see Lauer, 1965, and compare this view with the Titchenerian view of consciousness). Rollo May is among latter-day psychologists who have attempted to tie together phenomenological and psychological ideas. He writes (1966, p. 75):

Our science must be relevant to the distinctive characteristics of what we seek to study, in this case the human being. We do not deny dynamisms and forces; that would be nonsense. But we hold that they have meaning only in the context of the existing, living being.

It is clear that the modern conception of phenomenology and of the namesake of Titchener's and Wundt's psychology, existentialism, is really antithetical to their views. There is the surface similarity, the belief that consciousness is critical. Neither phenomenology nor existentialism seems susceptible to the current explosive technological changes which daily produce alterations in the methods of scientific investigation. Hence, phenomenology as a system of thought may last as long as thought itself.

DIMENSIONAL DESCRIPTIONS OF STRUCTURALISM

Structuralism, like associationism, is near the restrictive pole and stands very high in analytic and structural orientation. Despite its analytic and quantitative tendencies, it would not be judged high in objectivity. All would agree that the science of the "generalized human mind" was transpersonal in orientation and that it tended to emphasize exogenous factors. It would also be judged static, but that is a judgment imposed from the outside; we have seen that Wundt and Titchener tried to view consciousness as a process.

Again, the student would be well-advised to rank structuralism independently on Watson's eighteen dimensions and to select the three dimensions emphasized most heavily in the system. A comparison of city-block distances from the authors' values (Table 3-2) will inform the student of his understanding of the structuralist viewpoint.

The authors and students were in some disagreement as to the values assigned on the dimensions methodological objectivism-methodological subjectivism, nomotheticism-idiographicism, and staticism-developmentalism (Table 3-2). The authors justified their extreme value on the first of the above dimensions by the fact that introspection is supposed to be the prototype of subjectivism. The authors would argue that the structuralist emphasis on the "generalized" human mind makes structuralism one of the most clearly nomothetic schools. Finally, its critics, at least, emphasized its static character. The students seem not to have departed far from the mean values on these dimensions.

As judged by the twenty-three graduate students, the dimensional characteristics most heavily weighted by structuralism were conscious mentalism, structuralism, and empiricism. (The foregoing is a shorthand expression combining identification of the dimension with identification of the judged position on the dimension.)

SUMMARY AND CONCLUSIONS

Structuralism was launched in 1898 by E. B. Titchener as *the* psychology. Its problems were the discovery of conscious elements, their mode and laws of combination, and their relation to the nervous system. Its method was introspection, conceived by Wundt as the study of immediate experience and by Titchener as the study of experience as dependent upon the experiencing organism. Both Titchener and his teacher, Wundt, emphasized the indispensability of the experimental method for psychology. The structural school succeeded in winning academic recognition for psychology as an independent science. Titchener tried to free psychology as a method from metaphysics and in general established it as an empirical science, although structuralism as a school was not completely free from some problems that today would be considered metaphysical.

Structuralism was criticized for its methodology and its narrowness in general. The critics prevailed, and today modern psychology tends to accept only the basic scientific attitude of structuralism and the empirical results that were obtained in such a way that they were independent of systematic preconceptions. Various forms of introspection are still in use, but the systematic formulations of structuralism are of historical interest only.

Further Readings

Wundt's *Principles of physiological psychology* (1904) gives a good picture of the general structuralist systematic position, as the student has already seen in the quotations in the present chapter. This book, supplemented by Titchener's "Postulates of a structural psychology" (1898) and Boring's "History of introspection" (1953), is adequate to give a very good understanding of the tenor of the structuralist psychology early in the present century. The student might browse through issues of the *American Journal of Psychology* printed prior to Titchener's death in 1927. These issues give an insight into the everyday experimental implications of the structuralist metatheory which can be obtained today in no other way. Titchener's *Text-book of psychology* (1910); Boring's *Physical dimensions of consciousness* (1933); and Boring's short article with a long title, "A psychological function is the relation of successive differentiations of events in the organism" (1937), will then finish the picture, showing how structuralism developed and why it disappeared. R. I. Watson's *Great psychologists from Aristotle to Freud* (1968) is great browsing in connection with every system to be treated in this book. Watson is intellectually twice removed from Titchener (having dedicated his book to E. G. Boring) and is carrying on in that scholarly tradition, albeit in a readable manner. Like Wundt, he revises at a mad pace. His third edition, a bargain in paperback, followed his second by only three years (Watson, 1971).

TABLE 6-1   Important Men in American Functional Psychology

British Antecedent Influences	American Functionalists		
	Pioneers	Founders	Developers
Individual differences, mental tests, statistics			
Sir Francis Galton (1822-1911)	George T. Ladd— Yale (1842-1921)	John Dewey— Chicago (1859-1952) (Columbia)	Robert S. Woodworth— Columbia (1869-1962)
	Edward W. Scripture— Yale (1864-1945)		
	James McKeen Cattell— Columbia (1860-1944)		
	G. Stanley Hall—Clark (1844-1924)		
Evolutionary theory			
Charles Darwin (1809-1882)	James Mark Baldwin— Princeton (1861-1934)	James R. Angell— Chicago (1869-1949)	Harvey Carr—Chicago (1873-1954)
	William James— Harvard (1842-1910)		
Animal behavior			
George John Romanes (1848-1894)	Edward L. Thorndike— Columbia (1874-1949)		
C. Lloyd Morgan (1852-1936)			

6 Functionalism

Functionalism was the first truly American system of psychology. Its development in this country began with William James, who is apparently still regarded as the greatest American psychologist (Becker, 1959), and led directly to Watsonian behaviorism. Part of the early strength of functionalism was drawn from its opposition to structuralism, just as later part of the strength of behaviorism came from its opposition to structuralism and the less extreme functionalism.

Functionalism has never been a highly differentiated systematic position. In fact, according to Woodworth (1948): "A psychology that attempts to give an accurate and systematic answer to the question 'What do men do?' and 'Why do they do it?' is called a *functional psychology*" (p. 13). In terms of such a weak specification, functionalism could not die until our linguistic habits of asking what, how, and why had been replaced by others. But this is probably an inadequate specification of functionalism. Though its definition must remain as loose as the system, we can at least add that a functionalist is characteristically concerned with the function of the organism's behavior and consciousness in its adaptation to its environment. The functionalist is also likely to be concerned with functional, or *dependency*, relationships between antecedents and consequents; here function is used in its mathematical sense. American psychology, influenced by evolutionary theory and a practical spirit, has been concerned with the utilities of consciousness and behavior. Thus it has tended to be functional.

Table 6-1 (facing) shows that three groups of psychologists contributed to the development of functionalism. The *pioneers* are early psychologists who laid the groundwork for the later growth of functionalism by opening up a wide variety of new fields of inquiry, such as child and animal behavior. The *founders*, John Dewey and James Angell, established functionalism as a system. And the *developers*, Harvey Carr and Robert S. Woodworth, were responsible for the maturation and further elaboration of the system.

Three primary antecedent influences, all British in origin, are also shown at the left of Table 6-1. Charles Darwin (1872) engaged in the study of animal behavior as well as in the development of the modern theory of organic evolution.

Galton was influenced by evolutionary theory and initiated the scientific study of human capacity. Romanes and Morgan gave additional impetus to the study of animal behavior. James, Hall, and Baldwin were directly influenced by evolutionary theory, and Hall was also interested in testing and individual differences. Carr was more interested in animal studies than his most direct predecessor, Angell. Baldwin, Ladd, and Scripture are included because they had a hand in setting the stage for the development of functional psychology; they are not considered important enough to the basic tenets of functionalism to require treatment in the text. Early in his career E. L. Thorndike had strong interests in animal research and was related closely to both James and Cattell. His connectionism might have been included in this chapter as a special kind of functionalism rather than in Chapter 4 on associationism.

Table 6-1 excludes two men who, although originally trained by functionalists, were subsequently involved in the development of other schools. John B. Watson was functionally trained and later turned behavioristic; he took his degree with Angell. Bergmann (1956) goes so far as to regard Watson as the last and greatest functionalist. Walter S. Hunter is another product of the Chicago school, although he also tended to regard himself as a behaviorist. Nevertheless, his development and guidance of a small but very active and productive laboratory at Brown University justifies at least mention in the present overview. The research produced for many years at Brown had a strong functionalist flavor and would certainly rate with that produced at Columbia and Chicago in general excellence if not in quantity or scope.

As its own leaders have pointed out, there was never a single functional psychology in the same sense as there was a single structuralism. There were only the many functional psychologies, each a little different from the others. Today there are not even these; functionalism as a *school* disappeared, when Carr retired from Chicago, at a time when there seemed little need for systematic emphasis. If functionalism is viewed simply as a system opposing existentialism (structuralism), then it died with existentialism. If it is considered a methodology, independent of its subject matter, then it was superseded by the more forceful, extreme, and outspoken behaviorism. But functionalism conceived of as a fundamental set of values and procedures emphasizing adaptive acts and empirically demonstrated functional relationships has remained a strong influence in psychology, and even today represents much of the mainstream of American psychology.

ANTECEDENTS OF FUNCTIONALISM

Charles Darwin (1809-1882) created one of the greatest controversies in the intellectual history of mankind, one whose reverberations have not fully died out in the current year of our Lord. The Lord, of course, had a great deal to do with the controversy, since evolution shook religion to its foundations.

Ironically, Darwin was such a cautious scientist, not to say a timid and withdrawn recluse, that he might never have published and started the controversy had Alfred Russell Wallace (1823-1913) not sent him a report which outlined exactly the same theory of evolution on which Darwin had been working for twenty years. As Irvine says (1963, pp. 98-99):

Wallace's next letter, containing the famous paper on evolution and natural selection, struck him like a bombshell. Within a single week, while lying ill with malarial fever in the jungles of the Malay peninsula, Wallace had leaped from his earlier position to Darwin's most advanced conclusions. What Darwin had puzzled and wondered and worried and slaved over with infinite anxiety and pain for two decades, Wallace had investigated and explained—far less elaborately but still to precisely the same result—in some three years. The familiar ideas, the older man could not help noticing, were conveyed with un-Darwinian force and clarity.

Characteristically, Darwin was unable to resolve the dilemma presented by his receipt of Wallace's paper. Two friends of his, Lyell and Hooker, resolved it for him by reading both Wallace's report and a sketch of Darwin's ideas before the same meeting of the Royal Society. It is to the credit of both men that they were lifelong friends, their mutual respect emerging unscathed from a situation which could have become extremely acrimonious.

Darwin could not personally respond to the furor which arose over this paper and reached a crescendo with the 1859 publication of *The origin of species*. The battle fell to the lot of Thomas Henry Huxley (1825-1895), Darwin's fierce, brilliant friend and fellow biologist. That Huxley eventually carried the day for evolution (with the scientific community, at least) is now history. Darwin, when unpleasantness threatened, always found it necessary to withdraw to a spa for the sake of his uncertain health.

Despite his eccentricities, this English scientific bulldog was one of functionalism's most important antecedents. He was an acute observer of animal behavior as well as of animal morphology. His theory established a continuity between man and animal that was necessary to justify the extended study of animal psychology. Finally, the evolutionary emphasis on adaptation to the environment was imported directly as an "explanation" of behavior via instinct, and perhaps indirectly as the principle of reinforcement.

Sir Francis Galton (1822-1911) was inspired by his cousin, Darwin, to study the problem of heredity in human beings. It was his aristocratic wish to control heredity, but first he had to demonstrate its effectiveness as an agent of change. He was led by this necessity to study the inheritance of human intelligence, of which Galton himself is said to have had plenty (his estimated IQ was 200; see Boring, 1950, p. 461). His *Hereditary genius* contained studies of individual differences in intelligence and opened up the field of mental testing; this field has done a great deal to justify the existence of our young science throughout the years of its childhood.

Romanes (1848-1894) and Morgan (1852-1936) are important to psychology because of their work in the field of animal behavior. Each represents an attitude toward the relationship between man and the lower animals. Darwin was castigated by theologians because of their belief that he was bringing man down to the level of the animals; they admitted apelike ancestry only with great, high-collared resistance. From the contemporary point of view, however, it appears that both Darwin and Romanes were overgenerous in the other direction. Each of them was disarmingly willing to attribute human faculties to animals. Morgan would have none of their childish enthusiasm and demanded strict evidence before according man or animal a "higher" phyletic faculty on the basis of a particular performance. Romanes and Morgan thus defined a polarity which is still visible, but both men lent support to the study of animals.

Herbert Spencer (1820-1903) would be featured even in a catalogue of eccentric geniuses. He anticipated Darwin with a theory of evolution which had the misfortune of being Lamarckian and thus not influential for long. Also unfortunately, Spencer did not tend to base his views on a thorough perusal of the facts. According to Irvine (1963, pp. 287-288):

No modern thinker has read so little in order to write so much. He prepared himself for his *Psychology* chiefly by perusing Mansel's *Prologomena Logicae* and for his *Biology* by going through Carpenter's *Principles of Comparative Physiology*. He produced a treatise on sociology without reading Comte, and a treatise on ethics without apparently reading anybody. . . . He had discovered that his "head sensations," with their attendant ramifications, were due to an impaired circulation of the blood to the brain . . . therefore . . . Some of the most abstruse chapters of the *Psychology* were dictated . . . during the intervals of a tennis game near London. His rational life had not become less eccentric with the passing of years.

Despite his eccentricities (of which the foregoing is a very small sample), Spencer produced the first complete evolutionary psychology. Moreover, he did not hesita'e, as Darwin had, to make broad characterizations and draw analogies to society (Spencer, 1961). His influence was, accordingly, marked in social thought, sociology, and social psychology (cf. Hofstadter, 1955). Spencer saw clearly that the kinds of changes that occur through learning in the life of the individual could occur through selection in the life of the species. Unfortunately, his impatient tendencies showed up again is his decision to transmit learned behaviors quickly via a Lamarckian inheritance of acquired characteristics. Had he been more willing to wait for another kind of selection, he might have been considered a very great psychologist rather than one among many of psychology's antecedents. As it is, the idea of referring evolutionary changes and changes with learning to a common framework, but with a different time scale, is a very important one (see Fisher, 1966, for further development). We may hope that modern psychology and biology will eventually work out the relationship in much greater detail, perhaps by implicating genetic materials like DNA in the learning process.

THE PSYCHOLOGY OF JAMES

William James (1842-1910) was the leading American antecedent of functionalism, if we do not choose to regard him as its founder. His two-volume work, *The principles of psychology* (1890), was a classic virtually before it was published, since much of the book had appeared in periodical form as the chapters were completed. Watson (1968) is among those who have pointed out that the book is still read by people who have no necessity to do so—rare tribute for a textbook! Part of the reason for this popularity is James's urbane but enthusiastic personality, which led him to believe that ". . . the last book he read was always a great work and the last person seen a wonderful man" (Joncich, 1968, p. 434). Such a personality did not lead James to be a great experimentalist. His contribution to the growth and development of psychology was through his ability to synthesize psychological principles suggested by the experiments of others, to make intuitive guesses where knowledge was missing, and to present the results in an incredibly attractive verbal package.

Chronologically, James belongs between Wundt (who was ten years his senior) and Titchener (twenty-five years his junior). As has been pointed out (Heidbreder, 1933), he both precedes and succeeds Titchener—in the sense that his ideas reach further back into the past for metaphysical roots and at the same time have lost so little of their freshness that James is still not only readable but also surprisingly modern, although necessarily outmoded in most details. He had an unusual talent for being practical, readable, interesting, and popular—and at the same time commanding scientific respect. His writing was by no means mere popularization; a great deal of original thought and interpretation went into it.

James came from a well-known New England family. His brother, Henry James, was an eminent novelist. William James started out in medical training, but it was interrupted by a breakdown in health. At about the same time, he apparently experienced some serious conflicts between his religious and scientific beliefs. Nevertheless, he returned to his medical studies and received an M.D. degree at Harvard. He later became an instructor in anatomy there.

It was while he was teaching anatomy that he started to conduct informal psychological experiments, although he had no established laboratory. This venture into psychology occurred around 1875, a few years before the formal founding of the laboratory at Leipzig by Wundt. Shortly thereafter, James started to write the *Principles*, which he worked on for approximately twelve years before its publication.

As a result of this shift in interest from anatomy and physiology to psychology, James's title was changed first to professor of philosophy and later to professor of psychology (1889). Soon thereafter, however, strictly philosophical matters began to predominate, and the remainder of his career was spent in philosophy. The recognition of his basically philosophical rather than scientific bent apparently came early for James—in 1865, while he was in Brazil on a scientific expedition with the naturalist Agassiz. James is said to have expressed such feelings in a letter home (quoted in Kallen, 1925): "If there is anything I hate, it is collecting. I don't think it is suited to my genius at all" (p. 22).

James as a Critic

James rebelled against what he considered to be the narrowness, artificiality, and pointlessness of the German, or Wundtian, tradition in psychology, as exemplified in Titchener and the Cornell school. James was a most important factor leading to the more general protest that the functionalists were later to make. It is best to let James speak for himself, as in the following two quotations from the *Principles*, to demonstrate the forcefulness of his criticism as well as the fluency and persuasiveness of his literary style. Of Fechner, for example, he said (1890, I, p. 549):

But it would be terrible if even such a dear old man as this could saddle our Science forever with his patient whimsies, and, in a world so full of more nutritious objects of attention, compel all future students to plough through the difficulties, not only of his own works, but of the still drier ones written in his refutation.

And, speaking more generally of the subsequent Wundtian psychology (1890, I, pp. 192ff.):

Within a few years what one may call a microscopic psychology has arisen in Germany, carried on by experimental methods, asking of course every moment for introspective data, but eliminating their uncertainty by operating on a large scale and taking statistical means. This method taxes patience to the utmost, and could hardly have arisen in a country whose natives could be *bored*. Such Germans as Weber, Fechner, Vierordt, and Wundt obviously cannot; and their success has brought into the field an array of younger experimental psychologists, bent on studying the *elements* of the mental life, dissecting them out from the gross results in which they are embedded, and as far as possible reducing them to quantitative scales. The simple and open method of attack having done what it can, the method of patience, starving out, and harassing to death is tried, the Mind must submit to a regular *siege*, in which minute advantages gained night and day by the forces that hem her in must sum themselves up at last into her overthrow. There is little of the grand style about these new prism, pendulum, and chronograph-philosophers. They mean business, not chivalry. What generous divination, and that superiority in virtue which was thought by Cicero to give a man the best insight into nature, have failed to do, their spying and scraping, their deadly tenacity and almost diabolic cunning, will doubtless some day bring about.

The Positive Program

It would be a mistake to assume that James was merely a clever critic of elementarism and Wundtian introspectionism. On the contrary, he had an extensive positive program for psychology. While he himself preferred not to experiment, he recognized the value and the necessity of the experimental method, for psychology as well as for the older disciplines. More broadly, however, the keynote of his program is his emphasis on *pragmatism*, which implies that the validation of any knowledge must be in terms of its consequences, values, or utility. Useful knowledge for psychology, James felt, would come from a study of behavior as well as consciousness, of individual differences as well as generalized principles, of emotion and nonrational impulses as well as intellectual abilities.

Underlying all this kind of study was the general assumption that psychology must study *functions*—that psychology is a part of biological science and man must be considered in his adaptation and readaptation to the environment. In keeping with the newly influential evolutionary theory, James felt that man's behavior, and especially his mind, must have had some function to have survived. The effects of James's early medical training are also evident throughout his writings in his stress on the importance of the *conditions* of mind and behavior; conditions for him meant the nervous system. James retained an active interest, on a literary level at least, in neurophysiological theorizing. His most famous original theoretical contribution—his theory of emotion—is a nice illustration of this tendency, since James makes the sensory feedback from bodily actions the focal point of the emotional process.

James on Consciousness

The breadth of James's views on consciousness, when contrasted with that of Titchener, is especially instructive as a cue to the difference between the structural and functional approaches to psychology. First, James pointed out the *characteristics* of consciousness, which are studied only by psychology: It is *personal*, individualistic—belongs only to a single person; it is *forever changing*—is essentially a *process* and should be studied first as such (his famous phrase "stream of consciousness" was coined to express this property); it is *sensibly continuous*—in spite of gaps, individual identity is always maintained; it is *selective*—it chooses, with attention providing the relevance and continuity for choice; and it occurs in *transitive* as well as *substantive* form.

This last point, the dichotomy between clear content and so-called fringe states of consciousness, is one of James's more noteworthy emphases. James held that transitive conscious processes are less easily noticed but are very important and that they had not been given sufficient credit or study. He thought that all ideas enter consciousness as transitive, marginal in attention, and often fleeting and that they may or may not then proceed to substantive form, in which the idea has more stability, more "substance." In any case, transitive or fringe ideas (as of unfamiliarity, relation, and the like) account for much meaning and behavior.

Second, James emphasized the *purpose* of consciousness. Here, as suggested above, he was much influenced by the new evolutionary theory and felt that consciousness must have some biological use, or else it would not have survived. Its function is to make man a better-adapted animal—to enable him to choose. Conscious choice is to be contrasted with habit, which becomes involuntary and nonconscious. Consciousness tends to become involved when there is a *new* problem, the need for a *new* adjustment. Its survival value, as James reasoned, is in relationship to the nervous system (1890): "The distribution of consciousness shows it to be exactly such as we might expect in an organ added for the sake of steering a nervous system grown too complex to regulate itself" (p. 144).

Third, James thought that psychology had to study the conditions of consciousness. In contrast to Titchener, with his psychophysical parallelism, James felt that consciousness could not be considered apart from the body. In the *Principles* James examined in detail the mind-body solutions of his time and found that he had to reject them all. Later, as a full-fledged philosopher himself, he developed more fully a mind-body position of his own (James, 1909).

One product of his neurophysiological speculations was the notion of ideo-motor action. James felt that the nervous system functions in such a way that sensory processes tend to express themselves in motor processes unless something inhibits them; thus it is to be expected that any idea, unless inhibited by other ideas, will lead more or less directly to action. James's own example of the value of this hypothesis was that if one has trouble getting out of bed in the morning, one has simply to keep getting up in mind and clear out all conflicting ideas. According to the hypothesis, he will soon find himself standing up.

James seems to have experienced the usual textbook writer's disgust with his product, saying when he finished that his book proved only "that there is no such thing as a science of psychology" and that psychology is still in "an ante-scientific condition" (Boring, 1950, p. 511). Yet even today James seems sometimes to have had an incredible modernity. Herrnstein and Boring (1965, pp. 483-495) present a selection from James in which we see him brilliantly refuting the arguments that were to be produced by John B. Watson about twenty-five years later as the foundations of behavioristic psychology. This demonstrates that such issues were already in the air of 1890, but it also shows James at his usual high pitch of incisiveness, recognizing and surgically exhibiting the most critical methodological issues. We shall see the same characteristics again when we look for the antecedents of Gestalt psychology!

PIONEER AMERICAN FUNCTIONALISTS

G. Stanley Hall

Granville Stanley Hall (1844-1924) had one of the most amazingly varied careers of any professional psychologist. Hall did things in spurts of great interest, leaving others to fill in the details. He is important in a systematic sense because he opened up new fields and new activities, mostly of a utilitarian or functional nature. Although he did not contribute formally to the founding of functionalism, his contributions had an obvious functional flavor before there was a functional school.

Born a farm boy in Massachusetts, Hall went to Williams College to study for the ministry. However, his ideas seemed too liberal for this calling, and he turned to philosophy. He spent three years studying philosophy and physiology in Europe. Upon returning to the United States, he finally took his divinity degree, but preached for only ten weeks. After various minor academic jobs, Hall went to Harvard to study and took in 1878 under James the first American doctorate in psychology. The experimental work for his dissertation, which dealt with muscular cues in the perception of space, was performed in Bowditch's physiology laboratory. There were only two years' difference in age between Hall and James; however, there was a tremendous difference in temperament and in subsequent professional history.

After getting his doctorate, Hall returned to Europe to spend two more years in Germany, becoming Wundt's first American student at Leipzig in 1879. He sampled a variety of scholarly fields (studying physiology under Ludwig at Leipzig, for example, while living next door to Fechner). He then returned to the United States and proceeded to found a remarkable number of institutions. In 1883 he founded at Johns Hopkins University what has been called the first psychological laboratory in this country. R. I. Watson (1963, p. 327; 1968, pp. 374-375) has shown that the claim is hard to document; James seems to have earned the right to this "first" by starting a small laboratory at Harvard in 1875, even before the usual date given for the "founding" of psychology.

There is no disputing the fact that Hall founded, in 1887, the *American Journal of Psychology*. In 1888 he was called to the presidency of a new graduate school, Clark University, in Massachusetts. In 1891 he founded the *Pedagogical Seminary* (now the *Journal of Genetic Psychology*). In 1892, the same year that Titchener arrived in America, the American Psychological Association was planned in a conference in his study, and he became the first president.

Hall's development of psychology as a scientific academic discipline at Clark is of considerable interest; it resulted in the unusual situation of having the newest of the scientific disciplines assuming the most important part in this graduate school established primarily for scientific training. He brought in E. C. Sanford from Hopkins to head the laboratory and maintained an active personal interest in psychology. His wide range of interest is illustrated by his bringing Freud, Jung, and Ferenczi—leading psychoanalysts—to the Clark University celebration in 1909.

Hall continued to develop new areas in psychology, proceeding from child psychology—where he popularized the use of the questionnaire as a research tool—through adolescent psychology—where his two huge volumes, *Adolescence*, are probably his most influential publications—and on into the psychology of old age, publishing *Senescence* (appropriately, at the age of seventy-eight!). In addition, he worked in the fields of applied psychology; educational psychology; sex (after his discovery of Freud, in whom he took an early interest); religious psychology (his book *Jesus, the Christ, in the light of psychology* representing a revival of his early theological interests); and even alimentary sensations!

Hall's influence was felt mainly indirectly, in that he stimulated interest and activity in such a great variety of fields. All these fields were more applied than the strict introspectionism of Titchener. Although he turned out eighty-one Ph.D.s at Clark (as contrasted with the fifty-four produced at Cornell by Titchener), only a few of these became prominent in psychology. Lewis Terman, long an American leader in the field of testing and individual differences, is perhaps the best known of them. It is suggestive of Hall's personal influence that fully a third of his doctoral candidates eventually went, like himself, into administrative positions. In any case, the career of this most remarkable man had much to do with the variegated development of early American psychology and particularly with the strong tide toward functionalism.

James McK. Cattell

James McKeen Cattell (1860-1944) had an active and varied career, similar to Hall's. He was particularly active in editing and publishing. While he avoided philosophy and psychological systematizing, he helped lay the groundwork for functionalism by his development of mental tests and his long-continued interest in individual differences.

In 1883 Cattell went to Leipzig to become Wundt's first (and self-appointed) assistant in the new laboratory. Himself a very aggressive, opinionated, and forceful individual, he never completely accepted Wundt's definition of psychology and persisted even at Leipzig in working with an unorthodox subject, that of reaction times, After three years he returned to the United States to establish the psychology laboratory at the University of Pennsylvania; then he went to Columbia University in 1891, where also he founded the psychology laboratory. He was discharged in 1917, on account of his outspoken pacificism, and returned on a full-time basis to his editing and to The Psychological Corporation, a leading center for applied psychological research which he had founded in New York City.

The most important of Cattell's editorial accomplishments were the founding of the *Psychological Review* (with Baldwin, in 1894); the editing of the periodical biographical volume *American Men of Science*; and the editing of the journal *Science*, official organ of the American Association for the Advancement of Science. The latter publication was sold to the association by the Cattell family the year after his death.

Of more direct importance to the development of functionalism was Cattell's promotion of mental tests. He was giving mental and physical tests, of a relatively simple sort, to Columbia University students in the 1890's, before the Binet-Simon Scale had been produced. However, the success of this more comprehensive battery eclipsed the earlier work at Columbia. Cattell continued his activity in the field of individual differences and capacity (for example, in perception and reading, in psychophysics, and in free and controlled association), working in later years mostly through The Psychological Corporation.

THE FOUNDING OF FUNCTIONALISM

Functionalism as a formal school started at the University of Chicago under John Dewey and James Angell, both of whom came in 1894 to teach at the new university. Angell had previously studied under both Dewey, at the University of Michigan, and James, at Harvard.

John Dewey

John Dewey (1859-1952), a philosopher, educator, and psychologist, was one of the eminent Americans of recent times. He studied with Hall at Hopkins, taking his doctorate there, and taught at Minnesota, as well as at Michigan, before going to

Chicago. It was Dewey who sent Angell from Michigan to Harvard to study with James. Sometimes we are surprised at the many interrelationships which detailed study reveals among prominent figures in the history of psychology. This is probably not as true of the men just mentioned, who belonged to a common tradition, as it is of Watson and Titchener, discussed in the previous chapter. Our conceptual categories seem to make us visualize the American Psychological Association meetings of the past as though they took place in a great hall in which there were signs reading "Structuralists register and meet here," "Functionalists register and meet here," etc. Yet a moment's thought should tell us that were such a meeting held today, psychologists would be milling around, not knowing where to go. So would the last generation have done; although psychologists doubtless associated selectively to some degree, there was much mingling, and well-known psychologists knew one another's work well.

In 1886 Dewey published *Psychology*, the first such work by an American author. It was popular at first, but was soon overshadowed by the even more successful *Principles* of William James.

Ten years after his book appeared, Dewey made what was to be a more influential contribution to psychology in a short paper, "The reflex arc concept in psychology" (1896). The paper became a classic and is considered to be the most significant landmark in the beginning of the functionalist movement. Dewey objected to the reflex-arc analysis, which broke behavior down into the separate stimulus and response units and assumed that the sensory and motor nerves that participate in reflexes thus behave separately. According to the reflex-arc schema, the behavior chain can be broken down into (1) an afferent, or sensory, component, initiated by the stimulus and mediated by sensory nerves; (2) a control, or associative, component, mediated by the spinal cord and the brain; and (3) an efferent, or motor, component, mediated by motor nerves and culminating in a response.

Dewey took examples from James and from Baldwin to show the inadequacy of their formulations of behavior in terms of reflexes. He developed an organismic position, stressing behavior as a total coordination which adapts the organism to a situation. He followed the spirit of James when James urged the continuity of consciousness rather than when James talked about reflex action. Dewey regarded stimulus and response as convenient abstractions rather than as realities and pointed out the necessity for having a response before we can meaningfully say we have a stimulus; the overall reflex is not a composition made of successive stimulus and response, for there is no such successive relationship involved. The stimulus-response distinction is artificial; it is a result of the holding over of the old mind-body dualism. (Dewey said this in 1896!) The two main points Dewey made were that behavior should be considered as it functions and that molar units of analysis should be used in order to prevent too much elementaristic analysis. The first point marked the beginning of the Chicago school of functional psychology, and the second was a Gestalt point made twenty years before Gestalt psychology existed.

The functional side of Dewey's paper is revealed in the following statement (1896, pp. 365-366):

The fact is that stimulus and response are not distinctions of existence, but teleological distinctions, that is, distinctions of function, or part played, with reference to reaching or maintaining an end. . . . There is simply a continuously ordered sequence of acts, all adapted in themselves and in the order of their sequence, to reach a certain objective end, the reproduction of the species, the preservation of life, locomotion to a certain place. The end has got thoroughly organized into the means.

Unfortunately, the reflex-arc paper was one of the last of Dewey's contributions to psychology proper. During his stay at Chicago, he worked mostly in education and philosophy. He laid out the program for the progressive education movement in an address, "Psychology and social practice" (1900), delivered upon his retirement as president of the American Psychological Association. Dewey remained the titular head of this movement until his death. He, more than anyone else, was responsible for the application of pragmatism to education—the notion that education is life, learning is doing, and teaching should be student-centered rather than subject-centered. We should not hold Dewey responsible for the occasional excesses of his followers in the progressive education movement. Leaders are seldom asked by their followers to approve new interpretations and applications before they are put into practice. Dewey simply paid the usual price of fame in being saddled with the errors of others. In 1904, Dewey went to Columbia University Teachers College as professor of philosophy, and he remained there for the rest of his career.

Dewey's importance to psychology does not follow from his substantive contributions to the field. His best-known psychological work was an analysis of thinking in adaptive terms (Dewey, 1910). Dewey is remembered for his stimulation of others, particularly through his delineation of the philosophical foundations of functionalism.

James R. Angell

James Rowland Angell (1869-1949) took his M.A. in psychology at Michigan and studied with James at Harvard and with Erdmann at Halle in Germany. After a year at Minnesota, he came to Chicago in 1894. His first paper (1896), published jointly with A. W. Moore in the same volume of the *Psychological Review* in which Dewey's reflex-arc paper appeared, was an experimental study of reaction times. It attempted to resolve the controversy between Titchener and Baldwin. Titchener had held that reaction times are faster when the subject concentrates on the response (*motor* condition); Baldwin had claimed that, on the contrary, they are faster when the subject concentrates on the stimulus (*sensory* condition). Angell and Moore reported that there were wide individual differences in reaction times among naïve subjects, with some giving faster sensory times (supporting Baldwin), but that with continued practice motor times generally were faster (supporting Titchener). This resolution pointed up the basic difference between the structuralist position, with its emphasis on the highly trained observer, and the developing functionalist position, with its acceptance of data from naïve as well as from trained observers.

In his paper replying to criticism of his type of psychology, Titchener borrowed from James the term *structural psychology* as opposed to *functional psychology*. The terms *structural* and *functional* were used as the basis of the newly defined "isms" in psychology; Titchener was thus responsible for the naming of both systems.

As we have already observed, Titchener was fighting a losing battle. As the century ended, developments in educational psychology, animal psychology, mental testing, and related fields were helping to strengthen the basic functionalist position. It was James Angell who became the leading champion of the new trend. He published a paper on the relations between structural and functional psychology (1903), a textbook (1904), and finally the clearest expression of the functionalist position in his (1906) address as president of the American Psychological Association, "The province of functional psychology" (1907, pp. 61-94):

Functional psychology is at the present moment little more than a point of view, a program, an ambition. It gains its vitality primarily perhaps as a protest against the exclusive excellence of another starting point for the study of the mind, and it enjoys for the time being at least the peculiar vigor which commonly attaches to Protestantism of any sort in its early stages before it has become respectable and orthodox. The time seems ripe to attempt a somewhat more precise characterization of the field of functional psychology than has as yet been offered.

Angell proceeded in his address to outline three separate conceptions of functional psychology. First, functionalism might be considered a psychology of mental operations in contrast to a psychology of mental elements. This view presents a direct antithesis between the structuralist and the functionalist positions. From the functionalist point of view, Angell notes, the complete answer to the question "What?" with respect to the mind must include answers to the corollary questions "How?" and "Why?" Second, functionalism might be considered the psychology of the fundamental utilities of consciousness. Angell presents in this second connection a view very similar to James's, with the mind functioning to mediate between the organism and its environment and becoming active primarily in accommodating to the novel situation. Third, functionalism might be considered the psychology of psychophysical relations. Here functionalism is the psychology of the total relationship of organism to environment, including all mind-body functions. This third view leaves open the study of nonconscious, habitual behavior.

Angell believed that the first and second views were too narrow: each of them restricted functionalism to the study of conscious experience, and the first put too much emphasis on opposition to structuralism. The third view was most satisfactory, although Angell felt that the three views of functionalism were interdependent.

At Chicago, Angell built up the department of psychology and made it a center for functional studies. Then, in 1921, he went to Yale University as president. He remained there until his retirement in 1937; during his Yale years he gave up his active role in psychology and concentrated on administrative matters.

THE CHICAGO SCHOOL: HARVEY CARR

Harvey Carr (1873-1954) received his doctoral degree at the University of Chicago in 1905. He succeeded Angell as chairman of the department at Chicago, actually in 1919 and officially in 1921. Since it was under Carr that Chicago functionalism flourished and took on as much definition as it ever had, we shall consider his system in some detail as the most comprehensive representative of functionalism.

The attitude at Chicago under Carr was not such that it encouraged much systematic fuss or bother. What was being done at Chicago was regarded as *the* psychology of the time, and there was apparently little need felt for formal systematizing. Marx (1963, pp. 14ff.) has placed functional theorizing between the extremes of the large-scale deductive approach and the purely inductive approach. The functional tendency has been to construct very limited, data-bound theories. In this respect, the functionalists anticipated the modern trend toward mathematical miniature systems. Since the functionalists did not attempt to build a cohesive system, they had no need to ignore any particular data or approach to psychology.

The functionalists also tended to share the feeling that other "new" systematic positions like behaviorism, Gestalt psychology, and psychoanalysis had little to offer. These movements were seen as exaggerated, overdramatized emphases on relatively limited aspects of psychology. Thus the behaviorist, with his stress on, and use of, measurements of overt behavior, was merely taking up where the functionalist had already more quietly broken the ground. The Gestalt psychologist was emphasizing points about the stimulus field which the functionalist had been investigating all the while. The psychoanalyst was pointing to the great importance of motivation, a concept that had been basic all along to the functionalist stress on purposive and adaptive behavior. The functionalists felt that the new schools added little beyond what their own all-embracing psychology had always included in its scope.

Carr's functionalism as it appeared in his 1925 textbook, *Psychology*, will be considered according to the six systematic criteria of McGeoch. The stress throughout Carr's book is functional in the broadest sense; organismic adjustment is the central theme.

Definition of Psychology

Psychology is the study of *mental activity*, which is the generic term for adaptive behavior. According to Carr (1925, pp. 72ff.), the adaptive act is a key concept for psychology. It involves three essential phases: (1) a motivating stimulus, (2) a sensory situation, and (3) a response that alters the situation to satisfy the motivating conditions. The motive is a stimulus that dominates the behavior of the organism until the organism reacts in such a way that the stimulus is no longer effective. Motives, as thus defined, are not conceived of as necessary to behavior but as directive forces that in general determine what we do. There are three ways in which a motive may be resolved by an adaptive act: The act may remove the stimulus, disrupt it by introduction of a stronger stimulus, or resolve it through sensory adaptation to the stimulus.

Carr felt that adaptive behavior was the subject matter of both psychology and physiology. The two disciplines were to be distinguished, however, in terms of the kinds of variables studied. Carr made the following distinction (1925, p. 7):

Psychology is concerned with all those processes that are directly involved in the adjustment of the organism to its environment, while physiology is engaged in the study of vital activities such as circulation, digestion, and metabolism that are primarily concerned with the maintenance of the structural integrity of the organism.

On the role of a strictly introspective psychology, Carr took a definite stand. Consciousness, he held, is an artificial abstraction, an unfortunate and unnecessary reification; something is supposed to exist, whereas all that exists in reality is a set of processes. The concept of consciousness is similar to other abstract concepts like intelligence, willpower, and crowd mind; none of these concepts exist apart from the acts and processes that give them meaning, and none of them can serve directly as the subject of empirical investigation.

Postulates

The postulates of functionalism, as in the case of all early psychological systems, were not explicitly stated. However, several assumptions stand out clearly: (1) Behavior is intrinsically adaptive and purposive. (2) All sensory stimuli affect behavior—not just motives, as defined above. For Carr, there was no absolute difference between a motive and any other stimulus; a motive might become an ordinary stimulus after it was resolved as a motive. (3) All activity is initiated by some sort of sensory stimulus: no response occurs without a stimulus. (4) Each response modifies the stimulus situation. Behavior, as earlier pointed out by Dewey, is essentially a continuous and coordinated process.

Mind-Body Position

Here Carr followed Dewey, rather than James, and minimized the problem (see Table 2-2 for a summary of mind-body positions). He felt that there was no need for a detailed solution because there was no real problem. The psychophysical integrity, or integration, of the organism was simply assumed. Functionalism thus tends to adopt either a monistic or a double-aspect position, but has no elaborate or strongly held position of any kind. The earlier functionalists, like Angell, might tend toward a parallelism or might even take a position that seemed to imply interactionism, like James; but Carr felt that psychology as an empirical and natural science did not need to concern itself with metaphysical problems. Carr did point out the inadequacy of psychophysical parallelism as adopted by Titchener, and the general functionalist position was in turn vigorously attacked by Watson as being in reality interactionist. Angell had earlier made the point that an epiphenomenal position must be rejected if one accepts the functionalist belief that consciousness has adaptive value, a belief that does seem to imply interactionism.

Nature of the Data

Although in its stress on organismic adjustment to the environment, functionalism has a behavioristic flavor, functionalism does not eliminate introspection as a method of obtaining data. Its data are thus both objective and subjective, with increasingly more stress on the former kind as functionalism matured as a system.

There are ample studies of animals in the functionalist experimental literature to illustrate the use of objective data. On the other side, Carr's interests in perception and thinking illustrate his use of concepts that might not fit within a behavioristic framework. *Perception* as Carr used the word referred to the apprehension of the immediate environment through present spatial stimuli; *thinking* referred to apprehension of a situation that was not immediately present in the environment. Introspective data were acceptable in the study of either.

Principles of Connection

The principles of connection are the principles of learning and as such were the heart of the functionalist research program. Learning, basically, was a process of establishing associative connections or of organizing elements of behavior through association into new and larger units. Most functionalists, like Carr, were willing to take over associationistic principles in their explanations of learning. Much of the work that followed from the Chicago tradition could not be distinguished from work that might have followed from the associationistic tradition. Notable examples are the verbal learning work done by McGeoch, Melton, and Underwood (see below). Their work on nonsense syllables follows logically from the work of Ebbinghaus, who was listed as an associationist. The diffuse "schools" of associationism and functionalism are probably better distinguished by tracing their historical origins to the British empiricists or to evolutionary theory than by trying to distinguish them on the basis of an individual's current systematic beliefs.

The functionalists usually preferred the *relative* approach to the interpretation of learning. They avoided what Carr called the "quest for constants" and emphasized instead a *dimensional* analysis through structuring a total learning situation into specific continua which could eventually be measured. As Underwood put it (1949): "When any phenomenon can be demonstrated reliably (consistently) to vary in amount with respect to some specific characteristic, we have a *dimension*" (p. 7). His books on experimental psychology (1957, 1966) are generally illustrative of the functionalist approach. Carr's student and friend, J. A. McGeoch (McGeoch & Irion, 1952), also provides an excellent example of this general approach to the problems of learning. The position taken on the problem of the learning curve, which was a controversial and apparently exciting issue to the early generations of experimental psychologists, is representative. Until dimensional analyses could be completed, the functionalist was willing to accept gracefully the fact that there is no curve that can be called *the* learning curve; there is too much dependence of results upon the influence of the specific situation.

In a letter replying to a question about graphology (1934), McGeoch once expressed the functionalist willingness to suspend judgment until the facts were in:

Before your craving for information anent graphology I bow in ignorance . . . but until I know, I doubt with good and hearty doubt. In the meantime I shall hold unto my bias that, when another few hundred years of fundamental work has been done upon the complexities of the interwoven functions we call mind, it will be time to attack the hinterlands where molar forecasting and proximal necromancy abide. But by that time Robert may have become long since a saint and Mr. Rhine, who has recently sprinkled salt on the tail of telepathy, may be an archangel, while I am running memory drums in hell for their amusement.

Functionalist research has dealt with factors influencing the rate and course of learning rather than with the basic nature of the learning process; it has also dealt with problems of retention and transfer. McGeoch's (1942) attitude typifies the usual atheoretical stand, accepting the empirical law of effect as an adequate explanatory principle and refusing to take a stand on the theoretical necessity of effect. A summary of functionalist learning theory and research is given by Hilgard (1956) and Hilgard and Bower (1966).

Principles of Selection

The main agents of behavior selection for Carr were *attention, motives,* and *learning*. Attention is conceived of as a preliminary act or sensorimotor adjustment, whose major function is to facilitate perception. Motives, defined as persistent stimuli, direct action and so have a major role in determining which behavior occurs. Learning operates in three main ways: (1) Certain adaptive mechanisms must be acquired by necessity in living; (2) as adjustive mechanisms are thus acquired, other aspects of the stimulating situation come to be associated with the response (as in conditioning) and thus capable of eliciting it; and (3) certain associations are imposed by society (for example, fear of the dark or of thunderstorms and dislike of particular ethnic groups).

The Experimental Program

Laboratory experimentation, as we have suggested, was the keynote of functional psychology under Carr at Chicago. One example of Carr's own research interests stands as an important contribution in its own right and as an interesting indication of how the functional principles were actively implemented in the experimental program. Research on guidance, or tuition, was a persistent laboratory problem. The main problem here was under what conditions and at what time active guidance should be introduced. Research on the rat in the maze was utilized to develop important and far-reaching principles. For example, it was concluded that, as far as possible, the animal's own initiative should be utilized, with active guidance used sparingly, and that such guidance as is given should be administered early in training. Carr's attempt to apply such principles to human teaching and learning (1930) represents a good early example of how results on animals may, with caution, be generalized to human problems.

Besides Carr, the two most important figures in the experimental program at Chicago were Karl S. Lashley, an early behaviorist whose best-known contribution was his program of brain extirpation related to learning efficiency (see Chapter 11), and L. L. Thurstone, best known for his contributions to factor analysis and the study of primary human abilities. In addition, prominent psychologists from all over the country were brought into Chicago for short periods, especially during the summer sessions, so that during the 1930s, the university developed into one of the leading centers—if not the leading American center—of psychology.

THE COLUMBIA SCHOOL: ROBERT S. WOODWORTH

Robert Sessions Woodworth (1869-1962) was one of psychology's most remarkable men. His career spanned the period from Thorndike's early work with cats in puzzle boxes to the present era. He received the first American Psychological Foundation Gold Medal Award in 1956; published *Dynamics of behavior* in 1958, when he was eighty-eight; and started revising his popular *Contemporary schools of psychology*, no doubt in the midst of a busy schedule of other activities. Woodworth got his Ph.D. at Columbia with Cattell in 1899. After four years, one spent with the neurophysiologist Sherrington at Liverpool, he returned to Columbia and stayed until he "retired" in 1945. The list of his publications is long and includes several textbooks.

Woodworth's systematic viewpoint was first expressed in his *Dynamic psychology* (1918). There are many close resemblances between Woodworth's position and that of the Chicago functionalists; however, to a great extent he developed his position independently, and dynamic psychology might be considered an independent school. We shall follow the example of Boring (1950) and Hilgard (1956) in including it as a branch of functionalism.

Woodworth shares common antecedents with Chicago's functionalists: James and Dewey, Hall and Cattell. His system, like theirs, is moderate and unassuming, with no pretensions to finality or completeness. Both views are experimentally oriented, with very restricted theoretical superstructure. Woodworth shows the functionalist eclecticism in extreme form, seeking to take the best features from each system. Mowrer tells a story about Woodworth which illustrates this attitude (1959, p. 129):

There is a story, perhaps apocryphal, to the effect that a colleague once good-naturedly chided Professor Woodworth for having "sat on the fence" during much of his professional lifetime, instead of getting down and becoming involved in prevailing controversy. To which Woodworth, after a moment's reflection, is supposed to have replied: "I guess I have, as you say, sat on the fence a good deal.

But you have to admit one gets a good view from up there—and besides, it's cooler!"

This point of view may not be true of his 1958 book, but is certainly true of Woodworth's earlier eclecticism; he tended to accept contributions irrespective of their origins. Even in Woodworth's last work (Woodworth & Sheehan, 1964), one gets the impression that he evaluated new experiments as follows: "If it is good work, then it is functional. If it is functional, it is acceptable."

Woodworth's dynamic psychology was less a protest against Titchenerian structuralism than the Chicago functionalism was. Woodworth accepted introspective techniques to a greater extent and was even at times a staunch defender of introspection. Nevertheless, he rejected structuralism as well as behaviorism as providing an adequate methodology for psychology. He was less influenced by associationism and a strict stimulus-response approach. The S-R theorists have often talked as though the stimulus led directly to a response, without mediation of the organism or dependence upon the organism to determine the response; this is the basis of the complaint that much psychology deals with the "empty organism." Woodworth emphasized the importance of considering the organism and insisted upon putting the organism into the basic formula which expressed the relationship psychology dealt with. Thus he wrote not S-R, but S-O-R. As a partial corollary to his emphasis on the organism, Woodworth gave more emphasis to motivation than the Chicago functionalists did. Carr might define motivation as a persisting stimulus, but Woodworth insisted on considering the physiological events which underlie motivation.

The heart of Woodworth's system is his concept of *mechanism*, which has more or less the same meaning as Carr's *adaptive act*. Mechanisms for Woodworth were purposive responses or sets of responses. He made the same distinction as Sherrington (1906) between preparatory and consummatory reactions; the former prepare for oncoming reactions, while the latter carry out the intention. Thus we open our mouths (preparatory reaction) before we can receive the food and swallow (consummatory reaction).

Drives for Woodworth were closely related to mechanisms. Although drives are generally defined as internal conditions that activate mechanisms, Woodworth preferred to think of internal drive processes as being themselves kinds of responses. The reverse was also true: Mechanisms, the overt behavioral ways in which drives are satisfied, could become drives! Woodworth felt that practically all mechanisms could become drives and thus run under their own power, so to speak. G. W. Allport (1937) later advanced a similar notion in his theory of the "functional autonomy of motives."

A later contribution of Woodworth offers another illustration of this kind of thinking. This is his suggestion that the act of perceiving is intrinsically reinforcing, which was proposed in an unpretentious paper entitled "Reënforcement of perception" (1947). Perception is here interpreted as an adaptive behavior whose successful performance is reinforcing without the operation of either extrinsic drive conditions or extrinsic reward conditions. This paper and his latest book seem to put him more in the cognitive camp than in the S-R-reinforcement camp, since he does not see any necessity for external reinforcing operations in order that behavior be maintained.

CRITICISMS OF FUNCTIONALISM

Definition

It was said by some that functionalism was not a well-enough-defined position to constitute a meaningful system. A Titchener-trained psychologist, C. A. Ruckmick (1913), objected to what he saw as the vague and vacillating use of the term *function*. He found it used in two senses: first, to mean an activity or a use, and second, in the mathematical sense, to indicate a dependence of one variable on another (a functional relationship). Although it may be true that there was some vagueness in the functionalist's usage of the word *function*, there is nothing wrong with using a word in two different ways, as long as the two usages are generally acceptable and are not illegitimately interchanged. The two separate usages are quite closely related; both refer to the same process. The functionalist was interested in the process for its own sake (first usage) and for its relationships to other conditions (second usage). Carr said that the mathematical meaning could also be shown to include the others.

Applied Science

The fact that the functionalist, with his multiple interests in utilitarian activities, did not distinguish carefully between pure and applied science was disturbing to some of the early critics. Contemporary psychologists take a position much like that of the functionalists. It is now generally accepted that the essential scientific procedures are identical and that pure and applied science can be distinguished only with respect to the intent of the investigator (i.e., the degree to which he has an application in mind). Many important basic relationships have been discovered as a result of strictly applied efforts, and it is perhaps more significant that some of the *most* important applied findings have been incidental results of the carrying out of pure research. Thus the contemporary position would be that the pure-applied distinction is not absolute or even very important and that the functionalist should be congratulated rather than criticized for deemphasizing the distinction.

Teleology

The functionalist, with his interest in utility and purpose, was accused of using the ultimate consequences of behavior to explain behavior; in the absence of relevant evidence, such an explanation is generally referred to as *teleological*. This criticism may apply to some functionalists, but not to Woodworth or Carr; Carr was particularly careful to disclaim teleology and to postulate only proximate stimuli as causal. He recognized that an explanation in terms of the effects of behavior was incomplete at best, tending to stop investigation before the detailed nature of the relationship between the stimulating situation, the physiology of the organism, and the behavior was worked out. The tree-climbing behavior of certain larvae may be taken as an example. Their climbing has the effect of taking them up to a place where they feed on leaves. Thus the behavior may be an important factor in the evolutionary survival of the species; but if we say that they climb up the trees in order to eat leaves, we are giving a teleological explanation that really tells us nothing about the "why" of the behavior of the individual organism. As Carr said (1925, p. 81): "Each act must be explained in terms of the immediate situation and the animal's organization in reference to it." Thus, if we can point out that the larvae always make a positive response to light and that there is a gradient of brightness which leads them up the tree, we have escaped from the illusory finality of the teleological explanation and are on the way to an explanation of the behavior in terms of proximate factors.

There is some similarity between the teleological accusation made against the functionalist in this context and the accusation made against Thorndike and other reinforcement theorists that their explanation of reinforcement requires that a cause work backward to an effect that preceded it in time. In the case of both "instincts" and "behaviors learned through the action of reinforcement," however, the cause acts forward in time. When only the fittest survive, the effect is to select behaviors that are already adaptive. When reinforcement occurs, the effect is seen on subsequent trials and is presumed to be mediated through effects on activity contemporaneous with or following the reinforcement.

Eclecticism

Because functionalists have generally been willing to accept so many different kinds of problems and techniques of investigation, they have often been accused of being vapid and nondescript eclectics. Henle (1957) has criticized the eclectic position, directing her attention mostly to Woodworth. She maintains that an eclectic tends to accept the good features of contradictory positions at the expense of blurring the differences between them. However, she does not distinguish clearly between different possible types of eclecticism.

Henle is speaking of eclecticism at a theoretical level. She maintains that when there are alternative deductive systems for deducing empirical statements, we cannot afford to fall between them, lest we lose deductive capacity. Thus, the eclectic must choose a theory or devise one of his own. But there are other *levels* of eclecticism and other eclectic positions regarding theories even at this level.

First, one may be an eclectic at the level of rules for theory building as well as at the level of theory itself. That is, one may accept both Gestalt and behavioristic methodological pronouncements and do work typical of both schools. Both subjective and objective data may be accepted. An eclecticism of methodology we shall call a *metatheoretical eclecticism*. In the present state of uncertainty about the specifics of methodology, especially in psychology, a certain degree of tolerant but skeptical metatheoretical eclecticism is a necessity, not a handicap. We have already seen how too narrow a metatheory contributed to the downfall of structuralism. Failure to attack problems because they do not fit into a fixed methodological framework is always dangerous in science. Only the most basic and general premises of science, as discussed in our first three chapters, are sufficiently well established to accept even tentatively, and these are accepted within all systems.

Even at a theoretical level, eclecticism may be safe; that is, the eclectic may admire many theories for their successes and be sorry for their failures, ideally while trying to improve on them. The eclectic may accept *no* theory rather than all; since he belongs to no system, he is freer to reject than he might otherwise be. The eclectic misses some of the stimulation, as well as the acrimony, of controversy; his temperament will determine whether or not this is good.

Functionalists have tended to take a more inductive viewpoint than exponents of other systems. They have therefore tended to ignore theory construction, paying greater relative attention to empirical findings. Thus, if one does not like eclecticism, a criticism of functionalism on the grounds that it is too eclectic is justified. Henle is such a critic. However, eclecticism may be made the grounds for a compliment rather than a criticism. Certainly, the eclecticism of the Chicago and the Columbia functionalists must not be considered evidence of soft-mindedness or weakness. On the contrary, these functionalists generally tended to be very astute and tough-minded critics, particularly with regard to empirical problems.

Finally, there is an entirely different defense available against those who bemoan eclecticism. It is that functionalism is not necessarily eclectic. One can easily imagine an eclectic structuralism under the quiet and modest Carr and a rigid functionalism under the autocratic Titchener (once over the hurdle of imagining the two gentlemen in question switching other aspects of their systematic positions, that is). The point is that eclecticism is a function of the personalities of a school's leaders, as well as of the systematic precepts of the school. There is nothing in functionalism to make it permanently atheoretical, nor is there any stipulation that it must forever have a wider range of experimental interests than other schools. Eclecticism appears to have a partially subsidiary, partially accidental relationship to the functionalistic position.

THE CONTRIBUTION OF FUNCTIONALISM

Because of the moderation and lack of presumption with which functionalism has gone about its business, it is easy to overlook the importance of its contribution to psychology. True, it has erected no fancy theories; it has not even been much of a school or system, in a formal sense. But its early opposition to the stifling restrictions of structuralism provided a real service to American psychology at a time when the embryonic outlines of the new discipline were just emerging.

Nor should the obvious fact that functionalism has been pushed from the systematic spotlight by livelier schools and systems be taken to mean that its service to psychology is over. As a matter of fact, functionalists have continued actively to stimulate and perform experimental research in all the fields where the early functionalists pioneered: learning, animal as well as human; psychopathology; mental testing; and genetic and educational psychology.

Two research products may be cited as good illustrations of the functionalist program. Woodworth's scholarly manual, *Experimental psychology* (1938; Woodworth & Schlosberg, 1954), is a classic of its kind. It is a scientific handbook in the old style, dealing intensively and comprehensively with the data and theories of a large variety of experimental problems. The other example is the extended series of researches, lately reaching twenty-four in number, on the phenomenon of distributed practice in human verbal learning by Underwood (Underwood & Ekstrand, 1967). Underwood's persistent and patient productivity in research nicely illustrates the functionalist's tendency to deal intensively with interdependencies of empirical variables (even though, theoretically, Underwood himself may well be considered an associationist in functionalist's clothing).

Among the functionalists actively conducting research were some of the Chicago graduates who worked under Carr: John McGeoch, with his extensive set of human verbal learning and retention studies (and his own protégés and students, A. W. Melton, B. J. Underwood, and A. L. Irion); M. E. Bunch, with his long-time program of human and animal research on transfer and retention; Fred McKinney, who shifted his interests from learning to mental health and counseling, and subsequently to television instruction and the problem of values in teaching; and Henry N. Peters, who similarly shifted from early research on a judgmental theory of emotion to the application of basic learning techniques to the motivating of chronic schizophrenics. None of these men have produced anything like the elaborate theoretical superstructure characteristic of Hull and some others, but they have pursued empirical problems carefully and intensively.

Finally, there has been an exciting rebirth of a generally functionalist viewpoint within the fields of psychology and biology. The ethologists have generated this excitement. They have made their advances via the kind of careful, detailed, unbiased observation which should be characteristic of functionalism at its best.

A DIMENSIONAL DESCRIPTION OF FUNCTIONALISM

Functionalism does not fit so neatly at an end of Coan's dimensional system as structuralism and associationism. The difficulty begins immediately, with the consideration of whether it was basically restrictive or basically fluid in orientation. Certainly functionalism was an "open" system, with a functional orientation, but functionalists have tended to be analytic in their approach, and to be restrictive in their criticality toward experimentation, in the high standards they have set for acceptability of data. The six lower-level factors give less difficulty: functionalists have tended somewhat toward objectivism, somewhat toward elementarism (though this is not always true, for example, of James), and somewhat toward a quantitative approach with a slightly transpersonal orientation, an approach which is slightly toward the dynamic pole, with both endogenous and exogenous factors taken into account.

Even Coan's dimensions leave functionalism in an eclectic position. One of the difficulties is that functionalism was a diverse school. Carr was very different from James; if we take either as a prototypical functionalist, we get a position on Coan's dimensions which differs in several respects from a description of the other. However, functionalists did not tend to take extreme theoretical positions, and individual functionalists may therefore tend to fall closer to a middle position than members of more radical schools.

The rated positions on Watson's eighteen dimensions can be seen in Table 3-2; the student should again assign his own values and see how his ratings compare with those given in the table. The authors and graduate students differed significantly only on the values assigned to the monism-dualism dimension. The authors feel that William James definitely pushes functionalist tradition toward the dualistic end of the dichotomy. Other representatives of the school might well justify the more neutral position chosen by the students.

The dimensional characteristics chosen as most important by the graduate students were functionalism, utilitarianism, and molarism; the latter was rated just to the molar side of center, but the dimension was probably regarded as important by the majority of the students because it was dramatized by the contrast with structuralism.

SUMMARY AND CONCLUSIONS

We have been concerned in this chapter with the diverse origins and manifestations of functionalism in psychology. Functionalism has been described as a loose and informal systematic development, but one that represented, more than any other, the mainstream of American psychology. Its major antecedents and pioneers were William James, G. Stanley Hall, and James McK. Cattell; its founders were John Dewey and James Angell; its mature representatives were Harvey Carr at the University of Chicago, where the more formal development occurred, and Robert S. Woodworth at Columbia University, where a collateral branch flourished as dynamic psychology. Functionalism as a systematic movement arose in opposition to Titchener's structural psychology. It emphasized learning, mental testing, and other utilitarian subject matters. Functionalism declined in systematic importance as the need to oppose structuralism disappeared. However, its characteristics fit many psychologists, and functionalism has therefore continued to go its unpretentious way even after its systematic decline.

Functionalism, especially as represented in the psychologies of Carr and Woodworth, has been identified as basically experimental; concerned more with functional interrelationships of variables than with theoretical superstructures; accepting both introspective and behavioral data but utilizing mainly the latter; stressing adaptive behavior and purposive, motivated activity within either an S-R

(Carr) or an S-O-R (Woodworth) framework; and revealing always an active, systematic eclecticism in combination with a tough-minded approach to experimental problems. It has made and will continue to make a most important contribution to the advance of psychology as a science, but will do so largely in the absence of systematic pretensions.

Further Readings

Our frequent allusions to Irvine's delightful *Apes, angels, and Victorians* (1963) should already have convinced the reader that it furnishes an easy entrée to the world of functionalism's English antecedents. James's *Principles*, too, needs no further advertising from us as a source of information about our American genius. Dewey's paper (1896) is also brilliant and blessedly short, since it is not easy reading even for us sophisticated moderns. Carr's *Psychology* (1925), for the Chicago school, is a good historical source. For the Columbia development, Woodworth's early *Dynamic psychology* (1918) and his more recent *Dynamics of behavior* (1958) are excellent sources. In addition, Woodworth's systematic textbook, *Contemporary schools of psychology* (1948), expresses the functionalist, or middle-of-the-road, point of view very well. Woodworth's *Experimental psychology* (1938), revised by Woodworth and Schlosberg (1954), should also be mentioned; this book stands as a classic experimental approach to the older problems of psychology. For the more recent developments, Underwood's two books, *Experimental psychology* (1949) and *Psychological research* (1957), offer prime examples of a thoroughly functionalistic approach to experimental problems and methodological issues. McGeoch's *Psychology of human learning* (1942), revised as McGeoch and Irion (1952), summarizes much of the early type of functionalist research utilizing verbal human materials and subjects. Chapter 10 in Hilgard and Bower's *Theories of learning* (1966) treats the functionalistic approach to research and contains a number of examples from the learning literature. Finally, for the last reading, what could we suggest except the last word of the last great functionalist, Woodworth's *Contemporary schools of psychology* (Woodworth & Sheehan, 1964)?

TABLE 7-1   Important Men in Behaviorism

Antecedent Influences	Behaviorists		
	Pioneers	Founders	Developers
Evolution and animal behavior			
Charles Darwin (1809-1882)	James McKeen Cattell— Columbia (1860-1944)	John B. Watson— Hopkins (1878-1958)	Albert P. Weiss— Ohio State (1879-1931)
C. Lloyd Morgan (1852-1936)	Edward L. Thorndike— Columbia (1874-1949)		Walter S. Hunter— Brown (1889-1953)
Jacques Loeb (1859-1924)			Karl S. Lashley— Chicago (1890-1958)
Extensions of mechanistic explanations			
Descartes (1596-1650)	Ivan P. Pavlov— St. Petersburg (1849-1936)		Edward C. Tolman— California (1886-1961)
La Mettrie (1709-1751)	Vladimir M. Bekhterev— St. Petersburg (1857-1927)		Edwin R. Guthrie— Washington (1886-1959)
Cabanis (1757-1808)	James R. Angell— Chicago (1869-1949)		
Positivism			
Auguste Comte (1798-1857)	Max Meyer—Missouri (1873-1967)		Clark L. Hull—Yale (1884-1952)
			B. F. Skinner— Harvard (1904-)

7 Behaviorism

The system of objective psychology called *behaviorism* by its founder, John B. Watson, is by far the most influential and most controversial of all the American schools. Behaviorism came to play a prominent role not only in psychology but also in general cultural affairs, where its influence has rivaled that of the European import, psychoanalysis.

Watson had one main positive and one main negative interest. On the positive side, he proposed a completely objective psychology. He wished to apply the techniques and principles of animal psychology, in which he had been working, to human beings. This positive aspect of behaviorism has been called *methodological* or *empirical* behaviorism. His main methodological point—insistence on the primacy of *behavior* as the source of psychological data—has been dominant and is still well accepted today; however, the recent rise of phenomenology and existential psychology has again made it controversial.

Watson's negative emphasis was his inveighing against mentalistic concepts in psychology. He protested against both the introspective psychology of Titchener and what he considered the inadequacies of Angell's functionalism; Watson alleged that Angell had retained an interactionistic bias and still accepted introspective data. Though Watson deplored the prominence of metaphysical problems in psychology, he took a definite metaphysical position by denying, by implication at least, the existence of mind. This denial constituted his *metaphysical, or radical, behaviorism*, which has been less widely accepted. Radical behaviorism has been the center of much of the controversy that has raged around Watson and his ideas.

The present treatment begins with a consideration of the three major trends out of which Watsonian behaviorism developed: the philosophical traditions of psychological objectivism (whose direct influence on Watson is questionable), animal psychology, and functionalism. We then describe the founding of behaviorism; outline Watson's system, with special emphasis on the mind-body issue; consider some of the secondary characteristics of Watson's thinking; and discuss some of the more important of the early behaviorists other than Watson. We conclude with a treatment of the various criticisms offered against Watsonian behaviorism, an analysis of the factors responsible for the acceptance of behaviorism, and finally an evaluation of Watson's contribution.

Table 7-1 (facing page 165) lists the most important men in behaviorism.

EARLY TRENDS TOWARD PSYCHOLOGICAL OBJECTIVISM

Watson was by no means the first to stress the need for objectivity in psychology. There is a long history of such efforts, involving mainly philosophers (see Chapter 2 for a related trend). Our treatment of this history is indebted to the classic review by Diserens (1925), who defines psychological objectivism as including "any system in which the effort is made to substitute objective data and the universal method of science, direct observation, for subjective data and the special method of introspection" (p. 121).

We have already seen how Descartes and La Mettrie took some of the first steps toward the use of objective data in psychology by extending mechanistic explanations to the body, and finally the mind, of man. Cabanis (1757-1808) then attempted to define mind in terms of objective factors, especially physiological functions. According to him, "mental" events are functions of the total organism and not simply of the mind (see Boring, 1950).

The most important name in this series is that of another Frenchman, Auguste Comte (1798-1857), who founded a movement called *positivism*. All varieties of positivism emphasize positive (i.e., not debatable) knowledge; there is sometimes disagreement about what kind of procedure gives such knowledge. Comte believed that only social, objectively observable knowledge could be valid; introspection, which depends upon a private consciousness, could not provide valid knowledge. He denied the importance of the individual mind and vigorously criticized mentalism and subjective methodology. He believed that human critical thinking advanced through three stages, from the theological through the metaphysical to the positivistic, or scientific, mode of thought. Comte referred to traditional psychology as the last phase of theology. He stated (1896) that "In order to observe, your intellect must pause from activity, and yet it is this very activity you want to observe. If you cannot effect the pause, you cannot observe; if you do effect it, there is nothing to observe. The results of such a method are in proportion to its absurdity" (p. 11). More constructively, Comte emphasized two types of study of affective and intellectual functions: (1) determination with precision of the organic conditions on which they depend and (2) observation of the behavioral sequence. These two types of study certainly should provide data acceptable to Watsonian behaviorists.

Subsequent French and British materialists, followers of Comte, carried on in this tradition. The most important of these were Antoine Cournot, G. H. Lewes, and Henry Maudsley.

ANIMAL PSYCHOLOGY

We have already seen how important Darwinian evolutionary theory has been in the development of psychology as a science and particularly as a background factor determining the form of functional psychology. The theory also gave great impetus to the study of animal psychology, which in turn was perhaps the most important single factor which led Watson to formulate his behavioral psychology.

Animal psychology grew more or less directly out of evolutionary theory. Darwin's theory had a great influence among British intellectuals, but strong opposition to the theory arose, particularly among the clergy and theologians. A primary objection was to Darwin's assumption of mental continuity between man and the lower animals. The most effective answer to the objection was to demonstrate such mental continuity in somewhat the same way as Darwin's evidence had already demonstrated the physical continuity. This demonstration necessitated an animal psychology. One way to defend Darwin's theory was therefore to show the presence of mind in infrahuman organisms (contrary to Cartesian tradition) and to exhibit its continuity with the human mind.

Charles Darwin himself began the defense. His main theme in *Expression of emotions in man and animals* (1872) was that emotional behavior in man is the result of the inheritance of behavior once useful to animals but now useless to man. Darwin's great wealth of observation on animals was drawn upon for many examples. One of the most famous is man's curling of his lips in sneering; this was held to be a remnant of the baring of the canine teeth in rage by carnivorous animals. The tendency found in the dog to turn in a circle several times before sitting down was likewise held to be an evolutionary remnant of behavior once useful in the more primitive stage of his ancestors; presumably, the dog performed the motion as a precautionary measure against snakes and the like and to flatten out a bed.

We have already seen that one of Darwin's personal friends, George John Romanes, later undertook the defense. Romanes culled the literature for all sorts of stories, both scientific and popular, on animal behavior. He accumulated a great mass of material from which he wrote the first comparative psychology, *Animal intelligence* (1886). Romanes's method of gathering data is now called the *anecdotal method*. In spite of the fact that he had explicitly laid down rules for using the stories, Romanes was unable to avoid using some inadequately controlled observations, since he had no way of checking on the original sources. The tendency to anthropomorphize—to read human motives and abilities into animal behavior—played into Romanes's hands, since he wished to demonstrate a continuity between man and animal. Anthropomorphizing, like the anecdotal method, is today thoroughly disapproved of in psychology. In spite of the limitations of his methodology, Romanes deserves credit for stimulating the initial development of comparative psychology and preparing the way for the experimental methodology that followed.

C. Lloyd Morgan used a semiexperimental methodology and partly controlled observations in the field in his studies on lower animal forms. He is better known today for his methodological contributions than for his substantive findings. Morgan adapted the law of parsimony (also called, more picturesquely, *William of Occam's razor*) to comparative psychology. In what came to be known as *Lloyd Morgan's canon*, he expressed this position (1899): "In no case may we interpret an action as the outcome of the exercise of a higher psychical faculty, if it can be interpreted as the outcome of the exercise of one which stands lower in the psychological scale" (p. 59). This dictum was intended to counteract the tendency to anthropomorphize, and the point was well received. (See Newbury, 1954, for an extended discussion of Lloyd Morgan's canon in its various interpretations.)

If one does not anthropomorphize, how does one demonstrate the desired continuity? For one thing, Lloyd Morgan's canon applied not just to animals but also to man; in the latter case it implied that we have a tendency to "anthropomorphize" when interpreting the behavior of other men, in the sense that we may give them too much credit for higher mental functions. Romanes was demonstrating continuity by finding mind everywhere; Morgan also wished to demonstrate continuity, but suggested that it might be done as well if we could find mind nowhere. Morgan's appeal to simplicity and rejection of anthropomorphism would seem, from a modern perspective, to have made the development of a scientific behaviorism inevitable.

Morgan relied upon habits, rather than intelligence, as the main explanatory factor, and trial-and-error learning was stressed. He assumed that human and subhuman learning processes were continuous. Thorndike's later laboratory experimentation is closely related to Morgan's work in both content and outlook; Watson also was stimulated in his animal research by reading Morgan's reports. It is interesting that all three men tended to explain all learning in terms of a few simple principles which apply to man as well as to animals low on the phyletic scale. Others, like the Gestaltists, are more like Romanes in their tendency to see insight, characteristic of human learning, even in animals lower on the scale.

Lloyd Morgan's canon has been attacked by some psychologists who recognize, correctly we believe, that in many cases the more complex of two alternative interpretations is the appropriate one. However, this does not invalidate Morgan's canon or the principle of parsimony; these rules apply only to cases in which all the alternatives are about equally supported by the available data. Naturally, if there is a flaw in the simpler explanation, it is not acceptable, and there is no issue at all. But it is incumbent upon the proponent of the more complex account to show why his account must be accepted over the simpler one; if he cannot, the simpler account is preferable.

Jacques Loeb (1859-1924) is the next important man in the development of animal psychology. Loeb, a German biologist, came to the United States in 1891 and spent the greater part of his professional career here. Loeb is responsible for the wide acceptance of the concept of the *tropism*, or forced movement, as an explanatory factor in animal behavior. In a tropism, the response is a direct function of the stimulus and is in this sense forced. Loeb felt that all the behavior of the lowest of animal forms is tropistic and that a considerable proportion of the behavior of higher forms is also. One familiar example of a tropism is the apparently mechanical and irresistible movement of certain moths into light (positive phototropism), even though flight directly into a flame results in their destruction. Naturally, not all tropisms are so maladaptive.

Loeb was not reacting against Darwinism but against the anthropomorphic tendency which we have seen represented by Romanes. Despite the fact that Loeb felt tropistic factors could account for a great deal of the behavior of higher forms, he did not attempt to deal with human problems. He did, however, contribute to a problem arising from the human being—the problem of consciousness. He suggested an objective way to determine whether a given organism was conscious. His criterion was whether the organism manifested associative memory. Certainly this criterion is not very exclusive; protozoa, for example, have been said to show evidence of associative learning, though the evidence has also been seriously questioned. The question of what organisms are conscious can be given only an arbitrary answer; our operational criterion of consciousness in animals can be chosen at will, and we should be quite clear that various answers to the problem are possible. Any other attempt at solution would have to fall back on our tendency to anthropomorphize.

By this time the study of animal behavior within the biological sciences was becoming widespread. In support of Loeb's position, the biologists Thomas Beer, Albrecht Bethe, and Jacob J. von Uexküll came out strongly for the elimination of psychological terms and the substitution of objective ones. The biologist H. S. Jennings, on the other hand, obtained evidence for the modifiability of behavior in the protozoan *Paramecium* and opposed Loeb's mechanistic interpretations of animal behavior. Hans Driesch also opposed Loeb and maintained a vitalistic position (i.e., there is something qualitatively different about living organisms, and they are not reducible to physicochemical reactions). Sir John Lubbock was studying ants, wasps, and bees, and the Frenchmen Fabre and Forel were also studying insects. Albrecht Bethe published a mechanistic interpretation of the social life of ants and bees. Certainly animal psychology was a going concern. The pressure of these various researches was beginning to push objective psychology to the fore long before behavioristic psychology was founded as a school in America.

In America, we have already seen how systematically E. L. Thorndike was working with animals. In this he was not alone. Robert M. Yerkes (1876-1956) began his animal investigations in 1900. Yerkes studied crabs, turtles, frogs, dancing mice, rats, worms, crows, doves, pigs, monkeys, apes, and finally man. His research on the apes is the most significant; it is comprehensively summarized in *Chimpanzees: A laboratory colony* (1943). Yerkes at one time collaborated with Watson in the development of visual testing techniques for animals. However, Yerkes was not a behaviorist by persuasion, despite the fact that he did work in comparative psychology that was typically behavioristic in method. Yerkes was an admirer of Titchener and felt that the investigation of experience was one of the most interesting of psychology's problems. Yerkes's contribution to behaviorism was simply in strengthening the position of comparative psychology, especially through his establishment of the chimpanzee experimental station at Orange Park, Florida; the station was named the Yerkes Laboratories of Primate Biology when he retired from active administration in 1941. The main laboratory has since been moved to Atlanta, where it is associated with Emory University; there are several regional centers. Yerkes made a great contribution to the advancement of the application of psychology during World War I when he was a leader in developing the program of testing of Army recruits.

W. S. Small at Clark devised the first rat maze in the same year that Yerkes began his animal investigations—1900. The albino rat was so well adapted to being studied in the maze that it has ever since been the outstanding laboratory animal in psychology, and the rat-in-the-maze has been a standard situation for the study of learning. Since the 1930s, it has become clear that the rat is equally well adapted to life in the Skinner box (or, as Skinner seems to prefer, life in the operant chamber). Growth of the study of animals was so rapid between 1900 and 1911 that the *Journal of Animal Behavior* was founded then. Finally, Titchener's first doctoral student, Margaret Floy Washburn, published a compendium of animal psychology (1908). The book was essentially an analogical study of human and animal mental processes, but it contained a great deal of factual information and became a classic in the field. Thus, some of the impetus of a behavioral psychology came from the camp of the structuralists.

AMERICAN FUNCTIONALISM: 1910

American functionalism was the third of the important trends that led toward behaviorism. Several psychologists who were functionalists only partially or indirectly were also leaning toward an objective orientation. We have already mentioned Cattell and Thorndike; Herrnstein (Watson, 1967, pp. 18-20) even argues that Thorndike's position was more like that of modern behaviorists in some respects (the roles of learning and of reinforcement) than Watson's was. In 1904, Cattell said (as quoted by Woodworth & Sheehan, 1964, p. 114): "It seems to me that most of the research work that has been done by me or in my laboratory is nearly as independent of introspection as work in physics or in zoology...." Watson's old opponent, William McDougall (1871-1938), had even defined psychology as the positive science of conduct. He made experimental observations on color discrimination in infants in 1901, and his books (1905, 1912) contain objective data; the latter book was even named *Psychology: The study of behavior*. However, McDougall was an outspoken purposivist, accepted consciousness, and used introspective data—in short, he was the antithesis of Watson in the most critical respects one can think of, and thus he cannot be considered a serious rival to Watson in the formulation of an exclusively objective psychology.

Max Meyer (1873-1967) would be a more serious candidate. He published *The fundamental laws of human behavior* in 1911, a book which reflects his thoroughgoing objectivism. By 1921, he had indicated his behavioristic inclinations more overtly by titling another book *The psychology of the other one*. But Meyer was more an avoider than a seeker of publicity and never became known as Watson did. Meyer was content to pursue his research and writing without systematic aspirations.

We have also mentioned the Russian reflexology school, initiated by I. M. Sechenov and developed by Pavlov and Bekhterev; the latter entitled one of his major books *Objective psychology* (1913); the book was apparently published in Russia in about 1907. Sechenov (1965) published his *Reflexes of the brain* in book form in 1873 and in monograph form in 1863! This is truly amazing when one considers that Sechenov's basic philosophical and methodological position was nearly identical to Watson's in its objectivity.

In America, however, the most prophetic psychologist was probably James Angell, with whom Watson was associated at Chicago before 1908. We have already met Angell as a founder of functionalism. He seemed to recognize that psychology, already largely functional in character, was about ready for a further step in the direction of objectivity. Two expressions of his changing point of view preceded Watson's first published behavioristic pronouncements. In 1910, at the Minneapolis meetings of the American Psychological Association, Angell had this to say (1913, p. 255):

But it is quite within the range of possibility, in my judgment, to see consciousness as a term fall into as marked disuse for everyday purposes in psychology as has the term soul. This will not mean the disappearance of the phenomena we call conscious, but simply the shift of psychological interest toward those phases of them for which some term like behavior affords a more useful clue.

Two years later, at the Cleveland meetings of the association, he presented a paper on this topic which was written just before Watson's first systematic paper. He now spoke at more length (1913, pp. 256ff.):

The comparative psychologists have from the first been vexed by the difficulty of ascribing to animals conscious processes of any specific kind in connection with intelligent behavior. . . . Obviously, for scientists engaged in this field of investigation, it would from many points of view be a material gain, in convenience at least, if the possible existence of consciousness might be forgotten and all animal behavior be described objectively. Nor has there been, so far as I am aware, any general objection to this proposal. . . . It is furthermore not unnatural that finding it practicable and convenient, as undoubtedly it is, to waive reference to consciousness in matters relating to animal behavior, the tendency should manifest itself to pursue a similar line of procedure in dealing with human conduct. This tendency does not so much represent any formally recognized program like that of our world-reforming realists, as it does a general drift occasioned by several different sources. Its informal and unselfconscious character is probably indicative of a more substantial and enduring basis than belongs to movements more carefully and more purposely nurtured.

Boring has summarized the situation in American psychology just prior to Watson's founding of behaviorism (1950): "America had reacted against its German parentage and gone functional. ... Behaviorism simply took from functionalism part but not all of the parental tradition . . . the times were ripe for more objectivity in psychology, and Watson was the agent of the times" (p. 642).

THE FOUNDING: JOHN B. WATSON

John Broadus Watson (1878-1958) was born in South Carolina and took his M.A. at Furman University in 1900 after five years of college study. He was attracted to the University of Chicago by an interest in John Dewey, but was "steered into" experimental psychology as a major field by Angell. He also received training at Chicago in physiology and neurology under H. H. Donaldson and Jacques Loeb. After three academic years and three summers he took his Ph.D. in 1903.

Although he had developed an undergraduate interest in philosophy and had taken graduate work in it, apparently this kind of thinking "wouldn't take hold." Watson explained briefly (1936, p. 274):

I got something out of the British School of philosophers—mainly out of Hume, a little out of Locke, a bit out of Hartley, nothing out of Kant, and strange to say, least of all out of John Dewey. I never knew what he was talking about then, and unfortunately for me, I still don't know.

While at Chicago, Watson worked mainly with animal subjects. Some three decades later, he put his feelings this way (1936, p. 276):

I never wanted to use human subjects. I hated to serve as a subject. I didn't like the stuffy, artificial instructions given to subjects. I always was uncomfortable and acted unnaturally. With animals I was at home. I felt that, in studying them, I was keeping close to biology with my feet on the ground. More and more the thought presented itself: Can't I find out by watching their behavior everything that the other students are finding out by using O's [observers].

Watson's doctoral dissertation was accordingly done with animal subjects. Directed jointly by Donaldson and Angell, it involved the correlation between the increasing complexity of behavior in the young albino rat and the growth of medullation in the central nervous system. A somewhat better-known piece of research completed at Chicago was his analysis of the sensory cues used in maze learning by the rat. Here Watson followed the techniques of Small, Morgan, and Thorndike and concluded, after systematic elimination of the various senses, that kinesthesis (which he could not completely eliminate) was the most basic to maze learning.

In 1908, Watson accepted a professorship in psychology at Johns Hopkins University. There he continued his experimental laboratory research on animals, collaborating with Yerkes (who was for a short time at Hopkins in the medical school) on an apparatus for testing animals' visual abilities, taking course work and laboratory work with Jennings, and apparently making satisfactory professional progress.

According to his own statement, Watson had early begun to think in more thoroughly objective terms. His animal researches at Chicago stimulated him to his first formulation in connection with a colleague at the University of Chicago in 1903 (J. B. Watson, 1929, preface); this formulation was not encouraged. Apparently the chief objection at that time was that the formulation applied to animals but not to human beings. His first public expression came in a lecture given at Yale University in 1908, when he was again discouraged, this time on the grounds that his formulation was descriptive and not explanatory. Finally, in 1912, he gave a more definitive expression in the course of some public lectures delivered at Columbia University. The first published polemic, a paper entitled "Psychology as the behaviorist views it," appeared the following year in the *Psychological Review* and marked the official launching of the behavioristic school.

Here is the keynote of Watson's original position (1913b, p. 158):

Psychology as the behaviorist views it is a purely objective experimental branch of natural science. Its theoretical goal is the prediction and control of behavior. Introspection forms no essential part of its methods, nor is the scientific value of its data dependent upon the readiness with which they lend themselves to interpretation in terms of consciousness. The behaviorist, in his efforts to get a unitary scheme of animal response, recognizes no dividing line between man and brute. The behavior of man, with all its refinement and complexity, forms only a part of the behaviorist's total scheme of investigation. . . . The time seems to have come when psychology must discard all reference to consciousness; when it need no longer delude itself into thinking that it is making mental states the object of observation.

This first paper on behaviorism was followed shortly by a second one on the concepts of image and affect (1913a). He reduced images to implicit language responses and affect to slight vascular changes in the genitalia. We shall see later that he was severely criticized for these reductions. These two early papers were combined into the introductory chapter of his first book, *Behavior: An introduction to comparative psychology*, which appeared in 1914. This book has been reissued with an introduction by R. J. Herrnstein, who shows especially clearly how Watson first ignored and then embraced Pavlov. Herrnstein also outlines particularly well the relationship of Watson's thought to that of Tolman, Hull, and Skinner.

In 1919 Watson published another book, *Psychology from the standpoint of a behaviorist*. This volume completed the program outlined in his earlier papers. Objective methods were definitely extended into human behavioral problems. Verbal behavior was to be accepted as data, but introspection was rejected. (This distinction led his critics to heated charges of inconsistency.) The stress was on genetic factors, and the 1924 revision gave detailed results of Watson's work at the Johns Hopkins Hospital on infantile emotions and emotional conditioning.

Watson felt that psychology as a scientific discipline needed to make a complete break from the past. He declared (1929, p. 3):

[Psychology] made a false start under Wundt ... because it would not bury its past. It tried to hang on to tradition with one hand and push forward as a science with the other. Before progress could be made in astronomy, it had to bury astrology; neurology had to bury phrenology; and chemistry had to bury alchemy. But the social sciences, psychology, sociology, political science, and economics, will not bury their "medicine men."

In 1920 Watson obtained a divorce and married Rosalie Raynor, the girl with whom he did his famous experimental work on infants. The attendant publicity was sensational. He was asked to resign his professorship at Hopkins; he did, and never returned to academic life. He was displeased with the way the academicians had let their opinions of his personal life influence his career. He went into the field of advertising, where he stayed until his retirement from active life. For several years, however, he continued to lecture in New York City and to publish on psychological topics. In 1925 his *Behaviorism* appeared, as a series of lectures, with a strong environmentalist position and a positive program for the improvement of human beings. This was the book that provoked the most attention from the nonpsychological public, both favorable and unfavorable. Watson continued to publish occasionally, producing one book on child care and a number of popular articles. However, he was careful to point out the scientific inadequacy of these in his autobiographical statement (1936). Nothing new or significant was produced by him following the mid-20s; this man, whose systematic pronouncements did so much to influence the course of psychology, dropped completely out of professional activity. Whatever our systematic position, we must regret the untimely and unnecessary loss of a figure whose vitality and clarity of expression commanded so much attention and (depending on one's bias) admiration or amazement. Watson was essentially relegated to the scientific scrap heap at the age of forty-two, when many famous psychologists have just been reaching the height of their powers.

WATSONIAN BEHAVIORISM: SYSTEMATIC CRITERIA

Definition of Psychology

Psychology for Watson was (1929) "that division of natural science which takes human behavior—the doings and sayings, both learned and unlearned, of people as its subject matter" (p. 4). No mention need be made of the psychic life or consciousness—these are "pure assumptions." Watson clearly included verbalization as a kind of behavior (1925): "*Saying* is doing—that is, *behaving*. Speaking overtly or to ourselves (thinking) is just as objective a type of behavior as baseball" (p. 6).

Watson's behaviorism had two specific objectives: to predict the response, knowing the stimulus, and to predict (really *postdict*) the stimulus, knowing the response. The terms *stimulus* and *response* represented for Watson broader concepts than their usual definitions allow. Thus (1925, pp. 6, 7):

The rule, or measuring rod, which the behaviorist puts in front of him always is: Can I describe this bit of behavior I see in terms of "stimulus and response"? By stimulus we mean any object in the general environment or any change in the tissues themselves due to the physiological condition of the animal, such as the change we get when we keep an animal from sex activity, when we keep it from feeding, when we keep it from building a nest. By response we mean anything the animal does—such as turning toward or away from a light, jumping at a sound, and more highly organized activities such as building a skyscraper, drawing plans, having babies, writing books, and the like.

Postulates

Watson's assumptions were stated directly and carefully, although not necessarily in the form of postulates. The major ones may be summarized as follows:

1 Behavior is composed of response *elements* and can be successfully *analyzed* by objective natural scientific methods.

2 Behavior is composed *entirely* of glandular *secretions* and muscular *movements*; thus it is reducible ultimately to physicochemical processes.

3 There is an immediate response of some sort to every effective stimulus; every response has some kind of stimulus. There is thus a strict cause-and-effect *determinism* in behavior.

4 Conscious processes, if indeed they exist at all, cannot be *scientifically* studied; allegations concerning consciousness represent supernatural tendencies, and as hangovers from earlier prescientific theological phases of psychology must be ignored.

A number of secondary assumptions, having to do with the nature of thinking, the role of the environment, and the like, are discussed in a later section because they are not essential to the central behaviorist argument.

Nature of the Data

The character of the data for behaviorism has already been fairly well indicated in the material included under the two preceding criteria. Briefly, they are always objective reports—of muscular movements or glandular secretions in time and space; these must be, at least in principle, quantitatively analyzed, and stimulus-response relationships are the units of description (although they may be rather large-scale units, such as "building a skyscraper," and not merely "muscle twitches").

Principles of Connection

Here Watson adopted, at first, merely an older version of associationism—the laws of frequency and recency minus the "effect" aspect that Thorndike had added. Apparently he saw in effect too much of the old mentalistic attitudes, although, as we have noted, a strictly objective and operational interpretation is possible. Watson emphasized that the successful response must always occur and terminate the behavior; Thorndike's retort was that very often certain errors, such as entrances into the more popular blind alleys in a maze, were much more frequently made than the corresponding correct response. Watson subsequently shifted his emphasis to classical conditioning as demonstrated in the laboratory by Pavlov and Bekhterev (see Chapter 4). This he came to recognize as the basis for all learning; the most complex habits could be most appropriately conceived of as combinations and chainings of simpler reflexes. It is interesting, as Woodworth notes (1948, p. 88), that in spite of his enthusiasm for classical conditioning Watson apparently never recognized the very great similarity between Pavlovian reinforcement and Thorndikian effect; he continued to hold to an exercise law (frequency and recency factors) while accepting classical conditioning principles and even using them himself in his experiments on emotional conditioning in infants.

Principles of Selection

Watson assumed a large number of inherited reaction tendencies to stimulation and the "almost immediate" modification of these through conditioning into more and more complicated and individually differentiated tendencies. Thus he wrote (1925, p. 13):

One of the problems of behaviorism is what might be called the ever increasing range of stimuli to which an individual responds. Indeed so marked is this that you might be tempted at first sight to doubt the formulation we gave above, namely that response can be predicted. If you will watch the growth and development of behavior in the human being, you will find that while a great many stimuli will produce a response in the new-born, many other stimuli will not. At any rate they do not call out the same response they later call out. For example, you don't get very far by showing a new-born infant a crayon, a piece of paper, or the printed score of a Beethoven symphony. . . . It is due to conditioning from earliest childhood on that the problem of the behaviorist in predicting what a given response will be is so difficult.

Thus Watson maintained that selectivity of response and of the sufficient stimulus depends only on innate and acquired S-R connections. Selection does not constitute a unique problem. The older mentalistic concepts of purpose and value are eliminated as explanations.

THE MIND-BODY PROBLEM

The mind-body solution proposed by Watson is at the heart of what has been called *radical* or *metaphysical* behaviorism. Historically, the mind-body issue has been of considerable importance, especially with respect to the controversy about behaviorism. We therefore treat the problem at some length. Ten years ago the issue seemed to have become noncontroversial, with the behaviorist position completely dominant, at least within psychology. Today the issue has been revived (Wann, 1964) by phenomenologists and existentialists, and the completeness of the behavioral position is again an object of debate. Nevertheless, we agree with the weaker view (to which Watson sometimes subscribed) that there is presently no adequate methodology for making mind a direct object of study.

It is unfortunate that Watson's emphasis upon the mind-body issue tended to preserve it as a problem for psychology. Centuries of philosophical endeavor have netted little of scientific value concerning this philosophical problem. No one has formulated a concept of mind in such a way that it demands the attention of the scientist; its only legitimate meaning for scientific purposes is as a construct, which means that mind has no *unique* status as an object of study. Scientific issues fundamentally are questions of fact; this means that there must be some empirical basis for accepting or rejecting the statements made, with the result that the statements either gain scientific acceptance or can be discarded. There are not yet any factual statements on the mind-body issue. If eventually sufficient empirical data that demand a concept like mind for their examination and explanation become available, mind will become the concern of psychology. Today we are not in a position even to formulate scientifically useful questions regarding mind, let alone give their solutions. Until there are relevant data, the psychologist will continue to study whatever he can study, without concern for its classification or relation to the mind-body problem.

Avowed behaviorists, however, felt a need to accept some more positive position. They did not wish to study consciousness or mind and therefore wished to deny its importance; this they could do only if they accepted some appropriate mind-body position. Of the available positions (see Table 2-2), two were best fitted to their purposes. First, an epiphenomenal view would imply that consciousness had no causal efficacy and therefore little interest for science; it might or might not attend bodily events and would be of little importance. According to this position, mind would have a role comparable to that of a shadow; it would often, but not always, accompany and more or less follow the outline of the physical object (body) to which it related but would itself have no substance and accomplish no causal effects upon the physical objects producing it (i.e., would not interact). This analogy, like all analogies, is not perfect but is useful in clarifying the general nature of the epiphenomenal view.

Second, a completely physical monism would deny the very existence of mind and would from this point of view serve the purposes of behaviorism admirably.

Watson's early pronouncements were of a less extreme sort. For example (1913b, p. 174):

Will there be left over in psychology a world of pure psychics, to use Yerkes' term? I confess I do not know. The plans that I most favor for psychology lead practically to the ignoring of consciousness in the sense that that term is used by psychologists today. I have virtually denied that this realm of psychics is open to experimental investigation. I don't wish to go further into the problem at present because it leads inevitably over into metaphysics. If you will grant the behaviorist the right to use consciousness in the same way as other natural scientists employ it—that is, without making consciousness a special object of observation—you have granted all that my thesis requires.

Other expressions of this point of view may be found in papers by Walter Hunter and A. P. Weiss. Hunter, for example, said (1926, p. 89):

A brief inspection of the writings of any behaviorist will convince you that he is neither blind, deaf, anosmic, ageusic, or anaesthetic. He lives, and admits quite frankly that he lives, in the same world of objects and events which the psychologist and the layman alike acknowledge. Let us, therefore, hear no more from the psychologist that his opponent denies the existence of these things.

Weiss also accepted conscious processes as real, even if no more than epiphenomenal. He held (1917) that "... consciousness (the totality of our sensations, images, and affections) is a purely personal experience and has no scientific value or validity unless it is *expressed* in some form of behavior, such as speech or other form of representation" (p. 307). The general position here clearly stated is that the physical facts of behavior are sufficient; the "mental" correlates to these facts are unreliable and superfluous.

Acceptance of this methodological behaviorism put the behaviorist into the somewhat embarrassing position of admitting that experience exists, even if in a most shadowy manner, and yet cannot be attacked by scientific tools. Thus, faced with the dilemma of either admitting that there are some psychological facts which he cannot explain by natural scientific techniques or denying the existence of such alleged facts, the radical behaviorist, following Watson, chose the latter course: the explicit denial of the existence of any conscious correlates to introspective reports.

By 1924 Watson seems to have come to this alternative. For example, in his debate with McDougall (J. B. Watson & McDougall, 1929), he said that consciousness "has never been seen, touched, smelled, tasted, or moved. It is a plain assumption just as unprovable as the old concept of the soul" (p. 14). And, more at length (p. 26):

He then who would introduce consciousness, either as an epiphenomenon or as an active force interjecting itself into the physical and chemical happenings of the body, does so because of spiritualistic and vitalistic leanings. The Behaviorist cannot find consciousness in the test tube of his science. He finds no evidence anywhere for a stream of consciousness, not even for one so convincing as that described by William James. He does, however, find convincing proof of an ever-widening stream of behavior.

Another early behaviorist, K. S. Lashley, likewise supported an extreme position. In his single excursion into such polemic, he wrote (1923, pp. 351-352):

There can be no valid objection by the behaviorist to the introspective method so long as no claim is made that the method reveals something besides body activity. . . . The attributes of mind, as definable on introspective evidence, are precisely the attributes of the complex physiological organization of the human body and a statement of the latter will constitute as complete and adequate an account of consciousness as seems possible from any type of introspective analysis.

This view reduces mind entirely to physiological functions and thus represents a radical behavioristic position.

There were several common behavioristic arguments against the existence of consciousness. Though we present them, we do not vouch for their validity. First, the critics asked how the so-called gaps in consciousness, such as allegedly occur during sleep, can be explained? What is lost? What returns? There appears to be no measurable, physical loss. But there are behavior differences. The behaviorists answered that unconsciousness (as in sleep or anesthesia) simply means that certain neural pathways are blocked off so that the person is unable to report stimulation.

Second, the behaviorists maintained that the stimulus is really the important thing in introspection, not the alleged conscious correlates. Introspection is simply a way of reporting what has been learned by language training. Situations in which the "wrong" terms are learned are instructive: for example, the calling of a "red" stimulus "gray" by a color-blind person is wrong only because it is not consistent with most other language reports on the stimulus.

Third, and most important, the behaviorists argued that the assumption of nonphysical events interacting with physical events clearly violates the conservation-of-energy principle. Physics tells us that energy is neither created nor destroyed in physical systems; it is only transformed. All the energy within physical systems can be accounted for physically; none is gained from, or lost to, any nonphysical system. If conscious events affected the body or its physiological processes, they would have to do so by adding or subtracting energy or mass. But this is impossible, according to the conservation-of-energy principle, which is scarcely to be overthrown on the basis of old theological and philosophical dogma. Thus the fact of experiencing, the allegedly mental process, cannot influence even the muscular efforts necessary to speech. And if ideas *can* influence muscles, then they must themselves be physical events occurring in the nervous system—and therefore nonmental.

To follow up the implications of this argument, the radical behaviorist next disposed of both major dualistic positions in the following manner: If mind is granted, for the sake of argument, then it must either (1) affect behavior (interactionism) or (2) not affect behavior (parallelism). But if (1) is true, then the law of the conservation of energy, otherwise inviolate in physics, is violated. If (2) is true, how can one say that one has an "idea," unless so saying is induced by the "idea" itself, as according to (2) it cannot be. Belief in such a well-coordinated set of coincidences overstrains credulity, and the assumption of some outside coordinating force—such as God (occasionalism)—is scientifically unacceptable. Thus ideas cannot be proved unless they affect the nervous system, but to do this they must be within the physical system, and this is quite satisfactory to the behaviorist because it means that ideas are no longer "mental."

Finally, the behaviorists insisted, the conservation-of-energy principle can be applied to the epiphenomenal view. If conscious correlates are accepted as strictly noncausal events, they must nevertheless be produced by physical events. But this means that energy is used to produce them; how else could the physical events operate? Such expenditure of energy without demonstrable physical loss of energy or mass is likewise incompatible with generally accepted physical principles.

The radical behaviorist therefore turned to a strict physical monism, according to which "mental" is merely a description of the way the physical events function and consciousness has no independent or unique existence.

WATSON'S EXPERIMENTAL PROGRAM

Although Watson's early work was with animal problems, as indicated above, the best example of his experimental behavioristic program is probably the research he conducted on conditioning and reconditioning of emotional responses in infants. This work also represents the best example of the application of the conditioning techique by any of the early classical behaviorists. The early research is most comprehensively described by Watson in three papers in the volume *Psychologies of 1925*, from which the following exposition is mainly derived.

Starting from the vantage point provided by the extensive studies of behavior during the fetal and early postnatal periods in animals, Watson began the comparable study of very young human infants in an effort to determine the kind and variety of congenital behavior which could be reliably identified and which was presumably inherited. He states that "almost daily observation" was made of several hundred children through the first thirty days of postnatal life and of a smaller number for longer periods ranging into early childhood. The result of these observations was a catalog of the "birth equipment of the human young," as Watson called it. A long list of behaviors was developed, with objective descriptions for each, but the only experimental, or semiexperimental, observations at this time involved some interesting work with twenty babies on the causal factors in handedness. Watson's conclusion (1926a) was that ". . . there is no fixed differentiation of response in either hand until social usage begins to establish handedness" (p. 29).

Watson was also concerned with the genetic (longitudinal) study of the emotional life of the infant and child. Again the fully objective technique of behavior description was applied, this time intensively to a sample of three-year-olds. Watson found, not too surprisingly, that most three-year-old children are shot through with useless and actually harmful emotional reactions. Not content with what he described as the historically orthodox interpretation of such emotional behavior as inherited, Watson saw the need for new experimental techniques. He early discovered that children taken from typical homes did not make good subjects for the study of the origin of emotions. The obvious need for controlled emotional backgrounds in such subjects was met by use of "strong healthy children belonging to wet nurses in hospitals, and other children brought up in the home under the eye of the experimenters" (1926a, p. 42). With these subjects he instituted a prolonged series of simple tests, made primarily by the introduction of various kinds of animals, at the zoological park as well as in the laboratory. He was unable to find evidence of fear and concluded that accounts of the inheritance of emotional responses to such stimuli were false.

One of the best-known contributions of this phase of the research program was Watson's description, as a result of further semiexperimental observations, of the basic conditions that could be reliably depended upon to produce fear, rage, and love in infants. As most students of elementary general psychology have been told, Watson found fear produced by loud sounds and sudden loss of support; rage, by hampering of bodily movement; and love, by tickling, rocking, patting, and stroking of the skin.

This pioneer research of Watson's constituted an advance and a stimulation to further research. Bridges (1932) questioned the ability to discriminate different emotions in the infant, and her results showed that the only sure distinction is between a generally excited state and a quiescent one. It is now generally conceded that adults cannot make reliable judgments of the emotion being shown by an infant unless they have knowledge of the stimulating situation (e.g., pinprick versus stroking). Despite the modification of Watson's conclusions suggested by later research, his basic point that infants show very few varieties of innate emotional behavior has not been contradicted.

From 1918 on, Watson reported, he conducted experimentation designed to determine some of the factors underlying the acquisition and loss of emotional responses in children. "We were rather loath at first to conduct such experiments," he said (1926b), "but the need of this kind of study was so great that we finally decided to experiment upon the possibility of building up fears in the infant and then later to study practical methods for removing them" (p. 51). Watson found it relatively easy to establish fear in a subject through a simple conditioning procedure. This aspect of the research was completed by the demonstration of spread, or generalization, of the conditioned fear response to similar but previously neutral stimuli, in a manner comparable to that found for other kinds of conditioned responses without emotional components.

Finally, Watson turned to the problem of eliminating conditioned fears. A variety of commonly used techniques was first tried experimentally on subjects in whom conditioned fears had been produced: disuse, verbal appeal, frequent application of the fear stimulus, and use of a social (unafraid) model. None of these was effective. Then, in experimentation performed by Mary Cover Jones under Watson's direction, clear evidence for the effectiveness of the unconditioning, or reconditioning, technique was obtained from one subject with whom intensive work was done. This was achieved by bringing in the conditioned fear stimulus at some distance, so as not to elicit the fear response, while the child was eating. After daily introductions of the stimulus (a rabbit) at progressively closer points on the long lunchroom table, the child was finally able to handle it without fear while continuing to eat. Generalized fear responses to similar objects were also found to be eliminated by this procedure.

Watson concluded from the preliminary results of this research that emotional organization is subject to the same laws as other habits; he congratulated himself upon putting the study of emotion upon a natural scientific basis. No doubt he was correct in asserting that his formulation would lead to more research than James's earlier formulation of the problem of emotion had.

SECONDARY CHARACTERISTICS OF WATSONIAN BEHAVIORISM

Today, the methodological characteristics of the behavioristic position are felt to be the most basic because of the wide acceptance of the methodological point and the rejection of, or controversy about, the other points. The secondary aspects of Watson's thinking are not implied by the word *behavioristic*. However, much of the attack on behaviorism has been directed at these secondary points, and they are many times confused or mixed indiscriminately with the primary characteristics (see Koch, 1954, pp. 5-6).

It is safer to distinguish the critical and secondary propositions. For example, although it is natural for the behaviorist to view thinking as a peripheral process that is easily accessible to behavioral observation, it is not necessary that one accept Watson's peripheralism in order to remain a "good" methodological behaviorist. Characteristics like this one are treated as secondary. We shall discuss language development and thinking, the role of environmental factors in behavior, and determinism and personal responsibility as examples of the secondary characteristics.

Language Development and Thinking

Because of its use as an example of a behavioristic interpretation of a mentalistic concept, the theory of language development plays a key role in behavioristic thinking. It goes as follows: First, many separate syllables are naturally produced by the normal vocimotor apparatus of any human child. The normal instigation for the first of such mouthings—for example, the common sound *da*—is probably some obscure physiological stimulus. A *circular conditioned response* eventually becomes established as a result of the concurrence of the sound *da* with the saying of it. That is, the infant hears *da* as he says it, and the sound itself becomes a conditioned stimulus to the saying—circular because it is obviously self-perpetuating. The kind of babbling that is characteristic of early vocalization thus develops, with the infant stopping the sequence of repeated syllabizing only when distracted by some other stronger stimulus or when fatigued. Second, the mother or some other adult hears this kind of babbling and repeats the sound, thus producing the conditioned stimulus and causing the child to repeat it. In this manner the child soon learns to imitate many of the sounds the mother makes—or at least to approximate them.

Finally, the mother shows the child an object, such as a doll, while repeating the appropriate syllable. In this way new connections between visual stimuli and established sounds are developed. The further process of language development is a long-continued elaboration and refinement of this basic process.

Evidence for the soundness of this general interpretation was adduced from the case histories of deaf-mutes—babies born deaf whose initial babblings are not continued and who do not learn to speak, presumably because of the absence of normal auditory conditioned stimuli. Also, with normal children, the behaviorist can point to the common occurrence of parents using so-called baby talk in communicating with their infants.

In all this, the behaviorist takes pains to point out, there is nothing save brain connections and reconnections; no mental events are necessary. The child learns to say *blue* or *red* or *green*, or *loud* or *shrill* or *bass*, because of the conditioning of brain events and not because of sensory experience such as sensations. Watson himself preferred to avoid the old terminology as contaminated with mentalistic connotations, but Weiss and some of the less radical behaviorists were willing to use the old terms with new behavioristic meanings.

Watson extended this interpretation into the field of thinking, considered as implicit, or covert, behavior. Such behavior consists of tendencies toward muscular movements or glandular secretions that are not directly observable by the usual techniques of observation but may nonetheless play an important role in activating or mediating other, more overt behavior (e.g., *action currents* detectable in musculature by electronic devices in the absence of any overtly observable movements). As language functions develop in the young child, from two years or so on, much of his motor activity tends to be accompanied by a more or less complete language description. For example, the child will tend to say "Johnny eats"—or some approximation thereof—as he eats. Under parental and other adult pressures, however, he is gradually forced to reduce this overt speech, which is generally regarded with disfavor. It then tends to turn into silent speech—or thinking—in adulthood.

Past training in the form of conditioning accounts for both overt body behavior and language responses, overt and implicit. If the overt behavior aspects are inhibited, the implicit language responses may still be kept; the person is then said to be thinking. Thinking is thus primarily trial-and-error behavior of the laryngeal mechanism (or, as a humorist epigrammatically put it, Watson made up his windpipe that he had no mind). Watson further pointed out, however, that under certain conditions, language behavior of this sort might also be suppressed, and then thinking could continue in the form of either overt body activity or visceral reactions. A later Watsonian position was thus that we think with our whole bodies. Because of the poor connections between the visceral and the laryngeal series of muscle changes, visceral thinking responses are largely unverbalized. They are therefore fundamentally important in thinking of an unverbalized sort (determining tendencies, hunches and intuitions, and feelings of unfamiliarity, familiarity, approaching familiarity, certainty, and the like). Although thinking occurs primarily in verbal terms, it may go on in other forms.

Watson's position on the developmental control of unverbalized thinking is well summarized in the following statement (1926b, p. 56):

I want to develop the thesis sometime that society has never been able to get hold of these implicit concealed visceral and glandular reactions of ours, or else it would have schooled them in us, for, as you know, society has a great propensity for regularizing all of our reactions. Hence most of our adult overt reactions—our speech, and movements of our arms, legs, and trunk—are schooled and habitized. Owing to their concealed nature, however, society cannot get hold of visceral behavior to lay down rules and regulations for its integration. It follows as a corollary from this that we have no names, no words with which to describe these reactions. They remain unverbalized.

Although Watson held an essentially peripheral theory of thinking, with stress on muscular reactions and tendencies toward them as the basis of thinking, other behaviorists carried the assumption of progressive suppression of muscular actions on to its logical conclusion. This means a central theory of thinking, with only brain states involved. However this problem is eventually decided, it will not affect the methodological tenets of behaviorism, but only Watson's elaboration of them. B. F. Skinner's treatment of verbal behavior (1957b) shows that Watson's basic behavioristic position regarding language and thinking is very much alive today.

Emphasis on the Environment

Although in his earlier writing Watson accepted the importance of inherited behavioral tendencies, in his later work he placed the major emphasis on the role of the environment in the molding of adult human behavior. He declared that the concept of instinct was no longer needed in psychology, but took pains to make it clear that he did not doubt the important role of inherited *structures*. Performance, then, was dependent upon the way in which the environment acted on such structures. In the following example, he attempts to clarify his position (1926a, p. 2):

The behaviorist **would** *not* say: "He inherits his father's capacity or talent for being a fine swordsman." He would say: "This child certainly has his father's slender build of body, the same type of eyes. . . . He, too, has the build of a swordsman." And he would go on to say: ". . . and his father is very fond of him. He put a tiny sword into his hand when he was a year of age, and in all their walks he talks sword play, attack and defense, the code of duelling and the like." A certain type of structure plus early training—*slanting*—accounts for adult performance.

In his emphasis on the importance of the environmental factors, Watson pointed to the very great variety of human traits and habits associated with different climates and different cultures. Although recognizing the limitations of available data, he felt that every normal human baby has within it essentially similar potentialities. This presumption led him to make predictions for which he has been strongly attacked. For example, he stated (1926a): "I would feel perfectly confident in the ultimately favorable outcome of careful upbringing of a *healthy, well-formed* baby born of a long line of crooks, murderers, thieves and prostitutes. Who has any evidence to the contrary?" (p. 9). Then, admittedly going beyond the facts, Watson went on to state a challenge for which he is famous (1926a, p. 10):

I should like to go one step further tonight and say, "Give me a dozen healthy infants, well-formed, and my own specified world to bring them up in, and I'll guarantee to take any one at random and train him to become any type of specialist I might select—a doctor, lawyer, artist, merchant-chief and, yes, even into a beggar-man and thief, regardless of his talents, penchants, tendencies, abilities, vocations and race of his ancestors." . . . Please note that when this experiment is made I am to be allowed to specify the way they are to be brought up and the type of world they have to live in.

Determinism and Personal Responsibility

In the long-standing disagreement between science, with its acceptance of a strictly determined natural world, and theology and various types of philosophy, in which freedom of the will is generally accepted, there is no question at all about where Watsonian behaviorism stands. Since all behavior, including that called *voluntary* and involving choices, is interpreted in physical terms, all acts are physically determined in advance.

Watson's own interest was less in the theoretical problem of determinism per se than in the consequent or corollary question of personal responsibility. Along with many other behavioristically inclined psychologists and sociologists, he argued strongly against the assumption that individuals are personally responsible for their actions in the free-will sense. The implications of this belief are especially important in relation to such social problems as crime. The behaviorist would accept punishment of criminals as a part of a general system of social control but not on the basis of a theory of retribution. Instead of retributive treatment by which an errant individual is made to pay for his violations, Watson argued for treatment on the basis of the individual's need for reeducation. He conceded that if criminals could not be salvaged for society—that is, if satisfactory reconditioning could not be achieved—then they should be kept under restraint or destroyed.

Watson himself developed quite a visionary program for social improvement—a so-called experimental ethics to be based on behaviorism. His early training in functionalism (if we may apply a behavioristic dictum to Watson's own career) thus shows through particularly at the very end of his *Behaviorism*, where he states (1925, p. 248):

I think behaviorism does lay a foundation for saner living. It ought to be a science that prepares men and women for understanding the first principles of their own behavior. It ought to make men and women eager to rearrange their own lives, and especially eager to prepare themselves to bring up their own children in a healthy way. I wish I had time more fully to describe this, to picture to you the kind of rich and wonderful individual we should make of every healthy child; if only we could let it shape itself properly and then provide for it a universe in which it could exercise that organization—a universe unshackled by legendary folk lore of happenings thousands of years ago; unhampered by disgraceful political history; free of foolish customs and conventions which have no significance in themselves, yet which hem the individual in like taut steel bands.

OTHER PROMINENT EARLY BEHAVIORISTS

Although Watson was without question the first and foremost systematic behaviorist, he had a number of important and sometimes vociferous supporters. One, Albert P. Weiss (1879-1931), was born in Germany but came to the United States at an early age. He was appointed an assistant to Max Meyer, who himself had come from the University of Berlin in Germany to establish the psychology laboratory at the University of Missouri in 1900. Meyer has already been mentioned as an early objectivist whose "psychology of the other one" antedated Watson's behaviorism. Weiss took his Ph.D. with Meyer at Missouri in 1916 and pursued an active career at Ohio State University. Weiss's *Theoretical basis of human behavior* was first published in 1925. Weiss saw behavior as ultimately reducible to physicochemical terms. Psychology was thus a branch of physics. The first chapter of his book, for example, is entitled "The ultimate elements" and consists of a discussion of the structure of matter, the nature of energy, the concept of force, and the like.

The reader should not be misled into assuming that Weiss was merely a farfetched and unrealistic theorist. On the contrary, he was among the most careful and ingenious of the early behaviorists, certainly far more careful than Watson in the matter of defining terms and developing concepts. A single example will suffice to indicate this quality of his theoretical thinking: his attempt to explain voluntary activity (a problem whose resolution Watson did not bother to attempt). The problem for Weiss was to determine what kind of behavior is conditioned to the word *voluntary*. Whereas the mentalist says that the mind does the choosing, the behaviorist says that physiological brain states operate and that the term *voluntary* is applied when there is some conflict, or at least potential conflict, between the tendencies to action associated with different sets of stimuli. One set of stimuli eventually achieves a clear physiological channel, and the individual makes a "choice." This is of course determined by past experience as it has shaped the brain connections. "Willpower," which is allegedly exercised on difficult choices, was for Weiss merely the spilling over of brain excitations into motor tensions which build up because they are not allowed immediate outlet. The effort of the "will" is assumed from the muscular contractions that are themselves by-products of brain action. Voluntary behavior is thus basically no different from other types, but does have this apparently additional characteristic of muscular tension.

Weiss regarded psychology as a biosocial discipline because of the nature of the variables with which it was concerned. He set up an experimental program of research on child behavior, but his early death prevented its consummation.

Edwin B. Holt (1873-1946) was influential mainly through his books, in which he gave strong philosophical support to the behavioristic movement. As Boring (1950) has noted, Holt's greatest specific influence in contemporary psychology has probably come through his role in stimulating E. C. Tolman to a behavioristic combination of purposivism and cognitive theory. *The Freudian wish and its place in ethics* was published in 1915, and *Animal drive and the learning process* appeared in 1931. Holt was a philosophical neorealist who attempted to integrate the essential parts of the behavioristic and the psychoanalytic ("dynamic") movements. He took his Ph.D. at Harvard in 1901 and subsequently taught both there and at Princeton.

Walter S. Hunter (1889-1953) made some of the most important methodological contributions to the field of animal learning. Like Watson, Hunter was trained in functionalism at Chicago, taking his Ph.D. there in 1912 with Angell and Carr. After teaching at Texas, Kansas, and Clark Universities, he was at Brown University from 1936 until his death. At Brown, he developed and maintained a small but active department of experimentalists. His methodological innovations included the delayed-response and double-alternation tasks, which were devised for the investigation of higher symbolic abilities in animals. Hunter was interested primarily in laboratory research rather than in theory, but he did attempt to push his new name for the science of behavior, *anthroponomy* (1926). Like most terminological innovations, this one did not stick.

Karl S. Lashley (1890-1958) was a student of Watson and received his Ph.D. at Hopkins in 1915. He was later at the Universities of Minnesota and Chicago, then at Harvard, and finally at the Yerkes Laboratory of Primate Biology. Lashley was a leading physiological psychologist and ventured only occasionally into systematic problems. He is best known for his work on brain extirpation in the rat, which demonstrated the limits of localization.

Lashley's two famous principles of equipotentiality and mass action are generalizations based on this extirpation work. The first principle states that one part of the cortex is essentially equal to another with respect to its contribution to tasks like maze learning. The second states that the efficiency of learning depends upon the total mass of cortex left functioning.

Lashley moved away from a stimulus-response toward a field-theory frame of reference (see Chapter 11), partly as a consequence of the theoretical import of his own findings on brain functions. This shift should not be construed as implying that Lashley's attitude toward a basic behavioristic psychology changed; rather, he changed his position with respect to some of Watson's secondary points. He no longer believed that the most fruitful analysis was to be made in terms of discrete S-R connections which were strengthened via some kind of conditioning process.

Floyd H. Allport (1890-   ) took his Ph.D. in 1919 at Harvard and went on to popularize behavioristic concepts (for example, the circular conditioned reflex theory of language development, described above) in his social psychology text (1924). Allport has continued, at Syracuse University, to apply behavioristic principles to social psychology. More recently, he has turned to the psychology of sensory processes (Allport, 1955). He is perhaps best known because of his description of the J curve, which describes the distribution of responding when some social institution exerts pressure toward some prescribed mode of responding. In such cases, most people behave according to prescription, and the number responding in this way are responsible for the high part of the J. Others, however, scatter away from the modal response, as represented by the lower part of the J. A commonly cited example is the behavior of people at a stop sign: Most conform to social pressure and come to a complete stop, others nearly stop, and a few extreme cases continue onward without abating speed.

Z. Y. Kuo (1898-   ) is a Chinese psychologist who was trained in this country (Columbia University). He adopted an extremely environmentalistic position (1922, 1924), far more radical even than Watson's. All alleged instincts were to be explained on the basis of inherited structure and environmental influences. Kuo was far from an armchair speculator on the problem. He watched the development of behavior in the embryo chick by replacing part of the shell with a small transparent window (1932a, 1932b, 1932c, 1932d, 1932e). He found that much chick behavior which may appear to be instinctive is really learned during the embryonic period as a function of conditions within the egg. For example, the alternate stepping behavior of the normal newly hatched chick was shown to be dependent upon certain mechanically induced alternate hind-limb movements inside the shell. Cramping from the yolk sac often acted as a stimulus to the movements. Kuo differed from Watson in that he preferred to think of continuities in behavior rather than conditioning as a basic explanation of behavior changes.

In other research Kuo showed that the cat's reactions to rats are not strictly determined by heredity but can be easily altered from the normal predatory form by appropriate experiences (1930, 1938). These results all fit well into his environmentalism. Kuo concluded that inherited structures are important but that even these can be molded via environmental influences. He did not believe in any direct native behavior tendencies beyond those which are strictly the result of structural factors.

Kuo, now in Hong Kong, has recently come back into print (1967), apparently in response to the new ethological emphasis on inherited behaviors. His current view on exogenous and endogenous factors is considerably moderated relative to his earlier view, but he remains the hardheaded antimentalist. Even his moderated position on environmentalism emphasizes learning much more than is typical of the ethologists.

CONTEMPORARY BEHAVIORISTS

A list of contemporary psychologists who accept the behaviorist methodological point would be a large one indeed. There are four men, however, who have bridged the gap between Watson and the present; they were important during Watson's lifetime and are still important. These four men are E. C. Tolman, E. R. Guthrie, C. L. Hull, and B. F. Skinner. Their contemporary importance is such that their systems are discussed in the third part of the present book. Their past role has been one of winnowing Watson's behaviorism for the good that was in it and adding their own personal contributions. In addition, we note the important role of such men as C. H. Graham (1951, 1958) and W. R. Garner (Garner, Hake, & Eriksen, 1956) in applying the basic behavioristic notions to the experimental psychology of visual perception, and of D. O. Hebb (1949) and R. C. Davis (1953) in applying these notions to physiological psychology. The psychology that has emerged because of the creative efforts of all these men is far more sophisticated than anything Watson himself produced.

WATSONIAN BEHAVIORISM: CRITICISMS AND REPLIES

The critical attacks made upon Watson and his brand of behaviorism hit all aspects of the system. Since we cannot consider them all, we shall select those which refer to the methodological and metaphysical points that are most crucial. In addition, the criticisms of Watson's experimental ethics are presented as representative of the attacks upon the more peculiarly Watsonian aspects of behaviorism.

Methodological Behaviorism

Although psychology was reasonably well prepared for the stress on objectivity, not all psychologists were satisfied with Watson's pronouncements. An immediate objection was that Watson's extreme formulation left out important components of psychology. This point was made even by those who in general supported much of the objective program. Woodworth, for example, has complained that the early behavioristic emphasis upon strict objectivity hindered the development of research into sensory and perceptual processes by turning the attention of younger men away from this problem area. Acceptance by Watson of the "verbal report" was not satisfactory. For example, Woodworth criticized Watson for attempting to deal, within the strictly objective framework, with the phenomena of afterimages. He stated (1948, p. 84):

The "phenomena" which Watson finds so interesting and valuable in the after-image experiment are the after-images themselves, not the subject's speech movements. We may conclude that verbal report is not a behavioristic method and that Watson's use of it is practically a confession of defeat for methodological behaviorism.

A broader and more vigorous attack was made by McDougall, who presented himself, as we have noted, as an earlier proponent and user of the strictly behavioristic experiment. McDougall's strictures of this methodological incompleteness of Watson's position may be summarized in the statement that a completely objective approach cannot obtain an adequate account of (1) the functional relations of conscious experiences (e.g., their dependence on external or bodily conditions), (2) the accuracy of verbal report (e.g., whether or not a subject is malingering, as in military service), and (3) the meaningfulness of the verbal report (e.g., in regard to the analysis of dreams). He was particularly eloquent in regard to the incompleteness of the behavioristic account of the finer things in life, specifically music (J. B. Watson & McDougall, 1929, p. 63):

I come into this hall and see a man on this platform scraping the guts of a cat with hairs from the tail of a horse; and, sitting silently in attitudes of rapt attention, are a thousand persons who presently break out into wild applause. How will the Behaviorist explain these strange incidents: How explain the fact that the vibrations emitted by the cat-gut stimulate all the thousand into absolute silence and quiescence; and the further fact that the cessation of the stimulus seems to be a stimulus to the most frantic activity? Commonsense and psychology agree in accepting the explanation that the audience heard the music with keen pleasure, and vented their gratitude and admiration for the artist in shouts and handclappings. But the Behaviorist knows nothing of pleasure and pain, of admiration and gratitude. He has relegated all such "metaphysical entities" to the dust heap, and must seek some other explanation. Let us leave him seeking it. The search will keep him harmlessly occupied for some centuries to come.

Watson would argue that McDougall and Woodworth, despite their objections, must use behavior as their datum. Whenever their metaphysics makes them try to use something else, they get into trouble; and we find those who try to use consciousness as the basic datum involved in useless squabbles about what they find there. Consciousness is a tool for the scientist, not an object of study. He uses it to study *both* afterimages and concrete blocks, but does not study it in itself.

As an example of the behavioristic attitude, consider a blind man who is interested in studying visual afterimages. Given someone to set up the equipment, he could successfully conduct research by writing down the verbal responses emitted by his assistant and by his subjects. He would be unable to use his own experience directly to give him data; he would use the behavior of others. If he could himself respond to light, he might use his own responses as data, but he would not use his own experience directly. The blind man would be truly objective in collecting data, for anyone could study all his data, and he would have no private data stemming from his own response to light. If he were skeptical, he might doubt that his subjects' *consciousness* of their response to light differed in any respect from his own, though they respond differently. Even that belief would not change the data. As Washburn (1908) early pointed out, the situation is exactly the same for animals as for people other than ourselves; we can only *infer* that others are conscious, and the inference is of no scientific use.

On a somewhat different level of argument, Boring has also criticized Watson for his acceptance of verbal report (1950, p. 645):

[Watson] wished to let in discriminatory verbal report when it was accurate and verifiable, as it is, for instance, in the observation of difference tones, and to rule it out when it was unverifiable, as it is when it consists of statements about the nature of feeling or about the impalpable contents of imageless thinking. . . . The admission of verbal report was a damaging concession, for it made it appear that behaviorism was asking only for verbal changes and not for a reform in scientific procedures.

The modern behaviorist's answer to Boring's objection is simply agreement. The point basic to the whole behaviorist revolution was to use only verifiable, accurate data in psychology. The thing that furnishes such data is behavior and only behavior. Verbal behavior is behavior and constitutes valuable data if it is verifiable and repeatable. Not all behavior, and hence not all verbal behavior, furnishes useful data; the behaviorist is not obliged to accept data indiscriminately. Boring himself (1964) reports on a senseless controversy between Wundt and Stumpf concerning ". . . whether a perceived tonal interval is bisected psychologically by the arithmetic or by the geometric mean of its tonal stimuli" (p. 683). The behaviorists believed, rightly or wrongly, that these disagreements arose partly because of the type of data used.

Woodworth and Sheehan (1964) present the basic enigma in two moderate, eloquently understated paragraphs which quietly communicate despair of a final answer (pp. 3-4):

For one group of psychologists the proper content seemed reasonably to be man's conscious experience, which they held could be investigated through introspection. This is a method of self-observation which, as we shall see later, may take a variety of forms, ranging from the simple reporting of one's immediate sensory impression of a stimulus to long-extended probing, during analytical therapy, of one's emotional experiences. Unlike as these "introspections" may seem, they have in common a private quality which appears to distinguish them from the methods of physics or chemistry or biology. In these sciences any number of observers can report on what is visible in the test tube or under the microscope, whereas the psychological "experience" can be reported by only one observer.

How real this distinction is remains a perplexing epistemological problem. Does each observer see in the test tube or under the microscope a bit of the real external world, or does each merely report on his subjective experience resulting from some emanations of the real world? If the latter is the case a sharp line cannot be drawn between the data of the "objective" sciences and the subjective data of psychology. In all cases the observing subject would be reporting the private content of his own "consciousness."

Still more recently, O'Neil (1968) has tried to clarify the behaviorist's position on consciousness by relating behaviorism to realism in philosophy, and he does succeed in showing that consciousness is not a problem for radical behaviorists; but it may remain a problem for others.

Watson's initial attempts to translate some of the older mentalistic concepts of psychology into behavioristic language have been criticized from two points of view. On the one hand, some have contended that the acceptance of any mentalistic terms weakened his strictly objective system. On the other hand, Heidbreder has taken Watson to task for (1933, p. 275):

. . . a tendency to indulge in feats of translation, and apparently at times to regard translation as an explanation. It is difficult, when reading some of the behavioristic accounts, to escape the impression that the writers regard it as an explanation to say that a wish is an organic set, that a meaning is a bodily attitude, that thoughts are language mechanisms. Yet little is added to the knowledge of wishes, meanings, and thoughts by these statements, which after all consist largely in taking over what is known about these happenings from common sense and the older psychology and devising, often not on the basis of known facts, some possible physiological explanation of them.

Although we agree with Heidbreder that Watson actually did little with such translations, we think they can be regarded as starting points in the objectification of psychological problems. While Watson was guilty as charged of premature enthusiasm, final evaluations of the success of the fully objective program need to await more extensive applications of detailed research like that which Watson himself initiated on emotional conditioning in infants and children. No behaviorist would today rest content with such a purely verbal translation, and probably that is not what Watson really intended either. The point is that the mentalistic terms as they were used had no behavioral meaning, and the translation was really a definition. The concept was then not explained but defined and made workable. Wishes and thoughts did not need translating; they needed *some* meaning that would be useful in a natural scientific framework. Skinner's book *Verbal behavior* (1957b) makes its chief contribution through such a reformulation rather than through the presentation of new empirical results. This book presents many independent variables which seem likely to be useful in the explanation of verbal behavior. It does not, as one example, translate ideas into other terms; ideas are simply not part of the formulation. Watson himself was often content simply to let mentalistic terms disappear rather than translate them into some other language. This elimination of fruitless concepts and the hardheaded attitude toward all concepts were behaviorism's outstanding contributions.

Another line of methodological criticism involves the charge that Watson was backtracking on his own restriction of psychology to observables by including implicit behavior tendencies, which were not directly observed, albeit in theory observable. Woodworth, for example, has complained that Watson, even while postulating such implicit behavior, restricted his own research on emotion to the directly observable overt aspects of behavior and made no effort to investigate the presumably important visceral components.

The answer to this objection is similar to that given to the previous one. Certainly Watson, in his impatient enthusiasm to get to a new and thoroughly objective psychology, went beyond the available data in drawing conclusions and did not himself begin all the necessary research to back up his assumptions. Nevertheless, there is no necessary inconsistency in the assumption of implicit behavior tendencies and the holding to a strictly objective systematic and experimental framework. No one can do everything. Attempts were made to observe the implicit responses, for example, tongue, mouth, and larynx movements in implicit speech, and much later even muscle potentials in deaf-mutes. Watson's own research utilized observable responses for its data. It was only natural to make the explanatory system of behaviorism consistent with the data system, and the responses were not expected to *remain* unobservable.

This tendency may be seen throughout psychology. For example, Freud's explanation of the subconscious processes grows out of the kind of data available to the psychoanalyst, and Hull's theory of learning was taken directly from experimental results. Watson's theorizing about internal changes, especially with emotion, seems amply vindicated by results of recent studies on the learning of visceral and glandular responses (N. E. Miller, 1969). Such is the success of this work that society may, after all, eventually be able to regularize these responses, the ones whose freedom from control Watson seemed to be bitterly celebrating in 1926.

A related criticism has been developed strongly by another avowed behaviorist, E. C. Tolman, who finds in overt behavior a purposiveness that Watson did not admit. Tolman early criticized Watson's research on emotions and stated his position most succinctly as follows (1932, pp. 6-7):

In short, our conclusion must be that Watson has in reality dallied with two different notions of behavior, though he himself has not clearly seen how different they are. On the one hand, he has defined behavior in terms of its strict underlying physical and physiological details. . . . We shall designate this as the *molecular* definition of behavior. And, on the other hand, he has come to recognize . . . that behavior, as such, is more than and different from the sum of its physiological parts. Behavior, as such, is an "emergent" phenomenon that has descriptive and defining properties of its own. And we shall designate this latter as the *molar* definition of behavior.

Tolman's psychology is proof that he prefers the molar definition of behavior, that he thinks purposiveness must be introduced in order to have a useful psychology. Purpose generally alludes, in Tolman's usage, to some influence of the animal's behavior on the environment; for instance, we may speak of the purpose of an animal's behavior as being the release of a food pellet or the depression of a bar. Usually, the bending of a limb would not be considered a purpose, although this would be a purposeful description compared with the flexion of a muscle. Tolman contends that it is more useful to define responses in molar behavioral than in molecular physiological terms. Watson, like most psychologists before and after him, agreed in practice with this point. He wished to make the additional point that purposive behavior is in principle reducible to the physiological level, although he did not actually work on this level. Other behaviorists, like Guthrie (1952), have attempted to work on a more molecular level. If the problem of psychology is to explain the behavior of an animal in his environment, and if we define purpose in terms of the influence of the animal on the environment, then it seems that a complete psychology must consider purpose as so defined. Watson would no doubt be a purposivist when purpose is so defined. Tolman's quoted statement suggests that he believes Watson recognized this kind of purposivism, since he rightfully accuses Watson of using the term *behavior* in both senses. However, Watson would not agree, nor would most contemporary behaviorists, that purpose as an explanatory concept in the McDougallian sense is legitimate.

The Gestalt psychologists have been vociferous in their complaints against the allegedly molecular brand of S-R psychology, as we shall see in the following chapter. But, again, a particularly telling argument came from within the behavioristic camp itself. As suggested above, K. S. Lashley began his professional career as an avowed and enthusiastic behaviorist. His own research, however, convinced him that some of the behavioristic assumptions were in error. As he himself has told the story (1931, p. 14):

I began life as an ardent advocate of muscle-twitch psychology. I became glib in formulating all problems of psychology in terms of stimulus-response and in explaining all things as conditioned reflexes. . . . I embarked enthusiastically upon a program of experiments to prove the adequacy of the motor-chain theory of integration. And the result is as though I had maliciously planned an attack upon the whole system. . . . The conditioned reflex turned out not to be a reflex, not the simple basic key to the learning problem. . . . In order that the concept of stimulus-response should have any scientific value it must convey a notion of how a particular stimulus elicits a particular response and no other. . . . When viewed in relation to the problems of neurology, the nature of the stimulus and of the response is intrinsically such as to preclude the theory of simple point-to-point connection in reflexes.

Watson's own research efforts were certainly not of the muscle-twitch variety, with which he is so often identified; much of the debate over behaviorism has resulted from the discrepancy between the actual behavioristic experimental program and the theoretical framework. According to the theoretical framework of men like Watson and Weiss, all complex behavior is ultimately reducible to combinations and chainings of simple reflexes and even to the terms of physics and chemistry. It is this kind of aspiration that is responsible for much of the opposition. But it would be a mistake to assume that behaviorism is tied to a muscle-twitch view of psychology. It would even be a mistake to assume that Lashley became less a behaviorist because of his findings. In the methodological sense, one can be a field theorist and a behaviorist at the same time; a good example is Tolman himself. The issue between the orthodox S-R behaviorists on the one side and the S-S (Tolman) behaviorists and the field theorists on the other side is still a source of systematic controversy, but its outcome will have nothing to do with the acceptance of behaviorism.

Metaphysical Behaviorism

Criticisms of Watson's rejection of the introspective technique were blunted by his acceptance of the verbal report as behavior, as indicated above. The argument that he was neglecting useful data was therefore not valid. The brunt of the critical attack upon his system was transferred to the essentially metaphysical argument against interactionism and against his denial of the existence, and not merely the scientific usefulness, of mind. As we have already stated, we do not regard this issue as a legitimate problem for current psychology. Watson's defense of his position, therefore, is of no greater scientific value than the critical attacks of his detractors. Nevertheless, the arguments advanced are of something more than merely historical interest in that they are related to more strictly scientific methodological problems, as we shall attempt to show.

Early attacks upon the extreme behavioristic position on mind were made by behaviorists and nonbehaviorists alike. Angell, for example, cautioned (1913, p. 267):

After all is said and done, something corresponding to consciousness in its vague common reading does exist and it is within its compass that the problems of science arise. We must be cautious therefore that in seeking for bettered means of knowing human nature in its entirety we do not in effect commit the crowning absurdity of seeming to deny any practical significance to that which is its chief distinction—the presence of something corresponding to the term mind—the one thing of which the fool may be as sure as the wise man.

And the behaviorist Hunter (1924) likewise expressed doubt about the radical position in his conclusion that ". . . no mere denial of the existence of 'consciousness' can permanently win a wide following among psychologists" (p. 4). In this prediction Hunter would seem to have been fairly well borne out, since the radical behavioristic position has never been generally accepted.

Some of the attacks upon methodological behaviorism may be more or less directly traced to the underlying assumption of the monistic metaphysical position. A good example is the criticism by Heidbreder. She pointed out that if the behaviorist makes an outright denial of consciousness (1933, p. 281):

. . . he finds it extremely difficult to explain what he means by some of his terms. When he says that thinking is merely a matter of language mechanisms, or emotion an affair of visceral and glandular responses, he is at a loss to tell where he gets the terms "thinking" and "emotion." He cannot get them from his own awareness of his own inner speech or disturbed heart-beat, for, by hypothesis, such awareness is impossible. The heart and the larynx, to be sure, belong to the physical world, but one's immediate awareness of their action can be based only on one's personal and private sensations. Does the behaviorist mean, then, that a person cannot be aware of his own anger except by means of kymograph tracings, or blood-analysis, or some other evidence of his bodily reactions that is accessible to others as well as himself—by catching sight of his flushed face, in a mirror, for example, or by seeing directly his own clenched fist?

Heidbreder also pointed out (1933) that ". . . in actual practice, behaviorism rejects awareness that arises through the interoceptors and proprioceptors; awareness which arises through the exteroceptors it accepts without question. In this fact lies the clue to the acceptances and rejections that characterize behaviorism" (p. 218).

The behaviorist's reply would probably be to point out that it is difficult for anyone to say how he attributes meaning to words like *thinking* and *emotion*. Actually, the behaviorist would urge, they are not learned by some kind of connection to internal events; we learn to say *pain* in certain situations, such as when we observe blood on others or ourselves, or *thinking* when a problem has been presented and the person is oriented toward the problem but otherwise quiescent. We do not actually learn these things on the basis of the contents of our own consciousness alone; otherwise our language would be private. It is not surprising that the awareness which arises through the interoceptors is rejected, while that which arises through the exteroceptors is accepted. For the language of exteroceptors is based on public events, observable at the same time by anyone. The language of interoceptors is based on private events, observable only by one individual. Science is a public enterprise, and only a public language, only public events, are appropriate for its subject matter.

The more recent criticism of Watson's extreme metaphysical position is represented by Bergmann's professional philosophical evaluation (1956): "Watson's particular mistake was that in order to establish that there are no interacting minds, which is true, he thought it necessary to assert that *there are no minds*, which is not only false but silly" (p. 266). Bergmann suggests that Watson failed to keep out of trouble because he saw himself as a champion of the revolt not only against structuralism but also against functionalism; for this reason, presumably, he was not willing to stay with the more moderate metaphysical positions of the earlier systematists.

Bergmann's view is probably fairly representative of the modern attitude toward Watson's metaphysics. Watson seems to have felt it necessary to do more than divorce psychology from metaphysics; others within the school that he opposed had already tried to do that. He felt it necessary to destroy the very existence of mind in order that psychologists be freed from the methodological error of attempting to study this presumed entity. Part of Watson's contribution, then, is that he was wrong on a metaphysical point—wrong so courageously and forcefully that he was able to lead psychologists out of the wilderness on the planks of a false platform. (The above, of course, is not to be taken as a literal description of Watson's motivation.)

Criticisms of Secondary Properties

There has been a plethora of attacks upon the more specific positions that Watson himself took on psychological problems. One particular issue is of sufficient generality and interest to justify a detailed account as representative of such arguments. This is Watson's stand on determinism and personal responsibility as it relates to his espousal of experimental ethics.

To begin with, it was pointed out that there is a paradox in the situation where a strict determinist talks as though he is trying to tell people what they should do—as though they could choose for themselves! A related argument is directed against the assumption by the behaviorist of a strict S-R interpretation of behavior, which is seen as mechanistic and therefore of dubious explanatory value in practical problems. McDougall, for example, said (J. B. Watson & McDougall, 1929, pp. 71-72):

If all men believed the teachings of the mechanical psychology (and only beliefs that govern action are real beliefs) no man would raise a finger in the effort to prevent war, to achieve peace or to realize any other ideal. So I say that the mechanical psychology is useless and far worse than useless: it is paralyzing to human effort.

Before describing the behaviorist answer to such attacks, we should like to clarify one confusion that is well represented by the excerpt from McDougall. This is the confounding of determinism and mechanism. Now, the defense of mechanism aside, there is no good reason why a basically deterministic position should be any more mechanistic than nonmechanistic. It is true that men like Watson, who hold what appears to be a mechanistic view, are also determinists; but so are most field theorists, at least ones like Köhler and Lewin. They do share the general belief that behavior as a process is lawful, but they diverge markedly with respect to the type of lawfulness involved. Mechanism involves a belief that organisms behave in a machinelike fashion and therefore implies a particular subtype of determinism. Determinism requires only that events occur according to *some* kind of natural law, and hence it is not necessarily mechanistic.

The behaviorist would also note that the existence of practical difficulties such as McDougall mentioned does not break down determinism or establish free will. It might be true that man cannot work for his own betterment, undesirable as this may seem. The behaviorist would argue further that the claim of many opponents of determinism that they are for freedom is an illusory one; what they are actually for is not a true freedom but a determinism of another sort than the scientist endorses. Generally, at least in the case of most of those opponents who have a fundamentalistic theological background, this is a determinism by some divine force: the individual is free only in order that he can accept the fully determined rule of God.

Finally, the behaviorist would take note of one mistaken claim of those who hope to establish the existence of free will. The Heisenberg principle of uncertainty, or limited measurability, has often been invoked as a proof that free will must exist for the human being, since it presumably does so for the electron. But the Heisenberg principle involves no such assertion for the electron. It is simply a mathematical demonstration that the simultaneous precise measurement of the position and the momentum of an electron is impossible. There is disagreement within physics about the philosophical implications of this demonstration; Einstein, for example, would not forsake a strictly deterministic picture of even the behavior of the electron on the basis of this principle. Even if the behaviorist accepted his own positivistic medicine regarding the meaningfulness of determinacy in electrons under these circumstances, he would still have a way out. Before the principle could be applied to behavior problems, it would need to be shown that behavioral variables are influenced by the indeterminacy of electron behavior. It may be that the indeterminacy at the atomic level disappears in going to the far more molar level of behavior; certainly indeterminacy has only minute and utterly insignificant effects on molar physical events, such as the flight of golf balls. The behaviorist's conclusion would be that there is thus no really sound scientific basis at the present time for attempting to utilize the Heisenberg principle in relation to psychological problems.

We should like to add some final comments to this discussion. Determinism amounts mostly to a kind of faith, since at best our knowledge can be only partially complete. A test of complete determinism cannot be obtained. This does not constitute any support for the opposite contention that there is some kind of free will. Our own position on this problem is similar to that earlier stated in connection with the ancient mind-body issue: It will take a great deal more relevant data than we presently have or can even envisage before a sound scientific position can be taken on the problem.

To return to the problem originally posed by the paradox of the determinist attempting to influence people, we must concede that there is really no completely logical and satisfactory answer to it. The determinist will most probably agree with Thorndike's point of view as earlier presented (Chapter 4). Essentially, we are free only if determined; we can determine the behavior of other people and build a better world only if the world is lawful. Yet if everything is determined, including our efforts to make changes in nature, as we assume, the behaviorist can only hope that it is favorably determined and that the world will get better. Certainly McDougall's statement that mechanists (he really means determinists) will not raise a finger to prevent war, etc., is false. People who hold this view strongly, like Watson and Thorndike, *do* attempt to make the world better. This is simply a matter of observation.

Two other aspects of Watson's individual position suffered heavy attack. One was his environmentalism. Though there is nothing morally reprehensible about being an environmentalist, it is probably true that innate factors in behavior were neglected more than they needed to be during the period of ascendance of Watsonian behaviorism. We may be seeing that common phenomenon, the swing of the intellectual pendulum to the other side of center, with the rise of ethology. The second point of attack centered on Watson's use of the term S-R. His definitions were too casual and flexible and lent themselves easily to a certain amount of post hoc bending to account for results—whatever results there were! This issue will be discussed further in Chapter 10, where we shall examine the Skinner-Chomsky controversy over language.

To rebut these arguments against Watson, it might be argued that an infant science must sometimes exclude areas and be a bit cavalier about definitions if it is to get off the philosophical ground where it finds itself stranded. Here, too, Watson's prescriptions can be defended on the basis of their results.

THE APPEAL OF BEHAVIORISM

The response to Watson's plea for complete objectivity in the methods and facts of psychology was far from predominantly negative. Both within psychology and without, he was greeted with acclaim of the kind accorded outspoken men of great vision.

The primary reason for the appeal of Watsonian behaviorism is that American psychologists were ready and willing to leave the cramping confines of introspective study. Watson's call for an explicit extension of natural scientific methodology into the field of behavior was bound to be welcomed enthusiastically by many of the younger men. An indication of the extent to which this enthusiasm went is given by E. C. Tolman, who said (1927, p. 433):

This paper should have been called "The frantic attempt of a behaviorist to define consciousness." In fact, the doctrine I shall present seems to me quite unprovable and to you it will no doubt seem something far worse. And yet so great is my faith that behaviorism must ultimately triumph that I should rather present even the following quite doubtful hypothesis than hold my mouth and say nothing.

Tolman's faithful adherence to his doctrine shows that scientists do not always meet the standards of objectivity that they set up as ideal. In Tolman's case, however, his disarmingly human honesty tells us that, at a higher level, he has reached the ultimate degree of objectivity required to recognize the exercise of his own prejudices. This was typical behavior for the loyal citizen who, after serving his country in the Office of Strategic Services during World War II, resigned his position while in his sixties rather than sign a loyalty oath he regarded as unfair.

Strong supplementary support for the behavioristic doctrine came from the operational movement in physics, which was very quickly welcomed and adapted to psychology, and from the new positivism in philosophy as represented by the Vienna Circle. The relationships of these movements to behaviorism are well discussed by Stevens (1939). The relationship is roughly one of equivalence to methodological behaviorism. All result in an insistence upon the use of the same kind of data and the same attitude toward the data.

There are a number of secondary reasons for the striking success of Watson's call to arms. These have been well summarized by McDougall in his polemic directed against Watson. First, behaviorism was so simple as to be easily understood and undertaken, in contrast to Gestalt psychology and structuralism particularly; McDougall's further comment was that Watson's views (J. B. Watson & McDougall, 1929, pp. 41-42):

. . . abolish at one stroke many tough problems with which the greatest intellects have struggled with only very partial success . . . by the bold and simple expedient of inviting the student to shut his eyes to them, to turn resolutely away from them, and to forget that they exist. This naturally inspires in the breast of many young people, especially perhaps those who still have examinations to pass, a feeling of profound gratitude.

Second, in addition to its natural simplicity, Watsonian behaviorism had the advantage of being a peculiarly American product and so of being readily comprehended in this country. Third, Watson's own forceful personality was a factor in the spreading of his gospel.

Two additional factors were suggested by McDougall. First of all, behaviorism was said to be attractive because some people are attracted by anything which is bizarre and preposterous. Second, some were attached to behaviorism out of pity for what they saw as Watson's misguided efforts, especially if they themselves were well informed. These explanations of behaviorism's appeal are more entertaining than serious; McDougall, although he seems to have regarded behaviorism as bizarre enough, certainly showed it little pity. In this he was typical of behaviorism's opponents; there was little relenting on either side.

The response to Watson's appeal was in some ways even more striking outside psychology and the academic-scientific sphere. Woodworth (1948, pp. 93-94) gave some interesting specimen comments from newspaper and magazine reviews of Watson's *Behaviorism*, which called for social reforms. Most instructive are the brief quotations from the *New York Times* ("It marks an epoch in the intellectual history of man") and the *New York Herald Tribune* ("Perhaps this is the most important book ever written. One stands for an instant blinded with a great hope"). Woodworth concluded that Watson's behaviorism was "a religion to take the place of religion." There is no question but that in its fervor and faith it had some of the aspects of religion and that these were partly responsible for its great appeal.

THE CONTRIBUTION OF WATSONIAN BEHAVIORISM TO PSYCHOLOGY

By now we have probably made clear our opinion that, in spite of his shortcomings, Watson made a very great contribution to the development of a scientific psychology. The primary contribution is the one that we cited as responsible for the welcome reception with which many psychologists greeted behaviorism: It called out plainly and forcefully for a strictly objective study of behavior. The influence of Watsonian behaviorism in objectifying psychology, as to both methodology and terminology, has been enormous. Methodological behaviorism has been so well absorbed into American psychology that it no longer need be argued. As Bergmann said (1956): "Methodological behaviorism, like Functionalism, has conquered itself to death. It, too, has become a truism. Virtually every American psychologist, whether he knows it or not, is nowadays a methodological behaviorist" (p. 270).

An appreciably smaller number would care to be listed as Watsonian behaviorists. Woodworth's 1924 comment is still relevant and applicable to many psychologists (1924, p. 264):

In short, if I am asked whether I am a behaviorist, I have to reply that I do not know, and do not much care. If I am, it is because I believe in the several projects put forward by behaviorists. If I am not, it is partly because I also believe in other projects which behaviorists seem to avoid, and partly because I cannot see any one big thing, to be called "behaviorism"—any one great inclusive enterprise binding together the various projects of the behaviorist into any more intimate union than they enjoy from being, each and severally, promising lines of work in psychology.

Watson's extreme metaphysical position, which we believe was unnecessary, made a kind of contribution. Just as Titchener's strenuous effort to develop Wundtian structuralism gave a thorough trial to that brand of psychology, so

Watson's insistent laboring of the mind-body issue has helped to point up the scientific fruitlessness of the problem. There is no necessary relation between one's mind-body position and his experimental or theoretical research. One's mind-body position usually is not specific enough to direct research; however, the type of research a person engages in may influence his mind-body position. The latter, after all, is easier to change. Even Titchener apparently was little concerned with the problem and behaved as though he wished the issue would go away and leave him to his research on more strictly psychological problems. Watson helped to eliminate the problem for today's experimenters. A mind-body position seems to have little influence on research even in fields like psychosomatic medicine, where there is a superficial plausibility to such a relationship. Examination of the actual operations of the researcher, however, will soon indicate that the relationship is an illusory one.

Watson's own personal contribution was primarily, as Boring put it (1950), "as a dramatic polemicist and enthusiastic leader" (p. 645). In addition, we have described several pieces of important research, both with animals and with human young. Nevertheless it is true that he himself contributed little of importance in the way of new technique or new substantive theory; even his loosely formulated notions of thinking and the like were mostly revisions of older ideas. Bergmann went so far as to say of Watson (1956): "As I see him, Watson is above all a completer and a consummator—the greatest, though not chronologically the last, of the Functionalists" (pp. 267-268). It is difficult ever to say that a man is really an originator. But if he states issues for the first time clearly and unequivocally, as Watson did, he is at least in this much an innovator. Seldom has a man had such an impact upon the general method and formulation of a science.

Watson's emphasis on the noninteraction of the mind and body within an individual has been stressed by Bergmann as the major point in his behavioristic program, but in our opinion Watson's most important contribution rests on the scientifically more significant contention that there is no interaction *between minds*. Washburn believed that consciousness is a useful concept and introspection a useful method. Yet she recognized that the existence of consciousness in any other organism must rest upon an analogy. It must remain an inference based upon behavioral observations. The great import of the Watsonian revolution in psychology was to clarify and elaborate this point: The only interaction between minds is through physical events like words or other forms of overt behavioral cues. Since Watson wished to relegate the mystical minds to the dust heap, we would do him more justice to say that organisms interact only through physical processes. Since science is made by human organisms, and since they have defined it as *public* knowledge, the subject matter of science must be observable by more than one member of the species. It must be *objective*. This is the methodological contribution, a far more important point than the philosophical rejection of mind-body interaction.

In conclusion, Watson's own comments on his contributions are interesting. We quote both from his first polemic statement and from what is probably his last professional word (1913b, p. 175):

In concluding, I suppose I must confess to a deep bias on these questions. I have devoted nearly twelve years to experimentation on animals. It is natural that such a one should drift into a theoretical position which is in harmony with his experimental work. Possibly I have put up a straw man and have been fighting that. There may be no absolute lack of harmony between the position outlined here and that of functional psychology. I am inclined to think, however, that the two positions cannot be easily harmonized. Certainly the position I advocate is weak enough at present and can be attacked from many standpoints. Yet when all this is admitted I still feel that the considerations which I have urged should have a wide influence upon the type of psychology which is to be developed in the future.

And, in his brief autobiographical statement, he concluded (1936, p. 281):

I still believe as firmly as ever in the general behavioristic position I took overtly in 1912. I think it has influenced psychology. Strangely enough, I think it has temporarily slowed down psychology because the older instructors would not accept it wholeheartedly, and consequently they failed to present it convincingly to their classes. The youngsters did not get a fair presentation, hence they are not embarking wholeheartedly upon a behavioristic career, and yet they will no longer accept the teachings of James, Titchener, and Angell. I honestly think that psychology has been sterile for several years. We need younger instructors who will teach objective psychology with no reference to the mythology most of us present-day psychologists have been brought up upon. When this day comes, psychology will have a renaissance greater than that which occurred in science in the Middle Ages. I believe as firmly as ever in the future of behaviorism—behaviorism as a companion of zoology, physiology, psychiatry, and physical chemistry.

DIMENSIONAL PROPERTIES OF BEHAVIORISM

Behaviorism, as we have indicated, had the charm of clarity. Describing it in terms of Coan's figure (Figure 3-3) is delightfully simple. It tends toward the right-hand side of the figure with respect to all nine factors: the six first-order factors, the two second-order factors, and the one general factor. Modern psychologists of a generally behavioral persuasion as to the nature of the data may be less elementaristic, more quantitative, less exclusively transpersonal, less static, and less exogenous in emphasis than Watson was. They would tend, however, to be themselves at least slightly to the right of center; otherwise, why should we call them behaviorists?

The relative clarity of behaviorism's stance shows up in objective form in the student ratings on R. I. Watson's prescriptive dimensions. These ratings (Table 3-1) tend to be less variable (and thus to have a smaller standard deviation) in the case of behaviorism than in the case of any other system. It might be argued that the small variability can be accounted for by greater familiarity of students with the system, but this might be countered by the argument that psychoanalysis should be reliably rated if this were the explanation. It was not, and it seems reasonable to argue that psychoanalysis is methodologically less clear than behaviorism.

The student is again referred to Table 3-2 for the authors' ratings of behaviorism on Watson's dimensions and those of the graduate students. Once more, it would be advantageous for the student to assign his own values first and decide on the three dimensions most important to behaviorism.

The agreement between the students' and the authors' ratings of behaviorism was fairly close. An interesting point about which there was disagreement was the dimension conscious mentalism-unconscious mentalism. The students may have felt that the dimension does not really apply to behaviorism at all, since no mental structure of any kind is intentionally presented by behaviorists. The authors felt that if it is granted that mentalism is involved, it has to be unconscious. There is little doubt that behaviorists weighted unconscious factors heavily in the determination of behavior. Consciousness for a behaviorist plays no causal role, even if it exists. However, the authors freely admit that unconscious *factors* do not necessarily imply unconscious *mentalism*.

The graduate students most heavily weighted the dimensional characteristics of contentual objectivism, methodological objectivism, and determinism, in that order.

SUMMARY AND CONCLUSIONS

Behaviorism, like all other schools, has a long past. It goes back directly to Descartes, who viewed the body of man as a complex machine. Watson's real contribution was the consistency and extremity of his basic viewpoint; he simplified and made objective the study of psychology by denying the scientific usefulness of mind and consciousness. He espoused a metaphysics to go with his methodology and felt it necessary to deny the existence as well as the utility of consciousness, or at most to regard it as an epiphenomenon with no causal effects on behavior. His methodological point today is accepted, either wittingly or unwittingly, by nearly all experimental psychologists. Most other psychologists also are methodological behaviorists, but the indication at present is that unanimity is no longer being approached, and may be decreasing.

His metaphysical point, like most metaphysical points within science, is neither accepted nor rejected for scientific purposes, but simply called irrelevant. There seems to be little evidence that a mind-body position has a marked influence on the work done by a psychologist. Rather, the scientist seems more likely to accept a mind-body position which harmonizes with the work he is already doing.

Watson's secondary positions on issues like environmentalism and peripheralism have served to encourage research. However, they are today regarded as preliminary formulations and no longer useful or meaningful as originally phrased.

The reasons for the acceptance of Watsonian behaviorism are related to the clarity and force of Watson himself. The close relationship of his psychology to the American tradition also made his credo more desirable. Contemporaneous and somewhat later developments in physics (operationism) and philosophy (positivism) accorded so well with behaviorism that the conjunction of the three movements added power to all. The confining influence of structuralism also added impetus to any movement that was away from it.

Criticisms of behaviorism have been and continue to be vociferous. They have swept away most of the excesses of behaviorism and changed its form markedly. Metaphysical behaviorism, many of Watson's secondary tenets, and any mechanistic views that may have been associated with too rigid an S-R reflex formulation have disappeared in the storm of protest. The foundation stone, behavioristic methodology, has stubbornly resisted and must today be regarded as a solid and apparently enduring contribution of John B. Watson. However, a stone is not a house, and a methodological restriction is not a system; so today, as there is no structuralism, there is no complete system called *behaviorism*.

Further Readings

Diserens's (1925) paper on psychological objectivism is a classic historical treatment of behavioristic antecedents. The most useful primary publications of a behavioristic sort are Watson's *Behaviorism* (1930), Meyer's *Psychology of the other one* (1921), and Weiss's *Theoretical basis of human behavior* (1925). Watson's *Behavior: An introduction to comparative psychology* has been reprinted with an introduction by Herrnstein (1967). Tolman's *Purposive behavior in animals and men* (1932) represents an important broadening of the basic behavioristic doctrine. For the flavor of the early polemics, the student will do well to consult the interesting little volume reporting the debate between Watson and McDougall, *The battle of behaviorism* (1929). A comprehensive volume on the various facets of the mind-body problem is edited by Feigl, Scriven, and Maxwell (1958). Secondary sources, mostly critical, are Woodworth's *Contemporary schools of psychology* (1948), Heidbreder's *Seven psychologies* (1933), Murphy's *Historical introduction to modern psychology* (1949), and Roback's *History of American psychology* (1952). Stevens's classic (1939) paper, "Psychology and the science of science," relates the behavioristic trend to logical positivism and operationism and is a most useful historical treatment. An especially interesting and provocative paper, utilizing Kuhn's concept of paradigm clash, is that by Burnham (1968). Finally, a treatment of behaviorism from a highly sympathetic point of view is found in Spence's paper "The methods and postulates of behaviorism" (1948). Other more recent treatments are cited in Chapter 10.

8 Gestalt Psychology

Gestalt psychology was born with Max Wertheimer's (1880-1943) paper (1912) on apparent movement. The paper was a report of work by Wertheimer, Wolfgang Köhler (1887-1967), and Kurt Koffka (1886-1941), the co-founders of the new school. Like most new schools, Gestalt psychology cleared away some of the old problems in psychology and pointed the way to new ones. Its rejection of the artificiality of much of the psychological analysis of the day led to a collateral concern for problems closer to everyday-life experiences. The problem of the organization of elements into wholes and the laws of such organization were emphasized. The Gestalt type of examination and explanation of perceptual phenomena, such as afterimages and apparent movement, was begun. Learning theorists were forced to consider Gestalt principles, such as organization and insight, in the formulation of their theories. We have already seen Thorndike's belongingness as an example of such a concession to Gestalt principles.

Gestalt psychology was and is especially prone to be misunderstood. It was the product of European culture (see Table 8-1, which lists the names of the most important men in the school), with its credo originally published in a foreign tongue. Fortunately, Gestalt psychology had founders who remained active in psychology. The sojourns of the three founders in the United States after they fled Nazism helped to clarify the Gestalt position and to make its principles available in English. The early misunderstandings are beginning to dissipate. Köhler's book (1947) has been especially helpful. For example, he has pointed out (p. 168) that Gestalt psychology does not reject analysis in general. Many American psychologists had felt that the Gestalt derogation of artificial introspective analysis implied a rejection of all analysis. Köhler has also pointed out that the Gestalt opposition to quantitative statements was a prescription for psychology because of its youth, not an objection to the ultimate desirability of such formulations.

This improved understanding of the Gestalt position and the interaction of Gestalt psychology with the more Americanized brands have resulted in the general acceptance of several fundamental Gestalt ideas even in the relatively unfriendly climate of American psychology. An acceptance of the Gestalt point that there are

TABLE 8-1   Important Men in Gestalt Psychology

Antecedent Influences	Gestaltists		
	Pioneers	Founders	Developers
Franz Brentano (1838-1917)	G. E. Müller–Göttingen (1850-1934)	Max Wertheimer–Frankfurt (1880-1943)	Kurt Lewin–Berlin (1890-1947)
Ernst Mach (1838-1916)	Erich R. Jaensch–Göttingen (1883-1940)	Wolfgang Köhler–Frankfurt (1887-1967)	Raymond H. Wheeler–Kansas (1892-1961)
Christian von Ehrenfels (1859-1932)	David Katz–Göttingen (1884-1957)	Kurt Koffka–Frankfurt (1886-1941)	Kurt Goldstein–Berlin (1878-1965)
Alexius Meinong (1853-1920)	Edgar Rubin–Göttingen (1886-1951)		
G. F. Stout (1860-1944)			
William James (1842-1910)			
John Dewey (1859-1952)			

wholes which lose much of their identity and importance by an analysis into parts has helped make the study of relatively unanalyzed, global variables more respectable in experimental psychology. The size of the unit of analysis is now seen as arbitrary and a matter of convenience. This position is quite different from the Watsonian theoretical tendency to reduce every molar act to chained reflexes, using only relatively molecular units of analysis. An "atomistic reductionism" is no longer the exclusive concern of psychology. If the psychologist does analyze situations into a number of simpler variables, he recognizes the need for what may be called *combination laws*. These combination laws specify the relationships between the several simple variables and tell how they combine in the production of the final behavior. It is no longer considered sufficient to specify the relationships between single independent variables and the dependent variable, "other things being equal." Situations can be completely understood only when we know how the several relevant variables interact. The Gestalt point that new phenomena are created (*emerge*) in complex situations is accepted.

The Gestalt emphasis on phenomenology makes it difficult for present-day users of introspection to ignore the phenomenological contents of experience, that is, the direct, naïve reports of untrained observers. Since the phenomenological report contains meanings directly, it is no longer necessary to quibble about stimulus errors, which presumably arise from prior knowledge about the stimuli. The report, with its meaning, can be accepted as such. Since the wholes given in phenomenological experience are assumed to be legitimate phenomena in their own right, there is less concern with an attempt to break every experienced whole into its constituent elements. The concept of constancy in perception has been rethought. The old concept, which was based on constancy in response when local stimulation varied (as when you move away from a man and the retinal image changes, and yet he continues to appear to be the same height), was no longer meaningful. The Gestaltists insisted that *local* stimulation should not be expected to coincide with *local* response, for both are parts of a total field whose influence would be expected to change the nature of the response to every local stimulation present. Thus the man should be *expected* to remain the same perceptual height, for the field of which he is a part retains many of its relationships through the shift in distance.

J. J. Gibson has, over the years, worked out in impressive detail the nature of the properties that remain invariant under certain kinds of shifts. In his latest book, he presents his general theory of visual perception. His point of view is that the senses exist for getting information; they have evolved as effective systems for carrying out this function. One desirable property in an information-gathering system would be to have it extract constant features from the flux of experience. Along these lines, Gibson (1966) says: "Above all, it should be remembered that the informative variables of optical structure are *invariant under changes in the intensity of illumination and changes in the station-point of the observer*" (p. 242). If one considers the infinitude of changes in illumination and station-point that take place during the life of a human being, it is clear that a system which preserved the results of such changes would very quickly find itself overloaded. From this point of view, it becomes clear that the structuralist concern with the analytic details of local stimulation was misguided if scientific interest is to be focused on the same things that are important in the life of the organism. The organism, in order to function through a reasonable lifetime, must be constructed so that it focuses on invariants, and these invariants turn out to be fairly complex, relational properties of wholes. Thus efficient stimulus definition must be molar stimulus definition.

THE ANTECEDENTS OF THE GESTALT MOVEMENT

When one speaks of antecedents of modern psychological systems, Wundt comes readily to mind. He was the villain against whom the systematists rebelled, and his role was necessary. His elementaristic position was a target for Gestalt psychology just as it was for functionalism and behaviorism. However, he was an antecedent in a more direct sense; his principle of creative synthesis was an early concept that implied some recognition of the difference between wholes and the sum of their parts. This concept was much like John Stuart Mill's mental chemistry. Both ideas recognized that new characteristics might emerge from the combination of elements into wholes. Neither man, however, did enough about his notion to satisfy the founders of Gestalt psychology.

Franz Brentano, whom we have discussed in relation to Wundtian psychology (Chapter 5), believed that psychology should concentrate upon the process or act of sensing rather than upon the sensation as an element. He used introspection, but his introspection tended toward the naïve phenomenological variety. He considered Wundt's introspection artificial and strained. Thus he anticipated the Gestalt method of introspection and made the direct, naïve expression of experience respectable. However, he did not recognize the emergence of new phenomena with increasing complexity.

Carl Stumpf (1848-1936) was another antecedent of Gestalt psychology, but in a strange sense. Köhler dedicated a book (1920) to Stumpf, his teacher; Wertheimer and Koffka were also students of Stumpf. One would expect that the man who taught all the founders of Gestalt psychology must have given them many of their ideas for the new movement. Yet, according to Hartmann (1935, p. 32), Stumpf himself denied any direct systematic influence on the new movement. The three founders do not mention any such direct influence either. Stumpf's psychology did, however, represent some concession to phenomenology. Boring (1950, p. 595) reports that Husserl and Brentano won Stumpf over to phenomenology.

Most of the other antecedents had a more direct systematic influence. Ernst Mach (1838-1916) was a physicist who came into the history of psychology by the back door. He was interested, it is true, in the new psychology and contributed to it both in theory and in experiment. He insisted that sensations form the basis of all science. This was a point that a physicist could make as well as a psychologist, for it relates to the general question of epistemology. Yet in his specification of the nature of sensations, he was led to postulate the existence of two entirely new types of sensation: sensation of space form, as in a circle or any other type of geometrical form, and sensation of time form, as in a melody. These sensations of space form and time form Mach correctly (according to the Gestalt psychologists) stated to be independent of their elements. For example, circles can be red, blue, large, or small and lose nothing of their circularity. Similarly, the notes of the melody can be played in another key without any alteration of their time form.

Christian von Ehrenfels (1859-1932) shared with Mach an interest in the new psychology. Although he was a philosopher for the most part, he elaborated Mach's psychological notions of the new elements into a theory and called it *Gestaltqualität*. He is generally recognized as the immediate intellectual precursor of the Gestalt movement, although the Gestalt theorists have denied any direct influence. In his analysis of the new sensational elements, he was faced with the problem of whether they were really new. Could the new qualities be reduced to combinations of the other qualities? He decided that although the qualities depend upon the elements arranged in a certain pattern, they are nevertheless immediately experienced and do not inhere in any of the component elements. They are present in the mind and not in the physical events.

These men postulated new elements, but they were not Gestalt psychologists. We miss the point of the Gestalt revolution unless we see that its precursors, like Mach and von Ehrenfels, were in reality merely carrying on in the old atomistic tradition. They simply discovered new elements rather than eschewed elementarism, as the Gestaltists did. They pointed out the problem but gave an entirely wrong solution. They complicated rather than simplified. Primarily for this reason, the Gestaltists have disclaimed any direct relationship.

Alexius Meinong (1853-1920) gave the same wrong answer that von Ehrenfels had. He was a pupil of Brentano and the leader of the Graz school of psychology. He elaborated the ideas of von Ehrenfels and changed his terminology, but added nothing essentially new. His methodology tended toward the phenomenological, again anticipating Gestalt. The break of act psychology and the psychology of the Graz school with the academic tradition was not clean enough.

Helson (1969), in his article "Why did their precursors fail and the Gestalt psychologists succeed?" makes nearly the same point: "First and foremost, it was a radical movement. I once referred to the Benussi group as the left-wing Gestalters with their assumption of higher level processes to account for whole qualities, and Koffka said: 'No, we are the radicals in rejecting such processes,' and he was, of course, right" (p. 1007).

The Benussi group to which Helson was referring was made up of students and other associates of Benussi, who was himself a student of Meinong. They, like the other predecessors, failed to take the radical step; they failed to reject elementarism.

Thus these schools did not flourish and gain adherents as Gestalt psychology did later. They did not satisfy one of Kuhn's conditions for having a paradigm, and they established no real school, since schools need "students." And, although we can see them now as antecedents in the intellectual, systematic sense, there was no real continuity of the personnel of these earlier schools and the originators of Gestalt psychology. The origin of Gestalt psychology can therefore be thought of as occurring by the very process that Gestalt psychology later was to advocate as the basis of learning—an insight!

Several psychologists at Göttingen were important precursors and supporters of Gestalt psychology. G. E. Müller directed the laboratory there and supported a program of introspective research that savored of the Gestalt phenomenological approach. He was later to claim (Müller, 1923) that there was really nothing new in the Gestalt approach to perceptual theory. The research of three other men in his laboratory lent support to his contention. Had these men had the inspiration to make their results the ground for a school, the names of Gestalt psychology's founders might have been Erich R. Jaensch (1883-1940), David Katz (1884-1957), and Edgar Rubin (1886-1951). All three men were working on and publishing phenomenological investigations in 1911 or 1912, which was the year Wertheimer published his results and launched Gestalt psychology.

Jaensch was working with visual acuity, and he showed that large interacting systems had to be considered in the discussion of acuity; the elementary atomistic approach would not do. Katz had already published an investigation of color in 1907, and in 1911 he published an extensive monograph on color. It contained a careful phenomenological description of the different kinds of colors: surface colors, volumic colors, and film colors. He described the conditions under which each type of color could be observed and did *not* try to explain the different types of colors by recourse to the combination of sensations of color with some other elements, as the Wundtians would have. Rubin did not begin his work until 1912, the year the Gestalt school was founded. He developed the distinction between figure and ground in his phenomenological investigation. He noted that commonly part of the total stimulus configuration stands out, while part of it recedes and is more amorphous. He produced several demonstrations in which the figure and ground can be reversed. He did not publish until 1915; the Gestaltists pounced on his work immediately and appropriated it to their system, since it was another instance of evidence which required the consideration of the totality of stimulation for its explanation.

Meanwhile, others were being beckoned by problems similar to the one so ingeniously solved by the Gestalt triumvirate. In England, G. F. Stout (1860-1944) in 1896 raised questions about the whole-part relationship. He was concerned chiefly with form and concluded (1902) that ". . . an element which is apprehended first as part of one whole, and then as part of another, is presented in two different points of view, and so far suffers transformation" (p. 71). He had stated clearly the Gestalt point that there exist wholes which influence the mode of existence of the parts.

Even earlier, William James in the United States had challenged psychological atomism. He said (1890, Vol. I): "The traditional psychologist talks like one who would say a river consists of nothing but pailsful, spoonsful, quartpotsful, barrels-ful, and other moulded forms of water. Even were the pails and the pots all actually standing in the same stream, still between them the free water would continue to flow" (p. 255). Like the water, the stream of consciousness for James had a reality independent of its atomistic analysis.

Curiously, James also used an analogy that was almost exactly like one used by Köhler many years later (James, 1890, Vol. I, p. 279, footnote):

In a sense a soap bubble has parts; it is a sum of juxtaposed spherical triangles. But these triangles are not separate realities. Touch the bubble and the triangles are no more. Dismiss the thought and out go its parts. You can no more make a new thought out of ideas that have once served you than you can make a new bubble out of old triangles. Each bubble, each thought, is a fresh organic unity, sui generis.

Had James seen fit to elaborate his point sufficiently, Gestalt psychology might have had an earlier founding.

We have already met another American who was surprisingly close to Gestalt principles, although his point was made relative to quite another empirical area. John Dewey, in his reflex-arc paper (1896), was advocating a field approach, a study of the whole situation in itself, a discarding of the artificial analysis into stimulus and response. The reflex arc was seen to be an organic unity, losing its meaning and reality in the analysis (cf. Chapter 6).

The very atmosphere of thought just prior to the founding of Gestalt psychology seemed to be permeated with the notion of fields, the notion of organic wholes. And thought of this sort was not limited to psychologists and philosophers. For example, E. B. Wilson, a leading biologist, said that the cell must not be regarded as an independent unit, the only real unity being that of the organism.

THE FOUNDING OF THE GESTALT SCHOOL

In 1910, Max Wertheimer arrived at the Psychological Institute in Frankfurt am Main. Köhler and Koffka helped him to do research on apparent movement, serving as subjects, and the three of them had long discussions of the results of their research. The apparent-movement phenomenon, whose best-known everyday-life application is probably the motion picture, had long been a difficult problem for psychological interpretation. In essence, the problem was how to explain the perception of movement resulting from a series of still stimuli.

Wertheimer worked with two slits, one vertical and the other inclined 20 or 30 degrees from the vertical. When light was thrown first through one slit and then through the other, the slit of light appeared to move from one position to the other if the time between presentations of the two lights was within the proper range. Wertheimer worked out the range within which movement was perceived. The interval of around 60 milliseconds was optimal. If the interval between presenta-tions was longer than about 200 milliseconds, the light was seen successively first at one, then at the other position. If the interval was too short, 30 milliseconds or less, both lights seemed to be on continuously. Wertheimer gave one type of movement that occurred the name *phi*; he wished to give it a name that would emphasize its independent character as a phenomenon in its own right. It was a phenomenon which could not result from the summation of individual stimulations, for certainly an elementarist could not argue that the addition of a second stationary stimulation to a first stationary stimulation could yield, by summation, a sensation of movement. The founders of Gestalt psychology were perhaps fortunate in working with an experimental paradigm which made it so crystal clear that the overall situation was critical in determining what was perceived.

Wertheimer's monograph (1912) describing the research contained an explanation of apparent movement so simple, yet so ingenious, that it served as the basis of the new school of psychology. The explanation was essentially that apparent movement does not need explaining! It exists simply as a real phenomenon in its own right, a phenomenon irreducible to simpler sensations of any kind. An attempt to analyze it into simpler sensations, in the orthodox Wundtian manner, would destroy the reality of the phenomenon as such. Apparent movement would not be found to exist except in situations where prescribed *relationships* between elements held.

This apparently simple beginning of Gestalt psychology was really not so simple as it might now seem. Its principles were completely counter to most of the academic tradition of German psychology. To regard a complex experience as having an existence of its own amounted to revolution. To maintain, as Wertheimer did, that the *primary* data of perception are typically structures (*Gestalten*) was heresy to the German introspectionistic tradition and to its American counterpart, which was flourishing under Titchener. Structures, for these psychologists, were things to be broken down into the elements, which were primary.

In addition, Wertheimer maintained that it was legitimate for introspection to use simple, naïve descriptive words. He maintained that local sensations should not be expected to concur with local stimulation because both are part of a field, a whole, which influences the individual parts in a way depending on the structure of the whole.

Not only did Wertheimer advocate these things, but Köhler and Koffka advocated them vociferously. As Köhler said in his obituary for Koffka (1942, p. 97):

Those were years of cheerful revolt in German psychology. We all had great respect for the exact methods by which certain sensory data and facts of memory were being investigated, but we also felt quite strongly that work of so little scope could never give us an adequate psychology of real human beings. Some believed that the founding fathers of experimental psychology had done grave injustice to every higher form of mental life. Others suspected that at the very bottom of the new science there were some premises which tended to make its work sterile.

This last point concurs with one stated brilliantly by James and cited in Chapter 6 (see p. 144).

With such cheerful revolutionists, the movement gained momentum. There were many in Germany, as in America (e.g., Helson, 1925, 1926), who were dissatisfied with the artificiality and paucity of results of the older psychology. Gestalt psychology quickly gained support from them. Many psychologists were happy to find a way to avoid the proliferation of elements needed to explain each new complex experience. They did not believe that the legitimacy of the phenomenological approach, or of emergent real phenomena, could any longer be denied. This was the primary assumption of the developing school. Let us look further at the set of tenets developed by the new psychology.

THE TENETS OF GESTALT PSYCHOLOGY

The Whole-Part Attitude

Examples Illustrating the Problem. The attitude of Gestaltists toward wholes is one of the most difficult to grasp in all psychology. We must therefore devote the most careful attention to it. Certainly the distinction they make between a whole and the sum of its parts is not new. The Chinese sage Lao-Tse is said (G. W. Hartmann, 1935, p. 9) to have expressed in 600 B.C. the notion that the sum of the parts is different from the whole. Also, Skinner (1938, p. 29) has contended that the question of whether the whole is different from the sum of its parts is a pseudoproblem. On the other hand, Weiss (1967) has entitled a long and beautifully illustrated article "1 + 1 $\neq$ 2 (One plus one does not equal two)," and there is no doubt whatever that he considers it a meaningful problem. Many have been concerned with it, and it may justify as much investigation as that other long-lived puzzle, the mind-body problem, in order to find out whether it is a profitable question to ask.

Max Wertheimer had this to say about the whole-part problem as it occurs with respect to the given in experience (Wertheimer, 1938): *"The given is itself in varying degrees structured* (Gestaltet), *it consists of more or less definitely structured wholes and whole-processes with their whole-properties and laws, characteristic whole-tendencies and whole-determinations of parts. Pieces almost always appear as parts in whole processes"* (p. 14).

Wertheimer was here emphasizing the fact that the structure of experience, like the structure of a house, is important. The nature of the human being is such that our perception, though it may be based on unstructured aggregates of items, is itself to some extent structured. And experience as structured has a structure character that is unique to a particular structure; if it is structured in some other way, it will be quite different. Visualize, for example, six dots in a line as compared with the same dots in a circle. Here the different structures are given in the stimulus, but certainly there is a vast difference between the experiences. Orbison (1939) gave a demonstration which can be used as a clear and dramatic proof that the mode of appearance of a part is affected by the structure of which it is a part. The objectively identical squares in Figure 8-1 appear quite different because they are parts of different wholes, or patterns.

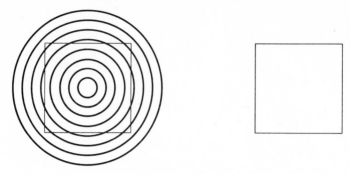

Fig. 8-1 An illustration of the dependence of perception of a part upon the pattern of the whole. (Adapted from Orbison, 1939, p. 42.)

Analogies from other fields which demonstrate the importance of structure and the difference between wholes and the sums of parts are common. One of the oldest and most familiar is water, which is quite different from a simple mixture of its elements, hydrogen and oxygen. Water has emergent qualities, that is, qualities that emerge only in the combination of its elements. We can know about the characteristics of the compound, water, only by studying water directly; the characteristics could not, at least until very recently, be predicted by a knowledge of the characteristics of the elements alone. Although new advances in theories and techniques of wave mechanics have made it possible to make such predictions, it can be argued that the advances could not even have occurred in the absence of observations of wholes.

C. S. Smith, a materials scientist, in a review of the status of his own field, makes several statements which indicate that physical scientists are increasingly being forced to recognize the importance of organized wholes in their study of materials (1968, p. 638):

The main characteristic of today's science of materials is a concern with properties and the dependence of properties upon structure. This is exactly where the story began. The history of materials has been a long journey in search of knowledge in strange and difficult terrain, finally to return to the familiar scene with vastly better understanding. . . . Matter cannot be understood without a knowledge of atoms; yet it is now becoming evident that the properties of materials that we enjoy in a work of art or exploit in an interplanetary rocket are really not those of atoms but those of aggregates; indeed they arise in the behavior of electrons and protons within a framework of nuclei arranged in a complex hierarchy of many stages of aggregation. It is not stretching the analogy much to suggest that the chemical explanation of matter is analogous to using an identification of individual brick types as an explanation of Hagia Sophia. The scientists' laudable striving to eliminate the evidence of the senses has sometimes produced a senseless result.

To eliminate any doubt that Smith is talking about the whole-part problem, look at a later excerpt (1968, pp. 643-644):

The immense understanding that has come from digging deeper to atomic explanations has been followed by a realization that this leaves out something essential. In its rapid advance, science has had to ignore the fact that a whole is more than the sum of its parts.

Polanyi (1968) has strongly argued that biology is not reducible to physics and chemistry since the existing morphology of an organism, which provides the boundary conditions within which the physical or chemical laws operate, is physically and energetically indistinguishable from other no less probable morphologies that have not happened to come into existence. This argument is valid and applies even to the much simpler aggregates of the materials engineer.

Köhler's *Die physischen Gestalten* (1920) is a relatively clear statement of the Gestalt view of the whole-part relationship, although such a complex problem with so many facets is never really simple. Here Köhler said in part (1920, as translated in Ellis, 1938, pp. 18-19):

Let us consider under what conditions a physical system attains a state which is independent of time (i.e., a state of equilibrium or a so-called stationary state). In general we can say that such a state is reached when a certain condition is satisfied for the system *as a whole*. The potential energy must have reached a minimum, the entropy a maximum, or the like. The solution of the problem demands not that forces or potentials assume particular values in individual regions, but that their total arrangements relative to one another in the whole system must be of a certain definite type. The state of process at any place therefore depends in principle on the conditions obtaining in all other parts of the system. If the laws of equilibrium or stationary state for the individual parts can be formulated separately, then these parts do not together constitute a *single* physical system, but each part is a system in itself.

Thus an electric circuit is a physical system precisely because the conditions prevailing at any given point are determined by those obtaining in all the other parts. Contrariwise, a group of electrical circuits completely insulated from each other constitutes a complex of independent, single systems. This complex is a "whole" *only* in the mind of one who chances to think of it as such; from the physical standpoint it is a summation of independent entities.

Weiss (1967) gives several commonplace examples of complexly interrelated systems best regarded as wholes. One is a spider web. Changes made by the spider near the center of the web have effects that literally *can be seen* to reverberate throughout the web, as when a garden spider vibrates his web in response to an intruder. Multiple interconnections between all parts of the web can be seen to account for its action, but these interconnections defy analysis into parts—hence, "the whole is different from the sum of the parts."

As a contrasting type of example, consider a collection of 500 marbles scattered on a floor. Assume that an outside marble hits one of the collection. Multiple hits would follow, provided the mass and velocity of the first marble were great enough. Nevertheless, this "system" is quite different from the first one, and the changes in marble position would seem to be potentially analyzable into a collection of interactions between individual pairs of marbles. In contrast, the spider web provides no place for sinking in our analytic teeth and constitutes a real system rather than the kind of pseudosystem provided by the marbles.

Implications for a World View. G. W. Hartmann has pointed out that there are two extreme views of the physical world and the role of systems in it. One view is that the world is composed of independent additive parts whose total constitutes reality. The other view is that everything is related to everything else, and there are no independent systems. The Gestaltists held neither of these extreme views, although they leaned toward the latter. They recognized that there are systems which may be considered independent for practical (including practical scientific) purposes. Hartmann has concluded (1935): "Both evils are avoided as soon as one recognizes that *the laws of science are the laws of systems*, i.e., structures of finite extent—a generalization applicable to both physics and psychology" (p. 42).

The Gestaltists, then, wished to extend these ideas about physical systems to psychology. They maintained that in biology and psychology as in physics, there are phenomena whose character depends on the character of the whole field. In visual perception, for example, the thing seen was thought to be a function of the total, overall retinal stimulation rather than of the stimulation of any specific local point. Unfortunately, the nature of the psychological field is not always clear.

In 1955, at the American Psychological Association meeting in San Francisco, the physicist Robert Oppenheimer (1956) said he had no idea what a "psychological field" could mean. The statement drew laughter and applause from the audience of American psychologists. Apparently many of them did not know either and felt either that there is no such thing or that it is an overworked and ill-defined concept. Yet Köhler's analogy, quoted above, seems simple and reasonable enough. The real question is whether or not the application can meaningfully be made to psychology. Let us examine this question: "What meaning can wholes, systems whose parts depend on the whole, or fields, have in psychology?"

One of the key issues is the determination of what constitutes an isolated system. The Gestalt contention has been that the fields or systems are widespread in psychology and that the elementaristic analysis of structuralism or behaviorism destroys the meaningful relationships these fields might have in psychological laws. At the same time, the Gestaltists have not denied that the proper use of analysis is necessary. How can we determine whether a particular field can be further analyzed without destroying the very relationships we intend to study? It seems that the only way to do so is by attempting both analysis and the use of the unanalyzed field in the construction of psychological laws. The decision about which should be used will eventually be made on a pragmatic basis. If the molar, Gestalt approach leads to more useful laws, and if no further analysis is necessary, then this approach will be adopted for the particular purpose. On the other hand, if this approach does not succeed, further analysis must be carried out.

A very important tool for determining the degree and kind of system one is dealing with is factor analysis. If various measures of system behavior can be taken, the matrix of intercorrelations may reveal significant aspects of the system's structure. In this book we have seen how Coan's analysis illuminates some of the structure of systematic issues. Moreover, there seems to be a trend in Germany for present-day psychologists to return to some of the qualitative Gestalt problems using multivariate analysis. Thurstone, though certainly not a Gestaltist, was well known for his multivariate analysis. Gulliksen says of him (1968, p. 800):

Neither could the experimenter hope to learn very much from an experiment involving only two or three variables. For the last 25 years of his study, Thurstone typically investigated 40-60 variables at a time in order to get good leverage on the interrelationships among them.

It may be said that this is the greatest legacy he has left us: the emphasis on both accurate experimentation and accurate analyses in the multivariate situation that is essential to psychology.

The Gestalt psychologist proceeds on the assumption that the unit of description should be chosen by the organism being studied; that is, the organism's responses determine what constitutes a meaningful whole. For example, if in a study of perception an observer reports that he sees a tree, then "tree" will become a unit of description, rather than some combination of greens, browns, textures, and the like. For this particular analysis, the tree as perceived will be assumed to be a reasonably isolated system and a meaningful unit of analysis. The acceptance of phenomenological description implies an acceptance of the units decided upon by the phenomenological describer.

Many times, the unit is chosen that seems most natural to the scientist; he makes a phenomenological decision himself. For example, he may decide to choose as a response unit any depression of a bar by a rat. This is the unit of response that seems most useful to the scientist. Since people make science, some such method seems inevitable. The Gestaltist, in his willing acceptance of phenomenological description, has recognized that knowledge will always depend in part on the nature of the perceiving organism and at the same time has decided to live graciously with that limitation.

GESTALT PSYCHOLOGY AND PHYSIOLOGY

Gestalt psychology has frequently used the concept of field, and most of its examples of fields have been borrowed from physics. From Oppenheimer's remarks, we may infer that field does not always mean the same thing in psychology that it does in physics, since he understands one kind and not the other. In physics, the field is an inference made directly from the movements of particles within a portion of space. The field is then given a mathematical description so that all such movements can be predicted from the description. The field has only these mathematical properties; it has no existential properties.

In psychology, a similar situation *may* obtain. By *perceptual field*, the careful psychologist may mean nothing more than certain antecedent-consequent relations and the verbal or mathematical description of a state of affairs which would allow the derivation of the observations. The concept of field is most likely to be used where the consequent (verbal report or other behavior) does not depend in a point-to-point fashion upon the local characteristics of the stimulus. If field is used in this strict sense, as a mathematical device for describing relationships, there is a considerable kinship between psychological and physical fields. Of course, if the psychological field does not allow predictions, it is essentially meaningless. A psychological field, used thus strictly, is many times more "physical" than most physiological fields, which are quite likely to be pure assumptions, especially when used by psychologists. That is, there will often have been no observations of any kind at the physiological level. If the physiological field is recognized as a model which helps in making predictions, there is nothing wrong even with this usage, for it makes no difference to its predictive power whether the field is thought of as physiologically localized or not. The unfortunate thing is that the reader may be misled into thinking that the physiological field is based on some physiological evidence.

As yet, the picture of cerebral action is quite incomplete. The early ablation work of Franz and Lashley, referred to in Chapter 7, demonstrated that the mode of action of the brain must be extremely complex, a conclusion that has never been brought into question. Lashley generally favored the view that a whole pattern of neural activity, rather than localized activity, determines behavior (see Chapter 11 for a fuller discussion of Lashley's views). Yet Lashley, Chow, and Semmes (1951) performed experiments whose results brought into question the whole Gestalt view that electrical field activity in the brain underlies perception. Lashley and his co-workers simply took the Gestalt position seriously and undertook to short out field currents in the visual cortex of the monkey by placing gold foil on the cortical surface or by placing metal pins in the striate cortex. They found no deterioration of visual discrimination and concluded that cortical fields are probably not related to visual perception. This type of experiment was later extended (Sperry & Miner, 1955; Sperry, Miner, & Myers, 1955), again without affecting visual discrimination.

Köhler (1958) did not think Lashley's experiments had been adequate to short out the cortical currents, but he was more concerned with the more thorough tampering which had occurred in the Sperry experiments. However, Köhler maintained that the latter results were not consistent with *any* theory of cortical mechanisms, since the damage had been so extensive that visual discrimination should have deteriorated. He suspected that some extraneous cues might have accounted for these results, with visual discrimination essentially bypassed.

The attempt to explain brain action without the invocation of a field concept has not been abandoned (Hebb, 1949, 1959). And, whatever the final explanation, there is certainly no detailed field explanation which is accepted at the present time. The description of brain fields given by the Gestalt psychologists depends largely upon data from perceptual, not physiological, experiments. Prentice (1958, p. 451) cites physiological research which provides some exceptions to the above statement, but the physiological results thus far are not overwhelmingly impressive.

We must conclude that the Gestaltists' physiological statements should be regarded as models which presumably make possible the predictions of results on the psychological (behavioral) level, although it is not clear that these predictions would actually be possible in all cases.

An instructive instance is the theory of cohesive and restraining forces. Cohesive forces are tendencies of excitations in the cortex to attract one another if nothing restrains them. Restraining forces prevent such movement and are generally the result of present stimulation. When stimulation is presented and then removed, cohesive forces are free to manifest themselves. Brown and Voth (1937) demonstrated cohesive effects in an experiment on apparent movement. Four lights were arranged in a square pattern and flashed on, one at a time, successively around the square. As the rate of succession increased, apparent movement was perceived from one position to the succeeding position. As the rate increased further, the path of the movement became curved until the path followed finally became circular. The perceived path of movement had a diameter too small for the path to intercept the actual positions of the lights! A circle, in order to pass through the lights, would have to have a considerably larger diameter than the path of the perceived movement.

This phenomenon was explained by invoking cohesive forces. The excitations begun by the flashes of light attract one another, thus constricting the path of the perceived movement. The locus of the attraction is presumably the brain. However, it is clear that the inference about cohesive forces is made from observation of a stimulus-response relationship, and the cohesive forces would be equally useful as an explanatory concept if they were presumed to occur in the stimulus field, or a psychological field.

Isomorphism

Gestalt theorists have tended to make easy inferences from stimulus-response observations to physiological events because they accept the principle of isomorphism. An isomorphism is a 1:1 relationship, assumed in this case to hold between brain fields and experience. The structural properties of brain fields and experience are assumed to be topographically identical; that is, we may think of the relationship between the two as being identical as to order.

Köhler stated an isomorphism with respect to experienced space as follows (1947): *"Experienced order in space is always structurally identical with a functional order in the distribution of underlying brain processes"* (p. 61). Woodworth (1948, p. 135) used an analogy to the relationship between a map and the country it represents to clarify what the Gestaltists mean by isomorphism. The map and the country are not the same, but their structure is identical in the sense that we can read off the characteristics of the country from the map, and vice versa. The identity is a very restricted one. All that the Gestaltist seems to demand is that the physiological and experimental fields have *some* identity, perhaps not one as strong as that between a map and a country. To extend Woodworth's analogy, the "scale of miles" involved in going from physiology to experience and back may not be the same for all parts of the map or country. In addition, the map may, of course, be folded or wadded up without destroying the isomorphism. Nevertheless, the Gestaltist assumes that we shall eventually be able to read off information about physiology from what we know of experience, and vice versa; we just need more directions for reading and need to open the physiological events to easier view.

The doctrine of isomorphism leads easily to another way of approaching the whole-part problem. To recapitulate, the Gestaltists emphasized whole properties and a phenomenal approach to perception. Gibson showed that the informational properties of our stimulus world require a complex "holistic" description. These facts have their counterparts in physiological observations made years after the doctrine of isomorphism was proposed. In their now classic article, Maturana, Lettvin, McCulloch, and Pitts (1960) described units in the frog's optic tract which responded when stimuli had certain complex characteristics, such as a particular degree of curvature, but which did not respond when those characteristics were absent. It is clear that a physiology or a psychology which studied only local responses to local stimulation would find it impossible to deal with such complex properties. There are probably large numbers of examples of such nerve nets that extract complex features from stimuli, in man as in frogs. These nets may extract precisely the kinds of information-bearing features that Gibson stresses.

Nativism-Empiricism and the Contemporaneity Principle

Both the components of the Gestaltists' isomorphism are components that presently exist. Both the physiology and the correlated experience are available for present study. Thus present experience is explicable solely on the basis of its relationship to the present state of the physiological field. It is only natural that this relatively ahistorical point of view led the Gestaltists to show less interest in past experience than the members of the other schools. They did not deny that past experience might play a role in perception and behavior, but they tended to deemphasize its role. They emphasized that the past experience must have modified the present condition of the organism before it could have any effect. Thus a complete knowledge of the present would leave nothing out of the immediate causal account, while a study of the past would be handicapped by the distortions worked upon earlier events by later ones as well as by the complexities introduced by the participation of the historical effect in the present field.

Köhler stated part of the case against past experience as an exclusive explanatory principle as follows (1938, p. 58):

It would be extremely unfortunate if the problem were thrust aside at this point as being after all only another case of the influence of past experience. No one doubts that past experience is an important factor in *some* cases, but the attempt to explain all perception in such terms is absolutely sure to fail, for it is easy to demonstrate instances where perception is not at all influenced by past experience. Fig. 1 is an example. We see a group of rectangles; but the figure may also be seen as two H's with certain intervening lines. Despite our extensive past experience with the letter H, it is, nevertheless, the articulation of *the presented object* which determines what we shall see.

Here is Köhler's figure 1:

Köhler was not insisting that past experience is irrelevant to present perception, nor was he insisting that perceptual behavior is innate. There are three types of variables that may influence perception: genetic, historical, and present. Nativism is commonly understood to be the position that genetic variables completely determine present perceptual responding. The Gestalt position is not nativistic in this sense. The Gestaltists have simply insisted that the historical variables do not completely determine perceptual responding and concomitantly have emphasized the two other classes of variables.

Egon Brunswik was a psychologist with Gestaltlike leanings (see Chapter 11). Yet he apparently did not see anything contradictory in the position that the Gestalt laws of organization, which were concerned with features of the presented stimulus, might be learned. Brunswik and Kamiya (1953) did a preliminary study of the stimuli furnished in photographs of natural objects to see whether it was conceivable that elements in proximity might be seen as parts of the same object because people had *learned* that elements in proximity belonged to the same object. If elements in proximity within the stimulus tended to belong to the same object, then people could learn to organize proximate objects into the same whole because other experiences had shown that they (the perceptual elements) probably arose from the same object. Brunswik and Kamiya found that there is a tendency, relatively weak, for proximate elements to belong to the same object. Their conclusion was that the principle of proximity could be learned by the individual, although to show that it is would require further investigation. The possibility that the visual system had "learned" the principle through the process of evolution would have to be eliminated.

The Attitude toward Analysis

Gestalt psychology began partly as a revolt against the allegedly artificial analysis of the introspectionist. Still, the Gestalt psychologists recognized that analysis is at the very heart of science. The objection was not to analysis as such but to a particular kind of analysis. Köhler (1947) said that if we analyze as the orthodox introspectionists do, then those experiences that are most important will be neglected completely. Common experience, the experience of everyday life, is not to be found in the introspectionist's psychology. Köhler did not argue that the introspectionist's findings are unreal, just that the reality is contrived and artificial. Gestalt psychologists have objected not to the artificiality of the laboratory as such but to the artificiality of a stilted type of method and a sterile conception. Gestalt psychology is not an applied psychology, but the Gestaltists have tried to make it a psychology whose results apply to real experience.

Gestaltists have also been interpreted as rejecting quantification within psychology. Their feeling was not that quantification is illegitimate or unnecessary, but that it is often premature. They have held that psychology should first concern itself with important qualitative discoveries. The attitude toward quantification *as such* was not negative, but the attitude toward quantification *for its own sake* was quite negative. The feeling is summed up in Köhler's statement (1947) that "... one can hardly exaggerate the value of qualitative information as a necessary supplement to quantitative work" (p. 49). He went on to say, of his own work on learning: "Everything that is valuable in these observations would disappear if 'results' were handled in an abstract statistical fashion" (p. 50). It is not often that an opportunity arises to point out an analogy between the attitude of the Gestalt psychologist and that of the operant conditioner, but here we find an exception!

Koffka (1935, pp. 13-15) gave a more thorough and sophisticated treatment of quantification, making essentially the same points. He destroyed the antithesis felt by some to exist between quantity and quality, concluding that "... the quantitative, mathematical description of physical science, far from being opposed to quality, is but a particularly accurate way of representing quality" (p. 14). Koffka would therefore agree that psychology must eventually express its laws in quantitative form in order to reach maximum precision.

EMPIRICAL STATEMENTS

Principles of Organization

The best-known empirical statements made by the Gestalt psychologists are the principles of perceptual organization put forth by Wertheimer (1923). These principles are typically given a demonstrational type of proof, and that precedent is followed here. Hochberg and McAlister have commented on the status of the laws of organization (1953): "Empirical study of the Gestalt principles of perceptual organization is, despite their great heuristic value, frequently made difficult by their subjective and qualitative formulation" (p. 361). Thus, if the reader sometimes has difficulty in understanding the following laws, he need not feel that the inadequacies are all his; even the more emphasized perceptual factors, outlined below, are lacking in precision of statement.

> (a) *Proximity.* Elements close together in time or space tend to be perceived together. For example, the lines in Figure 8-2*a* tend to be seen as three pairs of lines rather than in some other way.
>
> (b) *Similarity.* Like elements tend to be seen together in the same structure, other things being equal, as in Figure 8-2*b*.
>
> (c) *Direction.* We tend to see figures in such a way that the direction continues smoothly. This factor is illustrated in Figure 8-2*c*.

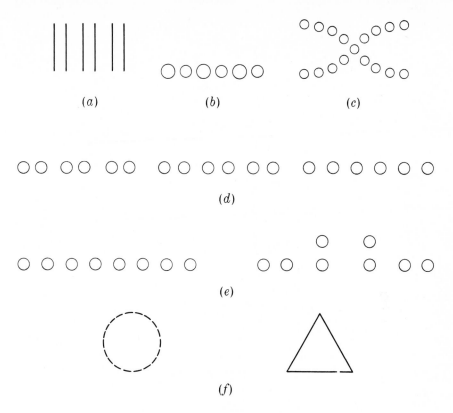

Fig. 8-2 Examples of perceptual factors in Gestalt psychology.

(d) Objective set. If one sees a certain type of organization, one continues to do so even though the stimulus factors that led to the original perception are now absent. Consider the series shown in Figure 8-2*d*. As one looks at the dots progressively from left to right, one tends to continue to see the pairs of dots as on the left, even though on the right the proximity factor no longer favors this organization.

(e) Common fate. Elements shifted in a similar manner from a larger group tend themselves to be grouped, as in Figure 8-2*e*.

(f) Prägnanz. Figures are seen in as "good" a way as is possible under the stimulus conditions. The good figure is a stable one. For example, as shown in Figure 8-2*f*, gaps in a figure are frequently closed because the resulting figure is more "pregnant" (subprinciple of closure). A good figure is one which cannot be made simpler or more orderly by a perceptual shift.

Wertheimer recognized the influence of past experience or habit. If we have frequently seen a given figure, we are more likely to see it again. However, the Gestaltists have generally deemphasized the influence of learning on perception (Köhler, 1947).

Wertheimer recognized that the laws of organization were far from final or even completely stated. He suggested by implication some of the work that needed to be done to improve them (1923, as translated in Ellis, 1938): "What will happen when *two* such factors appear in the same constellation? They may be made to cooperate; or, they can be set in opposition. . . . In this way, it is possible to test the strength of these factors" (pp. 76-77).

Koffka, writing twelve years later, could say (1935): "A measurement of the relative strength of these factors would be possible, as Wertheimer has already suggested, by varying these relative distances" (p. 166). Now nearly half a century after Wertheimer made his statement, there is still no quantitative formulation of the relative strengths of the factors in organization.

This kind of situation is, unfortunately, a common one in psychology. The effective variables, or at least some effective variables, are known, but the exact functional relationships relating the effective independent variables to the dependent variables concerned are not known. The Gestaltists proceeded in just the way they criticize in others. Demonstrations were constructed wherein the individual factors can clearly be shown to operate, *other things being equal.* The laws of combination of the factors, their relative strengths, and even precise definitions of the meanings of the variables were and are missing.

Learning Principles

Gestalt psychologists have not worked nearly so extensively in learning as in perception. However, they have done some highly suggestive studies. Köhler's *Mentality of apes* (1925b) was based largely on his study at the anthropoid station at Tenerife in the Canary Islands, where he had been marooned during World War I.

It was natural that Köhler saw the problem-saving process in quite a different way from the way the behaviorists and associationists or even the functionalists saw it. Gestalt psychology is based on the premise that perception is determined by the character of the field as a whole. What is more natural than that the Gestaltists should explain learning and problem solving in an analogous fashion? That is just what Köhler did. Problem solution for him became a *restructuring* of the perceptual field. When the problem is presented, something necessary for an adequate solution is missing. The solution occurs when the missing ingredient is supplied so that the field becomes meaningful in relation to the problem presented. For example, one of the chimpanzees in Köhler's experiment was given two sticks which could be joined, enabling him to reach a banana that could be reached in no other way. After many futile attempts to reach the banana with one stick by itself, the chimp gave up and continued to play with the sticks. When he accidentally (or at least idly) joined the two sticks, he immediately reached out and got the banana. The missing perceptual ingredient for the solution had been supplied. The perceptual field had been restructured. Just as "good" perceptual figures are stable, so learning, once achieved through this insightful restructuring, is stable. The Gestaltists regarded some kinds of learning as requiring a single trial, with the performance being easily repeatable without further practice.

Much Gestalt work has concerned problem solving rather than learning. The two areas are distinguished roughly. Problem solving involves the combination of already learned elementary elements in such a way that a solution is achieved. Learning is usually concerned with the acquisition of relatively simpler, more discrete responses. The distinction is to some extent arbitrary, as is certainly clear from Köhler's experiments with apes, which could be considered either learning or problem solving.

Wertheimer's *Productive thinking* (1945) suggested effective methods for problem solving. He applied the Gestalt principles of learning to human creative thinking. He said that thinking should be in terms of wholes. One should take a broad overview of the situation and not become lost in details. Errors, if inevitable, should at least be good errors, errors with a possibility of success, not blind errors made without regard to the limitations of the situation as a whole upon acceptable solutions. Just as a learner should *regard* the situation as a whole, so a teacher should *present* the situation as a whole. He should not, like Thorndike, hide the true solution or the true path and require errors. One should not be required or even allowed to take a single blind step, but rather should always be required to keep the goal and the requirements for success in view.

Duncker (1945) performed an extensive Gestaltist analysis of the problem-solving process. He analyzed the factors in the situation and in the problem-solving procedure which determine difficulty of solution. Like Wertheimer, he believed that the tendency of the subject to narrow the possible solutions is one of the most serious obstacles to successful performance. He devoted a great deal of attention to discussion of fixedness of response. Errors were regarded as helpful in the sense that thinking does not regress to the original ideas about possible solutions when leads are found to be false. Thus errors direct further responses, serving a positive function as well as simply being eliminated. The requirements of the problem situation "ask for" a solution with the required attributes; that is, responses are determined by the total situation, the problem field. Duncker's classic monograph contains many ingenious ideas and examples, but has the usual Gestalt characteristic of being largely nonexperimental and programmatic.

The Gestaltists have generally emphasized the *directed* character of behavior in problem-solving situations. Thorndike emphasized trial-and-error learning, as though the behavior of the animal in the situation were blind and random. Köhler and Wertheimer pointed out the blindness of Thorndike's situation. They believed that the random nature of the activity inhered not in the animal but in the situation. A good solution is possible only if the whole situation is available to the animal. In Thorndike's puzzle-box situation, only the experimenter can see the overall situation. The animal is *reduced* to trial and error by the situation, but to say that learning in general is by trial and error is itself an error.

Thorndike, a favorite Gestalt target (see Chapter 4), had stated that learning is a gradual process of elimination of errors with the accompanying fixation of the correct response. The Gestaltists said that more frequently, learning is not gradual at all, but is rather a process involving insight. We might think of insight as a sudden shift in the perceptual field. There seems to be no basic theoretical reason why the Gestaltists should say that the perceptual shift should be sudden rather than gradual, but Köhler's empirical observations indicated to him that sudden learning does occur. Four behavioral indices of insight learning are usually cited: the sudden transition from helplessness to mastery, the quick and smooth performance once the correct principle is grasped, the good retention, and the immediacy with which the solution can be transferred to other similar situations involving the same principle. Once the sticks had been joined to reach the banana, they would be joined in other situations for reaching other objects if insight were truly involved.

The disagreement about whether learning is continuous, as Thorndike thought, or sudden, as the Gestaltists stated is typically the case, gave rise to the continuity-noncontinuity controversy in learning. According to the continuity position, each trial or reinforcement contributes some increment of response strength. This assumption is denied by the noncontinuity position, which emphasizes sudden discontinuous increments, such as are associated with insights, rather than a slow building up of strength.

This controversy, like many such controversies, is no longer regarded as answerable in a simple yes-or-no fashion. Both continuous and discontinuous improvements in performance occur. A complete learning theory will define all the variables affecting learning and give their functional relations to performance. Both continuous and discontinuous learning curves will be possible, depending upon the values of each of the effective variables over successive trials.

Spence (1940) has shown that Hull's theory, which is a strict continuity theory, can predict sudden increments of performance if the constants in his equations are chosen properly. Then, if there is a sudden shift in a parameter like hours of deprivation from a trial to its successor, there will be a sudden increment in performance. The Gestalt assertion is just that such sudden changes can occur, although presumably as a function of other variables besides shifts in deprivation. The Gestalt learning theorist is now faced with the task of writing the equations needed to make a Gestalt learning theory as sophisticated as its competitors, which can now predict the same phenomena. The occurrence of insight, however, is not as critical as some of the more basic tenets of Gestalt theory.

Insight involves structuring, or restructuring, the situation as a whole. Thus it is predicted, from Gestalt theory, that there will be occasions when an animal will respond not absolutely to the local stimulus but to a relationship between stimuli. This is exactly the situation that is said to hold for perception, where the perception accords with the whole field rather than with the local, elementary stimulation. So behavior should depend on the situation as a whole.

The transposition experiment is an example of this principle. An animal is trained to respond to the darker of two gray cards; he always finds food behind it. The traditional associative explanation of what has happened in training is that the dark card is now associated with reward, so that the animal approaches it. The lighter card has no association, and the animal does not approach it. However, when the dark card is put with a still darker card, the animal under some conditions chooses the new darker card, even though responding to it has never been reinforced. Koffka (1935) said that in looking at the two cards, a *step* is perceived from lower to higher brightness, and the animal responds to the lower step. Thus, the whole field must be considered in making predictions.

Spence (1937b) has derived the observed relational responding by introducing gradients of generalization of reinforcement from the reinforced card to other values of gray and of inhibition from the lighter card to other values. If the generalization curves are given appropriate shapes, the animal should respond to the new card according to associative principles. The significant aspect of Spence's transposition demonstration is that it not only allowed for prediction of the Gestalt phenomenon but also predicted and found the "distance effect," which Gestalt theory could not handle. Hearst (1968) has obtained evidence that empirically derived gradients of inhibition and excitation *can* be used to predict discrimination behavior successfully. Even so, the general Gestalt point is again made—that the combination of simple elements presents a complexity requiring new laws for its description (in this case, new equations describing generalization gradients and methods for combining them). Perhaps the Gestaltists would themselves insist that any associative approach is inherently mistaken and wasteful, but it seems that they need not so insist.

Krechevsky (1932) noted that animals tended to persevere over a number of trials with systematic responses. For example, the animal might respond in terms of a position habit and then suddenly shift to a choice of the brighter of two stimuli. These consistent tendencies he called *hypotheses*, by analogy with a situation in which a human being tries out various alternative solutions until the correct one is found. This finding lent some support to the Gestalt contention that animals were not responding blindly or randomly in their solution of problems. Spence (1936) observed that *hypothesis* is just a name for a persistent response tendency whose history of reinforcement we do not know. Harlow (1951) pointed out that the typical paradigm for insight learning is one in which we do not know the past experience of the animal with the component parts of the problem. Insight did not occur in some experiments in which the subjects were animals without such previous experience. Gestalt psychology has pointed to a number of interesting phenomena in the field of learning, but it has not worked out many detailed answers, and the experimentation carried out has often lacked any control of critical background factors that might influence the outcomes. The Gestaltists' theorizing has been highly general, and their explanations usually ad hoc.

Lewin is a case in point. He is a field theorist, and his is the most sophisticated of the field theories of learning. Even so, examination of the theory (Estes, 1954b) has revealed that its usefulness is severely curtailed because of its failure to make specific predictions capable of verification or disproof. If the most sophisticated of the Gestalt learning theories suffers from this evaluation, the less sophisticated ones suffer still more from a lack of any predictive power. Lewin's theory will be treated in greater detail in Chapter 11 because it is of contemporary, as well as of historical, interest.

GESTALT PSYCHOLOGY AS A SYSTEM

Definition of Psychology

The Gestaltists tended to define psychology as the study of the immediate experience of the whole organism. They intended to include all the areas of psychology within their scope, but they began with perception and have thus far emphasized perception more than the other areas. Thus the Gestaltists and those following them have tended to pay more attention to the relationships between antecedents and perception than to those between perception and behavior. They contrast markedly with the behaviorists, who skipped the way station of perception to study the relationships between antecedents and behavior directly.

Postulates

We present here only the few postulates that we feel are most basic, and even these are divided into a primary and a secondary set. The reader can find a more complex list in Helson (1933) or in the original sources.

Gestalt psychology, like behaviorism, seems to have only one really primary postulate which relates to its name and which has finally commanded wide acceptance. This is the postulate related to the whole-part attitude. Any shorter discussion than the one given earlier in this chapter must fail to do it justice, but the following sentences indicate this attitude. The whole dominates the parts and constitutes the primary reality, the primary datum for psychology, the unit most profitable to use in analysis. The whole is not the sum, or the product, or any simple function of its parts, but a field whose character depends upon all of itself.

The secondary postulates, like those of behaviorism, are not necessary to a Gestalt psychology, although the founders made them a part of *the* Gestalt psychology that has developed. The most important of these is the isomorphism principle. A related principle, or perhaps a corollary, is the contemporaneity principle. More specific secondary principles related to the whole-part attitude are the laws of organization. The noncontinuity postulate regarding learning has been discussed as secondary.

None of the Gestalt postulates were entirely new. Even the basic postulate had been anticipated. The thing that made Gestalt psychology new was itself a Gestalt. It was the organization, pattern, or structure of things that Gestaltists said about the whole-part attitude that distinguished their psychology from the philosophical forerunners which had made a case for emergence and from the psychological forerunners which had made a case for phenomenology.

Mind-Body Problem

The Gestaltists, like most psychologists, tried to evade this issue by pointing to the unity of the organism and maintaining that there was no real problem. However, their recognition of experience and their use of the principle of isomorphism implied some kind of dualism, for isomorphism must be a relation between two different sets of events. Isomorphism itself says nothing about the particular subvariety of dualism that should be chosen. Since the Gestaltists attempted to make light of the problem, and since their whole-part attitude emphasized the emergence of new levels of description, new *aspects* of complex phenomena, the mind-body position that seems most consistent with their general position is a dual-aspect view. This view gives two aspects that can be isomorphic, and yet it allows the statement that there is somehow really only one basic reality seen in two views—that the organism is really unitary and integrated.

Prentice expressed the Gestalt desire to avoid the issue (1958, p. 435):

Let me say once for all that the concept of isomorphism is not an attempt to solve the mind-body problem in its usual metaphysical form. It takes no stand whatsoever on the question of whether "mind" is more or less "real" than "matter." Questions of reality and existence are not raised at all. Mind and body are dealt with as two natural phenomena whose interrelations we are trying to understand. . . . It comes nearest, perhaps, to what has sometimes been called the "double aspect" theory, the view that cortical events and phenomenal facts are merely two ways of looking at the same natural phenomenon, two faces of the same coin, as it were.

However, Prentice has apparently not been allowed to have his say "once for all," since R. I. Watson says (1968): ". . . by his statement of isomorphism Köhler was offering his particular solution to the age-old mind-body problem. Isomorphism was his way of integrating the mind with the rest of the world" (p. 448). Obviously, it is not easy to agree on just what kind of stand is required to constitute a mind-body position.

Nature of the Data

Immediate, unanalyzed experience obtained by naïve introspection furnished the bulk of the data for Gestalt psychology. The "given," as they called such experience, was used as data. Behavioral data were also used, notably in the fields of learning and problem solving, but behavioral data were less important because of the larger number of perceptual studies.

Because the behaviorists were making a different point and because they deemphasize experience, it is easy to miss the fact that both schools tended to accept the same types of data and that both schools were making a point that converged on the same criterion for acceptability of data. The behaviorists, although they rejected consciousness, accepted verbal behavior as data when there were consistency and agreement within the given experimental condition. The Gestaltists, although accepting experience and consciousness, rejected a certain kind of analysis of that experience. They retained the given in consciousness. Now, that given was generally very nearly coterminous with the class of verbal behavior which was acceptable to a behaviorist. Wertheimer, when he talked about the given, talked about trees and windows. Watson, when he wished to make the point that consciousness was not part of science, contrasted it with things that were—contents of test tubes, things that he could see and feel and lift. Both men were using primarily an object language, a language that a long history of verbal usage has endowed with a great amount of agreement about meaning. Thus, although the two schools started from quite different points, they tended to accept about the same kinds of data as being of interest in their kind of psychology. The Gestaltists were more tolerant; they could afford to accord a kind of reality to the results of the old introspection, while the behaviorists, whose whole existence was based on a methodological point, could not.

Principles of Selection

For the Gestalt psychologist, every part of the field played some role in perceptual structuring. Thus the problem for the Gestaltist was not so much how the given was selected as how it was structured. Why, out of all the possible alternatives, did the actual structure emerge? One principle was that in a given perceptual whole, part of the perception will be figure, and part ground. Rubin's laws governing the selection of the figure state how this segregation takes place. Wertheimer's laws of organization are also laws of selection in the same sense; they explain the particular form taken by the figure. Neither Rubin nor Wertheimer worked out the laws in great detail, as we have already seen in the case of Wertheimer. J. J. Gibson's (1966) later work has done much more to specify the properties of stimuli which make them available as invariants for the organism's stimulus processing. Maturana et al. (1960) used objective physiological responses to discover some of the properties of stimuli that were responded to by the frog's eye. Looked at from the other side, they were finding out what stimulus features were singled out and responded to. The work of these men fits nicely into the Gestalt tradition.

Principles of Connection

The form of the problem of connection was also different for a Gestaltist. Since elementarism was rejected, one form of the question of connection could also be ignored. It is not meaningful to try to reconstruct wholes by connecting elements which are supposed to be the parts of the whole. The Gestaltists believed that the *bundle hypothesis* was completely fallacious. The bundle hypothesis treated complex perceptions as though they were a bundle of simple perceptions and treated meaning as though it arose from such a bundling. Thus one of the Gestalt principles was negative; it was that the bundle hypothesis is invalid, and therefore one of the problems of connection is an artificial problem arising from an artificial analysis. The laws of organization are not principles of connection, for organizations are not elements connected. The laws state what structures will arise, not what elements will be connected.

Another form of the problem of connection cannot be avoided by any system. This is the problem of the connection or relationship between antecedents and consequents in laws. The Gestaltists have stated that the relationships are dynamic and that the significant relationships are between fields. Their experiments have illustrated a few of these relationships, and their principle of isomorphism states another relationship in advance. But the Gestaltists have not specified these principles, as indeed no system can at the present time.

CRITICISMS OF GESTALT PSYCHOLOGY

Gestalt psychology has been criticized chiefly for its nebulous character. Many hardheaded scientists have maintained that it does not really assert anything. This criticism seems to be at least partially justified. Harrower, one of Koffka's students, may be typical of the Gestalt school in her attitude toward the problem of definition of terms in psychology (1932, p. 57):

Much criticism has accrued to Gestalt theory for its use of the term "organization," which has not yet been sufficiently rigorously defined to meet the demands of many psychologists. And if, in the realm of perception, where as yet it has been predominantly employed, one meets with the criticism of its vagueness and ambiguity, how much more open to attack will be its preliminary appearance in investigations concerning the higher mental processes.

And yet we deliberately give no precise definition of our use of the term, for with Dewey we believe that "Definitions are not ends in themselves, but instrumentalities for facilitating the development of a concept into forms where its applicability to given facts may best be tested." And since we believe that the concept is already in such form as to make it applicable to our facts, we leave more precise definition until experimental results can contribute towards it.

Harrower shows a tendency to bow coolly in the direction of definition and afterward to ignore it. This does not furnish any help in bringing experimental facts to bear. The psychologist needs to have some way of distinguishing a situation that is an organization from one that is not if he is to carry out empirical investigations on the subject. We have seen nearly the same criticism raised in reference to the principles of organization, and the fields selected for criticism on this point are fairly typical of Gestalt psychology as a whole. However, the Gestaltist can certainly defend himself by pointing his finger at other psychologists, who are also often obscure or incomplete in their definitions, although presumably much concerned with problems of definition. The often conflicting usages of the basic words *stimulus* and *response* are examples; Koch (1954) gives a specific treatment of conflicting usage by a single author, which could easily be applied to many others. The Gestaltist, perhaps, has been more cautious, preferring to await more results before rigidifying meanings of words.

Gestalt psychology has been criticized for having too high a ratio of theory and criticism to experiment and positive empirical statements. Gestalt psychology has certainly been experimental, but the devastation wrought by its criticism has not always been repaired quickly by its positive statements. A closely related criticism is that Gestalt psychology has not often furnished a system with predictive power. Gates, in defending Thorndike's identical-elements theory of transfer of training, has presented a criticism which, if justified, invalidates the Gestalt theory of transfer (1942, p. 153):

The Gestaltists somewhat similarly insist that transfer depends upon "insight." The objection to these views is not that they are wrong, but merely that they are too vague and restricted. To say that one transfers his learning when he generalizes is not saying much more than "You generalize when you generalize." "You get transfer when you get it." We must go deeper than that. In a scientific sense, no theory of transfer is a full or final explanation, but the Thorndike formulations at least point to a number of factors, observation and study of which enable us to improve learning.

Gates's criticism can probably be generalized to other areas, but is especially true of learning, where the associationists, functionalists, and behaviorists have been able to present some fairly specific theories. The Gestaltist has said, in effect: "Your theory is necessarily inadequate for the following reasons, and an adequate theory must take the following form." But the Gestaltist has not often said what the specific statements of this programmatic theory shall be. Thus, the proponent of the theory attacked can often say that the Gestaltist may be correct in his criticism but that he has done no better or has in fact presented *nothing but* criticism. But this is true of most critics. They do not have time to present correct theories in detail, especially where such theories must wait upon empirical spade-work.

These first two criticisms picture Gestalt psychology as more nebulous and programmatic than most systems. Even if there is at least a grain of truth in these criticisms, the third one, that Gestalt psychology has been metaphysical and mystical, is certainly not justified. The feeling that it is mystical probably comes largely from the difficulty of presenting its central points clearly. This difficulty was initially compounded in the United States by problems of translation and by the fact that Gestalt psychology arose from a cultural background somewhat foreign to Americans. When Gestalt psychology is properly understood, it seems to be as much a natural science as behaviorism and often is more sophisticated. Gestaltists universally reject vitalism, which is often a mark of some degree of mysticism. Sometimes certain behaviorists who cannot think in other than mechanistic terms make the accusation that those who reject mechanistic explanations are vitalists, and certainly a part of Gestalt psychology's paradigm is a rejection of a simple view of mechanism.

Weiss sums up the source of, and reply to, this kind of objection as follows (1967, p. 801):

The unorthodox dissenters usually phrased their argument in the age-old adage that "the whole is *more* than the sum of its parts." Look at this phrasing and you will discover the root of the distrust, and indeed, outright rejection, of the valid principle behind it. What did they mean by stating that "an organism is *more* than the sum of its cells and humors"; that "a cell is *more* than its content of molecules"; that "brain function is *more* than the aggregate of activities of its constituent neurons"; and so on? As the term "more" unquestionably connotes some tangible addition, an algebraic plus, one naturally had to ask: "More of what? Dimensions, mass, electric charges?" Surely none of those. Then what? Perhaps something unfathomable, weightless, chargeless, nonmaterial? All sorts of agents have indeed been invoked in that capacity—entelechy, *élan vital*, formative drive, vital principle—all idle words, unpalatable to most scientists for being just fancy names for an unknown X.

Unfortunately, in their aversion to the supernatural, the scientific purists poured out the baby with the intellectually soiled bath water by repudiating the very aspects of wholeness in nature that had conjured up those cover terms for ignorance.

A common and serious objection to Gestalt psychology has involved its usage of "field" analogies from physics. These criticisms are discussed more fully in Chapter 11, where the central issue is the notion of field. Here we shall preview that discussion by pointing out that physicists (Oppenheimer, 1956) and psychologists (Estes, 1954b; Spence, 1948) alike have seriously questioned whether the analogy between the term *field* as it is used in physics and as it was used in psychology by the Gestaltists is close enough to be useful.

One of the specific objections to the speculation found in the Gestalt system has been to its physiological assumptions. As we have previously pointed out, the principle of isomorphism has made these speculations easy. However, speculation is a part, and a useful part, of every system. The Gestaltists have frankly admitted, in most cases, that their physiologizing is speculative. It has no effect on the validity of their experimental results and has in fact stimulated or suggested experimentation. (See Prentice, 1958, for a vivid account of the relation between theory and experiment.) Besides, orthodox physiologizing, like Thorndike's assumptions about synaptic changes with learning, is just as speculative and no more likely to be correct.

The criticism that Gestalt psychology is antianalytic has already been countered in the discussion of the Gestalt attitude toward analysis.

The experimentation of Gestalt psychologists has been criticized for being poorly controlled, nonquantitative, and nonstatistical. Experimenters have been accused of giving the subjects cues which affected learning in unknown ways and of ignoring possible effects of past experience. It is true that the Gestaltists' level of sophistication in experiments has not been up to the level of their criticism and metatheory construction. However, they consciously feel that qualitative results must come first. Thus the experiments have purposely been nonquantitative and nonstatistical. Since new areas have been explored, or old areas explored from an entirely new point of view, it is natural that the experiments performed have often been of a preliminary, tentative sort. Anyway, such a criticism of experimentation, if valid in some individual cases, is not a criticism of Gestalt psychology but of particular Gestalt psychologists. Gestalt psychology certainly does not advocate poorly designed experiments. Poor experiments have been done under the aegis of every school, but with the sanction of none.

Other criticisms can be treated very lightly. One is that Gestalt psychology is not new. This can always be said, but (1) Gestalt psychology is as new as any school ever is, a point almost too obvious to discuss, and (2) the criticism is not even relevant to the merits of the system as it stands. The criticism that Gestalt psychology sets up straw men to attack in each of the older systems is also irrelevant; it applies to Gestalt psychology as an objection to other systems, but not to its positive program.

THE CONTRIBUTIONS AND PRESENT STATUS OF GESTALT PSYCHOLOGY

The experiments done by Gestaltists are an unquestioned contribution to psychology. This is the statement that is safest about any system. Gestalt psychologists have often done experiments which challenged the cherished beliefs of others. For example, latent learning and Zeigarnik effects (see Chapter 11), experimentally demonstrated, contributed to the difficulties of associationistic learning theorists and stimulated much research. Sometimes Gestalt psychology itself could not have predicted the results, but a fresh-thinking upstart can afford to create difficulties for himself as well as for others.

There is no sign that Gestalt psychology has stopped in the experimental creation of difficulties. Hochberg (1957) reviewed some experimental results in a symposium on the Gestalt revolution and concluded that the perceptions of space, depth, and distance are largely unsolved problems. The discussion of experiments by Ivo Kohler (1951) is of particular interest. Kohler experimented with several types of disturbances to normal stimulation and observed perceptual and behavioral adaptations to the disturbances. In one rather representative experiment, the left half of each of a pair of spectacles was made blue, and the right half yellow. Then, when the spectacles were worn, white objects to the left of center were seen as blue, and white objects to the right as yellow. After long adaptation, objects remained constant in color despite eye movement. Then, when the glasses were taken off, the world appeared yellow with eyes left and blue with eyes right! This fact illustrates a relational determination of color which is *completely* independent of local stimulation. Gestalt psychology could hardly have asked nature to provide a clearer demonstration of the inadequacy of the "mosaic hypothesis."

Other experiments by Johansson (1950) have shown that perceived motion depends in complex ways upon the totality of stimulation, with common motion of parts often "partialed out" and seen as motion of the whole, and with the motion of individual parts contributing only the residual motion. Thus the seen motion of a part depends, as to the Gestaltists it should, upon the properties of the whole.

These experiments and others provide abundant illustration that local stimulation may not be well correlated with local sensation. Though Kohler's observations emphasize the importance of perceptual learning, this direction of emphasis is by no means diametrically opposed to Gestalt precepts. The Gestalt position tended toward nativism because an antidote was needed. The structuralists had tended too often to hide behind the skirts of past associations whenever empirical facts belied what their elementaristic analysis led them to expect. Now that structuralism is gone and the nebulous past associations are passé as a refuge, the Gestalt position on nativism-empiricism can relax to a more natural neutral position.

The evidence gathered by Land (1959), apparently independently of any systematic preconceptions, gives powerful support to the Gestalt antimosaic hypothesis. Color perception, according to Land, is to a large extent independent of the nature of the stimulation of the individual retinal receptors; the perception of color depends, rather, upon relationships over the whole retina. Land believed that information about colors is gathered, and that colors are therefore seen, because objects of different colors reflect different proportions of "warm" and "cool" light. Thus negatives exposed through filters that screen long (warm) and short (cool) parts of the spectrum differently contain information about the colors of the objects present. When the two negatives are superimposed and projected on a screen, the viewer sees a range of colors, *even though only black-and-white film was used*! Land's findings could not give better support to Gestalt psychology if they had been specifically made up to support the theory. This does *not* mean support in detail, for Land believed that his results demanded a reformulation of color theory, including theories held by members of the Gestalt school. Walls (1960) disagreed with Land, holding that traditional explanations in terms of principles like contrast and induction are adequate to explain the phenomena. Regardless of which explanations turn out to be most economical, Land's redirection of attention to these color phenomena again vindicates the general Gestalt methodological emphasis on field phenomena.

Gestalt psychology, then, is not a useful failure like structuralism. It is a going concern. It is more actively a school today than any of the systems we have discussed so far. One of its founders, Wolfgang Köhler, in 1956 received a Distinguished Contribution Award from the American Psychological Association; in 1959 he served as president of the American Psychological Association. One of the reasons Gestalt psychology still has some of its school character is probably that its main points are not quite as well assimilated into psychology as the main points of the older schools and the more native (to America) behaviorism. Until Köhler's death in 1967, it still had a founder to organize around. Its propositions, especially those which concerned the whole-part relationship, involved complexities that still require working out, and that has kept scientists interested. Modern systems theory is just developing some of the techniques required for dealing with organized wholes.

Köhler lived to see the Gestalt whole-part attitude accepted as at least theoretically correct. Psychology has also accepted the theoretical correctness of the contemporaneity principle, although many psychologists still study historical variables because of their easier availability. The primacy of perception and the methodological dependency of sensation on perception are also accepted. Moreover, Gestalt psychology has led directly to stimulating and significant work within orthodox areas of general psychology (e.g., Asch, Hay, & Diamond, 1960, on verbal learning; Katona, 1940, on memory).

Lastly, Gestalt psychology has contributed to psychology even where its tenets were rejected. Its sharp criticism has required some reexamination and revamping on the part of every system which wished to stand in opposition to it. It has pointed to phenomena which existing systems could not incorporate, and these systems were energized by an order of criticism and competition that they might not otherwise have had.

A DIMENSIONAL DESCRIPTION OF GESTALT PSYCHOLOGY

Gestalt psychology took rather clear positions on Coan's first-order factors. Certainly there is emphasis on conscious processes, and therefore Gestalt psychology has a subjectivistic flavor. Its basic tenet is that it is holistic, and so the second factor presents no problem. Köhler, Koffka, and Wertheimer are among the most positive theorists on the transpersonal orientation, and so there is no doubt about it either. The antiquantitative bias of the Gestaltists, at least for psychology's present stage of development, requires no further discussion. Wertheimer is listed among the negative (that is, more static) theorists on the next dimension, but that is hard for us to reconcile with the general Gestalt emphasis on field properties, which tend to be dynamic, to restructure, and to change throughout whenever their parts change or when the field is immersed in a different whole. We would therefore argue that the Gestalt psychologists are at least intermediate on the static-dynamic dimension, and perhaps even lean conceptually toward the dynamic pole. Coan does not find the Gestalt psychologists occupying any extreme position on the exogenous-endogenous dimension, but—at least in the context of opposing theories—they tended to look endogenous because of their emphasis on nativism, as compared with associationists and behaviorists.

On the second level, the Gestaltists would have to be taken as the prototype for the synthetic pole of the analytic-synthetic orientation (though we have seen that the issue is not simple). Their position on the functional-structural dichotomy is less clear, though they range toward the functional in some respects. This leaves their position generally fluid on the highest-order factor.

The ratings of Gestalt psychology on Watson's eighteen dimensions are given in Table 3-2, and the reader should find it interesting to refer back to them. It may be recalled (Table 3-3) that the authors' ratings differed sufficiently from the students' so that a classification which took the student averages as defining the prototypical points for each system would have misidentified the ratings and would have classified them with the student ratings of psychoanalysis. It is instructive to look at the reasons for this disagreement.

The largest discrepancies occurred on the dimensions nomotheticism-idiographicism, rationalism-irrationalism, staticism-developmentalism, and staticism-dynamicism. The authors rated Gestalt as highly idiographic, and the students rated it as slightly on the nomothetic side of center. Coan's placement of all three Gestalt psychologists among those with a transpersonal orientation argues that the student average is closer to the judgment of the experts than that of the authors is. They argued, probably speciously, that the Gestalt insistence on considering all variables and their interactions made them idiographic in their approach, since each individual whole or field would represent a unique concatenation of variables—or, better, a unique Gestalt.

Köhler's studies on Tenerife, too, were of *individual* performances, not statistically treated. A closer examination of what nomothetic-idiographic could be taken to mean reveals that several things may be confused in thinking about the dimension—the emphasis on group versus individual data, the quest for general laws versus an emphasis on explaining individuals (which, though it is supposed to be *the* main basis of distinction, does not seem to us to make sense), and the insistence on creating "realism" in experimental situations by including all variables versus an emphasis on controlled laboratory experimentation. On the first and third of these potential subdimensions, Gestalt psychology would be rated idiographic, but the second, "heavily weighted" one makes it nomothetic. It appears that Watson's dimensions may not all be unidimensional, at least not in practice.

In rating the rationalism-irrationalism dimension, the authors were considering a type of physiological rationalism. From this viewpoint an organism was built in certain ways, and therefore it responds in certain ways. Nativism usually tends to be associated with rationalism. Gestalt tradition produced books like Wertheimer's *Productive thinking* (1945), which stresses insight learning in preference to the more irrational trial-and-error learning.

The staticism-developmentalism disagreement may have occurred because the authors were thinking of the contemporaneity principle as making Gestalt psychology emphasize a static orientation, whereas the students may have been thinking of the general fluid character of the Gestalt approach. Actually, Gestaltists spent relatively little time on the study of the developmental processes.

The authors rated Gestalt psychology heavily toward dynamicism, while the students' rating fell right at the mean between staticism and dynamicism. It was the authors' opinion that the Gestalt emphasis was on the "whole" interpretation and interrelationships and that these imply dynamicism. Since all parts are interrelated, a change in one part requires a restructuring and change of the whole.

The dimensional characteristics most heavily weighted were molarism, centralism, and purism (though with a very moderate rating on the latter).

SUMMARY AND CONCLUSIONS

Gestalt psychology originated in Frankfurt am Main, Germany, between 1910 and 1912. Wertheimer, Köhler, and Koffka arrived at their basic position after an examination of the experience of apparent movement (phi phenomenon). Their psychology was more phenomenological than that of Wundt; they accepted introspection but changed its character. One of their basic objections to the old psychology concerned its artificiality of analysis. They disliked the quest for the elements of experience and noted that the simple combination of elements was inadequate to produce the features of the whole. The *whole* in psychology, as in physics, required laws of its own, and psychology should try to find these laws.

For the Gestaltists, the laws of science were the laws of systems. They set out to apply their points of view to the fields of perception and learning. In perception, they put forth the laws of organization. In learning, they found the same kinds of principles. They objected to the overuse of past experience as an explanatory concept both in perception and in learning. Learning and problem solving were seen in relationship to restructuring of the perceptual field. Only influences on this field that were presently active could be used in the explanation of perception and behavior. Gestalt psychology has been accepted in part in America. Many of its criticisms of structuralistic and behavioristic psychology have been accepted as cogent, and these criticisms have forced the reformulation of those theoretical positions. Gestalt psychology is still itself an active force.

Further Readings

G. W. Hartmann's *Gestalt psychology* (1935) is a fine source for the student who seeks information about, and appraisal of, Gestalt psychology in the same book. It gives excellent historical background and a good explanation of the basic position. Köhler's *Gestalt psychology* (1947) is the most readable of the primary sources by the three founders; Koffka's *Principles of Gestalt psychology* (1935), while less readable, is more thorough. Koffka's book is the most comprehensive treatment in English by one of the founders. Wertheimer is represented in English by the posthumous *Productive thinking* (1945), which is brief and incomplete. For translations of early papers, Ellis's *Source book of Gestalt psychology* (1938) is, as the title suggests, a classic source for some of the most important of the basic Gestalt writings. Henle's *Documents of Gestalt psychology* (1961) also provides a useful source for many of the basic Gestalt writings. Prentice's article entitled "The systematic psychology of Wolfgang Köhler" (1959) is an easily available summary. Köhler's *Task of Gestalt psychology* (1969), prepared for posthumous publication by Solomon Asch, Mary Henle, and Edwin Newman, presents a broad review of the Gestalt movement (including an introductory eulogy by Carroll Pratt). Henle has recently (1971) edited a new collection of papers by Köhler containing two that were previously unpublished, seven translated into English from German for the first time, and one newly translated from French. An article by Crannell (1970) is interesting for its description of Köhler's personal courage in the face of Nazi persecution. Fritz Heider (1970) provides some good background for Gestalt theory, including descriptions of Meinong and Benussi, which are not covered in our text. Hochberg's summary of the Cornell symposium (1957) is a succinct appetizer for those who are curious about the kind of perceptual work which is now being done with a methodology which is Gestalt in orientation. Finally, Weiss's (1967) article can be unhesitatingly recommended for those who still do not believe that, under some conditions, $1 + 1 \neq 2$.

TABLE 9-1   Important Men in Psychoanalysis

Antecedent Influences	Psychoanalysts		
	Pioneers	Founders	Developers
G. W. Leibniz (1646-1715)	Johann Friedrich Herbart (1776-1841)	Sigmund Freud (1856-1939)	Alfred Adler (1870-1937)
Johann Wolfgang Goethe (1749-1832)	Arthur Schopenhauer (1788-1860)		C. G. Jung (1875-1961)
Gustav Theodor Fechner (1801-1887)	Jean Martin Charcot (1825-1893)		Sandor Ferenczi (1873-1933)
Charles Darwin (1809-1882)	Joseph Breuer (1842-1925)		Otto Rank (1884-1939)
			Karen Horney (1885-1952)
			Harry S. Sullivan (1892-1949)
			Erich Fromm (1900-)

9 Psychoanalysis

Psychoanalysis is the most widely publicized psychological system, especially to the nonpsychologist. Although it has long been rejected by some academic psychologists, it has been more popular in other scientific and technical areas, in literary circles, and with the lay public. More recently, it has become a growing concern within some of the previously recalcitrant groups of academic psychologists.

The body of psychoanalytic writing is enormous. Freud's collected works alone, in their English translation, run to twenty-four volumes. No chapter of the scope of the present one can attempt to give a comprehensive picture of even one psychoanalytic theory; we therefore present a synoptic treatment, with emphasis upon certain of the more critical problems associated with the system.

The fact that a discussion of psychoanalysis has a critical tone cannot today be taken as a denial that Freud and his followers made an enormous contribution to psychology; the importance of that contribution is generally well accepted. The reader should bear this in mind when reading the critical parts of the present chapter, which, in themselves, might be taken as such a denial. These criticisms should be regarded, rather, as a pointing out of important flaws which would need to be eliminated if psychoanalysis were to be accepted in the scientific community.

Table 9-1 lists the more important names associated with psychoanalysis.

HISTORICAL ANTECEDENTS OF PSYCHOANALYSIS

Psychoanalysis fell upon the world like a bomb. The shock of some of its concepts and principles was so great that most people regarded it as entirely new. Yet it, too, had many antecedents—so many that they again resign us to the fact that there is rarely anything entirely new in the world of ideas.

In the development of psychoanalysis, there are two kinds of influences. There is an intellectual tradition in which Freud can be placed, as Bakan (1958) has suggested, and there is another set of more direct, personal influences on Freud. Let us consider the former first.

Early in the eighteenth century, Leibniz developed a theory about the elements of reality that differed in kind from most of the previous theories. His elements were called *monads*, and they were extremely unlike the mechanistic atoms of Democritus. They were not even material in the usual sense, but could better be described as centers of energy. Each such center was independent of the others, with a source of striving within itself; a monad might be regarded as a center of motivation, a self-moved entity. Activity was the basic condition for being. Freud took a decisive step in his career when he turned away from the mechanistic tradition, in which he had been nurtured scholastically, to the more dynamic tradition represented by Leibniz.

Leibniz also pointed to the unconscious and to degrees of consciousness. A century later, Herbart took over some of Leibniz's ideas and worked out a mathematics of the conflict of ideas as they strive to become conscious. Freud, then, was not the first to "discover" the unconscious; his unique contribution was his detailed characterization of the unconscious and its mode of operation. Freud (1938, p. 939) yielded precedence to Schopenhauer for the idea of repression into the unconscious and resistance to recognizing repressed material; however, he said that he developed the same ideas without having read Schopenhauer.

Freud attended the lectures of Franz Brentano, who was at the time a very popular lecturer in Vienna. No doubt Brentano introduced him to the Leibnizian mode of thought, for Brentano based his own psychological ideas on *activity* rather than on elements.

The German romantic scientific tradition played a somewhat more direct role for Freud. Schelling and Goethe were two of the most important men in this tradition. Freud apparently chose a scientific career after reading one of Goethe's essays on nature. Jones (1953) has suggested that Freud saw his way to power through a really deep understanding of nature.

However, Freud's formal training put him in quite another tradition, the more mechanistic school of Helmholtz. For Freud, its direct representative was Ernst Brücke, with whom he was closely associated for years at the Vienna Physiological Institute. Brücke, Ludwig, and Du Bois-Reymond had formed an antivitalistic pact with Helmholtz when all were in their twenties (Boring, 1950, p. 708). They intended to force acceptance of the notion that there are no forces within living bodies that are not to be found in nonliving bodies. Part of what motivated Helmholtz to write his earlier paper on the conservation-of-energy principle was a desire to show that there is no unique energy unaccounted for within the organism considered as a physical system. Perhaps contact with this tradition later helped Freud to view the dreams and fantasies, wit and errors, of man as determinate and to formulate his own version of the determinacy of man's behavior, which he called *psychic determinism*. It is possible that a familiarity with Helmholtz's concept of "unconscious inference," used as a way of describing how we reach conclusions in perception in the absence of identifiable cognitive processes, may have been of more direct help in pointing Freud toward the importance of unconscious processes.

Freud was no doubt reinforced in his determinism by his reading and discussion of Charles Darwin's evolutionary thesis with others in the institute and in the hospital where he studied during the course of obtaining his medical degree. He tended to take a biological view of man in accord with Darwin's biological view, and many of his ideas drew directly upon evolutionary theory; an example is the death instinct, which he said depends upon speculation about the origins of life.

Hughlings Jackson combined a physiological and an evolutionary outlook in his influence on Freud. He conceived the notion that nervous systems achieve, through evolutionary development, a hierarchical structure in which the higher structures are more complex, but less completely determined in structure. The precise interconnections of the higher structures are then developed during the life of the individual. In nervous diseases, Jackson thought there is a process which he called *dissolution*, the approximate opposite of the process of evolutionary development. Freud, in turn, apparently patterned his idea of regression after Jackson's dissolution (Herrnstein & Boring, 1965, p. 248).

Two somewhat conflicting traditions, which we may refer to as the romantic and the mechanistic, thus had some influence on Freud. The romantic and mystical side was strengthened by Freud's Jewish religious background, which contained strong mystical components. The Jewish writings also attributed a mystical significance to sex. Bakan (1958) has documented this influence.

One man, Gustav Fechner, seems to have shared the mechanistic-romantic conflict with Freud and finally to have solved it by being rigorously scientific about an essentially mystical, romantic problem—the mind-body issue. It seems that the kind of genius most peculiar to psychology has been of just this type. Among others who have "naturalized" some kind of theretofore mystical phenomena, we may mention Darwin (natural selection and evaluation), Ebbinghaus (memory), Pavlov (associations in behavior), and Skinner ("superstitious" behavior). Ellenberger (1956), among others, has shown in some detail that there was a direct relationship between Fechner and Freud. Freud confessed to an admiration of Fechner and was familiar with his writings. Freud's concern with the intensity of stimulation, with mental energy, and with the topographical concept of mind was related to Fechner's prior work.

THE LIFE OF SIGMUND FREUD

Sigmund Freud (1856-1939) is almost universally considered a giant among psychologists, even by those who think he was a misguided giant. The details of the life of such a man deserve more attention than those of the lives of less important psychologists. Furthermore, the kind of system which Freud evolved is more intimately related to his life than more academic systems are to those of their founders, and some understanding of his life is therefore of more than ordinary importance in evaluating his system.

Freud was born in what is now Pribor, Czechoslovakia, on May 6, 1856. The town was then Freiberg, Austria. His father, Jakob Freud, was a relatively poor wool merchant, and the family had moved to Vienna by the time Freud was four. Jakob Freud had a total of eight children; Sigmund was the eldest son by the young second wife. He early showed great academic aptitude and finally decided to become a physician, that being a profession more open to Jewish boys than many others were. Although he had decided upon medicine as a career, he did not like the practice of medicine, nor did he ever identify himself with the profession. He postponed the taking of the medical examinations while he spent his time working under Brücke in the institute on problems that were purely scientific and thus more friendly to his temper. He hoped eventually to become a professor of anatomy, rather than a physician. He finally gave up hope of academic advancement and decided to take his medical examinations and training at the hospital in order that he might enter private practice as a physician. Brücke had apparently helped him to arrive at this decision. Freud's Jewishness may have impeded his advancement, but another factor was apparently the great length of time that might elapse before a position became available.

Even prior to his taking the examinations for the M.D. degree, Freud felt an interest primarily in neurology or psychiatry among the medical specialties. In the hospital, his feelings were reinforced. From 1880 on, he wavered between study of the anatomy of the nervous system and study of psychiatry. He published many papers on anatomy, among them one concerning a new method of staining nervous tissue and a paper containing the germ of the neuron theory. At one time he became interested in cocaine and suggested its efficacy to one of his colleagues, who discovered its anesthetic properties; Freud seemed more interested in its potency as a tranquilizer and recommended its use to friends. At least one of his friends substituted a cocaine addiction for a prior addiction, and Freud's somewhat incautious attitude earned reprimands from colleagues who suspected the dangers of cocaine.

From the 1870s to the early 1890s, Freud was befriended by Josef Breuer, a practicing physician. Breuer gave his impoverished younger colleague money as well as advice and friendship. The two later were estranged at about the time Freud became closely attached to another physician, Wilhelm Fliess. The Fliess association led to an unusually close relationship during the years when Freud was first formulating his notions on psychoanalysis.

In 1885, Freud obtained a grant to study in Paris. He spent about half a year studying under Charcot, a famous Parisian hypnotist, teacher, and authority on hysteria. Freud already had some interest in hypnosis as a method of treatment, and the interest was strengthened by Charcot. Back in Vienna, he reported to his colleagues what he had seen and learned about hysteria and hypnosis. His report was poorly received, and the young pioneer was embittered. He continued, however, to use hypnosis in his practice to supplement massage, baths, and the mild kind of electrotherapy then in vogue. He later discontinued the latter, commenting that the only reason he disagreed with those who attributed the effects of electrotherapy to suggestion was that he did not observe any results to explain.

By 1895, Freud had lost interest in anatomy. He and Breuer had published together the work *Studies in hysteria*, which marked the beginning of the psycho-analytic school. He wrote no more articles or books on neurology, with the exception of one encyclopedia article in 1897.

It was about this time, too, that Freud became estranged from Breuer and established Fliess as his mentor—this in spite of the fact that Fliess was two years Freud's junior and intellectually his inferior. Freud was highly dependent upon Fliess during this most neurotic period of his life. He was at this time overdependent, jealous, sometimes domineering, overly concerned with death, and hypochondriacal; he never overcame some tendencies to the latter.

In 1897, Freud began a full-scale self-analysis. One of its results was the growth of his ability to stand on his own feet. Fliess and Freud had a disagreement in 1900, perhaps over some of Fliess's highly speculative ideas about the periodicity of behavior. Freud later attributed their alienation to an analysis he had made of Fliess's choice of occupation. The final separation followed several years later; Freud had been indirectly responsible for the plagiarism by one of his own patients of Fliess's ideas on bisexuality and had refused first to acknowledge any responsibility and then later to apologize.

Perhaps the greatest milestone in Freud's career was the publication of *The interpretation of dreams* in 1900, two years after the death of his father. According to Jones (1953, p. 324) and to Freud's own interpretation, the necessary freeing of the unconscious could occur only after the father was gone. Not long after this he began to gain recognition and soon had gathered around him a group of collaborators. His role became that of the father rather than of the son. Jung, Adler, Rank, and Ferenczi were first disciples and then rebels. Various difficulties in personal interaction usually started the rebellion, and the young group of psychoanalysts was intolerant of disagreement within its ranks. At one time a committee of the faithful was formed composed of Abraham, Eitingon, Ferenczi, Rank, Jones, and Sachs. The committee was to further analytic work. Freud gave each member a setting for a seal ring like the one he wore.

Through the committee and an ever-growing body of publications, Freud became successful and widely known. One of the first marks of his international recognition was G. Stanley Hall's invitation to speak at Clark University's twentieth anniversary celebration in 1909. Freud spoke, as did Jung; Ferenczi, Jones, and Brill were among the analysts present, while Titchener, Cattell, and James were among the famous academic psychologists who attended. James Putnam, a professor of neurology at Harvard University, became a steadfast friend of analysis at this time.

Jung later returned to the United States for further lectures and reported that he had little trouble in getting analytic doctrine accepted if he ceased to emphasize sex so heavily. This widened an already existing breach between Jung and Freud.

Despite growing recognition and success, Freud's personal difficulties were by no means over. There were the dissensions and defections within analytic ranks, and finances were always a matter of concern for Freud and his large immediate family, including six children and a sister-in-law. World War I brought anxiety and hardship, but he continued to work through it all, and his fame grew. He attracted an increasing number of English and American students who helped to keep him going in the years after the war when Austrian money was of little value. He continued to expand and modify his theories and to regulate the rapid expansion of psychoanalysis. One of his devices for control was his voluminous correspondence, wherein he admonished and praised his followers.

In the fateful year 1923, a cancer was discovered in Freud's mouth. It seems highly probable that Freud's cancer was connected with the fact that he characteristically smoked twenty cigars a day. Parts of the palate and upper jaw had to be removed, necessitating the wearing of a prosthesis to separate the mouth from the nasal cavity and to make eating and talking possible. Freud accepted the series of operations and almost continuous pain that attended the last sixteen years of his life with his characteristic blend of realism, pessimism, and fatalism.

Finally, the year 1938 brought the long-dreaded invasion of Austria by the Nazis. Freud was held there until his unsold books were burned. Ernest Jones, fearful that Freud might be persecuted, arranged for him to leave for England. That it is well he did is indicated by the fact that four of Freud's sisters were later killed.

Freud was well received in England but was unable to enjoy the last year of his life there very much because of his illness. He never really recovered from the last operation of a series of more than thirty and died on September 23, 1939.

THE FOUNDING OF PSYCHOANALYSIS

The germ of psychoanalysis appeared in a paper, *Studies in hysteria*, published by Breuer and Freud in 1895. Freud had met the older Breuer in the late 1870s, and they shared a strong scientific interest. Both were interested in hypnotism as a therapeutic device. Breuer had an interesting case, Fraulein Anna O., whom he treated until 1882; that fall he told Freud about it. The highly intelligent girl came to Breuer with multiple symptoms, including paralysis of three limbs, contractures, and a tendency to dual personality. In the course of treatment, it was found that if she related the origin of a symptom to Breuer while in a kind of transition state between the two personalities, the symptom would disappear. Breuer then began to hypnotize her daily so that she could rid herself of the symptoms faster. She christened the method they had discovered the "talking cure," or "chimney sweeping" (now commonly called *catharsis*). Breuer devoted an hour (or hours, according to R. I. Watson's 1968 account) a day for over a year to her and in the course of this time developed a strong affection for her. When he recognized the situation that was developing, he became concerned and terminated her treatment, finally by literally fleeing Vienna for a second honeymoon with his by then jealous wife.

Freud was greatly interested in the case and urged Breuer to publish it. However, the full-scale *Studies* followed the case by thirteen years, and even a preliminary report was eleven years in the making.

Meanwhile, in 1885, Freud spent his half-year with Charcot. Charcot was famous for his treatment of hysteria and other functional nervous diseases by hypnosis. After several months, Freud returned to Vienna and resumed private practice. It was at about this time that he abandoned electrotherapy. He also observed that not all his patients could be hypnotized, and, perhaps feeling that his technique was deficient, he went to study at Nancy with Bernheim for a few weeks. He took along a patient in whom he had been unable to induce a deep trance, but Bernheim also failed. However, Freud was impressed by his observation that posthypnotic suggestions could be carried out, and the suggestion forgotten; he was probably equally impressed with the demonstration that the patient would remember the suggestion after sufficient insistence on the part of the hypnotist.

Freud now began to modify his technique in cases where it was not possible to induce hypnosis. He was determined to save the talking cure; he insisted that the patient would remember the origin of symptoms even though not hypnotized, and he supplemented his insistence with suggestions that the patient would remember when Freud pressed upon his forehead. At this stage, Freud was exerting a great deal of guidance on the patient's processes of association. One patient told him that he was interrupting too much and that he should keep quiet. This suggestion was the final impetus that converted Freud from the hypnotic trance to free association as a method of treatment.

By the time the *Studies* appeared, Breuer and Freud were in possession of many of the ideas that were to provide the basis for psychoanalysis; several of the ideas had come from Breuer's observations of Anna O., and others from Freud's observations of hysterical patients. The first of these ideas was a conviction of the importance of unconscious processes in the etiology of the neuroses. This conviction came partly from the observation that symptoms often seemed to be expressions of events which the patient could not remember or of impulses of which he was unaware. The influence of posthypnotic suggestions, which the subject did not at the moment remember, may have contributed to the belief in the strength of unconscious processes.

Freud was himself convinced by this time that sex plays a predominant role in the psychic aberrations of the neurotic. Breuer did not share Freud's certainty on this point, and their disagreement seems to have resulted in some underplaying of the theme—according to Freud's tastes—in their publication. Charcot had apparently remarked at one time that a certain type of case always has a sexual basis. Freud also claimed that Breuer and a gynecologist named Chrobak had made similar remarks about nervous disorders. Freud himself observed that most of his hysterical patients reported traumatic sexual experiences, often with members of their own families, in their childhood. He concluded that no neurosis is possible in a person with a normal sex life.

The importance of symbolism was also recognized by Freud at this time. Symptoms seemed to be distorted, but symbolic, representations of repressed events or conflicts. In the case of Anna O., the symbolic relation between the origin of the symptom and the symptom itself was clear to the patient and to Breuer when the patient was able to recall the origin of a particular symptom. The symptoms were thus not arbitrary.

In every case, the situation at the time the symptom originated had involved strong impulses to do something, which had been opposed by forces preventing the girl from carrying out her wish. For example, she might want to cry in the presence of her father because of her grief over his illness and yet be unable to cry for fear he would become upset about his condition. The repressed impulse might later manifest itself, in symbolic form, as an inability to see. The existence of contradictory tendencies was evidence of the importance of conflict in the creation of symptoms and in the production of neuroses in general.

As the preceding discussion implies, an acceptance of the unconscious is intertwined with the notion of repression into the unconscious; undesirable impulses and memories are pushed into the unconscious and are forgotten and unavailable as conscious material under ordinary circumstances. Only through their recovery and working out (*abreaction*) can the patient be cured.

In the quest for the origins of symptoms, for the repressed material represented by the symptoms, Freud was forced further and further back into childhood; his belief in the importance of childhood experiences in the production of neuroses was growing. Many of these childhood experiences were sexual; in hysteria particularly, Freud found reports of early sexual experiences. However, he believed that these experiences gained their traumatic force only after the patient had reached puberty. He had not yet been driven to his later opinions about the early genesis of sexuality in childhood.

The last, and possibly most important, discovery was the transference relation. We have already seen how Breuer became fond of his patient (countertransference); it was also true that she became fond of him. It seemed that the patient transferred to her therapist the feelings that she earlier had for other people, especially her parents. At some stages of the therapeutic relationship, these feelings might be strongly positive, even sexual, in nature; later, the feelings might become as strongly negative. In either case, the patient was able to live through, to work out, the impulses that had earlier been incapable of expression. The transference could thus become one of the most useful tools of the therapist.

Transference, however, might evoke fear in the timid, as we have seen in the case of Breuer. It was probably his anxiety about the transference relations he found himself in that led to his leaving the field that the two were beginning to open up. There was also the storm that was breaking over the two men about the importance attributed to sexuality; Breuer, since he could not decide whether sexuality was really so important or not, chose what was for him the easier course and left psychoanalysis to Freud.

FREUD'S SYSTEM

We turn now to a presentation of Freud's system in its final form. A clear distinction should be made between this theoretical superstructure of constructs that Freud built, with which we are most directly concerned, and psychoanalytic techniques as (1) therapy and (2) producers of empirical data. These three facets of psychoanalysis need to be separately evaluated; much of the confusion in regard to criticism of psychoanalysis results from a failure to keep them separate. For example, methodological criticisms of the system need not apply to the therapy, and conversely, positive results of the therapy do not necessarily provide support for the system.

It should be understood that Freud did not suddenly develop the ideas to be presented, nor did he always continue to adhere to an idea if it seemed to contradict evidence that he himself gathered in his work. For example, a pronounced modification of his position on hysteria came about after he discovered that in many cases, the traumatic sexual incidents reported by the patients had not occurred at all; yet he had resisted all attempts by others to get him to change his position. R. I. Watson says of this incident (1968, p. 467):

A short time after he gave this paper the horrible truth began to dawn on him—these seductions in childhood, in most, but not all instances, had never actually occurred.

A lesser man might have hidden his mistake and tried to forget it. A less clinically acute individual might have "bravely" confessed his error and turned to other more profitable matters. Freud did neither. . . . Was not the very fact that their fantasies took the form of sexual matters evidence that there was a sexual tinge or basis to their thinking, and was he not, consequently, right in emphasizing the sexual basis of their difficulty even though the situations which they had described had actually never taken place? Despite the temporary setback, this "mistake" was actually later to be seen as an advance.

For a scientific investigator, he was extremely insensitive to criticism from the outside, especially from those unsympathetic to psychoanalysis; however, he was sensitive to self-criticism, and his system was accordingly flexible. Seldom did he present his theories as certainties; they were, rather, usually presented as tentative conclusions that seemed to be supported by his clinical data. It is largely his resistance to external criticism and his feeling that experimental support for his notions was not necessary that have given him the reputation of being cocksure and dogmatic about his conclusions.

Freud had a surprising attitude toward the reality of his conceptions. He might, when being self-consciously correct about methodology, admit that they were convenient fictions invented for explanatory purposes, but his usual attitude was that he was dealing with real things. For example, he once used Janet's statement that the unconscious was a "manner of speaking" as an example of Janet's low level of understanding (Jones, 1957, p. 214). It seems that Freud really regarded the unconscious as a country which he was exploring rather than as a system which he was constructing. We may be too prone to forget Freud's background in neurology, a background conducive to the belief that one is working with *real* structures.

The Psychic Apparatus

As we have already seen, Freud believed that he found two "states" within the "country," the conscious and the unconscious. Different kinds of laws determine what happens in these two states: The unconscious operates according to a set which Freud called the *primary process*, and the conscious according to the *secondary process.* Ordinary logic applies to the latter but not to the former; the mechanisms that can be observed in dreams characterize the action of the primary process. Some of the things that can occur are the *condensation* of several thoughts into a single symbol, the *displacement* of an impulse or affect from one symbol to another, the *timelessness* characteristic of dreams, the *conversion* of an impulse into its opposite, and so on. The illogicality of the dream is characteristic of the primary process as a whole.

Part of the energy for the mental apparatus is called *libido*; its source is in biological tensions, and certainly the most important of these to the mental economy is sexual. Most of the sexual energy derives from the erogenous zones, bodily areas especially sensitive to stimulation. The *id* is the primordial reservoir of this energy and, being unconscious, operates according to the primary process. Various instincts which reside in the id press toward the discharge of their libidinal energy. Each instinct, therefore, has a *source* in biological tensions, an *aim* of discharge in some particular activity, and an *object* which will serve to facilitate the discharge.

The id operates according to the *pleasure principle*. In general, the elimination of tension is what defines pleasurableness, although it is not always clear whether it is the elimination of all tension or the maintenance of a constant level of tension which is pleasurable. Departure from a low level of tension or any heightening of tension is unpleasurable. One should remember that the id operates *only* according to the pleasure principle; it does not, for example, distinguish between the hallucinatory fulfilling of a hunger need and the actual fulfilling of the need. However, the tension does not remain reduced except through contact with objects which are in reality appropriate.

Accordingly, another psychic structure develops and complements the id. It is called the *ego*. It operates according to the laws of the secondary process and, being in contact with reality, operates according to the *reality principle*; that is, it is an evaluative agency which intelligently selects that line of behavior which minimizes pain while maximizing pleasure. The ego is still in the service of the pleasure principle through the reality principle, but sometimes temporarily turns aside the direct gratification of needs in order that their overall gratification will be greater.

As a result of contact with the cultural realities, especially as embodied in the parents, a third mental agency develops. It functions as a suppressor of pleasurable activity in the same way that external agencies did at one time. It has two subsystems—a conscience, which punishes, and an ego ideal, which rewards behavior. The conscience brings about feelings of guilt, and the ego ideal brings about feelings of pride. The *superego* is unlike the ego (which serves the pleasure principle and only postpones gratification) in its attempts to halt completely certain pleasurable activities. The operation of the superego is largely unconscious; that is, a large part of its operation follows the laws of the primary process.

Freud himself came to the conclusion that the instincts active throughout the psychic apparatus could be divided into two groups: the life instincts and the destructive instincts. The latter were more commonly called the *death instincts*, since their aim is the death of the individual. Freud viewed the instincts as conservative; that is, they aim for a return to a previous state and thus explain the *repetition compulsion* which manifests itself in some behavior. Since living matter arises from dead matter, the ultimate previous state must be a state of complete quiescence, of death. The death instincts work for a disintegration of the individual, while the life instincts work for the continued integration of the individual. The death instinct is the part of Freud's theory least frequently accepted by other analysts; many articles written in analytic publications have been unfavorable to this Freudian conception (Jones, 1957, p. 276). The life and death instincts had the advantage for Freud of giving him a polarity, a pair of opposite elements in conflict. Jones (1957, p. 422) points out how fond Freud was of the dualistic mode of thought in preference to monistic or pluralistic conceptions.

The energy in the service of the life instincts was called by Freud the *libido*; no name was given especially to the energy that activates the death instincts. As the individual develops his ego, more and more of the available psychic energy comes under the dominion of the ego rather than of the id, which originally directs it. The ego attaches the energy to psychic representations of external objects; such an attachment is called a *cathexis*. The kind of object cathected depends upon the instinct which has energy available; the distribution of energy over the instincts is flexible. In the original version of the analytic theory, the distribution was assumed to change gradually, so that more and more energy was available for the self-preservative instincts of the ego, and less and less for the sexual instincts of the id. This version made the basis of conflict the self-preservation versus the sexual instincts rather than life versus death.

In the course of an individual's development, there is a stage in which much of the libidinal energy is cathected onto the parent of the opposite sex; in the case of the boy, this leads to the development of the Oedipal conflict. Like the mythical Oedipus, the boy loves his mother. He is also jealous and resentful of his rival, the father. His sexual feelings are directed to the mother, but the child is blocked from direct expression of the instinctual urges toward incest. Because of his impulses, which are repressed, the boy has a fear of castration by the father. It is at this time that the urges toward the mother are repressed into the unconscious, so strongly repressed that all sexual urges enter the latency period. They emerge again at puberty, when the increase in sexual tensions is sufficient to upset the psychic economy and allow the impulses to overcome the repressive forces. The Oedipal conflict was felt by Freud to be a major contribution of psychoanalysis; one of the presuppositions necessary for its acceptance is that sexuality is really developed very early in life.

Treatment of Neurosis

Let us now consider the implications of the psychoanalytic position for the treatment of neurotics. In doing so, we should keep in mind that we are reversing the process that actually occurred; in reality, the theory grew out of the therapy and the observations that attended it, rather than vice versa, as our discussion might erroneously suggest.

In the first place, ordinary methods of gathering information about the genesis of the symptoms will not do. We have seen how unwelcome memories and impulses are repressed by the ego at the behest of reality, or the superego. They are not conscious. They are not even in the in-between zone that Freud called the *preconscious*, where the simple application of sufficient effort may make them conscious. Any attempt at recollecting them will be met by *resistance*; accordingly, a special method, such as hypnosis or free association, is required. Dreams, since they are governed to a considerable extent by the primary process, provide an avenue to knowledge about the unconscious if they are interpreted correctly. Correct interpretation depends upon the knowledge that the function of dreams is to fulfill wishes; since the id does not recognize the difference between hallucinatory and actual satisfaction of wishes, the existing psychic tensions may press toward discharge in dreams. In order to determine the precise meaning of the dream—that is, in order to uncover the hidden (latent) impulses expressed—the patient is instructed to give his associations to the elements of the dream. In this way, the symbols in the dream can be related to their meanings and the repressed material brought to consciousness.

The analysis of resistance to recall of repressed materials is then one of the most difficult and most important tasks of the analyst. If the resistance is too strong, the patient continues to refuse to recognize the existence of the repressed material even when the analyst can present it verbally to him. It is only when the patient can overcome his inner resistance and accept the analysis that he can improve. By overcoming the resistance, he brings the impulses under the control of the ego, where they obey the laws of the secondary process. As the dominion of the ego is enlarged, the ego is strengthened, and the patient obtains rational control over his impulses. He cannot be freed from the rule of the pleasure principle, but he can obtain more overall gratification when the impulses must also conform to the reality principle.

The overcoming of the resistance is made possible, at least in some cases, by the transference to the therapist of a considerable portion of the libidinal energy. This energy is therefore available to the therapist for application of counterforce to the resistance. In turn, the transference itself becomes an object of analysis, and it must be overcome before the patient is independent and can be said to be cured.

In overcoming the resistance and tracing the significant repressed materials, the patient must be forced to recall material that goes further and further back into childhood. The childhood years are critical in the development of every individual; if he becomes fixated at some early stage of sexual development or returns (regresses) to an earlier stage in the face of later trauma, the scene is set for the development of neurosis. The early experiences that are most likely to be punished, and hence repressed, involve sex. Therefore, the significant material that will be recovered will concern sex. Even more specifically, we can say that the Oedipal conflict and its resolution will be central to the analysis, and insight into it by the patient central to his recovery.

In the discussion of the cure of neurosis, we see Freud's rather peculiar position on determinism at work. He believed in psychic determinism and is famous for his work on the determination of errors in speech and writing, on forgetting, and on losing objects. He showed that the apparently chance nature of these events conceals the fact that the error reveals the unconscious motivation of the person who has erred or forgotten. A published example (Freud, 1938, p. 75) concerns a member of the United Daughters of the Confederacy, who, in concluding her eulogy of Jefferson Davis, said "the great and only President of the Confederate States of America—Abraham Lincoln!" It would seem that she should have belonged to another organization.

The peculiarity in Freud's position arises from the fact that he seems to have felt that determinism can be abrogated if only the impulses can be brought under the sway of the secondary process. In this way the patient achieves *self*-control, rather than *impulse* control. He was relatively little concerned with the operation of determinism within the secondary process, although his followers (including his daughter Anna) have spent more time in the study of ego processes. For Freud, man's hope of improvement lay in becoming rational in the true sense. Although neither Freud nor his followers believed that the achievement of insight is a sufficient condition for effecting a cure, it is for them at least a necessary condition. Furthermore, the insight has to be "deep"; that is, there has to be a real emotional acceptance of the analysis, not just an intellectual parroting of his words.

THE REBELS

Four important early members of Freud's group first occupied a favored position and then disagreed with the Freudian beliefs and established rival analytic factions. They were, in order, Adler, Jung, Rank, and Ferenczi. Their defections have been used by opponents of psychoanalysis to demonstrate either that not all analysts agree among themselves or that Freud was a kind of despotic tyrant who brooked no opposition. As we might expect, the charges were neither wholly true nor wholly false. There were both fundamental agreements and fundamental disagreements among the five men presently being considered. As to the personality factors, these are difficult to assess; in every case, some of the blame can probably be laid at each doorstep. We shall say a few words on the subject as we discuss each individual. Perhaps it would be fair to apply Freud's own dictum to himself; he said (Freud, 1943) that when an individual is repeatedly "victimized" by the same kind of external circumstance, we may be fairly sure that his own psychological makeup is such that he is repeatedly putting himself into situations where he can be so victimized. With this foreword, we now turn to a brief exposition of the four men and the modifications they proposed.

Alfred Adler

Alfred Adler (1870-1937) was a Viennese physician who early attached himself to the Wednesday-night group that started meeting with Freud in 1902 to discuss psychoanalysis. Adler and Stekel were Freud's two oldest followers; they withdrew from the society in successive years (1911 and 1912). Stekel had contributed to the field of symbolism, but, according to Jones (1955, p. 135), had no scientific conscience and formed no school of his own after he left the fold of psychoanalysis.

Adler's case was quite different; he made a greater contribution to psychoanalysis, formulated a partially independent theory of behavior, and set up a rival school.

The difficulties between Freud and Adler became intense after Freud insisted that Jung be made president of the international association; the Viennese were jealous of their positions, since they had been the first followers. Then, the year after the international meetings in 1910, it was decided to hold discussions and debates about Adler's theories. After the discussions, the disagreements about theory seemed obvious, and Adler and his faction resigned from the Wednesday Society before the end of 1911. Adler formed a rival school which he finally named *individual psychology*.

Freud had at first tolerated or even welcomed Adler's contributions. Adler initially stressed organ inferiority in the backgrounds of neurotics. At first blush, this seems a more biological view even than Freud's. However, appearances are deceptive in this case, for Adler emphasized the psychological reaction to either real or *imagined* organ inferiority rather than the biological facts themselves. *Compensation* for this inferiority accounts for the nature of many neurotic symptoms and helps to determine the individual's *life-style*, the way in which he deals with problems in general. The analysis of the compensatory mechanisms was seen by Adler as the major task of both the theory and practice of analysis.

Although Adler emphasized the conflict between masculinity and femininity as very important, his views on sexuality were very different from Freud's. He saw the overcoming of femininity by both males and females ("masculine protest"), rather than sexuality in itself, as the important thing. The will to power was thought to be the most important motivating force in the lives of men, and sex at times was a symptom of this will, the sex act representing the domination of the female rather than the running off of truly sexual impulses.

The will to power and the need to overcome inferiority arise, according to Adler, because of the conditions of life that universally obtain for human infants. The infant is not a small sexual animal whose incestuous desires must be repressed, but a small and helpless organism whose every need must be ministered to by relatively powerful adults. Necessarily, then, the infant develops feelings of inferiority relative to these adults and must strive to overcome his inferiority and rise above his dependent status. The Oedipal conflict, if it exists at all, should be understood as a conquering of the mother rather than a direct expression of any infantile sexuality.

Adler thus shifted the emphasis away from inborn biological instincts and energies toward the social relationships within the family as the children grow up; he concluded that the position within the family (such as eldest son, second son, youngest child) is extremely important in determining how an individual deals with reality (i.e., his life-style). Sibling rivalry is bound to occur and affect the personality. In Adler's theory, we see that the important conflicts often occur between the individual and his environment, rather than within the individual, as Freud had held.

Adler presented a more hopeful view of man than the orthodox analysts did. He saw man not so much as a group of segments at war with themselves but more as an integrated, striving individual. He laid much less emphasis on the uncovering of the unconscious and its dark forces. He perceived man as largely conscious and creative, living partly by adherence to a "fictional future," which consists of precepts presently believed in. Such precepts, although not necessarily true, might nevertheless direct behavior, for example, the precept "your reward will be in Heaven."

Adler and his school made therapy a shorter process and, at least sometimes, dispensed with the Freudian couch. Practical applications of the Adlerian theory to educational and social problems helped to popularize the theory, as did the ease with which such terms as *inferiority complex* and *sibling rivalry* were assimilated in the lay language. Adler's theory is generally closer to common sense than Freud's and probably shares the strengths and weaknesses common to such theories.

Carl Jung

Relationship to Freud. Carl Gustav Jung (1875-1961) was a Swiss psychiatrist who became interested in Freud's theories after reading his *Interpretation of dreams* which appeared in 1900. Jung visited Freud and his Wednesday Society in Vienna in 1907, and the two men were immediately strongly attached to each other. Freud soon viewed Jung as the crown prince of the psychoanalytic movement. In 1909, as we have seen, Jung accompanied Freud to America for the Clark University lectures and later returned to America alone to give additional lectures. At the first meeting of the new International Psychoanalytic Association, Freud insisted over the Viennese opposition that Jung be elected president. He wanted a younger man who was not a Jew to head the new movement, for he felt that the resistance to Jews would impede the progress of the analytic movement were a Jew to lead the association. On these grounds, Jung seemed the logical choice. The Viennese, who were nearly all Jews, were jealous of their own priority in the movement and were also resentful because of Jung's own known anti-Semitism. But Freud overcame their objections, and Jung was elected.

Soon after, the relationship between Jung and Freud began to weaken. Jung was not performing his presidential duties as well as Freud had expected; he deemphasized sex in his lectures and in his therapeutic analyses, and he changed the concept of libido. Personal frictions were straining the relations between the two men. By the end of 1912, they had agreed to discontinue their personal correspondence. By 1914, Jung had withdrawn completely from the movement; he never resumed his former friendship with Freud, and he soon founded a new school which he called *analytic psychology*.

Basic Attitudes and Methodology. Jung had early assumed that there must be some physical changes which account for the development of schizophrenia. In this he was emphasizing a contemporaneous factor rather than a historical factor, as Freud was in the habit of doing. Although Freud at that time agreed with Jung about this particular point, he would not have agreed in general with Jung's emphasis on the present rather than on the past in the study of neuroses. Jung was more like the Gestaltists, and Freud more like the behaviorists, on this issue. Not only did Jung emphasize the *present* as important, but he also believed that one must understand the future, the potentialities, of man in order to make sense when talking about him. The goals and intentions of men were to Jung as important in directing man's behavior as his history. He deplored Freud's study of causality exclusively in terms of the past and thought Freud's theorizing too reductive and mechanistic. Jung later suggested (Jung & Pauli, 1955) a principle called *synchronicity* for those events which occur together in time but which do not cause one another; his archetypes, which are primordial images that entail inherited response tendencies, are supposed to fulfill themselves psychically and physically within the real world at the same time without the two manifestations being causally related. This view sounds like Hume's analysis of causality and contemporaneity, or the doctrine of psychophysical parallelism.

Jung changed his position on scientific methodology as time went on. At first, he was interested in bridging the gap between academic psychology and psychoanalysis via the association experiment. In this way he hoped to make psychoanalysis more scientific. Later, Jung lost interest in "proving" analysis through traditionally conceived experiments. He and his followers turned more to the study of mythology and art as more useful methods of revealing the form of the unconscious. Jung became the most negative of the leading analysts toward the traditional methods of empirical science.

Jung's therapy, in accordance with these basic views, put less stress upon the past of the individual and more upon his present situation and desires for the future. Jung saw man as more creative and less a passive recipient of environmental influences than Freud; Jung was accordingly more optimistic in his psychology. Freud saw Jung's therapy as something that might be expected from a priest, with moral exhortation, appeals to willpower, and an attempt to develop man's yearnings after the divine (Freud, 1938, p. 975). Jung believed that man's primitive urges might be channeled into a quest for self-actualization or for the divine; if the energy were not recognized and used properly by the ego, it might so warp man's functioning that he would become neurotic or psychotic.

Basic Energies and Instincts. Jung's views about the basic energy of man were closer to a commonsense conception than Freud's. He regarded the libido as a general biological life energy, not necessarily predominantly sexual. Where Freud saw sexual energy concentrated on different body zones at different stages (oral, anal, phallic, latency, genital), Jung saw the life energy simply manifesting itself in the form which was at the moment most important for the organism, for example, in relation to eating, elimination, and sex. The early concentration of gratification upon the oral zone was accounted for by the relation of the oral zone to eating rather than to the pleasurable sensations (conceived of by Freud as sexual in the broad sense) which arise from oral stimulation. Jung did not like Freud's lumping together of all pleasurable sensations as sexual.

Since he did not conceive of the basic energy as altogether sexual, he was free to reinterpret analytic observations that had previously been assumed to represent sexual strivings. The Oedipal conflict was reinterpreted, as it had been by Adler. This time the nutritive functions, as we might expect, become important in the child's attitude toward the mother. These become overlaid and combined with sexual feelings as the child develops in his sexual functioning. Combined with these feelings are certain primitive unconscious predispositions to react toward the mother. The Oedipal relationship is then not based, as Freud thought, almost exclusively on sexuality.

Jung transferred concepts from physics almost directly into dicta about psychic energy. He did not believe that psychic energy can be destroyed any more than physical energy can. If the energy is used in some psychic function, the amount available for that function will decrease, but will reappear in the form of increased energy available for some other function. If the energy disappears from some psychic system, it will reappear in some other. This view is not very unlike Freud's; he, too, talked of the reappearance of unused psychic energy in other forms, as when sexual energy is sublimated and used for artistic creativity. Jung did not believe that the sum of the available psychic energy remains constant, for energy can be exchanged with the external world through such things as muscular work and the ingestion of food. Energy, since it can flow from one psychic system to another, tends to move from the points of higher energy toward the points of lower energy. The system, in short, tends to reach a state of balance, although the tendency is never fully realized. Even were a balance to be reached, it would soon be upset by exchanges between some psychic system and the external world. For example, if most of the available energy were concentrated in the personal unconscious, it would tend to share energy with other systems, such as the ego. Then an exchange with the external world might occur. The ego would further increase the energy supply, and the direction would now be reversed.

Views on Psychic Structures. C. S. Hall and Lindzey (1957, p. 79) have given an excellent thumbnail summary of Jung's position:

The total personality or psyche, as it is called by Jung, consists of a number of separate but interacting systems. The principal ones are the *ego, the personal unconscious* and its *complexes*, the *collective unconscious* and its *archetypes*, the *persona*, the *anima*, or *animus*, and the *shadow*. In addition to these interdependent systems there are the *attitudes* of introversion and extraversion, and the *functions* of thinking, feeling, sensing, and intuiting. Finally, there is the *self* which is the fully developed and fully unified personality.

Jung's ego is something like the layman's conception of himself; it is the conscious mind in contact with reality, and it contains the conscious memories. It is felt to be the center of identity and personality. Jung's ego is not unlike Freud's ego.

The personal unconscious is the region just "interior" to the ego. Since it is in contact with the ego, materials may be repressed into it from the ego. The personal unconscious is not unlike a blend of Freud's unconscious and preconscious; the contents of the personal unconscious are available to consciousness and contain only materials which have come into the unconscious as a result of the personal experiences of the individual and the collective unconscious.

Deeper still than the personal unconscious is the collective unconscious. In this dark and misty region are those things which man has inherited phylogenetically. The things that are inherited are called *archetypes*; they are something between symbols and predispositions to perceive or act in a certain way. Archetypes are formed as a result of the universal experiences of man in his evolution; Jung thus accepted the doctrine of inheritance of acquired characteristics. Since the presumed experiences are universals, the archetypes too are universals. Jung discovered their existence as a result of his study of the myths and art productions of different ages and different cultures; he found certain symbols that were common to all, despite the fact that no direct exchange between the cultures could ever have occurred. Examples of archetypes are birth, death, the hero, the child, and God.

Four archetypes are better developed than any of the others: the persona, the anima, the animus, and the shadow. These are so well developed that they have become separate personality systems. The *persona* is the mask presented by an individual to his society. It is the part of himself which he wishes to publicize, and it may or may not serve the function of concealing the real personality.

The *anima* and the *animus* are Jung's recognition of man's bisexuality. The anima represents the feminine part of man; the animus, the masculine part of woman. These archetypes evolve, like any other, as a result of experiences: the anima, as a result of man's experiences with woman, and the animus, as a result of woman's experiences with man.

The *shadow* consists of that part of the unconscious which was inherited from man's prehuman ancestors; it is the animal instincts. Immoral and passionate impulses emanate largely from the shadow. When these impulses appear in consciousness, they may be expressed or repressed, with the result in the latter case that some of the materials of the personal unconscious originate in the shadow.

A fifth well-developed archetype is the most important one of all. It is the *self*. Jung found this archetype represented in various cultures by a symbol which was called the *mandala* or *magic circle*. It represented man's striving for unity, for wholeness, for integration of the personality. Jung made the self, accordingly, a separate system, changing from his earlier conception of the self as equivalent to the whole psyche. The self holds all the other systems together. It apparently strives for oneness of the individual with the world through religious experiences as well as oneness of the psychic systems within the individual. The self can appear only as the other psychic systems become separate enough to require integration, which does not occur until middle age. Some of Jung's disagreements with Freud were based on this "breaking point" in middle age; Jung thought Freud might be essentially correct about the importance of sexual motivation before middle age, but he believed that Freud had simply ignored what happened after this point had been passed, when the self had developed and when sex had become a subsidiary consideration.

The two attitudes toward the world distinguished by Jung, extraversion and introversion, are better known than any other part of his system. In extraversion, most of the individual's attention is directed to the external world; in introversion, the opposite is the case. Usually, the ego and the personal unconscious have opposite attitudes, since both attitudes are always present to some extent somewhere in the personality; the nondominant attitude, then, tends to be repressed. The stronger the conscious expression of one attitude, the stronger the unconscious development of the other. Sometimes an upset allows the libido attached to the unconscious attitude to overwhelm the repression, and the dominant attitude is overcome.

Finally, there are the functions, any one of which may be dominant. Jung's definitions of thinking, feeling, sensing, and intuiting do not differ from the common meanings. He did not think there was anything arbitrary about the statement that there are exactly four functions; it was a statement of fact as far as he was concerned. Generally, two of the functions predominate at the expense of the other two; the latter are then developed unconsciously, just as in the case of the repressed attitude. If an individual is described in terms of function and attitude, we have a sort of typology; thus a feeling-intuiting-introvert might be a prophet or a monk. All functions and both attitudes are necessary for successful living; accordingly, there are no pure types. The whole individual has all these factors in harmony. As pure types are approached, the pathological is approached.

Contribution and Evaluation. Jung is especially difficult to evaluate. When Freud was alive, Jung and all other analysts were in his shadow. In addition, it has frequently been pointed out that Jung is difficult to comprehend; as Jones has said (1957): "Then his mentality had the serious flaw of lacking lucidity. I remember once meeting someone who had been in school with him and being struck by the answer he gave to my question of what Jung had been like as a boy: 'He had a confused mind.' I was not the only person to make the same observation" (p. 32).

Although Jones may have been somewhat biased in his estimate because of his friendship with Freud, there does seem to be some justification for his attitude. Recently, a reviewer of the English translation of Jung's published works said that Jung's statement about one of his works seems applicable to many (Jung, 1956):

"It was written at top speed, amid the rush and press of my medical practice, without regard to time or method. I had to fling my material hastily together, just as I found it. There was no opportunity to let my thoughts mature. The whole thing came upon me like a landslide that cannot be stopped" (p. xxiii). A book so written could hardly be easy for the reader. In addition to the style problem, the English-speaking reader had the problem of translation until 1966, when the last of eighteen volumes was translated.

Even when the difficult problem of reading and understanding Jung is passed, many others remain. Jung's dislike for traditional scientific methodology makes his type of persuasion foreign to psychologists who like statistical or laboratory proof. If such proof is demanded, Jung can be dismissed at once.

It is even difficult to find any logical system to evaluate, for Jung was not a systematist. Whatever system there is must be distilled from his writing and then fitted together; Jung has presented no postulates or derivations. In this, he is in the company of the other analysts.

Yet Jung has seemed to grow in importance within recent years. He outlived Freud by twenty-two years, and his works are appearing in English. His ideas are novel and provocative. His view of man furnishes a refreshing antidote to Freud's. It is optimistic and consistent with the religious point of view. Jung was himself interested in both myths and religions, especially Oriental religions. His position affords a comfortable, compatible resting-place for those who are surfeited with the scientific approach and its results. Jungian psychology is an easy companion for the existentialist (modern variety). The perhaps accidental fact that interest in these subjects—Oriental religion, mysticism, existentialism—has enjoyed an upsurge has strengthened Jung's position.

It is significant that Jung's scientific training was not as long or intense as Freud's. Thus Jung was able finally to accept a consistently antiscientific view. Freud had faced many fearful tests of courage—childhood sexuality and his own error in believing his patients' stories of sexual episodes, for example—but he never conceived the possibility of flying completely and purposely in the face of organized science. Jung did. That will be his downfall or his salvation. Jung was erudite and enthusiastic, and his followers were loyal and impressed once they understood him. We would not care to bet on what the coming years will do to the popularity of Jung's psychology.

Rank and Ferenczi

These two men can be treated together because they published together and because their defections from Freud were somewhat related to each other. Rank's schism from Freud was earlier, more severe, and more complete than Ferenczi's. Neither man has yet assumed the stature of Freud, Adler, or Jung, although both have made significant contributions to the theory or practice of psychoanalysis.

In 1922, Otto Rank (1884-1939) began to present his ideas on birth trauma. In addition, he and Ferenczi were collaborating on a book entitled *The develop-*

ment of psychoanalysis (1925). The book advocated the possibility of shorter therapy and stirred considerable dissension among analysts later. Even more disturbing was the book Rank wrote alone, *The trauma of birth* (1929). Freud himself reacted quite positively to the book at first, but he was later ambivalent about it. Complicating the picture was Rank's aversion to Jones; Freud apparently did not know whose side to take in these disagreements. A series of declarations of independence by Rank, followed by declarations of friendship, finally resulted in Rank's complete separation from Freud and the orthodox analytic movement.

Initially, Ferenczi showed some hostility to the members of the committee and was disappointed at his treatment at party congresses; he was never elected president by a full congress. However, his final separation from Freud was neither so early nor so dramatic as that of Rank. He simply drifted away from the other analysts, partially because of his therapeutic beliefs. There was little or no real bitterness between him and Freud, at least until very near the end of Ferenczi's life in 1933; by this time Ferenczi's physical illness may have affected his mind (Jones, 1957, p. 176).

Rank's background contributed a professional issue to psychoanalysis. He had come from a technical school to the Wednesday Society and had been encouraged to attend the university. His application of psychoanalysis to cultural developments endeared him to Freud. Rank thereby swayed Freud in favor of lay analysts. Freud had never identified with the medical profession himself and did not see any absolute necessity to study medicine in order to practice analysis.

Rank's more direct contribution was connected largely with the birth trauma. In a sense, Rank was pushing Freud's concern with the early years to its logical conclusion. He saw the neuroses as originating in the trauma of birth, where the child experiences a forcible and painful expulsion from the comfort of the womb into the terrors of the world. This trauma, he believed, is never forgotten. The "separation anxiety" that results from the birth trauma is basic to neurotic symptoms. The clash of will between child and parent that later attends the growing-up process is also important. The job of the therapist, then, is to alleviate both the guilt of the patient over this clash and his anxiety over separation. In order to get the patient really to work during therapy and in order to ensure that he does not become overdependent on the therapist, a definite date is set for the separation of therapist and patient. The therapy is then terminated at the agreed time, and the patient develops in therapy the ability to function alone after this time.

There is one interesting sidelight on Rank's theory. Freud was ordinarily quite opposed to statistical treatment. The only known exception to this occurred when Freud was in a critical mood toward Rank's theory; he suggested (Jones, 1957, p. 68) that he would never have proposed the theory without prior statistical evaluation of the mentalities of those who were firstborn, had difficult births, or were delivered by Caesarean section.

Sandor Ferenczi (1873-1933) made no theoretical modifications as sweeping as Rank's. His chief defections were in therapeutic technique. He shared with Rank the belief that it is not always necessary to exhume the historical origins of neurotic symptoms; thus a briefer therapy should be possible. Ferenczi thought that the warm relationship with the mother was missing in the lives of most of his neurotic patients and that the therapist should supply this missing element. Accordingly, he coddled patients, holding them in his lap and kissing them at times (Jones, 1957, pp. 163-164). Freud saw this as opening the door to therapeutic techniques which could discredit psychoanalysis completely, and Ferenczi was hurt by Freud's doubts. However, he would not be dissuaded from his belief that *acting out* the unconscious problems is the way to mental health and continued to use his unique therapy until his health became so poor that he could no longer work.

This concludes the purely expository portion of the present chapter. It is in no sense a complete history of psychoanalysis even up to the time of Freud's death in 1939; it is a sample of highlights only. More recent developments will be presented later, but they too must be incomplete. Psychoanalysis is an organic movement that is forever growing and replacing parts of itself, so that no cross section can give a realistic or a complete picture. However, we now turn to some evaluation of the cross section we have presented here.

In view of the differences between those systems usually called *psychoanalytic*, psychoanalysis cannot be discussed as a single system. However, there are important commonalities even among the widely divergent systems, and we shall try to keep these commonalities in the focus of the discussion. Wherever we discuss a point which is not common to all systems, Freud's system will be used rather than any of the others. Even with these restrictions, it requires some forcing to fit Freud's system into the boundaries of criteria set up by an academic psychologist. Nevertheless, the questions raised by McGeoch's criteria are important ones for psychoanalysis.

Definition of Psychology

Although Freud was not within the tradition of psychology as such, psychoanalysis was to him perhaps the only psychology worthy of the name. He was interested in developing a systematic framework but not in stating definitions. His followers did not differ from him on this point. Freud *distinguished* psychoanalysis at one time by its concern with resistance and transference; at another time he said that the distinguishing mark of an analyst was his concern with sexual factors. But these were not definitions. We may attempt a definition "from the outside" based on what psychoanalysis seems to us to be. Psychoanalysis is that discipline which began in the study of neurosis through the techniques of hypnosis, dream analysis, and free association. It has emphasized unconscious motivational conditions. It has since broadened its fields and methods of study to include anthropological investigation, laboratory experiments, testing techniques, and the study of normal persons, cultures, and cultural records. Rapaport makes clear the fact that psychoanalysis does intend to define psychology in a way that allows psychoanalysis to encompass it (1959, p. 79):

Finally, in the late thirties, forties, and fifties, the influence of psychoanalysis and of the new psychoanalytic ego psychology expanded to the whole of psychology, first through projective techniques into clinical psychology, then into experimental clinical psychology, and finally into experimental psychology proper. Thus the original claim of comprehensiveness for this theory is gradually being realized.

Several basic assumptions are made by analysts, and these assumptions must be included as a part of the definition of the school; only those who accept some minimum number of them are accepted analysts. These assumptions are next examined.

Basic Postulates

According to Munroe (1955), nearly all varieties of analysts accept four basic assumptions. First, the psychic life is *determined*. Second, the *unconscious* plays a predominant role in determining the behavior of man, which previously had been thought to follow rational patterns of determination. Third, the most important explanatory concepts are *motivational* (i.e., "dynamic"). Many different behavioral manifestations can be explained by recourse to a single underlying motivational concept; the emphasis is on the purposiveness of action rather than on more mechanical S-R connections. Fourth, the *history* of the organism is of extreme importance in the determination of contemporary behavior.

In addition to these four primary postulates, more orthodox analysts usually accept several others which may be summarized as follows. The basic drive is sexual and has its foundation in the biology of the organism. The manifestation of this primal biological energy is seen in the various instincts. There is a basic conflict of life and death instincts (we have already seen that this is one of the least popular postulates). A structural, topographical model is needed to explain unconscious activity; Freud's id, ego, and superego are the usually accepted structures. Parental relationships to the young child account for the neuroses. The individual goes through various stages of libidinal development—oral, anal, phallic, latency, and genital. The defense mechanisms under the control of the ego protect the individual from psychological harm. Finally, dreams, slips of the tongue, wit, and various errors have symbolic meaning related to repressed sexual content.

Although we have included the above assumptions under the name *postulates*, this term should not be taken literally. Freud was an inductive thinker, at least as he conceived the process. He did not see himself as postulating at all but merely as reporting or summarizing the results of his observations. His reaction to Janet's saying the unconscious was a manner of speaking shows that Freud did not like to have his concepts put on a postulational level. The behavior of many of his followers indicates that they tend to think the same way. This is not necessarily a telling criticism, for it does not matter how concepts are viewed as long as they play a useful part in theory.

Nature of the Data

The basic data of psychoanalysis have been gathered in the therapeutic setting. They are the data of verbal report, or of introspection. The type of introspection is markedly different from the classic type, but the difficulties of the classic type are still present, often in aggravated form. If psychoanalytic introspection is supposed to give information about past events, then the original stimuli for the verbal report occurred months or years previously. Many of the hypotheses of psychoanalysis are about relationships between events in the history of the patient and his present behavior. In fact, some critics have felt (e.g., Skinner, 1954a) that one of the main contributions of psychoanalysis has been its emphasis on the causal importance of events in the life of the individual. Yet these events have been little studied in any direct way. The data are the *present* verbal productions of the patient. Freud was himself puzzled when he found by checking the reports of his patients against the reports of other family members that many of the reported events could not possibly have occurred. He decided that it made no difference whether the event had occurred; the fact that the event had been fantasied made it important for therapy. Ezriel (1951) has argued on the basis of such reasoning that analysis is *not* a historical method. It seems that he is right. The analyst really works on the assumption that *reports* about the past are important; operationally speaking, the analyst has nothing to do with the past of the patient. He studies the personality of the individual through an observation of his interaction with another person (the analyst), not through the reconstruction of the past. Psychoanalysis is a dynamic, not a genetic, method, working with contemporary rather than genetic data.

The relationship between the data and the theory of psychoanalysis is thus far from clear. If the theory is about genetic factors, then most of the data are highly questionable. The past events must be *inferred* from the kind of data collected. We remember from the criticisms of structural psychology that psychologists have generally not been content to trust the human memory for more than a few seconds, even under strictly controlled conditions. If the data are recognized for what they are—appropriate to statements about the present only—then the form of Freudian theory would seem to require modification. This kind of criticism is, of course, less appropriate to Jung or even to Adler, since they recognized more explicitly the importance of the present in their theoretical presentations. Even in their cases, however, many of the hypotheses are about the past—in Jung's case even the phylogenetic past, where no direct data at all are available.

A second difficulty arises necessarily from the nature of the therapeutic relationship. Many of the statements made by the patient must be kept in strictest confidence. The analyst must play the role of therapist during an analytic session and can take the detached role of scientist only after the session is over. He may forget or select only confirmatory data. What the patient says may be influenced by previous statements of the analyst. Freud himself taught his patients some analytic theory in the therapeutic process, although he did not do so to as great an extent in later years; suggestions may thus have inclined the patient toward those statements which would be confirmatory as far as the theory was concerned. The net result is that the data are not generally available even to the scientific public. Scientists generally, then, cannot evaluate their quality. The confirmation by a patient that an analysis of some of his productions (for example, a dream) is correct is of little scientific value. The patient himself participates to some extent in the interpretation, and his agreement or verification may be a result of unintentional suggestion by the analyst that the interpretation is correct. There is no outside source which can confirm or deny the correctness of the analysis.

One might wish to ignore the need for such data and demand only data on the success of therapy. Even data on therapeutic success are seldom available in any quantity. There are, of course, plenty of reports of patients who got better, but there are few studies with control groups, equal in other respects, which are given some other type of therapy or no therapy at all. Each analyst sees so few patients, even over a lifetime of therapy, that it is difficult to get a large sample. Even if one could get such control groups and such samples, it would be extremely hard to show that the individual analyst's application of the theory had been correct or that extraneous factors had not contributed to the outcome. Altogether, it is very difficult to demonstrate a tight logical relationship between the theory and the outcome of therapy. A therapeutic situation does not seem to be the place to prove a scientific theory.

Nevertheless, in one year Dittmann (1966) found five studies of the outcomes of therapy (usually not psychoanalytic therapy). Dittmann's review cannot be used to buttress any statements about psychoanalytic theory or therapy, but it does give some illustrations of the pitfalls involved in such research. One study is particularly instructive (Nash, Frank, Imber, & Stone, 1964). These investigators found, according to Dittmann, "an enormous effect of beginning treatment, an effect which started before any treatment was administered, and seemed unrelated to the type of treatment whether active or inactive medication." When effects like these are prevalent, it is not surprising that the best-intentioned therapists overvalue the effectiveness of their own work.

Observational data have come in from other situations. Kardiner (1939), Mead (1950), and Malinowski (1950) have gleaned relevant data from primitive societies. These data have sometimes bolstered the system and sometimes necessitated its modification; for example, the data have not supported the supposed universality of the Oedipal complex (Toulmin, 1948).

Hilgard (1952), among others, has reported data from human subjects in laboratory or classroom situations. These data are necessarily fragmentary. They are concerned with isolated portions of psychoanalytic theory, as nearly any closely controlled study must be at this stage. Still absent is the painstakingly detailed longitudinal study which would be needed to give sound underpinning to psychoanalytic genetic assumptions. Pumpian-Mindlin (1952) is typical of those who feel the need for a psychoanalytic institute to carry on such research.

Sears (1943) has reviewed the objective research prior to 1942 which attempts to verify psychoanalytic concepts. Many of these studies have been with animals, and a disproportionately large number have been tests of fixation or regression. Horwitz (1963) points out that psychoanalysts are most often sublimely uninterested in such experiments. Too often the hypotheses investigated are trivial, or the experimental investigator has not taken the trouble to get more than a most superficial knowledge of the theory he is attempting to test. Under these conditions, the attitude of the analyst is certainly understandable. Nevertheless, the experiments are relatively well controlled and indicate a salutary concern with the scientific acceptability of the concepts tested. The overconcern with limited concepts probably indicates a weakness in the theory; most of the analytic statements are too general or too ambiguous to allow easy testing. It is in most cases not possible to test predictions based on derivations from several postulates because there is never any quantitative statement and seldom even any statement of the relative qualitative importance of the several possible factors which might bear on a behavioral outcome. Thus the kinds of data and their relevance to analytic theory are partially limited by the condition of the theory.

Mind-Body Position

Freud was a modern in this respect; he did not much concern himself with the question. Jones (1953, p. 367) has said that passages could be quoted from Freud which would place him in any one of several philosophical mind-body positions; Freud self-consciously declared himself a psychophysical parallelist. He held that psychical processes cannot occur in the absence of physiological processes and that the latter must precede the former. He thus assigned some priority to the material, a priority that may have been held over from his student days when he espoused a radical materialism.

Principles of Connection

Since psychoanalysts are outside academic psychology, it is unnecessary for them to begin with the problem of connection as such. However, their basic method is the free-association method, and one can ask how it happens that the associations are connected in such a way that they provide, as Freud said of the dream, a "royal road to the unconscious." The principles of connection are of several kinds.

First, there are the classic principles of contiguity, similarity, and opposition. The elements that have been contiguous to each other in an individual's experiences tend later to be connected in an associative train. Also, elements which are similar for an individual or which are opposites may evoke or substitute for each other. Although the acceptance of these classic principles makes available a rudimentary learning theory, Rapaport explicitly says (1959): "If we must single out an outstanding limitation of this theory's claim to comprehensiveness, then we should choose its lack of a specific learning theory" (p. 79).

The more important principles of connection are those which relate to motivational factors. In an association, the similarity or opposition may be one of motive or feeling rather than of the objective stimuli. A recognition of this fact enables the analyst to recognize connections which are not apparent to the academic psychologist. The determination of associations by these factors also explains why the "free" associations of the patient involve material relevant to his basic problems; these problems beget motives which in turn control the associations.

Still other and more complex principles are needed to explain completely why certain symptoms arise from their problems and why certain manifest content arises from its latent content in the dream. These are the special principles of symbolism which have been mentioned earlier: distortion, displacement, and condensation are such principles. Finally, there are the defense mechanisms of the ego—rationalization, projection, etc.—which explain the connections between certain overt behaviors and their motivational bases. The complexity of these principles of symbolism and defense is such that they have long been the objects of extended analytic investigation.

Principles of Selection

Motivation provides the key to selection as well as to connection; it seems that in most systems, the principles tend to be simply the obverse of one another. Analysts have emphasized the selectivity exercised in the movement of material into consciousness from the preconscious or unconscious more than the selection of stimuli in the environment. The selection of an idea or memory is dependent upon the dynamic balance between repressive forces and those instinctual forces which strive for the expression of the repressed material. Repression acts selectively to remove material from consciousness, and resistances act to keep the emotionally toned material out. The job of the analyst is to redistribute the libidinal energy available so that the repressive forces of the ego or superego are lessened relative to the expressive forces. Often the libido attached to the repressed material is so strong that it forces its own selection for acting out in disguised form; for example, repressed hostility may be expressed through its projection onto other persons, who are then reported to be hostile. The ego is continuously selecting appropriate repressed materials for such symbolic expression. The principles of connection are also involved in selection; the ego must *select,* according to the principles of *connection,* the symbols that are needed to give vent to repressed impulses.

We see from such examples that a considerable part of Freud's contribution was the detailed development of principles of connection and selection in cases that had previously been regarded as arbitrary and lawless. He extended the principles to the unconscious, where different laws were required, and this extension is at the heart of his system.

Recently, research involving the so-called new look in perception has been concerned with the effects of motivation on the perception of objective stimuli. Such selective perception has been demonstrated in the laboratory and represents an extension of the kind of thinking typical of the analysts. Although the interpretation given the experiments is in doubt (e.g., Goldiamond, 1958), there can be no doubt that variables which were earlier thought inappropriate are now being studied in the perceptual context. An example of the observed results is the finding that more time is required for the perception of a guilt-arousing than a neutral word. The analytic interpretation would be that an ego-defensive mechanism is at work and tends to repress its perception.

CRITICISMS OF PSYCHOANALYSIS

Immorality

The lay and religious publics have been vindictive toward Freud and psychoanalysis because of its alleged irreligiosity, amorality, and emphasis on sex. It has been said that Freud reviled and desecrated religion and childhood. Freud was not personally religious, and he attempted to explain religiosity in natural, scientific terms. It is also true that Freud extended the concept of sexuality into childhood and that he advocated somewhat less repressive attitudes toward sex; he was, for example, in favor of sex education of a realistic sort.

Regardless of what Freud's personal feelings were or of what he said on these subjects, the arguments are altogether irrelevant to the truth or falsity of any scientific hypothesis. If one regards Freud's pronouncements on these subjects as philosophical rather than scientific, then his rejection can be on the grounds of value rather than truth. Thus if a reader does not like the pessimism of Freud as a philosophy of life, he can reject it for a more optimistic view. His acceptance or rejection will have nothing to do with science.

Origins

Several critics have pointed out relationships between Freud's personality or background and the theory that he evolved. For example, some might read Bakan's book (1958) as a denunciation of psychoanalysis, since it points out in a clear and scholarly way the relationship between Jewish mysticism and psychoanalysis, with side excursions into Freud's messianic feelings and their implications for theory. It is no rarity to see the Oedipal part of analysis explained by recourse to Freud's own relationship with his young mother or to see his tendency to oppose traditional views reduced to a reaction to his membership in the Jewish minority.

These criticisms, too, are fundamentally irrelevant. Nevertheless, psychoanalysis has been more often subjected to such criticisms than better-established disciplines. We have already seen that its data do not have the quality of conviction typical of most scientific data. Therefore, if a critic explains a part of analysis by recourse to mysticism, it is incumbent upon the defender of analysis to show that that part of analysis rests also upon some firmer foundation of scientifically acceptable data.

Theory

No system thus far discussed in this book has provided anything close to an adequate theory in Bergmann's sense (see Chapter 3), which is essentially the sense in which we have been using the word. Psychoanalysis is no exception. Only in an extremely broad sense of the word is there a psychoanalytic theory. There are a large number of empirical generalizations, and there are some parts which constitute a rudimentary model. Walker (1957) has outlined very clearly the nature of the unconscious as a scientific model. Freud regarded himself as a beginner only, his system as a beginning only. Perhaps the analogy between psychoanalysis and phrenology (see Dallenbach, 1955) is not so unfair as it would at first appear; both disciplines made important beginnings toward sciences, and Bakan (1968) has recently defended the virtue of phrenology, so that it is no longer necessary for us to be offended by an analogy between psychoanalysis and that scientific lady of questionable repute.

Since no psychological theory of any scope is at this time completely satisfactory, the only reasonable questions one can ask concern whether a particular theory is likely ever to *become* a good theory. Rapaport (1959) expressed pessimism by doubting that the theory could ever be confirmed by generating and testing predictions. Horwitz (1963) is more optimistic and does not see why this cannot eventually be done. A damning statement, if it continues to be true, was made in a review by Ford and Urban (1967):

Similarly, although 30 to 40 psychoanalytic articles and books have been examined, they are not emphasized here. Our examination of that literature gives the strong impression that little substantive development is underway.... There is little substantive novelty in these writings, and they are likely to be of interest only to followers of the particular view represented. . . . These books, the psychoanalytic literature this year, and our reading of that literature during the last few years lead us to the conclusion that the innovative steam has gone out of the psychoanalytic movement. Major theoretical and technical advances in the future will probably come from other orientations, although the theoretical contributions of the past will continue to be influential.

In view of these considerations, it is not surprising that there is really no such thing as a psychoanalytic theory. If one wished to test psychoanalytic theory, he would not know where to go to find the theory. Presumably the theory exists in the collected works of Freud or perhaps in such interpreters as Fenichel (1945), but nowhere is there a clear statement of what are postulates, what are theorems, what their relations are, what quantitative values are to be assigned; in short, one misses all the paraphernalia usually associated with a scientific theory. The data so far brought forward concern themselves with empirical generalization, not with deductions from any theory.

There are several reasons why the casual observer may be misled into thinking some theory exists. In the first place, there have been a great many statements made about matters of fact by analysts. The outsider may believe that these statements, some of which may be correct, are derived from some theory. The fact is that they are generally derived from observation; they are descriptive statements, or generalizations thereof. A second reason is that analysts have been willing to explain all sorts of behavior—dreams, forgetting, symptoms, and the genesis of given neuroses. Since there is a language and a set of statements available for explaining such otherwise inexplicable occurrences, the observer may believe that a scientific theory must be available. The unfortunate truth is that the *analysts' statements are so general that they can explain whatever behavior occurs.* A genuine scientific explanation cannot do this; it must predict one behavior to the exclusion of all other behaviors. Otherwise the theory is empirically empty and says, in effect, "Anything may happen."

As is usual with systems like psychoanalysis, empirical confirmation must apply itself to the limited, confirmable statements rather than to the theory itself. Yet, as Skinner (Hall, 1967) says, "You can't expect a Freudian to say, yes, I will admit that Freud's only contribution was in demonstrating some unusual causal relations between early experience and the present behavior. He loves . . . the various geographies of the mind and all of that stuff" (p. 69).

Farrell (1951) provided a list of propositions which at that time seemed confirmed: that infants obtain pleasure from oral stimulation or genital stimulation, that manual masturbation is more frequent among preschool boys than girls, and that small children exhibit extensive pregenital play. Other propositions he regarded as disconfirmed: that all small girls have penis envy and wish to be boys and that all children exhibit sexual attraction and attachment for the parent of the opposite sex and sexual jealousy of the parent of the same sex. A third class of propositions is regarded as untested or untestable, such as the hypothesis about substitutability of erogenous zones.

Whether or not one agrees with Farrell's classification of these few propositions, his procedure at least illustrates the necessarily piecemeal nature of the confirmation process. It is unrealistic to hope for any real confirmation or disconfirmation of the theory at the present time. We must agree with Farrell that "psychoanalytic theory is, qua theory, unbelievably bad." Although this is true of most psychological theory, analysts seem less concerned with this undesirable state of affairs than most academic psychologists. We have said earlier that theories are nearly always discarded not because they are wrong but because they are improved upon and replaced by superior theories. Kuhn (1962) makes the same kind of point in his discussion of scientific revolutions. Walker (1957) says that psychoanalysis fills the need for a model that will "go anywhere, do anything, and be good at dealing with people" (p. 122). Horwitz (1963) says, along the same lines, that it is the implicit feeling of clinicians "that psychoanalysis is not the best theory of human behavior; it is the *only* theory" (p. 429).

Even if this is the case, and we believe that there is beginning to be reason to doubt it, we are willing to argue that it is time to throw aside tradition and stop giving so much serious concern to psychoanalytic theory *even if there is nothing to replace it.* A hillbilly lady was once heard to observe, after drowning her infant in a mudhole into which it had fallen, that it would be easier to get a new one than to clean the old one up. Perhaps this is the case with psychoanalysis. Though Freud was undoubtedly a genius and made contributions of immense importance, he did not really leave behind a theory, nor did he leave behind anything enough like a theory for mortal man to be able to make it work. It is time, we believe, for us to go through the intellectual attic that is psychoanalysis, keeping the occasional rare pearl that can be validated by the current methods of science and boxing up for another 100 years or so, when they may have become valuable, the dusty love letters that are not really well understood by very many of our generation.

Criticisms of Therapeutic Outcomes

Toulmin (1948) said that ". . . if a fully-fledged analytic explanation is not part of a successful cure, we do not regard it as a 'correct' explanation; therapeutic failure is as fatal to an explanation in psychoanalysis as a predictive failure is to an explanation in physics" (p. 29). We must disagree with Toulmin on this point. A psychoanalytic explanation may be correct, but the course of the illness may nevertheless be irreversible because the independent variables which, if manipulated, would result in cure may not be under the control of the analyst. A somewhat analogous challenge might be to ask a physicist to change the orbit of Mars and refuse to accept his explanation of the laws of moving bodies if he were unable to do so. The lack of favorable therapeutic outcomes, therefore, may be a basis for criticizing the practicality or usefulness of the therapy, but in itself cannot be a basis for criticism of the theory. The theory could be criticized on the basis of therapeutic outcome only if it could be shown, first, that the theory was applicable and perfectly applied to the case and, second, that the therapist was able to manipulate all circumstances just as he pleased. We have already pointed out that there are few controlled data on therapeutic outcome; we may add here merely that a difficulty in getting such data is that there are no adequate and acceptable scientific criteria for improvement. The subjective judgment of the patient, analyst, or relatives may be used, but all are open to serious question.

It is interesting that regulatory agencies do not treat psychotherapy the way they treat chemotherapy. If a given drug cannot be shown to be effective, the government, through the Food and Drug Administration, steps in and stops its sale or restricts its advertising. Rigorous tests are required to show that the treatment has no harmful effects. Psychotherapy operates under no such restrictions, and the therapist need not even be licensed in some states. Until more adequate evidence is gathered, psychoanalytic therapy in particular stands vulnerable, an expensive and ill-defended anachronism.

Lack of Control

This criticism, to some extent, has already been met in all the other criticisms. It is the focal point of all the others. As discussed earlier (see Chapter 1), the control we are speaking of here is not the control the physicist might lack if he wished to change the orbit of Mars; it is the control of variables which would enable him to say what factors were at work in any given observation. The analyst lacks this control. He cannot isolate possible influences on a patient one by one, but must attempt to disentangle relationships from the complex matrix of life as the patient happened to live it. He cannot be sure that descriptions of the past, or even of the present, are adequate or, for that matter, accurate. He cannot back up and see what would have happened if events had been changed in some way; he cannot try out the effect of some single manipulation on the patient's future behavior, for there is no way of isolating people from a multitude of other influences. No wonder it has been said that the situation is uncontrolled!

A common answer to this criticism is that the analysts have proceeded through *clinical validation*. This seems to mean that successive confirmations of a theoretical prediction within the clinical setting constitute acceptable demonstrations of the accuracy of the principles involved. Such an argument is basically unsound. We have to know what alternative explanations are possible, and these alternatives must be eliminated by means of appropriate controlled changes in the situation. Otherwise, despite an infinite number of clinical validations, it is possible that the same artifacts continue to give the same outcomes, which happen to be consistent with the theoretical predictions. In reality, it is extremely improbable that clinical validation would ever be as systematic and careful even as we have pictured it; it is difficult to imagine a clinician finding enough cases appropriate to some prediction to permit him to repeat test after test of some good, operationally defined, clear hypothesis.

It is not easy to suggest improved methods for testing psychoanalytic propositions. This is clearly due to the state of the theory. A necessary step involving a huge amount of labor and ingenuity is the improved definition of terms and the formalization of the theory. A prior step, then, would be to try to define operationally the terms that occur in the isolated propositions so that these will be more experimentally testable. Mullahy (1948, pp. 316ff.) has given several examples of the need for clarification and elimination of contradiction. We have already indicated our opinion that the effort required would be misspent.

There are, nevertheless, probably many who will wish to make the effort. For them, we shall suggest the direction that confirmation, or attempted confirmation, of the theory might take.

There are several levels of behavioral observations and corollary realms of discourse involved in analytic theory and its testing. Most of the orthodox observations have been of verbal materials. Investigations at this level of observation might be improved by the use of more objective measures of the verbal behavior of the subject, as with psychological tests of various kinds. Stephenson (1953) has developed a technique, the Q sort, which is a compromise between the usual completely free analytic situation and the more strictly objective type of personality test, and has shown how the technique can be used to test analytic propositions. This technique has the advantage of dealing in a quantitative way with some of the attitudinal dimensions that are related to psychoanalytic theory.

A second level at which psychoanalytic propositions can be investigated is that of everyday-life behavior. Social caseworkers can make observations on the real-life characteristics of the individual and relate these observations to the events in therapy. These data would go beyond what is usually available to the analyst. We have already suggested that behavioral observations unrelated to therapy are also needed; although Freud felt that the best way to get information about the psychic apparatus was to study cases in which it was malfunctioning, we also need more information about the genetic events in the lives of normal people.

On a third level of investigation, studies within the therapeutic situation itself might well be improved in terms of both control and sophistication of approach. Horwitz reports as follows on some of these more ingenious and careful studies (1963, p. 431):

> The treatment situation, long the subject of post-dictive study, is now becoming the locus of predictive studies. Bellak and Smith (1956) have reported a carefully controlled study of short-term predictions concerning the expected developments in the analytic treatment of patients whose preceding hours had been carefully studied by a group of analyst-predictors who were not themselves treating the patient. Robbins and Wallerstein (1956, 1958, 1960) have initiated a long-range study of both process and outcome in which a major method is the formulation of predictions prior to beginning treatment. A key feature of this investigation is the formulation of the theoretical assumptive base for each prediction in an effort to validate and extend psychoanalytic theory.

A fourth level at which the propositions need further study is the fully experimental one in which full scientific abstraction and control are reached. Although many analytically inclined people doubt the possibility of testing the propositions in this way, we shall never know unless we try. We might even wonder whether the objectors question the possibility or fear the outcome. Furthermore, such investigations would be valuable in their own right, regardless of their bearing on psychoanalytic propositions. It would be surprising if any investigation produced results which were perfectly in keeping with the original speculations that instigated them. If they generally did so, experimentation would become unnecessary.

Dogmatism and Cultishness

We have already had some discussion of this point in other connections; for example, we saw the sense in which Freud was dogmatic and the sense in which he was not. We have met the "committee," composed of men who might almost be called disciples; Eitingon, for example, always made a pilgrimage to see Freud on his birthday. There are other points which suggest cultishness: "Only the analyzed can analyze," as though one had to be personally initiated in a trial by fire before one could carry the word.

A given psychoanalytic interpretation of a particular case is often accepted without question by its proponent; alternative views are simply not entertained. Finally, the adherence to a single systematic view is frequently combined with an emotional fervor such as is seldom seen in scientific circles.

These characteristics indicate why psychoanalysis from the outside has seemed almost as much a religion as a science. Again, this argument has nothing to do logically with the value of the theory or the therapy, but it has had something to do with the acceptance of the theory by scientists, who feel that science is not a cult. Agreement with a gospel or subjective evaluations of persons should have nothing to do with evaluations of scientific propositions, and psychoanalysts have sometimes seemed to use these criteria.

An interesting form of dogmatism is the criticism by analysts of the detractors of psychoanalysis. If a critic refuses to accept some aspect of psychoanalysis, he is said to be manifesting resistance. We can find such inherent dogmatism in Freud himself. When he wished to show why Adler was wrong, he said (Freud, 1938): "I shall, therefore, use analysis only to make clear how these deviations from analysis could take place among analysts" (p. 964). No doubt Adler analyzed Freud in return in order to show why Freud had resisted the new ideas.

CONTRIBUTIONS OF PSYCHOANALYSIS

Psychoanalysis is in the paradoxical position of being often rejected as a scientific system and yet accepted as an outstanding contributor to science. Freud is more often regarded as a pioneer, as a prescientist, than as a scientist; he called himself a conquistador. Whatever he is called, he is recognized even by his enemies as a great man and perhaps the greatest genius within psychology. He made contributions to many fields. Let us look at some of his contributions to psychology.

He stimulated thinking about, and observation of, many neglected areas of psychology: the significance of unconscious factors in determining behavior, the widespread importance of sex in normal and abnormal behavior, and the importance of conflict, of childhood, of the irrational, and of the emotional. He personally made acute observations throughout a long life of daily work and contributed hypotheses or facts—we cannot yet tell which are which—about broad areas of human behavior.

He developed highly provocative explanations of kinds of behavior previously considered outside the realm of scientific explanation, such as errors and dreams. The fact that such areas are examined and such explanations developed by a serious worker would have been an important contribution regardless of the eventual correctness or even usefulness of the explanations. A field of study was opened up that was virgin for all practical purposes when Freud touched it.

Even in technique and methodology, where psychoanalysis so often falls short of traditional scientific criteria, Freud either made contributions or reinforced points made by others. His development of the techniques of free association and dream analysis for the study of unconscious processes has been compared with the invention of the microscope for studying cellular processes. Equally important, his emphasis on the study of unconscious processes preceded and reinforced the behaviorist and Gestaltist point that the traditional methods of introspection are altogether inadequate for the development of a complete science of man. One could argue that Freud made incidentally a point that became a central thesis of behaviorism. In this sense, psychoanalysis has been the source of a great optimism; psychology is now viewed as a discipline that will certainly become a full-fledged science and develop whatever techniques are necessary. Without Freud, the conviction might have been slower in growing.

Psychoanalysis has contributed much empirical observation. Intensive studies of individual cases are available in the psychoanalytic literature as in no other place. Freud himself published only four case histories of his own patients, but other analysts have contributed, and the distillation of such observations presumably appears indirectly in analytic propositions. C. S. Hall and Lindzey (1957) believe that Freud's use of internal consistency as a method of testing hypotheses was one of his most important contributions to research strategy. As applied within psychoanalysis, internal consistency refers to the checking and cross-checking of a particular hypothesis by means of a large variety of different indicators; homogeneity of results is interpreted as supporting the hypothesis, much as a test is evaluated in terms of the extent to which the separate items can be shown to be positively correlated. Internal consistency becomes important as a research strategy only when there are a great many data on a single case. It makes possible a kind of reliability not otherwise easily obtained.

Another contribution is not easily weighed in a scientific scale: Psychoanalysis has contributed to the popularity of psychology and psychiatry with the lay public. The average man has analytic words and notions from all schools in his repertoire and uses some analytic modes of thinking about the behavior of others— and perhaps occasionally his own. Psychoanalysis has thus revealed the importance of psychology to the lay public in a way that other systems have not. It may be that money and talent are easier to recruit to the science of psychology because of the analytic contribution.

Psychoanalysis presents explanations of normal and neurotic behavior in a language and at a level that people are prone to believe they understand. For better or for worse, it deals with practical situations in an exciting and challenging manner. Its method and theory contrast markedly with the slow, tiresome, painstaking program characteristic of most scientific research and theory construction. Therein lie both its appeal and its weakness.

DIMENSIONAL ANALYSES OF PSYCHOANALYSIS

Psychoanalysis, in most respects, occupies the left end of Coan's diagram of theoretical variables. It could be characterized as subjectivistic, qualitative, personal, dynamic, functional, and fluid, without much controversy being likely. That takes care of all Coan's dimensions except for holism and endogenism. Psychoanalysis is holistic in the sense that an attempt is made to consider complex interactions of variables in explaining behavior. However, it is analytic in its attempt to reduce the patient's total personality to more manageable units like fixations (at stages), cathexes (to persons, objects, etc.), repressions, transferences, and so on. The analytic position on endogenism-exogenism is also unclear. Freud emphasized the instincts at a time when, in America at least, an extreme environmentalism made his position look very endogenous in emphasis. However, anyone who emphasized historical and developmental variables in his theoretical account as much as Freud did can hardly be said to have neglected exogenous variables, as we might usually think of them. Freud is listed among the endogenous theorists, and Coan (1968, p. 719) cautions:

A constitutional emphasis apparently tends to go with the former and an environmental emphasis with the latter, but the nature-nurture dichotomy evidently does not represent the central focus of the factor. Rather, the essential distinction seems to be between the contrasting orientations—toward the internal sources of behavior and toward the external sources—that find occasional expression in the nature-nurture controversy.

Freud would be an endogenist on such a factor because he tended to emphasize inner causation in *current* behavior, not because he emphasized inner causation as the ultimate account of the behavior. In fact, we have seen that Skinner felt that one of Freud's great contributions was his identification of the causal role of events in the history of the individual.

The reader should refer to Table 3-2 for the authors' ratings of psychoanalysis on Watson's eighteen dimensions and those of the students. The most disagreement occurred on the dimensions mechanism-vitalism, rationalism-irrationalism, and staticism-dynamicism. The standard deviations of the students' judgments on all three of these dimensions were high, as can be seen in Table 3-1. The students regarded psychoanalysis as much more vitalistic than the authors did. This is surprising because Freud was a great determinist and extended mechanistic thinking to unconscious processes such as dreams and slips of the tongue. He also seemed to support the viewpoints of Brücke and the others who made the antivitalistic pact.

The authors rated psychoanalysis as very irrationalistic, while the students rated it as neutral on this dimension. However, there was a great deal of disagreement among the students' individual ratings (Table 3-1). Their ratings on the rationalism-irrationalism dimension had a higher standard deviation than would be expected if the numbers 1 through 5 had been assigned randomly! Watson states that he has in mind for this dimension the extent to which emotional and conative factors intrude on intellectual functioning. The authors believe that psychoanalysis clearly belongs at the irrationalistic end of such a dimension. Had Watson not stated his definition explicitly, one might argue that the unique contribution of psychoanalysis is that it has made the apparently irrational rational by pointing to its genesis in the symbolic expression of repressed motives. In this special sense, psychoanalysis *is* rationalistic, but that is not what Watson meant. It should also be remembered that Freud's whole emphasis was upon the irrationality of man; in fact, this was one of the main points of complaint by critics.

On the staticism-dynamicism dimension, the authors and the students agreed as to the direction of the emphasis—dynamicism—but the authors' rating was much higher. Probably this was just another expression of the students' natural tendency to rate more toward the mean.

The students weighted unconscious mentalism, determinism, and irrationalism as the three most critical dimensional characteristics defining psychoanalysis.

SUMMARY AND CONCLUSIONS

Psychoanalysis deals with the interesting and mysterious, yet practical and important, regions of man's existence. Its adherents have hung together in a kind of cult; psychoanalysis is apparently thoroughly understood by few persons who are not analysts. Still, enough of its theory and practice has filtered out to others so that its terms enrich the lay vocabulary more than the terms from any other psychological system.

Psychoanalysis is more an art, a philosophy, and a practice than a science. The theory is loose and nebulous, sometimes even self-contradictory. The therapy has not demonstrated a greater effectiveness than other kinds of therapy, which in turn have seldom presented conclusive evidence that they are better than no therapy at all. The data and methodology which gave rise to analytic theory are markedly inadequate. Analysts have typically shown too little desire to improve the form of, or evidence for, the theory; this is not to imply that the theory does not show frequent changes as a result of new observations in therapy or, occasionally, in better-controlled studies, although examples of the latter would be hard to demonstrate.

Many of the modern variations on Freud's theory have followed Adler down the path of increased emphasis upon cultural factors, with some compensatory deemphasis upon biological factors. Much analytic effort has gone into increased specification of the nature and genesis of ego functioning; it is this area of study which probably gives the most promise of a rapprochement with academic psychology. Jung is typical of those who have placed increasing emphasis upon the unity and the creative potential of the self. The common rejection of the death instinct is typical of the less pessimistic outlook on human nature shown by modern analysts. Psychoanalytic theory has been a powerful force since 1900, and some of its basic ideas are receiving ever-wider acceptance. Among these ideas are the unconscious model and the importance of sexuality. There are still several training institutes for analysts within the United States. Yet there are those who say that psychoanalysis is dead or dying. It has glaring systematic and scientific defects. The effectiveness of its therapy has never been adequately demonstrated. If it is to remain a viable force, these defects must be remedied within the near future, before it is displaced by one of its increasingly effective competitors. If a competitive position enjoys dramatic success within the near future, psychoanalysis as a comprehensive theory will disappear as dramatically as it appeared.

In saying this we do not intend to derogate the positive side. Among its solid contributions to psychology are the opening up of new areas of investigation such as the unconscious and sex, the impetus to motivational research, the stress on childhood and genetic factors in personality, most of the empirical observations, and the findings concerning defense mechanisms, which are often accepted by otherwise unfriendly psychologists. A significant task of future behavioral scientists will be to convert the brilliant insights of Freud into scientifically acceptable propositions. In this process, it may well be that the peculiar flavor of psychoanalysis will be lost.

Further Readings

So much has been written on psychoanalysis that a reading list must be presented with great temerity. The books that follow are good, but are only a tiny fraction of the total number of good books. Jones's three volumes, *The life and work of Sigmund Freud* (1953-1957), are in many ways the best single source on psychoanalysis. These books can be read as absorbing biography and will infuse large quantities of knowledge painlessly into the unwary brain. Jones's formidable volumes have been abridged by Trilling and Marcus (1961). A fine little book which is just what it claims to be is C. S. Hall's *Primer of Freudian psychology* (1954). This book provides a solid basic introduction to Freud's system. C. S. Hall and Lindzey, in their *Theories of personality* (1970), do the same thing for all the important psychoanalytic theorists. Munroe's *Schools of psychoanalytic thought* (1955) is a friendly psychologist's look at psychoanalysis. If the student has taken a dislike to psychoanalysis and wants to find out how vitriolic critics can be, Ludwig's *Doctor Freud* (1947) will provide this extreme. On the other hand, Bakan's *Sigmund Freud and the Jewish mystical tradition* (1958) shows relationships which would otherwise be unsuspected by all except the most devout scholars and is worth reading just as an example of how the fine line between scholarship and readability can be navigated by a skillful writer. *A general introduction to psychoanalysis* (1943) is probably the most readable effort by Freud himself. The translations by Brill of *The basic writings of Sigmund Freud* (1938) are easily available and provide a good sample of Freud's work. A classic exposition of psychoanalytic theory is Fenichel's *Psychoanalytic theory of neurosis* (1945). Useful methodological criticisms, including some of a friendly sort, are to be found in a symposium on psychoanalysis in the November, 1954, issue of *Scientific monthly*; Skinner's (1954a) and Frenkel-Brunswik's (1954) papers are especially valuable. Rapaport's (1959) chapter in the Koch series has the same kind of systematic aims that we had in the present chapter, but Rapaport is more positively oriented toward psychoanalysis and more optimistic about its future. The interested reader will find many insights in Rapaport, and his references are a fine directory for further study.

PART THREE

CONTEMPORARY THEORIES

This final part of the present volume is concerned with some theoretical developments in contemporary psychology. Although our primary purpose is to present the theories, we have also attempted to show the relationship of contemporary theories to older systems.

We have selected those theories which have been most generally influential within American psychology and which relate to general systematic considerations, rather than those which concern specific subject matter. Therefore, some very important but more specialized theories (such as those in the field of color vision) have been omitted.

Contemporary theories have been treated in three groups, which can be more or less identified within the functional schema of stimulus-organism-response (S-O-R). Thus, the stimulus-response theories have been primarily response-centered; so-called field theories have developed largely from Gestalt psychology and have been primarily stimulus-centered (or perception-centered); and personality theories concentrate upon the organism and its characteristics. This simple schema cannot be pushed too far, since few theories deal exclusively

279

with any one of these categories, but it indicates primary emphasis.

The final chapter deals with a new and exciting development—the influences upon psychological theory of mathematical and engineering concepts and procedures. It can be predicted with some assurance that these influences will have an increasing effect on a wide range of psychological research and theory construction.

10 Varieties of S-R Theory

Anyone who tries to define S-R psychology should be prepared for an exercise in tolerance of frustration and ambiguity. It seems clear that we must first define stimulus and response if we are ever to define a stimulus-response psychology. Unfortunately, no agreed-upon definitions are available. We are in no position to legislate usage, but we can at least point to some of the alternative possibilities. The alternative chosen will determine what is taken to be S-R psychology.

One issue concerns whether the stimulus is to be defined independently or is to be only "that which produces a response." We have already seen that Dewey in 1896 deplored the artificial analysis of the reflex into stimulus and response. Skinner (1938) agreed in the sense that he thought it useful to consider a stimulus and a response to be any situational and behavioral aspects of a context that could be shown to enter into an orderly functional relation. J. J. Gibson (1960) was critical of this kind of formulation and pointed to the possibility that it would lead to circularity in some cases (that is, the stimulus might become whatever was needed to bring about the response, leaving no independent term to explain the response). Hocutt (1967) defended the meaningfulness of relational terms of this type. Among Hocutt's examples of such concepts are those of man and wife, neither of which can be defined independently of the marriage relation. Despite their lack of independence, it remains meaningful to speak of a wife as something like the "female partner in a marriage relationship." Even if a stimulus is conceptualized initially as independent of responses and is defined in terms of physical energies, it will be of eventual interest only if it does enter into some relationship with a response. It would seem, then, that the S-R psychologist need only be careful to have a means of identifying stimuli and manipulating them; he can then ascertain whether the independently identified stimulus enters into relationships with independently identified responses.

A second important question concerns the relative level of molarity of definition of stimulus and response. On the stimulus side, we have encountered a version of this problem in the contrast between the molecular view of the stimulus taken by the structuralists and the molar view taken by the Gestaltists. Brunswik's lens model (see Chapter 11) and his scheme of the organism in its surroundings are clear expositions of some of the possibilities both for stimulus and for response definition. Brunswik's general argument tends toward molar definitions for psychology, at least at the outset. The typical S-R psychologist is probably more molecular than Brunswik would wish and is in this respect a descendant of the more molecular and analytic associationistic school.

A third definitional question concerns what should be included in the definition of stimulus and response. The molar-molecular issue is related to the problem of inclusiveness, but more is involved than that. Specific questions related to the general issue would include, "Is deprivation a stimulus?" and "Is an injection of androgens a stimulus?" Because he believes that such things are *not* stimuli, Skinner does not think of himself as an S-R psychologist (Evans, 1968, p. 20; Skinner, 1966, p. xii). On the other hand, Kimble, because he uses the terms *stimulus* and *response* more inclusively, concludes (1967): "Thus the facts of psychology turn out to be Ss and Rs, a state of affairs which suggests with a certain insistence that the laws of psychology must be reducible to these terms and that an S-R psychology is an inevitability" (p. 76).

It is clear that there is disagreement about whether one must be an S-R psychologist because there is disagreement about what an S-R psychologist is. The latter disagreement follows, in turn, from the fact that stimulus and response are defined differently by different people. We shall leave this problem at this point and turn to an examination of some theories which are usually agreed to be S-R theories. This examination will reveal some of the properties generally shared by such theories. Contemporary S-R theory can be divided into two broad classes which differ in the role accorded the *reinforcement*, or response-strengthening, process.

The first of these classes may be called *S-R reinforcement theory*. Both of the two major subtypes of this theory afford reinforcement a central role, but they interpret the nature of this role differently. Many psychologists, like Hull, have interested themselves in the mechanism of the reinforcement process; some form of "need reduction" has been most often identified as the necessary and sufficient condition for reinforcement. Others, like Skinner, have stressed the importance of reinforcement without commitment to the underlying nature of the process. This view may be classed as *descriptive* S-R theory, since the fact of reinforcement is accepted in a descriptive or theoretically neutral sense.

The second class of modern S-R theory is generally called *contiguity theory*. Following Guthrie, contiguity theorists hold that all that is essential to learning is contiguity of stimulus and response. Reinforcement, in the sense of presentation of a so-called reinforcing stimulus such as food or money, is important only because it changes the stimulus situation and so preserves associations already established. From a historical point of view, modern contiguity theory is a highly refined associationism (see Chapter 4).

Several writers have suggested combinations of these two major views. These two-factor theories are treated briefly. With the exception of Mowrer's (1960a) version, they present few new theoretical positions, but rearrange the basic points already present in the two major positions.

All the different S-R theories have a great deal in common, probably more than theories of perception or personality. For one thing, they are all primarily *learning* theories.

Nearly all S-R theories now distinguish between learning and performance (Kimble, 1961) with some variables affecting only the latter, but learning remains central. Because of the important role that learning has played in these theories, it is often very difficult to distinguish between learning theory and general behavior theory. Hull, for example, considered himself a general behavior theorist and thought of learning constructs as central but not exclusive determiners of performance. To most psychologists, however, Hull has been a learning theorist because he has been concerned primarily with behavior *modification*. Similar statements could be made about most of the other theorists discussed in this chapter.

A second characteristic common to all S-R theorists is their neobehaviorism. The most marked difference between modern *neo*behaviorism and Watsonian behaviorism is the greatly increased theoretical sophistication of the former. Watson, Weiss, and Holt had to be content with making gross generalizations based on very limited empirical evidence. Today, however, detailed logical justification as well as empirical evidence is demanded by and of neobehaviorists.

S-R REINFORCEMENT THEORY: THE HULL-SPENCE SCHOOL

The main lines of modern S-R reinforcement theory were laid down by Clark L. Hull. In the development of this systematic effort he had the assistance of many psychologists, notably Kenneth Spence and Neal Miller. Both were associated with him for many years at Yale University, and both helped to determine the way in which Hull's theory developed. Spence especially has been consistently interested in the form of the theory and has trained and sent forth a large number of theoretical devotees. For these reasons we refer to the "Hull-Spence school." Miller not only worked directly with the theory but also extended it to the explanation of personality. This gives him a place in Chapter 12, as well as in this chapter.

Hull's Career

Clark Hull (1884-1952) was born in New York and reared in Michigan. Throughout his childhood and early adult years, he was beset by illnesses, and he suffered from very poor vision all his life. Polio left him crippled in one leg, and he himself believed that much of his motivation derived from his handicap; however, there is some reason to doubt that this is the whole story. His own "idea books" refer to a possible future greatness seven years before he contracted polio (Hays, 1962).

Hull's education was interrupted both by these physical problems and by lack of money; he had to teach both in one-room rural schools and in a Kentucky normal school for various periods. Nevertheless, he managed to earn his bachelor's degree at the University of Michigan, where Pillsbury was a dominant influence, and to complete his doctoral research at the University of Wisconsin. His dissertation was a study of concept formation (Hull, 1920). He was thirty-four by the time he completed his own personal obstacle course that led him to a Ph.D. His idea books (Hull, 1962) show that he was often concerned that his late start might prevent him from achieving the greatness to which he aspired. At one stage he expected to have only six creative years left; then he raised the estimate to eleven upon reading of the advanced ages at which men like Kant and Leibniz had created great works. When he made the eleven-year estimate, he actually had twenty productive years left!

After receiving his Ph.D., Hull stayed on at Wisconsin as a member of the psychology staff. One of his early research efforts concerned the effects of tobacco smoking on efficiency of behavior. These much-cited experiments (Hull, 1924) were marked for their especially good control of the sensory factors involved in smoking (such as the warmth of the air produced by a pipe). The control of suggestibility by concealing whether tobacco was actually present presaged Hull's later concern with the general problem of suggestion.

As a result of being assigned a course in tests and measures, Hull surveyed the literature in that field and eventually published an important early text, *Aptitude testing* (1928). He did not continue these activities, however, because of what he has called his "pessimistic view as to the future of tests in this field" (1952, p. 151). Here again Hull himself provides us with good justification for doubting his assessment of his own motives, since he says in an idea book of 1929 that he still plans to do "a grand experiment on a huge scale" (1962, p. 827) with the intention of constructing a universal aptitude battery. Hull's discussions there convey the clear impression that the aptitude work was merely being deferred until later because he thought of it as the kind of work that an older and less creative man than he then was might successfully do.

Hull's next persistent research interest was in suggestibility, hypnotic and otherwise. He became involved because he had to present academic lectures and laboratory work to medical students. He spent ten productive years in research on suggestion, supervising a large number of senior theses. By his own count, some twenty persons engaged in the research, which was reported in thirty-two papers. He has stated that his interest in hypnotic research was not encouraged after he moved to Yale because of medical opposition, which he had not encountered in the Middle West (1952). His publication of the book summarizing the research, *Hypnosis and suggestibility* (1933), marked the end of this phase of his research career. The book remains a classic in the field of hypnosis.

Hull's third and final major research interest was learning theory. He studied Anrep's translation of Pavlov's *Conditioned reflexes* (1927) and became progressively more interested in learning and general behavior theory. In 1929 he became a research professor at Yale's Institute of Psychology (which was shortly to become the Institute of Human Relations). Thenceforth he turned to the development of behavior theory on a full-scale basis. He continued zealous and devoted work on this most important part of his contribution to psychology, despite declining health during the last few years of his life, until his death in 1952. He left behind a band of students as devoted to him as he had been to them.

Development of Hull's System

The focal point of Hull's theoretical thinking was the conditioned reflex, as conceptualized by Pavlov. Hull regarded it as a kind of simplified learning situation which was admirably suited for experimental analyses. The findings could then be extended to other, more complex phenomena. Hull made the extension by basing the axioms of his system on experimental findings from conditioning experiments. For example, Hull's postulate II in his final system states the value of the "molar stimulus trace" as a function of time since stimulation.

Postulate II. Stimulus Reception

A. When a brief stimulus (s) impinges upon a suitable receptor there is initiated the recruitment phase of a self-propagating molar afferent trace impulse ($\dot{s}'$), the molar stimulus equivalent ($\dot{S}'$) of which arises as a power function of time ($\dot{t}$) since the beginning of the stimulus, i.e.,

$$\dot{S}' = 465{,}190 \times \dot{t}\, 7.6936 + 1.0,$$

$\dot{S}'$ reaching its maximum (and termination) when $\dot{t}$ equals about .450".

B. Following the maximum of the recruitment phase of the molar stimulus trace, there supervenes a more lengthy subsident phase ($\dot{S}'$), the stimulus equivalent of which descends as a power function of time ($\dot{t}'$), i.e.,

$$\dot{S}' = 6.9310\,(\dot{t}' + .01)^{-1.0796}$$

where $\dot{t}' = \dot{t} - .450"$.

C. The intensity of the molar stimulus trace (s') is a logarithmic function of the molar stimulus equivalent of the trace, i.e.,

$$s' = \log S'.$$

This postulate shows very clearly some characteristics of Hull's theory. It is stated formally and carefully. Symbols are introduced and defined, and they make mathematical statements possible. The mathematical statements are frequently quite precise, although the precision may be misleading in view of the uncertainty of the statements and the relative crudeness of the data which justify the postulates.

Postulate II, like many of Hull's postulates, arose rather directly out of the empirical relationships observed in conditioning experiments. Koch (1954, pp. 70ff.) has discussed the problems connected with inducing postulates from data; he believes that Hull erred in basing postulates too directly on data. Data may, of course, be limited or invalid, but that is not the main issue here. The more serious question is whether postulates based directly on data from particular experiments have any reasonable chance of being useful in a general theory. The history of science would suggest that the probability that such postulates would prove ultimately useful in a general abstract theory is extremely low. The more abstract postulate is usually several steps removed from the function forms seen directly in the data.

Such use of conditioning experiments as a source of axioms is a distinct and critical change from previous behavioristic practice; Watson, for example, used the conditioned reflex grossly, as an element from which complex behavior could be directly constructed by chaining elements together. It is clear that Hull's theorizing was a great leap forward within the behavioristic tradition, at least in sophistication of theoretical methodology.

In justifying his procedures, Hull published a series of brilliantly conceived theoretical papers on conditioning during the 1930s. Perhaps the best known of these was his presidential address before the American Psychological Association, entitled "Mind, mechanism, and adaptive behavior" (1937). The general purpose of these papers, exemplified in the title cited, was to show how basic conditioning principles might be extended to complex behavioral processes. As a methodological, rather than a metaphysical, behaviorist (see Chapter 7), Hull did not deny the existence of mental phenomena. However, he thought mental phenomena *needed explaining*, rather than themselves being useful as explanatory devices. He therefore proposed to give as complete an account of action as possible, and he hoped that this account would someday help to account for consciousness. Hull thought that the behavioral approach to mental phenomena had not had a thorough trial. He wanted to give it a trial that would either succeed or show that the approach could not work.

A brief excursion into the field of verbal rote learning followed this early theoretical work. Here Hull enlisted the aid of a set of mathematicians and logicians, as well as psychologists, and attempted a rigorous quantitative analysis of the kind of rote verbal learning first studied by Ebbinghaus (see Chapter 4). Although the book that emerged from this effort has been hailed as a landmark in the development of scientific psychology, it has been seldom read, less often understood, and unproductive of research. *Mathematico-deductive theory of rote learning* (Hull, Hovland, Ross, Hall, Perkins, & Fitch, 1940) thus remains an idealized but relatively fruitless model of psychological theory construction.

Hull's next major publication, *Principles of behavior* (1943), had quite the opposite effect. Its appearance marked the beginning of an era of psychological research in which Hull became the unquestioned leader of learning research in this country and one of the most controversial figures in the field. In *Principles of behavior* Hull attempted to lay down the framework for a comprehensive theory of all mammalian behavior. He outlined a set of postulates and corollaries, logically interlaced in the hypothetico-deductive style that he had come to consider a model of scientific theorizing.

Although many psychologists did not think the book fulfilled the great promise of Hull's early theoretical papers, *Principles of behavior* nevertheless had an enormous influence on research in the learning area. Hull became by far the most cited writer in the field. Untold numbers of master's theses and doctoral dissertations dealt with tests of various of the implications of Hull's theoretical system. Up to the time of his death in 1952, Hull remained the dominant figure in the field of learning theory.

A major factor in the success of *Principles of behavior* in stimulating research was its detailed spelling out of the postulate-corollary set. Hull deliberately laid the system out in as explicit a manner as possible in order to expedite continuous and persistent empirical checking. This characteristic was probably the most important feature of his systematic endeavor.

In terms of content, perhaps the most important aspect of Hull's theorizing was its attempt to reconcile the basic Thorndikian notion of effect with the conditioning paradigm and methodology of Pavlov (see Chapter 4). In essence, what Hull attempted to do was to incorporate the effect principle—now called *reinforcement* —into a conditioning type of framework. Unlike Watson, he did not think that frequency and recency of response were sufficient principles to account for learning. The emphasis on effect was evident in the last organization of his postulate set. Hull began with introductory postulates that dealt with "unlearned stimulus-response connections" (postulate I) and "stimulus reception" (postulate II). He then stated the key principle of reinforcement, first described as the *law of primary reinforcement* (1943, p. 80), as follows (1952, pp. 5-6):

Postulate III. Primary Reinforcement
Whenever an effector activity (R) is closely associated with a stimulus afferent impulse or trace (s) and the conjunction is closely associated with a rapid diminution in the motivational stimulus (S_D or S_G), there will result an increment (Δ) to a tendency for that stimulus to evoke that response.

Immediately following were corollaries dealing with secondary motivation and secondary reinforcement. Postulate IV stated the law of habit formation, utilizing the variable of number of reinforcements.

Hull's last books were *Essentials of behavior* (1951) and *A behavior system* (1952). The latter work attempted to extend the application of quantitative methods within the system and to extend the system to problems of individual behavior. A final contemplated work on social behavior was never begun. As a matter of fact, Hull, who was very ill during his last years, did not live to read the galley proofs of *A behavior system*.

Most of the modifications of the original (1943) system in Hull's final works were relatively minor, consisting mainly of rearrangements of postulates and corollaries and changes in details. The most important modification was the shift in the relationships of antecedent stimulus determinants to the constructs $_sH_R$ and $_sE_R$. This shift left the habit construct $_sH_R$ a function only of number of reinforcements and gave the reaction-evocation construct $_sE_R$ increased importance in that it was directly determined by the stimulus factors formerly held to affect $_sH_R$ (see Figure 10-1). After the shift, a relatively simple derivation of latent learning was possible (see Hilgard & Bower, 1966; Koch, 1954). Latent learning had been the most important of the experimental results produced by cognitive non-S-R theorists and advanced as especially embarrassing for Hullian S-R theory (cf. Chapter 11).

Hullian Methodology

Objectivity. Hull was first and foremost a behaviorist. He rejected metaphysical behaviorism, with its denial of consciousness (cf. Chapter 7), but fully and enthusiastically endorsed methodological behaviorism. Hull was considered the arch-objectivist of the 1940s by both his followers, who reveled in this identification, and his opponents, who chose it as a point of attack. In pursuing his behavioristic program, Hull tried to use concepts reducible, at least in principle, to physical terms.

Hull (1943) gave physicalistic definitions of stimulus and response; stimulus was defined in part as "stimulus energy in general, e.g., the energy of sound, light, or heat waves, pressure, etc." (p. 407). Koch (1954) does a nice job of showing that Hull's operations with stimuli did not at all conform to his definition. In practice, a stimulus was a part of the environment which the experimenter discriminated and responded to. Thus Hull, like most objectivists, did not really follow physicalistic definitions in his experimental work. However, even his critics have typically found Hull's data language objective enough.

Hull, with his more sophisticated behaviorism, was intensely concerned with some methodological problems not considered by Watson. Hull's theory contained a number of explicit intervening variables, while Watson's theorizing involved implicit intervening variables at most. Hull's intervening variables were functions of antecedent conditions like number of reinforced trials, stimulus intensity, or hours of deprivation. These intervening quantities then entered further equations that determined what the properties of the observed response should be (cf. Figure 10-1). It is often tempting in a psychological system to postulate intraorganismic variables whose quantity is appropriate to predict the response properties needed in the system. Hull was very careful to avoid this kind of trap; he insisted that every intervening variable be anchored in both antecedent and response conditions. To the extent that the anchoring was successful, the intervening variables were assured of having a clear meaning. If the predictions generated coincided with observed data, the intervening variables could be said to "summarize" the observed relationships.

Hypothetico-deductive Form. Hull was greatly impressed by the elegance of the formal mathematical and physical systems, such as those developed by Euclid and Newton. As his interest in developing a general behavior system grew, he determined to model it upon these examples. The result was that he attempted to build a highly formalized and comprehensive behavior theory in a hypothetico-deductive framework. Formal postulates and corollaries were advanced, together with theorems laid down as deductive consequences. Such a system is hypothetico-deductive because it begins with *hypotheses* which are sufficiently well connected in a logical system so that their consequences can be *deduced*. The deductions (theorems) are related by the theorist to statements of empirical observations which should be made under the conditions specified by the theorem. The validity of the empirical statements is then checked by the experiment. If the statements are true, the hypotheses are retained; if they are false, the hypotheses require modification or rejection.

In *Principles of behavior* (1943) Hull laid down sixteen primary principles, as postulates, and a large number of corollaries; in the revision of the system (1951) a total of eighteen postulates and twelve corollaries was produced. In accordance with the hypothetico-deductive procedure that Hull intended to follow, these primary principles were to be used deductively to predict secondary principles, such as the goal gradient and latent learning.

A single relatively simple example will serve to illustrate the way in which Hull used some prior empirical knowledge, one or more primary principles (postulates or corollaries), and some deductive derivation combined with a little quantification to produce theorems that could be tested empirically. Consider the problem of the order of elimination of blind alleys in maze learning, as by a rat. It had long been known that the blind alleys closest to the goal are eliminated first, a principle called the "goal-gradient hypothesis" by Hull (1932). Hull incorporated this empirical fact into a logical postulate by assuming that the response potential of any response is a function of its distance, in time, from the reinforcing event (in this case, the reaching of the food incentive in the goal box). Thus his corollary iii, delay in reinforcement (J), reads (1952): "A. *The greater the delay in reinforcement of a link within a given behavior chain, the weaker will be the resulting reaction potential of the link in question to the stimulus traces present at the time*" (p. 126).

This principle, the logical derivation of which was given (1952, Ch. 5), led to a number of empirical predictions, stated as theorems, for multidirectional maze learning (1952, Ch. 9). Among these, for example, were the propositions that a long blind alley, since it entails a greater temporal delay of reinforcement, will be eliminated more quickly than a short blind alley (theorem 104, p. 282) and that the rate of locomotion through the maze will become progressively faster for the later, compared with the early, parts (theorem 110, p. 286). Now it is important to note that neither of these two predictions could be generated directly from the first empirical result itself, the observation of a gradient of error elimination, but could be logically derived from the general principle concerning temporal delay of reinforcement which was developed from the empirical data. Such logical deduction of many new and different empirical predictions from a smaller number of key principles is considered to be a major contribution of a hypothetico-deductive system. Hull's *Behavior system* is full of such derivations, with quantitative calculations, and so represents a much closer approximation to hypothetico-deductive methodology than the more programmatic *Principles of behavior* does.

To Hull's credit, it must be said that he did not attempt to hold to a static or fixed system; indeed, his thinking was extremely fluid, and his formal theory went through an almost continuous series of revisions. He thus used the hypothetico-deductive system in the way it was intended. An indication of the extent to which he practiced the methodology he preached may be seen in his systematic writing of "idea books" and his distribution of mimeographed memorandums for criticism. His first idea book covered the period from 1902 to 1906, when he stopped writing until January, 1916. After that, he continued to write regularly until eighteen days before his death (Hays, 1962). There is an interesting disagreement about the number of these books; Hull stated (1951, p. 120) that there were twenty-five volumes, and Hays has said that at Hull's death in 1952, there were seventy-three! Perhaps Hull did not think that some of his handwritten notebooks were of high-enough quality to be considered among his idea books.

Quantitative Character. Hull felt very strongly that theoretical progress in psychology would come as a consequence of the successful extension of quantification. His own theory was supposed to be a primarily quantitative one. In *Principles of behavior* Hull's quantification was largely programmatic, and more apparent than real. Many postulates had no mathematical form or lacked numerical values for the constants. Hull was acutely aware both of the shortcomings of his 1943 system and of the difficulties associated with genuine quantitative statements. He immediately set out to achieve genuine quantification and published five articles which reported on this work. The basic experiment (Felsinger, Gladstone, Yamaguchi, & Hull, 1947; see also Koch, 1954) was a study of latency of response to a manipulandum; latency was measured from the time that a shutter was removed to make the manipulandum available. Thurstone's method of paired comparisons was used to estimate the amount of $_sE_R$ (reaction potential) giving rise to the response.

Whenever intervening variables which cannot be directly observed are involved in a theoretical chain, rational decisions involving an element of guesswork must be made as to the quantitative interrelationships between all the variables in the theory. There seems to be no escape from this conclusion. Guesses which produce a useful general theory require a high degree of creativity, plus some luck. Logan (1959, pp. 303-306) has given a concise example of the general method by which Hull proceeded to combine empirical observations with rational guesses to produce his version of a quantitative behavior theory.

Summary of the System

Essentially, as an S-R system, Hullian theory deals with three types of variables: the stimulus (antecedent or input), the intervening (intraorganismic), and the response (consequent or output). The following highly abbreviated account is intended to give something of the general nature and flavor of the system. The basic system is represented diagrammatically in Figure 10-1. For a more detailed exposition the reader is referred to one of the original sources (e.g., Hull, 1943, 1951, 1952) or to a secondary explanatory source (e.g., Hilgard & Bower, 1966; Spence, 1951a, 1951b).

The input, or stimulus, variables are such objective factors as number of reinforced trials, deprivation of incentive, intensity of the conditioned stimulus, and amount of reward. These various factors are directly associated with resulting

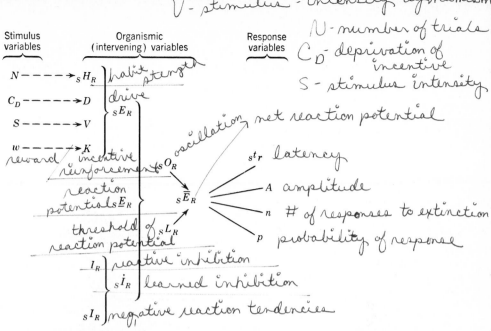

Fig. 10-1. Simplified diagrammatic representation of the Hullian system. See text for explanation of symbols and
relationships.

processes hypothesized to function within the organism: intervening variables of
the first order. Examples are habit strength $(_sH_R)$ as a function of number of trials
(N), drive (D) as a function of drive condition such as deprivation of incentive
(C_D), stimulus-intensity dynamism (V) as a function of stimulus intensity (S), and
incentive reinforcement (K) as a function of amount of reward (w).

Certain of these direct, or first-order, constructs are assumed now to coalesce
into a smaller number of second-order intervening variables. The major construct is
reaction potential or response evocation ($_sE_R$), which is a joint function of $_sH_R$,
D, V, and K. Also to be considered at this level are generalized reaction potential
($_s\bar{E}_R$), which is a function of the amount of similarity of the present conditioned
stimulus to ones previously experienced for which habit strengths have been established, and the aggregate of the negative reaction tendencies ($_s\bar{I}_R$). The latter
construct is a function of reactive inhibition (I_R) and conditioned or learned inhibition ($_sI_R$), both of which are the direct consequence of work performed in the
response.

At the final level, the higher-order intervening constructs then are net reaction potention ($_s\bar{E}_R$), a function of the two excitatory factors and the one inhibitory factor just mentioned, and two more speculative and less well-specified constructs which modify its action. These are the oscillation ($_sO_R$) and threshold
($_sL_R$) of reaction potential. Finally, on the output side, there are four major
measures of the effectiveness of response: latency ($_st_R$), amplitude (A), number of
responses to extinction (n), and probability of response (p).

Supplementary to the above descriptive account are a number of stimulus-trace concepts, such as the drive stimulus (S_D) and the fractional goal response (S_G), which are of primary importance in the system and also in more recent modifications of it, especially that of Spence (1956); these were omitted from the summarizing description so that the essential system could be presented in as simple a manner as is consistent with its character.

Also of great importance, but not included in the above summary, are a number of secondary or derived principles which Hull developed in an effort to bridge the gap between the normal complexities of molar behavior and the abstracted simplicity of his postulate set. Most important among these are the *habit family hierarchy*, the total set of habits which may occur in a given stimulus situation ordered in a hierarchy of strength, and the *goal gradient*, which has already been described.

Systematic Issues

Anyone who aspires to build a theory of behavior like Hull's must face a number of very difficult problems. There is a very low probability that these problems could be solved today, let alone when Hull was alive. However, we can defer criticism of Hull's aspirations until later and look at the nature of the problems which those aspirations led him to face.

Fairly early in the game, one must decide which independent and dependent variables will be discriminated by the theorist and used in the theory. Some guidance is available from experimental practice, but many decisions will remain. For example, will it be profitable to try to predict all response variables from the same theory? Hull emphasized the prediction of latency, amplitude, number of responses to extinction, and probability of responding. Skinner believes that rate of response is the best measure to use; he studies primarily free operants, responses which the animal is free to repeat "at will." Hull studied primarily controlled operants, wherein the experimenter controls opportunities for response emission, as in a runway. His decision to relate his final intervening variable—net generalized reaction potential—to four response measures made it legitimate to ask whether these measures were actually correlated as the theory said they should be. Hull could have avoided embarrassing issues of this kind by making predictions of only one response measure—but he would have lost a great deal of generality in so doing.

Similar problems had to be faced at the level of the intervening variables. For example, there is Hull's decision to have essentially only a single excitatory learning construct, $_sH_R$. If a theorist were working today, he might feel it necessary to have distinct constructs (or distinct theories) for different kinds of learning; for example, food-motivated learning might be distinguished from sex-motivated learning within the theory.

A very general problem connected with the intervening variables concerns what we might call their *reality status.* Hull and his colleagues no doubt had hundreds of discussions about whether it was wise to give the constructs of the theory a physiological interpretation. We have been characterizing Hull's intervening variables as "organismic," which implies some physiological commitment. A more neutral description would be simply that the intervening variables are intratheoretical—which they indubitably are—rather than intraorganismic, which they may or may not be. We shall discuss the characteristics of constructs in more detail in Chapter 13, since there are many facets to the problem.

Even after the constructs of a system are isolated and their general type decided upon, there remain problems concerning the definition of each construct and the specification of construct interrelationships. As an example of such problems, we might take the innocuous-looking N, the number of reinforced trials. What is a reinforced trial? Both Hull's earlier concept of reinforcement as need reduction and his later emphasis on drive-stimulus reduction as the necessary condition for reinforcement failed to eliminate the possibility of circularity. Thus, one could proceed to look for the need or drive-stimulus reduction *after* observing that behavior was strengthened in situations in which the experimenter did not intentionally reduce any need and in which no obvious drive stimulus was reduced. Hull's difficulty with the concept of reinforcement shows how hard it is to construct good definitions. The way in which looseness in the definition of reinforcement makes the concept of N imprecise illustrates the way in which problems with one definition can affect other concepts throughout the theoretical effort.

The specification of construct interrelationships is at least as fertile a source of problems. The habit construct $_SH_R$ can again serve as an example. In Hull's early theory, several variables, including drive (D) and incentive (K), influenced habit. Habit then influenced reaction potential. Since habit changed slowly and continously, it was not possible to derive sudden shifts in performance from the theory. Since such shifts occurred in the latent learning experiments (Hilgard & Bower, 1966), a change in the theory was obviously needed. Hull changed the construct interrelationships so that D and K affected $_SE_R$ rather than $_SH_R$, and the rapid change in response strength following changes in deprivation or incentive became possible. We are not implying that Hull changed the construct interrelationships *in order to explain* latent learning. Both Hilgard and Bower (1966) and Koch (1954) believe the change was made so that $_SH_R$ could more easily be quantified. It is clear, however, that the change in construct interrelationships did make it possible to explain some latent-learning phenomena, at least qualitatively.

The more precise statement of the relationship between constructs itself created additional controversies. Let us take $_SH_R$ as an example again. Its mathematical relationship to number of trials (N) was postulated to be as follows:

$$_SH_R = 1 - 10^{-aN}$$

Trials were assumed to be evenly spaced, and the constant a was thought to be approximately 0.03 in numerical value (Hull, 1951, p. 32).

This clear mathematical statement implies that each trial imparts an increment to the strength of $_SH_R$ and thus indirectly to the tendency to respond. Although this is not truly a continuous function, since N takes only discrete values,

Hull's theory was called a *continuity* theory to distinguish it from the view that learning is a basically sudden, or an all-or-none process. The latter view would be exemplified by the Gestalt position, which was that learning is sudden and insightful and thus noncontinuous. The starkness of Hull's mathematical statements made disagreements stand out nakedly and resulted in controversies like the continuity-noncontinuity controversy and the latent-learning controversy and led to questions about the generality of drives in activating habits.

Criticisms of Hullian System

Few psychologists have met such searching and often vehement criticism as Hull has. As a leading neobehaviorist, he inherited the kind of criticism that had earlier been accorded Watson. Much of this criticism has been polemic, or based on fundamental methodological or theoretical differences of opinion, and much seems to have been trivial or even personal in nature. Nevertheless, the solid critical points persistently lodged against Hull merit our attention.

Synthetic Approach. As we have seen, Hull attempted to work out a complete and comprehensive theoretical account of mammalian behavior almost at a single stroke. His systematic venture was essentially a synthetic one. He endeavored to fashion and put together the pieces of his puzzle in advance of much research. In Hull's defense, however, it must be said that he started with such empirical evidence as he could find and persistently tried to build up additional evidence.

Hull attempted to emulate the formal elegance of the systems of Euclid and Newton within a much shorter time than these beautifully integrated formal systems required for their development. The neatness and elegance of the final product in the case of such formal theory hide the fitfulness of actual development; it may be that theoretical progress is expedited by less ambitious efforts at the start. It is now generally conceded, even by many of those sympathetic to the Hullian brand of psychology, that his efforts represented an overly optimistic approach to an exceedingly complex set of problems.

Particularistic Approach. Perhaps the most persistent criticism from sympathetic sources has been that Hull relied too much upon certain particular values of critical variables within special experimental circumstances. The problem of generality, always a knotty one in behavior theory, was noted early by Koch (1944, p. 283) in his review of *Principles of behavior*; the point has more recently been made by Hilgard and Bower (1966, p. 186), who have cited the dependence of Hull's system upon particular constants from rat bar-pressing and human eyelid experimentation.

An indication of the extreme particularism of certain aspects of Hull's theorizing, in the sense of dependence upon particular experimental setups, may be seen in his provisional definition of the *wat* (honoring *Watson*) as the unit of reaction potential (1951, p. 100):

The wat is the mean standard deviation of the momentary reaction potential ($_sE_R$) of standard albino rats, 90 days of age, learning a simple manipulative act requiring a 10-gram pressure by 24-hour distributed trials under 23 hours' hunger, water available, with reward in the form of a 2.5-gram pellet of the usual dry dog food, the mean being taken from all the reinforcement trials producing the habit strength from .75 to .85 habs inclusive.

The improbability of successful generalization from such particular values of food weight and manipulandum pressure to other variables in animal behavior itself, let alone more complex behavioral functions of higher mammalian forms such as humans, should be quite evident. Thus while Hull's specificity is in some respects admirable, the aspirations of his theorizing seem rather far removed from the actual achievements. Reservations concerning the generality of his theory were made increasingly by Hull in his later writings (cf. Koch, 1954, pp. 167ff.) and are especially evident in the more restricted tone of his final work (Hull, 1952).

The only reasonable answer to these criticisms is simply that the results will determine the efficacy of the approach. More important, this is also the only answer to the more general criticism made of S-R theorists: that they oversimplify complex behavioral problems. Until we try, we cannot really be sure whether an approach such as Hull's will be adequate to account for the complexities of mammalian behavior, and the only scientific way to be sure is to try.

Logical Weakness. Probably the most telling critical attack upon Hull's theory involves the demonstration that his system was not at all the tightly knit, logical one that he intended it to be and that many for awhile after its publication believed it to be. Hull sometimes failed to build in logically necessary connections between his constructs. A number of careful critical attacks have appeared. Koch's (1954) critique is particularly devastating because of its extremely detailed documentation and logical sophistication (in spite of his unsympathetic and sometimes unfair attitude). The easy testability of construct relationships that Hull envisioned is now seen to be largely illusory. Cotton (1955) gives a persuasive and beautifully worked-out demonstration of the impossibility of making predictions from Hull's theory as it was presented. Difficulties remain even when "friendly" assumptions are made in the attempt to make derivations possible. We are forced to conclude that Hull's theory was not finished even in the logical sense.

Two reactions to the growing realization of the logical inadequacy of Hull's theorizing are typical: first, a marked swing to a purely descriptive kind of positivism, such as that provided by Skinner; and second, an intensification of the attention paid to so-called miniature systems, whereby more limited problem areas are more thoroughly attacked (cf. Chapter 3). Hull himself showed signs of limiting his approach in *A behavior system* (1952), where he systematically explored problem areas and emphasized the overall system less than previously.

Hull's Contributions

Objective Terminology and Methodology. Hull's own life was that of a scientist and scholar, a life of the mind. But in his psychology he determined to start with action, stay with action, and see how far action could carry him. His terms, therefore, were not new names for old concepts. *Inhibition, habit strength, reaction potential*—these words had some of their creator's active vitality, ringing forth with the promise of carrying out the evangelical behavioristic program thrust upon the incredulous world at Watson's psychological revival meeting. The type of methodology implied by these terms will not be forgotten, whatever the fate of the theory in which Hull embedded them.

We believe that Hull's most important contribution to psychology was his demonstration of the value of setting one's sights upon the ultimate goal of a thoroughly scientific and systematic behavior theory. He lived his own scientific life in pursuit of that goal and thereby influenced even those who disagreed most vehemently with the details of his work. Few psychologists have had so deep and enduring an effect on the professional motivation of so many researchers. He popularized the strictly objective behavioristic approach as it had never been popularized previously.

New Problem Areas. Hull opened new problem areas in a rather peculiar sense. He did not develop important new pieces of apparatus or initiate research in previously untouched areas. Rather, he reconceived ways of viewing problems and suggested new relationships to be studied. He was a theoretical psychologist, as some physicists are theoretical physicists. Unfortunately, he was a theoretician preceded by no Einstein, Newton, Copernicus, or perhaps even Archimedes in the field of psychology. Nevertheless, when he formulated a postulate or derived a theorem from his postulate set, other investigators were prone to perform experiments to test the stated relationships; for example, after Hull stated his belief about the shape of the generalization gradient, research focused on the empirical determination of the gradient. The very attempt to formalize a theory of behavior forced Hull and his followers to see what must be known before the formalization could be completed. Key concepts, such as stimulus, and processes, such as reinforcement, had to undergo intensive examination.

Although Hull was most strongly attacked by cognitive theorists and field theorists (cf. Chapter 11), in one respect his system was more fieldlike than the typical field theory. Hull specified as many of the relevant variables as he could reasonably conceive and also stated their hypothesized mode of interaction (cf. Figure 10-1). Not only is this high degree of theoretical specificity a far cry from the largely speculative utilization of conditioning by the early behaviorists, such as Watson, but it is also a good deal more concrete than anything offered by Hull's critics, who were more prone to counter the Watsonian speculation with their own speculation than to provide specification of the composition of the psychological field (cf. Estes, 1954b).

Finally, Hull has been criticized by some psychologists of other persuasions for giving too much direction to research effort. He and his system concentrated effort on the solution of those theoretical problems which he believed had to be solved before behavior theory could make significant advances. However, some have felt that we cannot, at the present time, afford to decide the direction of research on formal theoretical grounds. Rather, those empirical areas should be studied which are producing results that are interesting in themselves. We believe that there is value in both views and that it is fortunate there are large numbers of psychologists available to take both paths; Hull made a great contribution in providing one kind of guidance.

Hull's Place in History

Clark Hull's place in psychological history seems to be assured. He may have been one of those rare men who actively influence their times to such an extent that they can redirect a science. On the other hand, one may prefer the alternative view that this apparent influence is an illusion resulting from a man's merely moving within the historical stream of events and so actually moving *with* the times. The latter point of view is one that Boring (1950) has particularly emphasized (as stressed in the concept of *Zeitgeist*, or spirit of the times), in contrast to Carlyle's "great man" interpretation of history.

Whatever the causation, it is true that Clark Hull found psychology still wrestling hard with broad systematic issues, and he left large segments of it wrestling with criticisms of his postulates and theorems. In a sense both kinds of wrestling are misspent. The systematic issues were elusive foes for the psychologist, and Hull's system revealed gaps to the serious student that made criticism almost superfluous. Yet Hull taught psychology a new type of game, one so enthralling that now all but the strictest of positivists want to play.

It is paradoxical that Hull changed metatheory by being concerned with theory. His predecessors, the earlier behaviorists, had done their utmost to turn psychology away from verbal issues and toward more empirically meaningful problems. But this never quite came off. Hull brought it off with a positive effect. Hull was certainly deeply and intelligently concerned with metatheory, and his system is the grandest ever attempted in the behavioristic tradition. His distinction and his influence are based on the fact that he did not stop there. His attempt to push on into the tangled unknown where specific issues are resolved was largely unsuccessful. That was inevitable at the time. He did not come back with maps that were likely to be serviceable, but none before Hull had even given psychological explorers much of a feel for what a psychological theory should be.

Another paradox is Hull's lack of rigor. His system had the appearance but not the reality. He never had time to smooth out wrinkles. In this he is in the company of all psychology's greatest men. If there is in psychology a man excessively afraid of being wrong, that man has published no extensive theory. Hull, even while striving for a rigorous statement, had to stand with those who had no such fear. In this rather peculiar way, he carved his niche in history between the systematists and those following him who will construct more lasting behavior theories.

For a time, it seemed that Hull had made of psychology his own private yard. In the early fifties, he was cited far more often than any other psychologist in the *Journal of Experimental Psychology* (Ammons, 1962), and his *Principles of behavior* (1943) was the most frequently cited publication, with its nearest rival cited less than a fourth as often in the *Journal of Experimental Psychology* and three other journals included in the tabulation. Between 1930 and 1950, Hull was regarded as the leading psychological theorist (Coan & Zagona, 1962, p. 319). Recently, however, it would appear that his fall from favor has been rapid. The pendulum of theoretical style has swung rapidly toward primarily inductive procedures, but there are signs that it is swinging back. Mathematical modeling of a less grand scope is becoming popular (see Chapter 13), and there is no denying Hull's priority and early dominance in this type of endeavor.

Hull's Students

Kenneth W. Spence (1907-1967) was the most important successor to Hull, as far as the type of theory Hull was trying to develop is concerned. He took his doctoral training at Yale, where he was strongly influenced by his association with Hull, although he took his degree under Yerkes, and he worked for four years at the Yale Laboratories of Primate Biology in Orange Park. From 1938 to 1964, he was at the University of Iowa, where he worked very actively in research on learning and motivation. In 1964 he moved to the University of Texas, where he remained until his death at the relatively early age of 59. While at Iowa he published a number of theoretical papers with Gustav Bergmann, the philosopher. Spence's major works are *Behavior theory and conditioning* (1956) and *Behavior theory and learning: Selected papers* (1960). The former was based on the 1955 Silliman Lectures at Yale; Spence was the first psychologist to be honored by an invitation to deliver these lectures.

Spence's first important research and theorizing dealt with the problem of discrimination learning (1936; 1937a, 1937b). He produced a classic demonstration of how a conditioning theory involving positive and negative reaction tendencies interacting algebraically can account for the primary data of discrimination and transposition. His tilt with the Gestaltists on the explanation of these phenomena (cf. Chapter 8) is an excellent illustration of opposing approaches to psychological explanation. On one side we see Spence operating in the reductive mode characteristic of associationistic psychology, of S-R psychology as a more modern version, of Hull, and of Spence himself. Lloyd Morgan's canon is one of the first principles of theorizing for this tradition. Spence's theorizing on discrimination and transposition serves as an inspiring model of simplicity and clarity for exponents of this general approach. Hull's early work on the derivation of complex behaviors from conditioning was similar in this respect.

While recognizing his debt to basic Hullian theory, Spence was careful to point out the differences between his own theoretical efforts and those of Hull (cf. especially his 1956 book). He was less concerned with the comprehensive formality with which Hull endowed his work and more concerned with the quantification of variables. He did not share Hull's enthusiasm for physiological suggestions and speculations, feeling that until physiology has more to offer psychology, it can most profitably be kept out of behavior theory. He said (1956, p. 57) that he had not accepted the Hullian emphasis on need reduction as the essential component of the reinforcement process; he made no specific physiological assumption about the nature of the action of a reinforcer. Finally, he was much more cautious (1956) than Hull in regard to "hazarding a set of theoretical postulates on the basis of a minimum of empirical data" (p. 58). Spence also pointed out that, on the related question of generality, he intended his own work to be restricted to the particular experimental situations from which his data came. Spence adopted the basic Hullian approach and many of the theoretical constructs, but put less emphasis on the postulational approach and modified some of the postulates that he did accept.

Spence treated the key motivational variables somewhat differently from the way Hull did. Both men assumed that there was a multiplicative relationship between motivation and habit in the production of response (reaction potential). Spence, however, theorized that incentive and deprivation factors added to produce motivation; Hull had incentive and deprivation in a multiplicative relationship. Spence's formulation allowed for the occurrence of a response even when either incentive or drive was at zero, as long as the other factor was nonzero. Hull's multiplicative relationship called for a zero value of $_sE_R$ when either incentive or drive was zero; it is difficult to embarrass Hull on this point, however, since it is not easy to be certain that drive is completely absent. Neither is it easy to choose between the additive and multiplicative assumptions by doing a parametric study in which D and K are varied. The reason is that K is assumed to be related to fractional anticipatory goal responses and the stimuli produced by them. Thus motivation has come to have a learned component, and the relationship between drive, incentive, and reaction potential is further complicated. The two theories have, in a sense, been given a "side chain" which must be taken into account when making predictions. That is, suppose we are computing $_sE_R$ for a response after several trials. Its amount will depend on K. The amount of K will in turn depend on the $_sE_R$ of the fractional anticipatory goal responses conditioned to the cues present. Thus we must compute $_sE_R$ twice, the first time in the theoretical side chain that determines a value for K.

Spence also took quite a different view of reinforcement from that of Hull. In his later work, he assumed that habit formation was not dependent on reinforcement. He suggested a two-factor learning theory which is precisely reversed from the usual one. Usually, contiguity factors are assumed to account for classical conditioning, and reinforcement for instrumental conditioning. Spence's contiguity explanation for instrumental conditioning does not necessitate any change in the basic form of the theory; it simply changes the definition of what constitutes a trial for the purposes of the theory. For Hull, a trial was a *reinforced* trial. For Spence, reinforcement did not matter; it mattered only that the response was performed in the presence of the stimulus. On this matter, Spence's position resembled Tolman's (see Chapter 11); Spence was interested in Tolman's competing theory and was close to Tolman in some of his methodological attitudes (Kendler, 1967).

Following his early development of theory applicable to simple discrimination learning, Spence directed or supervised research projects on eyelid conditioning, latent learning, transposition, secondary reinforcement, and "anxiety" as measured by a questionnaire technique (see Spence, 1960). His work, much of it in collaboration with Janet Taylor Spence, on the relationship between anxiety and learning is widely quoted in articles on personality.

One of Spence's preoccupations in his later work was with the disentanglement of cognitive factors from the results of human eyelid conditioning studies. Earlier work had demonstrated apparent qualitative differences between eyelid conditioning in animals lower than man and in man. Human subjects typically extinguished conditioned eyeblinks in a very small number of trials, typically one or two, while animals might continue to make conditioned responses for hundreds of trials. Spence and his students used an ingenious masking task to conceal the true nature of the experiment, thereby apparently eliminating the influence of inhibitory cognitive factors and obtaining extinction behavior in human subjects that paralleled the behavior typically seen in animal subjects (see Spence, 1966).

This last work of Spence's ties in with the history of psychological systems in an interesting way. For one thing, the experimental situation is especially designed to reduce one aspect of the human subjects' functioning to the level of animal functioning. After Darwin, those working in a reductive tradition had often had to face the charge that they were in general trying to reduce human capabilities to the level of animal capabilities. Spence's work on eyelid conditioning thus exemplifies at the experimental level a reductive tendency which too frequently took place only at a theoretical level. At the same time, the attempt at reduction forced a clear recognition of a qualitative difference between human and animal functioning. The differences, like the similarities, have too often remained nebulous and theoretical. In following up on Hull's reductive program, Spence found factors which, at least at this time, cannot successfully be accounted for reductively. He thus, like many honest scientists, made a kind of contribution to those who hold opposing viewpoints about the nature of man.

Hull had a number of other students who became important theoreticians in their own right. We shall single out only two of them: O. H. Mowrer, who will be discussed briefly later in this chapter because of his development of a two-factor theory of learning, and Neal Miller (1909-   ), who has been almost incredibly productive, largely in empirical investigation but also to some extent in theoretical developments that grow rather directly out of the data. He worked with John Dollard to integrate learning theory with psychoanalytic theory in *Personality and psychotherapy* (Dollard & Miller, 1950). This work probably grew out of Hull's seminars of 1936 and 1937 on the relationships between these apparently diverse areas of psychology. In turn, there is little doubt that it helped to pave the way for more recent developments in behavior modification.

Miller has also done more than enough work to constitute a successful, complete career in physiological psychology. Some of these studies, and many of his behavioral studies, are reviewed in his article in the Koch series (N. E. Miller, 1959).

Some of Miller's experiments have involved electrical stimulation of brain centers; some, the effects of fistula feeding; and some, preloading the stomach with different substances before eating or engaging in instrumental behaviors. Still other studies were examinations of feeding without any nutritive consequences, and several have involved various behavioral effects of drugs.

It is not surprising that Miller has been led to a careful and sophisticated consideration of the starting and stopping of behavior. For one thing, he was aware of the fact that, under certain conditions, electrical stimulation of centers in the brain will be alternatively started and stopped by rats free to do both. For another, he knew that feeding may sometimes be started by brain stimulation or stopped by stomach loading and that feeding may *not* stop when it "should" after hypothalamic brain lesions.

Thinking about "go" and "stop" mechanisms may in turn have helped to lead Miller to his theoretical views on the nature of reinforcement. He was also exposed in 1954 to some of Sheffield's ideas (Haber, 1966, pp. 98ff.). Sheffield suggested that an *increase* in drive, produced directly or indirectly by reward, might account for learning better than the decrease in drive or drive stimulus typically assumed by earlier theories. Hull and Miller would both have, at one time, embraced the view that reinforcement is effective because it reduces the intensity of drive stimuli. It is reasonable to assume that Sheffield was instrumental in changing Miller's theory of reinforcement.

Miller suggested (1963) that reinforcing operations are effective because they activate a "go" mechanism. Responses occurring when the mechanism is activated are intensified and increase in frequency, according to Miller's view. Learning requires only contiguity between stimulus and response, but learning is increased by increases in the intensity or frequency of the pairing. Reinforcement (activation of the "go" mechanism) indirectly increases learning by increasing the opportunity for contiguity to produce learning.

This ingenious proposal is similar to the suggestions of several other theorists. It bears a striking resemblance to Guthrie's theory in that contiguity alone is supposed to suffice for learning (see the discussion later in this chapter). Thorndike's "confirming reaction" is something like Miller's "go" mechanism; the latter, however, is supposed to affect learning indirectly through increasing performance (which is the way Tolman would also have seen the problem), rather than directly through strengthening connections, as Thorndike had suggested.

Recently, Miller has been involved in a number of studies on whether autonomic responses can be conditioned through operant techniques (N. E. Miller, 1969). This work treats a problem which was central for Hull; we have seen that Hull accepted the Thorndikian principle of effect as a basic condition for learning. Hull had rejected his own earlier tentative commitment to contiguity (as in classical conditioning) as a sufficient condition for learning. Miller's work, which shows that the autonomic system is surprisingly susceptible to modification via effect learning, supports Hull's later formulation, albeit indirectly.

Ironically, at about the same time that Miller was enlarging the scope of behavior which could be modified through reward learning, Brown and Jenkins (1968) reported that key pecking could be shaped simply by illuminating the key prior to food delivery, that is, through a procedure very much like classical conditioning! It may be that we are about to lose one of our traditional distinctions, that between classical and operant conditioning. It may emerge rephrased as a distinction between response-independent and response-dependent schedules (Staddon & Simmelhag, 1971).

REINFORCEMENT THEORY: SKINNERIAN POSITIVISM

Skinner's Career

B. F. Skinner (1904-   ) has had a most remarkable career. It is similar to that of Sir Francis Galton in its demonstration of great breadth of interest and exceptional ingenuity of empirical operations. Skinner's contributions have been kaleidoscopic. His lively intellectual curiosity has refused to be contained within the narrow confines of a specialized area. He has concerned himself with an analysis of verbal learning, with missile-guiding pigeons, with teaching machines, and with the control of behavior by scheduled reinforcement. The ingenious apparatus to his credit includes an automatized baby-tending device, used with one of his own children and later marketed commercially. In his leisure time, Skinner has even managed to write a novel on a utopian theme, *Walden two* (1948b).

Skinner received his doctoral degree from Harvard in 1931. Following several years of postdoctoral fellowships he taught at the University of Minnesota (1936 to 1945) and at Indiana University (1945 to 1947), where he was chairman. He returned to Harvard in 1947. During the 1930s and 1940s Skinner's influence was less than that of Hull and Tolman, but it is now far greater (Coan & Zagona, 1962). His influence on younger psychologists has been especially impressive. Part of the reason for his ascendance is disillusionment with comprehensive theory of the Hullian type. Skinner's positivistic inclinations are at the opposite pole from Hull's fondness for the development of formal theories.

Methodological Emphasis

Skinner is best known for his insistence upon a strictly descriptive, atheoretical approach to behavior research. He has long felt that the state of knowledge in psychology is inadequate to justify elaborate, formal theorizing. Skinnerians often state that when theories are developed and espoused, personal satisfactions from confirmations and disconfirmations, rather than acquisition of facts, tend to become the issue. Skinner believes that more effective progress toward the prediction and control of behavior can be obtained through a careful collection of data. The "functional analysis of behavior" has been his objective. In this, experimental techniques are to be utilized, and the relationships between variables are to be established. Eventually, Skinner holds, sufficient empirical relationships will be established to justify the formation of some limited theories or more comprehensive generalizations, but these must be prepared with caution. Such integrative principles should be allowed to develop, not forced prematurely.

Skinner is not against all theory, and it may be that he believes psychology is more nearly ready for theory now than it was forty years ago, when he entered the field. At any rate, he has said (Evans, 1968): "But I look forward to an overall theory of human behavior which will bring together a lot of facts and express them in a more general way. That kind of theory I would be very much interested in prompting, and I consider myself to be a theoretician" (p. 88). In fact, Skinner has taken pains to emphasize his interest in theory, subtitling one of his books (1969) *A theoretical analysis* and detailing in its preface the numerous theoretical articles he has written. It is dangerous to overgeneralize with Skinner, just as it is with a Titchener or a Thorndike—or with any great figure in the history of psychology. Brilliant men seldom take positions as extreme as the positions ascribed to them by incautious critics.

A second important methodological emphasis of Skinner has been his insistence upon a thorough analysis of the behavior of a single organism and his disinclination to use large groups of subjects. Large numbers of subjects have too often been used, he contends, to cover up lack of experimental controls; with adequate controls, a single subject, or a very small number of subjects, should be sufficient. The use of large groups, he says, also leads indirectly to other difficulties. When a large group is used, the experimenter usually attends primarily or exclusively to certain statistical properties of the group, rather than to the behaviors of the individuals within it. Individual variations may then be lost, and the statistical measures may not describe the characteristics of *any* of the individuals within the group (Sidman, 1960). Skinner does not believe that such experiments are likely to lead to a science in which prediction and control of the behavior of individual organisms are possible. On the other hand, when large amounts of data from a single animal are collected under stringently controlled conditions, the results will be clearly replicable with other individuals. No statistical techniques will be necessary.

Third, Skinner has objected particularly to physiological speculation in the guise of theory. He has been against what he has considered excessive and futile physiologizing; when physiological data have more concrete points on which behavioral observations can turn, they should be permitted to influence psychology, but not before. This generally aphysiological attitude has been shared by Spence, and together they have contributed to the prominence of the so-called empty-organism era in recent psychological thinking. Even on this issue, it is easy to overdramatize Skinner's attitude. His opposition to too much physiologizing seems to be largely a matter of self-discipline. He says (Evans, 1968): "I have never said anything against the study of physiology, and I feel that I have done my best to facilitate it by clarifying the problems that the physiologist has to deal with. At the same time, I don't want to borrow support from physiology when my formulation breaks down." (p. 22).

A fourth major methodological characteristic of Skinner has been his emphasis on operant, as compared with respondent, behavior. Skinner early distinguished between responses made in direct response to stimulation (such as classical conditioned responses of a Pavlovian sort) and those emitted by the organism in the absence of any apparent external stimulation (the operant). The eliciting stimuli for the operant are unknown. The free operant is an operant whose emission does not directly preclude successive emissions of the same response; its study has been especially favored by Skinnerians. The free operant is best exemplified in the case of the bar pressing of rats and the key pecking of pigeons. Both animals usually respond in the Skinner box. These boxes are insulated against noise, and temperature and lighting are closely controlled. Data gathered under such controlled conditions tend to be more uniform than the data that are usually available. Skinner has typically used the rate of emission of a response as his dependent variable; the response is a simple one, and the measure, therefore, is relatively uncomplicated. A cumulative recorder which directly produces a cumulative frequency curve of responses, rather than the typical learning curve, has been used to record the data.

The free operant as the object of study, the use of rate as the primary datum, and the cumulative recorder as an instrument—these three, in Skinner's view, constitute a unique combination that makes for progress. Rate becomes a meaningful measure only when free operants are being studied, and the cumulative recorder shows rate characteristics over a long period of time. The experimenter can see what is happening to rate almost as soon as it happens, and he can change his procedures if that seems appropriate. Skinner (1966, p. 16) points out how important it was in chemistry to use dull, colorless weight as a measure in order to bring chaos to order in that field of study. He thinks the use of rate as a measure may have similar effects in psychology.

Major Contributions

Perhaps the most significant feature of Skinner's research and thinking has been his continuing work on the problem of reinforcement scheduling in operant conditioning. His early emphasis on intermittent reinforcement (1938) culminated in the exhaustive volume *Schedules of reinforcement* (Ferster & Skinner, 1957). He worked first with the rat in the Skinner box, subsequently with the pigeon in a comparable chamber, and ultimately with human subjects. Use of children as subjects in operant conditioning studies involving various reinforcement schedules has become a very important feature of behavioral research, involving psychologists of varying degrees of adherence to Skinnerian principles.

This research with children shades over into applied work with children (Risley, 1968); in the work cited, Risley and his co-workers used operant conditioning techniques to teach verbal and other behaviors to culturally deprived children. Ullman and Krasner (1965) present a host of cases in which behavior was modified in children and in adult psychotics by the application of operant techniques. Their book is only one of the earlier ones reporting what is happening in the behavior modification movement. The primary tool used by workers in this tradition is reinforcement systematically applied. This systematic application usually involves depriving the patient of the reinforcer and establishing a schedule in which reinforcement is strictly dependent on the behavior of the patient.

A number of examples may be cited from everyday-life situations to illustrate the effectiveness of intermittent reinforcement in controlling behavior. One of the most apt is the control of behavior exercised by the occasional payoff of the slot machine or by other gambling devices. Examination of other situations indicates that reinforcement is characteristically scheduled intermittently, rather than continuously, as it has more typically been scheduled in learning experiments. Thus the child's behavior produces approbation in the parent, but not invariably; the student succeeds on examinations, but also fails or misses particular items; and the typical fisherman returns home empty-handed from a very large proportion of his trips.

In laboratory investigations of the effects of different schedules of reinforcement, four major types have been used. These are *fixed interval* (FI), in which the first response made after some fixed period of time is reinforced; *variable interval* (VI), in which the first response made after some variable period of time is reinforced; *fixed ratio* (FR), in which the first response made after some fixed number of responses is reinforced; and *variable ratio* (VR), in which the first response made after some variable number of responses is reinforced. The two variable schedules (VI and VR) and the fixed-ratio schedule (FR) characteristically produce remarkably steady and high rates of responding. The FI schedule ideally produces more cyclical cumulative performance curves featuring bursts of responses just preceding the usual reinforcement time, with pauses or very low rates of response immediately following reinforcement. This pattern of responding gives the cumulative curve its so-called scalloped appearance.

Skinner's research with control of animal behavior is another long-standing contribution. He developed the method of *shaping*. Shaping is accomplished by giving an animal a reward if his response approximates the desired response. For example, if a rat is to be taught to climb a ladder, he would first be given food if he simply approached the ladder; then he might be required to reach up the ladder, then to get on it, and finally to climb it in order to receive his food reward. Skinner's method has been taken over by a large number of animal trainers. One of his early students, Keller Breland, left the academic field to become an animal trainer and has been very successful (Breland & Breland, 1951, 1961).

The observations made by the Brelands in the course of training many species of animals led them to depart in some respects from the Skinnerian views on operant conditioning. The Brelands noted (1961) numerous incidents of failure to teach the operant behaviors desired. For example (see Breland & Breland, 1966, pp. 67-68), raccoons, pigs, squirrel monkeys, and other animals often have trouble letting go of a token which they are learning to insert into a food dispenser, much as humans insert coins into machines. The Brelands believed that more primitive food-related behaviors were activated on earlier trials and that these more primitive behaviors interfered with the performance of the operant response. They described this "instinctive drift" as follows (1961, p. 684):

The general principle seems to be that wherever an animal has strong instinctive behaviors in the area of the conditioned response, after continued running the organism will drift toward the instinctive behavior, to the detriment of the conditioned behavior and even to the delay or preclusion of the reinforcement.

The Brelands, although they were nurtured by Skinner in the environmentalistic tradition which has been a common feature of the behavioristic outlook, have been prominent among psychologists partly responsible for the swing toward nativism, which the ethologists initiated and which is evident in American psychology today. Lockard (1971) has documented that part of the nativistic trend which is most closely related to animal behavior, detailing some of the contributions of the Brelands and of ethologists like Lorenz and Tinbergen. Lockard's conclusions come through clearly in statements like the following (1971, p. 171):

Scientifically speaking, only two pieces of information were needed to bring behavior into the modern synthesis of the new biology: the fact that behavior has a genetic basis, thus making it heritable and therefore subject to natural selection; and the fact that behavior, or rather, particular behaviors, are adaptive—that they bear intimate relationships to particulars of the environment such that some kind of advantage results. The genetic basis of hundreds and hundreds of particular behaviors has been demonstrated beyond doubt, and the adaptive significance of particular behaviors has been demonstrated in hundreds of cases.

During World War II Skinner conducted applied research on animals under the auspices of General Mills in Minneapolis. Apparently he was well along in the development of a training program whereby pigeons could be used in the guiding device in a bomb when the development of atomic weapons ended the war and removed the immediate urgency from this research. The project has been declassified, and a fascinating account given by Skinner (1960).

One of the most striking of Skinner's demonstrations of the potency of shaping in control of animal behavior is his research on "superstitious behavior" in pigeons (1948a). He demonstrated that clear-cut and uniquely individual responses could be quickly developed in hungry pigeons when they are given food at regular intervals regardless of their behavior. Such an arrangement, with the delivery of food not contingent on the animal's pressing a bar, pecking a key, or engaging in any specified behavior, constitutes a *noncontingent* schedule (also sometimes called an *incontingent* schedule). In such a situation some response, which just happens to precede a reinforcement early in the session, will generally be fixated and will predominate in the behavioral repertoire of the animal during the experimental period. This occurs because one or two early reinforcements increase the rate at which the particular response is emitted, thus making more and more likely its occurrence just prior to subsequent reinforcements. The particular response strengthened, such as wing flapping, neck craning, leg raising, etc., varies from one animal to the next. Probably the outcome of this procedure depends on the interaction between the animal's initial repertoire in the situation and the particular schedule of reinforcement delivery. Herrnstein (1966) reports on a study in which the animal is first taught a response on a fixed-interval schedule and then is shifted to a noncontingent schedule; this procedure gives the experimenter control over the animal's repertoire, at least in that it allows him to specify which response shall be of highest frequency when the noncontingent condition is initiated. Under these conditions, Herrnstein found that the high-frequency response was maintained at a rate well above the operant level over the course of many sessions. This result, however, probably depends on the relationship between the contingent conditions and the noncontingent conditions, since Edwards, West, and Jackson (1968) found that response rates fell fairly rapidly when noncontingent conditions were instituted.

The concept of superstitious behavior has been generalized to explain some aspects of the behavior that occurs under contingent conditions. For example, a number of different stereotyped responses may occur in different subjects, even though no particular topography is necessary to produce the reinforcement. It seems likely that some of the topographies are more effortful than necessary. The topographies may be said to be conditioned superstitiously because of their adventitious pairing with reinforcement.

Skinner has pointed out the fact that the connection between response and reinforcement in most operant work is simply a temporal relationship; as he says (1966): "The response produces food only in the sense that food follows it—a Humean version of causality" (p. 14). He is also aware that superstitious behaviors arise from response-reinforcement relationships not specified by the experimenter, and he has generalized this thinking to contingent conditions (1966): "It is characteristic of most contingencies that they are not precisely controlled, and in any case they are effective only in combination with the behavior which the organism brings to the experiment" (pp. 20-21). Schoenfeld, Cumming, and Hearst (1968) have suggested a classification scheme for schedules of reinforcement which characterized them in terms of strictly temporal variables; the critical properties of schedules dealt with were the length of the period during which reinforcement was available and the total "cycle length," which included the period of unavailability as well as the period of availability. If the animal responded during the period of availability, the reinforcement was delivered; during the remainder of the period, responding produced no results. They found a general response-rate increase when, for a fixed-cycle time, reinforcement availability time was increased. Conversely, rates tended to decrease when the reinforcement availability time decreased.

This work and Skinner's own thinking would seem to be pointing toward a description of contingencies couched in more basic terms than those currently used. Describing a schedule as "fixed-interval fifteen-seconds" leaves out critical properties of the relationship between reinforcement delivery and the organism's behavior. It also encourages a distinction between such a schedule and a fixed-ratio twenty-five-second schedule, whether or not such a distinction is important in a particular context. Finally, the similarities which may exist between intermittent reinforcement schedules and free food delivery on a noncontingent basis may tend to be obscured. A general description in terms of more basic properties of the various schedules as they relate to the organism's responses should make it possible to describe all the types of schedules in a common framework with noncontingent reinforcement delivery.

The first factor that comes to mind is the probability that a reinforcement will follow any specified response under study. For example, it is easy to specify these probabilities in a bar-pressing experiment with a traditional fixed-ratio five-second schedule, at least for the bar-pressing response. The probability that each of the first four responses following reinforcement will be itself reinforced is zero. The probability that the fifth response will be reinforced is 1. It is obvious that any desired distribution of probabilities could be scheduled for each cycle of five responses. Any such schedule based on five responses could be called a *cycle-five* schedule to express the fact that the same set of five probabilities repeats throughout a session. The five probabilities could be 0.2, 0.4, 0.6, 0.8, and 1.0, or they could be 0.92, 0.30, 0.61, 0.00, and 0.24. Similar reasoning applies to interval schedules, except that responses are described in terms of the *time* since the last reinforcement rather than in terms of the number of responses since the last reinforcement. In the typical schedule, these probability relationships with the response are kept simple and are specified only with respect to the response being recorded. In a general descriptive scheme, there should be no limitations on the probability distributions, on the property of the response of which the probability is a function, or on the number of responses to which the probability distributions can be attached. In the noncontingent situation the experimenter does not ordinarily specify in advance these probability distributions, but they nevertheless exist in the sense that the animal comes to the situation with various responses occurring at various rates. These rates, in conjunction with the noncontingent rate of delivery of the reinforcer, determine the probability that each of the responses in the repertoire will initially be the one that precedes reinforcement delivery. The delivery of the reinforcement would be expected to change the rates of all the responses in the repertoire and thus to affect the probability that each would precede the second reinforcement.

Two recent papers seem to bear out the expectation that the study of superstitious behavior may be particularly instructive and that it is revealing to consider all the responses in the animal's repertoire, or at least more than one. Staddon and Simmelhag (1971) studied the occurrence of a number of behaviors in a noncontingent reinforcement situation. They found, among other things, that highly characteristic sequences of behaviors occurred; component responses of the sequences never occurred "out of position." These authors compare the results of response-independent and response-dependent schedules and suggest a new view of the modification of adaptive behavior as a result of the comparison of multiple responses in the two situations.

Dunham (1971) uses a somewhat similar multiple-response base-line procedure to examine what happens to several responses in an animal's repertoire when punishment is introduced into an ongoing situation. His study enables him to question the dominant version of punishment theory: that responses are suppressed by punishment because alternative responses are strengthened and compete with them. Dunham also shows that only one of the several alternative responses is usually the beneficiary of the weakening of the punished response. There seems to be little doubt that much future progress will be made through more careful and detailed examination of the relationships between reinforcements or punishers and the animal's ongoing repertoire of behavior.

The average delay time between the reinforced response and the effective reinforcement would also seem to be an important property of a schedule of reinforcement. This delay time is usually held fixed and low in studies of schedules of reinforcement, but is not controlled in studies of the effects of noncontingent reinforcement. When there is a response-reinforcement contingency, the delay would be constant from trial to trial, except for minor variations due to variable equipment operating time or to variations in the time the subject takes to respond to the presence of the reinforcer. However, the response-reinforcement interval would be more variable when noncontingent reinforcements were being delivered and would be longer on the average than in the usual contingent case. It should be clear, however, that only the experimenter knows whether a contingency exists or not. To the animal, the whole situation might look like a game of "find the contingency, if one exists." He could be regarded by us as a causality-detecting machine which examines response-reinforcement relationships to determine whether any qualify as causal relationships. The characteristics of these relationships (which are assumed above to be described by the probability of reinforcement, and the properties of response-reinforcement delays) are *all* the experimental subject has to work with to inform him of the contingency.

The rat, like David Hume, cannot be certain that causality exists. Neither, in the superstitious case, can he be certain that causality does not exist. If Skinner has reduced the relationship to a temporal contiguity, how can the animal know that pressing a bar is more likely to be connected to the delivery of food than standing on his hind legs is? Let us consider the dilemma of our philosopher-rat "thinking" about a serious shock which he just received. At the time of shock onset, he was urinating leisurely in a quiet corner, having begun two seconds previously. The offset of urination was immediate, but the shock persisted while the rat leapt several times about the cage, and it stopped one second after he scratched desperately at the southwest corner. If the rat is well versed in the lore of psychology, he knows that the experimenter could be trying out shock as a punishment for urinating in the corner (and the definition of that response class might be very broad or very narrow). On the other hand, the shock might be serving as a negative reinforcer for the behavior of scratching the southwest corner. Only a further trial, or many trials, will give him the information about response-reinforcement relationships that he needs to sort out the various possibilities. The only difference between the aversive case and the positive-reinforcement case is that both onset and offset are dramatic for aversive stimuli, while we limit our interest for the most part to the *delivery* of positive reinforcement.

If the probability-delay descriptive scheme described above were accepted, the current distinctions between types of schedules might fall into disuse and be regarded as special cases within the more general framework. Precise realizations of such schedules might require computer control of reinforcement delivery and the use of brain stimulation as a reinforcer in order to bring delay under exact control.

The reduction of schedules to the status of special cases within a more general framework might be a precursor of the development of a more comprehensive theory of operant behaviors.

Another of Skinner's central and persistent interests has been research and systematic thinking about verbal behavior. His conceptualization of the important human behavioral problems of language has been influential in the field. This interest culminated in publication of a major work, *Verbal behavior* (1957b). According to Skinner's interpretation, language as verbal behavior is basically similar to other behavior and can be best understood when viewed in this general conceptual framework.

Skinner characterizes verbal behavior as behavior whose reinforcement is mediated by another organism that has been specifically conditioned to mediate such reinforcements. Verbal operants, like other operants, are recognized because of a relationship to an antecedent condition, typically a controlling stimulus. An example of a functional relationship between an antecedent variable and a verbal response would be one's writing "chair" as a response to the object on which he sits. Such responses are called *tacts* by Skinner because their controlling variable is *contact* with an object, event, or property of an object or event. If one says "coffee" because one is deprived of that substance, he is to Skinner emitting a *mand* because of his *demand* for the appropriate reinforcer. Skinner believes that the appropriate course of investigation of language involves just the functional analysis of the relationship between antecedents and verbal behavior. The organism makes no real contribution to verbal behaving, but is best regarded as a locus through which variables act.

Skinner usually receives credit for the great contemporary interest in programmed learning, much of which he probably deserves. We might consider the following, quoted in Boring and Lindzey, 1967, p. 322:

In a window of the little apparatus showed a four-choice question to which the student responded by pressing the key corresponding to the answer he thought right. If it was, the next question turned up, but if not, he had to try again until he did find the right answer—meanwhile a counter kept a cumulative record of his tries. Moreover (two features no device since has had) if a lever were raised, the device was changed into a self-scoring and rewarding testing machine: whatever key was pressed, the next question turned up, but the counter counted only rights; also when the set on a reward dial was reached, a candy lozenge was automatically presented. . . .

This quotation is not from Skinner's autobiography, but from Pressey's, and the machine described was exhibited in 1925. However, teaching machines did not catch on until much later. It is interesting to ask why. The machines themselves have undergone changes, but some highly successful ones are very simple—no more complex than Pressey's much earlier machine. Modern exponents of programmed learning would probably insist that the materials are now better organized and that the technical features of this organization are responsible for the current much greater success of programmed learning.

It is, nevertheless, interesting to contemplate the possibility that the reason for Skinner's success in popularizing this approach to learning, where Pressey had failed thirty years earlier, is that Skinner had better reasons to believe that the technique ought to work. Further, he had a cohesive and enthusiastic group of followers, and Pressey did not. The principles of operant conditioning were working in the control of animal behavior, and concurrent efforts indicated that they would work for the control of human behavior. Thus a *Zeitgeist* was developing within which programmed learning could thrive. It was probably Pressey's fate to be a little too far ahead of his time in 1925.

Most recently, Skinner's latest book, *Beyond freedom and dignity* (1971), threw down the gauntlet to our society. Vice-president Spiro Agnew picked it up (Goodall, 1972). Judging by the fact that the book has been high on the best-seller lists for a long time, the individual members of society are also picking it up. Skinner was no doubt issuing a deliberate challenge when he implied that freedom and dignity, two of our most holy cows, are in the way of progress toward a better world. Agnew, the prototype of a good American Hindu, is hardly ready to eat those cows, though the world starve. Your authors have no comment on whether those cows belong on the street or on the table; however, it seems likely that society is going to take psychology more and more seriously, and Skinner's book is one of the most important events in getting society's attention. It may be that, in the future, psychology will get support more commensurate with the importance of the problems we must deal with.

Criticisms of Skinner

The most persistent attacks have been concentrated on Skinner's positivism. Critics have maintained that Skinner is deluding himself if he believes theory has no value. Theory is inevitable. Every experiment and observation is in some way planned, based on hunches or ideas; therefore, say the critics, it is better to bring the presuppositions into the open and formalize them. Then they can be recognized and critically evaluated rather than hidden. In addition, formal theory in the older sciences has afforded a generality which Skinner's fact gathering alone can never achieve.

Skinner has several replies available. First, he is not antitheoretical; he is only against certain types of theories, either those which are premature or those which are attempts to avoid the necessity for empirical work or for genuine explanation. He does believe that theories may guide investigators into unprofitable efforts to confirm or disconfirm theories, when they might better devote themselves to the exploration of interesting empirical situations. Theories should be primarily inductive, not based on logical guesses. Theories *should* be an end product of scientific endeavor, but they should be proposed only as the data are ready to support them.

Second, Skinner would probably insist that presuppositions need to be kept to a minimum. Premature speculation, even if it is not misleading, is a waste of time. In the worst cases, it will be misleading, a waste of time both directly and indirectly, and a source of personal involvement and controversy.

Skinner has also been criticized for his peripheralism. This kind of argument has two major facets. One involves his aphysiological bias; this is largely a matter of taste. If one prefers not to think in physiological terms, surely this is his privilege. The other involves his refusal to posit intervening processes of a psychological sort (such as Hull's habit strength or inhibition, Spence's incentive motivation, and the like). Here too the issue is one of personal preference, but difficulties arise when one side attempts to force its views on the other.

We have already noted in passing Skinner's own contention that he is not against real physiological psychology. He is against only the practice of taking refuge in physiological terminology when behavioral accounts break down. The use of merely verbal explanations, whether physiological, mentalistic, or anything else, is discouraged by Skinner.

In some cases, Skinner or his followers may have waxed too enthusiastic in their efforts to purify psychological language by eliminating terms like *emotion*, *motivation, and perception*. These much-abused terms may be highly variable in meaning and yet might still have some core of useful meaning. If so, the critics would have a legitimate claim that certain problems were being neglected because of a positivistic insistence on purity of language. The reply might be that the problems of nature eventually insist that attention be paid to them. Meanwhile, there are plenty of problems suggested by concepts with demonstrated meaningfulness. Would the critic rather devote time to issues that are assuredly meaningful or to problems with no clear meaning?

Skinner has been criticized for extrapolating well beyond his data (cf. his proposals about complex human problems in *Science and human behavior*, 1953a). On this issue he seems to be somewhat vulnerable. The whole spirit of his methodology seems to revolve around the notion of sticking close to already observed facts. Yet his generalizations to human behavior very clearly go far beyond the observations of the laboratory.

There is a reply to this kind of criticism too. Bem and Bem (1968), in discussing the relationship between Skinner's *Verbal behavior* and Lenneberg's *Biological foundations of language*, indicate the direction such a defense might take: "Both works, in short, constitute plausibility arguments for particular views of verbal behavior" (p. 497). Skinner clearly stated that this was the way in which he viewed his analysis of verbal behavior, and he could easily extend this argument to his other extrapolations. If they are accepted as merely suggestions stemming from his conceptual framework, they may serve at least as an intellectual stimulant. The extent to which simple principles can be applied to apparently complex situations and processes is an empirical problem and cannot be safely prejudged.

With regard to Chomsky's attack on Skinner's treatment of verbal learning,

MacCorquodale (1969) has published a long and detailed defense and an explanation of Skinner's effort.

All the preceding criticisms involve broad methodological or attitudinal characteristics of Skinner's position. It is about as difficult to score heavily against Skinner on such points as it would be to criticize him effectively because he prefers a behavioristic approach to an existential one. These are the kinds of issues about which it is often said that the opponents "talk through" one another without making contact.

There are some issues which can be more closely joined, one of which concerns the use of statistics. Skinner and his followers are usually not interested in statistical tests; their attitude is probably best presented by Sidman (1960). Skinner himself says (Evans, 1968): "No student of mine to my knowledge has ever 'designed an experiment' " (p. 89). The Skinnerian methodology typically involves intensive and carefully controlled investigation of a small group of subjects. The search is for reliable functional relationships, and reliability is established by demonstrating the same functional relationship in several *individual* organisms, preferably under several different conditions. The statistical approach more typically uses larger groups of subjects and examines quantitative indices of the group's performance. Skinner does not believe that we are likely to arrive at laws which will help us predict and control the behavior of the individual unless we look at individuals. The issue is, like the more general issues, debatable, but the Skinnerians have certainly forced some important questions into the spotlight, where they can be more carefully considered. Some aspects of operant methodology are unquestionably useful, and on some issues concerning the relationships between group and individual functions the Skinnerians can be demonstrated to be correct. Those who advocate an overtly statistical approach are probably correct when they maintain that Skinnerians must make some statistical decisions, for example, about whether rate of responding has stabilized and about whether experimental manipulations have reliably been shown to have produced an effect.

The efficiency of the atheoretical approach has been questioned. The book *Schedules of reinforcement* (Ferster & Skinner, 1957) has been used as an example of the dangers of too inductive and positivistic an approach. It summarizes about seventy thousand hours of continuously recorded behavior of individual pigeons, during which time the pigeons emitted approximately one-quarter of a billion responses (Skinner, 1958b). The data are presented in a total of 921 separate figures with almost no interpretive, or even summarizing, comment. This procedure accords well with Skinner's belief that the scientist should be brought into direct contact with data, but it does not agree so well with the scientific temperament of those whose immediate interests are in general principles.

Cook (1963) has criticized Skinnerians for too literal an application of techniques appropriate in the operant conditioning chamber to programmed learning. For one thing, there is a great deal of evidence that humans need *not* make an overt response in order to learn, and in fact often do better if no overt response is required (Hillix & Marx, 1960; Rosenbaum & Hewitt, 1966; Rosenbaum & Schutz, 1967). Further, they often do as well when they are told in advance what the correct response is (prompted) as they do when they are reinforced after making the correct response. Both these errors in the application of operant techniques to humans are specific instances of the general criticism of premature extrapolation.

The best-known criticism of Skinner's extrapolations is by Chomsky (1959). In his famous thirty-two-page review of *Verbal behavior*, Chomsky analyzes Skinner's formulation with great care and criticizes it with great effectiveness. He devotes a great deal of attention to the terms *stimulus, response,* and *reinforcement,* since these are critical terms in Skinner's account of verbal behavior. Serious problems arise with the use of each of the three terms as they are employed in the analysis of verbal behavior. We shall note here only some difficulties with the use of *reinforcement.*

Chomsky notes that, in bar-pressing experiments, the reinforcer is an identifiable stimulus and that statements about reinforcement therefore have a meaningful referent, which in turn makes it meaningful to use the concept of reinforcement in the explanation of behavior. Chomsky contends that the extension to the explanation of verbal behavior is, however, completely unjustified. In support of his argument, he cites from Skinner a number of examples in which *reinforcement* does *not* refer to an identifiable stimulus. Skinner often uses automatic self-reinforcement (not identifiable as a stimulus!) as an explanation of why verbal behavior is maintained. Future reinforcements are also appealed to, as when a writer is said to be reinforced because of the effect his work will have upon future generations. Chomsky says of such usage (1959): "In fact, the term is used in such a way that the assertion that reinforcement is necessary for learning and continued availability of behavior is likewise empty" (p. 37).

Chomsky's review is reminiscent of Koch's review of Hull's work. Both are extremely sophisticated, careful, and thorough reviews. Both attack specific issues with great force and accuracy. Yet from one point of view both reviews are unjust. The reason is that Hull and Skinner were both being programmatic. Neither believed that he was correct in detail; in fact, it was Hull's explicit intention to set up hypotheses which could be proved wrong by others. However, Chomsky would probably rejoin that the defects in detail in Skinner are so great that the whole program becomes meaningless. At this time, the pendulum of history seems to be swinging in the direction of a verdict for Chomsky.

However, Skinner himself seems confident that the pendulum will, in the end, swing back and award the victory to him (M. H. Hall, 1967, pp. 69-70):

What the psycholinguists miss is any conception of a functional analysis as opposed to a structural analysis of verbal behavior. . . . They lean very heavily on the mentalistic psychology, and they are going to be let down because there is no such psychology. But as I said earlier, now they are postulating innate ideas, and that is next to worthless, if not a little bit comical. But I am in no real hurry, I have had my say. I am not interested in arguing with them at all. When all their mythical machinery finally grinds to a halt and is laid aside, discarded, then we will see what is remembered fifty or a hundred years from now, when the truth will have all been brought out in the open.

MacCorquodale (1969) agrees with Skinner. After chastizing Chomsky for what he sees as misunderstanding Skinner's purpose, MacCorquodale says (1969, p. 841):

Unfortunately for his purposes, Chomsky did not grasp the differences between Skinnerian and Watsonian-Hullian behaviorism, and his criticisms, although stylistically effective, were mostly irrelevant to *Verbal Behavior.*

He was simply wrong. This is a *great* book.

Skinner's Role in Contemporary Systematic Psychology

The extent of Skinner's systematic contributions to modern experimental psychology is nicely summarized in the formal citation accompanying the American Psychological Association's Distinguished Scientific Contribution Award granted him in 1958. This citation is as follows (*American Psychologist*, 1958):

An imaginative and creative scientist, characterized by great objectivity in scientific matters and by warmth and enthusiasm in personal contacts. Choosing simple operant behavior as subject matter, he has challenged alternative analyses of behavior, insisting that description take precedence over hypotheses. By careful control of experimental conditions, he has produced data which are relatively free from fortuitous variation. Despite his antitheoretical position, he is considered an important systematist and has developed a self-consistent description of behavior which has greatly increased our ability to predict and control the behavior of organisms from rat to man. Few American psychologists have had so profound an impact on the development of psychology and on promising younger psychologists.

Whereas in the period 1945 to 1950 there was no more enthusiastic band of psychologists than those working actively within the Hull-Spence systematic framework, today the same thing can be said of the Skinnerians, as they are often called. In addition to the group with Skinner at Harvard, there has been for years a tightly knit group trained under Fred Keller and William Schoenfeld at Columbia University. Skinnerian psychologists, resenting the orthodox restrictions of the American Psychological Association's journals (particularly the unwritten regulations concerning sample size and statistical tests), established the *Journal for the Experimental Analysis of Behavior* as their journal in 1958. Skinnerian techniques are almost universally accepted for some purposes even by opponents of the Skinnerian viewpoint. Young psychologists eager to help make the study of behavior an exact science continue to flock to the Skinnerian banner, often to the discomfiture of those holding opposing views. The popular press is coming to recognize Skinner as the greatest contemporary behaviorist (*Time*, 1969, p. 52) and his theoretical views as a serious competitor to Freud's. He has revivified and extended the strictly behavioral position. As one reviewer put it (MacLeod, 1959): "Watson's spirit is indestructible. Cleaned and purified, it breathes through the writings of B. F. Skinner" (p. 34).

CONTIGUITY THEORY: GUTHRIAN ASSOCIATIONISM

Guthrie's Career

Edwin Guthrie (1886-1959) was for several decades the leading exponent of a simple contiguity principle of learning. Throughout a long period, while first one and then another opposing school developed, Guthrie held steadfast to a small number of strict associationistic principles. This patience has finally paid off in the modern appearance of statistical models of learning based largely upon the Guthrian pattern. However, Guthrie's own contribution has remained that of a prophet and overseer more than that of an active experimentalist or detailed theorist.

Guthrie remained at one school, the University of Washington, throughout his entire academic career (1914 to 1956). He had less than the usual formal training in psychology, having been trained instead in philosophy and mathematics. He took his doctoral degree in 1912 at the University of Pennsylvania after having earned degrees earlier at the University of Nebraska. With one major exception (Guthrie & Horton, 1946), he preferred writing and argumentation to experimentation. His several books, especially *The psychology of learning* (1935, rev. 1952) and *The psychology of human conflict* (1938), are full of persuasive anecdotal supports for his general associationistic principles, but contain little controlled evidence.

Watson's doctrines so influenced Guthrie that he became a thoroughgoing behaviorist, although he differed from Watson on many points of theory. Guthrie's interest in psychology was apparently kindled during his graduate training by the philosopher E. A. Singer. He has stated that his year's collaboration on a textbook with the psychologist Stevenson Smith (S. Smith & Guthrie, 1921) gave him "invaluable training" in psychology. He retained his early interest in problems of philosophy of science throughout his career; his final major work (Guthrie, 1959) shows a continuing interest in general methodological questions, such as the relationship between logic, language, and scientific progress.

Guthrie's Basic Principles

Guthrie believed that a small number of primary principles are sufficient to account for the fundamental facts of behavior modification. His most famous principle is popularly referred to as *one-trial learning*. Guthrie held that S-R associations, as the basis of learning, are established by contiguity per se in a single pairing of stimulus and response. He early stated this principle as follows (1935): "A combination of stimuli which has accompanied a movement will on its recurrence tend to be followed by that movement" (p. 26). A related principle is (1942): "A stimulus pattern gains its full associative strength on the occasion of its first pairing with a response" (p. 30). Guthrie offered a final simplified version (1959): "What is being noticed becomes a signal for what is being done" (p. 186). This statement reflects his concern with the active role of the organism (the old problem of attention). In his final paper he also placed increased emphasis on the problem of patterning in stimulus complexes (cf. Guthrie, 1959, pp. 186ff.).

His early distinction between acts and movements enabled Guthrie to hold to his basic one-trial-learning principle and still account for the fact that behavior modification typically requires repeated pairings of cue and response before it can be reliably predicted that the response will occur in the presence of the cue. According to Guthrie, the basic connections are between stimuli and movements, but *acts*, rather than movements, are usually measured. An example of an act would be serving a tennis ball into the service court; every separate muscular movement which was necessary would serve well as an example of what Guthrie means by a movement. While observable in principle, these movements are not easily noticed and are generally overlooked in theorizing. However, anyone who has ever had tennis lessons is aware of the fact that these movements must sometimes be considered and carefully learned, especially when complex coordinations are involved.

This does not mean that movements are equivalent to the contractions of individual muscles. In a sense, what Guthrie means by movement is itself a kind of behavioral result; it is a result in terms of what is happening to a part of the organism, but it is not a result in terms of the environment. It is not the most molecular level of description which could be used. As Guthrie says (1959): "A description of the action of the individual muscles concerned would be hopeless confusion" (p. 183).

The situation is similar on the stimulus side. Guthrie regarded a complex stimulus as a collection of a great many stimulus components, with not all components present on every occasion. The net results of this complexity of stimulus and response components is that a large number of presentations of the gross stimulus and occurrences of the gross response (the act) are required before satisfactory regularity can be found in the behavior being measured. This is so because large numbers of the stimulus and response components need to be involved in the conditioning process. If exact replications of stimuli and responses could be achieved, single presentations would be sufficient to produce perfect conditioning.

For Guthrie, the process of conditioning is as follows: Aspects of the total stimulus situation present on a given trial become associated with a successful movement, that is, one which is part of the sequence constituting the successful "act." The successful movement causes movement-produced stimuli, which, along with external stimuli present in the environment as it may be altered by the movement, are associated with a subsequent successful movement. This chain of movements linked by movement-produced stimuli constitutes an act. When the act is terminated, it must result in the removal of the relevant stimuli if it is to be retained. Otherwise, other movements would become associated with the same stimuli.

On a subsequent trial in which different aspects of the total stimulus situation are present, the subject will engage in random behaviors until he again performs the act successfully. The movements constituting the act on that occasion are consequently associated with the stimulus complex present during the second trial. This associative process will recur on additional trials until successful movements are conditioned to all aspects of the stimulus situation. When this point is reached, conditioning is complete, and the act will occur smoothly, whatever aspect of the stimulus situation happens to be present.

Finally, it should be noted that Guthrie thought learning occurs through pure contiguity of stimulus and response. This might be considered a misguided view of the process of forming associations, since it is obvious that reinforcers have an important role in learning. Guthrie had no need to deny that reinforcers are effective; his theory simply accounted for their effectiveness in an ingenious and different way. The reinforcer was presumed to change the stimulus situation in which the response had just been made. The original stimulus situation (prereinforcer) therefore cannot be disconnected from the response just made and connected to a new response; the connection is thus preserved because of the stimulus change produced by the presence of the reinforcer. Unlearning, or extinction, is really the learning of different responses to the same stimulus, according to Guthrie. He is therefore able to present a beautifully parsimonious and consistent picture of the totality of behavior modification.

Evaluation of Guthrie

Guthrie's views have been most directly supported in the laboratory by his own investigation of stereotypy in the cat's behavior in the puzzle box (Guthrie & Horton, 1946) and by two investigations of Voeks (1948, 1954). Guthrie did not himself present any highly formalized theory; he stated (1959) that he did not think psychology was yet advanced enough to justify such theory. Voeks (1950) has nevertheless published a useful formalization of Guthrie's position. Her postulate of postremity, or recency, for example, states that only the last response made to a stimulus remains conditioned. Guthrie had said the same thing, but had made no effort to state it formally or to combine it with other postulates to form a system from which deductions could be made.

Although Guthrie did not leave any comprehensive theory, it is interesting to examine some experiments designed to test his statement that the last response made is the one that will be preserved and made again on the next presentation of the same cue. Voeks (1948) found that human subjects learning mazes made the postreme response far more often than the response which had previously been made most frequently. Postremity won out over frequency in predicting responses for fifty-six out of fifty-seven subjects, in cases where the two principles made opposing predictions. Seward, Dill, and Holland (1944), however, found that subjects in a multiple-choice situation usually made the response made earliest, rather than latest, to a particular cue (color). It would thus appear from these two studies that the principle of postremity works sometimes, but not always—a statement which is true with disturbing frequency when applied to psychological principles.

The most searching criticism of Guthrie's theory has been offered by Mueller and Schoenfeld (1954). They have indicated that the simplicity of Guthrian notions is more apparent than real and has been achieved only at the expense of failure to be explicit about key problems. They have also suggested that Guthrie has developed no real system at all, in clear contrast to many of the leading alternative theorists. He has been satisfied merely with repeating, over the years, certain of the key assumptions with which he started. Finally, they have raised some serious questions concerning the interpretation of the Guthrie and Horton (1946) data on stereotypy of behavior. Their treatment should be consulted, along with Guthrie's final authoritative paper (1959), by anyone interested in an evaluation of Guthrian theory.

Guthrie's success in maintaining his position as a leading learning theorist is surprising in view of the relative paucity of experimental support his theory received. This success has probably been due to a combination of several factors. Foremost among these is the apparent simplicity of his theory compared with the leading alternatives, such as Hull's. There is no difficulty in grasping at least the basis of Guthrie's views, and this simplicity appeals to many psychologists. A second factor has been the difficulty experienced by opposing theorists in presenting evidence which clearly contradicts the Guthrian theory. Finally, there is the fact that Guthrie and some of his adherents, notably Sheffield, have been consistently able to point to weaknesses and contradictions in the alternative accounts. Hull's need-reduction principle has been a special target (e.g., Sheffield, 1948; Sheffield, 1949; Sheffield & Roby, 1950; Sheffield, Wulff, & Backer, 1951). The fact that these successful attacks depend upon the greater predictive specificity of the alternative accounts does not seem to have reduced the effectiveness of the Guthrian attack. A consequence of this success in criticism has been that Guthrie's theory has remained a formidable alternative account, even though its laurels may have been won on largely negative grounds.

Despite these limitations, Guthrie has been more than merely an astute critic and propounder of simple generalizations supported by fluent anecdotal stories. He is one theorist who has stood by his theoretical guns, consistently espousing a contiguity principle as the basis of all learning. He has supported his emphasis on movements as the theoretical response elements by experimental studies of stereotypy and has shown how well stereotypy observed by other experimenters can be subsumed by his theoretical analyses. Guthrie has demonstrated the theoretical roles that can be played by mediating mechanisms like movement-produced stimuli. This ingenious mechanism is much like Hull's fractional anticipatory goal response in that both serve as the forgers of links in the chain of behavior. Finally, Guthrie has not said much because he did not believe he had enough information to say much. Thus he has made a small target. In 1958, the year before his death, Guthrie, the consistent psychologist, received the American Psychological Foundation Gold Medal Award in recognition of his distinguished contributions. These contributions have not stopped with his death; William K. Estes has modeled his statistical association theory on Guthrian principles. The Estes theory is discussed in Chapter 13, along with other mathematical developments.

TWO-FACTOR THEORIES

It has been clear for a very long time that the Thorndikian and the Pavlovian procedures for studying learning differ in the operations employed. In the Pavlovian procedure, the unconditioned stimulus follows the conditioned stimulus, whatever the subject in the experiment does. In the Thorndikian procedure, the reward is presented only if the subject has previously engaged in the behavior required by the experimenter. This basic difference in procedure implies some corollary distinctions. In the Pavlovian paradigm, the conditioned stimulus, which comes to elicit the conditioned response if learning occurs, is an identifiable stimulus and is manipulated by the experimenter. The unconditioned stimulus elicits an identifiable unconditioned response. The unconditioned response in the Pavlovian studies was always, or nearly always, an involuntary response mediated by the automatic nervous system. The conditioned response typically bears a close relationship to the unconditioned response, if it is not identical to it as measured in the experiment. The Thorndikian procedure is different in all the above respects: There is no experimentally identified conditioned stimulus; the response elicited by the reward is not of great interest, nor do the experimental arrangements "force" the performance of the unconditioned response to the reward; the response to be learned may not be at all related in form to the response made to the reward; and the responses of interest are mediated by the "voluntary" nervous system.

A consideration of these operational differences between Pavlovian (classical) conditioning and Thorndikian (instrumental) learning leads one fairly naturally to question whether different laws of behavior modification are involved in the two situations. For example, one might ask whether stimulus associations, as in Pavlovian conditioning, and stimulus-response associations, as emphasized by the Thorndikian procedure, are formed by different basic processes. Rescorla and Solomon (1967), in their review of the literature on two-factor learning theories, state that three different sets of variables are usually implicated by those who think there are two basically different processes. The three sets are the class of responses affected by the process, the effective reinforcers involved, and the results of the learning process. The most common distinction based on response characteristics has been that classical conditioning involves autonomic responses, while instrumental learning involves somatic (skeletal) responses, but a number of other distinctions have also been suggested. It is more difficult to find a basis for distinguishing the kinds of reinforcers, but it has been suggested that the "rewards" used in instrumental learning have to have an affective character, while Pavlovian reinforcers do not; again, several bases for a distinction between the reinforcers have been proposed. Finally, among the several possible distinctions between the "products" of learning is the suggestion that classical conditioning involves stimulus-stimulus connections, while instrumental learning produces stimulus-response connections. There is no highly convincing empirical evidence that compels adherence to any of these theoretical distinctions, but there is not sufficient evidence to reject them either.

The most popular theoretical strategy has been an attempt to reduce the two operationally different procedures to a common theoretical framework which can explain both. Hull, for example, accepted the laws of Pavlovian conditioning as basic, but modified the most common conception of the process in his emphasis on the necessity for drive reduction to occur if learning is to be successful. The more complex, and therefore less popular, solution is to assume that there are two different processes involved and to propose a theory which relates the two processes. If this approach is chosen, it is natural to assume that classical conditioning involves contiguity as a basic process and that instrumental learning involves reward as a basic component.

Kimble (1961) reports that Miller and Konorski presented an early version of two-factor theory in 1928, and that they were followed into the field by Schlosberg (1937) and by Skinner (1938). Skinner's distinction between type S and type R conditioning has since become part of the jargon of our discipline; the former was essentially Pavlovian, and the latter Thorndikian. Skinner was far more interested in the Thorndikian, operant variety, and he held the evidence for pure Pavlovian conditioning to be questionable.

Mowrer later became, and has remained, the best-known two-factor theorist because of the tightness of his reasoning, the empirical work which buttressed his suggestions, and the length and number of his publications on the subject (1947, 1951, 1954). He contrasted conditioning and solution learning. The acquisition of emotions, meaning, attitudes, and the like is mediated through simple contiguity of stimuli—conditioning. Overt instrumental learning—solution learning—occurs through reinforcement, or law-of-effect learning. Since Mowrer was originally a strong Hullian reinforcement theorist, his shift was an important one. His interpretation was criticized by his earlier collaborator, Neal Miller (1951), among others.

A suggestion for a different kind of two-factor theory has been made by Spence in his Silliman Lectures (1956). As he pointed out, one might develop his suggestions into a two-factor theory "exactly the opposite of the well-known two-factor theory espoused by Schlosberg, Mowrer, and others" (p. 151). Reinforcement would thus be accorded a determining role in the case of classically conditioned responses, which are emphasized in Spence's systematic theorizing, rather than in that of instrumental behavior.

By far the most ambitious effort at a two-factor theory has been provided by Mowrer (1956, 1960a, 1960b) in a drastic revision of his earlier two-factor theory. Actually, this theory is no longer "two-factor" in the original sense; Mowrer has come to accept now only conditioning or sign learning as the single basic learning process; solution learning is regarded as a special, derived case of conditioning. It is still a two-factor theory, however, in the sense that it stresses two *types of reinforcement*. *Decremental reinforcement* refers to the need-reducing type of process stressed by Thorndike and Hull in their theories; *incremental reinforcement* refers to the growth of "fear" with consequent avoidance behavior from excessive stimulation.

The present theory was developed mainly by means of an extension of the secondary-reinforcement principle. Mowrer assumes that when a hungry animal obtains food, response-produced stimuli become conditioned as secondary rein-forcers—as "promising" stimuli which arouse "hope." In this "feedback theory of habit," as Mowrer calls it, hope is thus conditioned in fundamentally the same manner as fear is conditioned in aversive learning. The parallelism is stated by Mowrer (1960b): "A conditioned stimulus not only makes the subject salivate: it also makes him *hopeful*, just as surely as a stimulus which has been associated with the onset of pain makes a subject *fearful*" (p. 8).

It is too early to say whether learning will eventually be subsumed under a single set of laws, under two sets, or under several. Rescorla and Solomon (1967) cite a number of empirical studies which demonstrate interactions between classical and instrumental conditioning. Changes in rate of instrumental responding can be produced by the introduction of conditioned stimuli previously used in the Pavlov-ian context. Such empirical demonstrations obviously do not prove that there are two kinds of learning, but they do show that it is profitable to study the relation-ships between situations in which stimulus *contiguity* is arranged (Pavlovian) and situations in which a response-reinforcement *contingency* is arranged. Two-factor theories may not turn out to be "correct," but they at least have the virtue of encouraging the study of such relationships.

SUMMARY AND CONCLUSIONS

In this chapter we have surveyed some theoretical positions loosely called S-R. In the main, these are neobehavioristic and concentrate on the problem of learning. They are distinguished on the basis of their treatment of the problem of reinforce-ment.

The reinforcement theory of Clark L. Hull represents a combination of the Thorndikian law of effect and the Pavlovian conditioning paradigm. This hypotheti-co-deductive system is highly formalized. It is by far the most ambitious theoretical and systematic effort of its kind. Compared with Watson, Hull was a sophisticated theorist, much concerned with logical as well as experimental specifications and empirical tests; he was a methodological, rather than a metaphysical, behaviorist. In spite of, or even perhaps partly because of, his high aspirations, Hull's direct sys-tematic influence has declined markedly in recent years. This decline has been a function both of the fundamental faults found in his system and of the increasing popularity of a more positivistic psychology of the kind advanced by B. F. Skinner. Today Hullian psychology is represented mainly in the theoretical efforts of Ken-neth W. Spence and his associates and, in much more modified form, in the work of Neal E. Miller.

Skinner has been much less interested in formal theory than Hull. He believes that theory should develop inductively and be determined by data, rather than from postulates which then determine what data are gathered. Skinner does seem to have either moderated or clarified his position, beginning from what seemed to be an antitheoretical position and developing toward a positive attitude toward certain limited types of theory.

In keeping with his metatheoretical beliefs, Skinner has maintained an atheoretical, descriptive view of reinforcement. His research has been some of the most provocative and stimulating to be found in psychology. His interests have ranged freely from baby boxes to utopian communities.

The major opposition within the S-R camp to the various reinforcement theories has been provided by the contiguity theorists, who hold to some kind of associationistic principle. They argue that reinforcement operates mainly to protect S-R connections formed through contiguity per se. E. R. Guthrie has been the most influential contiguity theorist over several decades. Within the past decade, however, the basic Guthrian contiguity principle has been cast in mathematical form by W. K. Estes and his associates. Their use of mathematical models has given a strong impetus to empirical research as well as to theoretical development.

A number of two-factor theories have also been developed. These have historically attempted to combine the reinforcement and contiguity positions. The most recent of these, by O. H. Mowrer, does offer something of a novel approach. It involves two kinds of reinforcement, both based upon the conditioning or contiguity principle.

An important conclusion to be drawn from the wide variety of theoretical approaches outlined is that no one procedure can be guaranteed in advance to be more productive than any other. Rather, all kinds of empirical and theoretical endeavors are to be encouraged, as long as the fundamental requirements of scientific procedure are met. Each approach that is given a thorough trial will help to motivate and organize research. Which kind of research will eventually be seen to be most significant must await the verdict of history.

Further Readings

For an understanding of Hull's system, the most useful of his books are probably *Principles of behavior* (1943) and *A behavior system* (1952). His 1937 paper on conditioning theory, cited in the text, indicates the fundamental development of his thinking, and his autobiographical statement (1952) is unusually frank in detailing personal factors in his career. Spence's adaptation of Hullian theory is presented in his *Behavior theory and conditioning* (1956) and in the volume of collected writings, *Behavior theory and learning* (1960). Of Skinner's many papers and books, the most important sources are his beginning text, *Science and human behavior* (1953a), and his collected writings, *Cumulative record* (1959). Two particularly influential books by psychologists writing in the Skinnerian framework are Keller and Schoenfeld's *Principles of psychology* (1950), which presents an integrated set of principles based on operant conditioning, and Sidman's *Tactics of scientific research* (1960), which is persuasive elaboration of the positivistic approach to experimentation. Guthrie is represented by his two basic books, *The psychology of learning* (1935) and *The psychology of human conflict* (1938). The simplest introduction to Estes' mathematical model is possibly his paper "Growth and function of mathematical models for learning" (1961). Two books are particularly valuable for material of special relevance to most of the S-R theories here considered: *Modern learning theory*, by Estes et al. (1954), which includes highly critical reviews of Hull (by Koch), of Skinner (by Verplanck), and of Guthrie (by Mueller and Schoenfeld), and Koch's *Psychology: A study of a science* (Vol. 2, 1958), which contains two papers on the Hullian system and its derivatives (by Logan and Miller), Guthrie's final systematic effort, Skinner's "Case history in scientific method," and an excellent detailed account of statistical theories by Estes. *Theories of learning*, by Hilgard and Bower (1966), describes all the above S-R theories, some field theories, and the most important contemporary developments.

11   Varieties of Field Theory

Several psychological theorists have been called *field theorists* because of a supposed analogy between their theories and the field theories of physics. We have already seen in Chapter 8 that Robert Oppenheimer, who presumably understood the nature of field theory very well, questioned the usefulness of the analogy. In the published version of his speech to the American Psychological Association, he put the matter quite politely (1956, pp. 133-134):

> But probably between sciences of very different character, the direct formal analogies in their structure are not too likely to be helpful. Certainly what the pseudo-Newtonians did with sociology was a laughable affair; and similar things have been done with mechanical notions of how psychological phenomena are to be explained. . . . I know that when I hear the word "field" used in physics and in psychology I have a nervousness that I cannot entirely account for.

As psychologists, we shall of course be quick to consider the possibility that we have here simply the case of an effete physicist throwing up a defense of his own territory. However, we might quickly find ourselves unduly swelling the ranks of the effete if we put all those who question this particular analogy into those ranks. For example, one of our own (psychologist William K. Estes) said in connection with his examination of Kurt Lewin's theory (1954b, pp. 318-319):

> Now we may ask what are the distinguishing characteristics of the enterprises which claim or at least permit the appellation field theory? It should be noted first of all that most of the attributes claimed by field theorists and sympathetic reviewers tend to vanish or at least become non-differentiating upon critical scrutiny. It is not clear to the present writer in what technical sense the term field theory is especially applicable to the systems of Lewin, Koffka, Köhler, or Tolman. The term field has been taken over from physics, but it is not easy to find a basis for the presumed analogy between field theories of physics and the so-called field theories of psychology.

Estes goes on to point out that many of the adjectives that are supposed to describe field theories in psychology apply equally well to S-R theories, for example, *dynamic* and *multiply determined*.

Two points can be extracted from the objections of Oppenheimer and Estes. First, there *is* no close technical or formal relationship between the field theory of physics and the field theory of psychology. We shall see that Lewin developed the most formalized field theory in psychology and that it used an altogether different formal system and an altogether different set of variables from those used by any extant field theory in physics.

The second point is that the metatheoretical program which was supposed to direct the efforts of field theorists in psychology did not produce theories which bore the distinctive marks of the metatheory. A detailed examination of this point would carry us too far from our purpose here, and Estes (1954b) has already documented this assertion.

What, then, is there left to discuss about field theory? There are two things. First, we can examine the analogy at the *metatheoretical* level between the field theories of physics and those of psychology, since there seems to be no valid analogy at a more technical level. Second, we can discuss the nature of the theories which have been called *field theories* in psychology, regardless of whether they are really any more fieldlike (in the sense of physics) than their competitors. We shall therefore be taking a friendly look at field theory, trying to assess it more in terms of its own aspirations than in terms of those of an outside critic. We believe that field theorists in psychology have made extremely important contributions to our methodology and that this justifies a close look at their suggestions and criticisms.

THE METATHEORETICAL ANALOGIES

Einstein's special relativity theory of 1905, and his general relativity theory of 1915, had unparalleled impacts on the view of the world held by physicists and philosophers alike. Related developments in quantum theory have further revolutionized man's world view. The awe with which these contributions are sometimes viewed is revealed by Gillispie (1960), who says: "And Lorentz lacked only that ultimate quality of something like divinity in Einstein's mind, which would take the same evidence and quite transform the shape of the world that physics sees in nature" (p. 506).

Even before the formulation of Einstein's special theory, Maxwell's field theory evoked great admiration. Under the circumstances, it was natural and desirable that the developing science of psychology try to emulate its more established fellow scientists by borrowing the lessons learned in the transformation from classical physics to relativity theory, the most prestigious representative of physical field theory.

The philosophy of relativity theory is a sea in which every man can find water beyond his depth. We must, nevertheless, try to extract from it those features which were taken over in the metatheoretical attitudes of field theorists in psychology.

Einstein's relativity theory, as modified by Minkowski, places events in a four-dimensional space-time field. The description of events is "holistic" in this and in other field theories in the sense that the theory inextricably interrelates the variables in describing the "trajectory" of events through this four-dimensional field. This general holistic property of field theories is taken over by field theorists in psychology as part of their metatheoretical equipment, whether or not it ever becomes visible as a characteristic of their theories.

A second supposed property of physical field theory, its dynamic character, is more controversial; that is, it is not agreed that relativity theory, at least, is really dynamic in the sense that it admits of change in a degree greater than the more "mechanistic" theories of classical physics. It has been argued that relativity theory provides for a complete and *static* view of existence, with past and future stretched out along the temporal dimension just as the sun and stars are arrayed in the spatial dimensions. Whether or not one agrees with this position (see Fraser, 1966, pp. 417-454, for both sides of the argument), it is hard to see why field theories in physics might be regarded as more dynamic than non-field theories. In psychology, "dynamic" has come to have a quite different connotation involving motivation, especially unconscious motivation, in addition to the more nearly physical meaning emphasizing change.

Field theories in physics do generally provide for continuity, for example, in space and time. The field properties may therefore change continuously, and this continuity of change—a mathematical continuity—may somehow connote dynamicism. It is, at least superficially, peculiar that Gestalt theory gave rise to a noncontinuity view of learning despite the close relationship of Gestalt metatheory to its precursors in physical field theory.

Einsteinian theory set sharp limits to the range of causality. Events which were too distant in space-time could not interact; no causal factors could propagate faster than the speed of light in a vacuum. The paths of the planets were reconceived as being along the shortest paths in the curved space produced by the presence of other bodies. There was no longer a gravitational attraction per se, since in some cases that attraction would have to take place instantaneously over vast distances. The field in which the planet moved at the time produced the movement of the planet. Action at a distance was no longer required. Psychological field theories seem generally to have taken over this view; they generally accept the "contemporaneity principle," which states that only conditions actually present at a given time can affect events occurring at that time.

There is a rather strange and contorted relationship between positivism and relativity theory. Mach was the positivist physicist and philosopher who furnished Einstein with the skepticism he needed to reexamine the foundations of physics and to eliminate, through his brilliant synthesis, the Newtonian notions of absolute space and absolute time. It was in the positivistic spirit that Einstein asked how one would determine, from two platforms moving with respect to each other, whether or not two events occurring somewhere else were simultaneous. It was therefore an outgrowth of Mach's thought that led Einstein to the conclusion that two honest and right-thinking men on the two platforms would necessarily arrive at opposite conclusions about the order of succession of events, provided certain conditions obtained.

Further, it was in the positivistic tradition when Heisenberg asked how one could go about determining the velocity and position of an electron; logic drove him to conclude that there was an irreducible uncertainty produced by the interaction of the electron with the measuring system. The electron, therefore, *does not have,* from the point of view of the positivist, a determinate position and velocity at the same time.

Now the contortions begin. Einstein, who started as a son of positivism, did not find it possible **to** remain an altogether loyal son. He did not wish to accept a basic indeterminacy at the heart of physics, even though it had been demanded by the same kinds of questions he had asked about the universe on a very large scale. Relativism could reign through the vast reaches of space, as long as its shady younger brother left the atom its determinate existence.

Another contortion comes from the fact that positivism, which started as a quest for *positive* knowledge, led inexorably to the conclusion that there are stringent limitations on what can be known. Some have concluded mistakenly that this means that subjectivism is now justified because of relativity or the indeterminacy principle. This is not true; the "facts" are perfectly objective in both cases, and will be agreed to by everyone making observations under the same physical conditions. Field theory in psychology seems to have, at least in some cases, substituted a version of subjectivism for relativism; we shall see that Lewin, like the Gestalt psychologists, accepts the causal efficacy of the "psychological field" of the individual; this psychological field seems to be insufficiently objectified for scientific purposes.

Apart from these metatheoretical considerations, there has been a high degree of commonality of theoretical content among field theories. Most important here are the widely shared interest in problems of perception and cognition and the correlated tendency to utilize perceptual and cognitive processes as explanatory factors. This is hardly surprising in view of the close relationship between modern field theories and classical Gestalt psychology, which was concerned primarily with similar emphases.

Principally, but by no means exclusively, field theory as used in psychology has come to refer to the metatheory of Kurt Lewin; his system is therefore the first of the several versions described in the present chapter. The unique combination of behaviorism and Gestalt psychology achieved in the purposivism of E. C. Tolman is included as the second important specimen of field theory. The theoretically more circumscribed but increasingly influential thinking of Egon Brunswik is next described. Then we turn to an examination of some of the contributions of Roger Barker, who combines some ideas of Lewin with those of Brunswik in some unique investigations. Finally, other systematists (K. S. Lashley, J. R. Kantor, and R. H.

Wheeler), whose work may be classified as falling within some kind of field-theoretical classification, are more briefly described.

VECTOR FIELD THEORY: LEWIN'S LIFE SPACE

The contributions to psychological theory made by Kurt Lewin (1890-1947) have been among the most significant of recent decades. On the one hand, Lewin was a brilliant researcher. Even his severest critics recognize him as a most ingenious experimenter; the series of experimental studies which he directed while at the University of Berlin in the 1920s is a model of theoretical creativity and imagination combined with sound experimental methodology. On the other hand, throughout his career he remained a strong advocate of the primacy of directive theory in research, and he is best known for his development of the motivational, or vector, system of psychology, most commonly referred to as *field theory*.

Although Lewin was associated with an active center of Gestalt psychology at Berlin, he retained little identification with the orthodox group, and his systematizing went well beyond the usual confines of the school. As a matter of fact, there was no formal relationship between his theories and those of the Gestaltists. Lewin's early efforts were concerned largely with motivational problems of the individual subject, which led to an interest in problems of personality organization; his later efforts were concerned mainly with a wide variety of problems in social psychology, including his initiation of the group-dynamics movement and his assistance in the development of *action research* (i.e., research directed at producing social changes). In between, he was peripherally concerned with problems such as the nature of learning, cultural factors in personality structure, and child development. But in all these diverse areas Lewin brought to bear on critical issues the same fundamental approach: an emphasis always upon the psychological, rather than the simple environmental, factors in the situation (or field). This emphasis is comparable to the earlier Gestalt distinction, most explicitly made by Koffka, between the "behavioral" and the "geographical" environment. The crux of the distinction is that the effective meaning of the environmental conditions depends upon more than merely physical attributes; that is, a description in terms of such factors alone is inadequate. It is the individual's *perception* of the physical attributes which determines how he will react.

Lewin's Career

Kurt Lewin was born in Prussia and received his higher education at the Universities of Freiburg, Munich, and Berlin (Ph.D., 1914). He was thus present during the early, formative years of the Gestalt movement. After a five-year interlude of military service, he returned to Berlin and remained in various academic capacities until 1932, when he came to the United States. He spent that year as visiting professor at Stanford and the following two years at Cornell. The decision to establish permanent residence in this country was made as a consequence of the rise of Nazi power in Germany, where his Jewish ancestry became a handicap. Lewin went to the Child Welfare Station of the State University of Iowa as professor of child psychology in 1935 and finally to Massachusetts Institute of Technology in 1944. In this last appointment he was director of the Research Center for Group Dynamics, a movement which he had only fairly well started at the time of his death in 1947.

Lewin's major publications were in the form of journal reports and contributions to various collections of papers. His own papers have been collected in four small volumes. The first two of these, *A dynamic theory of personality* (1935) and *Principles of topological psychology* (1936), represent the earlier European phase of his career; the last two collections, *Resolving social conflicts* (1948) and *Field theory in social science* (1951), relate to the later American phase.

Topology and Hodological Space

Lewin selected topology, a relatively new geometry, as providing a mathematical model upon which he could base his conceptual representation of psychological processes. In brief, topology is a geometry where spatial relationships are represented in a strictly nonmetrical manner. Positional relationships between areas or regions are maintained in spite of various kinds of changes in size and shape. The primary concern is with the connections between bounded regions and with their spatial relationships; for example, one area will remain inside another throughout a wide variety of stretchings and distortions. (See Brown, 1936, for a relatively simplified introduction to Lewin's use of the topological geometry.) Lewin felt that such positional relationships were the best way to conceptualize the structure of psychological relationships. There was, however, one serious limitation to topology: its lack of directional concepts. To represent the psychological concept of direction, Lewin then invented a new qualitative geometry (1938), which he named *hodological space* (from the Greek *hodos*, translated as "path"). He developed the characteristics of such a space that he felt were necessary for an adequate representation of the dynamic factors, usually called *vectors*, in psychological relationships.

Cartwright (1959, pp. 61-65) reports that recent researchers have substituted a new mathematical tool, the linear graph, for Lewin's topology plus hodology. On the planar maps which Lewin usually used to represent his life spaces, no more than four regions can have mutual boundaries. This limits the complexity of structure which can be represented on a two-dimensional, planar map. On a linear graph, an indefinite number of points (which replace regions in the life space) can be mutually interconnected. The linear graph also allows for the representation of asymmetrical relationships, as when movement can occur from region A to region B, but not back. There is no natural way to represent these asymmetries on the map.

Life Space

Lewin's objective in adapting and even inventing such geometries was to clarify his conceptualization of the psychological field, or *life space*. The life space is most

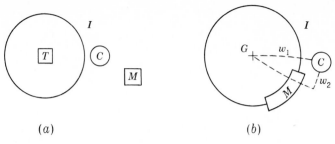

Fig. 11-1
Situation in which a young child wishes to reach a toy which lies inside a circular barrier. (*a*) Physical situation; (*b*) psychological situation. C, child; T, toy; I, barrier; M, mother; G, goal; w₁, w₂, paths. (From Lewin, 1936, p. 147.)

simply defined as the totality of effective *psychological* factors for a given person at some particular time. It consists of a number of differentiated *regions*, which represent significant conditions in the person's life. Although the totality of factors is emphasized in definitions such as the above, in actual practice only the most relevant ones are ordinarily included in diagrammatic presentations of the life-space concept.

Let us illustrate Lewin's distinction between physical and psychological representations by a relatively simple example from his writing. Figure 11-1*a* shows the physical situation, and Figure 11-1*b* shows the psychological representation, where a goal object (toy) is placed out of reach within a circular area. Direct physical approach to the goal via path w_1 is not possible, but psychological locomotion, via path w_2, is effective if mother can be persuaded to obtain the toy. Although the example pictured involves a physical barrier, the same psychological situation might obtain with a barrier produced by verbal restriction involving the toy, especially for an older child. Or, in somewhat similar situations, the barrier might consist of more strictly personal or intraorganismic factors such as politeness in a child trained not to take things without asking or timidity or even fear in some other child. In these cases the physical picture would show no barrier, but the psychological representation, for this slice of the life space, might look very much like that shown in the figure.

A somewhat more comprehensive example of a typical life space is shown in Figure 11-2. Here Lewin depicted a series of locomotions involving a particular occupational choice for a young man. Lewin (1936) pointed out that the passing of the college entrance examinations, while not a physical locomotion, represents a "real change of position in the quasi-social . . . life space. . . . Many things are now within his reach which were not before" (p. 48). It is this kind of crossing from one region to another that is emphasized in the life-space schema.

Important dimensions of the life space, as Lewin conceptualized it, are its temporal and reality characteristics. As the child grows older, not only does his life space become increasingly differentiated into regions as a function of his maturity

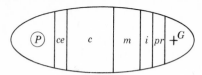

Fig. 11-2
Situation of a boy who wants to become a physician. P, person; G, goal; ce, college entrance examinations; c, college; m, medical school; i, internship; pr, establishing a practice. (From Lewin, 1936, p. 48.)

and expanding personal problems, but it also develops temporal and reality-irreality dimensions. For example, the child begins to plan for the future as well as to respond more effectively in longer time units. Further, he begins to use imagery and fantasy and thus to live, in some degree, on an irreality level; there he is less restricted in his behavior by the usual barriers of the real world.

The reality dimension is illustrated in Figure 11-3, in which Lewin showed three levels of this variable in the life space.

This dimension Lewin considered a prime significance in a psychological analysis, and so it was given considerable attention in his work. Lewin did not believe that an absolute reality or irreality dimension was tenable because of the continually changing field of experiences; that is, what at one instance may be considered absolute reality may be altered by new events and experiences. Furthermore, as the individual matures, the reality-irreality dimension broadens and becomes more differentiated (1936, p. 204).

Perhaps the most widely known Lewinian contribution within the life-space framework is his conceptualization of conflict. He stated that there are three basic types of conflicts producing frustration: approach-approach, approach-avoidance, and avoidance-avoidance. Approach-approach conflict occurs when an individual desires to achieve two goals, only one of which is obtainable (e.g., one has two invitations for the same evening). Approach-avoidance conflict is characterized by a goal which is both desired and undesired (e.g., one desires the money but not the effort entailed in a proffered job). An avoidance-avoidance conflict is present when anticipated consequences are both undesirable (e.g., one must accept an unwanted invitation or offend an esteemed friend). This type of conflict is characterized by a vacillation between the alternatives or by an attempt to escape the situation ("leave the field").

Lewin's System

It is impossible to describe any single integrated system constructed by Lewin (such as that described for Hull in Chapter 10). This is mainly because Lewin never attempted to produce such an integrated system; when not concerned with methodological problems in field theory, he worked on a variety of different problems. All

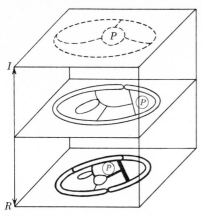

Fig. 11-3
Representation of different degrees of reality by an additional dimension of the life
space. R, more real level; I, more irreal level; P, person. In a level of greater reality
the barriers are stronger, and the person P
is more clearly separated from his environment. (From Lewin, 1936, p. 200.)

of them involved somewhat the same general type of working assumptions and
procedures and to a great extent the same constructs. However, no serious attempt
was made by Lewin to coordinate these concepts into one systematic framework
(cf. Cartwright, 1959).

The coordinated series of researches involving Lewin's assumption of the
tension system has been selected as the best example of his work; in some respects
it comes close to being an integrated system. A continuing series of experimental
studies, some of them described below, were all based upon implications of this
central concept. Lewin himself has provided a theoretical account of these researches, emphasizing the formal assumptions and derivations (Lewin, 1940, pp.
13-28; 1944, pp. 4-20). Our treatment follows this account as well as the more
informal description given by Deutsch (1954, pp. 199ff.).

The background for Lewin's development of the construct of the tension
system goes back to his first psychological research (1917). He was interested in
refining some of Ach's (1910) earlier research on the strength of the will. The
general procedure here was to establish associations of nonsense syllables through
repeated pairings and then to evaluate the strength of the voluntary factor, manipulated by instructions, by opposing it to the habitual tendency. (See Hilgard, 1956,
pp. 258ff., for a description of this research and the theoretical rationales.) Lewin
finally rejected Ach's attempt to supplement the association factor with such new
constructs as set and determining tendency, in the tradition of the Würzburg
school, to which Ach belonged (see Chapter 4). He felt that Ach had not gone far
enough in his interpretation. Rather than accept *both* association and voluntary

factors, Lewin concluded that the best conceptualization was to assume that there were simply two voluntary factors. He pointed out that association per se provided no motive power. As he later put it (1940, p. 14):

Dynamically, an "association" is something like a link in a chain, i.e., a pattern of restraining forces without intrinsic tendency to create a change. This property of a need or quasi-need can be represented by coordinating it to a "system in tension." By taking this construct seriously and using certain operational definitions, particularly by correlating the "release of tension" to a "satisfaction of the need" (or "reaching of the goal") and the "setting up of tension" to an "intention" or to a "need in a state of hunger," a great many testable conclusions were made possible.

The first formal effort to test the tension-system proposition thus developed by Lewin was the doctoral-dissertation research done by Zeigarnik (1927) under his supervision. Her experiments were based on the assumptions that (1) tension systems would be established in a subject when he was given simple tasks to perform and (2) if such tension systems were not dissipated, as would normally occur with the completion of the tasks, their persistence would result in a greater likelihood of subsequent recall by the subject of the names of the tasks. Her results in a variety of experiments substantially confirmed this prediction, since interrupted tasks were generally better recalled by subjects than completed tasks. There has been an extensive experimental literature (cf. Alper, 1948; Deutsch, 1954) concerning this interesting phenomenon, the so-called Zeigarnik effect.

The next experimental test of the tension-system construct was performed by Ovsiankina (1928). She showed that subjects would voluntarily resume interrupted activities more often than they would return to activities that had been completed.

Following the confirmatory results of these first two studies, a large number of further experimental tests were performed. Among the better known of these are the studies of Lissner (1933) and Mahler (1933) on the role of substitute activities as effective dischargers of tension; of Hoppe (1930) and J. D. Frank (1935) on success and failure, especially as these are related to the "level of aspiration" expressed by the subject; and of Karsten (1928) on "psychical satiation," which concerns the problem of the reduction in performance of an activity as a function of the continued repetition of the activity. A summary of these and other related studies is provided by Lewin (1935, pp. 239ff.). Although we do not have space here to present a further development of Lewin's contributions to research and theory via the tension-system construct, its fruitfulness is well attested by the manner in which these concepts and problems have been utilized in personality theory (cf. Deutsch, 1954).

Lewin's later concern with systematic problems of social psychology may be illustrated by his interesting, and somewhat unusual, wartime research on food habits of people (Lewin, 1943b; see also Lewin, 1951, Ch. 8). Here Lewin raised first the question of why people eat what they do. Interaction of psychological factors (e.g., cultural tradition, individual preference) and nonpsychological factors (e.g., food availability, cost) was investigated in the framework of a so-called channel theory. According to this viewpoint, most of the food that appears on the table is eventually eaten by someone or other in the family group, so that the primary question reduces to one that concerns the particular channels by which food is obtained for family use. The two major sources of food in this country during World War II were store purchases and gardening (minor channels were country buying, home baking and canning, and the like). Lewin emphasized the role of the "gatekeeper"—ordinarily the housewife—as the individual who determines for each channel how much of each foodstuff shall be procured and taken through the various stages of preparation for consumption (in the case of home gardening, of course, a larger number of steps are necessary before the final usable products are available for the table).

The psychology of the gatekeeper, as Lewin phrased it, thus became a focal point of this research. Although a large number of interesting questions were asked in the pursuit of the problem, we shall outline only one that received considerable empirical attention. That is the question of the most effective procedure for changing opinions. Here attention centered on individual versus group procedures. Lewin pointed out (1951, Ch. 10) that an a priori expectation might well be that single individuals, being "more pliable" than groups of like-minded persons, should be easier to convince. An opposite conclusion, however, is supported by the preponderance of much research (on a variety of social problems, such as alcoholism and prejudices, as well as food habits). Once the group standards themselves are changed, as by group rather than individual discussions, individual opinions are much more readily altered.

One illustrative study concerned increased consumption of fresh milk. No pressure was used in the individual or group discussions, and equal time was spent in each case. The results showed clearly that compliance by housewives with the requested change was greater following the group procedure. Similar results were found for other types of foodstuffs (such as evaporated milk and orange juice) and for quite different social problems (such as increased productivity among factory workers). A public commitment to a new course of action seems generally to produce more permanence of changed attitudes or behaviors. In some cases, the degree of change may even increase over a period of time following the experimental manipulations; when this happens there is said to be a "sleeper effect."

This research is a good example of the way in which Lewin's work combined theoretically important questions with practically significant problems and procedures. Food acceptability was of practical importance when Lewin started this research during wartime, and as the world's population increases, the problem promises to become of permanent practical significance. More generally, group processes are important to man's sense of well-being, and to his very survival. The contemporary upsurge in interest in T groups, etc., can be traced, to a very great extent, directly to the work of Lewin (see, for example, Bradford, Gibb, & Benne, 1964).

Criticisms of Lewin

Most of the critical objections to Lewin have been methodological ones, centering around his development and use of the field-theoretical approach.

One persistent criticism has involved Lewin's alleged misuse or misappropriation of topological concepts (London, 1944). The charge here is that Lewin has merely borrowed the terminology and certain of the gross conceptualizations from this geometry and has failed to utilize anything like the full set of fundamental topological relationhips. In answer to this objection, Lewin has argued that all that can legitimately be required of a psychologist who attempts to apply a mathematical model is that he coordinate some of the conceptual relations with empirical processes (1951): "There can be no other meaning and no other proof of the applicability of these geometries to psychology than the fruitfulness of predictions based on such coordination" (p. 22). If one accepts this modest objective as legitimate and sufficient, one can hardly argue with Lewin's appropriation and invention of geometries, at least as far as this aspect of his methodology is concerned.

Another criticism, voiced even by some who are strongly sympathetic to Lewin (Deutsch, 1954) as well as by less friendly critics, has been that he has failed to specify which of several possible interpretations he intended for key terms, such as *person*, or key relationships, such as *person* to *life space*. A related but much more fundamental criticism (Estes, 1954b) has been that Lewin has generally failed to indicate the empirical basis of his psychological concepts, such as life space, in spite of his admirable emphasis upon the necessity for strict operational coordinating definitions among concepts.

A corollary to the above stricture is the objection that Lewin in his emphasis upon the central cognitive aspects of behavior has tended to ignore the motor aspects. Field theorists generally, with their perceptual or cognitive orientation, have tended to undervalue the response side of the S-O-R formulation.

In a much-cited criticism, Brunswik has gone even further, holding that Lewin's "encapsulation into the central layer" means that his life space "is post-perceptual and pre-behavioral" (Brunswik, 1943). Lewin's reply to this particular comment has been that he did not think that psychology needs to study the objective physical and sociological factors which do not have implications for behavior. However, he was willing to include the study of those objective factors which are potential determiners of the life space; this kind of study he called *psychological ecology* (Lewin, 1943a). Cartwright's paper contains a carefully detailed formulation of this problem of the "boundary zone" of the life space (1959, pp. 69ff.).

Other critical evaluations of the more technical aspects of Lewinian field theory may be found in Leeper (1943) and Cartwright (1959). Comprehensive reviews by Deutsch (1954) and Escalona (1954) cover the contributions of his work to social psychology and child psychology, respectively.

Finally, a serious objection to Lewin has been that he failed to make his general conceptual system sufficiently precise and specific so that it can be disconfirmed by experimental test. To quote Estes (1954b, p. 332):

This informal development of coordinating definitions in use enables the theorist to give plausible accounts of concrete situations, but with no possibility of having the theory refuted by the outcome of the behavioral situation, since the correspondence between theoretical and empirical terms is adjusted in accordance with the empirical findings and is never formally incorporated into the system. Flexibility is obtained at the cost of testability.

It is necessary to recognize the important distinction between Lewin's effective experimental-theoretical research on specific problems, emphasized in the following section, and his theoretical efforts of a systematic sort, criticized in the preceding paragraph for their lack of adequate empirical specification. In particular, the life-space schemata seem to be of very limited value in setting up experiments. They serve as pedagogic devices and perhaps provide a general stimulating effect for the experimenter. Although it is impossible to identify the sources of a man's influence with certainty, it seems likely that Lewin's tremendous contemporary influence stems less from his formal theorizing than from his informal theorizing and the associated empirical work.

Lewin's Contributions

Lewin has few peers as a creative conceptualizer *and* an ingenious experimenter. It was largely this ability to implement his theoretical insights with concrete empirical situations that accounts for his preeminence. This ability was apparently based, at least in part, upon insightful observations of the everyday-life scene. For example, his conceptualization of the tension system in relation to memory (cf. the Zeigarnik effect, described above) is said to have been suggested by his observation that waiters in Berlin restaurants had a remarkably accurate memory for the detailed amount of each bill—until after it was paid (G. W. Hartmann, 1935, p. 221). Similarly, in his later career, his interest in problems of social interaction, such as the role of a social minority, was at least partially stimulated by his own keen awareness of the tragedies which he observed in the real world (Deutsch, 1954).

Second, Lewin's specific contributions to psychological theory were of great scope and depth. He developed concepts and experimental techniques, such as level of aspiration, that have enjoyed widespread acceptance in the fields of personality and motivation. These contributions to personality theory have had a strong, continuing influence.

Finally, Lewin's pioneering efforts in the field of social psychology would be sufficient to guarantee him a lasting and prominent place in the history of psychology. His early research in social psychology in this country is exemplified by the pioneer studies (Lewin, 1939; Lippitt, 1940; Lippitt & White, 1943) on behavior in social climates that were experimentally manipulated. For example, leadership techniques were experimentally varied in boys' clubs (laissez faire, democratic, autocratic), and various behaviors, such as aggression, were correlated with different social climates that resulted (Lippitt & White, 1943). These studies not only opened up an important new area of social research but also had some influence upon educational and social practices (Cartwright, 1959).

The final phase of Lewin's research, concerned mainly with group dynamics, found him taking more of an administrative and supervisory role and leaving to others the detailed working out of hypotheses and collection of data. In *Resolving social conflicts* (1948), Lewin reported on various experimental efforts to change social behavior in real, everyday-life situations (such as interracial factory workshops). It is unfortunate that his relatively early death prevented further contributions to this kind of research program.

The lines of work started by Lewin certainly did not stop with his death. He was one of those rare individuals who are in tune with the times twenty-five to fifty years after they are no longer alive. The problems connected with social influence and leadership are still under active study. Field observations, which so often gave Lewin his inspiration, are fast gaining respectability as a source of psychological information (Willems & Raush, 1969). His concern, late in life, with psychological ecology must have provided part of the impetus for Barker's work resulting in a book on precisely that topic (1968). Even his attempt to find parallels between different fields, best seen in his general attitude toward field theory and his attempt to use mathematical formalism, may have, at the least, provided part of the general background for the development of general systems theory (see Buckley, 1968, for papers in this area). To say that Kurt Lewin was one of the germinal figures for modern psychology is praise too faint.

COGNITIVE FIELD THEORY: TOLMAN'S PURPOSIVE BEHAVIORISM

The most important contribution of Edward C. Tolman (1886-1959) to the development of behaviorism has already been noted (Chapter 7). The emphasis which he early placed on a *molar* interpretation of behavior as *purposive* (1932) persisted throughout his long and illustrious career. Although Tolman cannot be said to have developed a definitive theory, his system of psychology, with its primarily cognitive, or S-S, position on learning, has been extremely influential. He has been the most acceptable of the major avowed behaviorists to nonbehavioristically oriented psychologists. His system represents the seemingly paradoxical combination of important elements of behaviorism and Gestalt psychology. His primary orientation has been stimulus-centered, or cognitive, rather than S-R; in his later papers especially (e.g., 1949a) he has not only professed a deep-seated admiration for the field-theoretical views of Kurt Lewin but also adopted an essentially Lewinian position with regard to fundamental theoretical problems. For these reasons Tolman is treated here as a kind of field theorist.

Tolman's Career

Edward Tolman was born in Massachusetts and took an engineering degree at the Massachusetts Institute of Technology. He switched to psychology and received his M.A. in 1912 and his Ph.D. in 1915 from Harvard. He served as an instructor in psychology at Northwestern University from 1915 to 1918. Tolman then moved to the University of California, where he established a rat laboratory. During World War II he served for two years (1944 and 1945) in the Office of Strategic Services. In 1950, at the age of sixty-four, Tolman demonstrated his patriotism in a different way by leading the fight against the state loyalty oath. During the next three years while the issue was being resolved, Tolman held appointments at the University of Chicago and at Harvard. His humanness, which made him beloved by his students, shows through even in the conclusion to his final published statement (1959, p. 152):

I have liked to think about psychology in ways that have proved congenial to me. Since all the sciences, and especially psychology, are still immersed in such tremendous realms of the uncertain and the unknown, the best that any individual scientist, especially any psychologist, can do seems to be to follow his own gleam and his own bent, however inadequate they may be. In fact, I suppose that actually this is what we all do. In the end, the only sure criterion is to have fun. And I have had fun.

Tolman the man was thus something of a maverick and a dissenter. We shall see, too, that the system produced by this man refuses to fit itself easily into the usual categories.

Tolman's System

The foundation of Tolman's purposive behaviorism was present in his first and major book, *Purposive behavior in animals and men* (1932), in a loosely formulated manner. Until recently, little effort was expended to organize the major ideas into anything like an integrated system. Predictions about experimental outcomes were not related to one another in any logically rigorous manner. In a word, Tolman has long been considered a programmatic theorist. A detailed attempt at a more definitive formalization of his major principles was made by MacCorquodale and Meehl (1954), and in a final work Tolman himself (1959) has endeavored to present a somewhat more organized picture of his system. We shall present here a summary of certain of his most salient principles.

The primary principle in Tolman's systematic thinking about behavior is that in its purposive or adaptive activities, the organism utilizes environmental objects and develops *means-end readinesses* with regard to them and their role in relation to his behavior. This phrase is but one of many awkwardly compounded terms which Tolman coined early in his career and used consistently in his writing; this one is particularly emphasized in his "Principles of purposive behavior" (1959). The term is roughly synonymous with *cognitions* or *expectancies*. It refers to the kind of learning which Tolman felt was central to behavior—sign learning. Briefly put, the organism learns "what leads to what." Like the Gestalt theorists, Tolman felt that the actual behavior is relatively unimportant; the primary determiners of action are central, not peripheral, as the typical S-R theorist would hold.

A more formal structure in Tolman's system was developed in his final comprehensive statement (1959). There he presented a systematic schema for each of five representative situations: simple approach to food, simple escape from electric shock, simple avoidance of electric shock, choice-point learning, and latent learning.

Without going into a detailed explication of these paradigms and the notation system used by Tolman, we may note several salient considerations suggested by the scheme. First, a somewhat superficial similarity to the Hullian system is evident. To some extent this logical interrelating of concepts was induced by the form of presentation requested by the editor of the book for which this particular paper was prepared; to some extent, perhaps, this kind of formalization was encouraged by the earlier effort of MacCorquodale and Meehl to put Tolman's thinking into Hullian form. In any case, it should also be mentioned, in fairness, that a somewhat comparable, though much simpler, tabular arrangement was early used by Tolman (e.g., 1936, 1938).

Second, and more important, Tolman's final formulation illustrates the central role played in his theory by the cognitive constructs. Here a little explanatory detail is in order. Two major cognitive constructs are involved. The means-end readiness is a relatively pure acquired cognitive disposition—pure in the sense that it endures independently of the present motivational state of the organism; that is, he may know where food is whether or not he is hungry. The expectation, on the other hand, is the concrete product of the means-end readiness—a cognitive event that applies directly and specifically to the present situation. Tolman summed up the two concepts (1959, pp. 113-114):

A means-end readiness, as I conceive it, is a condition in the organism, which is equivalent to what in ordinary parlance we call a "belief" (a readiness or disposition) to the effect that an instance of this *sort* of stimulus situation, if reacted to by an instance of this *sort* of response, will lead to an instance of that *sort* of further stimulus situation, or else, that an instance of this *sort* of stimulus situation will simply by itself be accompanied, or followed, by an instance of that *sort* of stimulus situation. Further, I assume that the different readinesses or beliefs (dispositions) are stored up together (in the nervous system). When they are concretely activated in the form of expectancies they tend to interact and/or consolidate with one another. And I would also assert that "thinking" as we know it in human beings, is in essence no more than an activated interplay among expectancies resulting from such previously acquired readinesses which result in new expectancies and resultant new means-end readinesses.

Tolman conceded the weakness of this formulation in terms of specific empirical measures. He recognized the difficulty of implementing such constructs operationally, but at the same time repeatedly pointed to what he saw as a comparable weakness in the Hull-Spence $r_g - s_g$ construct (see Chapter 10).

Although the concept of cognition, however phrased, is the key one in Tolman's system, he considered other types of concepts and other kinds of learning. In his effort (1949b) to cover the major types of learning processes, he pointed to the following six "types of connections": *cathexes*, which represent the affective properties acquired by objects (similar to Lewin's *valence*); *equivalence beliefs*, which are the cognitive representations of subgoals, secondary reinforcers, or impending disturbances; *field expectancies* (earlier called *sign-Gestalt-expectations*), which are representations of the environment that make possible latent learning, shortcuts, etc.; *field-cognition modes*, which are the higher-order functions that produce field expectancies through perceptual, memorial, or inferential processes; *drive discriminations*, which are the demonstrated abilities of animals to behave differentially under different deprivation conditions; and *motor patterns*, which are the responses and combinations of responses (skills) themselves.

Tolman made only the sketchiest effort to indicate the kinds of laws, or empirical relationships between variables, that might relate to these various kinds of learning. No laws were seriously suggested, for example, for the important field-cognition modes or for drive discriminations. A simple contiguity principle, following Guthrie, was accepted for motor patterns. Hullian need reduction was considered to be at least partially responsible for cathexes and equivalence beliefs. And no definitive interpretations were offered for the key concept of field expectancies, although the reinforcement principle here was specifically denied more than an incidental role.

Tolman's (1951b) model contained three major constructs: the *need system*, closely related to orthodox drive notions; the *behavior space*, closely related to Lewin's life space, described earlier in this chapter; and the *belief-value matrix*, which consists of hierarchies of learned expectations concerning environmental objects and their roles in relation to behavior.

These brief sketches of Tolman's approach should indicate the essentially tentative and preliminary nature of his system. He seldom felt certain enough of his ground to suggest lawful relationships, or even logical relationships, between the variables of his system. Tolman was himself acutely aware of the questionable status of some aspects of his system (1959): "... I think the days of such grandiose, all-covering systems in psychology as mine attempted to be are, at least for the present, pretty much passé.... I have an inveterate tendency to make my ideas too complicated and too high-flown so that they become less and less susceptible to empirical test" (pp. 93-94).

Tolman did not produce the kind of system he did because of his metatheoretical principles or his methodological ignorance, but because he was the kind of person he was. In his early works (1936, 1938), he had specified in some detail the particular variables which he felt were significant ones in behavior and had indicated the kind of "standard" experimental situation in which their values might be determined. He was also early concerned with a prototype of experimental design intended to identify the functional interrelationships of independent, intervening, and dependent variables. Thus Tolman espoused a strict empirical methodology designed to uncover lawful relationships between variables, but he never carried his beliefs over into practice. The amount of tedium involved may well make such a program impractical for anyone to carry out, and certainly it was not Tolman's kind of fun.

Tolman's Experimentation

The kind of experimental research performed by Tolman is well illustrated by an early study on insight learning in the rat (Tolman & Honzik, 1930). An elevated

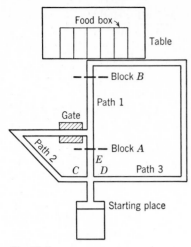

Fig. 11-4

Maze used to test insight in rats. The paths become established as a hierarchy according to length, path 1 preferred to path 2, and path 2 preferred to path 3. If path 1 is closed by block A, the rats run by path 2. If path 1 is closed by block B, the rats run by path 3 if they have insight that the barrier closes path 2 as well as path 1. (From Tolman & Honzik, 1930, p. 223.)

maze with three alternative paths to the goal box was used, as shown in Figure 11-4. The three paths varied in length. In preliminary training path 1, the shortest, was blocked, and the animals then learned to use the next shortest, path 2. It will be noted that paths 1 and 2 share the final part of the direct runway to the goal box. During training trials the block had been placed close to the starting place, well before the common segment of paths 1 and 2. For the test trials the block was moved to position B, toward the end of the common segment and close to the goal box. According to the insight prediction the animal would now turn to path 3, rather than to previously preferred path 2, since this was also blocked. A noninsight type of simple S-R view would presumably predict the mechanical running off of the next strongest response in the hierarchy established in training, that of running down path 2. Most of the animals tested in the study chose path 3, thus supporting Tolman's cognitive or expectancy position.

This experiment has been followed by several replications and modifications, not all of which have given clearly confirmatory results (cf. Hilgard, 1956, p. 195). It nevertheless stands as an important early research which not only supported Tolman's general cognitive theory but also served to stimulate further, more analytic researches. In these respects it is representative of much of Tolman's experimentation.

Even more characteristic of Tolman's research is the latent-learning experiment, originated by Blodgett (1929) in the California laboratory. The fundamental problem here is whether reward (or reinforcement) is essential for learning to occur. As a cognitive theorist, defining learning in terms of perceptual rather than response factors, Tolman insisted that learning will occur in the absence of reward but simply will not be demonstrated until the appropriate motivational conditions obtain.

In a typical latent-learning experiment, designed to test Tolman's cognitive position, a hungry animal is permitted access to a learning device, such as a maze, without being rewarded by food in the goal box. After a certain number of such trials, on which numerous errors are made and limited overt learning evidenced, the animal finds food in the goal box for the first time. The subsequent test trials generally show a remarkably improved performance, indicating that the animal had been learning something about the maze on the earlier trials but had not been motivated to perform appropriately (i.e., to take the true path to the goal box and avoid the blind alleys). When reward is introduced, the performance of such experimental animals quickly approximates that of controls which have had the same number of trials, all reinforced by food.

Although there is still some controversy on this issue, especially about the various subtle sources of reinforcement now suspected to operate (e.g., removal of the animal from the maze), the majority of the results seem to support Tolman's original position. (See Kimble, 1961; MacCorquodale & Meehl, 1951; and Thistlethwaite, 1951, for reviews of the pertinent literature.)

Criticisms of Tolman

The most persistent criticism of Tolman's work has already been indicated: his failure to develop anything like a logically integrated theory. In this respect certain of his own comments may be instructive. For example, in refusing to comment on a requested distinction between his use of immediate data language and construct language, Tolman noted (1959) that "I myself can neither get very interested in nor completely understand such more refined logical distinctions" (p. 149). Apparently his lack of interest in problems of logical relationships at least partly accounts for the programmaticity of his systematizing.

One particular and important criticism which Tolman has shared with Lewin is that he has paid insufficient attention to the problem of relating overt behavior to cognition and similar central states. Guthrie, for instance, has commented (1935) that Tolman leaves the rat "buried in thought" (p. 172). This weakness in Tolman's system may be seen as part of the overall inadequacy of specification, discussed above.

Finally, as a representative of a kind of commonsense approach to behavior, Tolman has come in for a variety of criticisms from the more tough-minded type of psychologist. An obvious point of attack has involved his alleged mentalism largely as a result of the kind of language Tolman has used and the centralist nature of his constructs. In answer to such attacks, he has stoutly and persistently defended his basic behaviorism. Even the more sympathetic of Tolman's critics, however, have entertained some doubt on this score. Thus MacCorquodale and Meehl have noted (1954) "a certain affinity for the dualistic" even while not meaning "even to suggest that he is anything else [than a behaviorist] consciously or unconsciously" (p. 185). In considering this criticism Tolman had at least a partial explanation, if not justification, to offer in terms of his initial exposure to objectivism. He has stated (1959) that ". . . although I was sold on objectivism and behaviorism as *the* method in psychology, the only categorizing rubrics which I had at hand were mentalistic ones. So when I began to try to develop a behavioristic system of my own, what I really was doing was trying to rewrite a commonsense mentalistic psychology . . . in operational behavioristic terms" (p. 94).

Tolman's Contributions

In spite of the undeniable programmaticity of his systematizing, Tolman has had a great influence upon the course of psychology over the past four decades. We shall describe several general forms of this influence and then mention some more specific contributions.

Tolman's role in leavening the behavioristic loaf in its early, formative period was a most significant one. Although his emphasis on a molar point of view and an acceptance of purposiveness was never quite accepted by some behaviorists, nevertheless this kind of interpretation served to make the system more readily understandable and acceptable to many others. Tolman thus saved for the consideration of the science of psychology concepts which might otherwise have been discarded completely because they were not easy to define operationally. The verdict of history has clearly favored Tolman, particularly in the case of "purpose"; the science of cybernetics has objectified and precisely defined what it is for a machine to have a purpose, so that there are few left in or out of psychology who would now maintain that the concept cannot be objectified.

The influence of his cognitive learning system has also been very great. For two decades Tolman's cognitive position offered the major alternative to the Hullian need-reduction theory. As a matter of fact, much of the learning experimentation and literature was directly concerned with one attempt or another to pit cognitive theory against reinforcement theory. Thus in reviewing the learning literature for the first issue of the *Annual Review of Psychology*, Melton (1950) could say that ". . . these past twenty years of experimental-theoretical development have been increasingly under the influence of the opposed theoretical systems of Tolman and Hull" (p. 9).

A different kind of general influence may be noted in Tolman's long-standing support of the rat as a laboratory animal and appropriate subject for even the field-theoretical and centralist thinking which he espoused. Such use of this favored laboratory animal by Tolman was undoubtedly responsible for a large amount of the acceptance generally accorded "rat psychology" in spite of the strong opposition of many psychologists. His position on this issue was very clearly and forcefully stated in his delightful (1945) essay. Here Tolman, always humorous and self-effacing, is at his best. The concluding sentences are especially noteworthy (1945, p. 166):

What, by way of summary, can we now say as to the contributions of us rodent psychologists to human behavior? What is it that we rat runners still have to contribute to the understanding of the deeds and the misdeeds, the absurdities and the tragedies of our friend, and our enemy—*homo sapiens*? The answer is that, whereas man's successes, persistences, and socially unacceptable divagations—that is, his intelligences, his motivations, and his instabilities—are all ultimately shaped and materialized by specific cultures, it is still true that most of the formal underlying laws of intelligence, motivation, and instability can still be studied in rats as well as, and more easily than, in men.

And, as a final peroration, let it be noted that rats live in cages; they do not go on binges the night before one has planned an experiment; they do not kill each other off in wars; they do not invent engines of destruction, and, if they did, they would not be so inept about controlling such engines; they do not go in for either class conflicts or race conflicts; they avoid politics, economics, and papers in psychology. They are marvelous, pure, and delightful. And, as soon as I possibly can, I am going to climb back again out on that good old phylogenetic limb and sit there, this time right side up and unashamed, wiggling my whiskers at all the silly, yet at the same time far too complicated, specimens of *homo sapiens*, whom I shall see strutting and fighting and messing things up, down there on the ground below me.

Of many particular contributions that Tolman made, two early ones need to be mentioned. One is his invention (1936) of the intervening-variable paradigm, later adopted and much more thoroughly implemented by Hull (see Chapter 10). An intervening variable is an intraorganismic function (e.g., hunger) that is postulated to account for a particular kind of behavior (e.g., eating) in a certain stimulus situation (e.g., presentation of food object after one day of food deprivation). Although Tolman apparently intended a purely abstractive usage of the intervening variable, he eventually renounced such a usage for the less operationally valid "hypothetical construct" (cf. Marx, 1963, Chs. 1, 5). He later stated (1959): "My intervening variables are generally speaking mere temporarily believed-in, inductive, more or less qualitative generalizations which categorize and sum up for me various empirically found relationships" (p. 97). He further observed (1959) that they are not "primarily neurophysiological . . . but are derived rather from intuition, common experience, a little sophomoric neurology, and my own phenomenology" (pp. 98ff).

Tolman is generally credited with having made the first effective distinction in the psychological literature between learning and performance. He early pointed out that learning alone is not sufficient to produce the learned behavior, that the motivational conditions must also be appropriate. The distinction between learning and performance has been a most important one in the development of learning theory and research. Tolman credited Blodgett, who performed the first latent-learning experiment, for having forced this distinction on him and also noted (1958, p. 149) that Lashley had anticipated him.

Finally, Tolman must be credited with having played a major role in the opening up of many significant areas of research. Of these, the most important are probably the latent-learning problem, which deals with the necessity of the reinforcement principle in learning; the transposition problem, which concerns the dependence of learning upon relative as contrasted with absolute cues; and the continuity-noncontinuity issue, which involves the question of whether each single reinforcement or nonreinforcement has an effect in learning (the continuity position). Each of these problem areas relates directly to the theoretical opposition between Hull and Tolman. While the large-scale systematic issues posed by these two views are no longer of prime concern to learning theorists, many of the particular problem areas developed in the theoretical controversy not only have produced much valuable research but also are still themselves of first importance in learning research. In this way Tolman, like Hull, has had a great and continuing influence on experimental-theoretical psychology.

FIELD THEORY OF ACHIEVEMENT: BRUNSWIK'S PROBABILISTIC FUNCTIONALISM

The probabilistic functionalism developed and propounded by Egon Brunswik (1903-1955) is difficult to categorize within the simplified theoretical framework which we have utilized for expository purposes in the present volume. Certainly Brunswik was not an S-R theorist, although under the influence of Tolman and others he very definitely moved in the direction of behaviorism after he came to this country. It is equally certain that he was in no obvious way a field theorist of the sort that Lewin represented. Although his research on the perceptual constancies was often related to orthodox Gestalt psychology, Brunswik himself (1949, p. 57) explicitly denied any such historical or conceptual relationship.

We have categorized Brunswik as a field theorist primarily because he so persistently and successfully considered the totality of interacting factors in his attempt to establish a meaningful systematic framework within which to evaluate psychological systems and behavioral problems. In this respect he outdid even Lewin, especially with his explicit emphasis upon distal, as compared with proximal, antecedent and consequent conditions. Furthermore, his insistence upon a representative, rather than merely a systematic, design for experimentation likewise indicates a deep concern for all the interacting factors involved in the determination of behavior. These statements should be clearer after the reader has grasped some of the basic points that Brunswik attempted to make and to implement in his own research.

Brunswik's Career

Egon Brunswik was born in Hungary, where he received an unusually varied education. After being trained in engineering and passing the first state examination, he shifted to the study of psychology at the University of Vienna. There he was much influenced by contacts with the logical positivists, in the Vienna Circle. He studied psychology under Karl Bühler, taking his doctorate in 1927. In the meantime he passed the state examination for teaching mathematics and physics.

Following several years of various academic appointments, a critical turning point in Brunswik's career occurred during the 1933-1934 academic year. E. C. Tolman, visiting in Vienna, met and was quite impressed with Brunswik. Two years later Brunswik received a Rockefeller Fellowship and, largely at Tolman's instigation, was invited to serve as visiting lecturer and research fellow in psychology at the Berkeley campus of the University of California. In 1937, he returned to Berkeley as assistant professor. He spent the remainder of his life there.

Brunswik's Research

Brunswik is best known in psychology for the breadth and intensity of his research on visual constancy factors, usually referred to as *thing constancy*. This research program was well begun in Europe and was a major factor in attracting Tolman to Brunswik. The heart of Brunswik's thing-constancy research is the dichotomy between the physical nature of an object and its sensory representation. The extent to which the perceptual effect tends to approximate the more remote physical (distal) or the more immediate sensory (proximal) value is the fundamental problem of this kind of research. For example, consider a wooden table. As a distal object, the table has a certain determinate physical length; as a proximate object, in perception, it also has a certain length, equivalent to the physical distance delimited on the appropriate receptor surface of the subject. It is the physical, or distal, dimension that remains relatively stable while a wide variety of other conditions, such as distance or angle of view, directly affect the proximal dimension.

The major finding of Brunswik's thing-constancy research was that there is almost inevitably a compromise in experience, or—more operationally—in the subject's reported judgment, between the distal and the proximal dimensions. Normally the subject tends to approximate more closely the distal, or real, characteristics of the object in spite of the various distorting conditions: hence the term *thing constancy*. Appropriate instructions, however can markedly reduce the influence of the distal factor so that the proximal dimension is more closely approximated. The index of this influence (Thouless's "regression to the real") is called the *Brunswik ratio*. This ratio is unity when constancy is perfect—that is, when perceived factors such as size, shape, and brightness are independent of distance, angle of tilt, luminous flux, etc. When the proximal (retinal) stimulus completely determines visual perception, the Brunswik ratio is zero. Thus the ratio indicates, on a scale ranging from zero to unity, the degree to which the constant aspects of the stimulus situation determine perception.

In subsequent research Brunswik extended this basic methodology to new problems of a somewhat wider interest. First, within the area of perception, he brought into his experiments such variables as monetary value. For example, in one experiment (Brunswik, 1934, pp. 147-150; see also Brunswik, 1956, p. 78) the experimenter asked subjects to make comparisons between cards containing varying

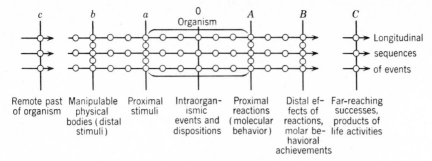

Fig. 11-5
Scheme of the organism in its surroundings. (From Brunswik, 1939a, p. 37.)

numbers of coins of varying sizes and monetary value. In accordance with the basic principle repeatedly demonstrated in the simpler research, judgments of equality between stimuli were compromised to some extent by each of the three variables. Later, under the influence of Tolman and American neobehaviorism Brunswik came to concern himself with instrumental behavior as well as perception (cf. the early collaborative paper, Tolman & Brunswik, 1935). In one important study (Brunswik, 1939b), he attacked the problem of what is now called *partial* or *intermittent reinforcement*. The all-or-none reward situation almost invariably used in American learning experimentation up to that time Brunswik felt to be quite unrepresentative of normal situations. Accordingly he varied the proportion of reward to total trials in the two ends of a standard T maze. The rat subjects cooperated and expressed preferences that were roughly correlated with degree of probability of reward in the two ends. This research is related, conceptually, to the earlier work in perception in that the primary concern is again with the degree to which the subject normally achieves a kind of constancy relationship.

Brunswik's System

The probabilistic functionalism which Brunswik came to feel most adequately systematizes psychological problems was a fairly direct and logical outgrowth of the research program outlined above. Brunswik's system is *probabilistic* since it holds that the perceptual and behavioral goals in the natural environment are related usually in an equivocal and rarely in a univocal manner to cues and responses. The system is a *functionalism* since it is concerned primarily with the degree of success, or achievement, in perception and instrumental behavior.

An illustration of Brunswik's systematic thinking is his conceptual framework (1939a) in which a succession of temporally and spatially ordered "levels" or "layers" of variables is envisioned. These range from the temporally most remote (those furthest back in the past of the individual) through manipulable physical objects (distal stimuli) to the outer physical areas of the organism (proximal stimuli) and thence to intraorganismic functions and states; on the response side, a comparable array is conceptualized, from proximal reactions through distal effects

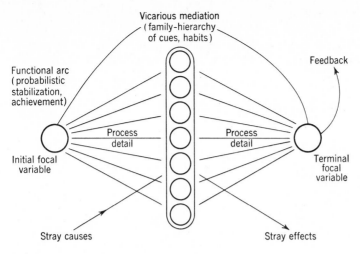

Fig. 11-6
The lens model: composite picture of the functional unit of behavior.
(From Brunswik, 1952, p. 20.)

(achievements in regard to environmental objects) to long-range successes and ultimate products of the individual's life-span. These relations are represented in Figure 11-5. Brunswik used his conceptual framework in the analysis, or characterization, of psychological systems. For example, both structural and Gestalt psychologists, according to Brunswik's analysis of the situation, confined themselves primarily to the study of the relationships between proximal stimuli (level *a* in the scheme) and intraorganismic events and dispositions (level O). Classical behaviorism studied *a-A* relationships for the most part. Psychoanalysis, viewed in a simplified manner, would be described as concentrating on *c*-O relationships. The concentration of a functionalism or a molar behaviorism would tend to be on *b-B* relationships (the O level may enter into nearly any systematic position, depending on whether or not the particular investigator is interested in physiology or in introspective analysis).

Brunswik's lens model (1952), shown in Figure 11-6, illustrates the way in which a great variety of different but interacting processes can be initiated from a single focal factor (such as an object in the stimulus situation in perception research or some aspect of a learning problem in instrumental behavior research) and also the way in which a similarly differentiated array of response processes mediated within the organism may focalize into a single perceptual or instrumental achievement. For an illustrative commonplace application of the lens model, consider the behavior of a baseball player who is attempting to catch a high fly ball (the "initial focal variable"). A number of different perceptual cues emanate from the ball in flight—its speed, height, etc.—and must be quickly taken into account by the fielder as he estimates its trajectory and ultimate destination. Such "stray causes" as the direction and force of the wind and position of the sun may also need to be taken into account. On the response side, the fielder needs to mobilize his energies so as to time his movement toward the ball properly without interference from other stray causes such as teammates, fences, and the like. "Stray effects" would then be exemplified by collisions with other fielders, bumping into fences, etc. An ultimate instrumental achievement such as catching a difficult fly ball (the "terminal focal variable") is thus seen as dependent upon the successful coordination of a variety of "process details" on both the perceptual and the response sides.

Brunswik felt that the double-convex model represents the manner in which an organism is able to mobilize its functions so as to maximize its utilization of cues emanating from distal stimuli and achieve a reasonable amount of success in its control of the environment. He felt that problems of distal relationships need to be studied first, before problems of mediation by intraorganismic detail processes are investigated. His own research presents as good an example of this kind of experimentation as any.

Hursch, Hammond, and Hursch (1964) followed up Brunswik's suggestion that the relationships represented in the lens model could be more precisely studied by using multiple correlation methods. Their techniques make it possible to determine how well a subject can do on the basis of various ecological cues and how well he actually is using the available cues. They show how their analysis can be applied to a case of probability learning and to a case of clinical inference. Although some additional experiments have used this type of analysis (for example, C. R. Peterson, Hammond, & Summers, 1965; Summers & Hammond, 1966), it is probable that the use of this particular derivation of Brunswik's thought has by no means reached its peak of popularity. With the increased respectability of naturalistic studies and the tremendous interest in ecology in general, it seems inevitable that applicable statistical techniques will be much in demand.

A major reason why Brunswik felt that problems involving particular mechanisms should wait until the fundamental achievement principles are worked out is the high degree of substitutability among such mechanisms. On the instrumental side, this may be simply illustrated by the variety of particular responses (habits) which a rat can use to depress a bar, or which a cat can use to tip a pole, and thereby open a restraining door, as in the Guthrie and Horton (1946) experiment. In these cases, the terminal–focal–effect is the same regardless of the particular mechanism used.

The same relationship of interchangeability among mechanisms may be illustrated, on the perceptual side, by the variety of cues that mediate visual depth perception (cf. Postman & Tolman, 1958, pp. 511ff.). The distal stimulus here is represented as a focal point, shown on the left in the double-convex lens model of Figure 11-6. A variety of different kinds of physical energies, represented by the diverging lines of the lens model, serve to produce the proximal distance cues (retinal disparity, accommodation, convergence, linear perspective, and the like), which are represented by circles in the center of the model. Intraorganismic mediating processes relate each proximal cue to the terminal perceptual event, in this case the distance judgment.

A number of interesting points are suggested by this kind of analysis. The *ecological validity* of cues (or habits) is defined as the degree of correlation between each such proximal condition and the value of the distal stimulus. For example, the ecological validity of retinal disparity is generally higher than that of accommodation or convergence as a cue to distance. This means simply that retinal disparity is a more effective cue, correlating more highly with physical distance. But it is not essential; other cues can substitute for it and mediate depth perception. In its normal adjustment to the flux of events in the environment the organism needs to have considerable flexibility with regard to which cues (or habits) are most often given the greatest weight. The necessarily probabilistic nature of the terminal focal events (perceptual and instrumental) is clearly indicated by this analysis. As Brunswik has put it (1955a, p. 207):

The general pattern of the mediational strategy of the organism is predicated upon the limited ecological validity or trustworthiness of cues. . . . This forces a probabilistic strategy upon the organism. To improve its bet, it must accumulate and combine cues. . . . No matter how much the attainment is improved, however, distal function remains inherently probabilistic.

Brunswik's Emphasis on Representative Design

Perhaps the most far-reaching aspect of Brunswik's conceptual formulation was his increasing emphasis on the necessity for psychology to use what he called *representative*, rather than systematic, design in its experimentation (Brunswik, 1956). This emphasis follows directly out of the probabilistic functionalism which he developed. As long as rigorous control of variables is practiced, in the orthodox systematic design used by most psychologists, there will be serious limitations on the degree to which experimental results are representative of the natural behavior of the subject. In order to permit a more adequate analysis of the organism's achievements in relation to the environment—seen by Brunswik from his functionalistic position as the primary problem for psychology—a wider sampling of effective variables must be utilized, even if this means less rigorous control in the usual sense.

As a corollary of this position, the highly general laws aimed at in orthodox systematic research would need to be replaced by statistical statements in which only probabilistic values can be expressed. Such statistical expressions concern the probabilities with which the various conditions sampled are found to correlate with the achievements of the organism in dealing with the environment. In representative designs correlational techniques thus replace the statistical tests of differences that are usual in systematic designs.

Although the positive side of these methodological proposals seems reasonably clear, since they follow directly from Brunswik's own research program, his criticisms of the orthodox type of systematic design may require further specification. Brunswik felt that any experiment which deals with only one variable at a time, in the classic manner, is hopelessly inadequate to present a realistic picture of the organism's behavior. Although the recent trend toward multivariate design was considered to be a step in the right direction, it has been nonetheless a

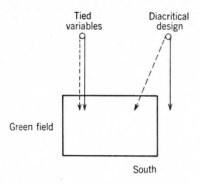

Fig. 11-7
Systematic design in the study of behavior constancy. See text for explanation. (From Brunswik, 1955a, p. 194.)

small and seriously limited one. Furthermore, the variables ordinarily manipulated
are proximal rather than distal ones, in the conceptual framework described above;
from Brunswik's point of view, this places the emphasis on the wrong kind of investigation.

Brunswik was also highly critical of the way in which variables are artificially
"tied" and "untied," as well as "interlocked," in orthodox systematic design. Although a detailed specification of these problems is beyond the scope of the present
book, the general point here is that a truly representative design should permit a
freer kind of covariation among factors (see Postman & Tolman, 1959, pp. 516ff.,
for an especially clear presentation of this argument). This point may be illustrated
by a relatively simple example which Brunswik (1955a, pp. 194ff.) developed on
the basis of a problem earlier suggested by E. B. Holt (1915). Imagine a flock of
birds flying (1) over a green field (dashed line) and (2) southward (solid line). As
shown in Figure 11-7, these two variables are confounded, or tied. Merely returning
the birds to point 0 does not resolve the confounding, nor does adding new subjects
from the same population. The typical technique used to untie these two variables
in systematically designed experimentation is called *diacritical* by Brunswik. It is
indicated in Figure 11-7 by the movement of the birds to a new position, so that
the two alternative interpretations may be clearly separated, that is, have different
consequences (birds either fly to the green field and not directly south or fly south
and thereby miss the green field). But, Brunswik pointed out (1955a, p. 195):

We soon discover that southwardness is still tied to such factors as the general area
of start, temperature and other climatic conditions, topographic landmarks, mag-
netic cues, and so forth; and so is the greenness of the field to its squareness or size.
What we have accomplished in diacritical design is to separate or "split" an original
encompassing cluster into two subclusters of tied variables; but we have not really
"isolated" our variable as it may have seemed at first glance, and therefore are not
yet entitled to speak of its attainment as a constant function.

For Brunswik the only satisfactory solution to this kind of problem would be a truly representative design in which a more adequate sampling of situational variables is possible. A partial solution would not be enough. A simple example of the inadequacy of such artificial untying of variables, in systematic design, has been provided by Brunswik (1956, p. 27). In an experiment on judgment of personality traits, subjects are placed in identical bodily positions and given identical clothes to wear. While this experimental procedure controls for the influence of these two variables, it also makes impossible the assay of any normal interaction between the personality traits estimated and such factors as body tone and dressing habits. This typical experiment is thus incompletely designed, according to Brunswik. For completeness, one would need to include a much wider range of important variables in the behavior sampling (e.g., have subjects take different positions or wear different clothes).

The problem posed is indeed like the problem posed for the pollster asked to assess public opinion. The pollster would like to sample the whole population, but that is impractical. He therefore settles for a "representative sample" of the population. In the same way, the experimenter might like to sample all the variables, and all the interrelationships between variables, in order to arrive at psychological laws. Then he could use a systematic design, and the design would give him all the interrelationships between variables. Such a procedure is far more difficult even than sampling a complete population. Thus the experimenter, too, must take a sample, and the most useful sample to take is not one that is arbitrarily chosen, but one that characterizes the variables and their values and interactions *as they occur in the actual environment*. Even if we could do a complete systematic experiment, we would not know what organisms would do until we studied the situations to which they would be exposed. Thus representative designs are necessary in principle as well as in practice.

Brunswik's Contribution to Psychology

Brunswik's logical analysis of design problems is almost certain to have more influence upon the future course of psychological science than is typical of such logical endeavors. Already there is evidence that his position is being implemented far outside the experimental study of perception in which it started. An outstanding example of this is K. R. Hammond's (1954, 1955) demonstration of the importance of considering representative design in clinical psychology. Research on the diagnostic use of test scores is criticized for not sampling adequately the personality characteristics of the examiners themselves and the situational variables involved in the test administration. As a matter of fact, frequently the range of examiners is severely limited, such as to a single person, for the express purpose of eliminating variability in results. Such application of the typical systematic design unfortunately has not prevented investigators from generalizing their results, at least implicitly, to a presumably wide range of examiners and situations, as well as to a population of tested individuals (the representativeness of whose selection in sampling is generally explicitly considered). Some extension of the principles of more fully representative design to other experimental and clinical situations would seem to be indicated, regardless of the extent to which one accepts Brunswik's strictures of orthodox systematic design.

Most of the criticisms of Brunswik's methodological points have centered around his apparent opposition to research on mediational mechanisms and his apparent assumption of a basic nonuniformity or nonuniversality in behavioral laws (cf. Hilgard, 1955; Postman, 1955). On the former point, Postman and Tolman (1959, p. 558) have attempted a clarification. They say that Brunswik was not so much opposed to the experimental analysis of mediational mechanisms as he was opposed to their being given priority over research on distal correlations involving perceptual and instrumental achievements. He was, of course, entitled to his opinion on this point, but, as we have pointed out before, it is difficult to say in advance which of several alternative procedures will be most effective; the safest position is simply to let each researcher follow his own inclinations on this issue, provided he is conversant with the alternatives. Brunswik's views must be admitted as among the most carefully reasoned and persuasive of those formulated by psychologists interested in general methodological problems. On the second point, Brunswik has taken pains to say that he did not think that behavioral laws are fundamentally probabilistic but only that their establishment is necessarily limited to statistical or probabilistic expression because of the limitations imposed by the great variety of interacting factors in behavior. As he has put it (1955b): 'The crucial point is that while God may not gamble, animals and humans do, and that they cannot help but to gamble in an ecology that is of essence only partly accessible to their foresight" (p. 236).

Apart from the ultimate significance of his methodological position, Brunswik has contributed substantially to the advancement of our understanding of the perceptual constancies. Secondarily, he has helped to free research on instrumental learning from certain of its early limitations, as described above. These achievements, added to his insightful analyses of design problems, are more than sufficient to ensure a prominent place for him in the history of systematic psychology.

MISCELLANEOUS RELATED THEORIES

Barker's Ecological Psychology

Roger G. Barker (1903-   ) received all his college degrees from Stanford University (Ph.D., 1934). When Kurt Lewin came to Stanford as a visiting professor in 1932, he and Barker began an association which led to the publication of the classic laboratory study of frustration and regression in children (Barker, Dembo, & Lewin, 1941), of which we shall have more to say later. After serving as an instructor at Harvard from 1937 to 1938, an assistant professor at the University of Illinois from 1938 to 1942, an associate professor at Stanford from 1942 to 1945, and a professor at Clark University from 1945 to 1947, Barker settled down as a professor at the University of Kansas. Barker and his colleague, Herbert F. Wright, established the Midwest Psychological Field Station in Oskaloosa, Kansas, in 1947. Barker's place in this volume is based largely on his first twenty years of work at the Midwest Station and at a station established in 1954, operated on a periodic basis, in Leyburn, Yorkshire, England. Comparisons between the findings at the two stations contribute to the fascination of the findings of Barker and his co-workers.

A cynic might claim that our inclusion of Barker as a field theorist can be based only on the rather bad pun between *field theory* and *fieldwork*, of which Barker has done a great deal. But we have already seen the meaning of *field* in physics and its meaning in psychology are so distant that the application of the same word to theories in the two disciplines is already almost a pun. In addition, there is a distant relationship between the metatheory of field theory and the encouragement of naturalistic—field—observations. Finally, there is the historical connection between Barker and Lewin, who was the paradigmatic field theorist in psychology.

Barker's work is a natural combination and extension of the interests of Brunswik and Lewin. Brunswik's most persistent interest was in perception, where he insisted on the importance of naturalistic studies of perceptual achievements in a representative sample of ecological situations. Lewin became interested in what one might call "social ecology" when he was forced to examine the mechanisms via which food finds its way to the table, in connection with his wartime research on the manipulation of attitudes toward particular foods. Although Brunswik at times overemphasized the disordered and probabilistic nature of the environment, at other times his intuitive evaluations were prophetic of the empirical findings of Barker (Brunswik, 1956, p. 39):

Ecological generality of experimental or statistical results may thus be established along with populational generality. In fact, proper sampling of situations and problems may in the end be more important than proper sampling of subjects, considering the fact that individuals are probably on the whole much more alike than are situations among one another.

The following statement by Barker, who was *not* guessing, is very closely related (1968, p. 4):

The environment is seen to consist of highly structured, improbable arrangements of objects and events which coerce behavior in accordance with their own dynamic patterning. When, early in our work at the Field Station, we made long records of children's behavior in real-life settings in accordance with a traditional person-centered approach, we found that some attributes of behavior varied less across children within settings than across settings within the days of children. We found, in short, that we could predict some aspects of children's behavior more adequately from knowledge of the behavior characteristics of the drugstores, arithmetic classes, and basketball games they inhabited than from knowledge of the behavior tendencies of particular children (Ashton, 1964; Barker & Gump, 1964; Raush et al.,

1959, 1960). It was this experience that led us to look at the real-life environment in which behavior occurs, with the methodological and theoretical consequences that are reported in this book.

One can only be grateful that Barker and his co-workers were led to look closely at this "real-life environment in which behavior occurs," for the results of that work have the kind of sturdy, unselfconscious beauty seen in the well-fed Hereford cows admired around Oskaloosa, Kansas. The data presented by Barker to illustrate molar units of individual behavior exemplify the general sturdy empiricism of the approach. Five-year-old Maud Pintner is in Clifford's Drugstore (1968, p. 146):

Maud sat at the fountain waiting to order the treat her mother had promised her. On the stool next to Maud was her two-year-old brother, Fred; her mother sat beside Fred.

2:48 P.M. From her jeans pocket Maud now took an orange crayon. She brushed it across her lips as if it were a lipstick.

Maud then leaned over, sliding her arms along the counter, as she watched a man serve a strawberry soda to his blond, curly-headed, three-year-old girl.

Maud seemed fascinated by the procedure; she took in every detail of the situation.

From this, two molar units of behavior, called *behavior episodes*, were abstracted: *pretending to use lipstick* and *watching girl eat soda*. The isolation of these units, which might at first appear to be a simple task, is both difficult and of critical importance if effective fieldwork is to be done. Barker (1968) says of behavior episodes: "Like crystals and cells that also have distinguishing attributes and limited size-ranges, behavior episodes have as clear a position in the hierarchy of behavior units as the former have in the hierarchies of physical and organic units" (p. 146).

Barker favors the gathering of data uncontaminated by the operation of the psychologist on the situation; the psychologist in the field can act simply as a transducer (and hence gathers T data, rather than the O data gathered by the psychologist who also operates in the situation). Barker illustrates the possible misleading conclusions that may be drawn from O data. His strictures are made doubly impressive by the fact that he uses his own classic study as the horrible example! Barker says (1968, pp. 144-145):

Experiments have provided basic information about the consequences for children of frustration, as defined and contrived in the experiments, e.g., Barker et al. (1941). But Fawl, who did *not* contrive frustration for his subjects, but studied it in transducer records of children's everyday behavior, reported (Fawl, 1963, p. 99):

The results . . . were surprising in two respects. First, even with a liberal interpretation of frustration fewer incidents were detected than we expected. . . . Second . . . meaningful relationships could not be found between frustration . . . and consequent behavior such as . . . regression . . . and other theoretically meaningful behavioral manifestations.

In other words, frustration was rare in children's days, and when it did occur it did not have the behavioral consequences observed in the laboratory. It appears that the earlier experiments simulated frustration very well as defined and prescribed in theories, but the experiments did not simulate frustration as life prescribes it for children.

This constitutes an indirect plea for a thorough study of the ecology in which man grows and behaves, a plea which Barker has certainly not hesitated to make directly in other places. He points out that it is ironic that we know the percentage of each element to be found in the earth's crust, but do not have similar knowledge about man's *behavioral* surroundings. Barker makes his contribution to this effort by cataloging the "behavior settings" of Oskaloosa, Kansas (the Midwest Psychological Field Station). His appendix lists 220 behavior settings, from abstract and title company offices to X-ray laboratories. These are all public behavior settings; one misses, for example, Maud Pintner's living room and awaits the Masters and Johnson of Oskaloosa, Kansas, to fill in the ecological picture.

In order to survey behavior settings, Barker had first to define a behavior setting—to discover or invent its identifying attributes. We shall list only the first three of seven attributes. First, a behavior setting consists of one or more standing patterns of behavior. Barker says that such patterns are clearly located in time and space, and he gives basketball games, worship services, and piano lessons as examples. Second, a behavior setting consists of standing patterns of behavior and milieu. That is, the setting includes the surroundings as well as the behavior, and the surroundings may be man-made (such as buildings) or natural (such as trees). Third, the milieu is circumjacent to the behavior—that is, the milieu surrounds the behavior, rather than vice versa. The interested reader is invited to consult Barker (1968) for the remaining defining characteristics, as well as for the details of other aspects of his data and theory.

Finally, Barker considers the interactions between behavior settings and the behaviors of the people who inhabit them. We might expect him to see the behavior setting as a field, and the persons in it as particles, on the basis of an analogy with physics. Instead, he borrows an almost opposite analogy from Heider and likens the behavior setting to a "thing" and the people who inhabit it to a "medium." An example of a thing is a stone, which can be thrown into a pond, the medium. The medium, although it has characteristics of its own, is more flexible than the thing and so adapts itself to it. People in general adapt themselves to behavior settings, partially because of the intervention of "environmental force units." But those are another part of the story, and we cannot tell it all. We shall conclude with the comment that Barker's work combines in a rare way the imaginative approach of the field theorist with the persistent empiricism which seems to have become connected more often with the image of the associationistic psychologist. Both his descriptive schemes and his theory of behavior settings show great promise for stimulating further work in ecological psychology. The availability of usable descriptive categories makes Barker one of the few psychologists rich enough to throw away the following tidbits, among others, on a single page (1968,

p. 141): Disturbances occur in a child's experience at a median rate of 5.4 per hour, half of the disturbances being occasioned by adults; the units of the Midwest children are shorter on the average than those of comparable "Yoredale" children; the Yoredale children receive four times as frequent devaluative input from adults as do the Midwest children.

Lashley's Neuropsychology

Karl S. Lashley (1890-1958) cannot be easily assigned to any single, simple category. We have already met him in Chapter 7, since he was one of the most enthusiastic of the early behaviorists. He belongs in this chapter also, however, since as his career developed, he moved more and more in the direction of a kind of field theory and could be found increasingly on the Gestalt or field-theory side of particular theoretical issues.

Lashley did his graduate work at the University of Pittsburgh and Johns Hopkins University, receiving his Ph.D. in psychology in 1914 at the latter school. His major teaching appointments were at the Universities of Minnesota and Chicago and at Harvard. He then became director, in 1942, of the Yerkes Laboratory of Primate Biology, the world-renowned chimpanzee-research station at Orange Park, Florida. In this capacity he retained his professorship at Harvard because the two institutions were then administratively related.

Lashley's earliest research was performed in collaboration with the biologist H. S. Jennings and the behaviorist John B. Watson at Johns Hopkins. His research interests ranged quite widely, from problems concerning the inheritance of size in paramecia to cerebral factors in migraine headaches in humans (see Beach, Hebb, Morgan, & Nissen, 1960 for these and many of his other papers). However, the problem of brain function related to behavior was his most important and most persistent interest and the one for which he is best known.

Lashley's interest in brain function was formed early in his training, but it was only in 1917, when he became associated with the eminent neurophysiologist Franz, that he embarked upon the line of research utilizing ablation of the rat brain as a technique to determine localization of function.

It is unfortunate that those who do not know Lashley's work well almost inevitably remember him for two vague principles with catchy names—*mass action* and *equipotentiality*. Even these names are not remembered precisely, for here is Lashley's statement of his famous principles (1929, p. 25):

Equipotentiality of parts. The term "equipotentiality" I have used to designate the apparent capacity of any intact part of a functional area to carry out, with or without reduction in efficiency, the functions which are lost by destruction of the whole. This capacity varies from one area to another and with the character of the functions involved. It probably holds only for the association areas and for functions more complex than simple sensitivity or motor co-ordination.

Mass function. I have already given evidence . . . that the equipotentiality is not absolute but is subject to a law of mass action whereby the efficiency of performance of an entire complex function may be reduced in proportion to the extent of brain injury within an area whose parts are not more specialized for one component of the function than for another.

A careful reading of these principles makes any comment on their vagueness (and even some possible circularity) unnecessary. Krech (1962), in his excellent review of the problem of cortical localization, credits Lashley with being aware of his own vagueness in stating these principles; Lashley stated the principles vaguely because the state of knowledge about brain mechanisms was vague!

Why, then, should Lashley be remembered? Pierre Flourens had reached similar conclusions on the basis of the results of similar ablations about one hundred years earlier. Lashley's unique contribution was that he brought far better, more analytic *behavioral* techniques into cooperation with the available physiological techniques. Lashley was not limited to the study of the effects of operations on naturally occurring behaviors; he experimentally created behaviors in mazes and discrimination problems, and he studied their retention and reacquisition after carefully planned ablations. His methodology was brilliant for his time, and his techniques excellent. He had been anticipated to some extent by his teacher, Franz, much as Isaac Newton was anticipated in the development of calculus by his teacher, Isaac Barrow; both pupils went far beyond their teachers.

There is no doubt, despite the vagueness of his statements, that Lashley strongly opposed the common belief in localization of function. The problem is by no means settled, but the "final" decision on this problem will probably favor more localization than Lashley believed likely. We still understand too little of the structure of behavior to know what a unitary "function" is; until we know, it is difficult to attack the localization problem. Lashley made a tremendous contribution to the beginning of the attack on the critical behavioral side of the question.

The extent to which Lashley was recognized by the physiologist as well as the psychologist is suggested by the tribute paid him by the neurologist Stanley Cobb, who said (Beach et al., 1960) that in the early days at Hopkins, Lashley "fascinated us by the breadth of his interest and by his flair for ingenious and adventurous experimentation" (p. xvii). Cobb added (Beach et al., 1960): "During the next forty years, Lashley was to be the psychologist most frequently chosen by neurologists and psychiatrists to come to their meetings to give a paper or to discuss the papers of others" (p. xviii). He concluded by saying (Beach et al., 1960): "And so, in paying Karl Lashley our homage, we claim at least a tithe of his work for neurology!" (p. xx).

But it is, of course, not only for his neurological contributions that Lashley is honored in psychology. In a twin introduction to the memorial volume of Lashley's selected papers (Beach et al., 1960), E. G. Boring reviewed his systematic contributions to psychological theory. The field-theoretical flavor of Lashley's interpretations is illustrated in certain quotations selected by Boring. For example, Lashley wrote that ". . . it is the pattern and not the localization of energy on the sense organ that determines the functional effect" (p. 492); and referring to brain action, that ". . . all of the cells of the brain are constantly active and are participating, by a sort of algebraic summation, in every activity" (p. 500).

Lashley's field-theoretical orientation is illustrated also by his position in support of a pattern, or relational, interpretation of transposition learning rather than the S-R, or connectionistic, position. In his presidential address to the American Psychological Association in 1930, he attacked the simple connectionistic view. He later presented a novel alternative to the orthodox S-R interpretation of generalization and discrimination learning. The Lashley-Wade hypothesis is that differential training on several values of a stimulus dimension is necessary for generalization to occur, denying the fundamental S-R assumption that reinforcement of a single stimulus value produces a generalization gradient whereby similar values of the stimulus automatically gain similar but reduced potency to elicit the conditioned response. The controversy thus created has stimulated a good deal of research. Kimble (1961, pp. 369ff.) presents one review of the issue. Terrace (1966) more recently reached a conclusion which favors Lashley and Wade: "A differential reinforcement procedure is necessary for the typical generalization gradient to emerge" (p. 339). Finally, Kalish (1969) reached something of a compromise position after a thorough and thoughtful review of the evidence.

Lashley made still other experimental and methodological contributions. For the former, his long series of researches on visual discrimination and the analysis of the visual cortex (see Beach et al., 1960) are perhaps the best examples; for the latter, his invention of the jumping stand, which forces an animal such as a rat to step or leap from a platform to one of two discriminable doors, is probably the most important contribution. This new experimental device enormously facilitated discrimination learning in the rat, presumably by forcing the animal to attend more directly to the relevant visual cues. Among the many subsequent users of the device, Norman R. F. Maier should be mentioned in the present context. Not only was he responsible for the most controversial utilization of the jumping stand (1938, 1949; see also Chapter 1), but he also has been a strong supporter of the field-theoretical position (e.g., Maier & Schneirla, 1935).

In conclusion, it is fitting to quote Boring's final tribute to Lashley's scientific perspicacity (Beach et al., 1960): "The impressive thing about the papers in this volume is the way in which discovery leads speculation, not speculation discovery" (p. xvi).

Kantor's Interbehaviorism

Jacob Robert Kantor (1888-   ) was born in Pennsylvania and educated at the University of Chicago, receiving his Ph.D. in 1917. He was an instructor in philosophy and psychology for two years at the University of Minnesota and then for three years at the University of Chicago following his obtaining the doctoral degree. In 1920, he went to teach at Indiana University and served as professor of psychology there from 1923 until his retirement. Kantor has been a consistent and prolific writer; his bibliography includes eighty-eight items, seven of which are books, some multivolume works. Kantor's scholarship is further attested by his publication of eighty-three book reviews. In fact, Kantor probably became the grand old man of American psychology with the death of E. G. Boring in 1968. Like Boring, he has remained active even though formally retired; the second volume of his historical study, *The scientific evolution of psychology*, appeared in 1969.

Kantor has been first and foremost a logical analyst and critic of the general scientific scene, with special reference to psychology. His major concern for over half a century has been, as he put it, "smoothing the path of psychology toward its goal of natural science" (1958, p. 223). Two favorite targets have been (1) "mental fictions" as represented in theoretical constructions within psychology and (2) major tenets of physiological psychology. These and related "errors" he attributed to the widespread acceptance in our culture of the dualistic heritage and the resultant failure of many scientists to look closely at their data. He has felt that the problems produced by the dualistic heritage are especially aggravated in psychology. Skinner, at least, appreciated Kantor's criticism of the surviving mentalism in psychology (1967): "Another behaviorist whose friendship I have valued is J. R. Kantor. In many discussions with him at Indiana I profited from his extraordinary scholarship. He convinced me that I had not wholly exorcised all the 'spooks' in my thinking" (p. 411).

Kantor does not have a system in the sense that Hull, or even Tolman or Lewin, had. Kantor has been above all else a metatheoretician, emphasizing a broad philosophical approach to behavior problems rather than specific solutions to such problems. He has written on physiological psychology (1947), language (1936), logic (1945, 1950, 1953), and history (1963, 1969), but has not concentrated his efforts in any one field in a way that might have made him preeminent in a particular area. He has offered what he calls a "formal logical system" (1958, p. ix). This last-mentioned book was prepared, as he noted, in order to present his ideas more efficiently and to avoid an excess of duplication from earlier works.

The heart of Kantor's logical system is the notion of the interbehavioral field, which is an interaction between the "response functions" of the organism and the "stimulus functions" of the environment. These two basic factors must always be considered together, in Kantor's view. The properties of the interaction between organism and stimulus are built up largely in the history of the interbehavioral relation. Both biological and cultural factors need to be considered.

Except perhaps for a lessened enthusiasm for S-R psychology, Kantor's critical views have changed little throughout the course of his long career, beginning with the publication of his *Principles of psychology* in 1924. He has continued to stress the psychological field and its constantly changing interactions, and he is included in this chapter for that reason. This aspect of his views is related to Dewey's views as expressed in the famous paper on the reflex arc, and even to the Gestalt doctrine of emergence. Kantor, however, would be anxious to distinguish his views from those of the Gestalt psychologists and most other field theorists, since he saw remnants of mentalistic fictions in their views.

Kantor's stress on holism led him to criticize the doctrine of localization of function (1947, pp. 80ff.) and to see language and logic as instances of the many products of, and participants in, interbehavioral relations. He also saw clearly that environmental objects participate importantly in social relationships (1929); his views in this respect are consistent with those of Barker, whom we have just discussed.

Many papers by Kantor and by sympathetic students (on whom he has had a remarkably strong and lasting influence) can be found in the journal _Psychological Record_, which Kantor founded. There is some evidence that Kantor's influence may be increasing, despite his failure to found an active experimental school; N. W. Smith (personal communication) has found that Kantor's work was cited about twice as often in the ten-year period ending in 1966 as it had been in the preceding ten-year period. Perhaps psychology, at last, is ready to acknowledge this tough old critic.

Wheeler's Organismic System

Raymond Holder Wheeler (1892-1961) was born in Massachusetts and educated at Clark University (Ph.D., 1915). He then taught at the University of Oregon (1915 to 1925). The most important part of his academic career was spent at the University of Kansas (1925 to 1947), which under his influence became a kind of Gestalt oasis in the otherwise generally behavioristic or at least functionalistic climate of the Middle West. This influence has persisted long after Wheeler's own departure from Kansas.

Wheeler developed a kind of Americanized Gestalt system. His formalization, on a programmatic level at least, of basic Gestalt principles was of a much greater scope than the comparable efforts made by the major German proponents, whose work tended to stay closer to the original visual-perceptual demonstrations (cf. Chapter 8). Köhler had related Gestalt psychological principles to physics; Wheeler attempted to relate them to biology. His particular reference was to the rapidly developing discipline of experimental embryology, where field principles found their greatest biological utility. (See Hilgard, 1948, Ch. 9, for a simplified review of these relationships as well as a thorough description of Wheeler's system and its applicability to learning and education especially.)

The dynamic laws that Wheeler laid down for his organismic, or holistic, system were centered largely around the basic concept of the whole. They were most simply presented in his early version (Wheeler & Perkins, 1932) and were only slightly modified later (e.g., Wheeler, 1940). These principles dealt directly with the functions of wholes and may be summarized as follows: Wholes are more than the sum of their parts; wholes determine the properties and activities of their parts; wholes evolve and function (adjusting to disturbances and responding to energy transactions) as wholes; and parts emerge from wholes rather than vice versa. One additional principle involves the law of least action: Minimal energy will be expended when alternative behaviors are available to the organism.

An interesting sideline in Wheeler's career was his research and speculation concerning the manifold ways in which climate affects behavior. In a literal sense, this application of a field approach to behavioral problems may be regarded as of the broadest possible scope. As a consequence of his historical research on the topic, Wheeler (1946) concluded that "... a culture pattern representing all important phases of human activity was fluctuating back and forth in rhythmic fashion as a vast, complex, but integrated whole or gestalt, each detail of which was related logically with the others in so intimate and clear a manner that, knowing one of them, the others could be predicted" (p. 81). In addition to his exhaustive historical and climatological research on the problem, Wheeler supervised laboratory investigations on the behavior of white-rat colonies maintained under hot, cold, and normal temperature conditions. The data from these studies are interpreted as supporting his general position (Wheeler, 1946, pp. 84-85).

Although Wheeler's organismic formulations were influential for a time, that influence has within the past decade greatly declined. A major reason for this decline is probably the strongly polemic character of their presentation and the failure of effective empirical research to follow from them. Like Tolman, Wheeler presented a large number of provocative and suggestive notions without definitive theoretical statements of the sort Hull attempted; but unlike Tolman, he was not successful in translating these into equally provocative experimental designs and empirical demonstrations. As one indication of Wheeler's declining influence, one might cite Hilgard's comment (1956): "Because Wheeler's theory is no longer influential, the chapter has been dropped from this edition, despite some provocative ideas contained in the theory" (p. 225).

SUMMARY AND CONCLUSIONS

The views of three theorists of "field" persuasion, and the work of several theorists with related attitudes, have been surveyed in this chapter. These theorists generally emphasize patterns of organization at the expense of discrete connections. Following from this general attitude are a general tendency to study molar variables and a tendency to resort to field observations in order to get the overall view of behavior and behavior laws.

The field-theoretical view has a tendency to drive people away from simple cause-and-effect thinking because of the large number of potential variables in fields or wholes. Further, the insistence on completeness and a tinge of subjectivism which often accompany field theory lead to the inclusion of central, cognitive variables which are often difficult to measure. The number of possible variables and interactions between variables, plus the vague, nonoperational character of some of them, tends to lose the potential experimenter in a maze of complexity and may paralyze experimental investigations. Yet the metatheoretical points made by theorists like Lewin and Brunswik are extremely persuasive.

The way out of the impasse seems to be shown by people like Kantor, who retains a general field orientation while providing a strong antidote for subjectivity and the dualism that may be associated with it. Even Skinner, who as far as we know has never been accused of being a field theorist, shows at least one attitude typical of field theorists when he attempts to let the experimental organism—rather than the experimenter—decide what the basic unit of analysis, the operant, shall be. A rapprochement with field-theoretical concerns with cognitive events is also represented by an increasing interest in the so-called S-R mediation theories. From the other side, we see people like Barker, who start from a more field-theoretical background, taking on some of the coloration of S-R theorists by making extremely careful and persistent empirical observations. Willems (1969) describes research activities in terms of a two-dimensional space, in which there is a place for the kinds of activities typical of the S-R psychologist and a place for the kinds of activities typical of the field theorist; his space forces the recognition that there is a continuity between the two kinds of activities, both of which contribute to the total scientific advance. Willems's two dimensions are degree of manipulation of antecedent conditions and degree of imposition of units. Field theorists have tended to be low on both dimensions, and S-R theorists high on both dimensions. Contemporary investigators tend to be spreading to many interesting intermediate positions, as well as occupying the old territories.

Still further rapprochement is represented by the increasing popularity of multivariate analysis, which combines the rigor typical of the S-R psychologist with the attempt to deal with complex interrelationships, which is demanded by the field theorist.

Brunswik was the field theorist most particularly insistent on the value of naturalistic, ecological study of the organism in its environment. Certainly such studies provide unique opportunities for discovering naturally occurring systems of interrelated variables, and they prevent the investigator from "wasting" time studying variables that do not have relevance to the world as it exists. However, an *exclusive* concern with naturalistic studies might prevent investigators from studying potential but nonexistent systems which could be artificially created with great benefit to mankind. As man determines more and more of his own environment, the charge of "artificiality" of psychological studies may become less and less significant.

The first of the three field theories considered was that presented by Kurt Lewin. Lewin's contributions have included a brilliant series of experimental attacks upon motivation and personality factors and the initiation of the group-dynamics movement; theoretically, however, he is best known for his conceptualization of life space. The second field theory considered was that of E. C. Tolman, who early espoused a molar, purposive behaviorism. His experimental and conceptual innovations leavened the behavioristic doctrine and gave cognitive psychology an experimental basis; for a time Tolman offered what seemed to be a clear contrast to Hullian, S-R doctrines. The third theory was Egon Brunswik's probabilistic functionalism, which offered alternatives to many otherwise unquestioned methodological assumptions in perception and learning.

Briefer consideration was given to Barker's ecological psychology, Lashley's neurophysiological theory, Kantor's interbehaviorism, and Wheeler's organismic theory.

The major strength of field theory comes from the fact that it has unhesitatingly concerned itself with some critical problems which orthodox S-R theory has tended to avoid. These are in general problems concerning central functions (cf. Hebb, 1949; G. A. Miller, Galanter, & Pribram, 1960) rather than peripheralistic ones, the latter having been the typical concern of the S-R theorist.

At the present time, the kind of approach to behavior problems represented by the field theorist is being increasingly supplemented by newer conceptual (e.g., the computer model of thinking) as well as experimental techniques. The major need in this kind of approach is to spell out more adequately the empirical referents for the central functions posited. To take one example from the present chapter, the concept of purpose, as conceived by Lewin and Tolman, is an obviously significant one in behavior, but little seems to have been done to develop anything like an adequate *experimental* attack upon it. Unfortunately, the stimulating lead initiated by Lewin, particularly in his tension-system research and conceptualization, has not as yet been fruitfully followed. When this kind of research is thoroughly developed, perhaps as a result of the amalgamation of field-theoretical and other more empirically oriented approaches, the promise implicit in the earlier field theories may well be fulfilled.

Further Readings

Volumes intended to illuminate cognitive, or field-theoretical, methodology are Kuenzli's *The phenomenological problem* (1959) and Bruner et al., *Contemporary approaches to cognition* (1957).

The best introduction to Lewin is provided by his four slender books published in English. *A dynamic theory of personality* (1935) and *Principles of topological psychology* (1936) summarize the earlier, European phase of his career. *Resolving social conflicts* (1948) and *Field theory in social science* (1951) are concerned with his later work in this country. His monograph, *The conceptual representation and measurement of psychological forces* (1938), is a more elaborate but difficult exposition of his metatheoretical position. An early critique by Leeper (1943), Estes' very critical evaluation (1954b), and two more sympathetic reviews by Deutsch (1954) and by Cartwright (1958) are among the more useful of the secondary sources on Lewin and his psychology. A recent addition to the literature on Lewin is Marrow's *Practical theorist* (1969). Tolman is well represented by his early book, *Purposive behavior in animals and men* (1932); his collected works, *Collected papers in psychology* (1951a); and his final systematic statement (1959). In addition, MacCorquodale and Meehl (1954) have provided an interesting and helpful formalization of Tolman's system. Although there is no easy road to Brunswik's thinking, the reader may be referred to his much-cited paper, "The conceptual focus of some psychological systems" (1939a); his more difficult methodological monograph, *Perception and the representative design of psychological experiments* (1956); and his two papers (1955a, 1955b) in the symposium on probability theory. The latter, in the May, 1955, issue of *Psychological Review*, contains several other important papers on the topic and should be consulted by any interested student. Brunswik's system is also intensively treated by Postman and Tolman (1958). Barker puts his own best foot forward in his interesting and readable *Ecological psychology* (1968). Lashley is well represented by *The neuro-psychology of Lashley*, edited by F. A. Beach et al. (1960). Kantor's *Interbehavioral psychology* (1958) is the best introduction to his systematic thinking. Wheeler's *Science of psychology* (1940) is probably the most useful single source for his work.

12 Varieties of Personality Theory

Personality theory is a kind of behavior theory. We have already considered two of the most important theories of personality: psychoanalytic theory and Lewinian theory. However, classic personality theory does have some general characteristics that set it apart as a subvariety of behavior theory. The very word *personality* tells us that, at least in the beginning, personality theory was based on the study of persons. In most personality theories, individual differences between persons are regarded as a very significant source of variance in behavior; information about the unique characteristics of persons is therefore expected to be very useful in making predictions about behavior.

There is great diversity of opinion and of emphasis on several issues connected with the study of the person. The first is the very basic set of opinions concerning the amount of variance which is attributed to persons, as compared with the amount attributed to situations. In the last chapter, we saw that Brunswik and Barker agreed that behavior could be predicted to a great extent from knowledge of the situation, regardless of the person in the situation. Rogers, who emphasizes the tendency of the person to develop his capacities "from within" (he calls this *self-actualization*), probably best represents the opposite extreme—he is the greatest optimist about the extent of an individual's ability to determine his own fate. In this respect Rogers is close to the existentialists, who believe that each individual has irrevocable responsibility for his own choices. S-R theorists generally emphasize the influence of the situation, or stimulus, and show less interest in the unique characteristics of the individual person. These theorists have a related tendency toward denying the generality and permanence of "traits" of personality; for example, it would be characteristic of S-R theorists to deny that honesty is a general trait or that it is likely to be a permanent characteristic of a particular person. This is consistent with the so-called empty-organism approach, which places little reliance either on assumed physiological functions or on assumed personality structures such as traits or attitudes. In this sense, S-R theories are general behavior theories, *not* personality theories in any restricted sense. However, we shall discuss one S-R theory below, partly to emphasize the continuity between behavior theories and theories which are more representative of theories of person-ality.

Still another question concerns the extent to which personality structure—whatever form it takes—is determined by nativistic factors and the extent to which it is determined by learning. The so-called self theorists are more likely to make a place in their scheme for nativistic factors than the S-R theorists, who quite naturally insist on the importance of learning. Later we shall see that there are still other questions related to the general question of the relative importance of individual differences, but, for the present, we shall turn to another set of distin-guishing characteristics of personality theories.

Theories of personality attempt completeness. This may be an increasingly distinctive characteristic because theorists in other areas of psychology are *less* enamored of attempts to develop "grand theories" than they used to be. Increas-ingly they limit themselves to partial or full explanations of things like one-trial learning by the method of paired associates in lists of nonsense syllables, auditory threshold effects, or some other closely circumscribed area. Not so the personality theorist. He has self-consciously chosen to explain the complex behavior of the total human organism. To some extent this has led to discouragement and diffusion of effort on the part of the personality theorist. Adelson (1969, pp. 136-137) says in this connection:

The impulse for synthesis, for finding unities, has for the moment been set aside. So, for example, the controversies we have—and there are surprisingly few—rarely center upon either large or substantive issues and usually involve internecine squabbling about this or that measure, method, or technique within a specific domain of research.

The sprawl and diversity in personality can be seen as both a cause and a consequence of the virtual abandonment of large theoretical ambitions.

The other distinguishing characteristics of personality theory are related to its usual attempt at comprehensiveness. First, the functional nature of personality theory should be noted. Theories of personality focus upon an understanding of the development, survival, and general adjustment of the organism. Second, an empha-sis on motivational ("dynamic") processes is characteristic of such theories. Third, the object of study is the whole person in his natural habitat. On this point, the study of personality clearly separates itself from the experimental tradition in psychology, which has typically advocated the study of more limited aspects of behavior. Fourth, personality theories are characteristically integrative, whereas much of psychology has moved in the direction of more specialized explanatory attempts. Fifth, personality theories frequently have rebelled against the prevailing psychological thought of the times. Certainly Freud's psychoanalytic theory offer-ed dissenting explanatory principles at the time of its inception. More recently, Gordon Allport has persisted in advocating the basic principles he felt necessary for an adequate theory of personality even when he seemed to stand alone. The fact that much of personality theory has developed outside the mainstream of academic psychology—frequently as a result of clincial observation—may account, in part, for its taking the highroad while the rest of psychology proceeded along the low road.

Thus we find in personality theories concern with variables typically left out of more limited theories. Psychoanalysis opened up the study of the unconscious determinants of behavior and offered a model of the structure of personality; Chapter 9 contains a more complete discussion of the empirical areas whose study was initiated by psychoanalysis. This personality theory and others have pointed to the need for detailed study of dynamic (motivational) variables, individual differences, heredity, biological factors, child and developmental psychology, abnormal and social psychology, and all the interrelationships between these and other fields. Every one of this formidable array of fields plays an important role in any attempt at a complete theory of personality.

Implied in the preceding discussion of the characteristics of personality theory are both its weaknesses and its strengths. The personality theorist is faced with a dilemma composed of, on the one hand, mounting needs to predict and control human behavior and, on the other hand, a distressing scarcity of knowledge about the basic laws needed for the task. Consequently, the structure of personality theory tends to be loosely cemented for lack of sufficient cohesive material in the form of empirical observables. The major weakness of such theory, and the shortcoming at which criticism is continually leveled, is its disproportion of explanatory principles in relation to the amount of empirical data at hand. Similarly, personality theories frequently fail to distinguish clearly between that which they assume and that which is empirically testable. Consequently, the derivation of predictions and empirical hypotheses from these theories is severely hampered.

In spite of these problems, however, there has been a good amount of research in the area of personality. Adelson (1969), in the review of a year's literature which he published in 1969, says that an extremely modest estimate of the year's volume is 500 citations; he references 210 of them in his paper. Dahlstrom, in his 1970 review, refers to 366 articles from some presumably larger set. The problem is not a lack of data, but a lack of a tight relationship between the data and a general theoretical framework. Even in this respect, one should not be altogether pessimistic; C. S. Hall and Lindzey, after examining seventeen theories of personality, conclude that twelve of them have been responsible for generating a considerable amount of research. Their comment on this finding is (1970, p. 595):

It is reassuring that, in spite of the limitations of theories of personality as generators of research, the large majority of such theories has been accompanied by a considerable quantity of research. Whatever procedural limitations may inhere in these investigations, the fact remains that they document the interest of the theorists in examining the effectiveness of their theories in the face of empirical data. It is hard to believe that in the long run this attitude will not lead to progressive changes that will result in more effective theories.

It is, indeed, comforting to encounter optimism about the future of personality theory, for even more weaknesses exist at present than we have yet men-

Table 12-1 Dimensional Comparison of Theories of Personality

	Purpose	Unconscious Determinants	Reward	Contiguity	Learning Process	Formal Analysis	Personality Structure	Heredity	Early Developmental Experience	Continuity of Development	Organismic Emphasis	Field Emphasis	Uniqueness	Molar Units	Homeostatic Mechanisms	Psychological Environment	Self-Concept	Group Membership Determinants	Biology	Social Science	Multiplicity of Motives	Multiple Mechanisms
																			Interdisciplinary Emphasis			
Freud	H	H	H	M	M	M	H	H	H	H	M	L	M	M	H	H	H	M	H	H	L	H
Jung	H	H	H	L	L	M	H	H	H	L	H	L	M	M	H	H	H	L	H	L	M	H
Adler	H	M	M	L	L	L	M	L	M	H	M	H	H	M	H	M	H	H	M	H	L	L
Horney	H	H	L	L	M	L	M	L	M	M	M	M	M	M	H	M	M	H	L	H	L	L
Fromm	H	M	M	L	M	M	M	L	M	M	M	M	H	M	H	M	M	H	L	H	L	M
Sullivan	M	L	M	H	M	H	M	L	L	H	L	H	H	L	L	H	M	H	M	M	M	M
Lewin	H	L	L	L	L	M	H	M	L	L	L	H	H	H	H	M	H	L	L	L	H	M
Allport	H	M	L	M	M	H	M	M	H	L	H	H	M	M	M	H	H	M	H	H	H	H
Murray	H	L	L	L	L	M	L	M	L	L	H	H	M	M	H	H	H	L	H	L	H	M
Angyal	H	M	L	L	M	L	H	M	L	H	H	H	M	M	H	H	M	L	H	L	L	H
Goldstein	L	M	L	L	H	L	H	H	L	L	H	M	L	L	L	L	M	L	H	H	L	M
Sheldon	M	M	M	M	H	H	L	L	M	M	L	L	M	M	L	L	L	L	H	L	L	L
Cattell	L	M	H	M	L	M	H	L	M	H	L	L	H	L	L	L	L	M	M	L	L	H
Dollard and Miller	L	L	H	M	H	L	L	L	L	H	L	L	L	L	L	L	H	M	M	M	L	M
Skinner	L	L	L	L	L	L	L	M	M	L	L	M	M	H	L	L	M	L	L	L	L	L
Rogers	H	L	L	L	L	L	L	L	M	L	H	H	M	H	H	H	H	M	L	M	L	L
Binswanger and Boss	H	L	L	L	L	L	L	L	L	L	M	H	H	H	M	H	H	L	M	L	L	L

KEY: H, high (emphasized); M, moderate; L, low (deemphasized).

SOURCE: C. S. Hall & G. Lindzey, *Theories of personality* (2d ed.), New York, Wiley, 1970, p. 592.

tioned. For example, personality theory may be criticized even on the basis of its self-stated criterion—completeness—when it is noted that few theories, to date, have attempted to handle adequately all the areas considered essential to a comprehensive theory. Table 12-1, adapted from C. S. Hall and Lindzey (1970, p. 592), indicates these authors' evaluation of the degree of attention paid to various factors by the theorists they review in their book. Freud, Sullivan, and Murray seem to deserve the highest "comprehensiveness" scores, and even they pay little attention to some issues.

As to other limitations, we can save a great deal of time by saying that Freud's psychoanalytic theory is in many ways the most influential theory of personality and that most of the criticisms leveled against the form of, and evidence for, his theory also hold for the other theories of personality. However, this judgment will be modified somewhat as the individual theories are discussed.

And what of the positive functions of personality theory? Curiously, its strengths often derive from the same characteristics which harbor its weaknesses. Through its rebelliousness and its attempts at integration and completeness, it has drawn attention to previously neglected problem areas. Motivation, which only recently has received widespread attention from psychologists, has long been heralded by personality theorists as basic to the understanding of behavior. In addition, personality theories have generated empirical investigation both directly and indirectly; directly, by providing a framework for research and parameters and dimensions suitable to the investigation of questions raised by theory; indirectly, by engendering either curiosity or conviction in those who encounter the personality theorists' efforts to describe the complex nature of human behavior.

S-R THEORIES

C. S. Hall and Lindzey (1970) list two S-R positions among their theories of personality: the theory of Dollard and Miller and that of Skinner and his followers. A look at Table 12-1 shows that Skinner pays little attention to fifteen of the twenty-two areas considered important by Hall and Lindzey and that Dollard and Miller ignore ten areas. We think this fact indicates that S-R theories are really not personality theories, but the hardheaded temper of our times has led many psychologists to ask whether personality theories are any more helpful to us in understanding personality than S-R theories, which can be at least partially applied to personality. The success of behavior modifiers in working with clinical problems has lent some credence to this view and has helpd to justify the inclusion of Skinner, especially, among the personality theorists. However, we have treated Skinner and his views rather fully in Chapter 10, and his views on personality are very close to his views on behavior in general. We shall therefore simply refer the reader to our earlier discussion for Skinner's "theory of personality," just as we do for Lewin, Freud, and to some extent others among the early psychoanalysts.

The work of Dollard and Miller in personality theory differs from that of Skinner in that the former authors did their work in personality as an effort somewhat distinct from what they did before and after that time. We shall therefore take them as our example of personality theorists whose theory is closest to traditional behavior theory. They, like Skinner, have tried to develop a personality theory based on experimental data, and with a minimum of concepts added to its basic principles of learning and behaving.

Dollard and Miller's S-R Theory.

John Dollard (1900-   ) and Neal Miller (1909-   ) began their collaboration at Yale's newly formed Institute of Human Relations in the 1930s. The institute—an innovation in cooperation among the behavioral sciences of psychology, psychiatry, sociology, and anthropology—provided an environment both receptive to psychoanalytic investigation and strongly influenced by Hull. We have already mentioned in Chapter 10 that Hull was himself interested in exploring the relationship between his concepts and those of Freud, and he conducted a seminar on the topic in the academic year 1936-1937. Dollard and Miller conducted research at the institute and soon started a series of joint publications. The first effort (with other co-authors) was *Frustration and aggression* (Dollard, Doob, Miller & Mowrer, 1939), in which S-R concepts were applied to the problem of frustration. Shortly thereafter, Miller and Dollard (1941) published a volume on social learning that provided a basic S-R framework in which complex behavior problems could be conceptualized. They subsequently explicated their joint theorizing further in *Personality and psychotherapy* (Dollard & Miller, 1959). Dollard remained at Yale, where he became a professor emeritus in 1969. Miller moved from Yale to Rockefeller University in 1966.

Aside from their joint theoretical effort, Dollard and Miller have contributed to different areas of psychology. Both received laboratory and clinical training. However, Dollard's work has been less centered on experimental problems than Miller's. Dollard received his Ph.D. in sociology at the University of Chicago and has taught both anthropology and sociology at Yale. Further training at the Berlin Psychoanalytic Institute crystallized his interest in psychoanalysis. Dollard has consistently dedicated himself to the unification of the social sciences and has published in the areas of anthropology and sociology (e.g., 1937). During World War II he conducted a psychological analysis of military behavior, published as *Fear in battle* (1943).

Miller took his Ph.D. at Yale and, shortly thereafter, became a Social Science Research Council traveling fellow. During his stay in Europe, he underwent training analysis at the Vienna Institute of Psychoanalysis. Miller directed psychological research for the Army Air Force during the war years and then returned to Yale. He is characteristically a careful experimentalist and theorist, having conducted numerous studies on drive acquisition, reinforcement, conflict, and, most recently, the effects of drugs and physiological variables on behavior (see Chapter 10 for more details).

In their collaborative work Dollard and Miller have come closer to a complete theory of personality than any other S-R theorists, though Guthrie (1938) and Skinner (1953a) have generalized their findings freely to the human case. Lundin (1969) provides a full explanation of the Skinnerian approach to personality. Mowrer (1950) has also be interested in personality as well as in learning; however, none of these men have developed an integrated S-R personality theory as thoroughly as Dollard and Miller have.

Dollard and Miller (1950; N. E. Miller, 1959) have not found the Hullian system, upon which their personality theory is ultimately based, adequate to the task without considerable interpretation. Both authors are interested in psychoanalytic theory as well as in S-R theory, and their interpretation takes the line of a reduction of many psychoanalytic concepts to S-R terms (e.g., N. E. Miller, 1948). Their aim is to combine the assets of the two systems; they need the scope of psychoanalytic theory in order to have anything like the desired coverage of dependent and independent variables. Where in Hull does one find a discussion of neurotic guilt or anxiety? At the same time, they prefer the greater precision of statement and degree of empirical confirmation found within the confines of Hullian theory. The drawing of precise parallels between theories as different as psychoanalysis and Hullian theory is always difficult, perhaps sometimes impossible. Yet Dollard and Miller have made an attempt at integration that is stimulating and worthwhile, though in their system it is possible to see the outlines of two distinct subsystems.

There are systematic similarities between psychoanalysis and Hullian theory which make a partial amalgamation easier than might at first appear. A version of the law of effect is found in both. Freud speaks of maintaining a fixed tension level or reducing the tension level as a goal of the organism. Hull speaks of drive reduction, or a reduction in the intensity of a drive stimulus, as a condition which strengthens behavior. Both formulations seem essentially the same on this point. There are also similarities in the attitude toward learning. Hull's basic learning construct, $_sH_R$, is conceived of as building up through repeated practice and staying at a high level; once $_sH_R$ builds up, it is not destroyed,. If the behavior which reflected $_sH_R$ stops, this happens because there is opposition to it by inhibitory factors or because there is no motivation left for the behavior. This account of learning, with its assumption of the permanence of the effects of experience, is in this way much like Freud's; he also seemed to believe that early experiences leave ineradicable effects, though the effects might not be easily seen because of repression, a concept which here plays the same role as Hullian inhibition.

The heart of the Dollard-Miller account is learning, or habit formation. They point out four significant features of the learning process: drive, cue, response, and reward. They give as an example a child looking for concealed candy in a room containing bookshelves. The initial *drive* is the hunger for candy; the *cues* are the instructions for playing the game plus the stimuli from the room; varied *responses* are made until the candy is found behind a book; and the response of moving the appropriate book is reinforced by finding and eating the candy *reward*. If the game continues with the candy in the same place each time, the drive gradually decreases; the significant, discriminative cues become only those helpful in making the correct response; and the response is now made more quickly and strongly. In this way *habits* are reinforced and become the basic and enduring elements of personality.

Dollard and Miller have not borrowed only the simplest concepts from Hull's (1943) theory; they have found a use for the hierarchy of responses, secondary reinforcement, the generalization gradient, and other more complex theoretical notions. They have also shown great ingenuity in relating complex concepts to simpler ones, thereby "explaining" what is involved. Their attempt to handle the problems of symbolic behavior is particularly valuable.

One of the contributions which Dollard and Miller have made, then, is the integration of two originally separate—if not opposed—theories in such a way that it becomes reasonable to apply the results of laboratory investigations with animals to practical human problems. Though Hull intended his theory to have such applications, he never personally took time to show how they could be made. Two such human problems which Dollard and Miller have treated are fear and conflict.

Fear in the neurotic human being may seem an irrational thing. Dollard and Miller, however, believe that this irrationality is a matter of appearance only; we as observers of irrational human behavior arrive upon the scene too late to observe the development of the fear, and we often do not know enough of the laws that determine the learning and spread of fear. Consider, in an analogous situation, a rat that is placed in a white box and shocked. If he is allowed to escape through a door to a black box, he will quickly learn to fear the white one. Furthermore, he will continue to respond in order to escape the white box even when there is no longer any shock present. The fear may even spread (generalize) to similar boxes. If we had not observed the learning process but only the fearful animal in a harmless white box, we should consider his fear irrational. Similarly, if we did not understand the process of generalization, we should consider fear of a *light gray* box irrational even if we had observed the process.

Dollard and Miller have given an equally stimulating account of the nature of conflict. Their analytic approach involves at least five assumptions derived from theory or from empirical observations. They assume that (1) the tendency to approach a goal increases as the distance to the goal decreases, (2) the tendency to avoid a negative stimulus (punishment) increases as the distance to it decreases, (3) the gradient for negative stimuli is steeper than the gradient for positive stimuli, (4) changes in drive increase or decrease the *level* (not the slope) of the appropriate gradients, (5) if two responses (say, approach and avoidance) compete at any point, the one associated with the stronger tendency will occur. Empirical studies of this model have typically involved white rats, shock, food, and a spatial scale, but the model has been freely applied to quite different situations, such as bachelors contemplating marriage. Summaries of experimental research on this problem have been provided by Miller (1944, 1958b). He has also reviewed the relationship between the experimental results on conflict and the conduct of psychotherapy in a short chapter (1964) which also examines other implications of modern behavior theory for psychotherapy. Finally, his work on the operant conditioning of autonomic responses (1969) has exciting implications for the acquisition and treatment of psychosomatic symptoms, and will need to be incorporated into the conceptual schemes of all personality theories.

This short sketch should be enought to indicate that the original contribution of Dollard and Miller shares the strengths and weaknesses of S-R theory more than it does those of psychoanalytic theory. Their approach tends more toward analysis and the application of laboratory principles to human behavior. They take Hullian theory as the methodological model; psychoanalytic theory is used because it is based on the content, the observations, they wish to explain. Dollard and Miller seem to be molding psychoanalytic *content* into S-R *form.* In doing so, it may be argued, they incorporate the elementaristic weakness of S-R theory. Their "personalities" become bundles of habits without the consistency and purposefulness which most other personality theorists see as guiding human behavior. In choosing a theory which treats learning much more thoroughly than other determinants of behavior, Dollard and Miller take a more environmentalistic position than many theorists think is justifiable.

In spite of these criticisms, the Dollard-Miller theory seems to have earned an important place in the history of the development of personality theory. Skinner has followed them through the door they opened into the club of personality theorists as a member—not necessarily in good standing. It is now respectable to apply concepts and procedures modeled after the outcomes of laboratory experiments in clinical situations; in fact, it is scarcely respectable to do anything else. Dollard and Miller in effect claimed that anything the psychoanalyst could talk about, they could talk about; and they made the claim by example, in detail. Their case was convincing to many, especially those who preferred the language of S-R reinforcement learning theory to the language of psychoanalysis. Much of the interest in the details of the Dollard-Miller theory has probably waned, for both the component theories on which the effort was based have fallen into some disrepute. Hull's theory no longer dominates the field of learning, and Freud's is under strong attack in the field of personality. Nevertheless, Dollard and Miller deserve a tremendous amount of credit for indicating the character, the scope, and the feasibility of synthesizing laboratory-derived and clinic-derived concepts in a theory of personality. *Personality and psychotherapy* was a milestone, as yet perhaps too little appreciated, in the history of psychology.

TRAIT AND FACTOR THEORIES

In addition to comprehensiveness, personality theories have another characteristic which generally sets them apart from other theories of behavior: Nearly all personality theories have within them a concept which serves to explain and emphasize the *consistency* of behavior per se. Nonpersonality theories typically predict such consistency only insofar as there is consistency of circumstances; that is, the same response should be observed only if the external stimuli are the same, if they are equivalent because experiences with each were the same, or if they are related closely enough via generalization to produce the same response. Obviously, the *if*s in the preceding sentence give the S-R theorist enough latitude to predict some consistency of behavior, but most personality theorists have not been content with this. They insist that the behavior is the same, or is consistent, because the behaving individual is the same. We pointed out at the beginning of this chapter that classic personality theorists generally maintain that much of the variance in behavior is attributable to individual differences; the corollary to this is that much of the consistency in behavior is attributable to *individual sameness*—that is, the same individual is behaving at different times or in different situations.

Two general classes of personality theory, not ordinarily categorized together, are alike in that they both give primary attention to the problem of consistency in behavior, albeit in markedly different ways. These are the trait theories best exemplified by the views of G. W. Allport, and the factor theories, represented by the work of Eysenck and Cattell.

The trait theorist believes that the job of the personality theorist is to isolate and describe certain properties of the individual which underlie and determine overt behavior, thereby giving the individual's behavior a consistent, integrated direction. These properties are called *traits,* and the traits may be very general, influencing all or nearly all the individual's behavior, or very specific, in which case only behavior in certain kinds of situations is influenced by the trait.

The factor theorist derives concepts (factors) from a statistical analysis of consistency observed in test performance. Like traits, factors may be general or specific, though the nature of their derivation makes them ususally less all-encompassing than a general trait.

Allport's Trait Theory

Gordon Willard Allport (1897-1967) was educated in a variety of fields and continued his interest in many of them. He received his A.B. at Harvard in economics, taught sociology and English in Istanbul, returned to Harvard for his Ph.D., and subsequently studied at three European universities—Berlin, Hamburg, and Cambridge. While in Europe Allport developed his persisting interest in international affairs. As a by-product of his stay abroad, he became one of the major interpreters of German psychology in the United States.

Allport taught in the Department of Social Ethics at Harvard upon returning to the United States and then moved for a short time to Dartmouth. In 1930 he returned to Harvard, where he remained until his death in 1967. At Harvard he helped to form the Department of Social Relations, in which psychologists, sociologists, and anthropologists combined their talents. Allport received high professional honors in 1963, when he received the gold medal of the American Psychological Foundation, and in 1964, when he received the American Psychological Association's award for distinguished scientific contributions.

Allport's publications reflect his diversity of interests and his recognition of the complexity and uniqueness of human behavior. A former editor of the *Journal* of *Abnormal and Social Psychology,* Allport wrote on subjects ranging from *The individual and his religion* (1950a) to *The psychology of radio* (G. W. Allport & Cantril, 1935). His major works in the area of personality theory are *Personality: A psychological interpretation* (1937), *The nature of personality: Selected papers* (1950b), *Becoming: Basic considerations for a psychology of personality* (1955), *Personality and social encounter: Selective essays* (1960), and *Pattern and growth in personality* (1961). Many of his important papers have been collected in *The person in psychology: Selected essays* (1968). Finally, in the area of test construction, Allport collaborated with his brother Floyd in the development of the *A-S reaction study* (G. W. Allport & Allport, 1928), and with P. E. Vernon to produce *A study of values* (1931).

Allport recognized that there are many factors which determine behavior. These form a hierarchy from most specific to most general, as follows: conditioned reflex, habit, attitude, trait, self, and personality. The more general factors generally dominate the more specific ones. The most general factor, personality, was defined by Allport as follows (1937): "Personality is the dynamic organization within the individual of those psychophysical systems that determine his unique adjustments to his environment (p. 48)."

Despite the dominating position of personality in the hierarchy of factors, Allport believed that the most profitable level for the personality theorist to study is the trait. He gave it its best-known definition (1937): "A generalized and focalized neuropsychic system (peculiar to the individual), with the capacity to render many stimuli functionally equivalent, and to initiate and guide consistent (equivalent) forms of adaptive and expressive behavior (p. 295)."

This comprehensive definition, though vague, points out clearly the role of the trait as a determiner of consistency in behavior and reveals Allport's emphasis on individuality as well as his interest in adaptive and expressive behavior. His studies of expressive behavior (G. W. Allport & Vernon, 1933) have afforded evidence for consistency; they also indicate his interest in idiographic rather than nomothetic investigation. Idiographic studies lead to intensive study of individuals. Nomothetic investigation is concerned with lawful regularities in the "typical" individual, and Allport believed that such studies tend to overlook significant features of behavior. Expressive behavior is that aspect of behavior which is related to an individual's own style of behaving rather than to the function of the behavior in adaptation; for example, two individuals writing or saying the same words in response to a question may do so in quite different ways, their individual ways expressing their own personalities.

Allport and Vernon studied the expressive aspects of several types of behavior, obtaining thirty-eight measures. They determined that there was satisfactory reliability for the measures when the behavior was repeated and when the same behavior was measured from different muscle groups. Then they examined the intercorrelations of their thirty-eight measures to see whether a few general traits or factors might account for the observed intercorrelations. They concluded that three general factors were indicated by the data: one was a kind of motor expansiveness indicated chiefly by the extensiveness of responses such as writing; a second was called the _centrifugal group factor,_ related to distance from the individual's center and having to do with outward tendency and extroversion; and the third had to do with emphasis, as indicated by gestures made while speaking, writing pressure, and so on.

Typically, Allport did not rest content with the group aspect of the study. He and Vernon then proceeded to an intensive study of four individuals and concluded that the expressive measures were quite congruent with the subjective estimates of personality study. This part of the study is typical of both the strength and the weakness of Allport's approach; the results are suggestive and provocative and yet somewhat unconvincing because of their subjectivity and the lack of specific predictions.

There are several aspects of Allport's psychology which deserve comment, aside from his definition and study of traits. Allport emphasized the complexity and individuality of behavior, together with the multiplicity of its determinants. Accordingly, he was not attracted by the aseptic laboratory studies which some others have used in the construction of their theories of personality. He felt very strongly that studies of group tendencies in a search for universal laws were overemphasized in American psychology; such studies he called _nomothetic._ Allport wished to foster intensive studies of the individual via methods which would reveal the uniqueness of that individual and thereby make it possible to predict his behavior; this approach he called _idiographic._ When Allport (1937) imported into personality discussions this nomothetic-idiographic distinction (originally made by Windelband [1921], a philosopher), he stirred up controversy (Skaggs, 1945) and further discussions of the issues (see Beck, 1953; Eysenck, 1954; Falk, 1956). Allport had struck a nerve.

The nomothetic-idiographic distinction is complex, and we cannot stop to discuss all the issues here. Allport's point has been made in the very limited sense that intensive study of individuals is now regarded as necessary. We have seen that even Skinner and his followers have arrived at this conclusion, but their reasons for doing so are diametrically opposed to those advanced by Allport. The operant conditioner studies the individual case intensively to make sure that every individual follows the same behavioral laws; that is, he studies individual differences to make sure they do not interfere with the functional relationships revealed by _every_ individual in the experiment. The operant conditioner studies individuals so that he can eliminate them from his laws; Allport would have us study individuals so that we can understand them in their uniqueness. In his detailed study of "Jenny" (1965), for example, Allport defends his idiographic approach by claiming to be able to predict her future behavior because of its consistency with what she had done in the past. Such limited generality over time would seem to be all the truly idiographic scientist can aspire to. Traditional science has generally sought laws with the widest possible range of generality; although every condition studied has some unique features, the scientist has attempted to abstract from unique situations those features which are general. Few psychologists have been willing to abandon this view for Allport's more idiosyncratic perspective.

R. R. Holt (1962), who did one of the later and more thorough analyses of the issue raised by Allport, tries to lay the whole issue to rest. First he shows how the idiographic opposition to natural science (characterized at that time as nomothetic) arose within the romantic movement. Holt then examines each idiographic assumption systematically and concludes that the phrase *idiographic science* is self-contradictory. However, he does *not* embrace the conclusion that science is therefore nomothetic (1962, pp. 399-400):

The nomothetic conception of science must be rejected as a caricature of what any contemporary scientist does. The only way to justify the application of the term nomothetic to the natural science of the present is to change the definition of the term so much that it no longer resembles its original meaning, and becomes an unnecessary redundancy ... the nomothetic is as dead a duck today as the idiographic, and neither term adds anything to contemporary philosophy of science.

Allport's thinking in another area was more widely accepted. Psychoanalytic theory made it fashionable to emphasize past experiences and unconscious influences in the determination of behavior. Allport provided a needed antidote by pointing out the necessity for determination of present behavior by present influences and by insisting that, in normal people at least, conscious influences on behavior are far more powerful than unconscious ones. It follows that the verbal report of an individual on the reasons for his behavior is likely to be the best single source of information about those reasons. In addition, the conscious *intentions* of an individual provide a better indication of how he will behave than any searching into the past (see especially G. W. Allport, 1955).

Allport's ideas on the functional *autonomy* of motives (Allport, 1937) have inspired more criticism (see Bertocci, 1940, for an early example) than any other single one of his ideas. Behavior, according to this view, may persist independently of the motive originally responsible for its occurrence. No other biological or primary motive need replace the original one; the behavior, once it has become functionally autonomous, may be engaged in for its own sake only. The old track star who in college ran for adulation or for pay may continue to run years afterward when there is no motive, external to the behavior itself, for continuing.

It is easy to see that such a concept invites critical attack. Allport cannot be saying that all behavior becomes functionally autonomous, or extinction could never be observed. He should then give an account of why some behaviors or motives become autonomous and some do not. This Allport attempted to do (1961). His account of the reasons for functional autonomy seems to constitute a moderation of his original position. For one class of autonomous behaviors, he accepts an account in terms of fairly traditional mechanisms, like unusual resistance to extinction. For the second class, he maintains that the behaviors continue because they are consistent with the acquired structure of the person. It seems that Allport's later position is more congruent with the views of learning theorists. Allport has again succeeded in drawing attention to a serious problem by somewhat overstating his case. Most psychologists would now at least agree that one should pay attention to the contemporary dynamics of any given behavior; one cannot rely exclusively on an account of the motives active when the behavior was originally acquired.

We have pointed out ways in which Allport sometimes opposed prevailing opinion. Yet in many ways Allport's theory is a prototype of most personality theory. He emphasizes structure and hierarchical arrangement of personality. He stresses the complexity and individuality of personality and the multiple determination of behavior. He opposes laboratory methods and nomothetic studies, preferring some looseness of conceptualization to oversimplification. For the tough-minded, these are serious defects; for the more tender-minded, the same attitudes are sources of inspiration and wisdom.

Factor Theories

Factor theories are conceptually related to Allport's trait theory though historically more closely related to a statistical technique called *factor analysis* (Spearman, 1931). The search of the factor analyst leads to something which accounts for an observed consistency of behavior, that is, a something much like Allport's traits. The rigor of the method of search, however, tends to set factor theory apart from trait theory and give it a kinship in spirit with S-R theories, though the two proceed toward the goal of precision via very different paths (Cattell, 1959).

Factor theories are more closely related to a particular method of study than other personality theories are. To understand them we must know something of the reasoning behind factor analysis as a statistical technique. In order to make the discussion concrete, we shall relate factor analysis to the study of intelligence, the context in which it actually developed.

We may look at the problem in this way. Say that we have observed, in a gross way, that some people consistently stand higher than others on some loosely defined dimension which we shall call *intelligence*. We understand little about either the dimension or the reasons for individual variations in amount of intelligence. Assume now that we are able to agree on a large number of measures of behavior which are related to this gross intelligence dimension. We can then find out how each of a large number of people scores on each of the measures. If there is a tendency for people who score high on one test also to score high on every other test, it is clear that these high-scoring people must possess a higher-than-usual amount of some general factor which plays a role in determining all the test scores. If smaller subgroups of the tests have a larger relationship than can be accounted for by the general factor, then there is a group factor present which underlies performance on just these groups of related tests. Any remaining variation in test scores must be attributable to factors useful only on the single test or to "errors" or unique circumstances surrounding the administration of the test. Burt (1941) has given a full description of these various types of factors.

There are generally several ways in which the tests can be associated so that mathematically reasonable factors can be isolated. In selecting a single one from the several available factor accounts of the observed correlations, a decision must be based upon some variety of psychological acumen.

Once the factors have been determined, the measures, or tests, can be looked at again. For an individual measure, we can ask how much its value has been determined by the general factor, how much by each of the group factors involved, and how much by specific and error factors. The pattern of determination for the measure is called the *factor loading,* or *saturation,* of the measure.

Finally, we can reexamine the gross concept, intelligence, and answer questions about its composition, its nature, and its usefulness as a concept. The outcome of the factor analysis will have suggested new ways to test intelligence and to conceive of intelligence; it may at this stage appear that intelligence is not what we thought it was or that our measures were not good measures of that which we wish to continue to call *intelligence.*

Although our discussion has been concerned with the more orthodox type of factor analysis in which scores from many individuals are analyzed, it is also possible to apply factor analysis to the correlations between different tests taken repeatedly by a single individual. Stephenson (1953, 1961) has combined factor analysis with his Q sort to obtain information about the unique attitudinal organization of individual persons. His subjects are required to make judgments concerning both themselves and others in a wide variety of situations, in order to provide data for the factor analysis. In this application of factor analysis to an individual, successive scores by a single individual can be treated as though they were made by different persons.

At this point it should be clear that factor analysis is a complex, sophisticated, and fascinating method for the study of multiple variables. As such, it is clearly applicable to the study of personality. But it, like any other method in any science, is no substitute for ingenuity and insight. It will not produce hypotheses or interpretations. Furthermore, it is important to remember that the results of a factor analysis can be no better than the data that are fed into it (see Anastasi 1958, pp. 335ff., for a simple, well-reasoned discussion of this problem).

Eysenck's Factor Theory. Hans Jurgen Eysenck (1916-   ), a German by birth, left his homeland during the rise of the Nazis and has spent most of his life in England. After taking his Ph.D. at the University of London, Eysenck served as a hospital psychologist during World War II. He then returned to the University of London and became director of the psychological department at the Institute of Psychiatry, where he conducted research in institute hospitals. Eysenck is presently associated with the University of London and serves as senior psychologist at two hospitals. During visits to the United States, he has taught briefly at the Universities of Pennsylvania and California.

Eysenck's contributions to personality theory are exemplified by *Dimensions of personality* (1947), *The scientific study of personality* (1952b), *The structure of human personality* (1953a), *The dynamics of anxiety and hysteria: An experimental application of modern learning theory to psychiatry* (1957), his editorship of the comprehensive *Handbook of abnormal psychology* (1961), and *The causes and cures of neurosis* 1965), of which Rachman is co-author. In addition to research in the areas of clinical psychology and personality, Eysenck has studied aesthetics, attitudes, and humor. Eysenck's publications, too, have strayed from his major field of interest into *The psychology of politics* (1954) and the *Uses and abuses of psychology* (1953b).

As an outstanding contemporary factor theorist, Eysenck tends to be tough-minded and operational in approach. He puts little credence in the dimensions of personality which have been initiated from outside the framework of quantitative method. His general attitude, with which most of those in the "behavior modification movement" enthusiastically agree, is well expressed in the following quotation (Eysenck & Rachman, 1965): "Learning theory does not postulate . . . 'unconscious' causes, but regards neurotic symptoms as simply learned habits; there is no neurosis underlying the symptom, but merely the symptom itself. *Get rid of the symptom (skeletal and autonomic) and you have eliminated the neurosis* (p. 10)."

The basic structure of Eysenck's theory is not unlike Allport's. He too recognizes a hierarchical arrangement of consistencies from least to most: the specific response, the habitual response, the trait, and the type. The trait is an observed consistency of action tendencies, while the type is a constellation of traits. Most of Eysenck's interest is directed to the types, though much of his research is necessarily concerned with traits; one cannot constellate regularities in behavior without first discovering them. Eysenck, with his operational orientation, does not accept traits unless they have been operationally validated.

In his early research on 700 neurotic soldiers, Eysenck (1947) uncovered two fundamental underlying variables, or typal polarities: introversion-extraversion and neuroticism. The first of these is recognized by Eysenck as almost exactly the introversion-extraversion earlier proposed by Jung as a basic personality dimension. It is different chiefly because it was extracted by Eysenck from the intercorrelations of a large number of ratings and classifications available on a large number of people. A major result of this study was that the neurotic type was found to be inferior in nearly every respect: intellectually, physically, emotionally, and especially with respect to the ability to sustain motivation.

Personality for Eysenck is divided, in the classic British tradition, into areas or sectors: the cognitive or intellectual, the conative, the affective, and the somatic. For the first three of these areas Eysenck is willing to suggest underlying general factors. For the first, of course, it is intelligence. Neuroticism is, in a sense, a conative or character defect, since it represents an inability to persist in the face of obstacles. Introversion-extraversion is a general factor in the affective area.

More recently (1952b) in a study of normal subjects and hospitalized mental patients, Eysenck discovered a third type, psychoticism. Somehow this does not seem surprising. Psychotics, like neurotics, tended to do more poorly than normals, though by no means on all tests. They were distinguished from normals and neurotics by a number of specific behavioral deficiencies.

Eysenck has made a methodological contribution which promises to be important. It is called the *method of criterion analysis* (1950). The method is simply a stipulation that the factor analyst should begin with two groups which are known to differ on some hypothesized underlying factor. Eysenck's normal and psychotic subjects would provide an example. When the measures are obtained from the two groups, only those which discriminate between the groups can justifiably be assumed to relate to the hypothesized factor. If Eysenck's criterion analysis is used, it ensures that the investigator will plan the investigation carefully in advance; he cannot simply administer a haphazard truckload of tests to a randomly selected flock of subjects and let the factors fall where they may.

Eysenck has been an extremely controversial figure. He is the kind of man who, if he were in India, might try to live on raw hamburger. He is a clinical psychologist who has characterized psychotherapy as a loose art form and has seriously questioned whether it does any good (1952a). Eysenck's forthright behavior has not endeared him to all his colleagues, who have not hesitated to apply the same high standards to his work that he has applied to theirs. Serious questions have been raised about both the empirical and the theoretical aspects of his research. It has been frequently noted that the evidence for his assertions is typically meager; he has also been criticized for overlooking alternative interpretations of his data in the absence of adequate controls to eliminate such factors (e.g., cf. Jensen, 1958, p. 300).

Nevertheless, Eysenck's influence on personality theory has been substantial, and his research looks very promising. He has tended to toughen thinking without eliminating valuable methods of observation. He has applied quantitative methods to the data of the clinic; this has been one of the crying needs of personality research. He has been quite as willing to eliminate a concept as to accept it; yet he is not at all antitheoretical. If these techniques result in further integration of the relatively fragmentary factors thus far isolated and tested, they will have made a most significant contribution to personality theory.

Cattell's Factor Theory. Raymond Bernard Cattell (1905-   ) was born and educated in England, where he was recognized as a leader in the field of personality research before coming to the United States. Cattell took his Ph.D. at the University of London and held both academic and clinical positions at that institution in close succession. His later career has been characterized by broad interests, encompassing both of these areas of psychology.

In the United States, Cattell has taught at Columbia Teachers College, Clark University, Harvard, and the University of Illinois, where he is now a research professor. His major works include *Personality and motivation structure and measurement* (1957) and two handbooks which he edited and to which he contributed chapters: *Handbook of multivariate experimental psychology* (1966) and *Handbook of modern personality theory* (1970). Besides other, older or less important work in personality theory, Cattell has to his credit work in the areas of measurement (1936, 1946) and experimental and social psychology (1952). Cattell has authored three widely used tests: The Culture Free Test of Intelligence (1944), The O-A Personality Test Battery (1954), and The 16 Personality Factor Questionnaire

(1950). These are only a few of the tests with which Cattell has been involved; Cattell and Warburton (1967) list over 400 tests devised by Cattell and his students!

Like Eysenck, Cattell is intellectually indebted to the factor analysts; this is not surprising, since he studied under Spearman, who developed the essential ideas for factor analysis, which he applied to the study of intelligence. Cattell's general personality theory shows similarities to McDougall's in its tendency to look for underlying dimensions of behavior; more directly, Cattell borrows McDougall's notion of the self-regarding sentiment. Cattell's developmental theory is markedly Freudian.

Cattell combines the qualities of tough-minded factor theorists like Eysenck with the qualities of more traditional personality theorists who stress comprehensiveness. His theory is therefore at once extensive and, in part, quantitative in emphasis and content. Eysenck has a far stronger tendency to limit himself to concepts derived from factor studies; Cattell sometimes allows himself more range in order to make his theory inclusive and to avoid ignoring data from other sources.

Cattell (1950) has defined personality as "that which permits a prediction of what a person will do in a given situation" (p. 2). This definition is consistent with our contention that a theory of personality is really identical with a general theory of behavior, for Cattell's definition would fit theories of behavior.

Traits are Cattell's basic elements of personality. He explicitly recognizes that traits are concepts used to explain observed consistencies of behavior, and he agrees with Allport and Eysenck that there are many levels of generality of traits, some applying only to particular individuals or circumstances, and others applying to very large groups. He has been concerned mainly, however, with the intraindividual organization of traits.

The chief distinction made by Cattell is between *surface traits* and *source traits*. The former are based simply on observed behaviors that occur together, while the latter underlie the surface traits, determining observed behavior consistencies through particular combinations. There is a rough correspondence between Eysenck's trait and Cattell's surface trait, and Eysenck's type and Cattell's source trait. The latter pair is in both cases more stable and more general, and both investigators have concentrated their interest more intensively upon such general factors.

Cattell also recognizes two kinds of traits according to their origins: constitutional and environmental-mold traits. He has performed some ingenious research in an attempt to discover to what extent traits are determined via these two influences. For example, in one study (Cattell, Blewett, & Beloff, 1955) a personality test was administered to identical twins, to fraternal twins, to siblings reared together and apart, and to unrelated subjects. The test measured traits established as significant personality factors in earlier factor studies. Study of the results obtained with subjects who thus differed to varying degrees in both hereditary and environmental similarity allowed the investigators partially to evaluate the relative contributions of heredity and environment to the factors studied. Such research is noteworthy within the personality area for its logical consistency and coordination with earlier research as well as for its ingenuity.

Cattell differentiates between source traits on the basis of their origins. The *erg* is a dynamic source trait with a constitutional origin; the *metaerg* is identical except for its environmental origin. Both determine patterns of behavior because they consist of motivational predispositions toward environmental objects. Meta-ergs are further subdivided into attitudes, interests, and sentiments. Sentiments are the most stable class.

The most powerful sentiment of all is the self sentiment. Cattell, like other personality theorists, introduces the self to explain the consistency that seems to suffuse all the behavior of an individual. Thus the self sentiment acts on all other sentiments and may strengthen or inhibit the tendency to action aroused by other sentiments. There are two selves, the real and the ideal. These have their obvious meaning, the former being the most realistic estimate an individual could make of himself, and the latter the individual as he would ideally like to be.

The development of personality depends upon the evolution of ergs and metaergs and the organization of the self through the process of learning. Cattell accepts both contiguity and reinforcement as principles of learning. Learning is conceived of as occurring via a series of stages, each involving alternative outcomes called *crossroads* by Cattell.

The framework within which personality development takes place is the social context. Cattell has turned his talents to the description of this context as well as to the description of personality. The dimensions of social institutions combine to form an analog to individual personality, the *syntality* of the institution. In several studies (e.g., Cattell, 1949; Cattell & Wispe, 1948) he has found factors which he believes are useful for the description of families and nations. The use of a variety of measures to derive social factors is still another example of Cattell's originality and enterprise.

Cattell has made greater efforts to synthesize his concepts explicitly than most personality theorists have. One example of this is his dynamic lattice (1950), which diagrammatically interrelates the ergs, sentiments, and attitudes which constitute the most important elements of a personality structure. This lattice portrays the connections between ergs (e.g., sex, protection, and security) and sentiments (e.g., toward a wife), which are in turn related to attitudes (e.g., toward a wife's hairstyle). In addition, elements at the same level may be interrelated (e.g., sentiments regarding one's wife and one's bank account).

Finally, Cattell suggests an explicit way to combine information about an individual in order to predict what he will do in a specific situation. This is done through the *specification equation:*

$$R = s_1 T_1 + s_2 T_2 + s_3 T_3 + \cdots + s_n T_n$$

Here s_1 represents the "weighting" of trait number 1 (T_1) in the situation in question, etc. The form of the equation is a simple linear sum. Cattell recognizes both that the form of the equation might need to be complicated to represent more complex interactions between traits and that a more elaborate type of model might eventually be needed. However, he also notes that one must walk before one can run and that his equation *can* be applied to prediction of things like academic performance (Cattell & Butcher, 1968); that is more than the opposition can say.

Allport, Eysenck, and Cattell have developed theories which have considerable logical similarity. All three men are alike in their vigor and iconoclastic tendencies—traits which psychology presently needs, especially in personality theory. Allport is very different from the other two in attitude and in method of study, having little sympathy for factor analysis or for the massive experiment. Eysenck and Cattell have shown unusual aptitude for originating experimental designs that wed quantitative methods to the study of personality. Their theories promise a long and happy marriage.

ORGANISMIC THEORIES

Many personality theorists start from a point of view systematically close to that of the Gestalt psychologists. Murphy, Rogers, Goldstein, Angyal, Maslow, Lecky, Murray, and Sheldon are members of this class. Any or all of these men might be included as organismic theorists. The decision must be based on the extent to which a holistic, Gestalt orientation toward the individual is a *central* feature of their personality theories. Quite arbitrarily, we are choosing Goldstein and Sheldon as organismic theorists and omitting the rest or treating them in a separate section. The choice of Goldstein needs no justification; Sheldon would often be put in another class because the really central feature of his theory is his preoccupation with constitutional influences on personality; he does, however, espouse a general organismic point of view, and his interest in organic effects qualifies him as an organismic theorist in the popular meaning of the term.

Goldstein's Holistic Theory

Kurt Goldstein (1878-1965) established his reputation as a neuropsychiatrist in Europe before coming to this country in 1935. Having received his medical degree from the University of Breslau, he associated himself with the Psychiatric Hospital at Köningsberg, At an early age, Goldstein became a professor of neurology and psychiatry and director of the Neurological Institute at the University of Frankfurt. He later held a similar position at the University of Berlin.

During World War I, Goldstein conducted the fundamental studies of brain-injured soldiers which laid the groundwork for his organismic theory (1942) and his most significant publication, *The organism* (1939).

In the United States, Goldstein held academic and clinical positions in a variety of institutions, in addition to maintaining a private neuropsychiatry and psychotherapy practice in New York City for many years. He delivered the William James Lectures at Harvard, discussing human nature in the light of psychopathology (1940), and was associated with the New York Psychiatric Institute, Tufts Medical School in Boston, Columbia University, Brandeis University, City College of New York, and the New School for Social Research. Goldstein died in 1965, and his posthumously published autobiography (1967) summed up the history of his intellectual development literally from beginning to end.

Aside from his theoretical and clinical work, Goldstein published works on language disturbances (1948) and, with Gelb (1920), on the Gestalt problem of figure-ground relationships (although Goldstein disclaimed any ties with Gestalt psychology).

To Goldstein, a primary feature of organisms is their organization. In behavior as in perception, processes are organized into figure and ground. The figure is the principal and outstanding feature of the ongoing activity, just as a perceptual figure stands out from its ground (cf. Chapter 8). In an organism's behavior, those features which are related to the strongest drives stand out.

The normal organism is structured but flexible, capable of tailoring its behavior to fit the needs of the ongoing stimulus situation. Its behavior can be understood only as part of an organic unity; the significance of its behavior can be assessed only as a contribution to the ongoing goal of the organism.

For Goldstein, the goal of the organism is unitary. It is self-actualization. Self-actualization sums up all the needs of the organism. A sexually driven organism actualizes itself in coitus, and a hungry one in eating; but the self-actualization of the complex human adult is expressed in many less organically driven acts. It is clear that on this point Goldstein is close to Carl Rogers, for whom self-actualization is also a crucial concept. Indeed, there is inevitably a close kinship at the core between all self theories and all organismic theories, for both emphasize the basic unity of the personality. The two types of theories differ, when they do, in that the self theorist has a greater tendency to analyze out subsidiary structures which have some degree of independent existence.

Goldstein believed that the strongly organized organism is capable of choosing a favorable environment or manipulating an unfavorable one to some extent. It is thus not the victim of blind forces or the pawn of fortuitous stimulus situations. But no organism is insulated from environmental effects; it must thus come to terms with its environment. Only through accepting those terms of the environment which cannot be avoided or changed can the organism continue in its attempt to actualize itself. This aspect of Goldstein's thinking puts him close to the phenomenologists and existentialists—a similarity which Goldstein himself did not fail to note when, in his eighties, he wrote about his life (1967, pp. 161-164).

Organismic theorists tend to avoid analysis; Goldstein was no exception. If it is necessary to study every behavior event within the context of the whole organism, it is tempting to stay on the level of generality without coming to terms with the problem of specificity of prediction. In this Goldstein was again no exception. His central concept, self-actualization, leaves one uncertain of the defining characteristics of such behavior and wondering whether there is much behavior which is not in some sense self-actualizing. Does this concept say very much more than that an organism will do what it will do, and that, if it does it, we assume that it needed to do it in order to actualize itself?

It is interesting that brain-injured patients and their symptoms led Goldstein to his holistic point of view. He found that the behavior manifested by a patient with a brain injury could be understood only in terms of an examination of the whole matrix of the patient's behavior. What at first appears to be a direct result of injury might, upon closer examination, turn out to be a quite indirect reaction stemming from an attempt to fit the results of injury into the mosaic of life. The same physical injury might lead to a variety of behavior syndromes, depending upon the patient's circumstances and personality structure. In general, a specific deterioration in some ability would lead a patient to be generally more sensitive, less self-confident, and more withdrawn; if one did not know this, he might uncritically attribute various performance decrements to direct results of injury rather than to these indirect manifestations.

With his background of clinical experience, it is natural that Goldstein should have preferred the intensive study of the individual to the group approach. Through his approach, Goldstein made his best-known discovery: The most characteristic difference between patients with extensive brain injury and normal individuals is that the former have lost the abstract attitude. Their ability to do concrete things and to react to concrete situations may be relatively unimpaired, but their ability to abstract is likely to be extremely limited. For example, the brain-injured patient may be unable to make statements that are obviously contrary to fact, such as "the moon is green." He cannot abstract common properties of dissimilar objects, such as a radio and a newspaper. This lack of abstract ability permeates his behavior. Goldstein and Scheerer (1941, 1953) developed tests to determine the extent to which abstract behavior is impaired; these tests therefore help to diagnose brain damage.

Goldstein was an example of an organismic theorist at his observational, clinical best. He was self-consciously antiexperimental, sharing the organismic belief that by thus restricting conditions and controlling behavior, we lose the significance which the activity might have in its natural context. But Goldstein was shrewd and industrious in taking advantage of the wealth of material which paraded before him in his psychiatric practice. Methodologically, he added few innovations to the organismic view, which has said in essence: "Take Gestalt principles from the study of perception and apply them to the study of the whole individual."

Sheldon's Typology

William H. Sheldon (1899-   ) is a trained physician, as his theoretical efforts to relate behavioral and body components might indicate. After receiving both his Ph.D. and his M.D. from the University of Chicago, he interned at a children's hospital. Sheldon taught at the University of Chicago, Northwestern University, and the University of Wisconsin before continuing his studies with two years of psychiatric training abroad. His visits with Jung, Freud, and Kretschmer contributed directly to his later theorizing, which owes most to constitutional theorists such as Kretschmer and Viola, but which also shows resemblances to Freudian, and particularly Jungian, theory.

At Harvard, Sheldon entered into a collaborative relationship with experimentalist S. S. Stevens, who brought to Sheldon's work a new sophistication in procedure and measurement. Together they published the basic works in constitutional psychology: *The varieties of temperament: A psychology of constitutional differences* (1942) and *The varieties of human physique: An introduction to constitutional psychology* (1940).

Sheldon's writing has been characterized by concern for the identification of, and relationships between, structural and temperamental factors, particularly as applied to the problem of delinquency (1949b). He has written a somatotyping guide, *Atlas of men: A guide for somatotyping the adult male at all ages* (1954). Always the taxonomist, Sheldon ventured away from personality theory temporarily, only to produce *Early American cents* (1949a)—a classification of coins!

Sheldon's road has not been an easy one. American psychology generally has been unfriendly to the idea that constitutional factors are important influences on behavior. Our democratic ideals and, more specifically, the extreme environmentalism of John B. Watson have made us unwilling to believe that innate predispositions really have a directive influence on our personality.

Despite this resistance, it has remained obvious to the man in the street that there are associations between constitutional factors and personality. To him, the fat man appears jolly; the skinny kid with glasses remains a withdrawn bookworm. It is not surprising, then, that the man who reinforced these long-held popular beliefs is one of the better-known theorists.

Sheldon is also well known to the beginning psychology student, perhaps because he stands out among the personality theorists as a man who has said something comprehensible to the beginning student. Regrettably, Sheldon has sometimes been presented as having made ludicrous or incautious statements. He may have advocated something unpopular or capable of misinterpretation, but not something ludicrous.

Sheldon's system is a modern version of statements running back at least as far as Hippocrates, who believed that there were associations between body fluids and temperaments and that there were two basic types of physique: short and fat or long and thin. Ernst Kretschmer, many years later, added a third body type—the muscular—between the two extremes and designated them as follows: pyknic, short and squatty; athletic, broad and muscular; and asthenic, tall and thin. He studied the relationship between these three types and the varieties of psychoses. Sheldon's continuity with his typological forebears has probably also contributed to his difficulty in getting a completely open-minded hearing from American psychologists. Hippocrates and his bilious temperaments are all too easy to laugh at, and some of this attitude toward humors has generalized to Sheldon. Psychology has been suspicious of typology as too easy a solution; even the description of personality in terms of patterns of traits is not above suspicion. Those familiar with the sad history of phrenology recognize both its similarity to trait psychology and its similarity to constitutional typology, for do not both phrenology and constitutional typology assess personality from physical measurements? It is easy to understand the rockiness of Sheldon's professional path. Fortunately, Sheldon seems well equipped to dish out punishment as well as to take it. He has written pungent criticisms of others, in addition to defending his own position.

Sheldon's contributions have been primarily an elaboration and tightening of Kretschmer's basic physical types and further empirical work in relating these types to behavioral variables. An important difference exists between his work and earlier theorizing, such as Kretschmer's. Sheldon has recognized that any given individual is marked by some *degree* of each type and thus is in this sense always a blend of types rather than a pure type.

Sheldon's attempt to establish a constitutional interrelationship between behavior and body build is anchored in the belief that the outward physical appearance (phenotype) is determined and guided by a hypothetical biological process (morphogenotype). Measurement of the physique is utilized by Sheldon in an attempt to evaluate indirectly the function of the morphogenotype. The obtained data fall into three categories of body types: endomorphy, mesomorphy, and ectomorphy.

This trichotomy was determined by evaluating 4,000 standardized photographs taken from three angles—front, back and side. These were sectioned into seventeen parts (Sheldon, 1940, p. 55), from which anthropometric measurements could be obtained. Sheldon is thus unique among personality theorists in being able to work with variables that can be, and have been, measured with a ruler. After analyzing the data, Sheldon concluded that all the physical characteristics could be grouped into three components according to the presumed embryonic origin of most of the individual's tissue in the outer (ectomorphic), middle (mesomorphic), or inner (endomorphic) layer.

The endomorph tends to be soft, fleshy, and round; the mesomorph is square, tough, muscular, dense, and athletic; the ectomorph is tall, thin, fragile, and small-boned. The endomorph is massive in relation to his surface area; the mesomorph, intermediate; and the ectomorph, more exposed to the world because of his high proportion of surface area to mass.

Besides the primary components of body type there are several which are classified as secondary. These are dysplasia (disharmony between the body parts), gynandromorphy (bisexuality denoted by the physique), and texture (as of hairiness of the body) (1940, p. 7).

Three components of temperament correspond, according to Sheldon, to the three components of the physique: visceratonia, somatotonia, and cerebrotonia. The visceratonic individual loves comfort, food, and affection, and is good-natured. The somatotonic person is active, vigorous, and aggressive. The cerebrotonic individual is a bookish, sensitive, shy individual who withdraws from social contacts.

If we assume that there are such identifiable components of consitution and of personality, are the two related or not? Sheldon (1942, p. 400) found a remarkably high correlation between the components that one would expect to find associated: endomorphy-visceratonia; mesomorphy-somatotonia; and ectomorphy-cerebrotonia. These correlations are all about .80! Personality theorists seldom find their expectations so gratifyingly corroborated.

It is easy to be dubious about Sheldon's components of personality, since they seem so close to the layman's stereotypes, until one discovers that the clusters of traits were derived from careful correlational studies using a large number of original traits rather than from the depths of the armchair (Sheldon, 1944, pp. 526-549). Sheldon's components of personality are each defined by twenty related traits (Sheldon, 1942, p. 26).

Sheldon seems to be on safe ground when he maintains that, descriptively, the postulated correlations exist. However, other experimenters generally find that the correlations are lower than those obtained by Sheldon (Child, 1950; Lindzey, 1967; Sanford, 1953; Seltzer, Wells, & McTernan, 1948). The inflated correlations between temperament and physique could be attributed to a "halo effect" since both sets of ratings were done by the same person; that is, there was no attempt at blind analysis. Although in *The varieties of temperament* (1942, pp. 411-425) Sheldon made an effort to justify his position, his attempt in no way negates the possibility that a subjective bias may have contaminated the results. The procedure, despite the possibility of subjectivism, remained unaltered.

An additional criticism has been made by Lubin (1950), who discovered that some of the coefficients found in the tables of intercorrelation among the temperamental traits (Sheldon, 1942, pp. 506-511) are not mathematically possible.

Sheldon has also been attacked on the grounds that he assumes that genetic, strictly biological factors account for the observed correlations. If Sheldon really maintained that these direct biological influences were *the* reason for the correlations, he would be open to attack. He does not; he recognizes, as do his detractors, that different cultural expectations or differential rewards related to different body builds might account for the observed personality differences. For example, a boy who is muscular by nature probably finds more reward in athletics than an endomorphic type. The rewards of sport would then increase both active competitive behavior and the accumulation of muscle tissue. Sheldon admits that, although the morphogenotype is invariant, the phenotype (from which measurements are taken) does fluctuate because of cultural and other influences. This admission forces him to relinquish partially his grasp on his basic theoretical relationship between the constitution and temperament. He says that the crucial relationship is between the morphogenotype and the temperament. The phenotype is only an attempt to measure the morphogenotype; this measurement is the best we have to date, despite its inexactness. It seems to us that operational criteria are highly applicable to this issue. Operationally, the morphogenotype has no meaning not exhausted by the measures of phenotype. The notion of morphogenotype may be lent *credibility* by analogy with other genetic characteristics, but no genetic observations directly justify the theoretical use of the morphogenotype. Therefore, we suggest, on grounds of parsimony, that the stated relationships be restricted to those holding between observed properties.

Sheldon is less willing to recognize the possibility that exclusively environmental factors, such as diet, might explain the observed relationships. However, Anastasi (1958) has pointed out that "Habitual overeating does lead to the accumulation of fat tissue. It is interesting to note in this connection that recent literature in abnormal psychology as well as in psychosomatic medicine contains many references to 'psychological overeating' resulting from frustration and other emotional problems" (p. 182).

Anastasi has also stated (1958) that "The original identification of the three temperamental components . . . can likewise be questioned because of inadequacy of data" (p. 177). That is, in the original study there were only thirty-three male college subjects, and although further attempts were made to revise the original twenty-two traits, the procedure for doing so was clearly dependent upon the original study and its results.

A major asset of Sheldon's theory is that it has kept public the fact that there is some type of relationship between physique and temperament; at the present time, however, we cannot ascertain its direction. Does the physique direct the temperament, or does the temperament determine the physique; or, more logically, is it a two-way process whose exact interrelations have not yet been ferreted out?

NEOANALYTIC PERSONALITY THEORIES

There are several closely related theories of personality that owe a great deal to psychoanalytic theory. Though they are by no means identical, their similarity of background and emphasis justifies their treatment under a single heading. The term *neoanalytic* is used to reflect their basic psychoanalytic framework as well as their modification of such principles in one way or another.

Karen Horney, Erich Fromm, Harry Stack Sullivan, and Henry Murray all developed their own personality theories as improvisations on the primary Freudian, Adlerian, and Jungian themes (see Chapter 9). In these newer theories social factors are emphasized. In playing up social factors, there has been a concomitant tendency to deemphasize biological factors. It is the relative neglect of the instinctive which sets these theories apart from Freudian analytic theory and which keeps at least the first three from having any basic commonality with Jungian theory.

All four of these theorists, and Sullivan especially, have contributed to the theory of ego functioning. This emphasis on ego functioning has been regarded as a strong point by sympathizers with the same point of view; on the other hand, some Freudians have regarded it as evidence that the theories represent an elaboration of Freudian theory rather than any really original contribution. Regardless of basic originality, each of these theorists has said unique things about the relationship of the individual to his society.

Horney's Social Theory

The training and contributions of Karen Horney (1885-1952) were entirely within the field of psychoanalysis, although she represented an important outbranching from orthodox psychoanalytic theory. German by birth, Horney studied medicine at the University of Berlin and received her psychoanalytic training at the Berlin

Psychoanalytic Institute, where she was analyzed by Karl Abraham and Hans Sachs.

In the United States, Horney served as associate director of the Chicago Psychoanalytic Institute, taught at the New York Psychoanalytic Institute, and conducted a private practice in psychotherapy. Her efforts to break away from orthodox psychoanalysis led to the formation of the Association for the Advancement of Psychoanalysis and the American Institute of Psychoanalysis, of which she was dean.

Horney's theoretical emphasis is reflected in the titles of three of her works on personality theory: *Neurotic personality of our times* (1937), *Our inner conflicts* (1945), and *Neurosis and human growth* (1950). Her theory is further explicated in *New ways in psychoanalysis* (1939) and *Self-analysis* (1942).

Horney's social theory flies the banner of *basic anxiety.* This essential factor in personality development (Horney, 1937) is "the feeling a child has of being isolated and helpless in a potentially hostile world" (p. 79). Horney's concept of helplessness as experienced by the infant does not have the universal flavor that Adler assigned to it. It provides a predisposition for the future development of pathological conditions; it does not lead to a striving for superiority, but merely accentuates a predilection for security.

The home environment and the social structure within the family receive by far the most emphasis in Horney's theory. In this structure and the child's reaction to it Horney believed she had the key to the development of an individual's personality structure. The predominant reason that basic anxiety develops from parent-child relationships is the absence of genuine love and affection, and this can almost invariably be traced to neurotic parents. It should be noted, however, that Horney defines neurosis as any deviation from normal, efficient behavior; the term is not used in a pathological context unless so indicated.

The child responds to his basic anxiety by developing some strategy of behavior, *neurotic trends,* in an attempt to overcome it. It is this character structure arising from the reaction to basic anxiety which accounts for neurotic symptoms; it is *not,* as Freud said, a frustration of the sexual instinct. Horney maintained that sexual difficulty is the result and not the cause of conflicts. Furthermore, it is not a compulsion to repeat experiences based on unchanged, repressed childhood experiences (Horney, 1939): "There is no such thing as an isolated repetition of isolated experiences; but the entirety of infantile experiences combines to form a certain character structure, and it is this structure from which later difficulties emanate" (p. 9).

The child also develops an idealized self-concept by internalizing the aspirational levels and ethics of others in his culture. This concept develops without regard for his own potentialities or limitations. Consequently, when he attempts to realize these ideational concepts, he is curtailed both by his own limitations and by those which are imposed upon him by the existing culture. In other words, a person's basic conflict is between self-realization and self-idealization. The idealized self becomes a crutch for the neurotic person. He comes to believe that he *is* his idealized picture. This solution brings a temporary reduction of anxiety, but in the long run increases it. The attempts of the neurotic to live up to his idealized, unrealistic picture of himself result in new conflicts and consequently greater tension. The only real conflict which Horney recognized is that of the present situation and the demands it makes upon the individual.

The devices the individual uses to face his conflicts (neurotic trends) are generally unrealistic and lead to some degree of neurotic behavior. These may be classified into two categories: (1) those which have their roots in the early developmental period of the child and which demonstrate a discernible etiology and (2) those which are a reaction to some situational stress and are usually transitory (Munroe, 1955). A vicious circle develops once these neurotic trends are initiated. Anxiety causes the original behavior, which in turn, because of its inadequacy, leads to further anxiety that initiates another cycle.

In a person's attempt to find security, he utilizes three types of behavioral patterns. He may move toward people, against them, or away from them (Horney, 1945). Fundamental to these three types of behavior are the need for affection, the need for self-sufficiency, and the need to exploit people. In respect to the type of behavior he selects there are corresponding personality types: compliant, aggressive, and detached. Again one must be cautioned not to assume that an individual utilizes only a single type. As the person vacillates from one situation to another, he utilizes the one most efficient for the specific situation. However, if one pattern is used exclusively, regardless of the situation, that is an index of neurosis.

The compliant individual relies upon other people; is ostensibly loving, kind, and loyal; and finds personal criticism devastating. Cynicism, a philosophy of the survival of the fittest, and extreme independence characterize the aggressive personality. The detached individual is perfectionistic, uncreative, and has a paucity of interpersonal relationships.

Horney emphasized only two of the many unconscious defense mechanisms: rationalization and externalization. Rationalization is used in the Freudian sense except that it is explained in the context of the social theory of Horney; that is, it is concerned with the whole organism and is not related to Freud's instinctual personality components. Externalization is merely a more general term for projection. The whole organism participates in an attempt to explain *every* motive and action externally, not just the undesirable ones.

Horney was optimistic about the possibility of avoiding neurotic reactions, as one tends to be when he believes that social factors are of preponderant importance. A secure and loving home would be insurance against the development of a neurotic character structure. Those, like Freud, who emphasize biological factors find it harder to be optimistic; if conflict is based on hereditary factors, change can come but slowly. Horney's more hopeful views have been welcomed by many as a relief from the oppressive pessimism of the orthodox Freudian assumptions. She has attempted to point the way to better families, to better societies, and, through them, to better people. Despite her long-term association with the training of analysts, Horney never formed a cohesive school of followers, nor did her theoretical views inspire research directly. As time passes, Horney's important contributions will probably become less associated with her name and more a part of the general *Zeitgeist* of psychology.

Fromm's Escape-from-freedom Theory

Erich Fromm (1900-   ) was born and trained in Germany. He studied sociology and psychology at the Universities of Munich, Frankfurt, and Heidelberg, where he took his Ph.D. His psychoanalytic training was conducted mainly at the Berlin Psychoanalytic Institute.

Fromm cannot be clearly identified by his affiliation with any one institution, although he has lectured at the Chicago Psychoanalytic Institute and has taught at numerous universities and institutes in this country since he emigrated here in 1933. Since 1951 he has been a professor at the University of Mexico, where he now lives. He is also director of the Mexican Psychoanalytic Institute.

Escape from freedom (1941), *Man for himself* (1947), and *The sane society* (1955)–Fromm's major contributions to personality theory–probably have drawn more cross-scientific and public attention than the works of any other neo–Freudian.

Fromm's primary interests lie in the larger segments of society as they affect the individual (Fromm, 1955, 1961b). As a matter of fact, Fromm is a greater admirer of Marx (Fromm, 1961a) than of Freud (Fromm, 1959) and might as accurately be labeled a Marxist personality theorist as a Freudian personality theorist (see C. S. Hall & Lindzey, 1970, p. 130). Such a labeling, however, does not fit well into the categorization system of American psychology!

However he is classified, Fromm believes that our political organizations no longer provide the firm direction and secure framework which they did when the units of political organization were smaller and man had less freedom to determine his own fate. Today, man suffers from a feeling of insecure aloneness engendered by his lack of a framework; that is, man desires to actualize his self-potential and develop a feeling of belongingness.

Fromm's basic premise that an individual attempts to escape from freedom and return to a more secure existence first gained public notice through his *Escape from freedom.* A child's physical condition at birth and shortly thereafter makes his survival dependent upon his environment in general and upon his mother in particular. The child is soon weaned from his early postnatal surroundings and gradually achieves more and more independence. However, the accompanying amount of strength necessary to augment his independence and to cope with the elements of society is conspicuously lacking. Moreover, man alone has the power to reason and imagine, and with the acquisition of this power he has lost the animal's ability to react instinctively, intimately, and directly to nature. Thus man finds himself in a unique position of being separated from his fellowman by political conditions and from the rest of nature by being a man. His first reaction to this situation is to try to recapture his earlier form of security. Upon finding this physically impossible and socially inefficient, he attempts other means. The two most common solutions are *authoritarianism* and *humanism.*

Broadly defined, authoritarianism is that which externally imposes a set of principles on society. It may be exemplified by a totalitarian state, or dictatorship, or belief in a supreme being. This solution is inadequate because it does not permit the individual an opportunity to realize his potentialities. Frustration and hostility against the imposed conditions are then mobilized.

Fromm believes that humanism is a better solution. All the actualities of human life have a chance to develop through love of fellowman and mutual cooperation. In a humanistic society, each man would be a brother to every man, and no man would be alone.

Fromm identified four ways of escaping the isolation and insecurity prevalent in modern society. He referred to them as types of orientation, or relatedness. They are receptive, exploitative, hoarding, and marketing. In addition, there is the healthy, or productive, orientation. No person exhibits a pure orientation. However, it is possible to manifest one type so that it subordinates all others.

The receptive orientation (Fromm, 1947) "is often to be found in societies in which the right of one group to exploit another is firmly established" (p. 79). Individuals with this type of orientation sacrifice everything in order to maintain their identification with the group or the leader. They expect to receive something gratis, and when adversity occurs they are extremely rebellious and aggressive, exhibiting behavior not unlike that of a spoiled child.

The philosophy of "might makes right" characterizes exploitative individuals. The value which they place upon an object is directly proportional to the value which others place on it. They would feel no compunction about taking some object for no other reason than that it is highly prized by another.

The hoarding orientation is what one might expect it to be: frugal, impecunious, and miserly. Security is evaluated in terms of tangible physical wealth.

The last orientation, marketing, is relatively new and is associated with the advent of modern capitalism. Here the emphasis is centered upon such superficial objectives as keeping up with the Joneses and social climbing.

Fromm (1964) later added the biophilous type, who is in love with life. If love of life is frustrated, the person may become necrophilous (attracted to death).

As society now stands, it is absolutely necessary to warp the individual to fit the needs of society. Though man will always have to fit into human society, Fromm see hope in a society which would give each man a chance to develop into a fully human creature. Fromm has named his ideal society a *humanistic communitarian socialism.* His desperate concern for the development of such a society, born at least partly out of his own flight from Nazism, has put him in the forefront of the science of psychology, which is only now undergoing its social awakening. If Fromm were thirty, instead of seventy, he would probably be a folk hero of youth in the United States. There can be little doubt that his thinking has influenced our recent social upheavals, although, as usual, it is impossible for us to assess the extent of that influence. It seems clear that Fromm is an important intellectual father of some extremely important events.

Murray's Need-Press Theory

Henry Murray (1893-   ) was a rigorously trained, productive biological scientist before turning to psychology. His academic degrees include an A.B. from Harvard in history, an M.D. from Columbia's College of Physicians and Surgeons, and an M.S. in biology from Columbia. Murray subsequently completed a surgical internship at Columbia's Presbyterian Hospital, taught physiology at Harvard, conducted embryological research at the Rockefeller Institute for Medical Research, and then journeyed to England to take his Ph.D. in biochemistry at Cambridge University.

While in Europe, a visit with Jung dramatically shifted Murray's interest to depth psychology. Shortly thereafter he took a position in academic psychology at Harvard and directed the Psychological Clinic there. He was on leave with the Office of Strategic Services during World War II, after which he returned to Harvard as a professor at the Psychological Clinic annex, where he remained until his retirement as professor emeritus in 1962. Murray's psychoanalytic training came under the direction of Franz Alexander and Hans Sachs; Murray paid his debt to psychoanalysis by helping found the Boston Psychoanalytic Society and by stimulating widespread interest in psychoanalytic research among his students. C. S. Hall and Lindzey (1970, p. 166) regret that Murray's conversations have not been preserved, since the richness of his thought and contribution is not fully represented in his published work. We shall see, however, that his published contributions are considerable! Murray, like another maverick, Gordon Allport, received the two highest awards his profession has to offer: the Distinguished Scientific Contribution Award of the APA and the Gold Medal Award of the American Psychological Foundation.

The Thematic Apperception Test (1943), which Murray developed, has become one of the most widely used empirical tools of clinicians and personality theorists. His major theoretical work is *Explorations in personality* (1938). However, his *Assessment of men* (Office of Strategic Services, 1948), written as a result of his work in the Office of Strategic Services during World War II, is also considered a significant contribution to the area of personality assessment. As an intellectual sideline, Murray has engaged in a twenty-five-year study of Herman Melville and has published an analysis (1951) of the psychological meaning of the novel *Moby Dick.*

One cannot read Murray (e.g., 1959) without receiving the impression that he is deeply preoccupied with the notions of process and field. Yet Murray is too well rounded to deny the importance of a controlled and reductive approach to psychology. The reductive approach is certainly foreign to Murray's own nature, for he sees too vividly the interactions that occur among all the processes that constitute a system. The system, to Murray as the Gestaltist, is the unit to be studied. Only systems maintain their boundaries and provide the hope for that stability which is so rare in nature but so necessary to scientific study. Murray sees science as operating not primarily with stable structures but with processes which may, with some probability, be predictable.

Murray has said of himself (1959): "But at no time, to the annoyance of my friends, was I a good Jungian, a good Freudian, a good Adlerian, or a good schoolman of any breed" (p. 13). Despite this independence of thought, Murray is close to Freud in many basic attitudes as well as in some of the details of his theory. Two of these attitudes are a belief in the great importance of the early history of the organism and an emphasis on the physiological processes accompanying the behavioral events in which the psychologist is interested. Murray allows for more changes of the personality by later events than Freud did. However, Murray still recognizes the possibility that the effects of infantile experiences may be so great that they lead to various complexes in adulthood. On the physiological issue, Murray is one with Freud in recognizing the independence of the science of psychology from that of physiology, while at the same time pointing out that there is a necessary relationship of dependence between the two types of events: without physiological processes, there can be no psychological processes. Some particular dominant configuration of processes in the brain always accompanies a particular conscious process.

Another theme in Murray's theorizing is his recurrent clear statement that the concepts of his theory are constructions, hypothetical entities, not reality. Murray is not the kind of man who believes that nailing a name onto the flow of process can make it hold still or behave like a convenient structure that the scientist can then deal with complacently. Murray is more like a man who builds a transparent map with rough lines and shadings, through which he can view reality more conveniently; he builds and rebuilds systems of classification, analyzes and re-analyzes processes as his understanding is enriched. His theory could be called a tool as much as a description.

Murray has presented one of the most elaborate taxonomies of needs (1938). He does not attempt to talk about needs as things isolated from the context of behavior. Although needs are related to internal states, they are also related to the presence of valued external stimuli which impel to action (presses). The need directs behavior to objects which can lead to a desired state; though this state may often involve the reduction of tension, it may sometimes involve an increase in tension. Murray does not believe that the normal person always seeks the numbness of no tension. Most needs have as accompaniments certain emotions and feelings.

Murray has redefined Freud's term *cathexis* to describe need-related objects; an object may have a positive or negative cathexis according to its ability to press the individual into responses of approach or avoidance. The individual's feeling for the object is called a *sentiment.* Cathexis and sentiment therefore refer to the same relationship between person and object; one is applicable when we are concerned with the properties of the object, the other when we are concerned with the properties of the person. Thus Murray has subdivided Freud's concept of cathexis into two parts.

Needs are interrelated as well as embedded in ongoing processes. Some needs are subsidiary to more global, superordinate needs, and the satisfaction of the subsidiary need is not an end in itself but only a step toward the greater satisfaction. Different needs may occur in the individual at the same time, in which case a conflict is engendered; one of the needs will be or become the strongest, in which case it is called *prepotent,* and will demand satisfaction before the concurrent needs can be attended to.

Closely related to Murray's acceptance of possible needs for tension increase is his description of two types of needs which do not involve a Thorndikian type of effect. He adds to the Thorndikian type of need *process needs* and *modal needs.* Process needs are needs to do; for example, the adult may need to exercise, or the infant may need to babble. Modal needs are needs to perfect some behavior and differ from process needs only in that the need to improve is involved.

Murray's thoroughness in his treatment of needs is also reflected in his full discussion of significant units of behavior. He has relatively little use for a formulation as molecular as S-R. His most analytic unit is the *proceeding,* which is an interaction involving a person and an object or a person and a person; the interaction must be long enough to be of dynamic significance. The proceeding need not be overt; it may be a daydream or plan.

Proceedings may follow one another in a coherent fashion, in which case they may constitute another unit, a *serial.* The serial involves planning and organization, and its nature imposes direction upon the proceedings which constitute it. A marriage is an example of a serial. Proceedings, and therefore serials, may overlap and intertwine; all of us are involved in many endeavors in a single day or even hour.

A *thema* is another of Murray's behavioral units. It lays more emphasis upon the press and need which determine the behavior in question and therefore is a more analytic and theoretical unit than the more descriptive proceeding. The thema, like the proceeding, may be serially organized. The thema is less fixed in scope than the proceeding and may persist over a longer period of time.

A serial program may also be considered a unit of behavior, but it lays emphasis upon the plans of the individual. He may plan a life goal, for example, college graduation, which involves a very large number of subgoals before it can be accomplished. A subgoal might be passing a course or completing a major.

We can see that Murray puts realism before precision, and creativity before compulsion, in his theory of personality. Though many of his ideas are basically psychoanalytic, there can be no doubt whatever that he is a thinker who is not afraid to modify or innovate whenever he feels that the evidence is in his favor. He has also devised new methods for getting evidence, as we know from his Thematic Apperception Test (TAT) (1943) and from the ingenuity of his wartime work in assessing men for special assignments (Office of Strategic Services, 1948).

C. S. Hall and Lindzey (1970) evaluate Murray's theory and his research as being out of tune with the times: "There is too much of the poet and too little of the positivist in his make-up" (p. 205). Murray has never shown a great desire to be in tune with the times and has had enough independent resources so that he has not had to be. His espousal of unpopular viewpoints may, as he thought, have been responsible for keeping him from getting tenure until he was fifty-five. At any rate, he was recently concerned that he might have achieved too much respectability (1967): "In due course the practice of introspection and the concept of motive force, in altered forms and disguised by fresh labels, surreptitiously regained their lost respectability; and after World War II, Freudian theory *in toto* overran large areas of American psychology as Napoleon overran Europe. . . . Murr found himself occupying a position of discomforting respectability" (p. 295).

As we have indicated in Chapter 9, we think that Freudian theory has met its Waterloo and is exiled to a quiet island in the ocean of academic psychology. Thus Murr (the name Murray uses for himself in his autobiography) can rest easy in at least a partial unorthodoxy, a condition that he has always found comfortable and productive.

Sullivan's Interpersonal Theory

Harry Stack Sullivan (1892-1949) was first and foremost a psychiatrist, although his contribution to psychology through his personality theory is undeniable and he was also influential as a scientific statesman and educator. After receiving his M.D. from the Chicago College of Medicine and Surgery, Sullivan became a medical officer for the Federal Board for Vocational Education. He was later affiliated with the U.S. Public Health Service; with Saint Elizabeth's Hospital in Washington, D.C.; and with the University of Maryland medical school, where he conducted investigations of schizophrenia.

As a scientific statesman, Sullivan served as consultant for the Selective Service System and the UNESCO Tensions Project. He helped plan the International Congress of Mental Health. He also edited *Psychiatry,* a journal whose publication was stimulated mainly by the need to publicize Sullivan's theory.

Neuropsychiatrist William Alanson White exerted a permanent influence upon Sullivan, who later was president of the William Alanson White Foundation and founded and directed its training institution, the Washington School of Psychiatry. The influences of Sigmund Freud and Adolph Meyer are also discernible in Sullivan's theory. Sullivan published only one book in the area of personality theory, *Conceptions of modern psychiatry* (1947). After his death, he became much more influential; that is, five books based on his notes and recorded lectures have been published (1953, 1954, 1956, 1962, 1964).

The interpersonal theory of Sullivan is less exclusively analytic than that of Horney or Fromm. Although Sullivan acknowledged intellectual indebtedness to Freud, his theory bears a closer resemblance to Adler's. Much of Sullivan's thinking is related to men who have a nonanalytic approach, for example, William Alanson White, Adolph Meyer, and George Herbert Mead. Moreover, Sullivan's closer relationship to psychiatry and to academicians (particularly social scientists) has resulted in a greater acceptance of his theory and may have something to do with its fuller statement (Sullivan, 1953); these features of his theory have, in turn, led to greater acceptance among clinicians.

Personality as defined by Sullivan (1953) is "the relatively enduring pattern of recurrent interpersonal situations which characterize human life" (p. 111). That is, it is regarded as an intervening variable inferred from an individual's behavior in relation to other people and objects. Personality exists only in interpersonal relationships. It follows that personality cannot be studied unless more than one person is interacting, although one of the persons need not be physically present; a person's interactions may be with an image, dream, fictional character, and the like. Sullivan has not entirely rejected the influences of heredity and biological factors; in fact, he has acknowledged their importance during infancy and at puberty. He proposed a hierarchy of physiological needs from which tension arises, which must be dissipated by satisfying the needs. However, he held that man's distinctively human characteristics are interpersonally developed and may directly affect the physiological needs.

Sullivan stated that three processes are evidenced in the development of the personality: dynamism, personifications, and cognitive processes. A dynamism is a prolonged behavior pattern which is revealed in characteristic interpersonal relationships. Dynamisms may also be described as classes of habits or personality traits which characterize an individual; toward certain people an individual may display a dynamism of hostility or of friendliness, depending upon his habitual behavior toward them. The self dynamism is the individual's picture of himself as he perceives it through his social interactions.

Personifications are images that an individual holds of other people or of himself. They are often products of his infancy. If they remain intact so that they influence his future opinion toward people, they are called *eidetic personifications*. An example of this might be a child's attitude toward a domineering father; this personification could influence responses toward other authority figures. However, when an image occurs solely in connection with a particular situation, only the word *personification* is used. A stereotype is any personification which is held by a group of people. It is interesting to note that these are in some ways a socialized and conscious version of Jung's archetypes.

Cognitive processes are subdivided into three classes: *prototaxic, parataxic,* and *syntaxic.* In the prototaxic mode, the individual simply experiences directly, without connecting the raw feelings or attaching meaning to them. It is not unlike what has been called a "stream of consciousness": all the thoughts, visions, ideas, sensations, and perceptions occurring at any given moment. This is followed by the parataxic mode, in which the individual connects his experiences as they occur and regardless of their logical relations: casual relationships between nonrelated events and experiences. Logical connections are accomplished in the syntaxic mode by the use of *consensually validated* symbols. Consensual validation is a Sullivanian concept which refers to any symbol to which a particular meaning has become attached and agreed upon by a number of people. It is used chiefly for communication, and words are the most common example of such symbols.

Sullivan proposed six stages in the development of the individual. These are roughly delineated into age groups corresponding to maturational levels. However, the importance of maturation is limited in the degree to which it enables the individual to achieve a new and higher level of interpersonal relationships.

Sullivan noted that in the development of the individual, it is often apparent that certain entities are outside his realm of awareness. Three major reasons may be posited for this: selective inattention, disassociation, and parataxic distortion. Selective inattention is merely the unwillingness on the part of the individual to perceive in the immediate environment that which contradicts his beliefs. Disassociation is approximately what the Freudians refer to as *repression.* Parataxic distortion occurs when an individual's personal and autistic meanings, rather than the socially validated meanings, accrue to a symbol and influence his thinking.

In sum, Sullivan held that the individual functions because he needs to secure satisfaction; his basic needs are not instinctual or biological, as Freud would have us believe, but are based on interactions with people.

It is indeed curious that so little criticism has been directed at Sullivan's position. Scrutiny of several very recent volumes (e.g., C. S. Hall & Lindzey, 1970; Levy, 1970; Maddi, 1968) failed to uncover any such criticism. Sullivan's system is an all-encompassing one that does not contain the outlandishly salient features (e.g., penis envy) that invite criticism in alternative positions such as Freud's. Also, he attempted to blunt criticism by incorporating many originally antagonistic views into his own system. Nevertheless, some critical comments can be made.

One immediately apparent omission is Sullivan's lack of direct attention to emotional factors in behavior. This omission is incongruous in such an otherwise comprehensive system, and especially in view of the fact that Sullivan depicts the adult personality as developing from a physiological base. Although he does speak of anxiety, this concept is not sharply defined.

Along with the other specially oriented personality theorists, Sullivan must be credited for having helped to add a most valuable, much-needed dimension to the basically biological theory of Freud. Like the others, however, Sullivan did not attempt to detail the manner in which the process of socialization occurs or the manner in which psychopathology is acquired.

Sullivan may also be credited with being the only social psychological theorist of his day who attempted to extend the Freudian developmental stages beyond puberty. Here again, however, he was programmatic: He failed to delineate the transition from one stage to another, the factors operating to produce smooth or difficult transitions, the role of the family setting (which is central in his theory, as it is in Horney's and Adler's), the role of the social order (which is focal in Fromm's theory), and how the latter two conditions interact.

Finally, Sullivan may be criticized for having failed to stimulate empirical research. This failure may be related to the somewhat vague and almost offhand manner in which he used most of his concepts (fruitful as these may have been in his clinical work). For example, it is often quite difficult for the reader to distinguish between two of his most crucial concepts, dynamisms and personifications.

Thus we have in Sullivan an enormously influential and comprehensive theorist whose strength is that he can accommodate what Freud on the one hand and the other socially oriented theorists on the other hand have been saying but whose weakness is that he has not provided the kind of precision in definition and theoretical specification of key concepts that is needed for the stimulation of important empirical research.

SELF THEORIES

Habits, traits and factors of varying degrees of generality, the organism, social interactions—we have already run quite a gamut of concepts that are used either to explain or to describe the consistency of an individual's behavior. The last organizer is the self. There are nearly as many definitions of self as there are self psychologists, and the definitions often seem to lack operational meaning; however, the common element in all definitions of self is the character of self as an organizer that imposes consistency on behavior.

There are three general ways in which self has been postulated to operate in achieving a harmony of diverse activities. The time-honored way was to use self as though it were a little man-inside-the-man who ordered all activities so that they pretty well suited his imperial selfship. Such a self, having his own sources of energy and will, is inaccessible to scientific investigation and is discredited in all scientific psychologies, including modern self theories.

A second way in which the self might organize behavior is as a kind of template or picture into which all ongoing behavior must fit. If the self is an objective, existing set of representations of an individual's past behaviors and experiences, these representations may somehow resist changes that would result from the impact of divergent new experiences on the old structure called self. We may think of this self as though it were a picture against which a contemplated new behavior is projected; if the discrepancy between the picture as it presently exists and the picture as it would have to be modified to accommodate the new behavior is too great, the behavior does not occur.

The third view of self is as a summary name for a set of psychological processes. The exact processes that are subsumed vary from theorist to theorist, but generally include evaluative and attitudinal functions. These processes, acting upon the materials that govern behavior, can thus themselves play a role in directing behavior.

A danger in self theories is that a regression from meanings 2 and 3 to meaning 1 may occur. Certainly no theorist will intend such a regression and will, when defining self for theoretical purposes, carefully exclude meaning 1. The reason for a push back toward meaning 1 may be that it is clearer than the other two. In the second case, one might still be curious as to how the discrepancies between the self and experience or behavior are resolved. Is it by a little man? If so, the regression is immediate. If not, then the structure which resolves discrepancies simply replaces the little man. In the case of meaning 3, the self-as-process shares the usual vagueness of such process concepts, and in addition it leaves one wondering why the concept is needed—at least it does if one has positivistic leanings. Self theorists, then, would seem to need logically to value fidelity of representation of complex human processes over strict positivism. In fact, they do.

Rogers's Self Theory

The career of Carl Ransom Rogers (1902-   ) has been marked by an interest in divergent fields, the first of which was scientific agriculture, which he encountered during his boyhood days on a farm (see Rogers, 1959, 1967a, for autobiographical information). Rogers subsequently attended the University of Wisconsin and Union Theological Seminary before terminating his education at Columbia Teachers College, where he took his Ph.D. and fell under the philosophical influence of John Dewey. Columbia also provided Rogers's first introduction to clinical psychology; he grew better acquainted with the field during his internship at the psychoanalytically oriented Institute for Child Guidance. While there he felt a definite conflict between psychoanalytic theory and the Thorndikian statistical influence which had prevailed at Columbia.

Rogers served as director of the Rochester Guidance Clinic, finding stimulation in the eclectic staff there. Their constant search for effective treatment was a problem Rogers turned to in *The clinical treatment of the problem child* (1939). He then shifted to academic psychology, teaching at Ohio State University, the University of Chicago, and the University of Wisconsin, but remained active in clinical activities. Rogers received the American Psychological Association's Distinguished Contribution Award in 1956. At Wisconsin, Rogers became progressively more disillusioned with what he thought were unduly stultifying rules imposed in the name of high standards by the psychology department. In 1963, he resigned from the department; in January, 1964, he joined the staff of the Western Behavioral Sciences Institute in San Diego, California, as a resident fellow; in 1968, he became a resident fellow at the Center for Studies of the Person in the same city.

The major stimulus for Rogers's personality theory came from his clinical therapeutic work, although he was strongly influenced by psychoanalyst Otto Rank. Rogers first advanced his views on personality in *Counseling and psychotherapy: Newer concepts in practice* (1942). That book was followed by his major theoretical work, *Client-centered therapy* (1951). He further explained his position in his chapter in Koch's *Psychology: A study of a science* (1959). Several of his more important papers were edited and collected in his *On becoming a person* (1961), and his most extensive research effort was published later (1967b).

The central concept of Rogers's theory is the self. The therapy which Rogers developed over a period of time is consistent with the belief that the patient has a self structure which he himself must change if improvement is to occur. Rogers believes that his observations demand both this kind of therapy and a concept of self like the one he evolved.

To Rogers, the self is a structure compounded out of the experiences which the individual is able to attribute to his own body or to the results of his own behavior; the self, then, is a self-picture, or self-awareness. The experiences come with value tags attached; that is, some aspects of the self-picture are positive, while others are negative. The self regulates behavior, for behavior that is not consistent with the self-picture either does not occur or is not fitted into the self-picture.

Though Rogers was at times subjected to psychoanalytic influences, he tends to reject the analytic emphasis on unconscious processes. He does recognize the possibility that self-inconsistent behaviors will occur as a result of unconscious influences, but he still feels that understanding of an individual can occur most easily if the therapist can enter the phenomenal field that appears to the patient. For Rogers, the consciousness of the individual contains most of what is needed for understanding his personality.

The self-picture is not supposed to be a static thing; although its structure has some stability, it can at times assimilate new experiences in such a way that the structure changes and the particular type of experience is subsequently experienced more easily. The threatened self is rigid and rejecting, but the secure self is fluid and tolerant. This single statement is the conceptual basis for Rogers's nondirective therapy.

Nondirective therapy sets a situation in which the patient can accept experiences into the self structure because the self is at no time threatened and reports of experiences are at no time rejected or devalued by the therapist. Studies have shown that, in therapeutic circumstances, the patients' conceptions of themselves and their ideal selves came into closer agreement (Butler & Haigh, 1954; Rudikoff, 1954, pp. 85-98). Whether the change occurs in the self-picture as such or in the ideal self, the observed changes in therapy should be helpful. The individual's experiences would be more easily assimilated as long as the real self was accepted as a satisfactory structure in relation to the ideal. The self would be less threatened and more subject to adjustment as necessitated by life experiences.

Rogers, like Goldstein, believes that the organism has a single goal. It strives to actualize, enhance, and maintain itself. The possible lines of actualization are laid down by heredity, and the organism has, as a part of its native equipment, a creative urge. Human beings, however, cannot actualize themselves effectively unless they can symbolize their experiences and choose the path that leads to self-enhancement.

It is the failure to symbolize all experience which makes Rogers's distinction between the objective world and the world as perceived by the individual so important. The individual responds to his perceived world rather than directly to the objective world; thus it is essential for his adjustment that the two worlds be as similar as possible.

Carl Rogers is a clinician's clinician. He has spent much of his professional life in his role as therapist, and his theory could hardly be other than closely related to his therapy. We should not expect the theory to be simple, static, dogmatic, or complete. It is the opposite of all these. His theory is, and will be, inductive.

A surprising and often-criticized aspect of Rogers's theory is its strong emphasis upon conscious processes; one might expect that he would follow more behavioristic or psychoanalytic lines, since he studied both at Columbia, where Thorndikian views were strong, and with Otto Rank. Though Thorndike was not a behaviorist, anyone familiar with his writing knows that he believed in the unconscious automaticity of the operation of the law of effect. Nevertheless, Rogers has preferred an attitude like that of Snygg and Combs (1949) and holds that the experienced world as available to the consciousness of the individual plays the preponderant role in the determination of his behavior. Rogers thus stands with Allport and many others in stemming the psychoanalytic tide, which seems today to run less strongly toward the depths of the unconscious. That Rogers's own views on the current status of psychoanalysis do not differ widely from ours is apparent from one of his statements describing a stay at the Center for Advanced Study in the Behavioral Sciences at Stanford (1967a, p. 372):

Another important influence was my contact with Erik Erikson, a splendid person whose very appearance is therapeutic, and several other psychoanalysts, foreign as well as American. From them I learned what I had strongly suspected—that psychoanalysis as a school of thought is dead—but that out of loyalty and other motives, none but the very brave analysts mention this fact as they go on to develop theories and ways of working very remote from, or entirely opposed to, the Freudian views.

Rogers differs from the psychoanalysts not only in that he assigns a small role to unconscious processes but also in that Rogers's self is a less differentiated entity than the psychoanalyst's mental apparatus. In fact, Rogers has been more concerned with personality *change* than with personality. It seems to us that he has contributed far more to therapeutic theory than to personality theory. Even when he discusses personality, his attention focuses on personality *development, breakdown,* or *functioning* (see Rogers, 1959, pp. 221-235), rather than on personality *structure.*

It is interesting to compare Rogers with Skinner, as we have compared him with Freud. Rogers and Skinner are usually regarded as being at opposite poles. American psychologists seem to regard getting Rogers and Skinner on the same symposium as better sport than baiting bears, and anyone who can succeed in setting up the game is assured of a huge audience and a lively time (see Rogers, 1956; Wann, 1964). Nevertheless, the contrast is in some respects overdrawn. Skinner himself says (quoted in Evans, 1968, pp. 67-68):

The whole thing is a question of method. That's the crux of my argument with Carl Rogers; I'd like people to be approximately as Rogers wants them to be. I want independent people, and by that I mean people who don't have to be told when to act or who don't do things just because they've been told they're the right things to do. . . . We agree on our goals; we each want people to be free of the control exercised by others—free of the education they have had, so that they profit by it but are not bound by it, and so on.

Skinner and Rogers, despite many disagreements on method, probably have some common attitudes even in this respect. Neither seeks to find out the details of the unconscious mental apparatus. Neither is greatly concerned to uncover the origins of the patient's symptoms in the past. Both would pay attention to current verbalizations, although the attitude toward the verbalizations would be different. Even some of Rogers's prescriptions can be translated into operant language, and the translation approved by Skinner. For example, Rogers, in outlining the necessary conditions for therapy, says a requirement is "That two persons are in *contact.*" Skinner could agree that only if the patient behaves in the presence of the therapist can the therapist effectively change his behavior. Rogers: "The therapist is *experiencing unconditional positive regard* toward the client." Skinnerian translation: "An organism which is showing a behavior deficit may be encouraged to behave if free reinforcement follows every identifiable behavior emitted." Finally, both Skinner and Rogers are optimistic about the possibilities for improving the lot of mankind.

We have no desire to gloss over the divisions between Rogers and Skinner (and thereby to ruin psychology's favorite spectator sport), and we have no illusions that Skinner and Rogers will suddenly experience unconditional positive professional regard for each other. However, it is worth noting that they have some fundamental agreements—such as shying away from complex inner structures—as well as some fundamental disagreements on other aspects of philosophy and method.

The fact that Rogers has shied away from the postulation of complex inner structures has made his ideas more amenable to empirical attack than the ideas of some other personality theorists. C. S. Hall and Lindzey (1970, p. 538) report a rather amusing finding from Rogers's (1967b) extensive study of therapy with schizophrenics. Several rating scales were being applied to the therapeutic interaction, and their reliability was being evaluated. One scale was to measure "unconditional positive regard," one of Rogers's key constructs (see, for example, 1959): "Putting this in simpler terms, to feel unconditional positive regard toward another is to 'prize' him (to use Dewey's term, recently used in this sense by Butler)" (p. 208).

Unfortunately, there was a *negative* correlation between the therapists' evaluation of the therapeutic interaction and the evaluations by patients or by independent raters. This is embarrassing enough in its implications concerning a therapist's ability to judge whether a therapeutic relationship is worth saving, but it becomes even more embarrassing if the finding is attributed to unconscious defenses on the part of the therapists!

It is to the credit of Rogers and his theory that they can be embarrassed. Few theories of personality are explicit enough to be tested, and the exponents of those which are that explicit seldom test them. Rogers has tried.

Rogers has recently turned his attention largely to intensive group experiences with normal individuals, thus starting to explore yet another field. He is using the same phenomenological, existential approach that he was using before those labels came into American psychology. His concern with groups, like his earlier work, fits perfectly into the "third force"—the humanistic alternative to behaviorism and psychoanalysis—which has emerged in psychology. Rogers is either *a* leader or *the* leader in this movement. Near the end of his autobiography, Rogers says (1967a): "I want to have *impact*. I am not a person who is ambitious in the ordinary sense. . . . But it is important to me to have influence. I want what I do to *count,* to make a difference somewhere" (p. 380). Rogers has his wish. He counts. How high history will carry him now depends on the fate of our third force. It could be high indeed.

Murphy's Personality Synthesis

Gardner Murphy (1895-   ) has brought to psychology a wide range of interests and has made professional contributions in each of his seemingly divergent fields of endeavor. Educated at Yale, Harvard, and Columbia, Murphy turned first to academic psychology. While teaching at Columbia, he collaborated with Likert to publish *Public opinion and the individual* (1938) on the subject of polling and attitude measurement. Murphy later became department chairman at City College of New York. For fifteen years, from 1952 to 1967, he was director of research at the Menninger Foundation. In 1967, he went to George Washington University as a visiting professor, and he is still visiting.

Long interested in parapsychology, Murphy has served as president of the London Society for Psychical Research and has been a strong and persistent exponent of the need for expansion of such research.

In the area of world peace and international relations, Murphy has studied social tensions in India as a UNESCO consultant and published *Human nature and enduring peace* (1945). He is also the author of two introductory psychology texts (1933, 1951) and has written on the history of psychology (1949), social psychology (Murphy & Murphy, 1931), perception (Solley & Murphy, 1960), and the effect of scientific choices today upon the world's tomorrows (1958). Murphy made his major contribution to personality theory in *Personality: A biosocial approach to origins and structure* (1947). Murphy has remained very productive, but his recent interests have been more in historical topics and in parapsychology than in personality.

It would seem that Murphy's personality theory could be treated under any heading. Murphy includes concepts from all important predecessors in his theory. His scholarship and literacy are highly esteemed. He exemplifies the fact that in personality theory, the eclectic needs to deal with the whole of psychology. It has been our contention that the final form of personality theory will be just a synthesis of all psychology; Murphy has come closer to this goal of selective synthesis than any other personality theorist. He has also introduced a number of key concepts which have been of wide influence.

Thumbnailing Murphy, then, is like thumbnailing a large part of the psychology of personality and does Murphy an even greater injustice than it does most other personality theorists. Murphy calls his approach *biosocial,* and one can say that he emphasizes everything: the biological organism, the individual personality, the society, the physical environment, the field nature of events wherein interchanges between organism and environment take place, the stages of personality development—all are treated by Murphy.

Murphy displays more critical selectivity than unique originality. His strength lies in synthesis. Still, there are striking aspects of Murphy's theory; for example, his definition of self is unexcelled for brevity and simplicity: "The individual as known to the individual" (1947). This definition stands as an island in an otherwise turgid sea.

One of Murphy's best-known concepts is called *canalization.* There is some similarity between canalization and Allport's functional autonomy. Murphy's word refers to the tendency individuals may develop to satisfy their drives in quite particular ways; for example, the hunger drive may always be satisfied by eating German food, or a particular kind of German food, when any food would satisfy the biological need as well. Murphy's canalization does not require that the activity be engaged in for its own sake, but it is as if something like Allport's functional autonomy tipped the motivational scales in favor of the preferred mode of need reduction.

Murphy's research cuts across the boundaries of psychology. It is often used by him to demonstrate the unity of the individual, whose functioning can be understood only by viewing his part processes as they are embedded in the whole. One of Murphy's best-known studies (Levine, Chein, & Murphy, 1942) has been widely cited as demonstrating that the tendency for hungry subjects to report more food objects in ambiguous pictures is a function of food deprivation. This, according to Murphy, demonstrates the general point that no aspect of behavior (such as perception) can be considered apart from other aspects (such as needs). Postman and Murphy (1943) similarly demonstrated that the degree to which pairs to be associated in memory fit into a subject's attitudinal framework has an important effect on his ability to learn and remember the associated pairs. Murphy later became involved at the Menninger Foundation in an extended program of studies in perceptual learning (Murphy, Santos, & Solley, 1968; Santos & Murphy, 1960).

There are numerous pitfalls in trying to be all things to all people, as Murphy in a sense has done. In his case, there are many benefits too. His theory, more than any other, tries to deal with all the facts in all their stubbornness, preferring to treat and relate all the features of personality theory rather than ignore factors which might not fit into any preconceived theory. In 1957, C. S. Hall and Lindzey (p. 548) credited Murphy and Sullivan, alone among seventeen personality theorists, with having given a medium or high degree of attention to each of the eighteen dimensions of personality considered (which illustrates the advantages of eclecticism). In 1970, Hall and Lindzey did not treat Murphy's theory of personality either in their table or in the rest of their book (which illustrates the pitfalls of eclecticism). Scholarly eclecticism tends to be unexciting. Iconoclasts, which many personality theorists have been, are exciting, but it is hard for a scholar—and Murphy is a scholar—to be iconoclastic.

We think honest eclectics deserve a better fate, especially when they combine enough iconoclasm to make a long-term, serious study of ESP. If extrasensory abilities eventually become some of the traits to be considered in descriptions of personality, as Murphy thinks they may, he will be the man of the hour. Meanwhile, we might remember Murphy's own cautious credo (1947, p. 927):

Despite all these lessons of the past we write and speak today as if the full concept and stature of man were known. But like our predecessors, we shall rectify mistakes not primarily by the minor readjustment of the lines of the argument but by the recognition of the fundamental limitations of the whole present system of conceptions. It is preparation for this destruction and rebirth of knowledge to which serious research should be directed.

SUMMARY AND CONCLUSIONS

The present chapter has attempted to give a broad overview of the major theoretical approaches to personality. We have classified these theories into five major categories: *S-R* (Dollard and Miller); *trait and factor* (Allport, Eysenck, Cattell); *organismic* (Goldstein, Sheldon); *neoanalytic* (Horney, Fromm, Murray, Sullivan); and *self* (Rogers, Murphy). Salient characteristics of each of these types of theory have been examined.

It is necessary to make some final comment concerning the contemporary status and future prospects of the type of theory generally labeled "personality." In doing so, we shall distinguish between two groups of personality theory; the S-R and factor theories will be considered in the first group, and all other types of theory in the second.

We have already indicated our belief that psychoanalysis is no longer a viable theory of personality. As to organismic and self theories, it seems that these theorists have the right point of view. Then the next comment is, "So what?" A point of view is not a theory, and we know of no real organismic or self theory with enough structure to qualify as a real theory. Trait theories are all right, but unless they are also factor theories, they do not seem to rest on a secure-enough empirical foundation to qualify as theories. Our guess is that in another twenty years, interest in all the preceding theories will be minimal in psychology as a scientific discipline. Humanistic psychology, which endeavors to stress human values in behavior study, is not now a full-fledged science. These theories may have a place—even, perhaps, a more important place than they now have—in humanistic psychology.

We have also indicated that S-R theories are not really theories of personality. S-R types of theories will, of course, continue to develop. Perhaps, as S-R psychologists work increasingly with clinical problems, someone of that persuasion will work out a theory of personality. It may be more likely, however, that some personality theorist of the future will simply incorporate S-R concepts in an independently developed theory of personality. S-R technology almost certainly will be used increasingly in therapy.

This leaves us with factor theories. Cattell's factor theory is the best worked out and is buttressed with the greatest amount of empirical data. It is comprehensive enough to qualify as a bona fide theory of personality. It takes account of both constitutional and environmental variables. The theory is flexible. Its present form is far from the final word, and the theory may not yet have had enough input from the clinic and from the therapy situation. Nevertheless, if any of the "grand theories" is to survive, it may well be Cattell's. It is fortunate that he has based his work on the methodology of factor analysis; that seems to provide a systematic approach and a discipline that are especially needed in the free-wheeling atmosphere of the field and clinic.

Meanwhile, much research goes on related to specific problems, as we pointed out early in this chapter. It may be that an entirely new theory, or even a new type of theory, will arise out of the dust of this empiricism. We are confident that future theories of personality will incorporate more fully the work of the laboratory with the work of the clinic. Such rapprochement would mark the real maturing of a scientific theory of personality.

Further Readings

The second (1970) edition of Hall and Lindzey's *Theories of personality* is probably destined to remain the classic introductory source. It provides a generally good, balanced, and critical overview, and this chapter is based to a considerable extent on their treatment. In *Interpreting personality theories,* Bischof (1970) sometimes seems awed by the magnitude of his task (as we certainly were), but his book supplements Hall and Lindzey's in treating some important theorists that they did not (Murphy and George Kelly, for example) and in presenting excellent lists of references. We recommend the two excellent review chapters already mentioned (Adelson, 1969; Dahlstrom, 1970) both for a picture of very recent trends and as sources of further references to the latest handbooks. For the individual authors treated in this chapter, the reader can refer directly to the references given.

13 Engineering and Mathematical Influences on Psychology

Psychology has undergone many revolutions. Revolution in a science becomes more difficult as the body of established knowledge increases, and psychology is developing enough confidence in its own internal worth so that it can react more coolly to new developments in other fields of knowledge. Nevertheless, psychology has undergone, over the past twenty-five years, a change in its point of view because of a technical explosion in the field of engineering. In retrospect, we see the genesis of this change in the field of mathematics, with the first relevant development occurring over one hundred years ago.

For the past few years, engineering has been increasingly concerned with the handling of information. In the more distant past, engineers were most interested in the production of devices whose chief output was work or heat or material. Today, engineers have turned their attention to devices that carry on humanlike activities, devices for data processing. Such devices are not entirely new, having developed over centuries from abacus to adding machine, but the scope of successes is now of a different order of magnitude. We must recognize that today is the age of automation, while yesterday was not. The names of computers become household words, but by the time they do, the Eniac has been overshadowed by the Illiac, and it in turn by the Univac. And, as man becomes familiar with the computer, his attitude toward the computer changes, First, perhaps, it was a technical feat, a curiosity, an object of amazement; then, as its potential was more widely appreciated, it became the source of extreme optimism—the omnipotent machine held the answer to the world's problems—or of extreme pessimism—the machine would subjugate man. Now that computers have been around for twenty-five years or so, the popular imagination seems to have subsided, and most people probably regard them as a mild threat or a small convenience.

What has this to do with psychology? Perhaps the implications of automation for psychology can be summed up by saying that the replacement of human function encourages the study of human function. If we wish to have a computer recognize speech, we are likely to begin by finding out how humans recognize speech. If a device is to detect signals, it may very well ape the human being in its detection. In deciding whether a given device is needed or useful, we compare its cost and performance with human cost and performance. A common quip in computer circles is that the human being is still the only general-purpose computer weighing in the neighborhood of 150 pounds which is mass-produced free. The comparative psychology of man and device is developing across the disciplinary line that divides psychology and engineering, much as the comparative psychology of man and animal developed out of biology and psychology about a century ago.

This new comparative psychology is related to the use of mathematical models, but it is more than that. It is a very far cry from the hodological space of Lewin (see Chapter 11) to the computer program which recognizes digits as they are spoken to a sensing device. The really serious and practical consideration of how a human function can be performed mechanically lends interest, urgency, and precision to the task of describing the process. The engineer who wants to automate a function forces the psychologist to recognize that he does not really know how the function is carried out. The actual testing of theory in devices gives an immediate knowledge of results which discourages fuzzy thinking.

The emphasis on devices should not lead one to the conclusion that it is the devices per se which are important for psychology. Rather, the important things are the conceptual sharpening which is likely to attend the development of the devices and their application to human functions, and also the impetus which the development lends to psychology. This impetus comes partly from engineers, whose primary intention is practical rather than scientific, and partly from psychologists who see in the computer and its program an unparalleled device for theory construction.

THE ROLE OF THE COMPUTER

There are two types of computers: analog and digital. The analog computer is designed to accept continuous variables as inputs and give outputs that are also continuous functions. The human being may behave like an analog computer in a number of respects; even the individual neural cells may show continuous variations over a range of values, rather than behaving strictly in an all-or-none manner. Nevertheless, there has been relatively little general intellectual interest in analog computers, and our attention will henceforth be confined to the digital computer.

The digital computer is so named because its inputs and outputs can take on only digital values, with no fractional values between numbers. We can therefore specify exactly the range of numbers that can be represented in a register of a particular digital computer. A representative register might hold ten decimal digits. An overwhelming majority of digital computers are electronic. The electronic digital computer can be quickly adapted to new problems without gross physical changes; the programs, or sequences of instructions to be performed, are changed. The presence of a program of operation distinguishes computers from calculators. The human operator "instructs" a simple calculating machine, one instruction at a time, by hitting keys. The operator instructs a computer, many instructions at a time, by writing down a sequence of operations which the computer is to carry out. Then, once the computer starts, it proceeds through the whole programmed task without outside intervention. It is this independence from the human operator which allows the computer to be so fast, for example, to add 200,000 numbers per second. Any figures that are given on speeds achieved by computers quickly become too conservative; engineers are already talking in terms of basic computer operations that occur in billionths of a second. It is no wonder that machines which perform such computational miracles capture the imagination.

It is not their speed, however, which makes computers of unique importance to psychology. Their speed makes them wonderful labor-saving devices and helps the psychologist, as it helps every other scientist. Data-reduction problems that would have taken years without a computer may take minutes with a computer, though writing the program may now take years. Problems that could not previously have been attacked can now be studied. However, this in itself would have no more theoretical significance than would the invention of an automatic cage-cleaning machine that made it possible to do more animal research. The fact that man has created the computer in his own image makes the computer uniquely fascinating to the psychologist. A computer is manlike, of course, in a functional rather than in a structural sense. We do not care whether the computer operates in a way which physically apes man, as long as the answers are "correct," that is, the same answers that a man would give to the same questions. This requires that the computer be the same as man in some logical sense.

N. Wiener (1948) and Von Neumann (1958) pointed to a logical similarity between man and computer even in the basic elements of their information-processing systems. That is, the classic view of the human neuron had it either responding completely or not responding at all (the "all-or-none" law), just as the computer element was either in one state or in another (usually called "on" versus "off" or "0" versus "1"). Physically, computer elements are larger, faster, fewer, and simpler—at the moment. La Brecque (1970) reports: "Today, microminiaturization has superceded miniaturization, and 100,000 integrated circuits can easily be placed on a single, half-dollar-sized silicon wafer ... other research aims at developing even more tightly integrated devices, some nearly as compact as the bioelectric system of the human brain" (p. 8). We should emphasize, however, that any physical similarity between computer elements and human neurons is unrelated to logical similarity, which is our main concern here.

Over a hundred years ago, George Boole (1854) developed an algebra which has turned out to be very useful in computer design. It is a two-valued logic, based on the notion that elements are either in or out of a set. This computer logic was developed by Boole as an expression of the laws of *human* thought; he had no intention of writing logic which would apply to *mechanized* thinking. Ironically, the symbols for *or, and, not*, etc., in Boole's algebra found their direct analogs in the "OR gate", "AND gate", etc., in the digital computer.

Digital computers use a two-valued number system which is compatible with Boolean algebra and with the two-valued character of computer elements. This so-called binary (two-valued) number system is worth looking at because of its almost universal use in digital computers and because an understanding of binary numbers is necessary for an understanding of information measures. The binary equivalents for the decimal numbers are $0 = 0$, $1 = 1$, $10 = 2$, $11 = 3$, $100 = 4$, $101 = 5$, $110 = 6$, $111 = 7$, $1000 = 8$, and $1001 = 9$. It is clear that only one of two things can occur in a particular binary column, 0 or 1. In the decimal number system, ten alternatives can occur in a given column, and so we can designate ten events by different symbols in a single column. Numbers for each of 10 times 10 events can be written in two decimal columns, 10 times 10 times 10 (10^3) events in three columns, etc. Correspondingly, two events can be symbolized in a binary column, 2^2 in two, 2^3 in three, 2^4 in four, etc. For example, numbers for 1,024 events clearly take four decimal columns (we could go up to 9,999 in the same space); writing the binary equivalent for 1,024 decimal numbers would take ten columns. Binary numbers use much more space on paper, but they can be represented physically with simpler, more reliable, cheaper elements. At least a part of the logical operation of animal brains seems to have been designed with the same qualities of reliability and low cost in mind!

Binary addition is easy to specify: $0 + 0 = 0$, $0 + 1 = 1$, $1 + 0 = 1$, and $1 + 1 = 10$. For example:

$$
\begin{array}{rl}
11110110 = 246 & \quad 111 = 7 \\
\underline{11101100 = 236} & \quad \underline{1111 = 7} \\
111100010 = 482 & \quad 110 = 14
\end{array}
$$

The multiplication table is equally simple: $0 \times 0 = 0$, $0 \times 1 = 0$, $1 \times 0 = 0$, $1 \times 1 = 1$. For example:

$$
\begin{array}{r}
11010 = 26 \\
\underline{1011 = 11} \\
11010 \\
11010 \\
00000 \\
\underline{11010 } \\
100011110 = 286
\end{array}
$$

The digital computer operates internally on binary numbers, and even the simple operations of binary addition and multiplication depend upon several operations at the Boolean algebra level; each summation carried out in an adder is the result of a number of "AND" and "OR" operations. For example, the computer puts a 0 in the first column after summing if the two components of the sum were both 0 *or* if both were 1; the second column has a 1 if one component in the second column had a 1 *and* both components in the first column had a 1 *or* if one component in the second column had a 1 *and* both components in the first column had a 0. The curious student can extend the translation of sums into the logical language of "ORS" and "ANDS" as an exercise (if he has had a good recent course in Boolean algebra).

The digital computer can do complex things because it is able to combine literally millions of elementary operations. The logical "ORS" and "ANDS" combine to make arithmetical operations possible. Numbers can therefore be combined, and the computer can compare these numbers with one another and perform different operations depending on the outcomes of such comparisons. Since alternative courses of action can be numbered, computers can, say, trigger a gun if its computations based on several sources of information indicate that some preset level of threat has been exceeded. The junior author vividly remembers one of his early encounters with the apparent intelligence of the computer. He was entering what was supposed to be a new program into a computer which already contained a program called a *compiler*. The compiler would translate the new program from the language in which it was written into a language the computer could use later. At the same time the new program was entered, the date of the computer run was supposed to be entered, but had been left out. The computer lights blinked for a tiny fraction of a second, and then the computer typed out, seemingly wearily, the query "Date?" on its automatic typewriter. Thus chastened, your programmer entered the date and again pushed the run button. The computer, following the dictates of its earlier program, examined the supposed new program which had been fed in and started revealing a stream of human errors, typing out indignant comments like "Undefined routine jumped to from Cell 27624." Several pages later the typewriter fell into a moody silence; one may imagine the computer waiting for a more intelligent programmer to give it a more reasonable program to compile.

After this exercise in projection (into the "indignant," "moody" computer), we hasten to say that the computer was not programmed to be either indignant or moody, and therefore we do not seriously propose that it experienced those emotions. A computer's sequence of operations is completely fixed by a set of operations prepared by a human computer programmer. Because of this, those with conservative viewpoints toward computer capabilities may maintain that computers are not capable of intelligent behavior, since they are merely slavishly following instructions.

One should not accept the conservative view too incautiously, since "what the computer is told to do" may be something like "learn to do this task better." For example, Samuel (1963) wrote a program instructing a computer how to play checkers and how to improve its game. After some practice, the computer played Robert W. Nealy, one of the country's strongest players. His comment, in part, was (Wooldridge, 1968, p. 105):

Up to the 31st move, all of our play had been previously published, except where I evaded "the book" several times in a vain effort to throw the computer's timing off. At the 32-27 loser and onwards, all the play is original with us, so far as I have been able to find. It is very interesting to me to note that the computer had to make several star moves in order to get the win, and that I had several opportunities to draw otherwise. That is why I kept the game going. The machine, therefore, played a perfect ending without one misstep. In the matter of the end game, I have not had such competition from any human being since 1954, when I lost my last game.

Wooldridge believes that such computer behavior is adequate evidence of intelligence. The reader can make his own decision as to the adequacy of the evidence. The evidence could, of course, be multiplied with examples of behaviors of other types—chess playing, musical composition, and the like—but the other examples exhibit essentially the same principles.

Some have suggested (e.g., Newell, Shaw, & Simon, 1958; Newell & Simon, 1961) that computer programs can constitute a theory of intelligent *human* behavior. However, there is a great danger in jumping to the conclusion that because a computer program operates in some particular way, so does the human being. The computer program is like the more traditional mathematical model in this sense; each may allow the correct prediction to be made, but neither is likely to describe how the human being accomplishes what he does.

Without its program, the computer "knows" nothing. The human worker who is given inadequate or incomplete instructions may manage to muddle through somehow or may even fall back on previous knowledge or experience and do perfectly well. It is quite likely that neither worker nor instructor will be able to say precisely and completely how the job was done. It is because of this that the complete moronic stupidity of a computer may sometimes be an advantage. If a computer is required to do a task with a program which is *in any way* incomplete, it simply cannot proceed. Imagine that some learning theorist is programming a computer to produce "behavior" that would be predicted from his theory. He may discover that some of his thinking is not sufficiently explicit for him to write the program, although until that time his theory had seemed perfectly clear. He may find that, when the program runs, the results do not conform with empirical findings in several unusual cases which he had previously not bothered to examine. In short, the stupidity of the unprogrammed computer demands complete foresight on the part of any person who wants the computer to do anything; no human taskmaster would be likely to exact such explicitness of statement. Yet the computer, once programmed, is so fast that it can afford to examine untoward conditions and is so rigid and thorough that it examines even those conditions which the human being would dismiss as "obviously" irrelevant for the purposes at hand (but which may turn out to be not only relevant but also critical).

The simulation of human functions is likely to lead the psychologist or engineer to take a particular series of steps. In any particular case, the series of steps is likely to be disjointed, unrelated, and undirected. It may be recognized only later, or perhaps never, that any simulation of human function was accomplished. However, if the process is self-conscious, the steps may occur as follows: A function needs to be carried out—for example, the detection of a target on a radar display. Man and device are regarded as substitutable for each other. The man is observed as he performs the task. His behavior is described mathematically. This behavior is compared with the behavior of existing or realizable devices that will do the same job. A new device is or is not made. If made, its behavior may be compared with human behavior.

Each of the several steps in this process is likely to be very interesting and instructive for the science of psychology. The mathematical description, however, is perhaps most likely to be useful. Its range of interest may turn out to extend considerably beyond the situation in which it was developed; we shall later see two excellent illustrations of this.

An increasing range of human functions can be performed by inanimate devices. The more complex functions are carried out less well; we have seen that computers can play checkers (a relatively simple game) at an extremely high level of competence. Chess, which is more complex, is played less well; Simon (1970) says: "No program yet plays expert, or even Class A, chess, but Greenblatt's program, perhaps the strongest in the field today, has won a Class C American Chess Federation rating on the basis of its performance in tournaments (against humans). This would place it, I am confident, well above the median strength of *Science*-reading chess players" (pp. 630–631). Computers have already shown enough promise so that Hilgard and Bower (1966) include a chapter on information-processing models in their book, *Theories of learning*. The authors describe most of the important types of program simulating human behavior.

How far can computer simulation be carried? There are two kinds of answers that can be given to this question. The first, empirical answer is "Wait and see." Extrapolating from the first twenty-five years, one would guess that the trend is going quite a way, until eventually it will include expert chess, good translation of natural languages, etc., but that the progress toward these things is not going to be very rapid. *Scientific* understanding of the human being has not yet been tremendously enhanced by computers, but the influence of "information-processing theories" has been, in our opinion, significant and positive.

The second kind of answer to "How far can it go?" is a logical one derived from mathematical and logical reasoning. There are three key logical findings which have an important bearing on the extent to which a machine may be expected to simulate a man. The first finding was by Turing (1937; see Arbib, 1964, for a discussion of the "second kind of answer"). To put it very crudely, what Turing showed was that *any* well-defined input-output relationship can be simulated by a simple type of machine (which came, of course, to be called a *Turing machine*). Thus any findings of S-R psychology could be simulated by a machine if those "findings" were in the form of well-defined S-R relationships. The second discovery was by McCulloch and Pitts (1943), who showed that the functions of a digital computer could be carried out by a nerve net, and vice versa. Thus it is reasonable to suppose that the logic of operation of the human nervous system can be simulated exactly by a computer. The third finding was by Kurt Gödel in 1931 (see Arbib, 1964, for an account in English). He proved a characteristic of formal systems which Arbib (1964) summarizes as follows: "His theorem states that *any* adequate consistent arithmetical logic is incomplete, i.e., there exist true statements about the integers which cannot be proved within such a logic (pp. 122-123). Gödel's theorem has been used to argue that there are limits on the extent to which human thought can be simulated by computers. The argument goes something like this: Digital computers are logical machines. As such, they are covered by Gödel's theorem. Human beings are not logical machines; hence they are not covered and thus not limited. Thus machines cannot completely simulate man.

We disagree that Gödel's theorem applies to computers but not to men. The theorem says nothing about how the logical system is represented—whether by transistors or by neurons, for example—and thus seems to have no force as limiting the extent of simulation. In any case, we, in keeping with the usual scientific practice, are far more impressed by empirical demonstrations of ability to simulate human behavior than by deductive proofs that simulation is or is not likely to be possible.

We can now turn to two specific influences which have straddled the boundary between engineering and psychology: information theory (cf. Attneave, 1959) and detection theory (cf. Licklider, 1959). The present chapter is not the place for a detailed substantive examination of either theory, but it is appropriate to look at each of them in broad perspective.

Both these theories grew in intimate association with engineering problems. Shannon (1951) did his work on information theory at Bell Telephone Laboratories, and no doubt much of the impetus for his work came from the desire of Bell Telephone to develop better devices for the transmission of information. Detection theory has emanated in large part from the Electronic Defense Group at the University of Michigan, and devices for detection are certainly desired products of this group. To date, a human being is likely to be a part of such a detection device.

INFORMATION THEORY

Information Measures

According to Norbert Wiener, no one man can be credited with the development of a measure of information (1948): "This idea occurred at about the same time to several writers, among them the statistician R. A. Fisher, Dr. Shannon of the Bell Telephone Laboratories, and the author" (p. 18). However, Shannon has worked most persistently on the theoretical development of information theory and has most widely disseminated information theory through his publication of both theory and data (e.g., Shannon, 1951; Shannon & Weaver, 1949). We may therefore give Shannon the primary credit.

The argument that underlies the definition of an information measure can be presented rather simply as long as we remain content with an approximate and intuitive treatment. Shannon was, as we have said, concerned with actual communication systems, containing at least a transmitter, communication channel, and receiver. What was desired was a measure of the capacity of channels to carry information. Shannon described one such measure.

First, assume that only a limited number of alternatives can be communicated via any communication system. For example, if an English-speaking radio announcer is transmitting, his set of messages is limited to the words of the English language. What he does in speaking is to choose from all the possible words a single word to transmit. Until he speaks, a person at the receiver is uncertain what word will be spoken. He does know that one of the set of English words will be chosen. The process of information transmission can be regarded as a process of reducing uncertainty. If there is no uncertainty remaining after a message is sent and received, then the amount of information transmitted is the same as the amount of uncertainty that existed initially. It seems reasonable to make the amount of uncertainty proportional to the number of possible messages that might conceivably be sent; the more alternatives there are, the harder it would be to guess which would be sent.

Shannon noted that it would be possible to number all the alternatives using the binary system, as we pointed out in our discusson of binary numbers. If there were 64 alternatives, we would number them from 0 through 111111 (which corresponds to a decimal 63). This requires a six-place binary number to complete the numbering.

We saw earlier that if we have some number N of columns of binary numbers, we can designate 2^N different alternatives. In the present case, $2^6 = 2 \times 2 \times 2 \times 2 \times 2 \times 2 = 64$. Shannon lets the number of columns of binary digits required to number the alternative messages equal the number of units of information. These units of information are called *bits*, an abbreviation for *bi*nary digi*ts*. If you are told which of 64 possible alternatives is true, you have received 6 bits of information. The logarithm of some number X is defined as the power to which some base number must be raised in order to obtain X; that is, base$^{log\ x} = X$. For example, if 2 is used as the base, $2^{\log x} = 64$. We just noted that $2^6 = 64$; therefore, log 64 to the base 2 equals 6. This is usually written $\log_2 64 = 6$. This suggests that we can find the number of bits involved in selecting one of a set of N alternatives by taking $\log_2 N$, and this is in fact the way the bit is defined, as $\log_2 N$. The student should remember that $\log_2 N$ equals the number of columns required to number a set of alternatives with binary digits.

A concrete example at this point may be useful. Consider a game in which a person has to discover which book from a shelf containing 16 books has been marked with a $10 bill inserted between the pages. His problem is to locate the book by asking the minimum number of indirect questions. (Of course, he cannot tell which book has been marked from the external appearance, and he cannot ask a direct question, such as "Which book is it?" The only questions permitted are ones that can be answered by "yes" or "no.") The proper procedure, from the point of view of minimizing the number of questions, is to ask first: "Is the book to the right (or left) of center?" After this question is answered, there will remain 8 rather than 16 possibilities. The same question, halving the possibilities each time, should then be asked until the marked book has been isolated. Four questions of this kind are required to make this determination, as one can easily verify by an empirical test. This number is exactly the number of columns of binary units required to designate 16 alternatives; also, $\log_2 16 = 4$, the number of bits of information transmitted. In this case, the information was transmitted, 1 bit at a time, by the four answers. Even if the statement "It's the thirteenth book from the left" were directly made, 4 bits would still have been transmitted.

The use of the simple definition of the number of bits, $H = \log_2 N$, is justified only if every message in the set of alternative messages is equally likely to occur. It seems intuitively obvious that the occurrence of unlikely events is more informative than the occurrence of very probable events. Thus, "man bites dog" is newsworthy, while "dog bites man" is not. The difference in information content as a function of the probability of occurrence of a particular alternative is considered in the more general formula, $H = \log_2 1/P$, where P is the probability that the message would have occurred. If an honest die comes up 4, the occurrence of this event transmits $\log_2 1/^1/_6$ bits $= \log_2 6$ bits $= 2.58$ bits. If the die is heavily loaded, the occurrence of a 4 may transmit almost no information. A die that always comes up 4 transmits $\log_2 1/1 = 0$ bits of information when it turns up 4.

Often the occurrence of a sequence of messages may present problems very similar to a gradual transition from a situation like throwing a fair die to one like throwing a loaded die; that is, the occurrence of a particular message in the first position may change the probabilities in the next position and so on through the whole series of messages. Language is an excellent example of this kind of relationship between the messages in a sequence. In English, the letter T is very likely to be followed by an H and not at all likely to be followed by an L. The effect of 100 letters on the 101st is so great that the 101st carries somewhere between 0.6 and 1.3 bits of independent information (it is not practical to make exact determinations). If every letter were equally probable, the occurrence of a letter or space at position 101 would carry $\log_2 27 = 4.76$ bits. It is clear, then, that a given amount of information transmitted via the English language is shared among many symbols. To put it another way, each symbol really carries *less* than the maximum information which it would be capable of carrying.

Systems of this kind are called *redundant,* and English would seem to be about three-fourths redundant. Redundancy is not all bad; if the information transmitted is shared among words, *the information* may be available even though part of the message is missed. For example, the blank in *psychol gy* can easily be filled in with an *o,* for the remaining letters give us sufficient information, and in effect we still have the whole message. If we reflect on the frequency with which children respond with "Huh?" to an attempt at communication, we shall no doubt be grateful for all the redundancy English contains. Probably the child's query is more often produced by an inferior ability to reconstruct missed parts of the message than by inferior hearing.

Empirical Studies

With this brief background, we can look at the psychological application of information measures and of the point of view afforded by information theory. We can ask how great man's channel capacity is, and some answers have been given.

Pierce and Karlin (1957) have reported one of the highest rates of continuous transmission. They had subjects read words aloud as rapidly as possible from a fixed vocabulary. The sequences of words were random; thus it was easy to calculate the amount of information involved in reading words, and information was not lost to the usual sequential effects. About 45 bits per second were transmitted. Husbands have long known that information is presented fastest verbally, but it is comforting to have quantitative evidence of this fact.

For a time it seemed that the rate of information transmission of the human channel might be almost independent of the nature of the transmission task, but it now appears that this is far from true. In reading words the information rate equals information per word times words per unit of time. Since information per word equals $\log_2$ (vocabulary size), larger vocabularies would have to be read more slowly than small vocabularies if the information-transmission rate were to remain constant. However, Pierce and Karlin—and, earlier, Sumby and Pollack (1954)—found that reading speed does not decrease markedly with increases in the size of the vocabulary. For a fixed number of syllables per word, the transmission rate increases almost linearly as vocabulary size increases.

In the reading task, subjects transmitted information continuously. It is also possible to have subjects observe a single brief presentation of a stimulus and then have them respond at leisure to what was observed. Here the measure is a measure of a kind of "absorption" rate rather than of what we would intuitively feel should be called a "transmission" rate. It may be considered a measure of the channel capacity of the sensory channel involved. G. A. Miller (1956) has reviewed the evidence from a number of studies of human abilities to discriminate between stimuli varying along some single dimension. Judgments of pitch, loudness, pointer position, and square size are examples of the tasks involved. Surprisingly, the number of values of stimuli which can be discriminated accurately is small, Miller's "seven plus or minus two"! This number is much smaller than the number of just-noticeable differences along these scales. The subject's task is very different in the situation Miller is discussing and in the situation where just-noticeable differences are being determined. In the latter case, a reference is presented so that the subject need only discern a difference. In studying information transmission, the subject is required to state which of several alternatives was presented; he has no reference present and must make an "absolute" discrimination. Very surprisingly, the number of absolutely discriminable values is insensitive to the spacing along the scale of the chosen values, at least to a considerable extent (Attneave, 1959, pp. 67ff.). Garner (1960) has indicated, however, that more information is transmitted by rating scales which use larger numbers of values; the total information transmitted increases with the number of scale values up to twenty.

Several experiments (Klemmer & Frick, 1953; Pollack & Ficks, 1953; Pollack & Klemmer, 1954) indicate that increasing the number of stimulus dimensions increases the number of bits that can be assimilated at a single observation. Klemmer and Frick, for example, got a transmission value for eight-dimensional stimuli of 7.8 bits, as compared with a value for single-dimensional stimuli of about 3 bits. Quastler, Osborne, and Tweedell (1955) investigated the best combination of number of scales and number of divisions and found that five or six scales, each divided into five or six scale positions, could be arranged to transmit 12 bits per look. Using three symbols in conjunction with a dial increased transmission to 17.6 bits. Other studies (Augenstine, 1958) indicate that most of the information uptake occurs in the first 40 milliseconds, with little additional information assimilated in the next 200 milliseconds.

MacKay (1952, 1969) made a distinction between two kinds of information content of stimuli which is useful in talking about this set of results. He called the information carried by the different values along a single scale the *metron content,* and the information carried by the different dimensions the *logon content.* It appears that the useful metron content, then, is limited to about eight values, and additional information can best be carried by increasing the logon content.

Information measures are useful in the study of memory as well as in the study of human information transmission. For example, Pollack (1954) found that immediate memory span is approximately constant at about seven units whether the units are binary numbers containing only 1 bit of information per digit, decimal numbers containing $\log_2 10 = 3.32$ bits, or letters of the alphabet containing 4.76 bits. It occurred to S. K. Smith and Miller (1952) that the information span might be increased for the smaller units if they were coded into units containing more information; then the larger units would be remembered and decoded back into the smaller units as they were reproduced. Binary digits could easily be coded three at a time as follows: 000 = 0, 001 = 1, 010 = 2, 011 = 3, 100 = 4, 101 = 5, 110 = 6, and 111 = 7. The code would then be remembered and finally reconverted into binary digits upon demand. For example, the stimulus digits 111011100010001 would be converted to 73421, which would be remembered easily. If the conversion-reconversion process were perfectly efficient, the memory span for binary digits would be increased threefold. Empirically, the improvement is not quite that marked.

Information measures have found further application in the description of the perceptual process. Attneave (1954) and Hochberg and McAlister (1953) pointed out the applicability of information measures to Gestalt concepts. For example, they noted that good figures contain less information. It is easier to predict the continuation of a line from a knowledge of previous portions of the line in a good figure than in a poor one. One can fill in a circle from a knowledge of any short arc, or a triangle from a knowledge of its three corners. Such figures are highly organized, redundant, and good. Similar informational descriptions can be given for many other Gestalt principles of organization. Information measures are more precise as measures of organization and accordingly should help to bring the heretofore qualitative Gestalt principles more fully into the province of quantitative psychology.

Garner (1962) discusses some of the difficulties in making a translation of Gestalt concepts into information terms; the problem arises because the Gestalt principles are supposed to apply to *single* stimuli, whereas information concepts are designed to apply to the characteristics of sets of stimuli. Later, Garner (1966) made a persuasive case for regarding stimuli as representatives of members of a class. He regarded perceiving as analogous to knowing the structure and organization of *sets* of stimuli. His series of experiments provides an excellent example of the usefulness of the viewpoint provided by information theory, even though little of the theory was directly involved.

The foregoing has been a summary review of completed work utilizing information measures or concepts. We have ignored such important problems as the determination of transmitted information when the transmitter and receiver are not in agreement, that is, when behaviors are less than perfectly correlated. Attneave (1959), Quastler (1955), Garner and Hake (1951), and McGill (1954) have given methods for calculating transmitted information from a knowledge of the inputs, outputs, and their relationships. We cannot deal with these more technical problems here, but we hope that the diversity of areas in which information theory plays a part has been indicated.

The strength of information theory is that its measure does not specify in any way whatever the nature of the message. It can be applied to things as different as binary digits, musical notes, and hormone flow from one part of the body to another. The generality is based on the simple but ingenious insight that any finite set of alternatives can be coded by numbering the alternatives. This same possibility is the basis for the variety of abilities which a digital computer can display. The generality of information theory makes it a very useful device for unifying the points of view of different sciences, for example, psychology and biology. One could ask whether the quantity of information which could be stored in a given number of RNA molecules was sufficient to represent a picture of a given size to a given resolution. Before information measures were available, such a question would have been considered nonsense.

During its formative years, information theory was regarded in psychology as a tremendously exciting development, perhaps one which would revolutionize the field. Some of the excitement seems to have died down. Information theory is now regarded as one of the basic mathematical tools for psychologists, just as calculus is. It is clear from the brief summary given here that information theory has already proved its worth and that it will have a useful future. It is still appropriate to conclude our discussion with the same cautionary paragraph we quoted some years earlier (Attneave, 1959, p. 88):

Although the techniques of information theory are useful in the study of the organism's information-handling processes, other techniques may often be more useful and more appropriate. That aspect of information measures which gives them so wide a range of application also limits their usefulness in any specific area. . . . The value of the concepts of information theory in leading us into new areas of investigation is not lessened, however, if in the pursuit of these investigations we find it possible to abandon information measures in favor of others more informative.

TABLE 13-1 Payoff Matrix for Detection Experiment

| signal presented? | subject's decision | |
	yes	no
Yes	10	−5
No	−1	1

DETECTION THEORY

During World War II, engineers developed a theory of detection which would apply to the detection of targets by radar receivers. Tanner and Swets (1953, 1954) and M. Smith and Wilson (1953) took over the mathematical treatment and applied it to human detection. These men and many others have since extended the theory.

Signal-detection theory is a special case of statistical decision theory. A detection involves a decision based on statistical considerations rather than a simple statement of the form, "Yes, I heard the signal," or "No, I did not hear the signal." Detection theory regards the experiment which attempts to determine a sensory threshold as a game between subject and experimenter. According to this view, the subject would always say he heard the signal, whether he heard it or not, if he knew in advance that it would be presented. This does not mean that subjects should simply be regarded as dishonest; it means that there is no sharp division between detecting and not detecting a signal. The subject is always making a decision based on probabilistic rather than certain information. There is an obvious compatibility of point of view between detection theory and Brunswik, with his probabilistic functionalism (see Chapter 11).

Since decisions must be based on probabilistic rather than certain information, they are often influenced by the values or costs that may be associated with making them and being right or wrong in the decision. The values and costs associated with being right or wrong about each possible decision determine a *payoff matrix*. If there are only two possible decisions—for example, "Yes, a signal was presented," or "No, a signal was not presented"—the payoff matrix will have only four entries. An example is given in Table 13-1. According to the matrix, the subject gains 10 units (say, 10 cents) if he says the signal was presented when it was, but loses 5 units (5 cents) if he says it was not when it was. If he makes an incorrect decision when a signal was not presented, he loses 1 cent, and he gains 1 cent if he makes the correct decision. It is intuitively clear that, given this payoff matrix, cases where the probability that a signal was presented is about equal to the probability that no signal was presented should be resolved in favor of signal. More will be gained if this turns out to be right than will be lost if it is wrong; putting it another way, more can be gained by saying "yes" correctly than by saying "no" correctly.

If at first this theory seems not to apply to real-life situations, consider some interesting examples of decision making under uncertain conditions, where values and costs are obviously involved.

Case 1. You are at a party, and you think you detect a possible sign of interest on the part of an attractive person of the opposite sex. The circumstances are such that there will be appreciable embarrassment if you are mistaken.

Case 2. Your wife thinks she hears a burglar downstairs. You do not think it is a burglar. Could you be looking at different value-cost matrices?

Another factor combines with the payoff matrix in biasing decisions. This is the advance, or a priori, probability that a signal will be presented. Again our intuition tells us that if we know in advance that signals will be presented in nine intervals out of ten, we should say "signal presented" in uncertain cases. The a priori probability, in conjunction with the payoff matrix, determines a criterion—a number—usually called *beta,* with which a number derived from the sensory observation should be compared in order to make the best decision. If the number derived from the sensory input exceeds the criterion, the ideal observer says "signal"; if it does not, the ideal observer says "no signal."

The criterion value is chosen so that some function is maximized. It is assumed that the ideal observer wishes to make decisions such that the greatest gain will be obtained, the most correct decisions made, or some other desirable goal achieved. W. W. Peterson, Birdsall, and Fox (1954) have discussed possible goals and have developed for each the equations which combine the a priori probabilities and payoff matrix to determine the optimum criterion value.

Two probabilities must be computed in order to derive the most useful number from the sensory observation. The first is the probability that *if* a signal had been presented, the observed sensory input would have occurred. The second is the probability that the observed sensory input would have occurred if no signal had been presented. The first probability is then divided by the second to form the *likelihood ratio.* This likelihood ratio is compared with the criterion in order to reach an optimal decision, as outlined above. It can be shown that the likelihood ratio contains all the information an observer needs to make an optimal decision. This fact vastly simplifies the decision process, as compared, say, with the necessity to remember exactly what the detailed signal was.

The reader may be wondering at this point what sense it can possibly make to consider the probability that a sensory input would occur if no signal were presented. Such a probability becomes reasonable on the assumption that there is always random stimulation, or noise, present in any sensory system. The name generally given to a sensory system within detection theory is *receiver.* As far as a receiver is concerned, there are two kinds of noise. One comes from the outside world, and the other from the receiver's own workings. In case the receiver is a human observer, the internal noise is usually called *neural* noise. Such internal

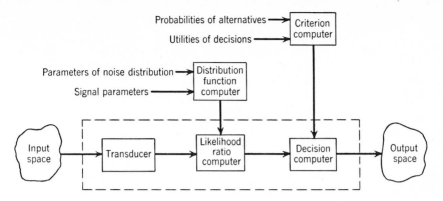

Fig. 13-1   Block diagram of ideal observer in detection theory. (From Tanner, 1961.)

noises can never be completely eliminated, even if it were possible to eliminate completely noise at the receiver input. The origin of the noise, as far as the performance of the detector is concerned, is irrelevant. Any noise will degrade the performance of the system. Most people have had the experience of hearing unearthly noises emanating from the television set, to which they respond, "Was that the set [internal noise] or the station [external noise]?" The reader by this time should also have noted the possibility that the "unearthly noise" might have been produced by, say, a rock music group—which gives us all the elements for a detection problem.

The determination of the necessary probabilities for the computations of likelihood ratio is not a trivial accomplishment. It is really this determination which distinguishes detection theory from decision theory, or the testing of statistical hypotheses, in general. The basic difficulty in characterizing the likelihood ratio associated with a given sensory input is that the input is initially given as a continuous wave form, while statistical decision theory is intended to work with discrete numerical measurements. If the wave form has certain properties, it can be characterized, without loss of information, by a limited number of measurements. The number of measurements required depends on the highest frequency present in the wave form (W) and the length of time (T) over which the wave form is to be measured; the number of measurements required is exactly $2WT$. Still other difficulties have to be overcome before the signal and noise can meaningfully be compared; the reader who is interested in the details of this problem may consult Licklider (1958). Green and Swets (1966) also treat this problem, as well as other psychologically relevant aspects of detection theory, in their excellent book.

Figure 13-1 is a general block diagram of the ideal observer as visualized in detection theory. Let us now examine an experimental situation in conjunction with this block diagram in order to get a clearer idea of how detection theorists think about signal detection.

Two general types of situations may be presented to the observer. Either he must say whether or not a signal was presented within a single fixed time interval, or he must say which of several specified intervals contained a signal, knowing that one of them did. It is simpler to talk about the former situation, although it is easier to relate the theory to the latter. In the multiple-interval case, the subject's task is just to choose the interval containing the sensory event with the largest likelihood ratio; the a priori probabilities, the payoff matrix, and hence the criterion are the same for all the intervals. Subject errors in assessing or combining the criterion factors therefore do not affect his decision.

In the other case, in which the subject must say whether or not a signal occurred in a single interval, a number of types of errors may occur. The subject might not use the correct a priori probabilities, he might not use the correct payoff matrix, he might not try to maximize the desired quantity, or he might not combine the factors correctly to do so. In addition, subjects under either condition may not compute the likelihood ratio correctly.

We shall consider the block diagram as it relates to the single-interval case. It is simplest to assume that the distribution-function computer is given the signal-plus-noise and the noise-alone distributions so that these need not be computed from experience. In either case, the distributions must be available so that the likelihood ratio can be computed from its component probabilities.

The a priori probabilities that signal plus noise, or noise alone, will be presented on a particular trial are needed by the criterion computer. The payoff matrix would also be necessary to its computation of the criterion.

With the distributions and the criterion in hand, the ideal observer is ready to begin its observations. An input is presented within an interval. The observer takes the sample through its transducer, which performs the necessary operations in order to obtain the $2WT$ measurements. The output of the transducer is fed into the likelihood computer along with the distribution functions for the two distributions. This information is sufficient for the likelihood-ratio computer to compute its output. The decision computer needs only to compare the likelihood ratio with the criterion computed by the criterion computer in order to make its decision.

How well can an ideal observer do in discriminating between signal plus noise and noise alone? This depends on just what properties describe the signal and noise, that is, what characteristics are available which determine the value of the likelihood ratio. If the *exact value* of the signal to be expected is known at every point in the observation interval, then the actual observation can be correlated point by point with the expected signal. Under these conditions, detection theory shows that the optimal performance possible depends on the relationship between the energy of the signal (E) and the power per unit bandwidth of the noise (N). To be more specific, the distance in standard deviation units between the means of the distribution of likelihood ratios for signal plus noise and noise alone, on a logarithmic scale, is the square root of $2E/N$. This distance between the distributions is called d'. The value of d' determines what performance can be achieved by the observer.

Figure 13-2 illustrates some of the concepts of detection theory. This figure is based on the assumption that the sensory events which occur under noise-alone (N)

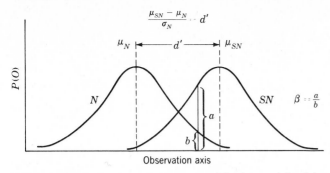

Fig. 13-2 A visualization of some concepts of the theory of signal detectability. See text for explanation.

conditions can be represented along a unidimensional "observation axis." Both the *N* events and the *SN* events (when signal plus noise is presented) are assumed to distribute normally with equal variances on this observation axis, that is, the relative probabilities of occurrences of various values along the observation axis are represented by normal probability distributions. Then d' is the distance between the means of the *N* and *SN* distributions, in units of the common standard deviation. (If the standard deviations are not equal, the standard deviation of the noise distribution determines the units.) At some point along the observation axis, the ordinate of the *SN* distribution (*a* in the figure) divided by the ordinate of the *N* distribution (*b*) will equal the criterion value of the likelihood ratio (β). For this case, all observations to the right of that point should be called *signal* and all observations to the left of that point *noise*. Since the two distributions overlap, even an ideal, perfect observer will only "hit" the signal when it occurs that proportion of the time represented by the area under the *SN* distribution to the right of the cutoff. He will mistakenly say that the signal is presented, though only noise is presented (called a *false alarm*), on that proportion of noise trials represented by the area under the *N* distribution to the right of the cutoff. The observer can, of course, move his cutoff to either the right or the left. If he moves it to the right, he will make fewer false alarms, but he will also have fewer hits. If he moves it to the left, he will have more hits, but also more false alarms. We shall see in a moment how movement of the criterion traces out a "receiver operating characteristic" curve. At this point, we should note that the sensitivity (measured by d') and the criterion (β) are separated by detection theory; thus measures of sensitivity are more likely to remain constant over situational changes that might affect a subject's criterion setting.

A perfect performance would be defined by the observation that the subject always said "signal" when a signal was in fact presented and never said "signal" when noise alone was presented. As we have seen, a perfect performance would be possible only if the *N* and *SN* distributions had no overlap. The goodness of imperfect performances must always be described as a certain relationship between the probability of a hit, $P_S(S)$, and the probability of a false alarm, $P_S(N)$. Since

$P_S(S)$ and $P_S(N)$ can be determined from the value of d', the reverse computation, plus certain assumptions, will give d' if one knows $P_S(S)$ and $P_S(N)$. This is indeed fortunate when d' is to be computed for the human observer, for in this case it is not possible to measure the noise distribution which is presented to the distribution-function computer or, for that matter, to measure the signal-plus-noise distribution. The neural noise cannot be directly measured. Therefore, it is impossible to compute d' from a knowledge of E and N as they come through the human transducer. Instead, the experimenter computes what d' would have to be in order that the ideal observer duplicate the observed values of $P_S(S)$ and $P_S(N)$. The required d' can then be compared with the higher value of d' computed from whatever physical measures the ideal observer would use. Actual observers can never perform better than (and probably never quite as well as) the ideal observer. Thus the theory is "normative" in that it allows us to say how well an observer "ought" to do. Further, the theory allows us to postulate that an ideal observer is limited to less-than-perfect information, and it also allows us to compare this limited performance with that of a human observer; if the limited ideal is very like the human, then we have a hint as to how the human may actually process his sensory information.

The d' values so far obtained for human observers have shown good consistency for a given individual over a considerable range of values of a priori probability and payoff matrix. It is this consistency which represents perhaps the greatest victory of detection theory, for this consistency cannot be achieved by the traditional theory based on thresholds. The threshold has been found to vary with conditions. Corrections for guessing cannot eliminate inconsistencies in threshold. Psychophysicists were coming to regard thresholds as significant only under the specified conditions in which the threshold had been determined. The d' measure, with its greater generality, escapes this limitation. If d' has been determined for a particular pair of values $P_S(S)$ and $P_S(N)$, then the pairing of other values of $P_S(S)$ and $P_S(N)$ can be given with greater generality (for a particular subject, as values in the payoff matrix and a priori probabilities are changed).

The ability to do this derives from the fact that d' determines a receiver operating curve, or ROC. Figure 13-3 shows a set of such curves. The diagonal line represents chance performance; we note that if the observer gives no false alarms, he cannot ever correctly call out "signal." However, if he is willing to call "signal" each time, he will always be correct *if* the signal is presented and always incorrect if the noise is presented. The diagonal line is the only possible ROC if d' equals 0; as d' increases, the ROC moves further from the diagonal line. There is never any sudden shift to a new level of responding as the signal and noise are made more discriminable, as a naïve view of the threshold concept might suggest. Swets (1961) reviewed several versions of threshold theory and showed that the modifications required to bring threshold theory into line with empirical results may so complicate it that it begins to look quite similar to detection theory. Swets (1964) has also collected many of the experimental papers on detection theory into an easily available set of readings.

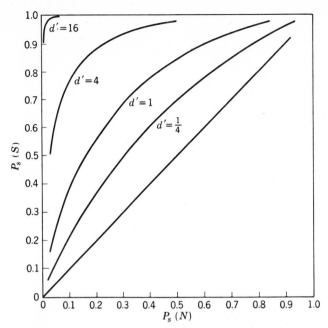

Fig. 13-3 Receiver operating curves of varying values of d'.
(From Peterson et al., 1954.)

Detection theory has been useful for predicting results in sensory psychology, particularly in vision and audition (Carterette & Cole, 1962). This is not surprising, since the theory was developed for handling "sensory" problems. An unexpected bonus, however, has been the application of detection theory to problems in memory, beginning with Egan (1958) and continuing to the present (e.g., Banks, 1970; Lockhart & Murdock, 1970). As we have mentioned, the theory has close relationships to the more general theory of statistical decisions and therefore applies in part to games and to statistical testing. Detection theory thus has surprisingly broad application, and its future importance in psychology seems assured. New techniques are being developed which make it possible to apply traditional tests of significance to the parameters of detection theory (Dorfman & Alf, 1968, 1969), thus integrating it even more closely with traditional statistics.

Let us now review what has been presented and note the relationships between the point of view of detection theory and some very general systematic considerations. We have already seen that Brunswik's probabilistic view of the organism-environment interchange is consistent with detection theory.

The primary datum for the detection theorist is a *decision* made by the observing organism (or observing equipment). The observer is playing a game (in the mathematical sense) which he tries to win, rather than describing a sensory experience. If the organism has information that the a priori probability that a tiger is present is equal to 1.00, the organism does not even listen to present stimuli; it does not introspect—it runs. The observer in the psychophysical experiment is regarded as a similar expression of a tendency for an adjustive organism to use whatever information *should* be related to a decision, with no prejudice that all relevant information is given on a sensory channel on a particular trial. This point of view resembles the functionalist point of view in its emphasis on adaptation, and it is behavioristic in its acceptance of the overt decision as the significant experimental datum. It is modern in its use of a mathematical system as a model; it shows the impact of another modern influence of mathematics on psychology in its relationship to game theory (see Birdsall, 1953). Its realm of relevance is limited, and its specificity is often very high; yet the theory has sufficient generality so that experimental results which had seemed to disagree can be related in a consistent and meaningful way. Despite the fact that the theory is specific and hence sensitive to experimental results, it is not so rigid that it must fall whenever any deviation of experiment from theory occurs; it can be modified to accommodate, to some extent, new and unexpected results.

Both detection theory and information theory represent what may be considered a new middle of the road for psychological theory. They strike a balance between specificity and generality, and between sensitivity and flexibility. Both bodies of theory are quite rigorous compared with the theory and systems of yesteryear, and neither takes all psychological knowledge for its province. Both theories have runners that cross into other gardens; or, to be more accurate, their roots are actually in engineering gardens and their runners in psychology. Finally, they are not isolated from each other or from other theories in terms of the people interested in them, the disciplines involved, or the problems treated. On one level of generality, they have much in common. Both theories deal with signals in a mathematical way, both originated in the study of equipment, and both apply in a most satisfying manner to the study of man. Both are heavy in considerations of probabilities of messages or signals, respectively. Neither is divorced from the study of cybernetics (here one could note again Wiener's discussion of information measures in his book entitled *Cybernetics*). As we saw earlier, computers play a role in the thinking of the men interested in all these areas. In fact, there is a very broad sense in which "information theory" or "information-processing theories" can be used to mean those theories which use concepts from all the fields discussed so far in this chapter: statistical communication theory (information theory in the narrow sense), computer simulation, detection theory, and cybernetics (which we did not discuss). All these theories must come together in the complete robot. If a complete robot existed, it would be a walking theory of human behavior.

There is a fairly cohesive group of scientists interested in the problems outlined in this section. They probably could be called a "school" of psychology with as much justification as, for example, the functionalists, who were a loose group. The contemporary engineering psychologists, like the operant conditioners, have a community of interest which is similar to that of the earlier schools of psychology, which we like to claim have disappeared in the last decades.

Before proceeding to consideration of mathematical models within psychology, we turn briefly to a related kind of development within experimental psychology: analysis of information-processing activities in the human subject.

INFORMATION PROCESSING

Posner (1964) is among those who have made extensive use of the information-processing view of human behavior. He suggests, for example, that such tasks can usefully be categorized as conservation tasks (in which the goal is to transmit information exactly as it is received, as in memory tasks), reduction tasks (as in addition of numbers, in which the goal is to map multiple stimuli into a single response), and creation tasks (in which the goal is to make multiple responses to a single stimulus, as in multiple associations). Posner finds predictable empirical relationships between the amount of information transformation required and the adequacy of behavior; for example, reaction time increases as the amount of information reduction increases. Fitts and Posner (1967) organize their book, *Human performance*, largely around the information model.

Neisser (1964) has conducted a series of studies of the process of searching for target words, numbers, faces, and the like in a background of similar items. He finds that the search process does not demand that all the information be processed fully and that different tasks may require several different levels of information analysis, from extremely gross to extremely careful. This conclusion can be reached because of the extremely different rates of examination of information under different conditions. One of Neisser's more interesting and counterintuitive findings is that experienced scanners can search information for multiple targets as quickly as they can search for single targets. For example, an experienced searcher can search a list for one of four names as quickly as he can search it for a single name.

Sternberg (1966) has developed an ingenious technique for studying the process of scanning memory, rather than external stimuli. After a subject memorizes a sequence of symbols, he is asked to give a "yes" response if a newly presented symbol was in the remembered sequence and to give a "no" response if it was not. Subjects are required to respond as quickly as possible. The time required for responding is an apparently linear increasing function of the number of items held in memory, and it is the same whether the symbol is present in the remembered set or absent from it. Sternberg concludes that the search process consists of serial comparisons between the "new" item and those held in memory and that the search is exhaustive even though a match is found.

MATHEMATICAL MODELS IN LEARNING THEORY

The Usefulness of Mathematics

Mathematics has always been a tool of the scientist. It has been said that mathematics lends to science rigor, precision, richness, logic, and other highly valued properties. We have ourselves said many laudatory things about two mathematical developments, information theory and detection theory. It is not surprising that psychology, which has been a sort of scientific second cousin, should turn increasingly to mathematics as a gateway to respectability. However, mathematics cannot be guaranteed to be such a gateway; before turning to some additional inroads of mathematics into psychology, let us consider briefly what mathematics can and cannot be expected to do.

Logic and mathematics are very closely related. We can say, at the very least, that any mathematical system has formal postulates at its foundations. These postulates are such that further statements (theorems) can be derived from them via rules for logical deduction. Mathematical theorems are thus derived from the postulates for the particular mathematical system.

Consider a mathematical system that can be used as a model for a physical system. New statements that are valid within the mathematical system can be generated. If these new statements turn out to be true of the physical system, the mathematical model is at that point a successful model. If the mathematically valid statement does not fit the physical system, the model fails. The possibility of checking statements in this way is the basis of the hypothetico-deductive approach and underlies the effort to construct mathematical models.

There are two extreme ways in which a theorist might proceed to relate a mathematical system to a physical system. He might select empirical relationships to which existing mathematics apply without modification. In one sense, this is not an unusual procedure; detection theory, for example, took a mathematical framework and specialized it to apply to an extant area of psychological investigation. Some degree of specialization is nearly always necessary, even though no real mathematical innovation is needed. The mathematical system would be complete, with postulates and most theorems worked out, in this case.

At the other extreme, the theorist might decide to take a defined empirical area and construct whatever model was necessary to fit that area. Hull and his collaborators (Hull, Hovland, Ross, Hall, Perkins, & Fitch, 1940) seem to have made an attempt of this kind. The postulational structure that was necessary to encompass the area of rote learning was so formidable that the model has aroused more amazement than interest on the part of psychologists. The model was too complex and unwieldy to be of much use, even if it had provided significant predictive advances over those possible from simpler empirical generalizations.

Rashevsky (e.g., 1948) and Lewin (see Chapter 11) provide further examples of mathematical brilliance that has been largely wasted as far as contemporary psychological interest is concerned. Rashevsky confined himself primarily to the adaptation of existing mathematics to physiological and psychological problems. Lewin modified the form of the mathematics, as we have seen, in an attempt to make it fit the empirical area better. Rashevsky appears not to have been in sufficiently close contact with an experimental program so that his ideas were given an adequate test. Lewin, although he certainly was closely associated with experimentation, experimented independently of the details of his mathematical formulation. The lesson of recent history seems to be that viable mathematical models must be developed and modified in an extremely intimate interchange with experimental results.

Mathematics is useful to science because it provides convenient and conventional deductive apparatus for prediction and generalization. There are many general types of mathematics as well as many possible models within a given type. One does not need to ask whether it is appropriate to use mathematics because the ability to predict and generalize is useful and because mathematics, conceived of very broadly, is just a tool for accomplishing these functions. Whether some new tools need to be invented for psychology's use remains to be seen.

The psychology student of today who neglects mathematics may in fact be agreeing to run his life's intellectual race on crutches. Platt (1962), in his discussion of creativity, supports this point of view: "The third component of intellectual prowess is the use of the best available equipment. It is the nylon tents and oxygen tanks, and the easy donkey train as far as possible, that make the difference in climbing Everest. A man should lose no opportunity to upgrade his intellectual manipulative equipment; that is, the symbolic apparatus with which he does his mental operations" (p. 123).

Mathematics and Measurement

Some people confuse mathematics and measurement, but the two are to a considerable extent independent. Measurement, as far as we are concerned, is a process that establishes a correspondence between mathematical systems and empirical systems. Manipulations within the abstract system of mathematics are possible whether any correspondence exists or not. Traditional measurement established a correspondence between some number system (usually the real numbers) and some property of an empirical system (like the deflection of a needle on an appropriate meter applied to a point in a physical system). Coombs (1964) has shown that the correspondence between numbers resulting from measurement operations and empirical events is not simple, direct, or free of assumptions.

It is clear that the problem of measurement is inextricably intertwined with the problem of constructing mathematical models, though measurement is not necessarily part of mathematics per se. As we shall see later in studying Estes' model, it is not necessary that all abstract elements be measured directly, but measurement in the sense of establishment of correspondences between model and empirical data is nevertheless an absolutely essential part of the process of modeling.

Properties of Mathematical Models

There is no single criterion defining what a mathematical model is. A single functional relationship between two variables can be considered a mathematical model, since it provides a method of deducing values of one variable from values of another. This function may hold only for a highly restrictive situation, as for rote learning of digits presented at a fixed rate under rigidly specified conditions, and only given several parameters of the equation.

At the other extreme, we might consider all Newtonian mechanics as another mathematical model. Here the model is of enormous scope and is far more complex.

One dimension of models, then, is their scope. In psychology we see at one extreme Ebbinghaus's empirical learning curve (see Hilgard, 1956) and at the other, Hull's theory of mammalian behavior (e.g., Hull, 1952). A related dimension is complexity. Though simplicity is desirable, it is not legitimate to criticize a model because of complexity, for it may be that even a complex model is the simplest one possible.

Another dimension of models has to do with their origins; the most common question asked is whether a portion of the model was derived empirically or rationally. Further questions then concern the adequacy of whatever grounds are produced. These are all legitimate questions, but they cannot have any bearing on the adequacy of the model. If the model had been, like commandments, simply handed to the theorist, there would be no formal grounds for criticism. The critic might justifiably be either skeptical or jealous (depending on his religious beliefs), but the final verdict on the model should in every case depend on its empirical adequacy rather than on its source.

Another broad category of dimensions is the mathematical and logical adequacy of the model. The model should meet the usual criteria, such as independence and consistency of assumptions, and the necessary correspondence between model and data must be established in order that mathematical operations be justified.

It is not likely to be easy to evaluate either the relative logical merits of a model or the degree of empirical verification of predictions made through the use of the model. Most models can make particular predictions with only a particular probability, and competing models may make the same prediction with a greater or lesser probability. It is not a simple matter to relate hypotheses to empirical outcomes; some excellent papers have been devoted to this problem (e.g., Watanabe, 1960). It will suffice for our purposes to say that a successful model must have predicted all outcomes to which it applies with some probability greater than zero and that in general, the higher the probability and the greater the number of outcomes predicted, the better the model.

A final property of mathematical models is the type of mathematical or logical system used. Lewin's work, discussed earlier in Chapter 11, is one illustration that the usual kind of mathematics taught in algebra and calculus courses is not the only type which has been tried in application to psychology. There is no a priori reason to prefer one type of mathematics to another. The type of mathematics to be preferred in psychology will be determined on other than a priori, logical grounds. It is clear that a model cannot be successful without diligent and prolonged effort. There is no ready panacea either in new and esoteric or in old and established mathematics.

A Representative Model

W. K. Estes has been a highly successful pioneer among contemporary psychologists who have attempted to develop mathematical models for learning (see also Chapter 10). His first statement of the preliminary version of his statistical association model was published in 1950. The scope of the effort that has gone into the development of his model is reflected in a comprehensive article (1959a). The present chapter can consider only some of the orienting attitudes involved, the basic assumptions underlying the model, and a sample of the techniques involved.

Estes is one of an increasing number of psychologists who are willing to pledge allegiance to the basic methods of the older sciences, especially physics. His orientation is quantitative, operational, physicalistic—generally hardheaded. This orientation seems typical of those who are or have been in the business of constructing mathematical models.

Estes is frankly behavioristic. His general orientation toward learning theory is similar to Guthrie's. His is an S-R theory which considers a stimulus to be decomposable into elements and which considers the termination of a situation a reinforcing event; it is a contiguity theory.

In this last respect, Estes' recent position is less clear than his initial one. He has said (1959b): "In brief, our answer to the question 'reinforcement or contiguity?' is simply, 'both.' Whether we can have our cake and eat it and still not grow fat is a much more difficult question" (p. 405). In spite of this apparent hedging, Estes leaned toward contiguity assumptions. He later (1959a, 1960; Estes, Hopkins, & Crothers, 1960) made a radical shift in the basic assumptions underlying his statistical association learning theory. The newer theory, backed by experimental results from human paired-associate learning, regards learning as an all-or-none process. The stimulus pattern to be learned either is or is not associated with the correct response on a particular trial. There is a certain probability test that the association will be forgotten, so that a correct response on one test will be followed by an incorrect response on a subsequent test. (As yet, it is not certain whether the correct-incorrect series should be attributed mostly to forgetting or to change in the stimulus pattern.) If the correct association is not learned on a particular trial, there seems to be no increase over the chance probability that a correct response will be made on a subsequent test.

Despite the drastic revision in basic assumptions that has occurred, we have elected to present Estes' more classic version of statistical association theory. More data have been collected in tests of the original theory, and the classic theory may still turn out to be more appropriate in the analysis of the free-response situation.

In his original model, Estes (1950; see also Hilgard & Bower, 1966) regarded learning as a basically statistical process. The stimulus is conceived of as a set of stimulus elements. Not all elements are available on any given trial; that is, on any given trial, the organism samples some proportion of the total set of elements. If an element is sampled on a trial, and some reinforced response terminates the trial, that element will be conditioned (connected) to that response as a result of that single pairing. Any stimulus element can be connected to only one response at a time. Extinction occurs, then, whenever the stimulus elements become connected to some other response than the previously reinforced one.

The response measure used is probability of response. Such a measure is simple enough to obtain when some fixed interval is given in which an organism can respond or not or in which the organism must choose one response from a set before a trial terminates. Some difficulties are encountered when the situation is a free-response situation and when multiple responses occur within a single experimental session.

Estes overcomes this difficulty by assuming some minimum time required to execute a response; let this be expressed in minutes by h. Then $1/h$ responses can occur per minute. For example, if the animal requires 1/60 minute to complete a response, the maximum rate of responding is 60 per minute. If the maximum rate is 60 responses per minute, but the probability that a response will occur in any one interval is only 0.25, then the rate will be only $0.25 \times 60 = 15$ responses per minute. At this point, the theoretical output, a probability, has made contact with an empirical measure, rate.

Other empirical relationships follow almost immediately from the initial computation. This situation contrasts markedly with Hull's method of handling response measures (see Chapter 10), in which each new response measure had to be linked to the reaction potential by means of a new postulated function. Let us look at how simple it is to relate probability to latency.

In any time interval T, there will be T/h intervals, or T/h possible responses. In our hypothetical case there would be $60 \times 10 = 600$ intervals or possible responses in a 10-minute period. Since the probability of responding in an interval is only P rather than 1.00, PT/h responses would be expected to occur. In our case, 150 responses would occur. Each response required h minutes, in our case 1/60 minute. These responses will require a total of $PT/h \times H = PT$ minutes (in our case 2.5 minutes), leaving $T - PT$ minutes (7.5 minutes) for intervals of no responding. Thus the average interval *between* responses for our example is 7.5/150, or 0.05 minute. For the sake of simplicity, Estes counts latency as the total period between the end of one response and the end of the next; this comes out to be just h/P. Finding latency and expected number of responses, given the probability, required no special assumptions. As Estes has said (1958a, p. 395):

We have no guarantee that our approach will lead to anything passable as a learning theory, but we can have some confidence that if we do arrive at a theory, it will not be found floating idly in mid-air while the constructors try belatedly to drop a few ad hoc mooring lines down to the plane of observables.

In the language of our earlier discussion, we might say that Estes took care of the problem of response measurement early in the process of theory construction.

Let us now return to the stimulus side of the model and see how almost equally simple assumptions and derivations lead to some predictions about the form of learning curves.

A critical question that must be answered concerns what proportion of stimulus elements is sampled by the organism on a particular trial. Let us ignore for a moment the problem of how this proportion is determined and assume that we know it. We shall call this proportion *theta* (θ). The question then is, "What effect will a single trial have on the probability of making a specified response?"

At any moment, we can divide the total number of stimulus elements S into two classes: those conditioned to the response in question and those conditioned to other responses. Let X be the number of elements conditioned to the response in question. If S is the total number, then there will be $S - X$ elements conditioned to some other response. Consider what this implies for a situation in which the response in question always occurs last and terminates a trial, that is, a correction procedure in which the trial does not end until the subject makes the correct response and is reinforced.

What number of elements do we expect to have conditioned as the result of a single reinforced trial? It would be the total number of initially unconditioned elements $(S - X)$ times the probability that any element would be conditioned on a trial (θ). To take a simple example with a finite number of elements, suppose there are 100 elements, 80 of which are not conditioned, with $\theta = 0.05$. Then the expected number of elements conditioned as a result of one trial would be 4. A "difference equation" in terms of the number of elements changed on each trial therefore reads $\Delta X = \theta(S - X)$. Since the probability of response is taken to be equal to X/S, we can write a difference equation in terms of the change in *probability*, rather than in terms of the change in number of elements conditioned, simply by dividing both sides of the preceding equation by S to obtain $\Delta P = \theta(1 - P)$. With this equation in hand, we can always say what, on the average, the probability of response would be if we know the probability of response on the previous trial. If P_n is the probability of the response on the nth trial and P_{n+1} is the probability of response on the next trial, then $P_{n+1} = P_n + \theta(1 - P_n)$. This is Estes' basic learning equation.

It is also relatively easy to derive a general equation for probability of response on any trial, given θ and the probability of response on the first trial; it is $P_n = 1 - (1 - P_1)(1 - \theta)^{n-1}$. Note that this equation represents one minus the probability that an element was not connected on trial 1 and remained unconnected (because it was not sampled) on any trial previous to the trial under consideration. One minus the probability that it was *not* connected is the probability that it *is* connected, which is just what we want. This equation has provided a good fit to acquisition data obtained from rats in runways, T mazes, and bar-pressing experiments (see Estes, 1959b).

This concludes our brief look at the early version of Estes' theory, but there are a few points that should be cleared up before we consider some additions to the theory. First, there is the question of determining θ, the proportion of elements sampled. The determination cannot be made directly by any sort of observation of a sampling process; for one thing, there is no correspondence established between the theoretical stimulus elements and elements of any experimentally defined stimulus. Even if such a correspondence existed, it is hard to visualize how one could determine what proportion of elements an organism sampled on a given trial. The determination of θ must, then, be indirect. That value of θ is chosen which provides the best fit of the theoretical curve to acquisition data. At this stage, the model becomes, for the moment, superfluous; that is, if success in fitting a curve to data were *all* the model provided, the theorist would be no better off than if he had started out directly in quest of a curve. However, if the value of θ obtained from a part of a set of data yields a good fit to the remainder, that is a gain over what might be expected from extrapolation of a curve. If values of θ obtained in one situation apply to others, that is a substantial gain. We saw in the earlier part of this chapter that the measure of separation d', used in the theory of signal detectability, provides this kind of predictability from situation to situation, whereas the threshold as a measure did not. It is too early to say what extent of generality can be expected of θ as a parameter, but the results to date are promising.

One of the most important modifications to Estes' theory has been the addition of a "barrier" which divides the total set of stimulus elements into two subsets. One subset is composed of those elements which are available for sampling. Over a period of time, elements move from one subset into the other. Since each subset is in turn divided further into two subsets on the basis of conditioning to a particular response, there are really four subsets altogether. It is clear that movement of unconditioned elements into the available subset may decrease probability of response, while movement of conditioned elements into the available subset will increase this probability. The overall set of stimulus elements has the property that the proportions of conditioned and unconditioned elements in the available and unavailable subsets tend to become equal over a period of time. The reader can verify that this complication of the model makes it possible to handle such phenomena as effects of interpolated learning, spacing of trials, spontaneous recovery, and forgetting. Estes has suggested (1958, 1961) that the effects of drive may also be amenable to this treatment.

SUMMARY AND CONCLUSIONS

A coherent group of ideas emanating from engineering and mathematics forms a nucleus which is serving to organize a new school in psychology. The organizing concepts are information transmission, decision and detection theory, feedback, and the computer's simulation of human function. In the present chapter, the basic concepts of information theory and detection theory have been presented. An indication of the relationships between computer technology and these theoretical developments has been given.

Finally, Estes' statistical learning theory has been examined in its earlier form. The mathematical development presented by Estes is a distant relative of detection theory and information theory; only the extensive use of statistical models relates them. This relationship, however, sets these statistical theories sufficiently apart from more traditional psychology so that they can be treated together.

Mathematical psychology burst out of its adolescence in the 1950s and 1960s. It now has its own multivolume handbook (Luce, Bush, & Galanter, 1963-1965), its own collections of readings (Atkinson, 1964; Luce, Bush, & Galanter, 1963), a choice of introductory textbooks (Coombs, Dawes, & Tversky,

1970; Restle & Greeno, 1970), and its own journal (the *Journal of Mathematical Psychology*). It has given up its grandiose adolescent notions of changing the world quickly and by fiat and has settled down to the long, hard grind which all the now-mature sciences have had to endure.

Further Readings

The difficulty in suggesting readings in mathematical psychology for today's average psychology student is in finding those which are relevant but not very mathematical. G. A. Miller, Galanter, and Pribram provide as good a place as any to start in *Plans and the structure of behavior* (1960), which shows how the feats of the computer have freed the psychological theorist to consider new cognitive types of explanations. Wooldridge, in *Mechanical man* (1968), ranges even further, in an even more popular tone. G. A. Miller's *Mathematics and psychology* (1964) is a beautifully chosen short paperback collection of articles covering the broad features of the subject—factor analysis, detection theory, information theory, and computers are all represented to some extent, as are mathematical learning theories and other topics with a longer history. Garner's *Uncertainty and structure as psychological concepts* (1962) is not mathematically demanding and illustrates how useful the point of view of information theory can be in psychological experiments and theories. Attneave's little book, *Applications of information theory to psychology: A summary of basic concepts, methods, and results* (1959), is still a model of concise clarity which should be read by every psychology major. The going is rougher in Green and Swets' *Signal detection theory and psychophysics* (1966), but that is simply the way it is with detection theory. Estes is still as well represented by his "Statistical approach to learning theory" (1959b) as by any other single article; an earlier article is reprinted in G. A. Miller's *Mathematics and Psychology* (1964), and Estes is also represented in *Handbook of mathematical psychology* (Luce et al., 1963-1965). This handbook is an excellent and essential reference for the mathematical psychologist and serves as an excellent road map to the literature even for the nonspecialist; however, it presumes considerable mathematical sophistication and is therefore not to be approached lightly by those of us who are only semiliterate in mathematics. Finally, we suggest further reading on a subject that we did not even cover, game theory. The reason is that the topic is important and the author of *Two-person game theory* (1969) and *N-person game theory* (1970), Anatol Rapoport, is one of those rare writers who combine brilliance and the patience necessary to bring mathematical topics to basically nonmathematical readers. He deserves our attention.

EPILOGUE

The Future of Psychology as a Science and as a Profession

The events of the ten years that have passed since the first edition was published have convinced us that we cannot look into the future. Even if we could, we would still hesitate to prognosticate; the events of today seem enough to frost the crystal balls of any number of seers. However, like most of those who make a business of foretelling the future, we can protect ourselves pretty well if we stay very general and, even at that level, state that anything is possible. In so doing, we also stay very close to our exemplars in psychological theory.

First, we must decide whether to be optimistic or pessimistic. There are signs that psychology continues a rapid and healthy growth. In 1963, when our first epilogue challenged the future, there were over twenty thousand fellows, members, and associates of the American Psychological Association. In 1970, there were over thirty thousand. We have continued to move smartly toward fulfillment of the joking prophecy that by the year 2000, there will be more psychologists than people. The way things are, we *need* more psychologists than people.

On the dark side of the ledger, we must enter the fact that the whole intellectual community is in considerable disfavor and that there are factors indicating that psychologists in particular will remain so for some time. Our liberal tendencies put us too close to radical students for the taste of society at large, at least in its present temper. Though psychologists are, of course, shrewd and balanced in perspective, that is not enough to keep us from being suspect in these troubled times. A few more years of static or decreasing funding of research and of the academic community will inevitably stop our growth. This is ironic in that society is cutting us back at the very moment when large numbers of psychologists have finally become convinced that they must turn their attention to societal problems, despite their long-standing disinclination to do so.

Although this political situation further complicates the already impossible job of forecasting, we shall choose a generally optimistic view of the future on the grounds that world problems are desperately urgent, that it is reasonable that psychologists be put to work on these problems, and that the public, despite its prejudices, will in the long run choose a rational path.

442   Epilogue

Though it is plausible that psychology should be able to contribute to the solution of our society's pressing problems, we certainly have no psychological atom bombs which we can drop on those problems. The tools we have will have to be made highly visible, and better ones will have to be discovered; otherwise, our plausibility arguments will grow progressively more hollow over the next twenty-five years, until we look around to find that most of our monies have been reallocated.

One special example of the difficulty of predicting what psychology's contribution will be is presented by clinical psychologists working with disturbed patients. The big story of the past ten years has been the increasing incorporation of behavior modification techniques into treatment programs. The simplest extrapolation would be, then, that this process will continue, and that would be the most comfortable extrapolation for the future of clinical psychology (though the process is certainly not free of its own tensions).

There is, unfortunately, a less simple and less comfortable extreme alternative, which is that there will be no psychotherapy aimed at the cure of psychosis by the end of the next twenty years. Psychiatrists often espouse an "illness model" of psychosis. If it were to be shown to be essentially correct through the discovery of physiological defects and cures for them, the demand for psychotherapy with psychotics would be greatly reduced. The psychologist, as might be expected, prefers the model of psychosis—a "social learning" model—which justifies the use of psychological talents. The model preferred by an individual seems to be more closely related to his profession than it is to any hard evidence available to him.

The prediction problem is posed by our guess that the level of methodological and theoretical sophistication now ready for application to the problems of psychosis is approaching that required for some fairly useful tests of the illness model. There is a possibility that schizophrenia, or some of its subvarieties, will be curable by chemical techniques within twenty years. It therefore behooves those who wish to avoid the fate of railroad firemen to be sure that their vocational wagon is not hitched to a particular model for psychosis. If the current feverish interest in group interactions continues, the skillful group leader will not need to worry about a decrease in the number of psychotics needing new social learning experiences, for the demands of normal people for psychological services will exceed the supply. The nature of our present society seems to create a great need for more intensive interpersonal interactions, and psychologists will continue to play an important role in providing them until other societal institutions evolve to provide the needed services.

THE PRESENT AND THE FUTURE OF EMPIRICAL STUDIES

It is hard to deny that most psychological studies strike the nonspecialist as a crashing bore. Nevertheless, the small percentage of exciting findings are so rewarding that we have no need for any greater excitement in the future. For one thing, areas that were previously taboo have come under careful empirical examination—

sex and death, for example. Masters and Johnson (1970), as a result of their research on sex, report remarkable rates of cure for sexual incompatibility. The results on death are not yet as remarkable.

The old taboos are being replaced to some extent by a new one. It is now very difficult to do any research in which the subject is being deceived, threatened, or made to feel pain or discomfort. We are not speaking for or against this taboo, but simply pointing to its existence. It is institutionalized in the form of research review committees, which are generally required in any research involving government funding. We only wish that it were possible to apply the same high standards for treatment of the individual in every area of life, not just to the area of laboratory research with human subjects. We also suspect that our concern with the laboratory subject is increased by the discomfort engendered by the *outcomes* of some experiments in which the subjects were made to feel uncomfortable. For example, Milgram (1963), in his controversial experiments, found that subjects "administered pain" in experimental situations to an extent not previously expected. These results could be taken to bolster the assertion that our behavior is more under the control of situations and less under that of our own personalities than we like to think—or perhaps to bolster the assertion that we have greater innate tendencies toward aggression than we care to admit.

Excitement is also generated when glaring holes in the research picture can be filled in because technological advances are made. The increasing sophistication of electrophysiology, plus an enlarged conception of what stimulus properties can be manipulated, has made it possible to study the behavior of assemblies of neural cells. Examples include the classical studies of the frog's eye "talking" about flies to its brain, studies of the centers of a moth's brain that direct its flight relative to sounds (like bat cries), studies of the receptive fields of particular cells (and the kinds of stimuli the cells respond to, like movement to the left), and studies of the different potentials evoked in the human brain when stimuli are in and out of focus on the retina. Bentley (1971) has recently reported on the genetic control of the calling song of the cricket; the songs differ in precise ways which are easily monitored and recorded. Further, the motor activity involved in the calling song is generated by a small neuronal network, and might be studied by electrophysiological techniques. Biochemical work should also be possible with the same preparation. Other examples could be given, but these are enough to show that we now have something which we have had very little of in the past: a physiological psychology which is beginning to be able to give a detailed description of the relationship between the behavior of identifiable groups of cells and meaningful behaviors in the organism. In the past, there were studies of the behavior of single neurons and—separately—studies of behavior. The only exceptions were very gross observations, as of the effects of ablations or of the gross EEG taken while the subject was asleep or awake. There is a tremendous amount of gap-filling to be done before we really understand the relationship between the neural microcosm and the behavioral macrocosm, but a solid start has at last been made. The empirical observation of "nerve nets" has been made more exciting because they were an essential part of Hebb's (1949) theory, and their logical capabilities had been worked out by McCulloch and Pitts (1943). The future will see, in our opinion, a considerable upsurge of studies at this level.

Related studies which encourage the inference that there are preorganized nerve nets are those which show that maternal or mating behaviors can be emitted by naïve rats in the presence of appropriate stimuli, given the appropriate hormonal stimulation.

Sperry (1961) and all those who participated in, or followed up, his initial "split-brain" experimentation have also generated tremendous excitement. It is not just that the function of the corpus callosum in interhemispheric transfer is understood; it is the fact that the two separate hemispheres show so much independence that we are tempted to say that two separate "minds" share the same body. Such findings may in the future be integrated into personality theories, particularly self theories.

Another area of study which is finally offering the high adventure which it only promised for so long is that of animal communication, particularly that old popular-imagination grabber, the communication of animals with man. The songs of the humpback whale are now for sale, though we do not know what they are saying, and Premack (1970) has given us some of the sayings of the chimpanzee Sara, though she does not sing. Porpoises, too, have been under study, but the results are equivocal. These animal studies, like the studies with chess-playing computers, further justify the assumed kinship between man and other logical entities, both animate and inanimate.

Despite this work on animal language and a rapidly increasing number of publications on human language—encouraged by the argument between Skinner (1957b) and Chomsky (1959)—psychologists still do not possess any neat keys to the relationship between man and his language. Pavlov's "second signal system" has belatedly become a fashionable topic for conversation, but it seems to possess about the same amount of theoretical power as the psychological field. The psychological study of language is in its infancy, as far as any deep results are concerned. The next few decades should see this situation change markedly. It may even be, with great luck, that new and unsuspected ideas about consciousness and the nature of self will emerge from future studies of man's language—which either was created by man or created him, or both. Segal and Lachman (1972) believe that the problems of language have put the finishing touches on neobehaviorism, after information theory and the psychological use of finite mathematics had started the trend toward a more cognitive approach. The result, they say, has been that "... the structure which was S-R behaviorism has no properties left. It, in short, has vanished" (p. 53).

Zimbardo's book (1969) on motivation supports the point of view expressed by Segal and Lachman. His point of view is cognitive, does derive from the information-theory-computer simulation point of view, at least partly, and does oppose the neobehavioristic picture of man. However, Atkinson and Birch (1970) present an ingenious theory of motivation which, although it is explicitly *not* an

S-R theory, has obvious affinities with the theories of Guthrie and those who have modified his basic theory. Atkinson and Birch treat images as covert *responses*; perception, which may attain consciousness, is correlated with overt behavior but does not cause it. Both covert and overt behavior are related to the same internal and external instigators of behavior. This view keeps man under ultimate environmental control and is behavioristic in its basic features. Thus it seems to us that the disappearance of S-R behaviorism is only partial; the S-R part has disappeared more completely than the behavioristic part, and even that has survived in greatly modified form.

The discovery of the mode of action of the genetic material DNA kicked off an era of great hopefulness in the field of learning. The search for the mechanism of memory storage had been long and until then fruitless. Nature's usual parsimony encouraged experimenters in learning to believe that DNA, or its relative, RNA, might be the memory molecule as well as the genetic molecule. Encouraging results were easy to produce but hard to replicate. Although there is still controversy about the memory-transfer experiments, it is very difficult for critics to see why the experiments should succeed even if DNA or RNA *is* the memory molecule. There is a Nobel Prize in the wings for the person or persons who someday trace the chemical pathways of memory, but the road to that prize is not going to be an easy one to tread.

Perhaps one tool to unlocking the keys to the engram will prove to be the consolidation experiment. Science usually proceeds to find out how things work by keeping them from working, and the disruption of memory by shock or chemical is bound to tell us something about the nature of a process that can be disrupted by these means. And if the disruption is *prevented* by other chemicals, what can those be doing? It is a beautiful problem, and the means of attack on it are coming to hand.

The areas we have discussed so far in this epilogue have been developed largely by American psychologists. Fortunately, we have not had to furnish ourselves with all our own intellectual awakenings. The Europeans have been only too happy to help us. Our appendix on European psychology details this. Here we can at least mention three very important influences: Jean Piaget (1952) and his theory of intellectual development, the ethologists and their contribution from the study of animal behavior, and the existential philosophers, who have had a great influence on humanistic psychology in America.

Piaget has given psychology a start toward a descriptive developmental cognitive psychology. Since his approach is cognitive, Piaget put himself in unintentional league with computer theorists and other centralists. Although he is not a nativist, he is not an environmentalist either, and hence everyone initially sees him as the enemy, and later as a friend. Most of his studies can be criticized as classics of naturalistic nonrigor or lauded as examples of brilliant intuitive efforts guided but not dominated by a general theory of intellectual development.

The second contribution, ethological, has Lorenz (e.g., 1970) and Tinbergen (e.g., 1967) among its leading names, with Hinde (1970) currently the outstanding systematizer and synthesizer. These men have supported the use of naturalistic research in the most meaningful possible way: with *findings* from such research. They include many tremendously detailed descriptions of species-specific behaviors and the circumstances eliciting them. To American psychologists, it looked like the return of the repressed—the banished—instincts and constituted a severe shock to the prudery of our environmentalism.

The third development, existential, stemming from Heidegger (1962), Sartre (1956), and others, has coalesced with the new humanistic movement in America. Existentialism challenges determinism, and hence the foundations of a mechanistic human science. Further, it elevates the human consciousness to a position of dark and pessimistic dignity. Existentialism fits in well with much of the temper of these times, but not well with the traditional view of science. One of the more interesting questions to be lived out in the next twenty years or so will be how existentialism will affect the development of psychology as a science and profession.

THE PRESENT AND THE FUTURE: GENERAL SYSTEMATIC ISSUES

Much that is new and exciting in psychology is quite independent of the issues raised by the older systems. This was a major theme of our first edition, published in 1963. Now there seems to be some deceleration of the trend toward the growing use of models and the as-if thinking which they characterize. Turner (1971) argues that we need the guidance of reality to help us choose between alternative models; thus we need theories whose components really correspond to something. Estes, whom we have seen as one of the leading model-builders, has recently (1970) found it worthwhile to return to some of the older and grander theories to see whether or not they had anything to contribute to the understanding of mental retardation. Atkinson and Birch (1970) say things like "...we ... share an understanding of the need for theory that has the twin virtues of scope and precision" (p. vii), and "We have had to make what we considered best guesses at many points" (p. ix). Atkinson and Birch are sounding like Hull! It is our guess that there will be less concern with an extreme operationism in the future and correspondingly less exclusive concern with miniature systems. There will be more theoretical development from above. Part of the reason for this reversal of the trend of ten years ago is an increasing historical and philosophical sophistication among psychologists; we now recognize that science has never been exclusively inductive and that even our best efforts in that direction could never eliminate presuppositions anyway. So we may as well put our presuppositions on the table and get on with our business.

Although psychologists are not inclined to hew to the line of thought of a particular traditional school or system, there is some evidence, at least for one case, that there is a modern counterpart of a school. Krantz (1972) found some evidence that operant and nonoperant psychology are mutually isolated from each other. Other candidates for mutual isolation, for example the computer simulation group, have simply not been studied. It might be objected that none of these psychologists see themselves as members of schools or as advocates of a particular systematic position, but the members of the traditional schools were probably no different in this respect.

Regardless of whether or not there are still general systematic allegiances, it is clear that one issue around which a great deal of controversy swirls is the nativism-empiricism controversy. In fact, some of the developments of recent years might be titled the "rebirth of nativism." Ardrey's books (1961, 1966), for example, have popularized a nativistic interpretation of man's aggression and of his alleged tendency to defend territory. Ardrey believes that many of modern man's aggressive tendencies can be traced back to a meat-eating, weapon-using ancestor, Australopithecus. Desmond Morris (1968) then joined the same general position with his image of man as the naked ape. Even before he did, the battle was well joined; Ashley Montagu (1968) has been one of Ardrey's most vociferous opponents, and a reading of Montagu would suggest that the only reason for renewed interest in nativism is Ardrey's ability to turn a dramatic phrase. More recently, Tiger and Fox (1971) have added *The imperial animal* to the group of books which argues that man's capabilities can be best understood by relating them to his biological heritage.

We would suggest, however, that even a writer of Ardrey's skill needs some favorable facts with which to bolster his argument and that he would not be listened to unless the psychological climate in which his readers exist was to some extent favorable. We have already mentioned in passing the work of the ethologists, who have marshaled strong evidence for innate determination of species-specific behaviors. It may not be legitimate for Ardrey (or for Lorenz when *he* writes on aggression) to argue from animal to man, but there is good evidence on animals per se, although the animals must be selected carefully.

There are other pieces of nativistic evidence recently gathered which Ardrey does not, to our knowledge, use. T. G. R. Bower (1966) has found striking evidence that form constancy is innate in human infants. A circle seen at an angle is responded to as a circle, not an ellipse. The Gibsons (e.g., Gibson & Walk, 1960) and others have related evidence indicating that depth perception is innate in many species. Thus in the perceptual field, where the nativism-empiricism argument has always been active, there is a swing toward the nativistic side.

Nativism's ultimate insult, however, is its recent invasion of environmentalism's old stronghold, the field of learning. Is nothing sacred? Seligman (1970) has suggested that nativistic factors underlie the relative associability of various stimulus-response combinations. Some combinations are *prepared* to be associated, and some are *contraprepared*. Rozin and Kalat (1971) play a similar refrain in their article "Specific hungers and poison avoidance as adaptive specializations of learning." Both lean heavily on the work of Garcia and his colleagues (for example, Garcia, McGowan, & Green, in press), who have shown repeatedly that some stimulus-response combinations are easy to associate, or can be associated despite extremely long S-R delays, and that other combinations are more difficult to associate, or cannot be associated over long delays. It is easy to see that the work of the Brelands, cited earlier, and of the ethologists, particularly on imprinting, are very relevant to the nativistic contribution to learning.

There is also some motivation which might lead us to find a nativistic position more comfortable than it used to be. For one thing, we now know something of how DNA codes genetic information. It is therefore possible to hope that one need not always be stuck with his genetic errors or imperfections; perhaps someday, if we do not like the codes we inherit, we can have them changed and become taller or slimmer or smarter. A belief in nativism has always been a comfort for conservatives, and our temper in this country may be now turning that way.

The temper of social science is far from conservative, however, particularly with respect to racial issues. If anyone dares to suggest that there may be racial factors related to intelligence, he seems destined to suffer abuse. Jensen (1969) has defended himself against those who attacked him severely for that very suggestion. Although there may well be valid scientific reasons for doubting any conclusion, the reasons for ignoring an area of study are seldom scientific. The present authors feel uncomfortable when social, cultural taboos prevent the study of sensitive issues. We could find ourselves being severely limited in our approach to psychology (as the Russians have been, when they have had to be very careful not to "deviate" from Pavlov or when they have had to accept the belief in the heritability of acquired characteristics).

Ghiselin (1972), in a review of a book by John S. Haller, Jr., repeats Haller's finding that no scientist during the 1880s and 1890s in the United States challenged the view that blacks were inferior. The question was the same as it is today, but the "answer" was the opposite. Today's liberals would revere a scientist who, in that day, challenged the consensus; but Jensen, who now at least raises questions about the consensus position, receives no such congratulations.

We do not mean to suggest that psychology is about to return to a naive instinct theory or to an extreme nativism. The general point that nature and nurture interact is too well understood for that to happen. What we are suggesting is that psychologists are again recognizing the importance of genotype; it is no longer only Tryon (1940), with his maze-bright rats, or Scott and Fuller (1965), with their variegated dogs, who pay attention to these matters. The study of the interrelationships of behavior and genetics is in full swing and is completely accepted as a field of study.

The nativism-empiricism issue is certainly not the only one being reevaluated, although its rethinking seems at the moment most dramatic. We certainly should note the renewed emphasis on the study of cognitive processes, and even some gain in respectability for the study of consciousness. When Kimble, long apparently an arch-behaviorist, writes an article on volition (1970) and Ryan (1970) writes a book on an intentional analysis of motives, it is certainly growing clear that psychology is loosening up its conceptual proscriptions.

The most exciting systematic development, however, and one which is in some ways disturbing, is the protracted critical examination of the very foundation of science. On the one hand, there are several scholars who are suggesting that the older picture of orderly and logical scientific progress was highly misleading; we have already cited Kuhn (1962; 1970) early in this book for his belief that progress in science must sometimes be cataclysmic. The old must be torn down and replaced with the new paradigm. Polanyi (1958) is a philosopher who believes that much of our knowledge is held and obtained on a far less logical basis than we would like to believe. In Chapter 1 we noted that Feyerabend is arguing for an anarchistic theory of knowledge, and he seems to be quite serious about it. He says ". . . I believe that a reform of the sciences that makes it more anarchistic and more subjective (in Kierkegaard's sense) is therefore urgently needed." All these men put a kind of subjectivity at the very base of the scientific edifice. Rosenthal (1966) adds experimental evidence of this subjectivity in the very generation of our data. Yet these four critics and their sympathizers are essentially friendly to science and probably accept the desirability of a somewhat objective and analytic approach. They point out errors and misconceptions so that they can be taken into account in the scientific process and so that science can thereby be improved.

Though these men are friends, we would be seriously self-deluding if we denied the presence of others less friendly. There are some psychologists who now seem to feel that science as we have understood the term in the past is lacking in a very fundamental way which does not admit of repair. There is therefore a developing schism within the ranks of psychologists, one which no longer involves the relatively trivial issue of how to optimize the simultaneous advance of the science and the profession of psychology. The schism within psychology reflects the larger schism between science and some parts of our society. So far, the number of psychologists on the ascientific or antiscientific side of the split is fairly small. Nevertheless, psychology *is splitting;* there are already organizations for those who regard the American Psychological Association as too softheaded (for example, the Psychonomic Society) and for those who regard it as too hardheaded (for example, the Society for Humanistic Psychology). We have always doubted that the formation of such groups would impede the progress of psychology as a science; on the contrary, they probably help to generate excitement and motivation for our tasks. The lesson of history is that solid progress comes as the products of groups which were at first regarded as extreme are incorporated into the mainstream.

We would be alarmed if large inroads were made by any essentially antiscientific group. There is currently a great deal of antiscientific sentiment in our general cultural milieu. However, it is still sentiment in search of a paradigm. For a time, it seemed to us nip and tuck whether science in general and psychology in particular were going to incorporate new points of view before a more attractive antiscientific paradigm was found. Now, Fischer (1971) has offered a "cartography" of states of consciousness; the new mapping conjoins concepts which may well interest the softheads with concepts that may satisfy the hardheads. At nearly the same time, Blackburn (1971) pointed to the sensuous intellectual complementarity which he thought science must recognize if it is to survive in the modern world. Blackburn, like Fischer, unites some interests from the counterculture with some interests of traditional science. With innovators like these men, and with the most prestigious general journal of science willing to publish their speculations, we now think that the institution of science is flexible enough to survive in our changing times. We doubt that a competitive philosophical position opposed to science is going to gain a large number of adherents in the next few decades—but finding out is going to be part of the fascination for psychologists in the near future.

REFERENCES

Ach, N. *Über den Willensakt und des Temperament: Ein experimentelle Untersuchung*. Leipzig: Quelle & Meyer, 1910.

Achinstein, P. *Concepts of science*. Baltimore: Johns Hopkins Press, 1968.

Adelson, J. Personality. *Annual Review of Psychology*, 1969, **20**, 217-252.

Allport, F. H. *Social psychology*. Boston: Houghton Mifflin, 1924.

Allport, F. H. *Theories of perception and the concepts of structure*. New York: Wiley, 1955.

Allport, G. W. *Personality: A psychological interpretation*. New York: Holt, 1937.

Allport, G. W. *The individual and his religion*. New York: Macmillan, 1950. (a)

Allport, G. W. *The nature of personality: Selected papers*. Reading, Mass.: Addison-Wesley, 1950. (b)

Allport, G. W. *Becoming: Basic considerations for a psychology of personality*. New Haven, Conn.: Yale University Press, 1955.

Allport, G. W. *Personality and social encounter: Selected essays*. Boston: Beacon Press, 1960.

Allport, G. W. *Pattern and growth in personality*. New York: Holt, 1961.

Allport, G. W. *Letters from Jenny*. New York: Harcourt, Brace & World, 1965.

Allport, G. W. *The person in psychology: Selected essays*. Boston: Beacon Press, 1968.

Allport, G. W., & Allport, F. H. *A-S reaction study*. Boston: Houghton Mifflin, 1928.

Allport, G. W., & Cantril, H. *The psychology of radio*. New York: Harper, 1935.

Allport, G. W., & Vernon, P. E. *A study of values*. Boston: Houghton Mifflin, 1931.

Allport, G. W., & Vernon, P. E. *Studies in expressive movement*. New York: Macmillan, 1933.

Allport, G. W., & Vernon, P. E. *A study of values*. (Rev. ed.) Boston: Houghton Mifflin, 1951.

Alper, T. G. Memory for completed and incompleted tasks as a function of personality: Correlation between experimental and personality data. *Journal of Personality*, 1948, **17**, 104-137.

American Psychologist, 1958, **13**, 735.

Ammons, R. B. Psychology of the scientist. II. Clark L. Hull and his "idea books." *Perceptual and Motor Skills*, 1962, **15**, 800-802.

Anastasi, A. *Differential psychology*. (3rd ed.) New York: Macmillan, 1958.

Anderson, R. J. Attribution of quotations from Wundt. *American Psychologist*, 1971, **26**, 590-593.

Angell, J. R. The relations of structural and functional psychology to philosophy. *Philosophical Review,* 1903, **12**, 243-271.

Angell, J. R. *Psychology: An introductory study of the structure and function of human consciousness.* New York: Holt, 1904.

Angell, J. R. The province of functional psychology. *Psychological Review,* 1907, **14**, 61-91.

Angell, J. R. Behavior as a category of psychology. *Psychological Review,* 1913, **20**, 255-270.

Angell, J. R., & Moore, A. W. Reaction time: A study in attention and habit. *Psychological Review,* 1896, **3**, 245-258.

Arbib, M. *Brains, machines, and mathematics.* New York: McGraw-Hill, 1964.

Ardrey, R. *African genesis.* New York: Atheneum, 1961.

Ardrey, R. *The territorial imperative.* New York: Atheneum, 1966.

Asch, S. E., Hay, J., & Diamond, R. M. Perceptual organization in serial rote-learning. *American Journal of Psychology,* 1960, **73**, 177-198.

Asch, S. E., & Lindner, M. A note on "strength of association." *Journal of Psychology,* 1963, **55**, 199-209.

Ashton, M. An ecological study of the stream of behavior. Master's thesis, University of Kansas, 1964.

Atkinson, J. W., & Birch, D. *The dynamics of action.* New York: Wiley, 1970.

Atkinson, R. C. *Studies in mathematical psychology.* Stanford, Calif.: Stanford University Press, 1964.

Attneave, F. Some informational aspects of visual perception. *Psychological Review,* 1954, **61**, 183-193.

Attneave, F. *Applications of information theory to psychology: A summary of basic concepts, methods, and results.* New York: Holt, 1959.

Augenstine, L. G. *Human performance in information transmission. VI. Evidence of periodicity in information processing.* Report R-75, University of Illinois, Control Systems Laboratory, 1958.

Bain, A. *The senses and the intellect.* London: Parker, 1855 (Republished: 1886.)

Bain, A. *The emotions and the will.* London: Parker, 1859.

Bakan, D. *Sigmund Freud and the Jewish mystical tradition.* Princeton, N.J.: Van Nostrand, 1958.

Bakan, D. Is phrenology foolish? *Psychology Today,* 1968, **1**, 44-51.

Banks, W. Signal detection theory and human memory. *Psychological Bulletin,* 1970, **74**, 81-99.

Barker, R. G. *Ecological psychology.* Stanford, Calif.: Stanford University Press, 1968.

Barker, R. G., Dembo, T., & Lewin, K. Frustration and regression: A study of young children. *University of Iowa Studies in Child Welfare,* 1941, **18**, 1.

Barker, R. G., & Gump, P. V. *Big school, small school.* Stanford, Calif.: Stanford University Press, 1964.

Beach, F. A., Hebb, D. O., Morgan, C. T., & Nissen, H. W. (Eds.) *The neuropsychology of Lashley: Selected papers of K. S. Lashley.* New York: McGraw-Hill, 1960.

Beck, S. J. The science of personality: Nomothetic or idiographic? *Psychological Review,* 1953, **60**, 353-359.

Becker, R. J. Outstanding contributors to psychology. *American Psychologist*, 1959, **14**, 297-298.

Bekhterev, V. M. *Objektive Psychologie: Oder Psychoreflexologie, die Lehre von den Assoziationsreflexen.* (Trans. from the original 1910 Russian ed.) (Republished: London, Jarrolds Publishers, 1933.)

Bellak, L., & Smith, M. B. An experimental exploration of the psychoanalytic process. *Psychoanalytic Quarterly*, 1956, **25**, 385-414.

Bem, D. J., & Bem, S. L. Nativism revisited: Review of E. H. Lenneberg's *Biological foundation of language. Journal of Experimental Psychology*, 1968, **11**, 497-501.

Benjamin, A. C. *Operationism.* Springfield, Ill.: Charles C Thomas, 1955.

Benjamin, A. C. *Science, technology, and human values.* Columbia: University of Missouri Press, 1965.

Bentley, D. R. Genetic control of an insect neuronal network. *Science,* 1971, **174**, 1139-1141.

Bergmann, G. The contribution of John B. Watson. *Psychological Review*, 1956, **63**, 265-276.

Bergmann, G. *Philosophy of science.* Madison: University of Wisconsin Press, 1957.

Bergmann, G., & Spence, K. W. The logic of psychophysical measurement. *Psychological Review*, 1944, **51**, 1-24. (Also in M. H. Marx [Ed.], *Psychological theory: Contemporary readings.* New York: Macmillan, 1951. Pp. 256-276.)

Berkeley, G. *An essay toward a new theory of vision.* Dublin: Jeremy Pepyat, 1709.

Berkeley, G. *Principles of human knowledge.* Oxford: Oxford University Press, 1710.

Berkeley, G. Theory of vision vindicated. In A. A. Luce & T. E. Jessop (Eds.), *Works.* Vol. 1. New York: Nelson, 1948. Pp. 251-279.

Berleyne, D. E. *Conflict, arousal, and curiosity.* New York: McGraw-Hill, 1960.

Beveridge, W. I. B. *The art of scientific investigation.* New York: Vintage Books, 1957.

Birdsall, T. An application of game theory to signal detectability. Technical Report 20, Electronic Defense Group, University of Michigan, 1953.

Blackburn, T. R. Sensuous-intellectual complementarity in science. *Science,* 1971, **172**, 1003-1007.

Blodgett, H. C. The effects of the introduction of reward upon the maze performance of rats. *University of California Publications in Psychology,* 1929, **4**, 113-134.

Boole, G. *An investigation of the laws of thought.* New York: Dover, 1854.

Boring, E. G. *The physical dimensions of consciousness.* New York: Appleton-Century-Crofts, 1933.

Boring, E. G. A psychological function is the relation of successive differentiations of events in the organism. *Psychological Review*, 1937, **44**, 445-461.

Boring, E. G. Mind and mechanism. *American Journal of Psychology,* 1946, **59**, 173-192.

Boring, E. G. *A history of experimental psychology.* New York: Appleton-Century-Crofts, 1950.

Boring, E. G. Vol. I, Murchison, C. (1930) Vol. II, Murchison, C. (1932) Vol. III,

Murchison, C. (1961) Vol. IV, Boring, E. G.; Langfeld, H. S.; Wernor, H.; & Yerkes, R. M. Vol. V, Boring, E. G., & Lindzey, G. (Eds.) *A history of psychology in autobiography.* Worcester, Mass.: Clark University Press, 1952.

Boring, E. G. A history of introspection. *Psychological Bulletin*, 1953, **50**, 169-187.

Boring, E. G. When is human behavior motivated? *Scientific Monthly*, 1957, **84**, 189-196.

Boring, E. G. Lashley and cortical integration. In F. A. Beach et al. (Eds.), *The neuropsychology of Lashley.* New York: McGraw-Hill, 1960. Pp. xi-xvi.

Boring, E. G. Cognitive dissonance: Its use in science. *Science*, 1964, **145**, 680-685.

Boring, E. G., & Lindzey, G. (Eds.) *A history of psychology in autobiography.* New York: Appleton-Century-Crofts, 1967.

Bower, T. G. R. The visual world of infants. *Scientific American*, 1966, **215**, 80-92.

Box, G. E. P. Non-normality and tests on variance. *Biometrika*, 1953, **40**, 318-335.

Bradford, L. P., Gibb, J. R., & Benne, K. D. *T-group theory and laboratory method: Innovation in re-education.* New York: Wiley, 1964.

Braithwaite, R. B. *Scientific explanation.* London: Cambridge, 1955.

Breland, K., & Breland, Marion. A field of applied animal psychology. *American Psychologist*, 1951, **6**, 202-204.

Breland, K., & Breland, Marion. The misbehavior of organisms. *American Psychologist*, 1961, **16**, 681-684.

Breland, K., & Breland, Marion. *Animal behavior.* New York: Macmillan, 1966.

Brentano, F. *Psychologie von empirischen Standpunkte.* Leipzig: Meiner, 1874, and Heiner, 1955, New ed.

Breuer, J., & Freud, S. *Studien über Hysterie.* Vienna: Franz Deuticke, 1895.

Bridges, Katherine M. B. Emotional development in early infancy. *Child Development*, 1932, **3**, 324-341.

Bridgman, P. W. *The logic of modern physics.* New York: Macmillan, 1927.

Bridgman, P. W. *The nature of some of our physical concepts.* New York: Philosophical Library, 1952.

Bridgman, P. W. *The way things are.* Cambridge, Mass.: Harvard University Press, 1959.

Bronk, D. W. The role of scientists in the furtherance of science, *Science*, 1954, **119**, 223-227.

Brown, J. F. On the use of mathematics in psychological theory. *Psychometrika*, 1936, **1**, 7-15; 77-90. Also in M. H. Marx (Ed.), *Psychological theory: Contemporary readings.* New York: Macmillan, 1951. Pp. 233-256.

Brown, J. F., & Voth, A. C. The path of seen movement as a function of the vector-field. *American Journal of Psychology*, 1937, **49**, 543-563.

Brown, P. L., & Jenkins, H. M. Auto-shaping of the pigeon's key-peck. *Journal of the Experimental Analysis of Behavior*, 1968, **11**, 1-8.

Brožek, J. Current status of psychology in the U.S.S.R. *Annual Review of Psychology*, 1962, **13**, 515-566.

Bruner, J. S., Brunswik, E., Festinger, L., Heider, F., Muenzinger, K. F., Osgood, C. E., and Rapaport, D. *Contemporary approaches to cognition: A symposium held at the University of Colorado.* Cambridge, Mass.: Harvard University Press, 1957.

Brunswik, E. *Wahrnehmung und Gegenstandswelt.* Vienna: Franz Deuticke, 1934.

Brunswik. E. The conceptual focus of some psychological systems. *Journal of Unified Science*, 1939, **8**, 36-49. Reprinted in M. H. Marx (Ed.), *Psychological theory: Contemporary readings*. New York: Macmillan, 1951. Pp. 131-143. (a)

Brunswik, E. Probability as a determiner of rat behavior. *Journal of Experimental Psychology*, 1939, **25**, 175-197. (b)

Brunswik, E. Organismic achievement and environmental probability. *Psychological Review*, 1943, **50**, 255-272.

Brunswik, E. Discussion: Remarks on functionalism in perception. *Journal of Personality*, 1949, **18**, 56-65.

Brunswik, E. The conceptual framework of psychology. *International Encyclopedia of Unified Science*, 1952, **1**, No. 10. Pp. 1-102.

Brunswik, E., & Kamiya, J. Ecological cue-validity of "proximity" and of other gestalt factors. *American Journal of Psychology*, 1953, **66**, 20-32.

Brunswik, E. Representative design and probabilistic theory in a functional psychology. *Psychological Review*, 1955, **62**, 193-217. (a)

Brunswik, E. In defense of probabilistic functionalism: A reply. *Psychological Review*, 1955, **62**, 236-242. (b)

Brunswik, E. *Perception and the representative design of psychological experiments*. Berkeley: University of California Press, 1956.

Buckley, W. (Ed.) *Modern systems research for the behavioral scientist: A sourcebook*. Chicago: Aldine, 1968.

Burke, C. J. Measurement scales and statistical models. In M. H. Marx (Ed.), *Theories in contemporary psychology*. New York: Macmillan, 1963. Pp. 147-160.

Burnham, J. C. On the origins of behaviorism. *Journal of the History of the Behavioral Sciences*, 1968, **4**, 143-151.

Burt, C. L. *The factors of the mind*. New York: Macmillan, 1941.

Bush, R. R., & Mosteller, F. A mathematical model for simple learning. *Psychological Review*, 1951, **58**, 313-323. (a)

Bush, R. R., & Mosteller, F. A model for stimulus generalization and discrimination. *Psychological Review*, 1951, **58**, 413-423. (b)

Bush, R. R., & Mosteller, F. *Stochastic models for learning*. New York: Wiley, 1955.

Butler, J. M., & Haigh, G. V. Changes in the relation between self-concepts and ideal concepts consequent upon client-centered counseling. In C. R. Rogers & Rosalind F. Dymond (Eds.), *Psychotherapy and personality change: Coordinated studies in the client-centered approach*. Chicago: University of Chicago Press, 1954. Pp. 55-76.

Butterfield, H. *The origins of modern science: 1300-1800*. (Rev. ed.) New York: Macmillan, 1957.

Cabanis, P. J. *Rapports du physique et du moral de l'homme*. Paris: Crapart, Caille et Ravier, 1805.

Capretta, P. J. *A history of psychology in outline*. New York: Dell, 1967.

Carr, H. A. *Psychology: A study of mental activity*. New York: Longmans, 1925.

Carr, H. A. Teaching and learning. *Journal of Genetic Psychology*, 1930, **37**, 189-219.

Carr, H. A. The question for constants. *Psychological Review*, 1933, **40**, 514-532.

Carterette, E. C., & Cole, M. Repetition and confirmation of messages received by ear and by eye. Technical Report No. 3, University of California at Los Angeles, Psychology Department, 1959.

Carterette, E. C., & Cole, M. Comparison of the receiver-operating characteristics for messages received by ear and eye. *Journal of the Acoustical Society of America*, 1962, **34**, 172-178.

Cartwright, D. Lewinian theory as a contemporary systematic framework. In S. Koch (Ed.), *Psychology: A study of a science.* Vol. 2. *General systematic formulations, learning and special processes.* New York: McGraw-Hill, 1958. Pp. 7-91.

Cattell, R. B. *A guide to mental testing.* London: University of London Press, 1936.

Cattell, R. B. *The culture free test of intelligence.* Champaign, Ill.: Institute of Personality and Ability Testing, 1944.

Cattell, R. B. *Description and measurement of personality.* New York: Harcourt, Brace & World, 1946.

Cattell, R. B. *A guide to mental testing.* (Rev. ed.) London: University of London Press, 1948.

Cattell, R. B. The dimensions of culture patterns by factorization of national character. *Journal of Abnormal and Social Psychology*, 1949, **44**, 443-469.

Cattell, R. B. *Personality: A systematic theoretical and factual study.* New York: McGraw-Hill, 1950.

Cattell, R. B. *Factor analysis: An introduction and manual for psychologist and social scientist.* New York: Harper & Row, 1952.

Cattell, R. B. *The O-A personality test battery.* Champaign, Ill.: Institute of Personality and Ability Testing, 1954.

Cattell, R. B. *Personality and motivation structure and measurement.* New York: Harcourt, Brace & World, 1957.

Cattell, R. B. Personality theory growing from multivariate quantitative research. In S. Koch (Ed.), *Psychology: A study of a science.* Vol. 3. *Formulations of the person and the social context.* New York: McGraw-Hill, 1959. Pp. 257-327.

Cattell, R. B. (Ed.) *Handbook of multivariate experimental psychology.* Chicago: Rand McNally, 1966.

Cattell, R. B. (Ed.) *Handbook of modern personality theory.* Chicago: Aldine, 1970.

Cattell, R. B., Blewett, D. R., & Beloff, J. R. The inheritance of personality. *American Journal of Human Genetics*, 1955, **7**, 122-146.

Cattell, R. B., & Butcher, H. J. *The prediction of achievement and creativity.* Indianapolis: Bobbs-Merrill, 1968.

Cattell, R. B., Saunders, D. R., & Stice, G. F. *The 16 personality factor questionnaire.* Champaign, Ill.: Institute of Personality and Ability Testing, 1950.

Cattell, R. B., & Warburton, F. W. *Objective personality and motivation tests.* Urbana: University of Illinois Press, 1967.

Cattell, R. B., & Wispe, L. G. The dimension of syntality in small groups. *Journal of Social Psychology*, 1948, **28**, 57-78.

Caws, P. *The philosophy of science.* Princeton, N.J.: Van Nostrand, 1965.

Child, I. L. The relation of somatotype of self-ratings on Sheldon's temperament traits. *Journal of Personality*, 1950, **18**, 440-453.

Chomsky, N. Review of *Verbal behavior* by B. F. Skinner. *Language*, 1959, **35**, 26-58.

Coan, R. W. Dimensions of psychological theory. *American Psychologist*, 1968, **23**, 715-722.

Cobb, S. A. Salute from neurologists. In F. A. Beach, D. O. Hebb, C. T. Morgan, & H. W. Nissen (Eds.), *The Neuropsychology of Lashley: Selected papers of K. S. Lashley*. New York: McGraw-Hill, 1960. Pp. xvii-xx.

Cohen, M. R., & Nagel, E. *Introduction to logic and scientific method*. New York: Harcourt, Brace, 1934.

Comte, A. *The positive philosophy*. (Trans. by H. Martin) London: G. Bell, 1896 (1824).

Conant, J. B. *On understanding science: A historical approach*. New Haven, Conn.: Yale University Press, 1947.

Conant, J. B. *Harvard case histories in experimental science*. Cambridge, Mass.: Harvard University Press, 1957.

Cook, J. O. "Superstition" in the Skinnerian. *American Psychologist*, 1963, **18**, 516-518.

Coombs, C. H. *A theory of data*. New York: Wiley, 1964.

Coombs, C. H., Dawes, R. M., & Tversky, A. *Mathematical psychology: An elementary introduction*. Englewood Cliffs, N.J.: Prentice-Hall, 1970.

Cotton, J. W. On making predictions from Hill's theory. *Psychological Review*, 1955, **62**, 303-314.

Crannell, C. W., Wolfgang Köhler. *Journal of the History of the Behavioral Sciences*, 1970, **6**, 267-268.

Dahlstrom, W. G. Personality. *Annual Review of Psychology*, 1970, **21**, 1-48.

Dallenbach, K. M. Phrenology versus psychoanalysis. *American Journal of Psychology*, 1955, **68**(4), 511-525.

Danto, A., & Morgenbesser, S. (Eds.) *Philosophy of science: A reader*. New York: Meridian Books, 1960.

Darwin, C. *Expression of emotions in man and animals*. (2nd ed.) London: J. Murray, 1872.

Darwin, C. *Origin of species*. (2nd ed.) London: Collier, 1909.

David, H. P., & Brengelmann, J. C. (Eds.) *Perspectives in personality research*. New York: Springer, 1960.

David, H. P., & von Bracken, H. (Eds.) *Perspectives in personality theory*. New York: Basic Books, 1957.

Davis, R. C. Physical psychology. *Psychological Review*, 1953, **60**, 7-14.

Dennis, W. (Ed.) *Readings in the history of psychology*. New York: Appleton-Century-Crofts, 1948.

Deutsch, K. W., Platt, J., & Senghass, D. Conditions favoring major advances in social science. *Science*, 1971, **171**, 450-459.

Deutsch, M. Field theory in social psychology. In G. Lindzey (Ed.), *Handbook of social psychology*. Reading, Mass.: Addison-Wesley, 1954. Pp. 181-222.

Dewey, J. *Psychology*. New York: Harper, 1886.

Dewey, J. The reflex arc concept in psychology. *Psychological Review*, 1896, **3**, 357-370.

Dewey, J. Psychology and social practice. *Psychological Review*, 1900, **2**, 105-124.

Dewey, J. *How we think*. Boston: Heath, 1910.

Diserens, C. M. Psychological objectivism. *Psychological Review,* 1925, **32,** 121-152.

Dittman, A. J. Psychotherapeutic processes. *Annual Review of Psychology,* 1966, **17,** 57-78.

Dollard, J. *Caste and class in a Southern town.* New Haven, Conn.: Yale University Press, 1937.

Dollard, J. *Fear in battle.* New Haven, Conn.: Yale University Press, 1943.

Dollard, J., Doob, L. W., Miller, N. E., Mowrer, O. H., & Sears, R. R. *Frustration and aggression.* New Haven, Conn.: Yale University Press, 1939.

Dollard, J., & Miller, N. E. *Personality and psychotherapy: An analysis in terms of learning, thinking, and culture.* New York: McGraw-Hill, 1950.

Dorfman, D. D., & Alf, E., Jr. Maximum likelihood estimation of parameters of signal-detection theory: A direct solution. *Psychometrika,* 1968, **33,** 117-124.

Dorfman, D. D., & Alf, E., Jr. Maximum-likelihood estimation of parameters of signal-detection theory and determination of confidence intervals-rating method data. *Journal of Mathematical Psychology,* 1969, **6,** 487-496.

Driesch, H. A. *The problem of individuality.* (A course of four lectures delivered before the University of London in 1913 by H. Driesch) London: Macmillan, 1914.

Duncker, K. On problem solving. (Trans. by L. S. Lews from the original 1935 ed.) *Psychological Monographs,* 1945, **58**(270).

Dunham, P. J. Punishment: Method and theory. *Psychological Review,* 1971, **78,** 58-70.

Ebbinghaus, H. *Uber das Gedachtnis,* 1885. (Reprinted as *Memory.* [Trans. by H. A. Ruger & C. E. Busenius.] New York: Teachers College, 1913.)

Edwards, D. D., West, J. R., & Jackson, V. The role of contingencies in the control of behavior. *Psychonomic Science,* 1968, **10,** 39-40.

Egan, J. P. *Recognition memory and the operating characteristic.* Technical Report No. AFCRC-TN-58-51, AD-152650, Indiana Univeristy, Hearing and Communication Laboratory, 1958.

Ellenberger, H. Fechern and Freud. *Bulletin of the Menninger Clinic,* 1956, **20,** 201-214.

Ellis, W. D. *A source book of Gestalt psychology.* New York: Harcourt, Brace & World, 1938.

English, H. T., & English, A. C. *A comprehensive dictionary of psychological and psychoanalytical terms.* New York: McKay, 1958.

Escalona, S. K. The influence of topological and vector psychology upon current research in child development: An addendum. In L. Carmichael (Ed.), *Manual of child psychology.* (2nd ed.) New York: Wiley, 1954. Pp. 971-983.

Estes, W. K. Toward a statistical theory of learning. *Psychological Review,* 1950, **57,** 94-107.

Estes, W. K. Models for learning theory. *Symposium on psychology of learning basic to military training problems.* Washington, D.C.: Committee on Human Resources, Research and Development Board, 1953, 21-38.

Estes, W. K. Individual behavior in uncertain situations: An interpretation in terms of statistical association theory. In R. M. Thrall, C. H. Coombs, & R. L. Davis (Eds.), *Decision processes.* New York: Wiley, 1954. Pp. 127-137. (a)

Estes, W. K. Kurt Lewin. In W. K. Estes et al., *Modern learning theory.* New York: Appleton-Century-Crofts, 1954. Pp. 317-344. (b)

Estes, W. K. Stimulus-response theory of drive. In M. R. Jones (Ed.), *Nebraska symposium on motivation.* Vol. 6. Lincoln: University of Nebraska Press, 1958.

Estes, W. K. Component and pattern models with Markovian interpretations. In R. R. Bush & W. K. Estes (Eds.), *Studies in mathematical learning theory.* Stanford, Calif.: Stanford University Press, 1959. Pp. 9-52. (a)

Estes, W. K. The statistical approach to learning theory. In S. Koch (Ed.), *Psychology: A study of a science.* Vol. 2. *General systematic formulations, learning and special processes.* New York: McGraw-Hill, 1959. Pp. 380-491. (b)

Estes, W. K. Learning theory and the new "mental chemistry." *Psychological Review,* 1960, **67**, 207-223.

Estes, W. K. Growth and function of mathematical models for learning. In R. A. Patton (Ed.), *Current trends in psychological theory.* Pittsburgh: University of Pittsburgh Press, 1961. Pp. 134-151. (Also reprinted in M. H. Marx [Ed.], *Theories in contemporary psychology.* New York: Macmillan, 1963. Pp. 132-146.)

Estes, W. K. *Learning theory and mental development.* New York: Academic Press, 1970.

Estes, W. K., & Burke, C. J. A theory of stimulus variability in learning. *Psychological Review,* 1953, **60**, 276-286.

Estes, W. K., Hopkins, B. L., & Crothers, E. J. All-or-none and conservation effects in the learning and retention of paired associates. *Psychological Review,* 1960, **60**, 329-339.

Estes, W. K., Koch, S., MacCorquodale, K., Meehl, P. E., Mueller, C. G., Jr., Schoenfeld, W. N., & Verplanck, W. S. *Modern learning theory.* New York: Appleton-Century-Crofts, 1954.

Evans, R. I. *B. F. Skinner: The man and his ideas.* New York: Dutton, 1968.

Eysenck, H. J. *Dimensions of personality.* London: Routledge, 1947.

Eysenck, H. J. Criterion analysis: An application of the hypothetico-deductive method of factor analysis. *Psychological Review,* 1950, **57**, 38-53.

Eysenck, H. J. The effects of psychotherapy. *Journal of Consulting Psychology,* 1952, **16**, 319-324. (a)

Eysenck, H. J. *The scientific study of personality.* London: Routledge, 1952. (b)

Eysenck, H. J. *The structure of human personality.* New York: Wiley, 1953. (a)

Eysenck, H. J. *Uses and abuses of psychology.* Baltimore: Penguin, 1953. (b)

Eysenck, H. J. *The psychology of politics.* London: Routledge, 1954.

Eysenck, H. J. *The dynamics of anxiety and hysteria: An experimental application of modern learning theory to psychiatry.* New York: Praeger, 1957.

Eysenck, H. J. (Ed.) *Handbook of abnormal psychology.* New York: Basic Books, 1961.

Eysenck, H. J., & Rachman, S. *The causes and cures of neurosis.* San Diego: Knapp, 1965.

Ezriel, H. The scientific testing of psychoanalytic findings and theory. *British Journal of Medical Psychology,* 1951, **24**, 26-29.

Falk, J. L. Issues distinguishing idiographic from nomothetic approaches to personality theory. *Psychological Review,* 1956, **63**, 53-62.

Farrell, B. A. The scientific testing of psychoanalytic findings and theory. *British Journal of Medical Psychology*, 1951, **24**, 35-41.

Fawl, C. L. Disturbances experienced by children in their natural habitats. In R. G. Barker (Ed.), *The stream of behavior.* New York: Appleton-Century-Crofts, 1963. Pp. 99-126.

Fechner, G. T. *Elemente der Psychophysik.* Leipzig: Breitkopf & Härtel, 1860.

Fechner, G. T. *Elements of psychophysics.* Vol. 1. Trans. by H. E. Adler, D. H. Howes, & E. O. Boring (Eds.) New York: Holt, Rinehart & Winston, 1966.

Feigl, H. The "orthodox" view of theories: Remarks in defense as well as critique. In M. Radner & S. Winokur (Eds.), *Analyses of theories and methods of physics and psychology.* Minneapolis: University of Minnesota Press, 1970.

Feigl, H., & Brodbeck, M. (Eds.) *Readings in the philosophy of science.* New York: Appleton-Century-Crofts, 1953.

Feigl, H., & Maxwell, G. (Eds.) *Current issues in the philosophy of science.* New York: Holt, 1961.

Feigl, H., & Scriven, M. (Eds.) *Minnesota studies in the philosophy of science.* Vol. 1. Minneapolis: University of Minnesota Press, 1956.

Feigl, H., Scriven, M., & Maxwell, G. (Eds.) *Minnesota studies in the philosophy of science.* Vol. 2. Minneapolis: University of Minnesota Press, 1958.

Feigl, H., & Sellars, W. (Eds.) *Readings in philosophical analysis.* New York: Appleton-Century-Crofts, 1949.

Felsinger, J. M., Gladstone, A. I., Yamaguchi, H. C., & Hull, C. L. Reaction latency (sta) as a function of the number of reinforcements (N). *Journal of Experimental Psychology*, 1947, **37**, 214-228.

Fenichel, O. *The psychoanalytic theory of neurosis.* New York: Norton, 1945.

Ferenczi, S., & Rank, O. *The development of psychoanalysis.* (Trans. by Caroline Newton) New York: Nervous and Mental Disease Publishing, 1925.

Ferster, C. B., & Skinner, B. F. *Schedules of reinforcement.* New York: Appleton-Century-Crofts, 1957.

Festinger, L. *A theory of cognitive dissonance.* New York: Harper & Row, 1957.

Feyerabend, P. K. Against method: Outline of an anarchistic theory of knowledge. In M. Radner & S. Winokur (Eds.), *Analyses of theories and methods of physics and psychology.* Minneapolis: University of Minnesota Press, 1970. Pp. 17-130.

Fischer, R. A cartography of the ecstatic and meditative states. *Science*, 1971, **174**, 897-904.

Fisher, R. Biological time. In J. T. Fraser (Ed.) *The voices of time.* New York: George Braziller, 1966. Pp. 357-382.

Fitts, P. M., & Posner, M. I. *Human performance.* Belmont, Calif.: Brooks/Cole, 1967.

Ford, D. H., & Urban, H. B. Psychotherapy. *Annual Review of Psychology*, 1967, **18**, 333-372.

Frank, J. D. Some psychological determinants of the level of aspiration. *American Journal of Psychology*, 1935, **47**, 285-293.

Frank, P. *Modern science and its philosophy.* Cambridge, Mass.: Harvard University Press, 1949.

Fraser, J. T. *The voices of time.* New York: George Braziller, 1966.

Frenkel-Brunswik, E. Meaning of psychoanalytic concepts and confirmation of psychoanalytic theories. *Scientific Monographs*, 1954, **79**, 293-300.

Freud, S. The history of the psychoanalytic movement. In A. A. Brill (Ed. & Trans.), *The basic writing of Sigmund Freud.* New York: Random House, 1938. Pp. 933-977.

Freud, S. *A general introduction to psychoanalysis.* (Trans. by J. Riviere) Garden City, N.Y.: Doubleday, 1943.

Freud, S. Beyond the pleasure principle. In J. Strachey (Ed. & Trans.), *The complete psychological works of Sigmund Freud.* Vol. 18. London: Hogarth Press, 1955.

Fromm, E. *Escape from freedom.* New York: Holt, 1941.

Fromm, E. *Man for himself.* New York: Holt, 1947.

Fromm, E. *The sane society.* New York: Holt, 1955.

Fromm, E. *Sigmund Freud's mission.* New York: Harper, 1959.

Fromm, E. *Marx's concept of man.* New York: Ungar, 1961. (a)

Fromm, E. *May man prevail? An inquiry into the facts and fictions of foreign policy.* Garden City, N.Y.: Doubleday, 1961. (b)

Fromm, E. *The heart of man.* New York: Harper & Row, 1964.

Fuchs, A. H., & Kawash, G. F. Prescriptive dimensions of five schools of psychology, Unpublished manuscript, 1972.

Garcia, J., McGowan, B. K., & Green, K. F. Biological constraints on conditioning. In A. Black & W. F. Prokasy (Eds.), *Classical conditioning.* New York: Appleton-Century-Crofts, 1972.

Garner, W. R. Rating scales, discriminability and information transmission. *Psychological Review,* 1960, **67**, 343-352.

Garner, W. R. *Uncertainty and structure as psychological concepts.* New York: Wiley, 1962.

Garner, W. R. To perceive is to know. *American Psychologist,* 1966, **21**, 11-19.

Garner, W. R., & Hake, W. H. The amount of information in absolute judgments. *Psychological Review,* 1951, **58**, 446-459.

Garner, W. R., Hake, W. H., & Eriksen, C. W. Operationism and the concept of perception. *Psychological Review,* 1956, **63**, 149-159.

Garner, W. R., Hunt, H. F., & Taylor, D. W. Education for research in psychology *American Psychology,* 1959, **14**, 167-179.

Gates, A. I. Connectionism: Present concepts and interpretations. *Yearbook of National Society of the Study of Education,* 1942, **41**, Part II.

Geissler, L. R. The measurement of attention. *American Journal of Psychology,* 1909, **20**, 473-529.

Gelb, A., & Goldstein, K. *Psychologische Analysen Hirnpathologischer Faelle.* Leipzig: Barth, 1920.

Ghiselin, M. T. A discarded consensus. *Science,* 1972, **175**, 506-507.

Gibson, E. J., & Walk, R. Visual cliff. *Scientific American,* 1960, **202**, 2-9.

Gibson, J. J. The concept of stimulus in psychology. *American Psychologist,* 1960, **15**, 694-703.

Gibson, J. J. *The senses considered as perceptual systems.* Boston: Houghton Mifflin, 1966.

Gibson, J. J. On the proper meaning of the term "stimulus." *Psychological Review,* 1967, **74**, 533-534.

Gillispie, C. C. *The edge of objectivity.* Princeton, N.J.: Princeton University Press, 1960.

Goldiamond, I. Indicators of perception. I. Subliminal perception, subception, unconscious perception. *Psychological Bulletin,* 1958, **55,** 373-411.

Goldstein, K. *The organism.* New York: American Book, 1939.

Goldstein, K. *Human nature in the light of psychopathology.* Cambridge, Mass.: Harvard University Press, 1940.

Goldstein, K. *After-effects of brain injuries in war.* New York: Grune & Stratton, 1942.

Goldstein, K. *Language and language disturbances.* New York: Grune & Stratton, 1948.

Goldstein, K. Kurt Goldstein. In E. G. Boring, & G. Lindzey (Eds.), *A history of psychology in autobiography.* Vol. 5. New York: Appleton-Century-Crofts, 1967. Pp. 145-166.

Goldstein, K., & Scheerer, M. Abstract and concrete behavior: An experimental study with special tests. *Psychological Monographs,* 1941, **53,** No. 2.

Goldstein, K., & Scheerer, M. Tests of abstract and concrete thinking. A. Tests of abstract behavior. In A. Weidler (Ed.), *Contributions toward medical psychology.* New York: Ronald Press, 1953. Pp. 702-730.

Goodall, K. Tie line. *Psychology Today,* 1972, January, 24-28.

Graham, C. H. Visual perception. In S. S. Stevens (Ed.), *Handbook of experimental psychology.* New York: Wiley, 1951. Pp. 868-920.

Graham, C. H. Sensation and perception in an objective psychology. *Psychological Review,* 1958, **65,** 65-76.

Green, D. M., & Swets, J. A. *Signal detection theory and psychophysics.* New York: Wiley, 1966.

Gulliksen, H. Louis Leon Thurstone, experimental and mathematical psychologist. *American Psychologist,* 1968, **23,** 786-802.

Guthrie, E. R. *The psychology of learning.* New York: Harper & Row, 1935.

Guthrie, E. R. *The psychology of human conflict.* New York: Harper & Row, 1938.

Guthrie, E. R. Conditioning: A theory of learning in terms of stimulus, response and association. *Yearbook of National Society of the Study of Education,* 1942, **41,** Part II, 17-60.

Guthrie, E. R. Psychological facts and psychological theory. *Psychological Bulletin,* 1946, **43,** 1-20.

Guthrie, E. R. *The psychology of learning.* (Rev. ed.) New York: Harper & Row, 1952.

Guthrie, E. R. Association by contiguity. In S. Koch (Ed.), *Psychology: A study of a science.* Vol. 2. *General systematic formulations, learning and special processes.* New York: McGraw-Hill, 1958. Pp. 158-195.

Guthrie, E. R., & Horton, G. P. *Cats in a puzzle box.* New York: Holt, 1946.

Haber, R. N. (Ed.) *Current research in motivation.* New York: Holt, Rinehart & Winston, 1966.

Hall, C. S. *A primer on Freudian psychology.* Cleveland: World Publishing, 1954.

Hall, C. S. & Lindzey, G. *Theories of personality.* New York: Wiley, 1957.

Hall, C. S., & Lindzey, G. *Theories of personality.* (2nd ed.) New York: Wiley, 1970.

Hall, G. S. *Adolescence.* New York: Appleton, 1904.

Hall, G. S. *Jesus, the Christ, in the light of psychology.* Garden City, N.Y.: Doubleday, 1917.

Hall, M. H. An interview with "Mr. Behaviorist" B. F. Skinner. *Psychology Today,* 1967, **1**, 21-23, 68-71.

Hammond, K. R. Representative vs. systematic design in clinical psychology. *Psychological Bulletin,* 1954, **51**, 150-159.

Hammond, K. R. Probabilistic functioning and the clinical method. *Psychological Review,* 1955, **62**, 255-262.

Hammond, K. R. (Ed.) *The psychology of Egon Brunswik.* New York: Holt, 1966.

Hammond, W. A. *Aristotle's psychology.* London: Swan Sonnenschien, 1902.

Harlow, H. F. Primate learning. In C. P. Stone (Ed.), *Comparative psychology.* Englewood Cliffs, N.J.: Prentice-Hall, 1951. Pp. 183-238.

Harlow, H. F. Learning set and error factor theory. In S. Koch (Ed.), *Psychology: A study of a science.* Vol. 2. *General systematic formulations, learning and special processes.* New York: McGraw-Hill, 1958. Pp. 492-537.

Harlow, H. F., Davis, R. T., Settlage, P. H., & Meyer, D. R. Analysis of frontal and posterior association syndromes in brain damaged monkeys. *Journal of Comparative and Physiological Psychology,* 1952, **45**, 419-429.

Harrower, M. R. Organization in higher mental processes. *Psychologische Forschung,* 1932, **17**, 56-120.

Hartley, D. *Observations on man, his duty, and his expectations.* London: W. Eyres, 1749.

Hartmann, G. W. *Gestalt psychology.* New York: Ronald Press, 1935.

Hartmann, H. Comments on the psychoanalytic theory of instinctual drives. *Psychoanalytic Quarterly,* 1948, **17**, 368-388.

Hartmann, H. Comments on the psychoanalytic theory of the ego. In A. Freud et al. (Eds.), *The psychoanalytic study of the child.* Vol. 5. New York: International Universities Press, 1950. Pp. 74-96.

Hartmann, H., & Kris, E. The genetic approach in psychoanalysis. In A. Freud et al. (Eds.), *The psychoanalytic study of the child.* Vol. 1. New York: International Universities Press, 1945. Pp. 11-30.

Hays, R. Psychology of the scientist. III. Introduction to "Passages from the 'idea books' of Clark L. Hull." *Perceptual and Motor Skills,* 1962, **15**, 803-806.

Hearst, E. Discrimination learning as the summation of excitation and inhibition. *Science,* 1968, **162**, 1303-1306.

Hebb, D. O. *The organization of behavior.* New York: Wiley, 1949.

Hebb, D. O. A neuropsychological theory. In S. Koch (Ed.), *Psychology: A study of a science.* Vol. 1 *Sensory, perceptual, and physiological formulations.* New York: McGraw-Hill, 1959. Pp. 622-643.

Heidbreder, E. *Seven psychologies.* New York: Appleton-Century-Crofts, 1933.

Heidegger, M. *Being and time.* New York: Harper & Row, 1962.

Heider, F. Gestalt theory: Early history and reminiscences. *Journal of the History of the Behavioral Sciences,* 1970, **6**, 131-139.

Heinsenberg, W. *The physicist's conception of nature.* (Trans. by A. J. Pomerans.) New York: Harcourt, Brace & World, 1958.

Helson, H. The psychology of Gestalt. *American Journal of Psychology,* 1925, **36**, 342-370, 454-526.

Helson, H. The psychology of Gestalt. *American Journal of Psychology,* 1926, **37**, 25-62, 189-223.

Helson, H. The fundamental propositions of Gestalt psychology. *Psychological Review,* 1933, **40**, 12-32.

Helson, H. Why did their precursors fail and the Gestalt psychologists succeed? *American Psychologist,* 1969, **24**, 1006-1011.

Henle, M. Some problems of eclecticism. *Psychological Review,* 1957, **64**, 296-305.

Henle, M. (Ed.) *Documents of Gestalt psychology.* Berkeley: University of California Press, 1961.

Henle, M. (Ed.) *The selected papers of Wolfgang Köhler.* New York: Liveright, 1971.

Herrnstein, R. J. Superstition: A corollary of the principles of operant conditioning. In W. K. Honig (Ed.), *Operant behavior areas of research and application.* New York: Appleton-Century-Crofts, 1966. Pp. 33-51.

Herrnstein, R. J., & Boring, E. G. *A source book in the history of psychology.* Cambridge, Mass.: Harvard University Press, 1965.

Hilgard, E. R. *Theories of learning.* New York: Appleton-Century-Crofts, 1948.

Hilgard, E. R. Experimental approaches to psychoanalysis. In E. Pumpian-Mindlin (Ed.), *Psychoanalysis as science.* Stanford, Calif.: Stanford University Press, 1952. Pp. 3-45.

Hilgard, E. R. Discussion of probabilistic functionalism. *Psychological Review,* 1955, **62**, 226-228.

Hilgard, E. R. *Theories of learning.* (Rev. ed.) New York: Appleton-Century-Crofts, 1966.

Hilgard, E. R., & Bower, G. H. *Theories of learning.* New York: Appleton-Century-Crofts, 1966.

Hillix, W. A., & Marx, M. H. Response strengthening by information and effect in human learning. *Journal of Experimental Psychology,* 1960, **60**, 97-102.

Hinde, R. A. *Animal behaviour: A synthesis of ethology and comparative psychology.* (2nd ed.) New York: McGraw-Hill, 1970.

Hobbes, T. *Leviathan.* London: Oxford University Press, 1651.

Hochberg, J. E. Effects of the Gestalt revolution: The Cornell symposium on perception. *Psychological Review,* 1957, **64**, 73-84.

Hochberg, J., & McAlister, E. A quantitative approach to figural "goodness." *Journal of Experimental Psychology,* 1953, **46**, 361-364.

Hocutt, M. On the alleged circularity of Skinner's concept of stimulus. *Psychological Review,* 1967, **74**, 530-532.

Hofstadter, R. *Social Darwinism in American thought.* Boston: Beacon Press, 1955.

Holt, E. B. *The Freudian wish and its place in ethics.* New York: Holt, 1915.

Holt, E. B. *Animal drive and the learning process.* New York: Holt, 1931.

Holt, R. R. Individuality and generalization in the psychology of personality. *Journal of Personality,* 1962, **30**, 377-404.

Holton, G. (Ed.) Science and the modern world view. *Daedalus,* 1958, **87**.

Holton, G. (Ed.) Science and technology in contemporary society. *Daedalus,* 1962, **91**.

Hoppe, F. Erfolg und Misserfolg. *Psychologische Forschung,* 1930, **14**, 1-62.

Horney, K. *Neurotic personality of our times.* New York: Norton, 1937.

Horney, K. *New ways in psychoanalysis.* New York: Norton, 1939.

Horney, K. *Self-analysis.* New York: Norton, 1942.

Horney, K. *Our inner conflicts.* New York: Norton, 1945.

Horney, K. *Neurosis and human growth.* New York: Norton, 1950.

Horwitz, L. Theory construction and validation in psychoanalysis. (Also in M. H. Marx [Ed.], *Theories in contemporary psychology.* New York: Macmillan, 1963. Pp. 413-434.)

Hull, C. L. Quantitative aspects of the evolution of concepts. *Psychological Monographs,* 1920, **28**, No. 123.

Hull, C. L. The influence of tobacco smoking on mental and motor efficiency. *Psychological Monographs,* 1924, **33** (No. 3), 1-160.

Hull, C. L. *Aptitude testing.* Yonkers, N.Y.: World, 1928.

Hull, C. L. The goal gradient hypothesis and maze learning. *Psychological Review,* 1932, **39**, 25-43.

Hull, C. L. *Hypnosis and suggestibility: An experimental approach.* New York: Appleton-Century, 1933.

Hull, C. L. Mind, mechanism, and adaptive behavior. *Psychological Review,* 1937, **44**, 1-32.

Hull, C. L. *Principles of behavior.* New York: Appleton-Century-Crofts, 1943.

Hull, C. L. *Essentials of behavior.* New Haven, Conn.: Yale University Press, 1951.

Hull, C. L. *A behavior system.* New Haven, Conn.: Yale University Press, 1952.

Hull, C. L. Psychology of the scientist. IV. Passages from the "idea books" of Clark L. Hull. *Perceptual and Motor Skills,* 1962, **15**, 807-882.

Hull, C. L., Felsinger, J. M., Gladstone, A. D., & Yamaguchi, H. C. A proposed quantification of habit strength. *Psychological Review,* 1947, **54**, 237-254.

Hull, C. L., Hovland, C. L., Ross, R. T., Hall, M., Perkins, D. T., & Fitch, F. G. *Mathematico-deductive theory of rote learning.* New Haven, Conn.: Yale University Press, 1940.

Hume, D. *A treatise on human nature.* London: Longmans, 1886 (1739-1740).

Hume, D. An enquiry concerning human understanding. (2nd ed.; L. A. Selby-Bigge [Ed.]) Oxford: Clarendon Press, 1902 (1748).

Hunt, W. A. Clinical psychology—science or superstition. *American Psychologist,* 1951, **6**, 683-687.

Hunter, W. S. The problem of consciousness. *Psychological Review,* 1924, **21**, 1-31.

Hunter, W. S. Psychology and anthroponomy. In C. Murchison (Ed.), *Psychologies of 1925.* Worcester, Mass.: Clark University Press, 1926 (Ch. IV). Pp. 83-107.

Hursch, C. J., Hammond, K. R., & Hursch, J. L. Some methodological considerations in multiple-cue probability studies. *Psychological Review,* 1964, **71**, 42-60.

Irvine, W. *Apes, angels, and Victorians.* New York: Time-Life, 1963.

James, W. A. *The principles of psychology.* New York: Holt, 1890. Vols. I, II.

James, W. A. *A pluralistic universe.* New York: Longmans, 1909.

Jeffress, L. A. (Ed.) *Cerebral mechanisms in behavior.* New York: Wiley, 1951.

Jensen, A. Personality. *Annual Review of Psychology,* 1958, **9**, 295-322.

Jensen, A. Input. *Psychology Today,* 1969, **3**, 4-6.

Jessor, R. The problem of reductionism in psychology. In M. H. Marx (Ed.), *Theories in contemporary psychology.* New York: Macmillan, 1963. Pp. 245-256.

Johansson, G. *Configurations in event perception.* Uppsala: Almquist & Wiksell, 1950.

Johnson, H. K. Psychoanalysis: A critique. *Psychiatric Quarterly,* 1948, **22,** 321-338.

Joncich, G. E. L. Thorndike: The psychologist as a professional man of science. *American Psychologist,* 1968, **23,** 434-446.

Jones, E. *The life and work of Sigmund Freud.* Vol. 1. New York: Basic Books, 1953.

Jones, E. *The life and work of Sigmund Freud.* Vol. 2. New York: Basic Books, 1955.

Jones, E. *The life and work of Sigmund Freud.* Vol. 3. New York: Basic Books, 1957.

Jones, E. *The life and work of Sigmund Freud.* L. Trilling & S. Marcus (Eds.) New York: Basic Books, 1961.

Jung, C. G. *Symbols of transformation.* New York: Random House, 1956.

Jung, C. G., & Pauli, W. *The interpretation of nature and the people.* New York: Random House, 1955.

Kalish, H. I. Stimulus generalization. In M. H. Marx (Ed.), *Learning processes.* New York: Macmillan, 1969. Pp. 205-298.

Kallen, H. M. (Ed.) *The philosophy of William James.* New York: Modern Library, 1925.

Kantor, J. R. *Principles of psychology.* Vol. 1. New York: Knopf, 1924.

Kantor, J. R. *Principles of psychology.* Vol. 2. New York: Knopf, 1926.

Kantor, J. R. *An outline of social psychology.* Chicago: Follett, 1929.

Kantor, J. R. *An objective psychology of grammar.* Bloomington: Indiana University Press, 1936. (Republished: Bloomington, Ind., Principia Press, 1952.)

Kantor, J. R. *Psychology and logic.* Vol. 1. Bloomington, Ind.: Principia Press, 1945.

Kantor, J. R. *Psychology and logic.* Vol. 2. Bloomington, Ind.: Principia Press, 1950.

Kantor, J. R. *Problems of physiological psychology.* Bloomington, Ind.: Principia Press, 1947.

Kantor, J. R. *The logic of modern science.* Bloomington, Ind.: Principia Press, 1953.

Kantor, J. R. *Interbehavioral psychology.* Bloomington, Ind.: Principia Press, 1958.

Kantor, J. R. *The scientific evolution of psychology.* Vol. 1. Bloomington, Ind.: Principia Press, 1963.

Kantor, J. R. *The scientific evolution of psychology.* Vol. 2. Bloomington, Ind.: Principia Press, 1969.

Kardiner, A. *The individual and his society.* New York: Columbia University Press, 1939.

Karsten, A. Psychische Sattigung. *Psychologische Forschung,* 1928, **10,** 142-154.

Katona, G. *Organizing and memorizing.* New York: Columbia University Press, 1940.

Katona, G. *The powerful consumer.* New York: McGraw-Hill, 1960.

Katz, D. Die Erscheinungsweisen der Faben. *Zeitschrift für Psychologie,* 1911, **7,** 1-3.

Keller, F. S., & Schoenfeld, W. N. *Principles of psychology.* New York: Appleton-Century-Crofts, 1950.

Kendler, H. H. Kenneth W. Spence. *Psychological Review*, 1967, **74**, 335-341.

Kimble, G. A. *Conditioning and learning*. (Rev. by E. R. Hilgard & D. G. Marquis), New York: Appleton-Century-Crofts, 1961.

Kimble, G. A. *Foundations of conditioning and learning*. New York: Appleton-Century-Crofts, 1967.

Klemmer, E. T., & Frick, F. C. Assimilation of information from dot and matrix patterns. *Journal of Experimental Psychology*, 1953, **45**, 15-19.

Kluver, H. Psychology at the beginning of World War II: Meditations on the impending dismemberment of psychology written in 1942. *Journal of Psychology*, 1949, **28**, 383-410.

Koch, S. Review of C. L. Hull, *Principles of behavior. Psychological Bulletin*, 1944, **41**, 269-286.

Koch, S. C. L. Hull. In W. K. Estes et al., *Modern learning theory*. New York: Appleton-Century-Crofts, 1954. Pp. 1-176.

Koch, S. (Ed.) *Psychology: A study of a science*. New York: McGraw-Hill 1958-1963. 6 vols.

Koch, S. Epilogue. In S. Koch (Ed.), *Psychology: A study of a science*. Vol. 3. *Formulations of the person and the social context*. New York: McGraw-Hill, 1959. Pp. 729-788.

Koffka, K. *Principles of Gestalt psychology*. New York: Harcourt, Brace, 1935.

Köhler, I. Uber Aufbau und Wahrnehmungswelt. *Oesterr. Akad. Wiss. Philos.-Histor., Kl.; Sitz-Ber.*, 1951, **227**, 1-118.

Köhler, W. *Die physischen Gestalten in Ruhe und im stationaren Zustand*. Erlangen: Weltkreisverlag, 1920.

Köhler, W. Gestaltprobleme und Anfänge einer Gestalttheorie. *Jahresbericht über die gesamte physiologie und experimentelle pharmakologie*, 1924, **3**, 512-539.

Köhler, W. *The mentality of apes*. New York: Harcourt, Brace, 1925.

Köhler, W. Some Gestalt problems. In W. D. Ellis (Ed.), *A source book of Gestalt psychology*. London: Routledge & Kegan Paul, 1938. Pp. 55-70.

Köhler, W. Kurt Koffka. *Psychological Review*, 1942, **49**, 97-101.

Köhler, W. Max Wertheimer, 1880-1943. *Psychological Review*, 1944, **51**, 143-146.

Köhler, W. Gestalt psychology: An introduction to the new concepts in modern psychology. New York: Liveright, 1947.

Köhler, W. The present situation in brain physiology. *American Psychologist*, 1958, **13**, 150-154.

Köhler, W. *The task of Gestalt psychology*. Princeton, N.J.: Princeton University Press, 1969.

Köhler, W., & Wegener, J. Currents of the human auditory cortex. *Journal of Cellular and Comparative Physiology*, 1955, **45**, 24-53.

Krantz, D. L. *Schools of psychology: A symposium*. New York: Appleton-Century-Crofts, 1970.

Krantz, D. L. Schools and systems: The mutual isolation of operant and non-operant psychology as a case study. *Journal of the History of the Behavioral Sciences*, 1972, **8**, 86-102.

Krech, D. Cortical localization of function. In L. Postman (Ed.), *Psychology in the making*. New York: Knopf, 1962. Pp. 31-72.

Krechevsky, I. "Hypotheses" in rats. *Psychological Review,* 1932, **39**, 516-532.

Kris, E. The nature of psychoanalytic propositions and their validation. In M. H. Marx (Ed.), *Psychological theory: Contemporary readings.* New York: Macmillan, 1951. Pp. 332-351.

Kubie, L. S. Problems and techniques of psychoanalytic validation and progress. In E. Pumpian-Mindlin (Ed.), *Psychoanalysis as science.* Stanford, Calif.: Stanford University Press, 1952. Pp. 46-124.

Kuenzli, A. E. *The phenomenological problem.* New York: Harper & Row, 1959.

Kuhn, T. S. *The structure of scientific revolutions.* Chicago: University of Chicago Press, 1952.

Kuhn, T. S. *The structure of scientific revolutions.* (2nd ed.) Chicago: University of Chicago Press, 1970.

Kulpe, O. *Outlines of psychology, based upon results of experimental investigation.* (Trans. by E. B. Titchener) New York: Macmillan, 1895.

Kuo, Z. Y. The nature of unsuccessful acts and their order of elimination. *Journal of Comparative Psychology,* 1922, **2**, 1-27.

Kuo, Z. Y. A psychology without heredity. *Psychological Review,* 1924, **31**, 427-448.

Kuo, Z. Y. The genesis of the cat's response to the rat. *Journal of Comparative Psychology,* 1930, **11**, 1-35.

Kuo, Z. Y. Ontogeny of embryonic behavior in Aves. I. The chronology and general nature of the behavior of the chick embryo. *Journal of Experimental Zoology,* 1932, **61**, 395-430. (a)

Kuo, Z. Y. Ontogeny of embryonic behavior in Aves. IV. The influence of embryonic movements upon the behavior after hatching. *Journal of Comparative Psychology,* 1932, **14**, 109-122. (b)

Kuo, Z. Y. Ontogeny of embryonic behavior in Aves. II. The mechanical factors in the various stages leading to hatching. *Journal of Experimental Zoology,* 1932, **62**, 453-489. (c)

Kuo, Z. Y. Ontogeny of embryonic behavior in Aves. V. The reflex concepts in the light of embryonic behavior in birds. *Psychological Review,* 1932, **39**, 499-515. (d)

Kuo, Z. Y. Ontogeny of embryonic behavior in Aves. III. The structure and environmental factors in embryonic behavior. *Journal of Comparative Psychology,* 1932, **13**, 245-272. (e)

Kuo, Z. Y. Further study of the behavior of the cat toward the rat. *Journal of Comparative Psychology,* 1938, **25**, 1-8.

Kuo, Z. Y. *The dynamics of behavior development.* New York: Random House, 1967.

LaBrecque, M. Very short circuits. *The sciences,* 1970, **10**, 8-10.

Lakatos, I. Falsification and the methodology of scientific research programmes. In A. Musgrave & I. Lakatos (Eds.), *Criticism and the growth of knowledge.* New York: Cambridge University Press, 1970. Pp. 91-195.

Lamarck, J. B. *Zoological philosophy: An exposition with regard to the natural history of animals.* (Trans. by H. Elliot) London: Macmillan, 1914.

La Mettrie, J. O. *De L'homme machine.* Leyden, 1748. (Republished as *Man a machine,* La Salle, Ill., Open Court, 1912.)

Land, E. H. Experiments in color vision. *Scientific American,* 1959, **200**, 84-99.

Laplace, P. S. *Essai philosophique sur les probabilities.* Paris: Gauthier-Villars, 1921.

Lashley, K. S. The behavioristic interpretation of consciousness. *Psychological Review,* 1923, **30**, 329-353.

Lashley, K. S. *Brain mechanisms and intelligence.* Chicago: University of Chicago Press, 1929.

Lashley, K. S. Cerebral control versus reflexology: A reply to Professor Hunter. *Journal of General Psychology,* 1931, **5**, 3-20.

Lashley, K. S., Chow, K. L., & Semmes, J. An examination of the electrical field theory of cerebral integration. *Psychological Review,* 1951, **58**, 123-136.

Lauer, Q. *Phenomenology: Its genesis and prospect.* New York: Harper & Row, 1965.

Lawson, R., & Marx, M. H. Frustration: Theory and experiment. *Genetic Psychology Monographs,* 1958, **57**, 393-464.

Leeper, R. W. *Lewin's topological and vector psychology.* Eugene: University of Oregon Press, 1943.

Leeper, R. W. Cognitive processes. In S. S. Stevens (Ed.), *Handbook of experimental psychology.* New York: Wiley, 1951. Pp. 730-757.

Levine, R., Chein, I., & Murphy, G. The relation of the intensity of a need to the amount of perceptual distortion: A preliminary report. *Journal of Psychology,* 1942, **13**, 283-293.

Levy, L. *Concepts of personality: Theories and research.* New York: Random House, 1970.

Lewes, G. H. *Study of psychology,* 1879.

Lewin, K. Die psychische Tatigkeit bei der Hemmung on Willensvorgangen und das Grundgestz der Assocization. *Zeitschrift für Psychologie,* 1917, **77**, 212-247.

Lewin, K. *A dynamic theory of personality.* (Trans. by K. E. Zener & D. K. Adams) New York: McGraw-Hill, 1935.

Lewin, K. *Principles of topological psychology.* (Trans. by F. Heider & G. Heider) New York: McGraw-Hill, 1936.

Lewin, K. *The conceptual representation and measurement of psychological forces.* Durham, N.C.: Duke University Press, 1938.

Lewin, K. Field theory and experiment in social psychology: Concept and methods. *American Journal of Sociology,* 1939, **44**, 868-896.

Lewin, K. Formalization and progress in psychology. *University of Iowa Studies in Child Welfare,* 1940, **16**, 9-42.

Lewin, K. Defining the "field at a given time." *Psychological Review,* 1943, **50**, 292-310. (a) (Also in M. H. Marx [Ed.], *Psychological theory: Contemporary readings.* New York: Macmillan, 1951. Pp. 299-315.)

Lewin, K. Forces behind food habits and methods of change. *Bulletin of the National Research Council,* 1943, **108**, 35-65. (b)

Lewin, K. Constructs in psychology and psychological ecology. *University of Iowa Studies in Child Welfare,* 1944, **20**, 1-29.

Lewin, K. *Resolving social conflicts.* New York: Harper & Row, 1948.

Lewin, K. *Field theory in social science.* New York: Harper & Row, 1951.

Lichtenstein, P. E. Psychological systems: Their nature and function. *Psychological Record,* 1967, **17**, 321-340.

Licklider, J. C. R. Three auditory theories. In S. Koch (Ed.), *Psychology: A study* of a science. Vol. 1. *Sensory, perceptual, and physiological formulations.* New York: McGraw-Hill, 1958. Pp. 41-144.

Lindzey, G. Behavior and morphological variation. In J. N. Spuhler (Ed.), *Genetic diversity and human behavior.* Chicago: Aldine, 1967. Pp. 227-240.

Lippitt, R. An experimental study of authoritarian and democratic group atmospheres. *University of Iowa Studies in Child Welfare,* 1940, **16,** 43-195.

Lippitt, R., & White, R. K. The "social climate" of children's groups. In R. G. Barker, J. S. Kounin, & H. F. Wright (Eds.), *Child behavior and development.* New York: McGraw-Hill, 1943. Pp. 485-508.

Lissner, K. Die Entspannung von Bedurfnissen durch Ersatzhandlungen. *Psychologische Forschung,* 1933, **18,** 218-250.

Lockard, R. B. Reflections on the fall of comparative psychology: Is there a message for us all? *American Psychologist,* 1971, **26,** 168-179.

Locke, J. *An essay concerning human understanding.* Vol. 2. (Reprinted from the 20th London ed.) Boston: David Carlisle, 1803.

Lockhart, R. S., & Murdock, B. B. Memory and the theory of signal detection. *Psychological Bulletin,* 1970, **74,** 100-109.

Logan, F. A. A micromolar approach to behavior theory. *Psychological Review,* 1956, **63,** 73-80.

Logan, F. A. The Hull-Spence approach. In S. Koch (Ed.), *Psychology: A study of a science.* Vol. 2. *General systematic formulations, learning and special processes.* New York: McGraw-Hill, 1958. Pp. 293-348.

Logan, F. A. *Incentive.* New Haven, Conn.: Yale University Press, 1960.

London, I. D. Psychologists' misuse of the auxiliary concepts of physics and mathematics. *Psychological Review,* 1944, **51,** 42-45.

Lorenz, K. *On aggression.* New York: Harcourt, Brace & World, 1966.

Lorenz, K. *Studies in animal and human behaviour.* Volume 1. R. Martin (Trans.) Cambridge, Mass.: Harvard University Press, 1970.

Lorge, I. D. (Comp.) Edward L. Thorndike's publications from 1940 to 1949. *Teachers College Record,* 1949, **51,** 42-45.

Lowry, R. *The evolution of psychological theory 1650 to the present.* Chicago: Aldine-Atherton, 1971.

Lubin, A. A note on Sheldon's table of correlations between temperamental traits. *British Journal of Psychology and Statistics,* 1950, **3,** 186-189.

Luce, R. D. (Ed.) *Developments in mathematical psychology.* New York: Free Press, 1960.

Luce, R. D., Bush, R. R., & Galanter, E. *Handbook of mathematical psychology.* New York: Wiley, 1963-1965. 3 vols.

Luce, R. D., Bush, R. R., & Galanter, E. *Readings in mathematical psychology.* Vol. 1. New York: Wiley, 1963.

Ludwig, E. *Doctor Freud.* New York: Hellman, Williams, 1947.

Lundin, R. W. *Personality: A behavioral analysis.* New York: Macmillan, 1969.

Luria, A. R. *The role of speech in the regulation of normal and abnormal behavior.* New York: Lippincott, 1961.

MacCorquodale, K. B. F. Skinner's *Verbal behavior:* A retrospective appreciation. *Journal of the Experimental Analysis of Behavior,* 1969, **12,** 831-841.

MacCorquodale, K., & Meehl, P. E. On a distinction between hypothetical constructs and intervening variables. *Psychological Review*, 1948, **55**, 95-107.

MacCorquodale, K., & Meehl, P. E. On the elimination of cul entries without obvious reinforcement. *Journal of Comparative Physiological Psychology*, 1951, **44**, 367-371.

MacCorquodale, K., Meehl, P. E. Edward C. Tolman. In W. K. Estes et al., *Modern learning theory*. New York: Appleton-Century-Crofts, 1954. Pp. 177-266.

MacKay, D. M. The nomenclature of information theory. In H. von Foerster (Ed.), *Transactions of the eighth conference on cybernetics: Circular causal and feedback mechanisms in biological and social systems*. New York: Josiah Macy, Jr., Foundation, 1952. Pp. 222-235.

MacKay, D. M. *Information, mechanism, and meaning*. Cambridge, Mass.: M.I.T. Press, 1969.

MacLeish, A. Why do we teach poetry? *Atlantic Monographs*, 1956, **197**(3), 49-51.

Macleod, R. B. Review of B. F. Skinner, *Cumulative record. Science*, 1959, **130**, 34-35.

Maddi, S. R. *Personality theories: A comparative analysis*. Homewood, Ill.: Dorsey Press, 1968.

Mahler, V. Ersatzhandlungen verschiedenen Realitatsgrades. *Psychologische Forschung*, 1933, **18**, 26-89.

Maier, N. R. F. Experimentally produced neurotic behavior in the rat. Paper presented at the meeting of the American Association for the Advancement of Science, Richmond, 1938.

Maier, N. R. F. *Frustration: The study of behavior without a goal*. New York: McGraw-Hill, 1949.

Maier, N. R. F., & Schneirla, T. C. *Principles of animal psychology*. New York: McGraw-Hill, 1935.

Malinowski, B. *Argonauts of the western Pacific*. New York: Dutton, 1950.

Malmo, R. B. Activation: A neuropsychological dimension. *Psychological Review*, 1959, **66**, 367-386.

Mandler, G., & Kessen, W. *The language of psychology*. New York: Wiley, 1959.

Margenau, H., Bergamini, D., & Editors of *Life. The scientist*. New York: Time-Life, 1967.

Marrow, A. J. *The practical theorist: The life and work of Kurt Lewin*. New York: Basic Books, 1969.

Marx, M. H. (Ed.) *Psychological theory: Contemporary readings*. New York: Macmillan, 1951.

Marx, M. H. Spread of effect: A critical review. *Genetic Psychology Monographs*, 1956, **53**, 119-186.

Marx, M. H. Gradients of error-reinforcement in a serial perceptual-motor task. *Psychological Monographs*, 1957, **71**, 1-20. (a)

Marx, M. H. Gradients of error-reinforcement in normal multiple-choice learning situations. *Journal of Experimental Psychology*, 1957, **54**, 225-228. (b)

Marx, M. H. (Ed.) *Theories in contemporary psychology*. New York: Macmillan, 1963.

Masters, W. H., & Johnson, V. E. *Human sexual inadequacy*. Waltham, Mass.: Little, Brown, 1970.

Maturana, H. R., Lettvin, J. Y., McCulloch, W. S., & Pitts, W. H. Anatomy and physiology of vision in the frog (Rana pipiens). *Journal of Genetic Physiology*, 1960, **43**, 129-175.

Maudsley, H. *Physiology of mind.* New York: Appleton, 1899. (Republished: Appleton-Century-Crofts, New York, 1953.)

May, Rollo (Ed.) *Existential psychology.* New York: Random House, 1966.

McClelland, D. C., et al. *The achievement motive.* New York: Appleton-Century-Crofts, 1953.

McCulloch, W. S., & Pitts, W. A logical calculus of the ideas immanent in nervous activity. *Bulletin of Mathematical Biophysics*, 1943, **5**, 115-133.

McDougall, E. *Physiological psychology.* London: Dent, 1905.

McDougall, E. *Psychology: The study of behavior.* London: Williams & Norgate, 1912.

McGeoch, J. A. The formal criteria of a systematic psychology. *Psychological Review*, 1933, **40**, 1-12.

McGeoch, J. A. Letter to Charles Mullett. Unpublished, 1934.

McGeoch, J. A. *The psychology of human learning.* New York: Longmans, 1942.

McGeoch, J. A., & Irion, A. L. *The psychology of human learning.* (2nd ed.) New York: Longmans, 1952.

McGill, W. J. Multivariate information transmission. *Psychometrika*, 1954, **19**, 97-116.

McMullin, E. The history and philosophy of science: A taxonomy. In R. H. Stuewer (Ed.), *Historical and philosophical perspectives of science.* Minneapolis: University of Minnesota Press, 1970.

Mead, M. *Coming of age in Samoa.* New York: Morrow, 1928. (Republished: Garden City, N.Y., Doubleday, 1950.)

Meehl, P. E. On the circularity of a law of effect. *Psychological Bulletin*, 1950, **47**, 52-57.

Mehrens, W. A., & Ebel, R. L. (Eds.) *Principles of educational and psychological measurement: A book of selected readings.* Chicago: Rand McNally, 1967.

Melton, A. W. Learning. *Annual Review of Psychology*, 1950, **1**, 9-30.

Mendnick, S. A., & Freedman, J. L. Stimulus generalization. *Psychological Bulletin*, 1960, **57**, 169-200.

Merleau-Ponty, M. *The structure of behavior.* Boston: Beacon Press, 1963.

Meyer, M. *The fundamental laws of human behavior.* Boston: R. G. Badger, 1911.

Meyer, M. *The psychology of the other one.* Columbia: Missouri Book Store, 1921.

Milgram, S. Behavioral study of obedience. *Journal of Abnormal and Social Psychology*, 1963, **67**, 371-378.

Mill, J. S. *Analysis of the phenomena of the human mind.* Vol. 1. London: Longmans, 1829.

Mill, J. S. *A system of logic.* London: Longmans, 1843. (Republished: 1956.)

Miller, G. A. The magical number seven, plus or minus two: Some limits on our capacity for processing information. *Psychological Review*, 1956, **63**, 81-87.

Miller, G. A. *Mathematics and psychology.* New York: Wiley, 1964.

Miller, G. A., Galanter, E., & Pribram, K. H. *Plans and the structure of behavior.* New York: Holt, 1960.

Miller, N. E. Experimental studies of conflict. In J. McV. Hunt (Ed.), *Personality and the behavior disorders.* Vol. 1. New York: Ronald Press, 1944. Pp. 431-465.

Miller, N. E. Theory and experiment relating psychoanalytic displacement to stimulus-response generalization. *Journal of Abnormal and Social Psychology,* 1948, **43**, 155-178.

Miller, N. E. Comments on multiple-process conceptions of learning. *Psychological Review,* 1951, **58**, 375-381.

Miller, N. E. Central stimulation and other new approaches to motivation and reward. *American Psychologist,* 1958, **13**, 100-108.

Miller, N. E. Liberalization of basic *S-R* concepts: Extensions to conflict behavior, motivation, and social learning. In S. Koch (Ed.), *Psychology: A study of a science.* Vol. 2. *General systematic formulations, learning and special processes.* New York: McGraw-Hill, 1959. Pp. 196-292.

Miller, N. E. Some reflections on the law of effect produce a new alternative to drive reduction. *Nebraska symposium on motivation.* Lincoln: University of Nebraska Press, 1963. Pp. 65-112.

Miller, N. E. Some implications of modern behavior theory for personality change and psychotherapy. In P. Worchel & D. Byrne (Eds.), *Personality change.* New York: Wiley, 1964. Pp. 149-175.

Miller, N. E. Learning of visceral and glandular responses. *Science,* 1969, **163**, 434-445.

Miller, N. E., & Dollard, J. *Social learning and imitation.* New Haven, Conn.: Yale University Press, 1941.

Mintz, A. Recent developments in psychology in the U.S.S.R. *Annual Review of Psychology,* 1958, **9**, 453-504.

Mintz, A. Further developments in psychology in the U.S.S.R. *Annual Review of Psychology,* 1959, **10**, 455-487.

Montagu, M. F. A. (Ed.) *Man and aggression.* London: Oxford University Press, 1968.

Morgan, C. L. *Introduction to comparative psychology.* London: W. Scott, 1891. (2nd ed., 1899.)

Morgan, C. L. *Animal behavior.* London: E. Arnold, 1900.

Morgan, C. T., & Morgan, J. D. Auditory induction of an abnormal pattern of behavior in rats. *Journal of Comparative Psychology,* 1939, **27**, 505-508.

Morris, D. *The naked ape.* New York: McGraw-Hill, 1968.

Mowrer, O. H. On the dual nature of learning: A re-interpretation of "conditioning" and "problem solving." *Harvard Educational Review,* 1947, **17**, 102-148.

Mowrer, O. H. *Learning theory and personality dynamics.* New York: Ronald Press, 1950.

Mowrer, O. H. Two-factor learning theory: Summary and comment. *Psychological Review,* 1951, **58**, 350-354.

Mowrer, O. H. Learning theory: Historical review and re-interpretation. *Harvard Educational Review,* 1954, **24**, 37-58.

Mowrer, O. H. Two-factor learning theory reconsidered with special reference to secondary reinforcement and the concept of habit. *Psychological Review,* 1956, **63**, 114-128.

Mowrer, O. H. Review of R. S. Woodworth, *Dynamics of behavior. Contemporary Psychology,* 1959, **4**, 129-133.

Mowrer, O. H. *Learning theory and behavior.* New York: Wiley, 1960. (a)

Mowrer, O. H. *Learning theory and the symbolic behavior.* New York: Wiley, 1960. (b)

Mueller, C. G., Jr., Schoenfeld, W. M., & Guthrie, E. R. In W. K. Estes et al., *Modern learning theory*. New York: Appleton-Century-Crofts, 1954. Pp. 345-379.

Mullahy, P. *Oedipus: Myth and complex*. New York: Hermitage House, 1948.

Müller, G. E. Komplextheorie und Gestalttheorie: Ein Beitrag zur Wahrenemungs-psychologie. *Göttinger,* 1923.

Munroe, R. *Schools of psychoanalytic thought*. New York: Holt, 1955.

Murchison, C. (Ed.) *A history of psychology in autobiography*. Vols. 1-3. Worcester, Mass.: Clark University Press, 1930-1936.

Murphy, G. *General psychology*. New York: Harper, 1933.

Murphy, G. *Human nature and enduring peace*. Boston: Houghton Mifflin, 1945.

Murphy, G. *Personality: A biosocial approach to origins and structure*. New York: Harper & Row, 1947.

Murphy, G. *Historical introduction to modern psychology*. New York: Harcourt, Brace & World, 1949.

Murphy, G. *Introduction to psychology*. New York: Harper & Row, 1951.

Murphy, G. *Human potentialities*. New York: Basic Books, 1958.

Murphy, G., & Likert, R. *Public opinion and the individual*. New York: Harper & Row, 1938.

Murphy, G., & Murphy, L. B. *Experimental social psychology*. New York: Harper & Row, 1931.

Murphy, G., Murphy, L. B., & Newcomb, T. M. *Experimental social psychology*. (Rev. ed.) New York: Harper & Row, 1937.

Murphy, G., Santos, J. F., & Solley, C. M. Development and transfer of attentional habits. *Perceptual and Motor Skills,* 1968, **26**, 515-519.

Murray, E. Peripheral and central factors in memory: Images of visual form and color. *American Journal of Psychology,* 1906, **17**, 225-247.

Murray, H. A. *Manual of thematic apperception test*. Cambridge, Mass.: Harvard University Press, 1943.

Murray, H. A. In nomine diaboli. *New England Quarterly,* 1951, **24**, 435-452. (Reprinted in *Princeton University Library Chronicle,* 1952, **13**, 47-62.)

Murray, H. A. Preparations for the scaffold of a comprehensive system. In S. Koch (Ed.), *Psychology: A study of a science*. Vol. 3. *Formulations of the person and the social context*. New York: McGraw-Hill, 1958. Pp. 7-54.

Murray, H. A. Henry A. Murray. In E. G. Boring & G. Lindzey (Eds.), *A history of psychology in autobiography*. Vol. 5. New York: Appleton-Century-Crofts, 1967. Pp. 283-310.

Murray, H. A., et al. *Explorations in personality*. New York: Oxford University Press, 1938.

Nafe, J. P. The psychology of felt experience. *American Journal of Psychology,* 1927, **39**, 367-389.

Nagel, E. Methodology and philosophy of science. Stanford, Calif.: Stanford University Press, 1962.

Nagel, E. The nature and aim of science. In S. Morgenbesser (Ed.), *Philosophy of science today*. New York: Basic Books, 1967. Pp. 3-13.

Nagel, E., Suppes, R., & Tarski, A. (Eds.) Logic, methodology, and philosophy of science. *Proceedings of the 1960 International Congress.* Stanford, Calif.: Stanford University Press, 1962.

Nash, E. H., Frank, J. D., Imber, S. D., & Stone, A. R. Selected effects of inert medication on psychiatric outpatients. *American Journal of Psychotherapy,* 1964, **18**, Suppl. 1, 33-48.

Natsoulas, T. Concerning introspective "knowledge." *Psychological Bulletin,* 1970, **73**, 89-111.

Neel, A. F. *Theories of psychology: A handbook.* Cambridge, Mass.: Schenkman, 1970.

Neisser, U. Visual Search. *Scientific American,* 1964, **210**, 94-102.

Newbury, E. Current interpretation and significance of Lloyd Morgan's canon. *Psychological Bulletin,* 1954, **51**, 70-74.

Newell, A., Shaw, J. C., & Simon, H. A. Elements of a theory of human problem solving. *Psychological Review,* 1958, **65**, 151-166.

Newell, A., & Simon, H. A. The simulation of human thought. In W. Dennis et al. (Eds.), *Current trends in psychological theory.* Pittsburgh: University of Pittsburgh Press, 1961. Pp. 152-179.

Newman, E. B. Public relations—for what? *American Psychologist,* 1957, **12**, 509-514.

Office of Strategic Services Assessment Staff. *Assessment of men.* New York: Holt, 1948.

Olds, J. Physiological mechanism of reward. In M. R. Jones (Ed.), *Nebraska symposium on motivation.* Lincoln: University of Nebraska Press, 1955. Pp. 73-139.

Olds, J. High functions of the nervous system. *Annual Review of Physiology,* 1959, **21**, 381-402.

O'Neil, W. M. Realism and behaviorism. *Journal of the History of the Behavioral Sciences,* 1968, **4**, 152-160.

Oppenheimer, R. Analogy in science. *American Psychologist,* 1956, **11**, 127-135.

Orbison, W. D. Shape as function of the vector field. *American Journal of Psychology,* 4, 1939, **52**, 31-45.

Ovsiankina, M. Die Wideraufnahme von unterbrochenen Handlugen. *Psychologische Forschung,* 1928, **11**, 302-379.

Pavlov, I. P. *Conditioned reflexes.* London: Oxford University Press, 1927.

Pavlov, I. P. *Lectures on conditioned reflexes.* New York: Liveright, 1928.

Pavlov, I. P. The reply of a physiologist to psychologists. *Psychological Review,* 1932, **39**, 91-127.

Pavlov, I. P. *Lectures on conditioned reflexes.* Vol. 2. *Conditioned reflexes and psychiatry.* (Trans. & ed. by W. H. Gantt) New York: International Publishers, 1941.

Pavlov, I. P. *Selected works.* (Trans. by S. Belsky; ed. by J. Gibbons, under supervision of Kh. S. Koshtoyants) Moscow: Foreign Languages Publishing House, 1955.

Perky, C. W. An experimental study of imagination. *American Journal of Psychology,* 1910, **21**, 422-452.

Peterson, C. R., Hammond, K. R., & Summers, D. A. Optimal responding in multiple-cue probability learning. *Journal of Experimental Psychology,* 1965, **70**, 270-276.

Peterson, W. W., Birdsall, T. G., & Fox, W. C. The theory of signal detectability. *Transactions of Professional Group on Information Theory, Institute of Radio Engineers,* 1954, PGIT-4, 171-212.

Piaget, J. *The origins of intelligence in children.* (Trans. by M. Cook from the original 1936 French edition) New York: International Universities Press, 1952.

Pierce, J. R., & Karlin, J. E. Reading rates and the information rate of a human channel. *Bell System Technical Journal,* 1957, **36**, 497-516.

Platt, J. R. *The excitement of science.* New York: Houghton Mifflin, 1962.

Polanyi, M. *Personal knowledge.* Chicago: University of Chicago Press, 1958.

Polanyi, M. *The tacit dimension.* New York: Doubleday, 1966.

Polanyi, M. Life's irreducible structure. *Science,* 1968, **160**, 1308-1312.

Pollack, I. The assimilation of sequentially-encoded information. *HFORL Memo Report,* TR-54-5, 1954.

Pollack, I., & Ficks, L. Information on multidimensional auditory displays. *Journal of the Acoustical Society of America,* 1953, **25**, 765-769.

Pollack, I., & Klemmer, E. T. The assimilation of visual information from linear dot patterns. *Air Force Cambridge Research Center, Technical Report,* 1954, **54**, 16.

Popper, K. *The logic of scientific discovery.* New York: Basic Books, 1959. (Original: *Logik der Forschung.* Vienna: Springer, 1935.)

Posner, M. I. Information reduction in the analysis of sequential tasks. *Psychological Review,* 1964, **71**, 491-504.

Postman, L. The probability approach and nomothetic theory. *Psychological Review,* 1955, **62**, 218-225.

Postman, L. Spread of effect as a function of time and intraserial similarity. *American Journal of Psychology,* 1961, **74**, 493-305.

Postman, L. (Ed.) *Psychology in the making.* New York: Knopf, 1962.

Postman, L., & Murphy, G. The factor of attitude in associative memory. *Journal of Experimental Psychology,* 1943, **33**, 228-238.

Postman, L., & Tolman, E. C. Brunswik's probabilistic functionalism. In S. Koch (Ed.), *Psychology: A study of a science.* Vol. I. *Sensory, perceptual, and physiological formulations.* New York: McGraw-Hill, 1959. Pp. 502-504.

Pratt, C. C. *The logic of modern psychology.* New York: Macmillan, 1939.

Premack, D. The education of Sarah. *Psychology Today,* 1970, **4**, 54-58.

Prentice, W. C. H. The systematic psychology of Wolfgang Köhler. In S. Koch (Ed.), *Psychology: A study of a science.* Vol. 1. *Sensory, perceptual, and physiological formulations.* New York: McGraw-Hill, 1958. Pp. 427-455.

Pumpian-Mindlin, E. The position of psychoanalysis in relation to the biological and social sciences. In E. Pumpian-Mindlin (Ed.), *Psychoanalysis as science.* Stanford, Calif.: Stanford University Press, 1952. Pp. 125-158. (a)

Pumpian-Mindlin, E. (Ed.) *Psychoanalysis as science.* Stanford, Calif.: Stanford University Press, 1952. (b)

Quastler, H. (Ed.) *Information theory in psychology: Problems and methods.* New York: Free Press, 1955.

Quastler, H., Osborne, J. W., & Tweedell, K. Human performance in information transmission. III. University of Illinois Report R-68, Control Systems Laboratory, 1955.

Rank, O. *The trauma of birth*. New York: Harcourt, Brace, 1929.

Rapaport, D. The structure of psychoanalytic theory: A systematizing attempt. In S. Koch (Ed.), *Psychology: A study of a science*. Vol. 3. *Formulations of the person and the social context*. New York: McGraw-Hill, 1959. Pp. 55-183.

Rapoport, A. *Two-person game theory*. Ann Arbor: University of Michigan Press, 1969.

Rapoport, A. *N-person game theory*. Ann Arbor: University of Michigan Press, 1970.

Rashevsky, N. *Mathematical biophysics*. Chicago: University of Chicago Press, 1938.

Rashevsky, N. *Mathematical biophysics*. (Rev. ed.) Chicago: University of Chicago Press, 1948.

Rashevsky, N. *Mathematical Biophysics*. (Rev. ed.) Chicago: University of Chicago Press, 1961. 2 vols.

Raush, H. L., Dittmann, A. T., & Taylor, T. J. Person, setting, and change in social interaction. *Human Relations,* 1959, **12**, 361-378.

Raush, H. L., Dittmann, A. T., & Taylor, T. J. Person, setting, and change in social interaction. II. A normal control study. *Human Relations,* 1960, **13**, 305-332.

Razran, G. Stimulus generalization of conditioned responses. *Psychological Bulletin,* 1949, **46**, 337-365.

Razran, G. The observable unconscious and the inferable conscious in current Soviet psychophysiology: Interoceptive conditioning, semantic conditioning and the orienting reflex. *Psychological Review,* 1961, **68**, 81-147.

Reese, T. W. The applicaton of the theory of physical measurements to the measurement of psychological magnitudes, with three experimental examples. *Psychological Monographs,* 1943, **55**, 1-88.

Reid, L. "Comment of Grubo Psychology." *Psychological Bulletin,* 1967, **67**, 226.

Reinforcement therapy: short cut to sanity? *Time,* 1969, **94**(2), 52-54.

Rescorla, R. A., & Solomon, R. L. Two-process learning theory: Relationships between Pavlovian conditioning and instrumental learning. *Psychological Review,* 1967, **74**, 151-182.

Restle, F., & Greeno, J. C. *Introduction to mathematical psychology*. Reading, Mass.: Addison-Wesley, 1970.

Risley, T. Learning and lollipops. *Psychology Today,* 1968, **1**, 28-31, 62-65.

Roback, A. A. *A history of American psychology*. New York: Library Publishers, 1952.

Rogers, C. R. *The clinical treatment of the problem child*. Boston: Houghton Mifflin, 1939.

Rogers, C. R. *Counseling and psychotherapy: Newer concepts in practice*. Boston: Houghton Mifflin, 1942.

Rogers, C. R. *Client-centered therapy: Its current practice, implications, and theory*. Boston: Houghton Mifflin, 1951.

Rogers, C. R. Some issues concerning the control of human behavior. (Symposium with B. F. Skinner) *Science,* 1956, **124**, 1057-1066.

Rogers, C. R. A theory of therapy, personality, and interpersonal relationships, as developed in the client-centered framework. In S. Koch (Ed.), *Psychology: A study of a science*. Vol. 3. *Formulations of the person and the social context*. New York: McGraw-Hill, 1959. Pp. 184-256.

Rogers, C. R. *On becoming a person.* Boston: Houghton Mifflin, 1961.

Rogers, C. R. Carl R. Rogers. In E. G. Boring & G. Lindzey (Eds.), *A history of psychology in autobiography.* Vol. 5. New York: Appleton-Century-Crofts, 1967. Pp. 341-384. (a)

Rogers, C. R. (Ed.) *The therapeutic relationship and its impact: A study of psychotherapy with schizophrenics.* Madison: University of Wisconsin Press, 1967. (b)

Romanes, G. J. *Animal intelligence.* London: Kegan Paul, Trench, Trubner, 1886.

Romanes, G. J. *Mental evolution in animals.* New York: Appleton, 1898.

Romanes, G. J. *Mental evolution in man.* New York: Appleton, 1902.

Rosenbaum, M. E., & Hewitt, O. J. The effect of electric shock on learning by performers and observers. *Psychonomic Science,* 1966, **5**, 81-82.

Rosenbaum, M. E., & Schutz, L. J. The effects of extraneous response requirements on learning by performers and observer. *Psychonomic Science,* 1967, **8**, 51-52.

Rosenthal, R. *Experimenter effects in behavioral research.* New York: Appleton-Century-Crofts, 1966.

Rosenthal, R. Experimenter expectancy and the reassuring nature of the null hypothesis decision procedure. *Pychological Bulletin Monograph Supplement,* Part II, 1968, 48-62. (a)

Rosenthal, R. Self-fulfilling prophecy. *Psychology Today,* 1968, **2**, 44-51. (b)

Rosenthal, R., Kuhn, R., Greenfield, R. M., & Carota, N. Data desirability, experimenter expectancy, and the results of psychological research. *Journal of Personality and Social Psychology,* 1966, 3(1), 20-27.

Rosenthal, R., & Lawson, R. A longitudinal study of the effects of experimenter bias on the operant learning of laboratory rats. *Journal of Psychiatric Research,* 1964, **2**, 61-72.

Royce, J. R. Factors as theoretical constructs. *American Psychologist,* 1963, **18**, 522-528.

Rozin, R. & Kalat, J. W. Specific hungers and poison avoidance as adaptive specializations of learning. *Psychological Review,* 1971, **78**, 459-486.

Rubin, E. *Syncopleoede figurer.* Kobenhavn: Gyldendalske Boghandel, 1915.

Ruckmick, C. A. The use of the term function in English textbooks of psychology. *American Journal of Psychology,* 1913, **14**, 99-123.

Rudikoff, E. C. A comparative study of the changes in the concepts of the self, the ordinary person, and the ideal eight cases. In C. R. Rogers & R. F. Dymond (Eds.), *Psychotherapy and personality change: Coordinated studies in the client-centered approach.* Chicago: University of Chicago Press, 1954. Pp. 85-98.

Russell, B. *A history of western philosophy.* New York: Simon & Schuster, 1945.

Ryan, T. A. *Intentional behavior: An approach to human motivation.* New York: Ronald, 1970.

Samuel, A. L. Some studies in machine learning using the game of checkers. In E. Feigenbaum & J. Feldman (Eds.), *Computers and thought.* New York: McGraw-Hill, 1963. Pp. 71-105.

Sanford, R. N. Physical and physiological correlates of personality structure. In C. Kluckhohn, H. A. Murray, & D. Scheider (Eds.), *Personality in nature, society, and culture.* (2nd ed.) New York: Knopf, 1953. Pp. 100-103.

Santos, J. F., & Murphy, G. An odyssey in perceptual learning. *Bulletin of the Menninger Clinic,* 1960, **24**, 6-17. (Reprinted in C. S. Hall, & G. Lindzey [Eds.], *Theories of personality: Primary sources and research.* New York: Wiley, 1965. Pp. 521-527.)

Sarton, G. *A guide to the history of science.* Waltham, Mass.: Chronica Botanica, 1952.

Sartre, J. P. *Being and nothingness.* (Trans. by H. Barnes) New York: Philosophical Library, 1956.

Schaub, A. deV. On the intensity of images. *American Journal of Psychology,* 1911, **22**, 346-368.

Schlosberg, H. The relationship between success and the laws of conditioning. *Psychological Review,* 1937, **44**, 379-394.

Schoenfeld, W. N., Cumming W. W., & Hearst, E. On the classification of reinforcement schedules. In A. C. Catania (Ed.), *Contemporary research in operant behavior.* Glenview, Ill.: Scott, Foresman, 1968. Pp. 113-118.

Schultz, D. P. *A history of modern psychology.* New York: Academic Press, 1969.

Scott, J. P., & Fuller, J. L. *Genetics and the social behavior of dogs.* Chicago: University of Chicago Press, 1965.

Sears, R. R. *Survey of objective studies of psychoanalytic concepts.* New York: Social Science Research Council, 1943.

Sebestyen, G. S. *Decision making processes in pattern recognition.* New York: Macmillan, 1962.

Sechenov, I. M. *Reflexes of the brain.* Cambridge, Mass.: M.I.T. Press, 1965 (1863).

Segal, E. M., & Lachman, R. Complex behavior or higher mental process: Is there a paradigm shift? *American Psychologist,* 1972, **27**, 46-55.

Seligman, M. E. P. On the generality of laws of learning. *Psychological Review,* 1970, **77**, 406-418.

Seltzer, C. C., Wells, F. L., & McTernan, E. B. A relationship between Sheldonian somatotype and psychotype. *Journal of Personality,* 1948, **16**, 431-436.

Seward, J. P. An experimental study of Guthrie's theory of reinforcement. *Journal of Experimental Psychology*, 1942, **30**, 247-256.

Seward, J. P., Dill, J. B., & Holland, M. A. Guthrie's theory of learning: A second experiment. *Journal of Experimental Psychology,* 1944, **34**, 226-238.

Shannon, C. E. Prediction and entropy of printed English. *Bell System Technical Journal,* 1951, **30**, 50-64.

Shannon, C. E., & Weaver, W. *The mathematical theory of communication.* Urbana: University of Illinois Press, 1949.

Sheehan, J. G. *Stuttering: Research and therapy.* Cambridge, Mass.: Schenkman, 1970.

Sheffield, F. D. Avoidance training and the contiguity principle. *Journal of Comparative Physiological Psychology,* 1948, **41**, 165-167.

Sheffield, F. D. "Spread of effect" without reward or learning. *Journal of Experimental Psychology,* 1949, **39**, 575-579.

Sheffield, F. D., & Roby, T. B. Reward value of a non-nutritive sweet taste. *Journal of Comparative Physiological Psychology,* 1950, **43**, 471-481.

Sheffield, F. D., Wulff, J. J., & Backer, R. Reward value of copulation without sex drive reduction. *Journal of Comparative Physiological Psychology,* 1951, **44**, 3-8.

Sheldon, W. H., with the collaboration of S. S. Stevens & W. B. Tucker. *The varieties of human physique: An introduction to constitutional psychology.* New York: Harper & Row, 1940.

Sheldon, W. H., with the collaboration of S. S. Stevens. *The varieties of temperament: A psychology of constitutional differences.* New York: Harper & Row, 1942.

Sheldon, W. H. Constitutional factors in personality. In J. McV. Hunt (Ed.), *Personality and the behavior disorders.* New York: Ronald Press, 1944. Pp. 526-549.

Sheldon, W. H. *Early American cents,* 1793-1814. New York: Harper & Row, 1949. (a)

Sheldon, W. H., with the collaboration of E. M. Harth & E. McDermott. *Varieties of delinquent youth: An introduction to constitutional psychiatry.* New York: Harper & Row, 1949. (b)

Sheldon, W. H., with the collaboration of C. W. Dupetuis & E. McDermott. *Atlas of men: A guide for somatotyping the adult male at all ages.* New York: Harper & Row, 1954.

Sherif, M. Social psychology problems and trends in interdisciplinary relationships. In S. Koch (Ed.), *Psychology: A study of a science.* Vol. 6. *Investigation of man as socius: Their place in psychology and the social sciences.* New York: McGraw-Hill, 1963. Pp. 30-93.

Sherrington, C. S. *The integrative action of the nervous system.* London: Constable, 1906. (Republished with a new foreword and a bibliography of Sherrington's publications: New Haven, Conn., Yale University Press, 1947.)

Sidman, M. *Tactics of scientific research.* New York: Basic Books, 1960.

Silverstein, A. The Grubo Psychology: Or can a science over 95 be happy without reductionism? *Psychological Bulletin,* 1966, **66**, 207-210.

Simon, H. A. Letters. *Science,* 1970, **169**, 630-631.

Skaggs, E. B. Personalistic psychology as a science. *Psychological Review,* 1945, **52**, 234-240.

Skinner, B. F. *The behavior of organisms.* New York: Appleton-Century-Crofts, 1938.

Skinner, B. F. "Superstition" in the pigeon. *Journal of Experimental Psychology,* 1948, **38**, 168-172. (a)

Skinner, B. F. *Walden two.* New York: Macmillan, 1948. (b)

Skinner, B. F. Are theories of learning necessary? *Psychological Review,* 1950, **57**, 193-216.

Skinner, B. F. *Science and human behavior.* New York: Macmillan, 1953. (a)

Skinner, B. F. Some contributions of an experimental analysis of behavior to psychology as a whole. *American Psychologist,* 1953, **8**, 69-78. (b)

Skinner, B. F. Critique of psychoanalytic concepts and theories. *Scientific Monthly,* 1954, **79**, 300-305. (a)

Skinner, B. F. The science of learning and the art of teaching. *Harvard Educational Review,* 1954, **24**, 86-97. (b)

Skinner, B. F. A case history in scientific method. *American Psychologist,* 1956, **11**, 221-233.

Skinner, B. F. The experimental analysis of behavior. *American Scientist,* 1957, **45,** 343-371. (a)

Skinner, B. F. *Verbal behavior.* New York: Appleton-Century-Crofts, 1957. (b)

Skinner, B. F. Teaching machines. *Science,* 1958, **128,** 969-977.

Skinner, B. F. A case-study in scientific method. In S. Koch (Ed.), *Psychology: A study of a science.* Vol. 2. *General systematic formulations, learning and special processes.* New York: McGraw-Hill, 1959. Pp. 359-379. (a)

Skinner, B. F. *Cumulative record.* New York: Appleton-Century-Crofts, 1959. (b)

Skinner, B. F. Pigeons in a pelican. *American Psychologist,* 1960, **15,** 28-37.

Skinner, B. F. The flight from the laboratory. In *Current trends in psychological theory.* Pittsburgh: University of Pittsburgh Press, 1961. Pp. 50-69.

Skinner, B. F. Operant behavior. In W. K. Honig (Ed.), *Operant behavior: Areas of research and application.* New York: Appleton-Century-Crofts, 1966. Pp. 12-32.

Skinner, B. F. B. F. Skinner. In E. G. Boring & G. Lindzey (Eds.), *A history of psychology in autobiography.* New York: Appleton-Century-Crofts, 1967. Pp. 385-413.

Skinner, B. F. *Contingencies of reinforcement: A theoretical analysis.* New York: Appleton-Century-Crofts, 1969.

Skinner, B. F. *Beyond freedom and dignity.* New York: Knopf, 1971.

Smith, C. S. Matter versus materials: A historical view. *Science,* 1968, **162,** 637-644.

Smith, M., & Wilson, E. A model of the auditory threshold and its application to the problem of the multiple observer. *Psychological Monographs,* 1953, **67,** No. 9. Pp. 1-35.

Smith, N. K. *The philosophy of David Hume.* London: Macmillan, 1949.

Smith, S., & Guthrie, E. R. *General psychology in terms of behavior.* New York: Appleton, 1921.

Smith, S. K., & Miller, G. A. The effects of coding procedures on learning and memory. Quarterly progress report of Research Laboratory of Electronics, M.I.T., to Air Force Human Resources Research Laboratories, 1952.

Snygg, D., & Combs, A. W. *Individual behavior.* New York: Harper & Row, 1949.

Sokal, M. M. The unpublished autobiography of James McKeen Cattell. *American Psychologist,* 1971, **26,** 626-635.

Solley, C. M., & Murphy, G. *Development of the perceptual world.* New York: Basic Books, 1960.

Solso, R. L. Recommended readings in psychology during the past 17 years. *American Psychologist,* 1971, **26,** 1083-1084.

Spearman, C. E. *Creative mind.* New York: Appleton, 1931.

Spence, K. W. The nature of discrimination learning in animals. *Psychological Review,* 1936, **43,** 327-449.

Spence, K. W. Analysis of the formation of visual discrimination habits in chimpanzees. *Journal of Comparative Psychology,* 1937, **23,** 77-100. (a)

Spence, K. W. The differential response in animals to stimuli varying within a single dimension. *Psychological Review,* 1937, **44,** 430-444. (b)

Spence, K. W. Continuous vs. non-continuous interpretations of discrimination learning. *Psychological Review,* 1940, **47,** 271-288.

Spence, K. W. The methods and postulates of "behaviorism." *Psychological Review,*

1948, **55**, 67-78. (Reprinted in M. H. Marx [Ed.], *Theories in contemporary psychology.* New York: Macmillan, 1963. Pp. 272-286.)

Spence, K. W. Theoretical interpretations of learning. In C. P. Stone (Ed.), *Comparative psychology.* (3rd ed.) Englewood Cliffs, N.J.: Prentice-Hall, 1951. Pp. 23-291. (a)

Spence, K. W. Theoretical interpretations of learning. In S. S. Stevens (Ed.), *Handbook of experimental psychology.* New York: Wiley, 1951. Pp.69-729. (b)

Spence, K. W. *Behavior theory and conditioning.* New Haven, Conn: Yale University Press, 1956.

Spence, K. W. *Behavior theory and learning: Selected papers.* Englewood Cliffs, N.J.: Prentice-Hall, 1960.

Spence, K. W. Cognitive and drive factors in the extinction of the conditioned eye blink in human subjects. *Psychological Review,* 1966, **73**, 445-458.

Spencer, H. *The principles of psychology.* New York: Appleton, 1855.

Spencer, H. *The study of sociology.* Ann Arbor: University of Michigan Press, 1961.

Sperry, R. W. Cerebral organization and behavior. *Science,* 1961, **133**, 1749-1757.

Sperry, R. W., & Miner, N. Pattern perception following insertion of mica plates into visual cortex. *Journal of Comparative and Physiological Psychology,* 1955, **48**, 463-469.

Sperry, R. W., Miner, N., & Myers, R. E. Visual pattern perception following subpial slicing and tantalum wire implantations in the visual cortex. *Journal of Comparative and Physiological Psychology,* 1955, **48**, 50-58.

Staddon, J. E. R., & Simmelhag, V. L. The "superstition" experiment: A re-examination of its implications for the principles of adaptive behavior. *Psychological Review,* 1971, **78**, 3-43.

Stengel, E. The scientific testing of psychoanalytic findings and theory. *British Journal of Medical Psychology,* 1951, **24**, 26-29.

Stephenson, W. *The study of behavior: Q-technique and its methodology.* Chicago: University of Chicago Press, 1953.

Stephenson, W. Scientific-creed—1961: Philosophical credo, abductory principles, the centrality of self. *Psychological Record,* 1961, **11**, 1-18.

Sternberg, S. High speed scanning in human memory. *Science,* 1966, **153**, 625-654.

Stevens, S. S. Psychology and the science of science. *Psychological Bulletin,* 1939, **36**, 221-263.

Stevens, S. S. (Ed.) *Handbook of experimental psychology.* New York: Wiley, 1951.

Stevens, S. S. On the averaging of data. *Science,* 1955, **121**, 113-116.

Stevens, S. S. Measurement, statistics, and the schemapiric view. *Science,* 1968, **161**, 849-856.

Stout, G. F. *Analytic psychology.* New York: Macmillan, 1902.

Stuewer, R. H. (Ed.) *Historical and philosophical perspectives of science.* Minneapolis: University of Minnesota Press, 1970.

Sullivan, H. S. *Conceptions of modern psychiatry.* Washington, D.C.: William Alanson White Psychiatric Foundation, 1947.

Sullivan, H. S. *The interpersonal theory of psychiatry.* New York: Norton, 1953.

Sullivan, H. S. *The psychiatric interview.* New York: Norton, 1954.

Sullivan, H. S. *Clincial studies in psychiatry.* New York: Norton, 1956.

Sullivan, H. S. *Schizophrenia as a human process.* New York: Norton, 1962.

Sullivan, H. S. *The fusion of psychiatry and social science.* New York: Norton, 1964.

Sumby, W. H., & Pollack, I. Short-time processing of information. HFORL Report TR-54-6, 1954.

Summers, D. A., & Hammond, K. R. Inference behavior in multiple-cue tasks involving both linear and nonlinear relations. *Journal of Experimental Psychology,* 1966, **71**, 751-757.

Swets, J. A. Is there a sensory threshold? *Science,* 1961, **134**, 168-177.

Swets, J. A. (Ed.) *Signal detection and recognition by human observers: Contemporary readings.* New York: Wiley, 1964.

Swets, J. A., Green, D. M., & Tanner, W. P. On the width of critical bands. *Journal of the Acoustical Society of America,* 1962, **34**, 108-113.

Tanner, W. P., Jr. Physiological implications of psycho-physical data. *Annals of the New York Academy of Science,* 1961, **89**, 752-765.

Tanner, W. P. & Swets, J. A. A new theory of visual detection. Technical Report 18, Electronic Defense Group, University of Michigan, 1953.

Tanner, W. P., & Swets, J. A. A decision-making theory of visual detection *Psychological Review,* 1954, **61**, 401-409.

Taylor, C. *The explanation of behavior.* New York: Humanities Press, 1965.

Terrace, H. S. Stimulus control. In W. K. Honig (Ed.), *Operant behavior: Areas of research and application.* New York: Appleton-Century-Crofts, 1966. Pp. 271-344.

Thistlethwaite, D. A. A critical review of latent learning and related experiments. *Psychological Bulletin,* 1951, **48**, 97-129.

Thorndike, E. L. *The elements of psychology.* New York: A. G. Seiler, 1905.

Thorndike, E. L. *Animal intelligence.* New York: Hafner, 1911.

Thorndike, E. L. *Educational psychology.* Vol. 2, *The psychology of learning.* New York: Teachers College, 1913.

Thorndike, E. L. *Human learning.* New York: Century, 1931.

Thorndike, E. L. *The fundamentals of learning.* New York: Teachers College, 1932.

Thorndike, E. L. An experimental study of rewards. *Teachers College Contributions to Education,* 1933, No. 580. (a)

Thorndike, E. L. A theory of the action of the after-effects of a connection upon it. *Journal of Psychology,* 1933, **40**, 434-439. (b)

Thorndike, E. L. *The psychology of wants, interests, and attitudes.* New York: Appleton-Century-Crofts, 1935.

Thorndike, E. L. *Selected writings from a connectionist's psychology.* New York: Appleton-Century-Crofts, 1949.

Thorndike, E. L. E. L. Thorndike. In C. Murchison (Ed.), *A history of psychology in autobiography.* Vol. 3. Worcester, Mass.: Clark University Press, 1936. Pp. 263-270.

Thorndike, E. L., & Rock, R. T., Jr. Learning without awareness of what is being learned or intent to learn it. *Journal of Experimental Psychology,* 1934, **17**, 1-19.

Thorndike, E. L., & Woodworth, R. S. The influence of improvements in one mental function upon the efficiency of other functions. *Psychological Review,* 1901, **8**, 247-261, 384-395, 553-564.

Thurstone, L. L. Primary mental abilities. *Psychometric Monograph,* 1938, **1**. Pp. IX-121.

Tiger, L., & Fox, R. *The imperial animal.* New York: Holt, Rinehart & Winston, 1971.

Tinbergen, N. The evolution of signalling devices. In W. Etkin (Ed.), *Social behavior and organization among vertebrates.* Chicago: University of Chicago Press, 1964. Pp. 206-230.

Tinbergen, N. *The herring gull's world.* Garden City, N.Y.: Anchor Books, 1967.

Titchener, E. B. *An outline of psychology.* New York: Macmillan, 1899.

Titchener, E. B. *Lectures on elementary psychology of feeling and attention.* New York: Macmillan, 1908.

Titchener, E. B. *Text-book of psychology.* New York: Macmillan, 1910.

Titchener, E. B. Prolegomena to a study of introspection. *American Journal of Psychology,* 1912, **23**, 427-488 (a)

Titchener, E. B. The schema of introspection. *American Journal of Psychology,* 1912, **23**, 485-508. (b)

Titchener, E. B. Psychology as the behaviorist views it. *Proceedings of the American Philosophical Society,* 1914, **53**, 1-17.

Titchener, E. B. *Systematic psychology: Prolegomena.* New York: Macmillan, 1929.

Titchener, E. B. The postulates of a structural psychology. *Philosophical Review,* 1898, **7**, 449-465. As reported by W. Dennis (Ed.), *Readings in the history of psychology.* New York: Appleton-Century-Crofts, 1948. Pp. 366-376.

Tolman, E. C. A behaviorist's definition of consciousness. *Psychological Review,* 1927, **34**, 433-439.

Tolman, E. C. *Purposive behavior in animals and man.* New York: Appleton, 1932.

Tolman, E. C. Operational behaviorism and current trends in psychology. *Proceedings of the Twenty-fifth Anniversary Celebrating Inauguration of Graduate Studies.* Los Angeles: University of Southern California Press, 1936. (Also in M. H. Marx [Ed.], *Psychological theory: Contemporary readings.* New York: Macmillan, 1951. Pp. 87-102.)

Tolman, E. C. The determiners of behavior at a choice point. *Psychological Review,* 1938, **45**, 1-41.

Tolman, E. C. A stimulus-expectancy need-cathexis psychology. *Science,* 1945, **101** 16-166.

Tolman, E. C. The psychology of social learning. *Journal of Social Issues, Supplement Service,* 1949, **3**, 5-18. (a)

Tolman, E. C. There is more than one kind of learning. *Psychological Review,* 1949, **56**, 144-155. (b)

Tolman, E. C. *Collected papers in psychology.* Berkeley: University of California Press, 1951. (a)

Tolman, E. C. A psychological model. In T. Parsons & E. A. Shils (Eds.), *Toward a general theory of action.* Cambridge, Mass.: Harvard University Press, 1951. Pp. 279-361. (b)

Tolman, E. C. Principles of purposive behavior. In S. Koch (Ed.), *Psychology: A study of a science.* Vol. 2. *General systematic formulations, learning and special processes.* New York: McGraw-Hill, 1958. Pp. 92-157.

Tolman, E. C., & Brunswik, E. The organism and the causal texture of the environment. *Psychological Review,* 1935, **42**, 43-77.

Tolman, E. C., & Honzik, C. H. "Insight" in rats. *University of California Publications in Psychology,* 1930, **4**, 215-232.

Toulmin, S. The logical status of psychoanalysis. *Analysis,* 1948, **9**, 23-29.

Tryon, R. C. Genetic differences in maze-learning ability in rats. *Thirtieth Yearbook, National Society for Studies in Education,* 1940.

Turing, A. M. On computable numbers, with an application to the Entscheidung's problem. *Proceedings of the London Mathematical Society,* 1937, **42**, 230-265; 1937, **43**, 544-546. Also in M. Davis (Ed.), *The undecidable.* Hewlett, N.Y.: Raven Press, 1965.

Turner, M. *Philosophy and the science of behavior.* New York: Appleton-Century-Crofts, 1967.

Turner, M. B. *Realism and the explanation of behavior.* New York: Appleton-Century-Crofts, 1971.

Ullman, L. P., & Krasner, L. *Case studies in behavior modificaton.* New York: Holt, Rinehart, and Winston, 1965.

Underwood, B. J. *Experimental psychology.* (Rev. ed.) New York: Appleton-Century-Crofts, 1966.

Underwood, B. J. *Psychological research.* New York: Appleton-Century-Crofts, 1957.

Underwood, B. J., & Ekstrand, B. R. Studies of distributed practice: XXIV. Differentiation and proactive inhibition. *Journal of Experimental Psychology,* 1967, **74**, 574-580.

Underwood, B. J., Keppel, G., & Schulz, R. W. Studies of distributed practice: XXII. Some conditions which enhance retention. *Journal of Experimental Psychology,* 1962, **64**, 355-363.

Valentine, W. L., & Wickens, D. D. *Experimental foundations of general psychology.* (3rd ed.) New York: Holt, 1949.

Verplanck, W. S., & Skinner, B. F. In W. K. Estes et al., *Modern learning theory.* New York: Appleton-Century-Crofts, 1954. Pp. 267-316.

Voeks, V. W. Postremity, recency, and frequency as bases for prediction in the maze situation. *Journal of Experimental Psychology,* 1948, **38**, 495-510.

Voeks, V. W. Formalization and clarification of a theory of learning. *Journal of Psychology,* 1950, **30**, 341-362.

Voeks, V. W. Acquisition of S-R connections: A test of Hull's and Guthrie's theories. *Journal of Experimental Psychology,* 1954, **47**, 137-147.

Von Neumann, J. *The computer and the brain.* New Haven, Conn.: Yale University Press, 1958.

Von Neumann, J., & Morgenstern, O. *Theory of games and economic behavior.* Princeton, N.J.: Princeton University Press, 1953.

Walker, N. Science and the Freudian unconsciousness. In T. Reik (Ed.), *Psychoanalysis and the future.* New York: National Psychological Association for Psychoanalysis, 1957. Pp. 117-124.

Wallerstein, R. S., Robbins, L. L., et al. The psychotherapy research project of the Menninger foundation. *Bulletin of the Menninger Clinic,* 1956, **20**, 221-276.

Wallerstein, R. S., Robbins, L. L., et al. The psychotherapy research project of the Menninger foundation: 2nd report. *Bulletin of the Menninger Clinic,* 1958, **22**, 115-116.

Wallerstein, R. S., Robbins, L. L., et al. The psychotherapy research project of the Menninger foundation: 3rd report. *Bulletin of the Menninger Clinic,* 1960, **24**, 157-216.

Walls, G. L. "Land! Land!" *Psychological Bulletin,* 1960, **57**, 29-48.

Wann, T. W. (Ed.) *Behaviorism and phenomenology.* Chicago: University of Chicago Press, 1964.

Warren, H. C. (Ed.) *Dictionary of psychology.* Boston: Houghton Mifflin, 1934.

Washburn, M. F. *The animal mind.* New York: Macmillan, 1908.

Watanabe, S. Information: Theoretic aspects of inductive and deductive inference. *IBM Journal of Research & Development,* 1960, **4**, 208-231.

Watson, J. B. Image and affection in behavior. *Journal of Philosophy,* 1913, **10**, 421-428. (a)

Watson, J. B. Psychology as the behaviorist views it. *Psychological Review,* 1913, **20**, 158-177. (b)

Watson, J. B. *Behavior: An introduction to comparative psychology.* New York: Holt, 1914.

Watson, J. B. *Psychology from the standpoint of a behaviorist.* Philadelphia: Lippincott, 1919.

Watson, J. B. *Behaviorism.* New York: Norton, 1925.

Watson, J. B. Experimental studies on the growth of the emotions. In C. Murchison (Ed.), *Psychologies of 1925.* Worcester, Mass.: Clark University Press, 1926. Pp. 52-53. (a)

Watson, J. B. Recent experiments on how we lose and change our emotional equipment. In C. Murchison (Ed.), *Psychologies of 1925.* Worcester, Mass.: Clark University Press, 1926. Pp. 59-81. (b)

Watson, J. B. What the nursery has to say about instincts. In C. Murchison (Ed.), *Psychologies of 1925.* Worcester, Mass.: Clark University Press, 1926. Pp. 1-35. (c)

Watson, J. B. *Psychology from the standpoint of a behaviorist.* (3rd ed.) Philadelphia: Lippincott, 1929.

Watson, J. B. *Behaviorism.* (Rev. ed.) New York: Norton, 1930.

Watson, J. B. J. B. Watson. In C. Murchison (Ed.), *A history of psychology in autobiography.* Vol. 3. Worcester, Mass.: Clark University Press, 1936. Pp. 271-281.

Watson, J. B. *Behavior: An introduction to comparative psychology.* New York: Holt, Rinehart & Winston, 1967.

Watson, J. B., & McDougall, W. *The battle of behaviorism.* New York: Norton, 1929.

Watson, R. I. Psychology: A prescriptive science. *American Psychologist,* 1967, **22**, 435-443.

Watson, R. I. *The great psychologists from Aristotle to Freud.* Philadelphia, Lippincott, 1963.

Watson, R. I. *The great psychologists from Aristotle to Freud.* (Rev. ed.) Philadelphia: Lippincott, 1968.

Watson, R. I. *The great psychologists.* (3d ed.) Philadelphia: Lippincott, 1971.

Weiss, A. P. Relation between structural and behavior psychology. *Psychological Review,* 1917, **34**, 301-317.

Weiss, A. P. *A theoretical basis of human behavior.* Columbus, Ohio: Adams, 1925.

Weiss, A. P. 1 + 1 ≠ 2 (one plus one does not equal two.) In G. C. Quarton, T. Melnechuk, & F. O. Schmitt (Eds.), *The neurosciences.* New York: Rockefeller University Press, 1967. Pp. 801-821.

Weitzenhoffer, A. M. Mathematical structures and psychological measurement of psychological magnitudes with three experimental examples. *Psychological Monographs,* 1943, **55**, 1-88.

Weitzenhoffer, A. M. Mathematical structures and psychological measurements. *Psychometrika,* 1951, **16**, 398-496.

Wertheimer, M. Experimentelle Studien uber das Sehen von Bewegung. *Zeitschrift für Psychologie,* 1912, **61**, 121-165.

Wertheimer, M. Untersuchungen zur Lehre von der Gestalt. II. *Psychologische Forschung,* 1923, **4**, 301-350.

Wertheimer, M. The general theoretical situation. In W. D. Ellis (Ed.), *A source book of Gestalt psychology.* New York: Harcourt, Brace & World, 1938. Pp. 12-16.

Wertheimer, M. *Productive thinking.* New York: Harper & Row, 1945.

Wheeler, R. H., & Perkins, F. T. *Principles of mental development.* New York: Crowell, 1932.

Wheeler, R. H. *The science of psychology.* (2nd ed.) New York: Crowell, 1940.

Wheeler, R. H. Climate and human behavior. In P. L. Harriman (Ed.), *Encyclopedia of psychology.* New York: Philosophical Library, 1946. Pp. 78-86.

White, R. W. Motivation reconsidered: The concept of competence. *Psychological Review,* 1959, **66**, 297-333.

Whittaker, R. H. New concepts of kingdoms of organisms. *Science,* 1969, **163**, 150-160.

Wiener, N. *Cybernetics, or Control and communication in the animal and the machine.* Cambridge, Mass.: Technology Press [c1948], New York: Wiley, 1948.

Wiener, N. *Cybernetics, or Control and communication in the animal and the machine.* (2nd ed.) Cambridge, Mass.: M.I.T. Press, 1961.

Wiener, P. P. (Ed.) *Readings in philosophy of science.* New York: Scribner, 1953.

Willems, E. P. Planning a rationale for naturalistic research. In E. P. Willems & H. L. Raush (Eds.), *Naturalistic viewpoints in psychological research.* New York: Holt, 1969. Pp. 44-71.

Willems, E. P., & Raush, H. L. (Eds.) *Naturalistic viewpoints in psychological research.* New York: Holt, 1969.

Windelband, W. *An introduction to philosophy.* (Trans. by J. McCabe) London: T. Fisher Unwin, 1921.

Wolfensberger, W. Ethical issues in research with human subjects. *Science,* 1967, **155**, 47-51.

Woodworth, R. S. *Dynamic psychology.* New York: Columbia University Press, 1918.

Woodworth, R. S. Four varieties of behavior. *Psychological Review,* 1924, **31**, 257-264.

Woodworth, R. S. *Experimental psychology.* New York: Holt, 1938.

Woodworth, R. S. Reinforcement of perception. *American Journal of Psychology,* 1947, **60**, 119-124.

Woodworth, R. S. *Contemporary schools of psychology.* New York: Ronald Press, 1948.

Woodworth, R. S., & Schlosberg, H. *Experimental psychology.* New York: Holt, 1954.

Woodworth, R. S. *Dynamics of behavior.* New York: Holt, 1958.

Woodworth, R. S., & Sheehan, M. R. *Contemporary schools of psychology.* New York: Ronald Press, 1964.

Wooldridge, D. E. *Mechanical man: The physical basis of intelligent life.* New York: McGraw-Hill, 1968.

Wundt, W. *Human and animal psychology.* New York: Macmillan, 1894.

Wundt, W. *Principles of physiological psychology.* New York: Macmillan, 1904.

Wundt, W. *Völkerpsychologie.* Vols. 1-10. Leipzig: Engelmann, 1900-1920.

Yamaguchi, H. G., Hull, C. L., Felsinger, J. M., & Gladstone, A. I. Characteristics of dispersions based on the pooled momentary reaction potentials (sEr) of a group. *Psychological Review,* 1948, **55**, 216-238.

Yerkes, R. M. *Chimpanzees: A laboratory colony.* New Haven, Conn.: Yale University Press, 1943.

Zeigarnik, B. Das Behalten erledigter und unerledigter Handlungen. *Psychologische Forschung,* 1927, **9**, 1-85. (Trans. and cond. as "On finished and unfinished tasks" in W. D. Ellis [Ed.], *A source book of Gestalt psychology.* New York: Harcourt, Brace & World, 1938. Pp. 300-314.)

Zeigler, B. Uber das Behalte von erledigten und unerledigten Handlungen. *Psychologische Forschung,* 1927, **9**, 1-85.

Zeigler, H. G. Electrical stimulation of the brain and psychophysiology of learning and motivation. *Psychological Bulletin,* 1957, **54**, 363-382.

Zimbardo, P. G. *The cognitive control of motivation.* Glenview, Ill.: Scott, Foresman, 1969.

PSYCHOLOGY IN EUROPE, AUSTRALIA, AND CANADA

John Brebner and James Drever,
University of Adelaide, Australia, and
University of Dundee, Scotland

EUROPE

In reviewing European psychology it is tempting to lay claim to all those trends with European origins. However, even restricting the task to current work inside Europe, it is impossible in a short survey of this kind to do justice to the variety of research going on in any one country, let alone Europe as a whole. Nor would it be particularly helpful, even if it were possible, to produce an annotated bibliography which had any claim to completeness. Moreover, the publication by the **APA** of *International opportunities for advanced training and research in psychology* (1966) gives a coverage of European institutions and the psychological courses they offer which could not be matched here. Instead, we have picked out a few key figures. The theoretical position of each of them is briefly indicated, and in a number of cases an example is given of the kind of data upon which the position rests.

Although World War II interrupted the theoretical development of psychology in Europe, the major trends were conserved and reconstituted under psychologists whose reputations were firmly established before the war. The death or retirement of giants of this generation, like Piéron, Michotte, and Von Frisch, together with an expansion in the subject, has brought many younger psychologists into senior positions. It is probably true that none of these has yet achieved "giant" status, but for many, like Broadbent, Ekman, and Fraisse, it is a considerable time since they could be regarded as psychological striplings.

In describing European psychology it is convenient to use linguistic rather than national boundaries. A common tongue means a common research literature, and other kinds of affinities soon develop. For our purposes German, French, and English are the most important languages. Psychologists belonging to the smaller linguistic groups, such as those of Scandinavia or the Low Countries, try to publish in one or another of the three major languages. For example, the *Scandinavian Journal of Psychology* is published in English. The most notable exception continues to be the Italian research literature, which is considerable.

Germany

Psychological work in Germany may be given first place if only on historical grounds. World War II had a particularly crippling effect on research in Germany and Austria as a result of the great losses suffered through exile in the previous decade. Partly, too, this was due to the fact that German psychologists had for so long been accustomed to influence others and had thought of the outside world as a sort of academic colony. Under these conditions isolation was not felt to be a hardship, however serious its effects. The impact on American psychology of the flow of German immigrant psychologists has been described by Wellek (1964) and Bühler (1965). The full effect upon German psychology is difficult to assess, but intensification of certain rather characteristic kinds of German work followed—in particular, verbal, descriptive studies of personality—that nowadays seem to belong to literature rather than science. In its earlier manifestation this approach was important, and it continues to have an influence, especially in its typological forms. Spranger's *Types of men* (1928) led to *The study of values* (1951), by Allport and Vernon. Jung's *Psychological types* (1924) gave our language *extravert* and *introvert*. Kretschmer's *Physique and character* (1925) is the early formulation of a classification which has influenced, among others, Eysenck. Finally, the typological elements in Rorschach's *Psychodiagnostics* (1942), though much less prominent, are sufficiently definite to make it clear that he too belonged to this important German-speaking movement. His work has given rise to a whole research literature of its own.

It is easy to see how arbitrary and intuitive typologies could become under unfavorable circumstances, such as those provided by national socialism. Some good work continued, however, and since the later 1940s it has steadily become more empirical. A useful survey of the whole area, with comparisons between the German and other approaches, is to be found in *Perspectives in personality theory* (David and von Bracken, 1957).

There are, fortunately, clear signs that German psychology is breaking away from its former insularity. For example, the Deutsche Forschungemeinschaft has commissioned a review of the redevelopment of German psychology since the war (Hoyos, 1961). More recently, direct comparisons between psychology in Germany and psychology in America have been made (Merz, 1960; Murch & Wesley, 1966; Russell & Roth, 1958; Wesley, 1966), and textbooks written in German which present some of the recent work outside Germany are appearing (Foppa, 1965).

It is clear from Hoyos's review that German psychologists still approach personality with a split-level treatment, which is nomothetic when typological and ideographic in the study of character. A recent text in the study of character is Wellek's book (1966). The German typological approach has perhaps been most clearly continued by Eysenck in Britain, with his recent attempts to find a genetic and physiological basis for introversion-extraversion (1963; 1963-1964).

Another field in which German psychology has held a distinctive position is perception. The Gestalt psychologists, first in Frankfurt-am-Main and then in Berlin, exercised a far-reaching influence from 1920 until 1934. The senior members of the group—Wertheimer, Köhler, Koffka, and Lewin—went into exile, but one or two good experimentalists among the younger generation stayed on. Of these, Metzger has been the most productive. His book *Gesetze des Sehens* appeared in a second edition in 1953 with many new data. In general, Metzger's work resembles most closely that of Koffka (1936), but increases the degree of stimulus complexity. In particular, there are some very interesting data on the kinds of perceptual organization which occur when we are presented with visual stimuli in motion.

The extent of current work on perception in Germany which is cast in the Gestaltist mold may surprise anyone who believes that information theory has swallowed up Gestalttheorie. Whether it ever could is a question raised by Green and Courtis (1966). Their argument is that attempts to apply information theory to figure perception have concentrated on the properties of a figure, rather than on the perceptual process, and that in so doing, they have failed to define the ensembles of signs and their associated probabilities of occurrence, which are essential for any measure of association such as our measures of information.

Fairly typical of the bulk of recent perceptual studies in Germany are the papers by Farne (1965) on figural aftereffects, Graefe (1964) on the effect of inner contours on form discrimination, and Schmitt (1966), who lays claim to a new perceptual illusion. Kiekheben's (1966) paper, in which he presents work on a "motivating effect of non-prägnanz," although couched in Gestaltist terms, has affinities with Berlyne's work on perceptual novelty and inspection.

A record of the work of the much smaller "Ganzheit" school of psychology at Leipzig—Ganzheiten are distinguished from Gestalten by including in the "whole" the effects of previous experiences—has been published (Volkelt, 1963).

More original, and at present more influential in the field of perception, has been the work going on at Innsbruck. Ivo Köhler has made a number of visits to the United States, and some of his experiments are well known. What Köhler does, as he puts it, is to place his laboratory on the bridge of his subject's nose—that is, he uses prisms and filters in a spectacle frame which allows an experiment to run for several weeks.

In such a frame, 10-degree prisms may be inserted with the same orientation, so as to produce a horizontal displacement of visual objects. The prisms are not corrected spherically or chromatically. At first the subject bumps into obstacles, sees vertical straight lines as curved, and finds that the world has become curiously elastic when he moves his head. In addition, all sharp vertical gradients of illumination show a marked fringe of blue or orange. Over a period of three days of continuous wear, these effects largely disappear. Some of the changes had already been described by Gibson (1933). The chromatic adaptation is unusual, however, since complementary aftersensations are obtained when the prisms are removed. These are not retinal, but may remain anchored to the vertical gradients of illumination, although the eyes may move. The theory which Köhler puts forward to account for these, and many other phenomena like them, which he has demonstrated, is not unlike Helson's adaptation level (1958). The organism establishes over time a null point for any constant feature of the stimulus milieu (Köhler, 1963). Köhler's work, originally published in two parts in 1951 and 1953, has more recently appeared in monograph form in English (1964). A useful discussion of Köhler's and other work on displaced vision is that by Harris (1965).

Further work along the same lines (Hajos & Ritter, 1965) has shown that some negative aftereffects are observed in both eyes even though one eye has been covered while the other has been seeing the world through a prism. Using prisms in opposed directions on the two eyes, the same workers have also demonstrated that each eye can develop its own adaptation independently of the other. Using a rather more conservative estimate, Ebenholtz (1966) found rather less interocular transfer.

Another feature of Köhler's work is his demonstration of "gaze-contingent" effects which are adapted to, and aftereffects which are produced by, prismatic transformation. Light falling on a subject's eye through a prism enters the prism at different angles, depending on the direction of the subject's gaze. Hence, if adaptation occurs, the subject must adapt to variations in the characteristics in the transformation which occurs when the eyes are moved, or even when the gaze direction is held constant and the subject moves his head. One recent study, has, however, failed to find gaze-contingent color aftereffects (Harrington, 1965).

Köhler's cybernetic interests are indicated, in an elementary fashion, in his outline of a simple electromechanical analog for classical conditioning (1962).

The third, and during the postwar decades the best-known, area of German research has been that of animal behavior. While American psychologists were coming more and more to depend upon the maze and the Skinner box, German biologists, protected against methodological insecurity by a great tradition, went on observing animals in their natural surroundings. Their observations were systematic, and nowadays a good deal of controlled experimentation goes on; however, the emphasis has always been upon the reactions of a particular species to the various characteristics of its natural environment.

The literature is a big one, and one or two striking studies must represent it. Von Frisch, whose work on bees had long been famous, made some observations during World War II that aroused a good deal of skepticism. He claimed that workers returning to the hive after discovering a new source of honey can indicate both the direction and the distance to their fellows. They do this by dancing. There are two dances—the "round" dance and the "waggle" dance. Round dances consistently indicate food 50 meters or less from the hive, and waggle dances are used for longer distances, but there is a range between 50 and 100 meters when either may

the notion of an ordered sequence as long as they are allowed to lay their test string alongside the model and check the items one by one against each other. It is clear from the types of errors made that the second stage is reached because the child has become able to maintain a constant order of progression. At first, however, it is very easy to disrupt the ordered sequence by moving the model to one side or by having the child reproduce a vertical order on a horizontal string. The perceptual pattern is necessary to maintain the constant direction. Between five and six years new possibilities begin to emerge. The child can maintain the sequence and even reverse it without a point-to-point comparison. He is then given the model with the items arranged in a circle and is asked to produce the order on a straight line. Here he must work at a more abstract level, and the perceptual separation of the two ends of the line causes trouble. It is not until he is six or seven years old that the child is able to handle spatial order as such and to reproduce or reverse models presented to him vertically, circularly, or even twisted into a figure eight.

One can see how this patient, rather informal exploration could be used as the basis for test construction or a more rigorous experimental design, but Piaget's own interests seem to be moving in the direction of a theoretical analysis of thinking as such. *The growth of logical thinking from childhood to adolescence* (1958) and, more recently, his work on classification and seriation (Piaget & Inhelder, 1964) give some indication of Piaget's activity in the field of thinking. *L'image mentale chez l'enfant* (1966) is one of Piaget's most recent works on thinking and symbolic processes in children. Piaget's work up to about 1960 is discussed in Flavell's useful book *The developmental psychology of Jean Piaget* (1963).

The extent of Piaget's influence is clearly seen in *Psychologie et épistémologie génetiques: thèmes Piagetiens* (Bresson & Montmollin, 1966). The contributors to this volume, published in Piaget's honor, include Berlyne (Canada), Smedslund (Norway), and Fraisse (France). Piaget's latest writings are *Biologie et connaissance: Essai sur les relations entre les régulations organiques et les processus cognitifs* (1967a) and, in translation, *Six psychological studies* (1967b).

Despite Piaget's stature as an innovator, it would be wrong to think of the work at Geneva as in any way isolated from French psychology as a whole. There are many links with Michotte's work through studies of causality, movement, and speed as understood by children, while Fraisse at the Sorbonne in *Les structures rhythmiques* (1957) shares with Piaget an interest in the development of the perception of time. An introduction to the work of Piaget and Fraisse which could be useful to someone who has no previous knowledge of Piaget's work on cognitive schematizing and perception or of Fraisse's work on time perception is given in Vol. 6 of *Traité de psychologie expérimentale* (Fraisse & Piaget, 1963).

The history of psychology in Belgium, and an assessment of recent trends there, is available in Nuttin's monograph (1961a). Nuttin's own experimentally based attack upon the Thorndikian view of the law of effect (1961b) has been largely neglected in the United States. His work on the spread of effect demonstrates this attack. Here, Nuttin sets out to demolish Thorndike's connectionist interpretation of the spread-of-effect phenomenon, which accepted that S-R bonds are strengthened by reward and weakened by punishment.

Nuttin (1949) suggests that more than one factor acts to produce the spread-of-effect result, and he demonstrates a similar phenomenon which is attributable to "spread of recall." What Nuttin demonstrates is that *if one rearranges the order* of a list which has been presented once to a subject, items are now recalled as having been rewarded if, on the second (test) presentation, they are close to items which were rewarded. That is, recalling items as having been rewarded, occurs significantly more frequently for those items now nearest rewarded items than for items which were nearest on the first presentation of the list.

Marx (1956), who at the time seems to have been alone among American psychologists in considering Nuttin's work, found it difficult to distinguish Nuttin's interpretation of the phenomenon from Thorndike's. Greenwald (1966) points out clearly that Nuttin is trying to disentangle the effects of rewards as strengthening associations on the acquisition trial and, alternatively, producing mistaken recalls of having been rewarded—as a function of nearness to rewarded items, even when the list order is rearranged—on the test trial.

Nuttin's spread of recall is certainly not how Thorndike saw the spread of effect operating and can be viewed as complementing rather than supplementing Thorndike's view. But Marx is right to wonder how Nuttin would define the strength of a response, rejecting, as Nuttin explicity does, increase in the frequency of response repetition in the course of a learning experiment. Perhaps the issue here is that, for Thorndike, reward acts on the connection between stimulus and response items; for Nuttin the effect of reward generalizes from the rewarded item to other nearby items.

Nuttin might have postulated a gradual decay of reward effect to explain why in his experiments, there is still some tendency in the test trial for items nearest rewarded ones in the acquisition trial to be wrongly recalled as having been rewarded even though they are now furthest from a rewarded item. However, Nuttin appears to prefer the alternative that both spread of effect and spread of recall may underlie the phenomenon.

Nuttin's work is damaging to Thorndikian connectionism, but the connectionist standpoint keeps cropping up in psychology. Fairly recently, for example, Broadbent (1958, p. 298) states that for the long term, the organism stores the conditional probabilities of past events. These, it can be argued, are precisely what Thorndike was manipulating through reinforcement in his "selecting and connecting."

This somewhat unlikely line of descent for Broadbent's idea of what is learned—which, in fact, probably derives from information-theory approaches—might also have included Skinner's response probability in the family tree. Technically, the main difference between Thorndike and Skinner is simply that, accepting the possiblity of rewarding smaller segments of behavior, Skinner achieves a faster and more precise control of his subject's behavior than Thorndike did.

British psychology tends to look across the Atlantic just now, but it still retains a few distinctive features. Oddly enough in the country of the "English" empiricists and associationists, one of these features is a lack of interest in associationism (Drever, 1965). This is probably the result of historical accidents. Empirical psychology as formulated at the beginning of the present century by the philosophers Ward (1918) and Stout (1913) had been transformed by post-Kantian German thought. Bartlett, who more than anyone else determined the present nature of British psychology, was a pupil of Ward. This did not make him a philosopher—he has always been impatient of armchair theorizing—but it did make him suspicious of a simple S-R approach. It is important for psychologists in the United States, or in Russia for that matter, to realize that the rather general European indifference to associationism springs from the fact that it is an "old-fashioned" point of view and can be found quite fully developed in the eighteenth century. While the Kantian reformation of Hume's position did not deal with associationism as such, it did imply the existence of cognitive structures other than those based upon contiguity and frequency. Since that time, all variants of the simple S-R theme have appeared too easy. This prejudice is held to have been justified by events, and there is a strong suspicion that the amount of information generated per rat-mile during the last fifty years has not been great.

Bartlett's *Remembering* is a study of perception and thinking as well as memory, and his more recent *Thinking* does no more than develop some of the themes in the earlier work. But Bartlett has been much more influential through his teaching than through his writings. The Cambridge laboratory was for many years a leading nursery for experimental psychologists. At one time more than two-thirds of the chairs in Great Britain were held by Bartlett's pupils. They may not all have been docile, but most of them show identifiable characteristics. Prominent among these are a preference for human rather than animal subjects and a tendency to use cognitive types of explanation. The latter are more often stated nowadays in neurological or electronic than in logical terms.

A key figure in the development of British psychology in the fields of perception and thinking was Craik, who died, still a young man, as the result of a road accident in 1945. He was a philosopher by training, an experimentalist by inclination, and a genius at inventing apparatus. Some of the basic ideas of cybernetics owe their origin to him. A short statement of his theoretical position is to be found in *The nature of explanation* (1943), and selected papers by Craik have recently been published (Craik, 1966).

Broadbent (1958) has described important experimental work which follows up some of Craik's ideas. According to Broadbent, two of the basic problems in perception as related to skilled performance are channel capacity and selectivity. How much information can the human operator handle, and how can he protect himself against overloading or from unwanted signals? In vision many of the necessary adjustments are carried out peripherally, but in hearing they must be done centrally. Thus Broadbent uses auditory stimuli in experiments where the subject has to listen selectively to one of two simultaneous messages or to a message accompanied by irrelevant noise; the filtering process which takes place is central rather than sensory. It depends upon the amount of information, as one might expect, but it also depends to a marked extent upon the sequential probability values within the two messages. It is this that makes the word *stimulus* about as specific and psychologically useful as the word *thing*. The theoretical position which emerges from Broadbent's work resembles that advocated by Bruner (1957) and others in the United States.

Broadhurst (1966), who is himself largely responsible for the recent redevelopment of interest in experimental psychogenetics in Britain, has seen in Broadbent's interest in introversion-extraversion "a hint of the merging interests of . . . Broadbent and Eysenck which, should it come to collaborative effort, might result in British psychology developing an impact born of coherent thought, the like of which it has not previously exerted." This, however, appears to ignore the fact that Broadbent (1958) relates introversion-extraversion to the length of "sample" of incoming data used by the individual. It also disregards the fact that predictions from Broadbent's model of introversion-extraversion have sometimes conflicted with predictions from the Eysenckian model (e.g., Broadbent, 1958; Griew & Lynn, 1960).

The work of the Applied Psychology Research Unit at Cambridge under Broadbent's direction is very much in the mainstream of Bartlettian influence. Some of the aspects of the unit's work are described by Poulton (1966) in his chapters on engineering psychology in the *Annual Review of Psychology* and on tracking in Bilodeau's *Acquisition of skill* (1966). This latter book betrays the fact that skilled performance in the United States is still, to a large extent, studied as a subdivision of learning. This is also true of the Soviet approach to skill, and it is not irrelevant that in both these countries monolithic theories of learning, which accept the conditioned response as a fixed behavioral unit, have held sway for long periods. In the United States the full extent of Watson's and Hull's influence may be seen in the fact that even authors who have rejected the conditioned response (for example, Tolman and Skinner) still discuss the (fixed) behavioral unit (Skinner, 1959; Tolman, 1932). Berlyne (1965) goes to some trouble to deny these fixed units: ". . . contemporary S-R psychology concerns itself with associations not between single stimuli and single responses (whatever those would be!) but between classes of stimulus situations and classes of behaviour (p. 8)." The temptation is to add "whatever those would be" again, but the main difference is that we retain freedom to *define* and, if necessary, *redefine* classes empirically rather than trying to force our behavioral analysis into inappropriate classes.

The Cambridge tradition in the study of skilled performance contrasts with this, asking the question: "How is complex purposive behavior organized?" and working by induction from finding to model, rather than deductively from theory to prediction. The barrenness, for Hullians, of the prediction which is unconfirmed is no more admitted by them than the precariousness of Skinner's theoretical approach is admitted by Skinnerians.

The Cambridge tradition in the study of skilled performance is seen in Vol. 27 of *Acta Psychologica,* which is a special volume on attention and performance dedicated to the remembrance of Paul Fitts.

Other important work which lies outside the mainstream of Bartlett's influence is also being carried out at Cambridge. Two sets of studies are noteworthy: first, the work by Gregory on perception (Gregory, 1966a, 1966b; Gregory & Wallace, 1963). Gregory's size-constancy theory of the illusions, in particular, has produced great interest among, and a good deal of criticism from, other European workers (Virsu, 1967; Zanforlin, 1967). Second, the work at Cambridge on the effects of cortical ablation in primates (Cowey, 1967; Cowey & Weiskrantz, 1967; Humphrey & Weiskrantz, 1967) derived its initial impetus from Zangwill's active interest in the effects of specific lesions on behavior. How far the recent Cambridge interest in creativity (Hudson, 1966) derives from Bartlett is not clear, but he has certainly advocated a change in the usual form of intelligence test (1954): "Intelligence is at least as much a matter of the ways by which an issue, or an answer to a problem is reached, as of whether the issue, or the answer, can be called 'correct'."

Hudson's work is on convergent and divergent thinking following Guilford (1950). He has shown that the tendency is for divergers to seek arts specialisms and for convergers to choose the physical sciences. Hudson rejects the facile identification of creativity with divergent thinking, pointing out that in the physical sciences, which attract convergers, the creative people still tend to be convergers, although they may be rather more like divergers than their less creative counterparts. The roots of convergent and divergent thinking Hudson suggests are to be found in the child's upbringing. Convergers may be made by parents who are unable to show affection easily. These parents, it is suggested, may typically find it easier to offer an academic sort of approval of more impersonal skills, thus leading the child to acquire these and find his security in them. The diverger's parents, on the other hand, tend to disregard the importance of practical achievements and to reserve their approval and affection for personal relationships. Such parents, Hudson argues, produce children who are "addicted to people," seeing them as the source of their security.

A second strand in British psychology can be traced back to Galton through Spearman, Thomson, and Burt. It was to the study of individual differences and the development of appropriate statistical techniques that Britain made its most distinctive psychological contribution during the first quarter of the present century. Spearman stated his hierarchical theory of intelligence in *The nature of "intelligence" and principles of cognition* (1923), followed by *The abilities of man* (1927). Thomson waited until 1939 to publish *The factorial analysis of human ability,* but the two had long been engaged in a lively academic duel. Thomson's attitude toward Spearman, and later toward Thurstone, was on the whole one of skepticism. In particular he doubted Spearman's claim that factor analysis could be used to prove the necessity of one particular solution. Burt is still active in statistical psychology, and his book *The factors of the mind* (1940) is an objective summing-up of the earlier controversies and the statement of the still distinctive British position in the factor-analysis field. Burt was also the first psychologist who applied Mendelian genetics to the study of mental inheritance, and it is from him that the current interest in psychogenetics in Britain stems (Broadhurst, 1959).

The application of mental testing in British education has been surprisingly wide for a country with such a reputation for conservatism. Until the present government indicated their intention to alter the educational system, most children in the state school system were given the so-called 11-plus examination, which is an intelligence and achievement test. What happens educationally thereafter is determined, perhaps too much, by the results. As a consequence, much present-day British research in this area has a marked practical and educational bias, and theoretical issues are no longer being raised. Of the workers whose main contribution belongs to the period since World War II, P. E. Vernon has been most influential. He is a pupil of Bartlett who belongs to the school of Burt. In *The structure of human abilities* (1950) he shows an empirical and cautious approach with the marked practical bias that has just been mentioned. A book published in 1964 is a critical survey of personality assessment. The main theoretical conclusions of this book are summarized in an article (Vernon, 1965) appearing in a volume of essays by Burt's former pupils and others, compiled in recognition of his formidable contribution to psychology.

The British view of the nature of intelligence differs from the American in being hierarchical. Thorndike (1914) thought of intelligence as a multitude of specific skills. Thurstone (1938) later worked with a relatively large democratically ordered collection of abilities. British workers in the field, though differing among themselves, have moved toward analysis of intelligence which starts with a general factor. Once the general factor has been removed from the matrix of test intercorrelation, it is found that two large group factors tend to show up—one of them verbal-numerical-educational in nature, and the other spatial-practical-mechanical. Below these again are smaller group factors corresponding roughly to the primary mental abilities of Thurstone, with specific factors deriving from particular skills and circumstances at the bottom. The differences between the British and the American views are not basic, but depend to some extent upon method. For example, Thurstone has a second-order general factor which in some respects resembles Spearman's original "g" factor.

To the outside observer, Eysenck might seem to belong here too, but the impression is misleading. It is true that his early work was based on the factor analysis of personality tests, and at one stage he was influenced by Burt, but his statistical procedures are only part of a wider strategy. More recently Hullian learning theory has been utilized in the same way. As has been suggested, Eysenck has much in common with the German typologists, though his methods are much more rigorous than theirs tend to be. Even so, there are those who feel that he sometimes uses his data in a forensic rather than a scientific way. At all events, his output is much greater than that of any other British psychologist just now and ranges all the way from highly technical to popular works. Perhaps *The scientific study of personality* (1952) gives the best general statement of his theoretical position. He is concerned, on the basis of objective test data, to rate his subjects on a number of dimensions, of which introvert-extravert and normal-neurotic are the most important. Having done this, he hopes to identify the underlying neurological variables for these dimensions. Much of his work has been done in a clinical setting, and he has edited a handbook of abnormal psychology (1960) in which most of the contributors are present or former colleagues.

It is a strength of Eysenck's that his attempts to relate together the numerous and diverse results on introversion-extraversion appear receptive to new trends in psychology. That the *Zeitgeist* stalks the corridors of the Maudsley is used equally often as a criticism by Eysenck's antagonists, who point to his rather loose interrelating of Hullian reactive inhibition, Pavlovian cortical inhibition, Pavlovian "strength" of the nervous system, and, more recently, the tonic activity of the reticular formation of the brainstem.

It has been suggested by Eysenck (1963), with a hesitancy which many might judge uncharacteristic, that the ascending reticular formation has affinities with psychological concepts of excitatory and inhibitory potential. Certainly, experiments with stimulant and depressant drugs which work through the reticular formation have shown that more introverted behavior follows administration of the former and that more extraverted behavior follows administration of the latter.

This is a suggested basis for the apparently genetically constituted tendency toward introversion or extraversion shown by Shields (1962). Shields compared the personalities of monozygotic and fraternal twins reared separately or together. The correlation on extraversion scores for identical twins brought up apart was +.61 (forty-two pairs), and for identical twins brought up together it was +.42 (forty-three pairs), whereas for fraternal twins brought up together it was −.17. While twin studies are always hedged about with difficulties, these data seem to point to a genetic basis for introversion-extraversion.

It is unnecessary to do more than note in passing that the naturalistic study of animal behavior, which was a feature of British biology at the end of the nineteenth century, is again becoming more prevalent as a result of influences from the Continent. Reference has already been made to works by Tinbergen, now at Oxford, and by Thorpe, of Cambridge. Recent work by Tinbergen has appeared on the evolution of signaling devices (1964), and both Tingergen (behavior and natural selection) and Thorpe (development of behavior) have contributed chapters to *Ideas in modern biology* (Moore, 1965). Another contribution has been made by Thorpe and Davenport (1964) to the study of learning in invertebrates. Other publications in this field include *Brain and behaviour in cephalopods,* by Wells (1962), whose work has more in common with that of J. Z. Young than with that of Tinbergen. This kind of approach seems more congenial to British psychologists than the use of mazes and Skinner boxes but a good deal of animal research on quantitative lines is going on as well.

Scandinavia

Scandinavia, which is seemingly geographically remote, is often associated with scientific and cultural developments of an advanced kind. Psychology as a profession has obtained more official recognition here than elsewhere in Europe, and in Norway particularly an admirable scheme of training and certification has been worked out.

On the research side there is widespread activity in most fields of psychology. Piaget's influence is apparent in Scandinavia, as elsewhere in Europe (see Smedslund, 1964), and some interest in human learning is evident. Bjorgen's book on rote learning (1964) is an attempt to relate both meaningfulness and learning speed to some mediator which allows the item to be learned to be integrated into the subject's store of experiences. But perception continues to be by far the most active field of Scandinavian psychological research. Katz, though he came late to Stockholm, was very influential. The phenomenological point of view, which he shared with Rubin, is well stated by von Fieandt, of Helsinki (1958). Johansson, at Uppsala, is more an experimentalist than a theoretician (e.g., Johansson & Ottander, 1964), but both his work (1958, 1964) and that of von Fieandt (von Fieandt & Gibson, 1959) show affinities with that of Gibson at Cornell. The importance of psychophysics in Scandinavian psychology may be seen in the fact that a major link between Scandinavian and American psychology occurs through the work of the latter-day psychophysicists—Gibson, Helson, and Stevens. This is not to say that there is always agreement between the two sets of workers; Ross's book on psychological measurement and its underlying logic (1964) claims that in his direct scaling methods, Stevens (in whose laboratory Ross had worked for a year) develops a subjective psychology. Ross's argument is not supported by the earlier work of Goude (1962), and the question is fully discussed by Eisler (1965). Helson's influence may be seen in the work of von Wright and Mikkonen (1963).

Much of the current work on psychophysics in Scandinavia has its direct origin in the laboratories at Stockholm, where Ekman is a figure of international reputation in the fields of psychophysics and scaling. Ekman's chapter, written with Sjoberg, on scaling (Ekman & Sjoberg, 1965) gives some idea of the contribution he and his co-workers made in this field. On the physiological side, excretion rates of adrenaline and noradrenaline in cognitive tasks under stress have been the subject of a series of experiments by Frankenhaeuser and her colleagues (Frankenhaeuser, 1966a, 1966b).

There also appears to have developed a Scandinavian school with a common approach to problem solving which lays emphasis on the restructuring of past experience (J. Jensen, 1960a, 1960b; Raaheim, 1960, 1961, 1962; Szekely, 1958, 1959).

Holland

Holland nowadays has much in common with Scandinavia. Applied psychology is quite advanced, particularly in the industrial and cultural fields, but there is no distinctive theoretical position. Social psychology is highly developed in Holland, as it is in Belgium and France, but as yet there is no sign of any European challenge to Michigan. Although the universities contribute a proportion of the current research on perception, as Amsterdam does under Duijker (e.g., Moed, 1964, 1965, 1966), the Institute for Perception R.V.O.-T.N.O. at Soesterberg is claiming a growing share of the output (e.g., Michon, 1965; Sanders, 1963, 1966), and already one good monograph (Levelt, 1965), on binocular rivalry, has emerged from the institute. Some of the institute's work is presented in the special volume of *Acta Psychologica* mentioned above (Vol. 27).

Italy

Italian psychology retained its philosophical charcteristics longer than the psychologies of the more northerly European countries. A notable early development of experimental work occurred at the Catholic University at Milan. Here Gemelli rivaled Piéron in the extent of his output and excelled him in diversity. In recent years there have been many signs of direct American influence upon Italian psychology, but earlier Gemelli played a twofold role. Not only was he a productive research worker and policy maker, but he also maintained a closer contact with the psychological world as a whole than any of his colleagues did.

Applied work in Italy, as at the National Institute of Psychology at Rome, derives mainly from Gemelli but also to a lesser degree from Ponzo's contributions to aptitude testing and selection and the recognition his efforts obtained for applied psychology in education, industry, and vocational guidance (see Misiak & Staudt, 1953).

Much of the psychological research in Italy either has an applied orientation—there is, for example, widespread interest in areas like accident prevention (Cesa-Bianchi & Di Naro, 1966; Iacono, 1966; Migliorino, 1965)—or is performed in areas where applied and theoretical issues come close to each other, for example, Tretini's (1966) formulation of a culturalization rate, expressed as culture-free intelligence over culturalized intelligence, for use with socially deprived children; the work on risk-taking behavior by Spaltro (1965), comparing group and individual decisions; and that of Chiari (1966), who studied attitudes and risk perception in adolescents in everyday and occupational activities.

Some theoretically orientated research is, however, carried on, and even now, as in Battachi and Montanini's (1965) work on syntactic structures, it is possible to detect echoes of Gemelli's earlier original research, in this case his work on the acoustic analysis of language. In the north, in Trieste under Kanizsa and in Padua under Metelli, pure research flourishes in the field of perception (e.g., Flores d'Arcais, 1965). These perceptual studies show the influence which German psychology, and particularly Gestaltists like Köhler, has exerted in Italy.

AUSTRALIA

Historically, psychology in Australia had its beginnings in education. Once psychology was under way in its own right, the bias of Australian psychologists, like A. H.

Martin and H. T. Lovell, was toward applied and, specifically, vocational psychology. There are now vocational guidance divisions in each state run by the Commonwealth (Federal) Labour Department, but Australian psychology has developed so rapidly that there is no disproportionate trend in current work to indicate its origins.

There are three main streams of current development in Australian psychology. The first, stemming perhaps from the influence of Champion and his colleagues at Sydney, is a widespread behavioristic approach to animal learning.

The second, deriving originally from the influence of A. J. Marshall at Western Australia and O'Neill at Sydney, is the present activity in perception. Here, as in Scandinavia, there is some identification with Gibson's approach. The strongest research line is undoubtedly the study of aftereffects led by Day at Monash and his collaborator Singer at Maquarie. Two particularly interesting examples of this work are Day's work with Power and the explanation of sensory adaptation and aftereffect advanced by Day and Singer. Day and Power (1965) bring together under one interpretation rotary movement reversals, shown, for example, by Ames's window; apparent reversals in orientation of static figures, of which the ambiguous windmill is an example; and the kinetic depth effect. All these effects are explained in terms of "an identity of retinal projections for two or more motions or orientations of an object in space." Day and Singer, following Barlow and Hill (1963), suggest that the neural coding of stimulation is represented by the difference in firing levels between groups of neurons which are specific to a particular form of stimulation, e.g., clockwise or anticlockwise movement and blue or yellow light. What is suggested is that with prolonged stimulation, the activity of the stimulated neuron group diminishes—producing adaptation—so that on cessation of the stimulation, there is relatively greater activity by the nonstimulated neuron group, thus giving rise to an aftereffect or negative afterimage until the firing levels of both neural groups again balance.

There are some problems with this approach, particularly where intersensory effects on aftereffects have been observed (e.g., Day & Singer, 1964a, b), but it seems not at all impossible that eventually a common processor group of neural units will be identified which accepts and integrates similar information from different modalities (e.g., Morrell, 1967). Certainly the existence of cross-modal effects on aftereffects makes this seem entirely likely.

The third stream of psychological research has its roots in an environment where social influences on personality not only were considered to be an important area of academic interest but also were conceived of as a field of applied social engineering. Most of this sort of work centered on Melbourne (e.g., Oeser & Emery, 1954; Oeser & Hammond, 1954; Oeser & Harary, 1964; Oeser & O'Brien, 1967).

It is possible to discern that there may soon be a fourth major trend in Australian psychology, relating to physiological psychology and particularly to perceptual processes. The origins of this work probably go back to Eccles himself, but currently the work includes Bishop's interest in vertebrate vision and, more lately, but also at Canberra, Horridge's work on invertebrates. What is presently lacking is a sufficient number of psychologists interested in attempting to relate this work to perception.

Outside the major trends, the main impression one gets of psychology at most Australian institutions is that it has a high degree of eclecticism. Hence, Sydney is a center not only of behaviorism in Champion's work but also of psychometrics (Sutcliffe, 1964, 1965; Sutcliffe & Bristow, 1966), and Canberra combines social psychology and an active Piagetian group with an essentially British approach to human performance. Adelaide's two universities are complementary in their coverage. The older university of Adelaide had its initial impetus from M. A. Jeeves's interest in cognitive psychology and shows strength in physiological and comparative psychology (e.g., Glow, Richardson, & Rose, 1967; Glow & Rose, 1966; Munn, 1964) and operant studies, together with a growing involvement with the cultural and social problems of Australia's Aboriginal population. More recently, however, under A. T. Welford, there has been an increasing emphasis on a Bartlettian approach to both theoretical and practical issues in the organization of human skilled performance. The newer Flinders University, on the other hand, is geared to work in personality and social psychology; e.g., Feather's studies on persistence and achievement motivation extend the original work of McClelland and Atkinson. Feather's contribution is seen in his book, written jointly with Atkinson, entitled *A theory of achievement motivation* (Atkinson & Feather, 1966).

Clinical and personality psychology is probably best represented outside the older universities at New South Wales (e.g., Hammer & Johnson, 1965) and Western Australia (e.g., Sarbin, Taft, & Bailey, 1960; Taft, 1959, 1966; Yates, 1962, 1966). Australian work goes beyond the particular biases mentioned, of course (e.g., Lafitte, 1957; O'Neil, 1962), but no major psychological innovation has yet originated in Australia.

CANADA

There is currently a great volume of psychological research in Canada, with widespread interest in two fields. The first is verbal learning and memory research (Earhard & Earhard, 1967; Earhard & Mandler, 1965a, 1965b; Jung, 1967; Marshall, 1967; Murdock, 1967; Murray, 1967). The second field is motivation. Appley, who with Cofer wrote *Motivation: Theory and research* (Cofer & Appley, 1967), and Bindra, the author of *Motivation: A systematic reinterpretation* (1959), were both at Canadian universities Malmo's work on motivation at McGill relates the notion of a generalized nondirected drive and physiological arousal (Malmo, 1958), and he tends to try to use physiological indicators of drive and emotion rather than more traditional behavioristic measures (1957, 1965). Berlyne's work on "novelty" or "surprisingness" (1954, 1960, 1961, 1963) relates the internal state of the animal, which may be called *attentional* and which includes level of arousal, and learning. He may be loosely grouped among the Canadian motivational workers, although his interests seem to have swung toward giving the neoassociationists a firm foothold in the field of thinking. Berlyne's book *Structure and direction in thinking* (1965) is an attempt to understand the "implicit responses" of intellectual processes in terms of the behaviorist's principles of overt behavior.

What is most distinctively Canadian in psychology, however, still derives from Hebb (1949). There appear to be two main lines of descent in Canadian psychology. The first involves work on sensory isolation (Bexton, Heron, & Scott, 1954) which is being carried on by Zubek and his co-workers, (Schutte & Zubek, 1967; Zubek & MacNeill, 1967). Work on perceptual isolation is not confined to Canada (see Fuller & Clark, 1966a, 1966b; Mason & Sponholz, 1963; Schultz, 1965), but Zubek's project is a systematic analysis of the separate effects of factors present in the original studies.

The second involves studies which are perhaps not immediately recognizable as being closely related to one another but which nevertheless have a link in their descent from Hebb's work. Hebb (1949, pp. 49-50) quoted the (then) unpublished work of Mishkin and Forgays (1952), showing that when words are tachistoscopically exposed in either left or right visual fields, they are more readily recognized in the right visual field. Hebb used these data in his attack upon Lashley's work on equipotentiality. Heron (1957) found results which went against Mishkin and Forgay's hypothesis that "a more efficient neural organization" is established in the left cerebral hemisphere for verbal material. Heron preferred to explain the data in terms of a post exposure attentional process, involving learned eye movements, which is developed in learning to read. This work has sparked off a large number of other studies, mainly using tachistoscopic techniques on the effects of retinal location, cerebral dominance, and directional reading habits (Bryden, 1965, 1967; Bryden & Rainey, 1963; Hirata & Osaka, 1967; Kimura, 1961).

CONCLUSION

Stepping back to look at psychology in these three parts of the world as a whole allows a few impressionistic comments. As a result of the use of computer techniques, information theory, and statistical decision theory, the discovery of a common language among experimental psychologists, and between psychologists and mathematicians and communications engineers, exemplified in Cherry's *On human communication* (1961), continues. Cherry himself (1957) gave a salutary reminder of the limitations of communication theory as a tool of experimental psychology, but the gains for theoretical development, which derive from this approach, are not yet exhausted. Other cognitive systems are being used in other contexts. Piaget's analysis of children's thinking is logical as well as descriptive.

What is conspicuously absent from the European scene is systematic learning theory of the Hullian type. This was largely an American phenomenon, just as a rigid conditioned reflex theory had to be characteristic of Russia. The East-West political division apart, the biggest gulf in the psychological world is still that between America and Europe. For reasons which are probably linguistic, an exception can be made in the cases of Britain and Scandinavia. For other European countries, however, what traffic there is in research and ideas seems to be largely one-way, with Europe following America's lead. This trend tends to reduce further the influence of European psychology, even inside Europe itself, and delays the assimilation of European discoveries within American psychology.

Nevertheless, the geographical peculiarities of psychology are slowly giving way before the current American move toward mediation types of formulation and the growing Russian interest in symbolic processes, shown, for example, by Luria (1959).

Skinner's influence, never very great in European research, is increasing slightly in applied fields, as in the use of autoeducational devices or in clinical work. But research into operant conditioning as a therapeutic procedure is still uncommon in much of Europe, where most clinicians pin their faith firmly to the advance of physical methods, particularly for the treatment of schizophrenia and the depressive illnesses.

Skinner's particular legacy to psychology will be a few valid and important generalizations and several useful techniques. In Europe at least, these may be incorporated into psychology without producing the research effort which usually surrounds a largely untested and complex theory such as Hull, for example, bequeathed to us.

Finally, it seems true that the major new trends in psychology are international. The move toward computer simulation as the new tool of psychology, toward psycholinguistics as a rapidly expanding field, and toward Piaget's thinking as, possibly, the main growing source of influence may be seen throughout most of the psychological world. This process is another important step in the maturation of psychology as an experimental science.

REFERENCES

Allport, G. W., & Vernon, P. E. *The study of values: A scale for measuring the dominant interests in personality.* (Rev. ed.) Boston: Houghton Mifflin, 1951.

American Psychological Association. *International opportunities for advanced training and research in psychology.* Washington, D.C.: A.P.A., 1966.

Annual Review of Psychology, 1949, **1**.

Atkinson, J. W., & Feather, N. T. *A theory of achievement motivation.* New York: Wiley, 1966.

Barlow, H. B., & Hill, R. M. Evidence of a physiological explanation of the waterfall phenomenon and figural aftereffects. *Nature*, 1963, **200**, 1345-1347.

Bartlett, F. C. *Remembering.* London: Cambridge University Press, 1932.

Bartlett, Sir F. C. Intelligence tests. *Times Science Review*, Summer, 1954.

Bartlett, F. C. *Thinking.* London: Methuen, 1958.

Battachi, M. W., & Montanini, M. M. Strutture sintattiche e modelli di ordinamento seriale. *Rivista de Psicologia Sociale*, 1965, **32**,193-205.

Berlyne, D. E. A theory of human curiosity. *British Journal of Psychology*, 1954, **45**, 180-191.

Berlyne, D. E. *Conflict, arousal, and curiosity.* New York: McGraw-Hill, 1960.

Berlyne, D. E. Conflict and the orientation reaction. *Journal of Experimental Psychology*, 1961, **62**, 8-13.

Berlyne, D. E. Motivational problems raised by exploratory and epistemic behaviour. In S. Koch (Ed.), *Psychology: A study of a science.* Vol. 5. *The process areas, the person, and some applied fields: Their place in psychology and in science.* New York: McGraw-Hill, 1963. Pp. 284-364.

Berlyne, D. E. *Structure and direction in thinking.* New York: Wiley, 1965.

Bexton, W. H., Heron, W., & Scott, T. H. Effects of decreased variation in the sensory environment. *Canadian Journal of Psychology*, 1954, **8**, 70-76.

Bilodeau, E. A. (Ed.) *Acquisition of skill.* New York: Academic Press, 1966.

Bindra, D. *Motivation: A systematic reinterpretation.* New York: Ronald Press, 1959.

Bjorgen, I. A. *A re-evaluation of rote learning.* Oslo: Oslo University Press, 1964.

Bresson, F. & de Montmollin, M. (Eds.) *Psychologie et épistémologie génetiques: Thèmes Piagetiens.* Paris, Dunod, 1966.

Broadbent, D. E. *Perception and communication.* London: Pergamon Press, 1958.

Broadhurst, P. L. Application of biometrical genetics to behaviour in rats. *Nature,* 1959, **148**, 1517-1518.

Broadhurst, P. L., & Broadhurst, A. Psychology in Britain today. *Indian Psychological Review,* 1966, **3**, 1-12.

Bruner, J. S. On perceptual readiness. *Psychological Review,* 1957, **64**, 123-152.

Bryden, M. P. Tachistoscopic recognition, handedness, and cerebral dominance. *Neuropsychologia,* 1965, **3**, 1-8.

Bryden, M. P. A model for the sequential organization of behaviour. *Canadian Journal of Psychology,* 1967, **21**, 37-56.

Bryden, M. P., & Rainey, C. A. Left-right differences in tachistoscopic recognition. *Journal of Experimental Psychology,* 1963, **66**, 568-571.

Bühler, C. Die Wiener Psychologische Schule in der Emigration. *Psychological Rundschau,* 1965, **16**, 187-196.

Burt, C. *The factors of the mind.* London: University of London Press, 1940.

Cesa-Bianchi, M., & Di Naro, C. Ricerga sugli atteggiamenti verso i mezzi di protezione individuali. *Securitas,* 1966, **51**, 89-126.

Champion, R. A. The latency of the conditioned fear-response. *American Journal of Psychology,* 1964, **77**, 75-83.

Champion, R. A. Reduced stimulus intensity as a CS in GSR conditoning. *Journal of Experimental Psychology,* 1967, **73**, 503-508.

Champion, R. A., & Allen, G. An acquired drive based on conflict. *American Journal of Psychology,* 1966, **79**, 111-115.

Champion, R. A., & Leung, S. Amount of reinforcement in human learning. *Australian Journal of Psychology,* 1964, **16**, 185-189.

Champion, R. A., & Smith, L. R. Predicting discrimination learning from differential conditioning with amount of reinforcement as a variable. *Journal of Experimental Psychology,* 1966, **71**, 529-534.

Cherry, E. C. On the validity of applying communication theory to experimental psychology. *British Journal of Psychology,* 1957, **48**, 136-188.

Cherry, E. C. *On human communication.* (3rd ed.) New York: Science Editions, 1961.

Chiari, S. Concetto di pericolo e percezione del rischio nell'etá evolutiva: Un sondaggio preliminare. *Securitas,* 1966, **51**, 127-141.

Cofer, C. N., & Appley, M. H. *Motivation: Theory and Research.* (2nd ed.) New York: Wiley, 1967.

Cowey, A. Perimetric study of field defects in monkeys after cortical and retinal ablations. *Quarterly Journal of Experimental Psychology,* 1967, **19**, 232-245.

Cowey, A., & Weiskrantz, L. A comparison of the effects of inferotemporal and striate cortex lesions on the visual behaviour of rhesus monkeys. *Quarterly Journal of Experimental Psychology,* 1967, **19**, 246-253.

Craik, K. J. W. *The nature of explanation.* London: Cambridge University Press, 1943.

Craik, K. J. W. *The nature of psychology.* London: Cambridge University Press, 1966.

David, H. P., & von Bracken, H. *Perspectives in personality theory.* London: Tavistock Publications, 1957.

Day, R. H., & Power, R. P. Apparent reversal (oscillation) of rotary motion in depth. *Psychological Review,* 1965, **72**, 117-127.

Day, R. H., & Singer, G. A. Spatial aftereffects within and between kinesthesis and vision. *Journal of Experimental Psychology,* 1964, **68**, 337-343. (a)

Day, R. H., & Singer, G. A. A tactile spatial aftereffect. *Australian Journal of Psychology,* 1964, **16**, 33-37. (b)

Day, R. H., & Singer, G. Sensory adaptation and behavioural compensation with spatially transformed vision and hearing. *Psychological Bulletin,* 1967, **67**, 307-322.

Décarie, T. *Intelligence and affectivity in early childhood: An experimental study of Jean Piaget's object concept and object relations.* New York: International Universities Press, 1966.

Drever, J. The historical background for national trends in psychology: On the non-existence of English associations. *Journal of Historical Behavior Science,* 1965, **1**, 123-130.

Earhard, B., & Earhard, M. Role of interference factors in 3-stage mediation paradigms. *Journal of Experimental Psychology,* 1967, **73**, 526-531.

Earhard, B., & Mandler, G. Mediated associations: Paradigms, controls and mechanisms. *Canadian Journal of Psychology,* 1965, **19**, 346-378. (a)

Earhard, B., & Mandler, G. Pseudomediation: A reply and more data. *Psychonomic Science,* 1965, **3**, 137-138. (b)

Ebenholtz, S. M. Adaptation to a rotated visual field as a function of degree of optical tilt and exposure time. *Journal of Experimental Psychology,* 1966, **72**, 629-634.

Eisler, H. On psychophysics in general and the general psychophysical equation in particular. *Scandinavian Journal of Psychology,* 1965, **6**, 85-102.

Ekman, G., & Sjöberg, L. Scaling. *Annual Review of Psychology,* 1965, **16**, 451-474.

Eysenck, H. J. *The scientific study of personality.* London: Routledge, 1952.

Eysenck, H. J. (Ed.) *Handbook of abnormal psychology.* London: Pitman, 1960.

Eysenck, H. J. Biological basis of personality. *Nature,* 1963, **199**, 1031.

Eysenck, H. J. The biological basis of criminal behaviour. *Advancing Science,* 1963-1964, **20**, 1-11.

Farne, M. Figural after-effects with short exposure time. *Psychologische Forschung,* 1965, **28**, 519-534.

Flavell, J. H. *The developmental psychology of Jean Piaget.* Princeton, N.J.: Van Nostrand, 1963.

Flores d'Arcais, G. B. Über die Wirkung figuraler Merkmale auf die enstehende "induzierte Bewegung." *Psychologische Forschung,* 1965, **28**, 153-178.

Foppa, K. *Lernen Gedächtnis, Verhalten.* Cologne and Berlin: Kiepenheurer und Witsch, 1965.

Fraisse, P. *Les structures rhythmiques.* Paris: Presses Universitaires de France, 1957.

Fraisse, P., & Piaget, J. (Eds.) *Traité de psychologie expérimentale.* Paris: Presses Universitaires de France, 1963.

Frankenhaeuser, M. Experimental approaches to the study of psychological stress. *Symposium on higher nervous functions and occupational health.* Vienna: Viennese Academy of Medicine, 1966. (a)

Frankenhaeuser, M. Physiological, behavioural and subjective reactions to stress. *Proceedings of the Second International Symposium on Environmental Problems of Man in Space.* Vienna: Springer, 1966. (b)

Fuller, J. L., & Clark, L. D. Effects of rearing with specific stimuli upon postisolation behaviour in dogs. *Journal of Comparative Physiological Psychology,* 1966, **61**, 258-263. (a)

Fuller, J. L., & Clark, L. D. Genetic and treatment factors modifying the postisolation syndrome in dogs. *Journal of Comparative Physiological Psychology,* 1966, **61**, 251-257. (b)

Gibson, J. J. Adaptation, after-effect, and contrast in the perception of curved lines. *Journal of Experimental Psychology,* 1933, **16**, 1-31.

Glow, P., Richardson, A., & Rose, S. The effect of reduced cholinesterase activity on the maintenance of an operant response. *Journal of Comparative Physiological Psychology,* 1967, **63**, 155-157.

Glow, P., & Rose, S. Some relationships between enzyme activity levels and behaviour. *Proceedings of the Eighteenth International Congress of Psychology.* Moscow, 1966.

Goude, G. *On fundamental measurement in psychology.* Stockholm: Almquist and Wirksell, 1962.

Graefe, O. Qualitative Unterseuchungen über Kontur und Fläche in der optischen Figurwahrnehmung. *Psychologische Forschung,* 1964, **27**, 260-306.

Green, R. T., & Courtis, M. C. Information theory and figure perception: The metaphor that failed. *Acta Psychologica,* 1966, **25**, 12-35.

Greenwald, A. G. Nuttin's neglected critique of the law of effect. *Psychological Bulletin,* 1966, **65**, 199-205.

Gregory, R. L. *Eye and brain.* New York: World University Library, 1966. (a)

Gregory, R. L. Visual illusions. In B. M. Foss (Ed.), *New horizons in psychology.* Baltimore: Penguin, 1966. Pp. 68-96. (b)

Gregory, R. L., & Wallace, J. G. Recovery from early blindness. *Quarterly Review of Experimental Psychology,* Monogr. 2, 1963.

Griew, S., & Lynn, R. Constructive "reactive inhibition" in the interpretation of age changes in performance. *Nature,* 1960, **186**, 182.

Guilford, J. P. Creativity. *American Psychology,* 1950, **5**, 444-454.

Hajos, A., & Ritter, M. Experiments on the problem of interocular transfer. *Acta Psychologica,* 1965, **24**, 81-90.

Hammer, A. G., & Johnson, L. Overinclusiveness in schizophrenia and organic psychosis. *British Journal of Social Clinical Psychology,* 1965, **4**, 47-51.

Harrington, T. L. Adaptation of humans to colored split-field glasses. *Psychonomic Science,* 1965, **3**, 71-72.

Harris, C. S. Perceptual adaptation to inverted, reversed and displaced vision. *Psychological Review,* 1965, **72**, 419-444.

Hebb, D. O. *Organization of behavior.* New York: Wiley, 1949.

Heider, F., & Simmel, M. An experimental study of apparent behavior. *American Journal of Psychology,* 1944, **57**, 243.

Helson, H. Adaptation-level theory. In S. Koch (Ed.), *Psychology: A study of a science.* Vol. 1. *Sensory, perceptual, and physiological formulations.* New York: McGraw-Hill, 1958. Pp. 565-621.

Hernandez-Peon, R., & Sterman, M. B. Brain functions. *Annual Review of Psychology,* 1966, **17**, 363-394.

Heron, W. Perception as a function of retinal locus and attention. *American Journal of Psychology,* 1957, **70**, 38-48.

Hirata, K., & Osaka, R. Tachistoscopic recognition of Japanese letter materials in left and right visual fields. *Psychologia,* 1967, **10**, 7-18.

Hofstätter, P. R. (Ed.) *Psychologia.* Frankfurt am Main: S. Fischer Verlag GmbH, 1965.

Hoyos, C. *Denkschrift zur Lage der Psychologie.* Wiesbaden: Steiner, 1961.

Hudson, L. *Contrary imaginations.* London: Methuen, 1966.

Humphrey, N. K., & Weiskrantz, L. Vision in monkeys after removal of the striate cortex. *Nature,* 1967, **215**, 595-597.

Iacono, G. Osservazioni sulla prevenzione degli infortuni in aziende siderurgiche statunitenzi. *Securitas,* 1966, **51**, 119-126.

Jensen, D. D. Operationism and the question, "Is this behaviour learned or innate?" *Behaviour,* 1961, **17**, 1-18.

Jensen, J. On functional fixedness: Some critical remarks. *Scandinavian Journal of Psychology,* 1960, **1**, 157-162. (a)

Jensen, J. On the Einstellung effect in problem solving: Some critical remarks *Scandinavian Journal of Psychology,* 1960, **1**, 163-168. (b)

Johansson, G. Rigidity, stability, and motion in perceptual space. *Acta Psychologica,* 1958, **14**, 359-370.

Johansson, G. Perception of motion and changing form. *Scandinavian Journal of Psychology,* 1964, **5**, 181-208.

Johansson, G., & Ottander, C. Recovery time after glare. *Scandinavian Journal of Psychology,* 1964, **5**, 17-25.

Jung, C. G. *Psychological types.* London: Routledge, 1924.

Jung, J. Cued versus non-cued incidental recall of successive work associations. *Canadian Journal of Psychology,* 1967, **21**, 196-203.

Kiekheben, F. Der einfluss eines kaleidoskopischen figurwandels auf das er-kundengsverhalten. *Psychologische Forschung,* 1966, **30**, 105-150.

Kimura, D. Cerebral dominance and the perception of verbal stimuli. *Canadian Journal of Psychology,* 1961, **15**, 166-171.

Koffka, K. *Principles of Gestalt psychology.* London: Kegan Paul, Trench, Trubner, 1936.

Köhler, I. Pavlov and his dog. *Journal of Genetic Psychology,* 1962, **100**, 331-335.

Köhler, I. The concept of adaptation in perception. Paper presented at the Seventeenth International Congress of Psychologists, Washington, D.C.: August, 1963.

Köhler, I. The formation and transformation of the perceptual world. *Psychological Issues,* 1964, **3**, 1-173.

Kretschmer, E. *Physique and character.* London: Kegan Paul, Trench, Trubner, 1925.

Lafitte, P. *The person in psychology: Reality or abstraction.* London: Routledge, 1957.

Levelt, W. J. M. *On binocular rivalry.* Soesterberg: Institute for Perception R.V.O.-T.N.O., 1965.

Lorenz, K. Z. *King Solomon's ring,* London: Methuen, 1956.

Lorenz, K. Z. *Evolution and modification of behaviour.* Chicago: University of Chicago Press, 1965.

Lorenz, K. *On aggression.* New York: Harcourt, Brace, & World, 1966.

Luria, A. R., & Vinogradova, O. S. An objective investigation of the dynamics of semantic systems. *British Journal of Psychology,* 1959, **50**, 89-105.

Malmo, R. B. Anxiety and behavioural arousal. *Psychological Review,* 1957, **64**, 276-287.

Malmo, R. B. Measurement of drive: An unsolved problem. In M. R. Jones (Ed.), *Nebraska Symposium on Motivation.* Lincoln: University of Nebraska Press, 1958. Pp. 229-265.

Malmo, R. B. Physiological gradients and behaviour. *Psychological Bulletin*, 1965, **64**, 225-234.

Marshall, G. R. Effect of total association and conceptual cohesiveness among words on recall, clustering, and recognition association. *Psychological Reports*, 1967, **20**, 39-44.

Marx, M. H. Spread of effect: A critical review. *Genetic Psychology Monographs*, 1956, **53**, 119-186.

Mason, W. A., & Sponholz, R. R. Behaviour of rhesus monkeys raised in isolation. *Journal of Psychiatric Research*, 1963, **1**, 299-306.

Meili, R., & Rohracher, H. (Eds.) *Lehrbuch der experimentellen Psychologie.* Berne: Hans Huber, 1963.

Merz, F. Amerikanische und deutsche Psychologie. *Psychologie und Praxis*, 1960, **4**, 78-91.

Metzger, W. *Gesetze des Sehens.* (2nd ed.) Frankfurt: Waldemar Kramer, 1953.

Michon, J. Studies on subjective duration. II. *Acta Psychologica*, 1965, **24**, 205-219.

Michotte, A., et. al. *Causalité, permanence et réalité phénoménales.* Louvain: Publications Universitaires, 1962.

Michotte, A. *The perception of causality.* [Translation by T. R. Miles and Elaine Miles] New York: Basic Books, 1963.

Migliorino, G. La percepcion visual en relacion a la conduccion de vehiculos rapidos. *Revista de Psicologia General y Applicada*, 1965, **20**, 15-28.

Mikkonen, V., & von Wright, J. M. Changes in reproduction as a function of adaptation level. II. *Report of the Psychological Institute, University of Turku*, 1963, No. 8.

Mishkin, M., & Forgays, D. G. Word recognition as a function of retinal locus. *Journal of Experimental Psychology*, 1952, **43**, 43-48.

Misiak, H., & Staudt, V. M. Psychology in Italy. *Psychological Bulletin*, 1953, **50**, 347-361.

Moed, H. K. W. Constancy and contrast. I. *Acta Psychologica*, 1964, **22**, 272-320.

Moed, H. K. W. Constancy and contrast. II. *Acta Psychologica*, 1965, **24**, 91-166.

Moed, H. K. W. Constancy and contrast. III. *Acta Psychologica*, 1966, **25**, 222-292.

Moore, J. A. (Ed.) *Ideas in modern biology.* New York: Natural History Press, 1965.

Morrell, F. Electrical signs of sensory coding. In G. C. Quarton, T. Melnechuk, F. O. Schimitt, & Associates & Staff of the Neurosciences Research Program (Eds.), *The Neurosciences: A study program.* New York: Rockefeller University Press, 1967. Pp. 452-469.

Munn, N. L. Discrimination-reversal learning in kangaroos. *Australian Journal of Psychology*, 1964, **16**, 1-8.

Murch, G. M., & Wesley, F. German psychology and its journals. *Psychological Bulletin*, 1966, **66**, 10-15.

Murdock, B. B. Distractor and probe techniques in short-term memory. *Canadian Journal of Psychology*, 1967, **21**, 25-36.

Murray, D. J. The role of speech responses in short-term memory. *Canadian Journal of Psychology*, 1967, **21**, 263-276.

Nuttin, J. R. "Spread" in recalling success and failure. *Journal of Experimental Psychology*, 1949, **39**, 690-699.

Nuttin, J. R. *Psychology in Belgium.* Louvain: Publications Universitaires, 1961. (a)

Nuttin, J. R. *Tâche réussité et échec: Théorie de la conduite humaine.* (2nd ed.) Louvain: Publications Universitaires, 1961. (b)

Oeser, O. A., & Emery, F. E. *Social structure and personality in a rural community.* London: Routledge, 1954.

Oeser, O. A., & Hammond, S. B. (Eds.) *Social structure and personality in a city.* London: Routledge, 1954.

Oeser, O. A., & Harary, F. A mathematical model for structural role theory. II. *Human Relations,* 1964, **17**, 3-17.

Oeser, O. A., & O'Brien, G. A mathematical model for structural role theory. III. *Human Relations,* 1967, **20**, 83-97.

O'Neil, W. M. *An introduction to method in psychology.* (2nd ed.) Melbourne: Melbourne University Press, 1962.

Piaget, J. *The language and thought of the child.* London: Routledge, 1926.

Piaget, J. *Judgment and reasoning in the child.* London: Routledge, 1928.

Piaget, J. *The child's conception of number.* London: Routledge, 1952.

Piaget, J. *The growth of logical thinking from childhood to adolescence.* London: Routledge, 1958.

Piaget, J. *L'image mentale chez l'enfant.* Paris: Presses Universitaires de France, 1966.

Piaget, J. *Biologie et connaissance: Essai sur les relations entre les régulations organiques et les processus cognitifs.* Paris: Editions Gallimard, 1967. (a)

Piaget, J. *Six psychological studies.* New York: Random House, 1967. (b)

Piaget, J., & Inhelder, B. *The child's conception of space.* London: Routledge, 1956.

Piaget, J., & Inhelder, B. *The early growth of logic in the child: Classification and seriation.* New York: Harper & Row, 1964.

Piéron, H. (Ed.) *L'année psychologique.* Paris: Presses Universitaires de France, 1898.

Piéron, H. *Thought and the brain.* New York: Harcourt, Brace, 1927.

Piéron, H. *Les problèmes fondamentaux de la psycholophysique dans la science actuelle.* Paris: Herman & Cie, 1951.

Piéron, H. *The sensations.* New Haven, Conn.: Yale University Press, 1952.

Poulton, E. C. Engineering psychology. *Annual Review of Psychology,* 1966, **17**, 177-200.

Raaheim, K. Problem solving and the ability to find replacements. *Scandinavian Journal of Psychology,* 1960, **1**, 14-18.

Raaheim, K. Problem solving: A new approach. *Acta Universitaires de Bergensis,* Ser. Hum. Litt., No. 5, Bergen, Norway, 1961.

Raaheim, K. Problem solving and the awareness of the missing part. *Scandinavian Journal of Psychology,* 1962, **3**, 129-131.

Rorschach, H. *Psychodiagnostics.* New York: Grune & Stratton, 1942.

Ross, S. *Logical foundations of psychological measurement.* Copenhagen: Scandinavian University Books, 1964.

Russell, W. A., & Roth, E. Psychologie in Deutschland und in Amerika: Eine Studie in Gegensätzen. *Psychologie und Praxis,* 1958, **2**, 223-231.

Sanders, A. F. *The selective process in the functional visual field.* Soesterberg: Institute for Perception R.V.O.-T.N.O., 1963.

Sanders, A. F. Expectancy: Application and measurement. *Acta Psychologica,* 1966, **25**, 293-313.

Sarbin, T. R., Taft, R., & Bailey, D. E. *Clinical inference and cognitive theory.* New York: Holt, 1960.

Scandinavian Journal of Psychology. Stockholm: Almquist & Wiksell, 1960.

Schmitt, G. F. Eine neue wahrnehmungstauschung. *Psychologische Forschung,* 1966, **30**, 200-240.

Schultz, D. P. *Sensory restriction: Effects on behaviour.* New York: Academic Press, 1965.

Schutte, W., & Zubek, J. P. Changes in olfactory and gustatory sensitivity after prolonged visual deprivation. *Canadian Journal of Psychology,* 1967, **21**, 337-345.

Schutz, F. Homosexualität und Prägung. *Psychologische Forschung,* 1965, **28**, 439-463. (a)

Schutz, F. Sexuelle Prägung bei Antiden. *Zeitschrift für Tierpsychologie,* 1965, **22**, 50-103. (b)

Shields, J. *Monozygotic twins.* London: Oxford University Press, 1962.

Singer, G., & Day, R. H. The effects of spatial judgements on the perceptual aftereffect resulting from prismatically transformed vision. *Australian Journal of Psychology,* 1966, **18**, 63-70. (a)

Singer, G., & Day, R. H. Interlimb and interjoint transfer of a kinesthetic spatial aftereffect. *Journal of Experimental Psychology,* 1966, **71**, 109-114. (b)

Singer, G., & Day, R. H. Spatial adaptation and aftereffect with optically transformed vision. *Journal of Experimental Psychology,* 1966, **71**, 725-731. (c)

Skinner, B. F. *Cumulative record.* New York: Appleton-Century-Crofts, 1959.

Sluckin, W. *Imprinting and early learning.* London: Methuen, 1964.

Smedslund, J. "Educational Psychology." In P. R. Farnsworth, O. McNemar, and Q. McNemar (Eds.), *Annual Review of Psychology.* California: Annual Reviews, 1964.

Spaltro, E. An analysis of risk-taking behaviour. *Archivio di Psicologia, Neurologia e Psichiatria,* 1965, **26**, 7-25.

Spearman, C. *The nature of "intelligence" and the principles of cognition.* London: Macmillan, 1923.

Spearman, C. *The abilities of man: Their nature and measurement.* London: Macmillan, 1927.

Spranger, E. *Types of men.* Halle: Niemeyer, 1928.

Stout, J. F. *Manual of psychology.* London: University Tutorial Press, 1913.

Sutcliffe, J. P. Some aspects of rank ordering and scaling with paired comparisons data. *Australian Journal of Psychology,* 1964, **16**, 137-149.

Sutcliffe, J. P. A probability model for errors of classifications. I. General considerations. *Psychometrika,* 1965, **30**, 73-96.

Sutcliffe, J. P., & Bristow, R. A. Do rank order and scale properties remain invariant under changes in the set of scaled stimuli? *Australian Journal of Psychology,* 1966, **18**, 26-40.

Szekely, L. Some comments on problem solving, availability and test magic. *Nordisk Psychologi,* 1958, **10**, 108-113.

Szekely, L. The problem of experience in Gestalt psychology. *Theoria,* 1959, **25,** 179-186.

Taft, R. Multiple methods of personality assessment. *Psychological Bulletin,* 1959, **56,** 333-352.

Taft, R. Accuracy of empathic judgements of acquaintances and strangers. *Journal of Personality and Social Psychology,* 1966, **3,** 600-604.

Thomson, G. H. *The factorial analysis of human ability.* London: University of London Press, 1939.

Thorndike, E. L. *Educational psychology* Vol. 3. New York: Teachers College, 1914.

Thorpe, W. H. *Learning and instinct in animals.* London: Methuen, 1956.

Thorpe, W. H. *Learning and instinct in animals.* (2nd ed.) London: Methuen, 1963.

Thorpe, W. H. The ontogeny of behaviour. In J. A. Moore (Ed.), *Ideas in modern biology.* New York: Natural History Press, 1965. Pp. 483-518.

Thorpe, W. H., & Davenport, D. (Eds.) Learning and associated phenomena in invertebrates. *Animal Behaviour,* Suppl, 1, 64.

Thurstone, L. L. Primary mental abilities. *Psychometric Monograph,* 1938, **1.**

Tinbergen, N. *A study of instinct.* Oxford: Clarendon Press, 1951.

Tinbergen, N. The evolution of signalling devices. In W. Etkin (Ed.), *Social behaviour and organization among vertebrates.* Chicago: University of Chicago Press, 1964.

Tinbergen, N. Behaviour and natural selection. In J. A. Moore (Ed.), *Ideas in modern biology.* New York: Natural History Press, 1965. Pp. 519-542.

Tolman, E. C. *Purposive behaviour in animals and men.* Los Angeles: University of California Press, 1932.

Tretini, G. Quotient of acculturalization and adjustment classes in the actual social-scholastic situation in Italy. *Archivio di Psicologia, Neurologia e Psichiatria,* 1966, **27,** 243-310.

Vernon, P. E. *The structure of human abilities.* London: Methuen, 1950.

Vernon, P. E. *Personality assessment: A critical study.* London: Methuen, 1964.

Vernon, P. E. The personality system. In C. Banks (Ed.), *Stephanos; studies in psychology presented to Cyril Burt.* London: University of London Press, 1965.

Virsu, V. Contrast and confluxion as components in geometric illusions. *Quarterly Journal of Experimental Psychology,* 1967, **19,** 198-207.

Volkelt, H. *Grundfragen der Psychologie.* Munich: Beck, 1963.

Von Fieandt, K. Towards a unitary theory of perception. *Psychological Review,* 1958, **65,** 315-320.

Von Fieandt, K., & Gibson, J. J. The sensitivity of the eye to two kinds of continuous transformation of a shadow pattern. *Journal of Experimental Psychology,* 1959, **57,** 344-347.

Von Frisch, K. The dances of the honey bee. *Bulletin of Animal Behaviour,* 1947, **5,** 1-22.

Von Frisch, K, *The dancing bees.* London: Methuen, 1954.

Von Wright, J. M., & Mikkonen, V. Changes in reproduction as a function of adaptation level. I. *Report of the Psychological Institute, University of Turku,* 1963, No. 1.

Von Wright, J. M., & Mikkonen, V. Changes in reproduction as a function of adaptation level. III. *Report of the Psychological Institute, University of Turku,* 1964, No. 12.

Ward, J. *Psychological principles.* London: Cambridge University Press, 1918.

Wellek, A. Der Einfluss der Deutschen Emigration und die Entwickling der Americanischen Psychologie. *Psychologische Rundschau,* 1964, XV, 1-4.

Wellek, A. (Ed.) *Gesamtverzeichnis der deutschsprachigen psychologischen Literatur der Jahre 1942 bis 1960.* Göttingen: Verlag für Psychologie, 1965.

Wellek, A. *Die Polarität im Aufbau des Charakters: System der Konkreten Characterkunde,* Berlin: Franke, 1966.

Wells, M. J. *Brain and behaviour in cephalopods.* London: Heinemann, 1962.

Wesley, F. Assessing German psychology. *Journal of Genetic Psychology,* 1966, **75,** 273-277.

Yates, A. J. *Frustration and conflict.* London: Methuen, 1962.

Yates, A. J. Psychological deficit. *Annual Review of Psychology,* 1966, **17,** 111-144.

Zanforlin, M. Some observations on Gregory's theory of perceptual illusions. *Quarterly Journal of Experimental Psychology,* 1967, **19,** 193-197.

Zubek, J. P., & MacNeill, M. Perceptual deprivation phenomena: Role of the recumbent position. *Journal of Abnormal Psychology,* 1967, **72,** 147-150.

SOVIET PSYCHOLOGY

Josef Brožek,
Lehigh University,
Bethlehem, Pennsylvania

INTRODUCTION

The aim of this chapter is to familiarize the readers with the contemporary Soviet scene in psychology. Soviet psychology is still largely a *terra incognita* in the West. At first contact, it is puzzling as well. Two recent American "explorers" (Cole & Maltzman, 1969, p. 37) have described their initial reactions in vivid terms:

Coming upon Soviet psychology and physiological psychology [the authors' term for the Pavlovian physiology of higher nervous activity] for the first time is a little like Darwin first visiting the Galapagos. Different forms of species have evolved, as a result of isolation and interbreeding, which are adaptable to their environment.

Cole and Maltzman also shatter the all too frequent American stereotype of psychology in the Soviet Union (1969, p. 37):

All too often Soviet psychology has been characterized as a rigid adherence to Pavlovian conditioning. This is simply not the case; but Pavlovian conditioning research and theory is itself far more sophisticated and complicated than the stereotyped and grossly oversimplified picture presented in most American [introductory] textbooks.

Since the chapter on Soviet psychology for the first edition of this book was written, in 1962, much has changed. For one thing, many of the individuals whose work was discussed—K. M. Bykov, N. I. Krasnogorskii, N. N. Ladygina-Kots—have died. Profound alterations, for the better, have taken place in the status of psychology in the U.S.S.R. While party ideology and the rigidly standardized formulations of dialectical materialism continue to reign unchallenged in journal editorials and introductions to textbooks, psychological research and theory have moved forward vigorously.

For all these reasons, a few touch-ups of the earlier chapter simply would not do. This presentation is a "supplement," endeavoring to reflect the recent developments and the current scene, not a "revision." Special attention will be given to the publications translated into English.

SOME METATHEORETICAL CONSIDERATIONS

The investigative work of the scientist is embedded in a network of concepts and concerns going beyond (*meta,* in Greek) specific facts and "miniature theories" relating the facts within a circumscribed area. The complexes of ideas lying outside the domain of concrete facts placed in short-range perspective have a variety of functions. They may serve as a source of inspiration ("new world, brave and free," "socialism with a human face," "Communist society"); as a guide in the selection of research problems; as ethical and methodological norms; as a clarification of the philosophical foundations of science (be they concerned with ontological or epistemological questions, i.e., the nature of reality or the nature of scientific knowledge); and as an interpretative framework (theory of evolution, cybernetics).

These considerations—ideological, philosophical, and metatheoretical—are a matrix in which the collection of data and the building of microtheories are immersed.

The matrix is universal, in the sense of being present both East and West. It is not identical either in its content or in the degree to which psychologists are concerned with these matters.

In America, concern with "metatheories" is less intensive and less widespread. The temper is (or has been) largely aphilosophical. Characteristically, the opinion has been widely held that the research scientist performs most effectively if he keeps his nose to the grindstone and operates strictly within the framework of empirical data and miniature theories. This does not mean that psychologists do not hold, in fact, although tacitly for the most part, certain metatheoretical assumptions. Watson (1967) labels them *prescriptions.*

In the Soviet Union the presence of the metatheoretical considerations is made more palpable by the fact that the country has been governed for over fifty years by a single political party, with a single-minded, vocal ideology, and an allegiance to the philosophical heritage of Marx, Engels, and Lenin.

It may be useful to point out that Marxism-Leninism (Anonymous, 1961) is many things: a theory of reality and knowledge (dialectical materialism); a philosophy of history (historical materialism); a socioeconomic theory of capitalism, socialism, and communism; and the theory and tactics of the international Communist movement.

In Nikita Khrushchev's words of 1959, "The ideas of Marxism-Leninism [are] the ideology which has a complete sway over the Soviet society" (Blakely, 1961, p. 147). Importantly, not only are these ideas binding for the Soviet philosophers, but they also "are the guiding stars for the consideration of all theoretical problems of science" (Blakely, 1961, p. 98). Consequently, they constitute "the philosophical basis of Soviet psychology" as well (Blakely, 1961, p. 103). In time, I. P. Pavlov's work on "higher nervous activity" was added as an essential ingredient of Soviet psychology's metatheoretical base.

Philosophico-Theoretical Views on the Nature Of the Mind and Its Relation to Matter

The synthesis of the Marxist-Leninist philosophy and of Pavlov's "physiology of the highest nervous activity" was accomplished only after a long period of discussion and debate, at times acrimonious. Because of their fundamental importance for Soviet psychology, the principles of "dialectical" and "Pavlovian" psychology will be presented in some detail, with specific reference to Rubinshtein's formulation. In our presentation we shall depend heavily on Payne's (1968) well-documented monograph.

In the thirties Rubinshtein sought a reunification of psychology, then split into warring "schools." His special concern was the achievement of a synthesis between the points of view, apparently irreconcilable, of the introspectionists, who regarded the immediate data of consciousness as the only legitimate subject matter of psychology, and the behaviorists, who disregarded consciousness and limited psychology to the study of objectively recorded reactions of the organism, animal and human. Rubinshtein conceived a reunification of psychology based on the principle of a "dialectical unity" of consciousness and behavior, embodied in Marx's concept of human activity (Payne, 1968, p. 50):

Through activity the subject reveals itself, objectivizing the inner world of its consciousness. . . . At the same time man, by his activity, forms and develops his subjective world. [This activity] is not merely individual but is above all social. Man's consciousness, which is the guide of his activity, evolved originally in the process of social activity, and the external world with which man enters into synthesis by his activity, is not only the world of nature but, at the same time, of society. In consequence, human activity always remains a socially conditioned phenomenon.

Consciousness and behavior are not viewed as separate aspects of the human organism, the one entirely "internal" and subjective and the other entirely "external" and objective. On the contrary, they represent a two-way interaction with external reality, from object to subject and from subject to object. Consciousness is a form of activity of the organism required for its adaptation to the demands of the constantly changing environment. It directs man's actions through which he modifies and changes the environment.

In *Fundamentals of general psychology* (in Russian), Rubinshtein formulated three principles he regarded as basic:

1 The principle of psychophysical unity. The mind forms a twofold dialectical unity: with its organic substrate, the brain (of which it is a function), and with the external world (of which it is a reflection).

2 The principle of mental development. The mind (*psyche*) develops along with the changes in the structure of the organisms and the mode of life.

3 The principle of "historicity." Human consciousness changes with man's social conditions.

The fourth principle, noted by Payne (1968, p. 52), the principle of the unity of theory and practice, is a general principle of Marxism-Leninism applicable to all sciences and not specific to psychology.

In the early fifties Rubinshtein responded to the critique that the philosophico-theoretical foundations of psychology are inadequate and must be reconstructed by taking into account the implications of the Pavlovian heritage. In his 1952 paper, Rubinshtein acknowledged that the chief defect of the *Fundamentals of general psychology* was its failure to follow the path laid down by Pavlov, and its uncritical acceptance of certain principles of foreign psychology.

The factual scope of the Pavlovian "reconstruction" of psychology, in Rubinshtein's hands, was less than one might have expected. The primary change was the replacement of the principle of psychophysical unity by the principle of *materialist monism,* emphasizing the primacy of the material, including the physiological brain processes. Mental processes are now *identified* with the "higher nervous," "reflex" activity of the brain.

The principle of psychophysical unity apparently came to be viewed as too "dualistic," implying that mental activity is *based* on higher nervous activity, which in turn is a direct function of the brain. In other words, the principle seemed to (or did) imply that the mental activity and the higher nervous activity represent two closely related but distinct series of events. According to materialist monism, the mental activity and the higher nervous activity constitute a single process.

Yet Rubinshtein continues to insist that mental activity is characterized not only by its physiological mechanisms but also by its content, i.e., by the fact that it is a reflection, by the brain, of the (external) material world.

This gives specificity to the mental phenomena which cannot be reduced, "without a remainder," to the processes studied by the neurophysiologist. Physiology abstracts from certain aspects of the process of man's interaction with the outer world. It is these "subjective" aspects that form the specific object of psychology. Mental phenomena, such as perceptions, thoughts, and feelings, represent a new, original "form of manifestation" (*forma proyavleniya*) of physiological phenomena.

The "reflection" of the world by man is not a passive process, a passive reception of images, but involves cognitive activity of the subject; the four basic cognitive operations are analysis and synthesis, abstraction and generalization. Second, knowledge of outer reality is conditioned by the personal characteristics (personality) of the subject (Payne, 1968, p. 143). Personality is defined as "a totality (*sovokupnost'*) of the inner conditions [of the human organism] through which all external influences are refracted."

In the current formulation (Leont'ev, 1967), psychology is defined as the study of mental phenomena (such as sensation, perception, thought, and emotions), viewed as processes of an active reflection of objective reality. Leont'ev states categorically that the philosophical prerequisites (*predposylki*) for the development of psychology as an objective science were provided by dialectical materialism. A "reconstruction" (*perestroika*) of psychology on this basis was initiated, in the U.S.S.R., only in the 1920s.

Mind (*psikhika*) is tied closely to the development of the "living matter." It serves to orient organisms in regard to their environment, and it regulates their behavior. The development of the specifically human mind, in the course of the evolution of man, is viewed as a product of social activities connected with human work, requiring interpersonal communication (verbal designation), and facilitating the development of consciousness (*soznanie*) as a special form of "reflection" of reality. Language becomes the medium (*nositel'*) of "social consciousness" and the "substrate" of the consciousness of individuals.

There is a two-way relation between external and internal activites: External operations (behavior) are transformed into internal, mental operations (process of interiorization), but also the internal, mental operations are expressed in external activities (process of exteriorization).

While, so far, Leont'ev's presentation has been a good deal more "Marxist-Leninist" than "Pavlovian," he does not neglect to point out that the study of the mind is closely bound to the physiological study of the activities of the brain. Yet mind is not reducible to "higher nervous activity"; mental "reflection" of reality—the very subject of psychology—is brought about by an active interaction of the individual with his environment, fashioned in the course of mankind's sociohistorical development. In this process man as a biological being is transformed into a bio-social being. The reflection of reality has a specific content.

SOVIET PSYCHOLOGY IN THE WESTERN LOOKING GLASS

Soviet psychology is distinct as regards the "metatheory," although, in part, this is a difference of vocabulary, framework, manner of presentation, and insistence. On the other hand, there is no single theory which would characterize scientific psychology in the Soviet Union as a "school" or "system." The field is more diversified than is frequently realized.

The total of the then current Soviet psychology was surveyed on several occasions (Brožek, 1964; Brožek & Hoskovec, 1966). No attempt will be made to do so again here, especially since our concern is to familiarize the reader with selected, "significant" aspects.

Like beauty, the historical significance of men, events, and ideas is, in part, in the eyes of the beholder. In order that we may arrive at a more objective portrait, unencumbered by one man's idiosyncrasies, and so that the reader may pursue, firsthand, his interests beyond our summary and comment, this section is based on Soviet monographs translated into English and published commercially outside the

Soviet Union. The selection of materials to be translated involves appraisal by many individuals. It provides the best available objective criterion of significance, although *significance* is defined pragmatically and from the "Western" point of view.

Admittedly, the resulting portrait is not representative. The bias emerges clearly when the topics are matched with the factual spectrum of current Soviet psychological research (Brožek, 1969). The dominance of the physiologically oriented research and a gross underrepresentation of such areas as educational psychology and the psychology of sports (like caviar, a Russian specialty) become patent.

Historical Roots

I. M. Sechenov's multifaceted work included contributions to psychology as well as to neurophysiology, physiology of work, and physiological chemistry (Koshtoyants, 1964, Chs. 11-15). Sechenov's *Autobiographical notes* (1965a) provides an informative, personal account of the life (1829-1905) of one of the moving spirits of Russian science in the second half of the nineteenth century. Sechenov's forward-looking work, entitled *Reflexes of the brain* and first published in 1863, was made effectively available to the English-speaking scientific public about one hundred years after it appeared in Russian (Sechenov, 1965b).

In his postscript (Sechenov, 1965b, pp. 143-145), W. A. Rosenblith stresses three aspects of Sechenov's work:

1 His pioneering reflexological approach to the study of behavior, as a prelude to Pavlov's research.

2 His discovery of the phenomenon of central inhibition, antedating neurophysiological investigations on reticular formation—one of the central topics of modern brain research.

3 His anticipation of physiological cybernetics and his role as a "too little appreciated intellectual forebear of Norbert Wiener," the author of *Cybernetics, or Control and communication in the animal and the machine* (1948).

In his *Reflexes of the brain* Sechenov views man's mental activity as a function of the brain, manifested externally by muscular movements, whether they involve muscle groups controlling physical activity or those controlling verbal behavior.

Both types of external manifestations of cerebral activity, i.e., "actions" and "words," can be reduced, ultimately, to a single phenomenon—muscular movements. The scientist's task is to determine the ways in which these movements originate in the brain regarded as a very intricate machine.

It has been well known that simple ("pure") reflexes can be elicited by stimulation of appropriate sensory nerves. Sechenov demonstrated experimentally, in 1862, the existence of mechanisms in the frog's brain which *inhibit* spinal reflex movements initiated by skin stimulation.

The concept that reflex movements can be both inhibited and intensified by the stimulation of different parts of the brain has important consequences for Sechenov's theory of "mental" phenomena. Thus in fright the effects of sensory stimuli are intensified by processes taking place in the cerebral hemispheres.

In human behavior an important part is played by responses (reflexes) acquired by learning: mental development is based on memory, which preserves, in the central nervous system, sounds and images in a latent state. These responses include speech, which involves formation of the associations of auditory sensations with kinesthetic, visual, and tactile sensations. Words are "conditional sounds."

In silent thinking, the motor response (the last member of a reflex initiated by sensory stimulation which evokes central processes and, at times, sensations) is inhibited. Put the other way, to Sechenov a thought is "the first two thirds of a mental reflex." Similarly, other mental phenomena, such as intentions or wishes, may be viewed as reflexes without external manifestation. In contrast to mental reflexes with an "inhibited end," emotions represent mental reflexes with an "intensified end."

In regard to what appears as a "voluntary" action, Sechenov's point of view is rigorously deterministic: Given the same internal and external conditions, man's action will be similar.

Sechenov was aware of the limitations and deficiencies of *Reflexes of the brain,* but felt that he did demonstrate the feasibility of what was indicated by the initial title of the essay: "An attempt to establish the physiological basis of psychological processes."

Individual Differences

One of the few areas in which the call for the "Pavlovization" of psychology, heard in the early 1950s, resulted in a large volume of innovative, empirical research is the study of individual differences carried out in Moscow in one of the laboratories of the Institute of Psychology, U.S.S.R. Academy of Pedagogical Sciences. The series of volumes, beginning in 1956 and edited by B. M. Teplov, in which the results were reported was initially called *Typological features of higher nervous activity in man.* A more Pavlovian title could hardly have been found. The change in the title of the series, as of the sixth volume, to *Problems of differential psychophysiology* is highly significant. The editor (Nebylitsyn, 1969) points out that in part, the change in the title reflects an endeavor to attune it to a more contemporary scientific terminology. More importantly, the change indicates a shift in emphasis toward the study of the relation between the "properties of the nervous system," emotional behavior, and performance in prolonged work and under the impact of other stresses.

In the Pavlovian tradition the *type of the nervous system* refers to two different concepts:

1 A complex of specific characteristics of the two basic, opposed nervous processes (excitation and inhibition), i.e., the "strength" of the excitatory

processes, "equilibrium" between excitatory and inhibitory processes, and "mobility." The opposite poles of the three dimensions are weakness, disequilibrium, and inertness.

2 Characteristic patterns of animal and human behavior.

The type in the first sense (a complex of specific properties of the nerve processes) was viewed as genotype and was referred to, in Pavlov's terminology, also as *temperament, nervous constitution,* or *type of higher nervous activity.*

The type in the second sense (habitual pattern of behavior) represents a *phenotype,* referred to also as *character.* In Pavlov's formulation of 1930, referring to man (Teplov, 1964, p. 36):

Human personality is determined both by biological inheritance and by the environment, i.e., the conditions of upbringing. The strength [i.e., the type] of the nervous system (temperament) is an innate property; character or the form of behavior consists to a large extent of acquisitions, habits formed during the individual's lifetime.

In later statements Pavlov spoke of the properties of the nervous system as "innate" or "congenital" rather than "inherited," though still retaining the term *genotype.* In this Pavlov was affected by Kupalov's findings that the properties of the nervous system may be modified during intrauterine development.

Historically, the individual differences between dogs were first described in terms of the animals' general behavior (i.e., the visually observed motor responses in the experimental stand and "at liberty"). Gradually, reliance came to be placed on strictly experimental indicators derived from the study of the salivary conditioned responses.

The *strength* of the nervous system refers to "the working capacity of the cerebral cells," defined as the ability of the nerve cells to withstand long, concentrated excitation or the action of an "ultrastrong" stimulus, without passing into inhibition.

Mobility is defined in terms of the speed with which a stimulus produces a response. An important aspect of mobility is the ability of the organisms to adapt their responses to a reversal of the sign—positive (excitatory) or negative (inhibitory)—of the conditioned stimuli.

The specific tests for the characterization of the typological properties of the animal nervous system are described in detail (Teplov, 1964, pp. 59-112).

Teplov (1964, p. 127) regards it as futile, and perhaps even harmful, to attempt to find quick methods of determining the type of nervous system in man, i.e., methods which would require only a few days or even a few hours. This would amount to a "testological approach," for which he has no sympathy.

The five reports of experiments from Teplov's laboratory, selected by Gray (1964, pp. 367-464) deal with the dimension of strength of the nervous system in man.

Gray (1964, pp. 157-287) summarized the results of the then available research, carried out in Teplov's laboratory, on strength of the excitatory processes (strength of nervous activity, strength of the nervous system), including a 1960 factor analysis of intercorrelations between twenty-one measures. In addition, he provided a reinterpretation (pp. 289-364) of the empirical findings obtained in Teplov's laboratory. Gray's interpretation employs concepts more familiar to Western psychologists than those of Pavlov, and it places reliance on more recent neurophysiological findings. Specifically, he sees merit in substituting for the dimension of strength of the nervous system that of arousability (levels of arousal), and he expresses (1964, p. 289) the belief that by making such a substitution, we can link together two different areas of research and so suggest fruitful lines of new research.

A Vast Memory

While studies on preschool and school-age children abound in Soviet psychology (Cole & Maltzman, 1969, pp. 41-273), Luria's (1968) volume extends the segment of the life cycle under observation from adolescence to maturity, exploring the ways in which imbalance in mental functioning affects the formation of personality.

In several ways, the "little book about a vast memory" is a fascinating case study. First, it covers a period of thirty years. Second, it deals with a remarkable individual. Third, it examines the individual broadly, as a person, not just as a mnemonic virtuoso.

The subject's memory was, indeed, fabulous, as documented by his capacity to reproduce long tables of numbers, letters, and nonsense syllables as well as complex formulas. The mechanisms of memorization varied. The subject was able to form and retain, for years, images of the tables, simply "reading off" the digits or letters. Words were converted into graphic images. Later, when he gave public performances as a mnemonist, he strengthened the accuracy of his performance by "enlarging" the dimensions of his images, making sure that the graphic images were clearly visible ("clearly illuminated") and suitably arranged spatially (e.g., along an imaginary street). Eventually, he developed a system of simplified images, a kind of visual shorthand.

The single most outstanding feature of his perceptual processes was their multisensory nature (synesthesia). Sounds produced immediately an experience of light and color, and frequently, of taste and touch as well. Words had not only their meanings but also "shapes" and colors. Thus *wine* was perceived as a "dark word." In putting his baby brother to sleep, he had to "sing in a *loud* voice, since it has to be *foggy* if one's going to fall asleep."

The synesthetic features of perception were important in his recall since they provided extra cues during remembering.

The duration of the subject's retention of what he memorized and the fact that traces left by one stimulus did not inhibit the recall of other, similar stimuli were amazing. At the same time, his memory was not equally excellent for all kinds of material. Specifically, he complained that he had a poor memory for faces, seen as ever-changing patterns of light and shadow.

His dominant sense was vision, and his "thinking" was primarily a manipulation of his vivid visual images. Once he commented: "Other people *think* as they read, but I *see* it all." Or again: "I can understand only what I can visualize." Overwhelmed by the richness of visual imagery, he found abstract thought difficult or impossible. He had difficulty understanding poetry and metaphoric expressions in general. In conversation the steady stream of emerging images led him into endless digressions.

His vivid imagination enabled him to control some of his body's autonomic functions, such as heart rate and body temperature. His images were so vivid that they took on the feel of reality. This resulted in lifelong daydreaming, which became a substitute for action. His attitude toward life was characterized by the expectation that something wonderful would happen to him, leading him to view all factual events as "temporary," as a prelude—a prelude to something that never materialized.

Thought Pathology in Mental Diseases

In the 1920s Blyuma V. Zeigarnik, author of *The pathology of thinking* (1965), was a student of Kurt Lewin in Berlin. At the tender age of twenty-seven years (tender, that is, for psychology's hall of fame) she became an eponym, giving name to the *Zeigarnik phenomenon* (Zeigarnik, 1927), which refers to a better recall of tasks that have not been completed and, more loosely, to an individual's concern over unresolved problems. Upon her return to the Soviet Union, she worked in the field of abnormal psychology with the many-sided L. S. Vygotskii. Pathology of thought became her speciality.

Her work fits the pattern of the long-standing, though not uninterrupted Russian tradition of close ties between scientific psychology and psychiatry, stressed by S. S. Korsakov, V. M. Bekhterev, and V. Kh. Kandinskii, the founders of modern Russian psychiatry. In the framework of Korsakov's neuropsychiatric clinic, A. A. Tokarskii established a laboratory of psychology in 1894. For many years Zeigarnik has been in charge of the laboratory of experimental psychology associated with the Moscow Research Institute of Psychiatry, Ministry of Health.

Zeigarnik refers to the application of psychological methods in the psychiatric context as *pathopsychology.* This is a narrower concept than *medical psychology,* which includes, importantly, psychotherapy. Pathopsychology is a branch of psychology. In Western terms, it may be regarded as a sector of clinical psychology concerned with the psychological characterization of individuals who are mentally ill. Zeigarnik's book is focused on one aspect of mental functioning, the thought processes.

The task of pathopsychology is viewed as twofold:

1 To meet the needs of psychiatric practice by contributing to the establishment of diagnosis: other authors would include also patho-

psychology's contribution to the appraisal of the effectiveness of therapy and, specifically, the evaluation of drug therapy.

2 To utilize the information acquired in dealing with these practical problems for further development of psychological theory. It is the latter aspect that is of direct interest here.

Thinking is defined by Zeigarnik (1965), in Leninist framework and terminology, as "a generalized and indirect reflection of the outside world" (p. 67), manifested in practical life as acquisition and assimilation of facts and utilization of knowledge. Thinking refers to the processes of analysis and synthesis in which sensory and rational cognition is combined into a single activity: Stressing the dialectical unity of these two stages of cognition (sensory and rational), the founders of Marxism-Leninism point out that it is the rational stage which makes it possible to probe into the essence of things and events in nature and society.

Only conceptual thinking provides a full reflection of reality, enabling us to understand the internal connections between phenomena.

The thesis concerning the two stages of cognition is seen as being in harmony with Pavlov's theory of the two signal systems, sensory and symbolic. Symbols, of which words are the most important category, are "signals of signals." Speech provides the means for the analysis and synthesis of the sensory impressions received by the human organism from the outside world and of images.

The core of Zeigarnik's (1965) volume is an account of a study on the disturbances of thought in psychiatric patients. The patients are grouped into nine disease categories, with the size of the groups varying from fifteen to well over one hundred.

Using a variety of testing procedures, Zeigarnik examined the disturbances in three aspects of thinking: (a) abstraction and generalization, (2) logical trend of thought, and (3) the purposive and critical character of thought.

Zeigarnik's data indicate that specific forms of disordered thought are not strictly limited to particular nosological categories. The conclusion is drawn that the results of psychological examinations of thought disturbances can aid in the establishment of a diagnosis, but are not specific enough, in themselves, for diagnostic purposes.

Zeigarnik suggests that the presence of a given type of thought disturbance in a group of mental diseases indicates a common underlying mental dysfunction: asthenia, with fatigability and emotional lability (in patients with cerebrovascular diseases and post-traumatic psychosis) and inertia (in oligophrenics and epileptics, who lack capacity for generalization and are absorbed by details).

While the study was focused on disturbances of the thought processes, Zeigarnik stresses that thinking cannot be regarded as an isolated "mental function," existing apart from man's needs and attitudes. What appears to be an impaired capacity for critical thought may reflect an attitude of indifference toward the tasks presented to the patient.

Zeigarnik disagrees with the view of adult mental dysfunction as a regression to an earlier stage of mental development and insists that, despite some external similarities, there exist qualitative differences between the thinking of a mentally defective adult and the thinking of a child (Zeigarnik, 1965): "The disintegration of mental activity is not the antithesis of its development" (p. 193). In the Pavlovian framework, such manifestations of adult mental dysfunction as fluctuation in the level of mental performance and hyperresponsiveness to extraneous stimuli are interpreted as consequences of impaired cortical inhibition. On the other hand, the distractibility of the child is viewed as a manifestation of a powerful orienting reflex, indicative of a high level of cortical activity.

Brain and viscera

In Pavlov's view, the function of the brain is to maintain the adaptation of the organism to the changing environment (principle of the unity of the organism with the environment). The environment is twofold: external and internal. Under the influence of the French physiologist Claude Bernard (1813-1878), the internal environment (*milieu intérieur*) was viewed, narrowly, as the fluids bathing the tissue cells of multicellular organisms. Exploration of the function of receptors located in the viscera, their cortical representation, and viscerocerebral and cerebrovisceral interaction has been pursued vigorously by the Russian physiologists, as indicated by the numerous references cited in Chernigovskiy's monograph (1967). In the monograph the interoceptors are grouped into four classes (mechanoreceptors, chemoreceptors, thermoreceptors, and osmoreceptors), and the mechanisms of their functioning are analyzed.

L. A. Bekkers and V. M. Shumovskii reported in 1862 that stretching the walls of the urinary bladder by filling it with liquid, introduced through a thin catheter, initiated contractions of the bladder. This response is an example of a "natural" (or systemic) reflex. Increased stimulus intensity gives rise to "conjugate" (concomitant, intersystemic) reflexes involving the activity of a number of effectors and manifested, for example, in the changes of respiration and a rise in blood pressure. Interoceptive stimulation can affect also sensory functions, e.g., the light threshold of the dark-adapted eye.

While the afferent impulses generated by the stimulation of interoceptors have also been studied electrophysiologically, it is the method of conditioned reflexes that served as the principal research tool in the Russian studies designed to clarify the two-way connections, through afferent and efferent pathways, between the internal organs and the central nervous system. Both aspects are of relevance to psychology.

It should be noted that, in man, conditioned visceral responses can be produced by conditioned stimuli of the first signal system (e.g., acoustic or tactile stimuli) as well as by words, regarded by Pavlov as conditioned stimuli belonging to the second (symbolic) signal system. The afferent and efferent chains may include the participation of the subcortical centers as well as of the endocrine system.

In Bykov's formulation (1959, p. 335), reflecting Pavlov's views:

The cortex is clearly a masterful organ dedicated to the performance of complicated tasks, not only as regards information reaching it over external receptors but also with the analysis, synthesis and organization of impulses from the internal organs. It is the prime system for channelizing the host of divergent and insistent signals, and of integrating them into the complex of action called behavior.

The interaction between the brain and the internal organs is a two-way process. Let us begin by considering the viscerocerebral relations.

In regard to the afferent impulses originating in the interoceptors of the viscera, psychologists are interested in the effects of the signals of the state of the internal organs on the function of the higher regions of the central nervous system and the activity of the organism as a whole (behavior).

Bykov showed, in 1928, that wetting of the gastric mucosa, paired with the application of an electrical shock to the hind limb of a dog, eventually elicited, when presented alone (i.e., without the shock), a lifting of the limb. This demonstrated that an interoceptive stimulus could elicit external behavior (a conditioned motor response). The development of complex (behavioral) reaction patterns involves an interaction of exteroceptive and interoceptive signals.

While for the most part we are not conscious of the afferent nervous impulses initiated by the interoceptors or the resulting sensations are "vague," they do affect importantly our moods, our feeling of well-being, and our self-awareness ("consciousness of one's body," in Bykov's terminology) and are an important part of the biological drives (hunger, elimination).

It was the remarkable I. M. Sechenov who, in 1863, wrote that the "dark" (obscure) sensations which accompany events taking place in the cavities of the chest, stomach, etc., "form one of the most potent motivation forces" (cited in Bykov, 1959, p. 405).

In the closing chapter of his monograph Chernigovskiy (1967) reviews experiments indicating that interoceptive signaling plays a role in the feeding behavior of animals, search for food, food selection (food consumption) and suggests that the study of the function of the interoceptors may contribute to an objective analysis of some forms of instinctive behavior.

The study of cerebrovisceral interactions, concerned with cerebral (and, in particular, cortical) regulation of visceral activities under conditions of health and with the role of malfunction of this regulation in the etiology of certain diseases, represents the Russian analog of Western psychophysiology and psychosomatic medicine.

Cerebrovisceral impulses can initiate or modify the activity of visceral organs. We speak of activating and regulating mechanisms, respectively.

The first data on the formation of urinary conditioned reflexes (diuresis elicited by a sound) were reported by K. M. Bykov and I. A. Alekseev-Berkman in 1926. Bykov's monograph (1957, 1959) documents the extension of the technique of conditioned reflexes to many other internal organs, in addition to the kidney.

Bykov and Kurtsin (1966) showed the importance of the disturbances of the cerebral (especially the cortical) regulation of gastric and duodenal function (secretion of gastric juice, trophic processes in the gastric and intestinal wall, resistance to digestion of the tissues by gastric juice) in the development of peptic ulcer.

Varieties of Behavior

Fragments of the work of I. S. Beritashvili (Beritov, in Russian), the outstanding Georgian neurophysiologist and student of animal behavior, are contained in the proceedings of scientific conferences (Beritashvili, 1963; cf. also Beritashvili, 1968a, 1968b). A systematic presentation of his physiological analysis of animal behavior, published originally in 1961, is now available in English (Beritoff, 1965).

Beritashvili differentiates four varieties of behavior: innate (instinctive), conditioned, image-controlled, and conscious. The first three varieties characterize higher vertebrates. The latter variety is present only in adult normal man who formulates goals and plans action. However, the lower levels of behavior may also be in evidence. Furthermore, initially conscious behavior, through repetition, may be automatized and may resemble a conditioned chain reflex. Under these conditions the conscious control is reduced but not entirely eliminated.

In animals, the basic varieties are the instinctive behavior, dependent upon the inborn organization of the central nervous system and serving specific organic needs, and the individually acquired behavior. While the instinctive behavior represents predetermined sequences of operations, it is susceptible, in a measure, to modification by experience (learning, conditioning). The individually acquired animal behavior falls, in its turn, into two categories: conditioned and image-directed.

The concept of image-directed behavior, as a separate category of individually acquired behavior, basically different from conditioned behavior, was a truly revolutionary departure from the Pavlovian interpretative framework.

A typical experiment demonstrating image-guided behavior proceeds as follows: A dog is taken out of his cage, is led to a place in the experimental room where he sees food being placed behind a screen, and is brought back to the cage. When released from the cage, he runs to the place where he had seen the food. While interpreting this behavior as the result of an integrated, multilevel activity of the nervous system, Beritashvili assigns the leading role to "psychoneural" activity of the cortex. This involves activation of a neuronal complex which reproduces images of vitally important aspects of the environment (goal objects). The images guide the behavior.

The morphological substrate of image-guided behavior is identified with the ste ate (star-shaped) neurons of the neocortex.

A high level of excitability of the stellate neurons is maintained by impulses arriving from the nonspecific reticular formation in the lower brainstem. In agreement with I. M. Sechenov (1829-1905), Beritashvili views images as the main regulator of behavior of higher vertebrates. The images regulate animal behavior in essentially the same way as the direct perceptions of the environment do. Thus in the illustrative experiment described earlier, the hungry dog runs to the place at which the food was located, behind a screen, as he would if he actually saw it there. The image *guides* the behavior, while an inborn drive to get food *motivates* the behavior.

Man exhibits conscious behavior, characterized by awareness of goals and planning of action. The results of action are anticipated prior to the actual onset of the action. Conscious behavior is characteristic only of adult man, not of animals or human infants, and represents the product of social interaction involving verbal communication. The young child's behavior is image-driven. Under certain conditions the behavior of adult man can revert to this lower level or even to the level of conditioned reflexes.

An extensive, updated account of Beritashvili's views on the structure and function of the cerebral cortex and the subcortical structures, with emphasis on the highest, "psychoneural" activity of the brain, appeared in Russian at a time when the author, eighty-four years young, was still busily engaged in research on memory (Beritov, 1969).

Experiments on Monkeys

The first of the three parts constituting the volume edited by Utkin (1960) is devoted to the study of conditioned reflexes ("the physiology and pathology of highest nervous activity," in the Russian parlance).

L. N. Norkina used lever pressing as the preferred method of studying conditioned motor reflexes in monkeys. She discussed the procedures, the formation of conditioned reflexes, their ready disturbance (external inhibition) by a variety of extraneous stimuli, and their "internal inhibition" (e.g., extinction through nonreinforcement of the conditioned positive stimuli). A stable differential inhibition (inhibition of responses to nonreinforced stimuli) could be established only with difficulty.

Norkina also reported studies on the "type of highest nervous activity," along Pavlov's line, but replacing the salivary method by the study of conditioned motor reflexes. One of the observations concerned the high "mobility" of the processes of excitation and inhibition in the monkeys, manifested in a ready adaptation to changes in the sign (meaning) of the conditioned stimuli (from positive or excitatory to negative or inhibitory, and vice versa).

D. I. Miminoshvili produced experimental neurosis in monkeys by overstraining the cortical excitatory processes. This was achieved by prolonging the conditioned stimulus (red light reinforced by electrical stimulation of the skin). The animals ceased to eat, exhibited persistent motor excitement, and failed to discriminate between positive and negative (inhibitory) feeding signals, responding with a prolonged pressure on the lever. The rate of respiration was increased dramatically (from twenty-eight to seventy-five respiratory movements per minute).

An additional form of stress was the collision between a conditioned stimulus, reinforced by electrical shock, presented simultaneously with, or shortly after, a conditioned stimulus reinforced by feeding. This resulted in a violent general motor excitement or, on the other hand, a general torpor (catalepsis) and drowsiness.

In some monkeys, stress was induced by exposure to "natural conditioned stimuli," as when a sexually mature rhesus monkey, first kept together with the females, was later placed in a solitary cage located next to a group of female monkeys headed by a male "rival."

Development of Animal Behavior

Krushinskii's *Animal behavior* (1962) is not a comprehensive textbook but an exploration, in depth, of selected themes, such as the integration of innate and individually acquired components of behavior. His approach involves the combination of laboratory methods for investigation of the Pavlovian "physiology of highest nervous activity" with the observation of behavior under natural conditions.

As regards heredity, Krushinskii views only unconditioned reflexes as inherited. Behavioral acts vary widely in regard to the role of the individually acquired components. Instincts are defined not simply as unconditioned reflex behavior, but as behavioral acts with a high proportion of innate components. The animal's behavior is adapted to the concrete conditions of its existence through the formation of conditioned reflexes. Habits represent a form of behavior in which the individually acquired components predominate.

The "excitability" of the nervous system of dogs exhibits large interindividual differences, with the scores in the two-minute test used by Krushinskii varying from 10 to 360 movements. Positive correlations were established between excitability and effectiveness in forming motor conditioned reflexes.

The "strength" of the nervous system is defined as its working capacity (endurance). Again, in dogs the criterion of strength correlated positively with the capacity to learn, though the reported rs were very low, varying from .06 to .33.

Hyperthyroidism results in an increased excitability of the nervous system, while extirpation of the thyroid gland or chemical blocking of its function has an opposite effect. Male dogs tend to have somewhat "stronger" nervous systems than females and to exhibit slightly more marked "active defensive reactions."

The appearance of epileptiform fits in rodents ("reflex epilepsy," in Krushinskii's terminology), elicited by sound stimuli, is interpreted in terms of the irradiation of excitation produced in the auditory projection area of the cortex and not effectively inhibited. By the method of selection Krushinskii developed a line of experimental animals (rats) with a low threshold of motor excitation and convulsive fits.

"Extrapolation reflexes" refer (Krushinskii, 1962, p. xv) to behavior by means of which some species of animals are able to grasp elementary cause-and-effect relationships between phenomena in the outside world. A nonlaboratory example of such behavior is as follows: A crow is crossing a road, at a given pace. Then, "extrapolating" the speed of movements, it hurries up and avoids being hit by an oncoming car, thereafter resuming its initial rate of movement. A variety of laboratory test situations were devised for studies with various species of birds and with rabbits. Krushinskii viewed this behavior as one of those types of reflex activity of the brain which may be characterized as elementary rational activity.

Varia

Limitations of space make it necessary to refer *briefly* to several additional monographs. We shall consider, in turn, the following topics: eye movements and vision, neurophysiological mechanisms of voluntary human movements, orienting reaction, set, thought and language, the role of speech in the regulation of human behavior, mental retardation, and disturbances in mental functions resulting from brain lesions.

Eye Movements and Vision. A. L. Yarbus (born in 1914) was trained as a physicist. For many years he was associated with the Institute of Biophysics, U.S.S.R. Academy of Sciences. His extensive investigations are summarized in a volume (Yarbus, 1967) edited by L. A. Riggs, a fellow student of eye movements in the United States.

In 1956 Yarbus developed a miniaturized optical system, attached by suction to the human eye, which facilitates the study of eye movements. Eye movements were studied in a wide variety of conditions, including fixation on stationary objects, perception of moving objects, and perception of complex objects (pictures, optical illusions, text to be read). From the records of the eye movements one can determine which features of an object, such as a portrait of a person, attract the observer's eye, in what order, how often, and for how long.

When we view a picture, the eyes fixate primarily on the components which contain or may contain information essential for the comprehension of the meaning of the picture (Yarbus, 1967): "Eye movements reflect the human thought processes" (p. 190). In observing human scenes, the eye movements will be markedly affected by the questions the experimenter asks the observer. The patterns of eye movements during such a "directed scanning" help to clarify the significance of the eye-movement records obtained during a free examination of the same picture.

During prolonged viewing of a given object the observer's eyes repeatedly return to the features yielding the primary information about the object.

Yarbus confirmed and enriched the earlier observations made by Western authors who reported that visual impressions, unchanging and stationary relative to the retina, become rapidly (within one to three seconds) invisible. Yarbus speaks of the formation of an "empty field" and suggests, in accordance with the electrophysiological data obtained in animals, that in man the immobility of retinal images sharply reduces or abolishes impulses entering the optic nerve from the eye.

Mechanisms of Movements. The study of the neurophysiological mechanisms of human bodily movements was for many years the speciality of Nicholas Bernstein (1896-1966). He contributed to the development of photographic methods of motion analysis (so-called cyclography), mathematical characterization of movements, and their novel physiological interpretation. With P. K. Anokhin, he was Russia's pioneering physiological cyberneticist and in 1935, thirteen years before the publication (in 1948) of N. Wiener's *Cybernetics,* was concerned with the functioning of self-regulating systems and stressed the crucial role of "feedback" for the control of man's voluntary movements. A "reflex circle" (or "ring"), not a reflex arc, represents the proper model of the fundamental unit of human activity. Bernstein (1967, pp. 115-116) speaks of "circular control" of human movements.

Bernstein's approach to the organization of goal-directed behavior incorporates the concepts of the factual (present) value of a situational parameter Iw (*Ist-wert,* in German), the required (future) value of the parameter Sw (*Soll-vert*), and the discrepancy $\Delta w = Iw\text{-}Sw$. Thus, in picking up an object seen on a table, the position of the object which must be reached by the hand corresponds to Sw, the actual position of the hand at a given moment corresponds to Iw, and the diminishing distance between the object and the hand corresponds to Δw.

Orienting Reaction. The "orienting reaction" (or investigatory, "what is it?" reflex) is another phenomenon in which physiologists and psychologists share interest. The phenomenon was described by Pavlov as far back as 1910 and, in greater detail, in 1922, but psychologists became involved in research on orienting reactions only in the last twenty years. The materials available in translation inform the reader about the status of the field in the late 1950s. The volume edited by L. G. Voronin et al. (1965) constitutes the proceedings of a conference held in February, 1957.

The orienting reaction is a phenomenon of broad biological and psychological significance. For one thing, there is a link between the orienting reflex, as a nonspecific generalized reaction, and arousal, as a function of the reticular activating system. Second, orienting reaction interacts, in complex ways, with other activities of the organism. It may inhibit ongoing acts; on the other hand, it may enhance the dominant activity of the organism, such as an unconditioned defensive reflex. Third, seen in a more "psychological" perspective, the study of orienting reactions opens the possibility for empirical investigations of cognitive processes.

Sokolov's (1963) monograph, first published in 1958, is focused on the role of conditioned reflexes in perception. Orienting reflexes are viewed as responses which bring about increased sensory sensitivity in animals during such activities as listening, sniffing, and watching. New stimuli give rise to peripheral vascoconstriction and cephalic vasodilation. Both responses decrease in intensity and eventually cease upon the repetition of a given stimulus. The weakening of an orienting reaction (*diminished reactivity*) is associated with a rise in threshold values (*diminished sensitivity*).

The orienting reaction can be brought about not only by a new stimulus but also by a change in the given stimulus, such as a change in the stimulus intensity, in either direction. In this case the intensity of the reaction is proportional to the intensity of the *change* in stimulus intensity.

The vasomotor responses represent only one component of the orienting reaction. The galvanic skin reflex (a fall in the resistance to electrical current passing through the body), recorded from the skin of the palm of the hand, is another component of the orienting reflex that was studied by Sokolov (1963, pp. 53-64). Latent period, magnitude, and duration of the reaction were measured. The response was similar to the vascular component of the orienting reaction, with a gradual extinction upon repeated presentation of the stimulus. In addition to the autonomic components noted above, orienting reactions involve somatic (movements of the body, head, eyes, ears), other autonomic (respiratory), and electroencephalographic (changes in the alpha rhythm) components.

The orienting reaction is viewed as a system of responses promoting, directly (through effects on cortical activity) or indirectly (by affecting cerebral blood supply), conditions favorable to stimulus reception (Sokolov, 1963, p. 285).

Sokolov uses a "neuronal model of the stimulus" to interpret physiologically the generation and extinction of orienting reactions. He postulates that the nervous system stores the information concerning the stimulus that is being presented repeatedly (its intensity, duration, and interstimulus interval) and compares the forecasts of future stimuli with the stimuli actually present. An orienting reaction takes place when the stimulus presented at a given time differs from the "neuronal model" of the stimulus.

Sokolov's neuronal model of the stimulus is closely related to P. K. Anokhin's concept of the "acceptor of action."

Set. In the South, in faraway Tbilisi in Georgia, D. N. Uznadze (1886-1950) and his co-workers have been engaged for many years in experimental investigations of "set" (*Einstellung*, in German; *ustanovka*, in Russian). Two of Uznadze's monographs were translated and published in a book entitled *The psychology of set* (Uznadze, 1966).

In contrast to the prevailing Russian point of view, to Uznadze the human mind is not identical with consciousness. It includes, importantly, the nonconscious factors to which he refers as "sets." Sets are defined as states of an organism, activated by the organism's needs, which give direction to the organism's activity in specific environmental situations. Usually, he (man) is not aware of these sets. But this does not stop them from being the active forces controlling his activity (Uznadze, 1966, p. 243).

The concept of set has important implications for all forms of behavior, from perception through the functioning of the normal personality to abnormal behavior.

Thought and Language. L. S. Vygotskii's (1896-1934) monograph was first published, in Russian, in 1934. It was regarded as important enough to merit a translation almost thirty years after it was written (Vygotsky, 1962). In one sense, it may be viewed as an early contribution to psycholinguistics and, specifically, to that segment of psycholinguistics which deals with the interrelations between intellective and verbal activity. But Vygotskii's work has broader implications for psychology. In the author's formulation (1962, p. 153):

Thought and language, which reflect reality in a way different from that of perception, are the key to the nature of human consciousness. Words play a central part not only in the development of thought but in the historical growth of consciousness as a whole. A word is a microcosm of human consciousness.

Just as physical work is performed by means of tools, mental activities involve the use of symbols, primarily verbal symbols (words). In the child's mental development a crucial role is played by internalization of overt behavior and, in particular, of the external dialogue transformed into inner speech and thought.

Regulation of Human Behavior. A. R. Luria, of the contemporary Russian psychologists the best known in the West, was a close associate of Vygotskii, many of whose interests he shares, including an interest in speech (cf. Luria, 1960b, p. 142).

In his study of the development of voluntary action in children, Luria (1960a) takes as a point of departure Vygotskii's theory that speech—first external, later internal—is the chief mechanism of voluntary behavior.

One of Luria's first books published in English after the war is a report of a study on the development of speech in a pair of identical twins, undertaken in cooperation with F. Ia. Yudovich (Luria & Yudovich, 1959). Having placed the twins in separate, parallel groups in a kindergarten, the authors observed the changes from a primitive, "synpractic" speech, closely tied to specific activities, to speech used by the twins for communication with others and for formulating the aims of their own activities.

In the course of the development of the child, the regulatory function of speech is carried out less and less by words as direct impulses to action and more and more by words as carriers of meaning (Luria, 1961). There is in the child a simultaneous shift, around the age of five years, from the external to the internal speech. At this stage of development, Luria notes, the internal speech comes to constitute the essential component both of thought and of voluntary behavior.

Mental Retardation. The role of speech in the control of behavior is also one of the topics explored in a volume edited by Luria (1963a) and dealing with various aspects of the functioning of mentally retarded children, such as electrical activity of the brain, orientation reflexes, formation of conditioned reflexes, and verbal associations. The book is introduced by a revealing chapter entitled "The problem of mental retardation and its study." Rejecting the concept of inheritance of mental abilities, the Soviets view *all* instances of mental retardation as a consequence of a serious brain disease during the intrauterine or early postnatal period of development (Luria, 1963, p. vii). The reader will also find some choice bits of misinformation about the use of mental tests in the "capitalist countries" (Luria, 1963a, pp. 1-3). Mental testing is one area in which ideological conflict continues to create barriers to comprehension and the possibility of a reasoned dialogue.

Brain and Behavior. Several of Luria's books are the outcome of his investigations on the impact of brain lesions on mental functions. They represent important contributions both to applied psychology and to the theoretical interpretation of brain-mind relationships.

Luria's views differ from the concepts of traditional "morphopsychology," whether they had postulated rigid localization of complex mental functions in specific "centers" or regarded mental activities as products of the brain operating as a whole. According to Luria, complex activities (such as locomotion or writing), are executed by a group of integrated structural units, central and peripheral (1966a, p. 468):

We adopted as our starting point the idea of a dynamic, systemic localization of functions, originally proposed by Pavlov and subsequently developed and applied to the higher mental functions of man by Vygotskii. We regard the higher cortical processes as complex, dynamically localized, functional systems.

Another book by Luria, published in Russian in 1948 (Luria, 1963b), is concerned with recovery after localized injury to the brain. The material on which the book is based was collected during and following World War II. The basic fact is that while the damaged brain cells do not regenerate, there is a partial restoration of the impaired brain function. The functions specifically considered by Luria include movements, visual perception, speech, thinking, and motivation.

Luria differentiates three types of mechanisms for the restoration of brain function: (1) restoration of temporarily inhibited functions (spontaneous deinhibition, restoration of synaptic transmission by pharmacological means, deinhibition by a change of mental orientation); (2) substitution of the opposite hemisphere; and (3) formation of new, compensatory functional connections between different areas of the cortex. In this way a new "functional system" is created involving areas of the brain that previously did not participate in a given activity (such as multiplication of numbers), impaired by focal brain lesions. Impairment of such complex activities as writing, reading, memorization, or spatial orientation can be compensated by the introduction of auxiliary visual, acoustic, or kinesthetic processes.

Luria's two large recent works (Luria, 1966a, 1966b) deal with a variety of topics in the area of neuropsychology, which connotes, in Luria's hands, largely the study of disturbances of behavior in the presence of brain lesions, whether they are due to gunshot wounds or tumors.

The first volume (Luria, 1966a) is a collection of ten essays, most of which were revised in 1962, written over a period of some thirty years. Sequelae of lesions of the anterior parts of the human brain represent the dominant theme. In the opening chapters the author discusses the more general problem of the functional organization of the human brain.

The second volume (Luria, 1966b) is similar in organization and content, with the first part concerned with the problem of localization of mental functions, and the second part dealing with the disturbances of "higher cortical functions" in the presence of focal brain lesions. The third part is new and describes a variety of methods used by Soviet clinical psychologists. Since in the Soviet journal publications the description of methods is frequently cursory, this detailed account is a welcome source of information.

Because of the importance of Luria's point of view on brain and behavior—one of the basic issues of physiological psychology—we shall close this section by quoting him directly (1966a, p. xvii):

Human mental processes are to be understood as complex functional systems, having a social-historical origin. . . . These processes take place as a result of the combined activity of several cortical zones, each of which plays its own specific role, and supplies an essential factor for the normal working of the system as a whole. A local brain lesion, directly causing the loss of one of the factors concerned in the construction of mental processes, thus leads to a secondary disturbance of the functional system as a whole; however, every disturbance has its own individual character depending on which link of the functional system is affected by each particular local brain lesion.

A LOOK INTO THE FUTURE

In our attempt to "look around the corner," we could hardly ask for a more competent guide than A. N. Leont'ev, dean of Moscow University's College of Psychology (Leont'ev, 1968).

Leont'ev points out that in the past, much of Soviet psychological research was associated with problems of education—the instruction and upbringing of children. There is need for broadening the scope of the research in this area, tied in the past too one-sidedly to methods of teaching specific school subjects. Educational psychology needs an atmosphere conducive to the exploration of *psychological* ideas from which genuine innovations in "educational technology"—such as programmed instruction—may emerge.

In view of the rapid and continuing advances in science and technology, it is essential not so much to impart to students ready-made knowledge and skills as to create in them the capacity to assimilate the new advances. This calls for a fundamental reexamination of the learning processes. First and foremost, the problem must be viewed, in Leont'ev's opinion, as a problem of psychology, not primarily or solely as a pedagogical problem.

Systematic attention must be given to the psychological aspects of the acceleration of child development, including the impact of the changes in the source of information transmitted to the child (direct contact with other persons versus speech transmitted by radio), the markedly increased amount of information entering the child's brain via the mass media, and the changes in the technological aspects of the child's environment.

In recent years the general scope of Soviet psychology has been substantially broadened, in several directions, including engineering psychology, medical psychology, research on personality, and social psychology. These are the areas in which important further growth of Soviet psychology may be expected to take place in the foreseeable future.

In a way, all these fields may be viewed as areas of "borderline research" in which psychology has been confronting the data, conceptual systems, and terminology of other sciences—biological, social, and technological. Soviet psychological papers are beginning to be replete with neurophysiological, technological, and cybernetic terms and mathematical formulas.

One of the problems that call for rethinking concerns the relations between psychology and neurophysiology. Such a rethinking must go beyond the general discussions of reducibility or the impossibility of reducing the mental to the physiological. Leont'ev is impressed by the fact that such processes as perception and memory represent multilevel phenomena. Thus subliminal sensory processes cannot be viewed legitimately as "purely physiological" since under certain conditions they may affect (regulate) complex human activity. Research on memory is being carried out at levels varying from molecular and cellular to that of the intact human organism. This approach reveals the lack of validity of the conception of the physiological and the mental as two separate "realms" (or entities). Leont'ev views as a task of prime importance the bringing about of a "vertical synthesis" of the different horizontal layers, i.e., the clarification of the relationships between the processes taking place at different levels of multilevel phenomena and the investigations of the interlevel transitions.

The study of the multilevel systems involved in behavior facilitates the rapprochement between the conceptualization of the function of organisms and adaptive (cybernetic) machines, and it enhances our intellectual and technological mastery of man-machine systems.

The steadily advancing automation of industrial operations has shifted the focus of the study of human factors from psychophysiological concern with movements and physical work environment to the more "psychological" level of perception, memory, and thought. Psychology is faced with the task of describing mental operations in terms which permit their modeling and their transfer to machines (and a more effective linkage between man and machine).

In the last ten years, engineering psychology and "psychological bionics" experienced rapid development in the U.S.S.R. and constitute, at present, an important segment of Soviet psychology. Furthermore, these fields exercise a profound effect on the development of Soviet psychology as a whole, interacting closely with other sectors of psychology, especially general experimental psychology.

The application of social psychology in the industrial setting is in its beginnings. Leont'ev cites problems of motivation of the workers and of interpersonal relations in industry as topics calling for research. He refers also to the problem of alienation of the workers.

The political and economic differences between the Soviet Union and the "capitalist West" lend potential interest and importance to research in the field of industrial social psychology. On the other hand, this is a sensitive area, and it remains to be demonstrated that significant, objective research in this area is, in fact, possible in the U.S.S.R. We wish to make clear that this comment is ours, not Leont'ev's.

The situation of social psychology as a whole is designated by Leont'ev as "complicated." In the past, social psychology was almost totally neglected in the U.S.S.R. as a special branch of psychology. One of the roots of this neglect was the ideologists' horror that the pursuit of social psychology might lead to a tendency to "psychologize social phenomena," "to implant subjectivist conceptions in sociology." This, again, is our interpretation, not Leont'ev's.

Leont'ev feels that there exists a legitimate complex of sociopsychological problems (such as the creation of the "sense of community") which can be properly singled out as the subject matter of social psychology. At the same time he admits that an adequately formulated program for sociopsychological research does not yet exist in the Soviet Union.

The field referred to in the West as *clinical psychology* does not have a true homolog in the Soviet Union. B. V. Zeigarnik refers to the psychological study of patients with neuropsychiatric disorders as *pathopsychology*. A segment of this field which received much attention in the Soviet Union is concerned with the psychological impact of focal brain injuries and the restoration of mental function impaired as a result of these injuries. A. R. Luria refers to this sector as *neuropsychology*. The concept of *medical psychology* is broader and less clearly defined. It includes psychotherapy [which was not cultivated systematically, intensively, or imaginatively by Soviet psychiatrists and seems to be "out of bounds" for psychologists] and such problems as the psychological response of patients to actions of a physician. Of greater importance for psychology is the fact that in this context, psychologists come face to face with problems of personality. It should be clear, notes Leont'ev (1968, p. 114) with refreshing frankness, that Soviet psychologists

... cannot avoid such questions as the problem of conflict experiences, emotional trauma, the role of the unconscious, and mental compensation—i.e., precisely those questions that in the past years have been ignored in the USSR not only in pathopsychology and general psychology, but also in child psychology.

REFERENCES

Anonymous. *Fundamentals of Marxism-Leninism.* Moscow: Foreign Languages Publishing House, 1961.

Beritashvili, I. S. The characteristics and origin of voluntary movements in higher vertebrates. In G. Moruzzi, A. Fessard, & H. H. Jasper (Eds.), *Brain mechanisms.* Amsterdam: Elsevier, 1963. Pp. 340-348.

Beritashvili (Beritov), I. S. Central inhibition according to I. M. Sechenov's experiments and concepts and its modern interpretation. In E. A. Asratyan (Ed.), *Brain reflexes.* Amsterdam: Elsevier, 1968. Pp. 21-31. (a)

Beritashvili, I. S. A modern interpretation of the mechanisms of I. M. Sechenov's psychical reflex medium member. In E. A. Asratyan (Ed.), *Brain reflexes.* Amsterdam: Elsevier, 1968. Pp. 252-264. (b)

Beritoff (Beritashvili), J. S. *Neural mechanisms of higher vertebrate behavior.* (Trans. from the 1961 Russian ed. and ed. by W. T. Liberson) Boston: Little, Brown, 1965.

Beritov, I. S. *Struktura i funktsiya kory bol'shogo mozga [Structure and function of the cerebral cortex].* Moscow: Mauka, 1969.

Bernstein, N. *The coordination and regulation of movements.* (Trans. from Russian and German.) New York: Macmillan, 1967.

Blakely, T. J. *Soviet scholasticism.* Dordrecht, Netherlands: D. Reidel, 1961.

Brožek, J. Recent developments in Soviet psychology. *Annual Review of Psychology,* 1964, **15**, 493-594.

Brožek, J. Spectrum of Soviet psychology: 1968 model. *American Psychologist,* 1969, **24**, 944-946.

Brožek, J., & Hoskovec, J. Current Soviet psychology: A systematic review. *Soviet Psychology and Psychiatry,* 1966, 4(3-4), 16-44.

Bykov, K. M. *The cerebral cortex and the internal organs.* (Trans. by W. H. Gantt) New York: Chemical Publishing, 1957.

Bykov, K. M. *The cerebral cortex and the internal organs.* (Trans. from the 1954 [3rd] Russian ed. by R. Hodes) Moscow: Foreign Languages Publishing House, 1959.

Bykov, K. M., & Kurtsin, I. T. *The corticovisceral theory of the pathogenesis of peptic ulcer.* (Trans. by S. A. Corson) Oxford: Pergamon Press, 1966.

Chernigovskiy, V. N. *Interoceptors.* (Trans. from the 1960 Russian ed. by G. Onischenko; ed. by D. B. Lindsley) Washington: American Psychological Association, 1967.

Cole, M., & Maltzman, I. (Eds.) *A handbook of contemporary Soviet psychology.* New York: Basic Books, 1969.

Gray, J. A. (Ed. & Trans.) *Pavlov's typology.* (Intro. by H. J. Eysenck) Oxford: Pergamon Press, 1964.

Koshtoyants, Kh. S. *Essays on the history of physiology in Russia.* (Trans. from the 1946 Russian ed. by D. P. Boder, K. Hanes, & N. O'Brien.) Washington: American Psychological Association, 1964.

Krushinskii, L. V. *Animal behavior: Its normal and abnormal development.* (Trans. by B. Haigh from the 1960 Russian ed.) New York: Consultants Bureau, 1962.

Leont'ev, A. Psikhologiya [Psychology]. In *Filosofskaya entsiklopediya [Philosophical encyclopedia].* Moscow: Sovetskaya Entsiklopediya, 1967. Pp. 420-422.

Leont'ev, A. N. Some prospective problems of Soviet psychology. *Soviet Psychology*, 1968, **6**(3-4), 112-125.

Luria, A. R. Experimental analysis of the development of voluntary action in children. In H. P. David & J. C. Brengelmann (Eds.), *Perspectives in personality research.* New York: Springer, 1960. Pp. 139-149. (a)

Luria, A. R. *The nature of human conflicts.* (Trans. by W. H. Gantt.) New York: Grove Press, 1960. (1st ed. 1932) (b)

Luria, A. R. *The role of speech in the regulation of normal and abnormal behavior.* (Ed. by J. Tizard) New York: Pergamon Press, 1961.

Luria, A. R. (Ed.) *The mentally retarded child.* (Trans. by W. P. Robinson from the 1960 Russian ed. English trans. ed. by B. Korman) New York: Macmillan, 1963. (a)

Luria, A. R. *Restoration of function after brain injury.* (Trans. from the 1948 Russian ed. by B. Haigh) New York: Macmillan, 1963. (b)

Luria, A. R. *Higher cortical functions in man.* (Trans. from the 1962 Russian ed. by B. Haigh) New York: Basic Books and Consultants Bureau, 1966. (a)

Luria, A. R. *Human brain and psychological processes.* (Trans. from the 1963 Russian ed. by B. Haigh) New York: Harper & Row, 1966. (b)

Luria, A. R. *The mind of mnemonist.* (Trans. from the 1968 Russian ed. by L. Solotaroff) New York: Basic Books, 1968.

Luria, A. R., & Yudovich, F. Ia. *Speech and development processes in the child: An experimental investigation.* (Trans. from the 1956 Russian ed. by O. Kovacs & J. Simon; intro. by O. Zangwill) London: Staples Press, 1959.

Nebylitsyn, V. D. (Ed.) *Problemy differentsial'noi psikhofiziologii [Differential psychophysiology].* Moscow: Prosveshchenie, 1969.

Payne, T. R. *S. L. Rubineštejn and the philosophical foundations of Soviet psychology.* Dordrecht, Netherlands: D. Reidel and New York: Humanities Press, 1968.

Rosenblith, W. A. Postscript. In I. M. Sechenov, *Reflexes of the brain.* Cambridge, Mass.: M.I.T. Press, 1965. Pp. 143-145.

Rubinshtein, S. L. I. P. Pavlov's theories and some problems of the reconstruction of psychology. (In Russian) *Voprosy filosofii*, 1952, **5**, 197-210.

Sechenov, I. M. *Autobiographical notes.* (Trans. from a text, completed around 1904, by K. Hanes) Washington: American Psychological Association, 1965. (a)

Sechenov, I. M. *Reflexes of the brain.* (Reprint of a 1961 trans. by S. Belsky, printed in Moscow, of a work first published in Russian in 1863.) Cambridge, Mass.: M.I.T. Press, 1965. (b)

Sokolov, Ye. N. *Perception and the conditioned reflex.* (Trans. from the 1958 Russian ed. by S. W. Waydenfeld) New York: Macmillan, 1963.

Teplov, B. M. Problems in the study of general types of higher nervous activity in man and animals. In J. A. Gray (Ed.), *Pavlov's typology.* Oxford: Pergamon Press, 1964. Pp. 3-153.

Utkin, I. A. (Ed.) *Theoretical and practical problems of medicine and biology in experiments on monkeys.* (Trans. by R. Schachter) New York: Pergamon Press, 1960.

Uznadze, D. N. *The psychology of set.* (Trans. by B. Haigh) New York: Consultants Bureau, 1966.

Voronin, L. G., et al. (Eds.) *Orienting reflex and exploratory behavior.* (Trans. from the 1958 Russian ed. by V. Shmelev & K. Hanes) Washington: American Psychological Association, 1965.

Vygotsky, L. S. *Thought and language.* (Intro. by J. S. Bruner; Trans. from the 1934 Russian ed. by E. Hanfmann & G. Vakar) Cambridge, Mass.: M.I.T. Press, 1962.

Watson, R. I. Psychology: A prescriptive science. *American Psychologist,* 1967, **22**, 435-443.

Wiener, N. *Cybernetics, or Control and communication in the animal and the machine.* New York: Wiley, 1948.

Yarbus, A. L. *Eye movements and vision.* (Trans. from the 1965 Russian ed. by B. Haigh; English trans. ed. by L. A. Riggs) New York: Plenum Press, 1967.

Zeigarnik, B. V. Über das Behalten von erledigten und unerledigten Handlungen. *Psychologische Forschung,* 1927, **9**, 1-85.

Zeigarnik, B. V. *The pathology of thinking.* (Trans. from the 1962 Russian ed. by B. Haigh) New York: Consultants Bureau, 1965.

FURTHER READINGS

Anokhin, P. K. Ivan P. Pavlov and psychology. In B. B. Wolman (Ed.), *Historical roots of contemporary psychology.* New York: Harper & Row, 1968. Pp. 131-159.

Bowden, D. Primate behavioral research in the USSR: the Sukhumi medicobiological station. *Folia Primatologica,* 1966, **4**, 346-360.

Brožek, J. (Ed.) Selected aspects of contemporary psychology in the USSR: A symposium. *Medical Reports* (Fordham University Institute for Contemporary Russian Studies), 1964, **6**(1), 1-21.

Brožek, J. Contemporary Soviet psychology. *Transactions of the New York Academy of Science,* Ser. II, 1965, **27**, 422-438.

Brožek, J., & Herz, A. P. Recent Russian books in psychology. *Contemporary Psychology,* 1971, **16**, 726-729.

Brožek, J., & Slobin, D. I. (Eds.) *Psychology in the USSR: An historical perspective.* White Plains, N.Y.: International Arts and Sciences Press, 1972.

Leont'ev, A. N., & Luria, A. A. The psychological ideas of L. S. Vygotskii. In B. B. Wolman (Ed.), *Historical roots of contemporary psychology.* New York: Harper & Row, 1968. Pp. 338-367.

Leont'ev, A., Luria, A., & Smirnov, A. (Eds.) *Psychological research in the USSR.* Vol. 1. Moscow: Progress Publishers, 1966.

Misiak, H., & Sexton, V. S. Psychology in the Soviet Union. In *History of psychology: An overview.* New York: Grune & Stratton, 1966. Pp. 258-280.

Molino, J. A. Is there a new Soviet psychology? In A. Simirenko (Ed.), *Social thought in the Soviet Union.* Chicago: Quadrangle Books, 1969. Pp. 300-327.

O'Connor, N. Report on Soviet science: Psychology. 2. Trends past and present. *Survey* (London) 1964, No. 52, 125-134.

O'Connor, N. (Ed.) *Present-day Russian psychology: A Symposium by seven authors.* Oxford: Pergamon Press, 1966.

Pick, H. L., Jr. Perception in Soviet psychology. *Psychological Bulletin,* 1964, **62**, 21-35.

Razran, G. Russian physiologists' psychology and American experimental psychology: A historical and systematic collation and a look into the future. *Psychological Bulletin,* 1965, **63**, 42-64.

Razran, G. *Mind in evolution: An East-West synthesis of learned behavior and cognition.* Boston: Houghton Mifflin, 1971.

Slobin, D. I. (Ed.) Handbook of Soviet psychology. Special issue of *Soviet Psychology and Psychiatry,* 1966, 4(3-4), 1-146.

Slobin, D. I. (Ed.) Special issue on Soviet psycholinguistics. *Soviet Psychology,* 1969, 7(3), 1-56.

USSR Academy of Sciences. *Social sciences in the USSR.* New York: Basic Books, 1965.

Woodworth, R. S., & Sheehan, M. H. Soviet psychology as a "school." In *Contemporary schools of psychology.* New York: Ronald Press, 1964. Pp. 90-110.

Yaroshevskii, M. G. I. M. Sechenov: The founder of objective psychology. In B. B. Wolman (Ed.), *Historical roots of contemporary psychology.* New York: Harper & Row, 1968. Pp. 77-110.

Zangwill, O. I. Report on Soviet science: Psychology. 1. Current approaches. *Survey* (London), 1964, No. 52, 119-125.

ORIENTAL PSYCHOLOGY*

Shinkuro Iwahara,
Tokyo University of Education,
Tokyo, Japan

Psychology in the Orient has been little known to the West (Europe and America) largely because of the language barrier. However, the language problem is one-sided; the Asian scientist is likely to know English, German, and French, but the scientist in the West is very unlikely to be familiar with Asian languages. India, Pakistan, and Ceylon are exceptions since their scientific output is written mostly in English.

According to the *International Directory of Psychologists* (1966), about 17 percent of all the psychologists in the world, exclusive of the United States, continental China, and a few other countries, are from Asian nations; of these, 67 percent are Japanese, and 12 percent are Indian.

CLASSIC PSYCHOLOGY IN INDIA AND CHINA

The ancient Hindu and Buddhist literature contains various systematic approaches to human nature and experience. An abundanceof psychological information is contained in the most ancient Rig-Vedas and especially in the Upanishads, which were composed around 800 B.C. "after the period of the exuberant Vedic hymns, as life became stabilized in the Indian peninsula and as a warrior caste gave itself more and more to contemplation and to cultivation of the inner life" (Murphy & Murphy, 1968, p. 51).

*The author is greatly indebted to Dr. Koji Sato, editor of *Psychologia: An International Journal of Psychology in the Orient,* for his valuable criticisms and suggestions, and also to Dr. D. L. Jayasuriya, of the University of Ceylon, for his detailed information on Indian, Pakistan, and Ceylonese psychology.

According to one of the Upanishads (literally "secret teaching"), four states of the mental processes are differentiated: sleeping, dreaming, the waking state, and the superconscious (Akhilananda, 1953). The first two states, which belong to the subconscious, are considered by Hindu philosophers to be important aspects of human experience. This is in contrast with some of the classic Western psychological systems such as English associationism, Wundtian structuralism, and Brentano's act psychology. Although these Western systems are considerably different from one another, they all deal with the intellectual and cognitive aspects of human experience as the subject matter of psychology. In addition, it is interesting to notice that Hindu workers differentiated sleeping from dreaming, since recent neurophysiologists generally support the dual theory of sleep: classical "slow" sleep and "paradoxical" sleep with dreaming (Thompson, 1967).

The Hindu psychologist, like the psychoanalyst, places special importance upon the subconscious (*samskara*) because it is believed to be an integration of past experiences, impressions, and tendencies of the individual. However, unlike psychoanalysis, Hindu psychology does not assume sex and death urges as the basic human instincts; the basic urge is, according to the Hindu theory, directed to eternal happiness or complete freedom from bondage. Notice its similarity to the Rogerian theory which postulates a drive toward growth, health, and adjustment of the individual.

The superconscious (*samadhi*) has no exact correlate in Western culture. It is an experience of spiritual enlightenment in which the individual is neither conscious nor subconscious, and it is quite different from hallucination or pathological states, since in such states spiritual insight cannot be attained. It is a mystic experience only in the sense that it is not intellectual, but is a whole mind-body experience or a holistic integration of the self and the world. The study of the superconsciousness is not unscientific. It can be experienced by the normal person. It does not matter whether he is Hindu, Buddhist, Christian, or atheist.

The Hindu and Buddhist thinkers not only have performed a detailed analysis of our inner life but also have shown a number of methods for attaining spiritual insight or samadhi, among which yoga (literally *union*) and Zen (a Japanese word, derived from *dhyāna*, meaning *meditation* in Sanskrit) are well known. Yoga and Zen appear quite different, but their underlying principles are similar. Zen is often said to be a blending of Indian rationalism, Chinese realism, and Japanese sentiments. In addition to yoga and Zen, a Burmese method of attaining meditation founded on Satipatthana sutra is now practiced in Burma, Thailand, and Ceylon (Dumoulin, 1962; Pe, 1966).

In ancient China, the universe was believed to consist of heaven, the earth, and man, where heaven and the earth obey natural law, while man observes moral law. According to Confucius (551-479 B.C.), morality is based on the three faculties of wisdom, benevolence, and valor. Later, Mencius (ca. 372-289 B.C.) divided morality into five elements: benevolence, righteousness, propriety, wisdom, and sincerity.

Like Aristotle, the ancient Chinese believed that mind lies in the center (heart) of the body. Besides mind and body, Mencius assumed *chi'i,* which corresponds roughly to spiritual energy or pneuma in classical Western psychology. Body is filled with *chi'i,* which is controlled by mind. Later scholars argued that *li* and *chi'i* make personality; *li* is innate and identical in all human beings, while *chi'i* can be modified by learning and environment and thus is the main source of individual differences and temperament.

Personality traits were systematically investigated by Liu-shao in about 220. His theory was based on the then current doctrine of the five elements of the universe (wood, fire, earth, metal, and water) and assumed that body, temperament, duty, and morality each have five different characteristics corresponding to the five elements and that when all these are mixed in proper proportion, an ideal personality is attained (Kuroda, 1948). The Chinese typology bears a remarkable resemblance to the Hippocratic theory of temperament.

ZEN BUDDHISM AND PSYCHOLOGY

Among various Oriental philosophical positions, Zen Buddhism is probably one of the best known in the West. It was early introduced to the West by Dr. Y. Motora, of Tokyo University. He presented a paper entitled "The concept of self in the Oriental philosophy" at the Seventh International Congress of Psychology at Rome in 1905. There he criticized English associationism as mechanical and devoid of an active self. The essential nature of mind, according to him, is a dynamic psychic potentiality into which the subject-object dichotomy is melted—*tathata* in Zen theory (Motora, 1905).

Otsuka (1960) uses Kuroda's (1931) definition of psychology as a science of consciousness and comprehension (*kaku*). Our usual experience is that volitional acts are eventually automatized with practice and become unconscious or half-conscious unless special attention is paid to them. This mental state is an example of comprehension. Another illustration of it is the knack, hunch, or *kan,* which refers to the occasional experience which we know but cannot make clear. Although comprehension is a naïve, preanalytic mental state, it evidently directs our behavior and plays an important role in our life. The purest form of comprehension, according to Kuroda, is the Zen enlightenment. Kuroda conducted a number of experiments on the exact nature of comprehension. A similar position has been taken by Chiba (1960).

Morita therapy, developed by the Japanese psychiatrist Dr. S. Morita, is a unique psychotherapy in the Zen mode of thought (Kora & Sato, 1958). According to Morita therapy, neurasthenia (or *nervosis,* in its own terminology) is attributable to a hypochondriac disposition and a mechanism of psychic interaction. The hypochondriac individual is overconscious of himself and feels that he is unusual or maladjusted; consequently, he concentrates attention upon his physical condition, especially upon his sensations, and thus his sensations become keener and in turn attract his attention. The interaction between sensation and attention exaggerates the hypochondriac tendency and consumes a great deal of mental energy with consequent behavior disorders.

In order to break up this vicious circle, the patient must accept the sufferings and worries as they are and must become carefree. Morita therapy starts with an absolute bed-rest period, during which the patient is prohibited from reading, writing, and even talking with others and is instructed to leave himself to the dynamics of his present situation. Through a light-work period to a hard-work period, the patient is gradually guided to lead a realistic daily life. Unlike psychoanalysis, Morita therapy involves no free association or interpretation (Kawai & Kondo, 1960). Another characteristic point of the Oriental therapy is the absence of labeling during treatment.

Evidently, Morita therapy is closely related to Zen philosophy in that both emphasize the present situation, "letting-be," spontaneity rather than etiology, and direct guidance and interpretation (Kora & Sato, 1958). Doi (1962) compared Morita therapy with psychoanalysis and argued that the difference may be attributed to the cultural difference between Japanese and Western societies, especially in terms of their attitudes toward dependency.

In spite of all these works, Zen has only recently been introduced to the West, mainly through English publications by the late D. T. Suzuki and Dr. Koji Sato. According to Suzuki (1956), Zen is "the art of seeing into the nature of one's being and it points the way from bondage to freedom . . . [and] liberates all the energies properly and naturally stored in each of us, which are in ordinary circumstances cramped and distorted so that they find no channel for activity" (p. 3). The final goal of Zen is the experience of spiritual enlightenment, or *satori*, which is a kind of trance having direct contact with reality.

Sato has written a number of introductory papers on Zen for Western readers in *Psychologia: An International Journal of Psychology in the Orient,* of which he is editor. One of his articles gives a brief description of *zazen,* or seated Zen, which is one of the commonest means of attaining satori. In zazen, the individual sits squarely on his seat with half-opened eyes and breathes quietly with his whole body, sometimes adjusting respiration by counting it. Then, applying a strain to the abdomen, he starts with a calm cry and gradually increases the voice level, ending with a vigorous shout, which results in high muscular tension in face, shoulders, and arms. In the meantime, he is able to meditate deeply into himself without diverting his attention. Meditation is characterized by a condition of no mind, nothingness, or "being one with the world." If the practice is successful, satori occurs rather suddenly with the release of tension. One of Sato's students described his own Zen experience as follows (Sato, 1959): "The mind became clear and serene, and a kind of joy was felt, with a force coming up from the bottom of the belly" (p. 112).

According to recent psychophysiological studies (e.g., Kasamatsu & Hirai, 1966), zazen produces dominant and continuous alpha waves which are not easily blocked, as in the normal waking state. The pulse is normal, or slightly faster, and there occurs no change in perception. The EEG changes during zazen are classified into four stages: appearance of alpha waves, increase of alpha amplitude, decrease of alpha frequency, and appearance of the rhythmic theta train. These stages are found to correlate with the degree of meditation. No such EEG changes are shown during hypnotic trance.

The Japanese Zen literature has appealed to some Western scientists, including psychologists, psychoanalysts, existential psychotherapists, and general semanticists. Erich Fromm, for example, has enumerated several similarities between Zen and psychoanalysis. According to him (1959), the "description of Zen's aim could be applied without change as a description of what psychoanalysis aspires to achieve" (p. 86), and "Zen can have a most fertile and clarifying influence on the theory of psychoanalysis" (p. 98), even though the two methods are quite different.

Hora (1959) has discussed the close kinship between Taoism, Zen, and existential psychotherapy in their common emphasis on nonteleological, nonintellectual, and existential aspects as well as on openness and "letting-be." Morris (1951) stated that Zen therapy, although it may appear mystic, can be legitimately accepted by current general semantics, and Holmes (1957) pointed out the transactional aspect of Zen.

The French psychotherapist Hubert Benoit has emphasized the thoroughgoing naturalism and realism of Zen in contrast with the idealistic position of Christianity. In Christianity, said Ando (1965), the basic idea is original sin, or the absolute difference between man and God, while in Zen doctrine man's essential self is identical in root and nature to the universe.

Recently, some American scientists profess to have experienced satori with the use of LSD (Rogers, 1964; Van Dusen, 1961). Van Dusen (1961), for example, argued that LSD acts as a new method of arriving at the Zen experience of sudden enlightenment. However, Suzuki clearly differentiated between Zen and psychedelic experience since the goal of Zen centers on the *person* himself and not on the objective situation that the person *sees* or *hears* (Sato, 1967). But Sato (1967) stated that LSD and other psychotropic drugs may help develop the process of Zen training if properly used.

After his comprehensive review of the psychological literature on Zen Buddhism, Maupin (1962) concluded that Zen experience is an adaptive type of regression in the service of the ego and that although the true satori takes years of training, the Zen meditation or zazen can still be used as a unique and powerful psychotherapeutic method which can be applicable for those patients who are inaccessible to other types of psychotherapy.

INTRODUCTION OF WESTERN SCIENTIFIC PSYCHOLOGY AND CURRENT PSYCHOLOGICAL ACTIVITIES IN THE ORIENT

India

Psychology has been included in philosophical courses in the Indian universities from the very beginning, but it was not until 1916 that the first psychological department and laboratory were started by Dr. N. N. Sengupta at the University of Calcutta (Pareek, 1957). Presently about thirty universities offer both undergraduate and graduate courses in psychology.

From 1950 to 1960, educational, industrial, social, and personality psychology seemed to attract the attention of Indian workers much more than the other fields of psychology (Krishnan, 1961). According to Jayasuriya (personal communication), the psychometric tradition in India has been geared to the practical problems of guidance and selection, and this is perhaps the strongest feature of Indian psychology.

Among more than a dozen psychological journals now published in this country, *Journal of Education and Psychology* (founded in 1942), *Journal of Vocational and Educational Guidance* (founded in 1954), and *Indian Journal of Psychology* (founded in 1926) contain valuable contributions in various fields of psychology. Content analysis of the issues of the *Indian Journal of Psychology* that appeared between 1964 and 1966 reveals that as much as 87 percent of the total number of articles deal with educational, personality, social, or industrial problems. A great number of psychometric tests and inventories have been either originally devised or adapted from foreign sources for Indian populations. Hundal (1966), for example, has standardized a group test of general mental ability by means of which he found the invariant factorial organization of mental abilities across different grade levels. Application of the Maudsley Personality Inventory showed some salient differences between various occupational groups as well as between students with different majors (Rao, 1966), and Krishnakanth and Prasad (1967) studied socioeconomic differences on a reasoning test.

Although experimental studies have appeared less often in Indian journals, this area was the most popular in terms of the number of papers presented to the Indian Science Congress between 1925 and 1963; 27 percent of the total psychological papers were devoted to experimental studies. Of the rest, 14 percent dealt with educational psychology, 12 percent with general and theoretical psychology, 11 percent with abnormal and clinical psychology, 10 percent with psychometry, 9 percent with vocational and industrial psychology, 6 percent with social psychology, and 5 percent with personality. The remaining papers were on Indian psychology, criminal psychology, religious psychology, and aesthetic psychology (Joshi, 1965).

The traditional Indian concern with depth psychology and mental hygiene gave birth to the Indian Psychoanalytic Association as early as 1922, and its official journal, *Samiksā*, started in 1947. The mental hospital at Calcutta and the All-India Institute of Mental Health, Bangalore, have a number of clinical psychologists working in collaboration with the medical staff.

India is probably the only country in Asia which attaches a special importance to the classical thought characteristic of the country. Adequate acquaintance with the traditional psychological systems is recommended at the graduate level (Sen, 1958). For many of the same reasons, there has been a long-standing interest in paranormal and psychic phenomena. This is well exemplified by a separate department of parapsychology at the University of Rajasthan. According to Dhairyan (1961), ". . . there is a wealth of applied clinical psychological concepts in the Yogi practices and philosophy which has yet to be explored and made to enrich modern science" (p. 159).

Pakistan, Ceylon, Burma, and Thailand

Pakistan psychologists are also oriented toward educational psychology, social psychology, personality, and other applied fields, as Indian psychologists are. Psychological research in this country is published mainly in *Pakistan Philosophical Journal, Journal of Psychology, Psychology Quarterly, and Pakistan Journal of Psychology*. The University of Dacca and the University of Punjab have the oldest and best-organized psychological laboratories, and the University of Karachi has just initiated a program in counseling psychology.

There are a number of complicated sociopsychological problems in this country which need the immediate attention of social scientists. Zaidi (1964) assumed that ". . . most of the social issues of Pakistan society can be explained in terms of the observed conditions in a transitional society undergoing a stressful experience" (p. 19), and then he proposed a model predicting a number of stages involved in the adjustment of a group to a stressful situation with frustration and conflict.

A similar psychological trend is observed in Ceylon. Racial stereotypes, family relationships, vocational guidance, and personality and intelligence testing have been most intensively studied among Ceylonese psychologists. For example, both Ceylonese and foreign scientists have conducted a number of cross-cultural studies using the Rorschach and intelligence tests. However, Jayasuriya (1965) warned in evaluating their results that many so-called culture-free tests are actually culture-bound unless they are equally standardized and meaningful for all groups concerned.

In Burma, the current research interests cover vocational guidance, counseling, and sociopsychological problems. The Universities of Burma and of Mandalay are the centers of the psychological activities in this country (Thwin, 1962).

The Psychological Association in Thailand, with administrative offices at Chulalongkorn University, was started in 1961, and it has been publishing a journal called *Psychology* under the editorship of Professor B. Chareanying, of the Institute for Child Study. The major areas of research interest and activity are child-rearing practices, problem children, and the development of various intelligence, achievement, and personality tests. In addition, cross-cultural projects are now being discussed between Thailand and Japan (Gardiner, 1968).

Indonesia, the Philippines, Hong Kong, and the Republic of Korea

The orientation and approach in Indonesian psychology are mainly European, although American books are also used. Most Indonesian psychologists are associated with the Faculty of Psychology, University of Indonesia, and with the Armed Forces, and their interest lies mainly in sociocultural and anthropophilosophical problems (Hassan, 1963).

The Psychological Association of the Philippines was established in 1962 (Lagmay, 1963), and its activities are in such areas as intelligence, achievement, personality testing, clinical psychology, social perception, attitude, and guidance (Guthrie & Bulatao, 1968).

In Hong Kong, the University of Hong Kong is the center of research and teaching in psychology.

The Korean Psychological Association was founded in 1946 and has its central offices at Seoul National University. The research output appears in a number of periodicals, including *Studies of Psychology,* of Seoul National University, and *Psychological Studies,* of Ewha Women's University. The main interest of the Korean psychologists is oriented toward industrial, clinical, counseling, and social psychology, as well as toward experimental studies. The Korean Psychological Association, in cooperation with the Pedagogical Association, offers in-service seminars in counseling once a year for those who are planning to be counseling specialists (Takahashi, 1967).

Continental China and Taiwan

The most drastic change in psychological thought occurred on the Chinese continent soon after the last world war. Before the war, Chinese psychologists had been indebted to American functionalism because of their realistic nature. The Chinese Association of Psychological Testing (ChAPT) was begun in 1930, seven years before the Chinese Psychological Association was first established. After the war, the ChAPT disappeared in continental China, but has survived in Taiwan.

The new continental psychologists have attempted to reconstruct a scientific psychology based on Pavlovian theory and Marxist principles (Shuh, 1959). To attain this objective, in 1956 they published the *Translation Journal of Psychology,* which contained articles selected from the Russian journal *Voprosy Psikhologii (Problems of Psychology)*, but this translation journal was discontinued in 1958.

Acta Psychologica Sinica, (established in 1956) has been an official journal of the newly reconstructed (1955) Chinese Psychological Society. About half of the total articles in the issues of the journal appearing between 1956 and 1959 were either theoretical or political, such as "Problems on the object of psychology" (C. S. Chu, 1956) and "How psychology can be of service to the socialistic reconstruction" (D. J. Chen, 1959). According to the new Chinese view, psychology is a science whose aim is to explore the material basis of psyche and the functional laws governing the activities of the brain, as well as the physiological mechanisms underlying them (Shuh, 1959).

Both classical behaviorism and neobehaviorism were criticized from the Chinese Communist viewpoint. According to Ni (1957) and Ching (1965), behaviorism is a product of American capitalism. In order to secure greater profits, the capitalist class, then flourishing in America, attempted to make the laborer like a machine or a man without consciousness. Thus, behaviorism is fundamentally reactionary. What is worse, the behaviorist pretended to be a scientist by borrowing Pavlov's conditioning theory for his system, and so he deceived people. Z. Y. Kuo, a widely known animal psychologist who introduced behaviorism to China, is criticized as being one of the most reactionary propagandists of American capitalism.

Although behaviorism and Communist psychology are both based on a kind of materialism, they are otherwise entirely different. First, behaviorism is mechanistic, while Communist theory is dialectic. Second, the behaviorist erroneously limits the subject matter of psychology to stimulus and response, neglecting the important functions of the higher nervous systems, which are the bases of the psychic activities. Consciousness is denied by Watson, but is accepted by the Communist psychologist as a reflection of the objective world. Third, Watson confuses human psychology with animal psychology. According to the Chinese psychologist, man and animal are different in quality rather than in quantity; human behavior is developed with a social and historical background, which is lacking in animals. Fourth, thinking in behavioristic terms is nothing but inner speech or muscular activity. On the contrary, Communist theory maintains that thinking and speech or language are basically different; language, according to Stalin, is simply an instrument of thinking.

A critical evaluation of Gestalt theory was attempted by H. L. Chu (1958). According to him, Gestalt theory was born when capitalism had turned to imperialism and subjective idealism had been dominant in Europe. First, Gestalt theory, which emphasizes totality and the risk of analysis, fails to recognize the fact that the brain has both analyzing and synthesizing functions, as was proved by Pavlov. The Pavlovian theory is based on dialectic materialism, but psychological theories colored by capitalistic idealism cannot understand it. On the one hand, associationistic psychology puts too much emphasis on analysis and thus deviates from our daily experience, while Gestalt psychology concerns itself only with synthesis and consequently regresses to transcendental idealism. Second, isomorphism, proposed by Köhler, has no relationship to the Pavlovian theory. It is merely a mystic speculation based on misunderstood neurophysiology. Third, the Gestalt concept of insight in chimpanzees is criticized as being anthropomorphic. Animal mentality must be differentiated from human mentality because only the latter develops the second signal system, making dialectic thinking possible. Lastly, such terms as *behavioral environment* (Koffka) and *psychological environment* (Lewin) are criticized as being typical examples of subjective idealism. Incidentally, it is interesting to note that the same Gestalt theory is still supported by Eastern German psychologists (K. Gottschalt, for example) who are related by blood to the advocates of Gestalt theory (Lun, 1958; Razran, 1958).

In 1962, the Congress of Educational Psychology was held, and in the next year the first academic meetings of the Chinese Psychological Society took place for ten days in Peking. A total of 203 papers were collected, 75 percent of which were educational in a broad sense, and 15 percent of which were theoretical. In addition, a number of symposia were held at the meetings (C. K. Chen, 1964). Evidently, the interest in educational psychology has rapidly increased, while theoretical papers have decreased in number. For example, in the 1965 issues of *Acta Psychologica Sinica,* only 10 percent of the total articles are theoretical or political, while 53 percent deal with educational problems, and 23 percent are purely experimental articles, mainly on perception.

Educational and child psychological studies are both practical and experimental rather than basic and theoretical, although the underlying principles must be based on Chinese communism (J. C. Tsao, 1965). For example, C. Y. Tsao and Shen (1965) conducted a series of experiments on the learning and recognition of Chinese characters in primary school children, and Chou (1965) experimentally analyzed errors made in learning the resolution of factors in junior middle school algebra.

The basic experimental research covers such areas as visual perception of size and velocity, interference in memory, and the EEG. Lambda waves in the human EEG were investigated by Tsai and Liu (1965), who found that they appear more frequently in young subjects than in adults, that they occur more during visual perception than during visual imagination, and that the same waves are more easily recorded for those who manifest "on responses" or "driving responses."

Medical psychology and industrial psychology are also well investigated in Communist China. K. C. Liu (1957) has proposed a therapeutic method, similar to Japanese seated Zen, which aims to cure mental diseases, and J. C. Tsao, Li, Ching, Chang, Yü, Feng, and Chu (1966) studied the man-machine system in the control room of an electric power station.

In the Republic of China in Taiwan, the National Psychological Association was established in 1963 (Su, 1963). Although the association has no official journal, the National Taiwan University has been publishing *Acta Psychologica Taiwanica* since 1958, and the Taiwan Normal University started *Psychology and Education* in 1967 (Iwahara, 1967). A content analysis of the 1966 and 1967 issues of the two journals reveals that about 50 percent of the articles concern experimental studies in learning, perception, and physiological psychology and that the rest are in the areas of personality and of clinical, educational, and social psychology. For example, Yen and Cheng (1966) studied binocular disparity and related parameters in depth perception, and Liu and his co-workers examined whether Weber's law can be applied to the perception of angles, circles, and cubes (I. M. Liu & Hu, 1967). The values of Taiwan college students, as measured by the Edwards Personal Preference Schedule (EPPS), showed higher scores in deference, order, succorance, abasement, nurturance, and endurance and lower scores in exhibition, intraception, dominance, change, and heterosexuality, as compared with the American standards (Hwang, 1967). Roughly correspondent results were reported between Japanese and American students (Berrien, 1964).

In addition to the Chinese Psychological Association and the Chinese Association of Psychological Testing, Taiwan has the Chinese Guidance Association, which aims to promote sound counselor education (Brammer, 1965).

Table C-1. Major areas of research interest, based on content analysis of papers presented at the 1968 JPA convention and appearing in two JPA journals

Research Area	JPA Convention, 1968, percent	*Japanese Journal of Psychology*, and *Japanese Psychological Research*, 1967, percent
General and statistics	4	9
Physiological	11	5
Perceptual	14	31
Learning	11	28
Personality and clinical	15	14
Education and developmental	18	7
Social	11	7
Industrial	9	0
Criminal	2	0
Other	5	0
Total	100 (*N* = 524)	101 (*N* = 58)

Japan

The Japanese Psychological Association (JPA) held its first annual meeting in 1927 with sixty-one papers presented; in 1968 it had a membership of about three thousand and more than five hundred papers were read at the annual convention. The JPA has three official periodicals: the *Japanese Journal of Psychology* (1926, bimonthly), *Japanese Psychological Research* (1954, English, quarterly), and *Japanese Psychological Monographs* (1965, quarterly).

Table C-1 indicates the distribution of major areas of research interest as indicated by the papers presented at the 1968 JPA convention and in two JPA journals. There are more experimental studies in the journals than were presented to the convention, partly because nonexperimental articles are published in other journals in specific fields of psychology, as shown in Table C-2.

Among the experimental fields, perception has attracted the attention of Japanese psychologists for more than forty years, and it is still one of the major research areas at most Japanese universities. Recently Yuki (1965) and Tanaka (1966) overviewed Japanese perceptual studies for American readers. Some of the most intensively studied areas are optical illusions (Morinaga, Noguchi, & Ohnishi, 1962), figural aftereffects (Sagara & Oyama, 1957), constancy phenomena (Akishige, 1968), visual induction (Obonai, 1957), color vision (Kaneko, 1968),

Table C-2. Current psychological periodicals in Japan

Periodical	Publisher or Editor
Annual of Animal Psychology (1943)	Japanese Association of Animal Psychology
Annals of Japanese Social Psychology (1960)	Japanese Association of Social Psychology
Japanese Journal of Clinical Psychology (1960)	Japanese Association of Clinical Psychology
Japanese Journal of Counseling Science (1967)	Japanese Association of Counseling Science
Japanese Journal of Criminal Psychology (1963)	Japanese Association of Criminal Psychology
Japanese Journal of Educational Psychology (1952)	Japanese Association of Educational Psychology
Japanese Journal of Educational and Social Psychology (1960)	Japanese Association of Group Dynamics
Japanese Journal of Psychology (1926)	Japanese Psychological Association
Japanese Psychological Monographs (1965)	Japanese Psychological Association
*Japanese Psychological Research** (1954)	Japanese Psychological Association
Japanese Psychological Review (1957)	Psychological Review Publisher (Kyoto University)
*Psychologia** (1957)	Psychologia Society (Otemongakuin University)
*Tohoku Psychologica Folia** (1933)	Tohoku University

*Published mostly in English.

NOTES: In addition to the psychological associations listed above, there is the Japanese Association of Applied Psychology, which publishes only the proceedings of the annual meetings. There are also interdisciplinary associations such as the Japanese Medical and Psychological Association of Hypnosis, the Japanese Association of Ergonomics, the Japanese Medical and Psychological Association of Aerospace Science, the Japanese Association of Conditioned Reflex, the Japanese Association of Electroencephalography, the Japanese Association of Color Studies, and a few others.

psychometry of odor (Yoshida, 1964) and of taste (Indow, 1966), and binocular vision (Kakizaki, 1960).

Japanese perceptual psychologists are proud of their original works, but unfortunately many of them have been buried unknown to foreign workers because of a language barrier and lack of international communication. For example, the converse of the tau effect was discovered independently by two Japanese psychologists, Abe (1935) and Abbe (1936), but the same effect was reported by Cohen, Hansel, and Sylvester (1953), about two decades later, as a new phenomenon.

As for theoretical aspects, Obonai (1957) has been criticizing Gestalt theory as philosophical romanticism and as being devoid of sound empirical basis. Scientific psychology, according to him, should be studied analytically and elementalistically like physics and physiology. On the basis of his voluminous and energetic works on visual perception, Obonai has proposed a theory called *psychophysiological induction*. Its basic idea is that the stimulation of a receptor will induce both excitation and inhibition around the stimulated area and that the resulting effect is an algebraic summation of these antagonistic functions, leading to actual perception. The induction occurs temporally and spatially. Obonai claims that some perceptual phenomena which are treated separately can be integrated by this theory. For example, the simultaneous contrast-confluence illusion and the figural aftereffect are only different aspects of the same phenomenon (Ikeda & Obonai, 1955).

The Japanese physiologist K. Motokawa and his co-workers, including a number of psychologists, have investigated many aspects of visual perception. Using his own ingenious techniques, Motokawa found that the electric excitability of the retina changes as a function of time after cessation of illumination and that the time function is characteristic of the wavelength of the light used for illumination. According to Motokawa (1953): "As . . . the retina is ontogenetically a part of the brain, and its structure resembles that of central nervous system . . . it is not surprising that psychological phenomena such as optical illusions should be interpreted in terms of retinal processes [p. 369]."

Yokose (1957) has proposed an electromagnetic model of visual perception. In his theory, the field potential of a visual figure, as measured by the stimulus threshold around it, is principally the same function of a number of variables as predicted by Bivot Savart's law in electromagnetism. His isomorphic field theory has been confirmed by a series of experimental findings concerning the change of threshold around a segmental line, a square, a triangle, and other geometric figures.

The second most popular research area in experimental psychology is learning and memory. Umemoto (1959), Motoyoshi and Iwahara (1960), and Iwahara and Fujita (1963) wrote English reviews of Japanese studies in human and animal learning. One of the original works on memory is concerned with the function of stimulus and response words in paired-associate learning. Kuraishi (1937) established the relative difficulty of recalling a foreign word from the corresponding Japanese word, compared with the difficulty of recall in the reverse order, and explained the phenomenon in terms of Gestalt theory. This study was followed by those of Umemoto (1959) and Morikawa (1959), who argued that the stimulus item is learned as a cue to the response item, while the response item is acquired as the goal to be responded to, and that backward recall is thus inferior to forward recall.

I. Ishihara and his co-workers have intensively studied paired-associate learning, especially in relation to word association. For example, they proposed a new kind of association value, defined in terms of frequency of appearance as associated items in a given free-association situation. A series of experiments on verbal learning has been conducted on the functions of the new association value and other related problems (I. Ishihara, 1960).

Other areas of main interest in human learning and behavior are mediated association (Kitao, 1967), massed and spaced practice (Akita, 1966), discrimination reversal (Sugimura, 1967), spread of effect (Iwahara, 1958), information theory (Takada, 1960), and mathematical models of motor learning (Ono, 1966).

In the field of animal behavior, S. Ishihara (1966) has found, in a series of her experiments, a decrement of response variability and facilitation of running response following nonreinforced trials; she called the phenomenon *induction* after Pavlov. Sukemune (1963) found that resistance to extinction in rats is a positive function of number of trials when both total amount of reinforcement and total number of reinforced trials are kept constant. Imanishi and his colleagues have been conducting a large-scale project on the social behavior of primates both in Japan and abroad (Imanishi, 1957). Other interesting data have been reported on spontaneous alternation (Fujita, 1961), conditioned avoidance response (Matsuyama & Tsukioka, 1964), successive versus simultaneous discrimination learning (Motoyoshi, 1956), and incentive motivation (Imada, 1964).

Another trend in experimental psychology is a marked increase of activities in physiological psychology. For example, Niki (1964) reported the inhibitory control of the hippocampus upon operant behavior in the rat, and Hirano (1965) investigated the effect of functional disturbance of the limbic system on memory consolidation. In another study, facilitation of running response due to partial reinforcement in the runway situation was found to be inhibited by a tranquilizer (chlordiazepoxide), but resistance to extinction after the same partial reinforcement was not affected by the drug (Iwahara, Nagamura, & Iwasaki, 1967).

Recently, a number of workers have been engaged in psychophysiological studies of sleep and wakefulness. Fujisawa (1960) has attempted a detailed analysis of EEG sleep patterns. Iwahara, Takeuchi, and Nagamura (1967) were interested in a multivariate analysis of EEG in both man and animals, and Niimi and his co-workers (Niimi, Kubota, & Iwama, 1968) studied spontaneous variation of the skin potential and skin-potential reflex during natural sleep in the cat.

The Japanese Association of Educational Psychology is the second largest psychological association, with a membership of about 1,500. Some of the most active research areas in educational psychology are personality adjustment in pupils and students, school counseling, developmental studies, teaching machines, and tests and measurements.

Most members of the Japanese Association of Clinical Psychology (membership of 1,300) have clinical experience, and they are interested in school refusal, early infantile autism, therapeutic processes, hypnotic therapy, emotionally disturbed children, projective and personality tests, and the legal status of the clinical psychologist.

The Japanese Association of Applied Psychology (membership of 1,000) has recently been discussing such problems as school curricula, traffic safety, public nuisance, industrialization and labor, physical education, and world peace and welfare.

Members of the Japanese Association of Social Psychology (membership of 550) and of the Japanese Association of Group Dynamics (membership of 200) are generally interested in human relationships in family, school, and other social situations; mass communication; attitudes and values; and person perception. The Japanese Association of Criminal Psychology (membership of 550) has no very close parallel in the United States. Most members of the association belong to juvenile delinquency detection and classification homes located in all prefectures of Japan. The current activities of the criminal psychologists are in such areas as diagnosis and prognosis of delinquent behavior, therapeutic treatments, mechanism of criminal behavior, psychedelic and hypnotic drugs, personality studies of violators of traffic regulations, and minority groups.

There are a few other associations of psychological science (see Table C-2), among which the Japanese Association of Animal Psychology (founded in 1933) has the longest history.

CONCLUSION

It is hard to summarize Oriental psychology in a few lines, but it may be stated that Asian countries as a whole have common interests in applied psychology, especially in educational and social fields. In addition, the theoretical-political aspects of psychology are discussed in continental China, and experimental psychology flourishes in Japan.

Although Oriental psychology still remains relatively unknown in the West, there is a growing tendency in the Orient to publish psychology journals in English, as well as to add English abstracts when the original articles are written in the native language.

The Twentieth International Congress of Psychology is scheduled to be held in Japan in 1972, which will be the first time this body has met in the Orient. This will offer excellent opportunities for Asian psychologists to meet with non-Asian psychologists and to discuss their common problems.

REFERENCES

The author has tried to restrict the references to those written in English. Unavoidably, however, some references are in other languages, which are indicated immediately after the titles.

Abe, S. Experimental study of the interrelation between time and space. *Tohoku Psychological Folia*, 1935, **3**, 53-68.

Abbe, M. Der räumliche Effekt auf die Zeitauffassung. *Japanese Journal of Experimental Psychology*, 1936, **3**, 1-52.

Akhilananda, S. *Hindu psychology*. London: Routledge, 1953.

Akishige, Y. Studies on constancy problem. IIA. *Psychologia*, 1968, **11**, 43-55.

Akita, K. Effect of the gradual change of distribution of practice in motor learning. *Japanese Psychological Research*, 1966, **8**, 18-29.

Ando, S. Zen and Christianity. *Psychologia*, 1965, **8**, 123-134.

Berrien, F. K. Values of Japanese and American students. Technical Report No. 14, Department of Defense, Office of Naval Research, Group Psychology Branch, Washington, 1964.

Brammer, L. M. Counselor education in the Republic of China: An outsider's view. *Psychologia*, 1965, **8**, 220-222.

Chen, C. K. The 1963 annual psychological society. (In Chinese) *Acta Psychologica Sinica*, 1964, **8**, 109-112.

Chen, D. J. How psychology can be of service to the socialistic reconstruction. (In Chinese) *Acta Psychologica Sinica*, 1959, **3**, 142-145.

Chiba, T. On proper consciousness (Koyū-ishiki). *Psychologia*, 1960, **3**, 65-72.

Ching, C. C. The behaviorism of J. B. Watson. (In Chinese) *Acta Psychologica Sinica*, 1965, **9**, 361-374.

Chou, H. S. Analysis of mistakes made in learning resolution of factors by first grade junior middle school pupils. (In Chinese) *Acta Psychologica Sinica*, 1965, **8**, 223-229.

Chu, C. S. Problems on the object of psychology. (In Chinese) *Acta Psychologica Sinica*, 1956, **1**, 11-19.

Chu, H. L. Critical comments on Gestalt psychology. (In Chinese) *Acta Psychologica Sinica*, 1958, **2**, 85-98.

Cohen, J., Hansel, C. E. M., & Sylvester, J. D. A new phenomenon in time judgment. *Nature*, 1953, **172**, 901.

Dhairyan, D. Research needs for development of psychotherapy in India. In T. K. N. Menon (Ed.), *Recent trends in psychology*. Orient Longmans, 1961. Pp. 154-161.

Doi, L. T. Morita therapy and psychoanalysis. *Psychologia*, 1962, **3**, 117-123.

Dumoulin, H. Methods and aims of Buddhist meditation: Satipatthana and Zen. *Psychologia*, 1962, **5**, 175-180.

Fromm, E. Psychoanalysis and Zen Buddhism. *Psychologia*, 1959, **2**, 79-99.

Fujisawa, F. The psycho-physiological studies of sleep. *Japanese Psychological Research*, 1960, **2**, 120-134.

Fujita, O. Studies of spontaneous alternation in rats. VIII. The effect of food deprivation, reward and intertrial interval. (In Japanese) *Japanese Journal of Psychology*, 1961, **32**, 303-310.

Gardiner, H. M. Psychology in Thailand. *Psychologia*, 1968, **11**, 122-124.

Guthrie, G. M., & Bulatao, J., S. J. Psychology in the Philippines. *Psychologia*, 1968, **11**, 201-206.

Hassan, F. Letter to Dr. Koji Sato. *Psychologia*, 1963, **6**, 179-180.

Hirano, T. Effects of functional disturbances of the limbic system on the memory consolidation. *Japanese Psychological Research*, 1965, **7**, 171-182.

Holmes, S. W. Zen Buddhism and transactional psychology. *Etc.*, 1957, **14**, 243-249.

Hora, T. Tao, Zen, and existential psychotherapy. *Psychologia*, 1959, **2**, 236-249.

Hundal, P. S. Organization of mental abilities at successive grade levels. *Indian Journal of Psychology*, 1966, **41**, 65-72.

Hwang, C. H. A study of the personal preference of Chinese university students by Edwards Personal Preference Schedule. *Psychology and Education*, 1967, **1**, 52-68.

Ikeda, H. & Obonai, T. Studies in figural after-effects. IV. The contrast-confluence illusion of concentric circles and the figural after-effect. *Japanese Psychological Research*, 1955, **2**, 17-23.

Imada, H. "Vigor" of water drinking behavior of rats as a function of thirst drive. *Japanese Psychological Research*, 1964, **6**, 108-114.

Imanishi, K. Social behavior in Japanese monkeys, *Macaca fuscata. Psychologia*, 1957, **1**, 47-54.

Indow, T. A general equi-distance scale of the four qualities of tastes. *Japanese Psychological Research*, 1966, **8**, 136-150.

Ishihara, I. *Psychology of verbal behavior*. (In Japanese) Tokyo: Kobunkan, 1960.

Ishihara, S. Growth and decay of induction. IX. Several aspects of behavior in the semicircular apparatus. (In Japanese) *Japanese Journal of Psychology*, 1966, **37**, 1-11.

Iwahara, S. Studies of the "spread of effect." V. The spread of verbal punishment and the meaningfulness of cue stimuli. *Japanese Psychological Research*, 1958, **5**, 38-50.

Iwahara, S. Psychological activities at the University of the Ryukyus, the National Taiwan University and Taiwan Normal University. *Psychologia*, 1967, **10**, 223-225.

Iwahara, S., & Fujita, O. Behaviorism in Japan. *Psychologia*, 1963, **4**, 59-64.

Iwahara, S., Nagamura, N., & Iwasaki, T. Effect of chlordiazepoxide upon experimental extinction in the straight runway as a function of partial reinforcement in the rat. *Japanese Psychological Research*, 1967, **9**, 128-134.

Iwahara, S., Takeuchi, E., & Nagamura, N. EEG patterns during natural sleep in the rat and their multivariate analyses. (In Japanese) *Bulletin of Faculty Education, Tokyo University of Education,* 1967, **13**, 41-57.

Jayasuriya, D. L. Recent psychological research in Ceylon. *Psychologia,* 1965, **8**, 169-174.

Joshi, M. C. Psychological researches in India. *Jalota Commemoration Volume,* 1965, 25-34.

Kakizaki, S. Binocular rivalry and stimulus intensity. *Japanese Psychological Research,* 1960, **2**, 94-105.

Kaneko, T. *Science of color: Its psychophysiology.* (In Japanese) Tokyo: Misuzu-Shobo, 1968.

Kasamatsu, A., & Hirai, T. An electroencephalographic study of the Zen meditation (Zazen). *Folia Psychiatrica et Neurologica Japonica,* 1966, **20**, 315-336.

Kawai, H., & Kondo, K. Discussion on Morita therapy. *Psychologia,* 1960, **3**, 92-99.

Kitao, N. Effects of mediated association on paired-associate learning. VIII. About the degree of prior learning and instruction. (In Japanese) *Japanese Journal of Physiology,* 1967, **38**, 137-147.

Kora, T., & Sato, K. Morita therapy: A psychotherapy in the way of Zen. *Psychologia,* 1958, **1**, 219-225.

Krishnakanth, A., & Prasad, J. N. Socio-economic differences on a reasoning test. *Indian Psychological Review,* 1967, **3**, 119-122.

Krishnan, B. A review of contributions of Indian psychologists (1950-1960). In T. K. N. Menon (Ed.), *Recent trends in psychology.* Orient Longmans, 1961.

Kuraishi, S. On the reproduction of simple thought-configuration by using the method of paired comparison. (In Japanese) *Japanese Journal of Psychology,* 1937, **12**, 578-602.

Kuroda, R. Stereopsychology: Its scope and method. *Acta Psychologica Keijo,* 1931, **1**, 69-82.

Kuroda, R. *A history of Chinese psychological thought.* (In Japanese) Tokyo: Koyama-shoten, 1948.

Lagmay, A. V. Letter to Dr. Koji Sato. *Psychologia,* 1963, **6**, 179-180.

Liu, I. M., & Hu, W. The cube and Weber's Law. *Acta Psychologica Taiwanica,* 1967, **9**, 87-89.

Liu, K. C. *Practice on the breathing therapy.* (In Chinese) Hopei People's Press, 1957.

Lun, S. H. Researches in perception in Democratic Germany. (In Chinese) *Acta Psychologica Sinica,* 1958, **2**, 45-52.

Matsuyama, Y., & Tsukioka, S. The intertrial-interval response in relation to amount of warning signal, and restraint time. *Japanese Psychological Research,* 1964, **6**, 1-9.

Maupin, E. W. Zen Buddhism: A psychological review. *Journal of Consulting Psychology,* 1962, **26**, 362-378.

Morikawa, Y. Functions of stimulus and response in paired-associate verbal learning. *Psychologia,* 1959, **2**, 41-56.

Morinaga, S., Noguchi, K., & Ohnishi, A. The horizontal vertical illusion and the relation to spatial and retinal orientation. *Japanese Psychological Research,* 1962, **4**, 25-29.

Morris, C. W. Comments on mysticism and its language. *Etc.,* 1951, **9**, 3-8.

Motokawa, K. Retinal traces and visual perception of movement. *Journal of Experimental Psychology*, 1953, **45**, 369-377.

Motora, Y. *An essay on Eastern philosophy*. Leipzig: Voigtländer, 1905.

Motoyoshi, R. Simultaneous and successive discrimination under three types of jumping platform. *Japanese Psychological Research*, 1956, **4**, 50-61.

Motoyoshi, R., & Iwahara, S. Japanese studies on animal behavior in the last decade. *Psychologia*, 1960, **3**, 135-148.

Murphy, G., & Murphy, L. B. (Eds.) *Asian psychology*. New York: Basic Books, 1968.

Ni, C. F. A preliminary criticism on the behaviorism of J. B. Watson. (In Chinese) *Acta Psychologica Sinica*, 1957, **1**, 194-200.

Niimi, Y., Kubota, K., & Iwama, Y. Spontaneous variations of the skin potentials and skin potential reflexes during natural sleep in the cat. *Japanese Journal of Physiology*, 1968, **18**, 190-197.

Niki, H. Response perseveration following the hippocampal ablation in the rat. *Japanese Psychological Research*, 1964, **6**, 108-114.

Obonai, T. The concept of psychophysiological induction: A review of experimental works. *Psychologia*, 1957, **1**, 3-9.

Ono, S. A mathematical analysis of motor learning: A control system model. *Japanese Psychological Research*, 1966, **8**, 72-89.

Otsuka, N. Stereopsychology and studies on k'an by Ryo Kuroda. *Psychologia*, 1960, **3**, 73-79.

Pareek, U. Psychology in India. *Psychologia*, 1957, **1**, 55-59.

Pe, W. Mindfulness of sensation. *Psychologia*, 1966, **9**, 195-198.

Rao, S. Occupational role and personality: A comparative study of a few occupational groups in India. *Indian Journal of Psychology*, 1966, **41**, 59-64.

Razran, G. Psychology in Communist countries other than the U.S.S.R. *American Psychologist*, 1958, **13**, 177-178.

Rogers, A. H. Zen and LSD: An enlightening experience. *Psychologia*, 1964, **7**, 150-151.

Sagara, M., & Oyama, T. Experimental studies on figural aftereffects in Japan. *Psychological Bulletin*, 1957, **54**, 327-338.

Sato, K. How to get Zen enlightenment: On Master Ishiguro's five-days' intensive course for its attainment. *Psychologia*, 1959, **2**, 107-113.

Sato, K., & Zuzuki, D. T. Zen and LSD 25. *Psychologia*, 1967, **10**, 129-132.

Sen, I. Teaching of personality in Indian universities. *Indian Journal of Psychology*, 1958, **33**, 129-133.

Shuh, P. China's recent research work in psychology. *Psychologia*, 1959, **2**, 193-202.

Su, H. Y. Letter to Dr. Koji Sato. *Psychologia*, 1963, **6**, 176.

Sugimura, T. Intradimensional and extradimensional shifts as a function of stimulus change and overtraining. *Japanese Psychological Research*, 1967, **9**, 78-84.

Sukemune, S. Effects of total number of acquisition trials under partial reinforcement schedules on running speeds. *Japanese Psychological Research*, 1963, **5**, 183-187.

Suzuki, D. T. *Zen Buddhism*. Garden City, N.Y.: Anchor Books, 1956.

Takada, Y. Reaction time and information in the discrimination of length of lines. *Japanese Psychological Research*, 1960, **2**, 14-24.

Takahashi, S. The present status of psychological activities in Korea. *Psychologia*, 1967, **10**, 225-226.

Tanaka, Y. Status of Japanese experimental psychology. *Annual Review of Psychology*, 1966, **17**, 233-272.

Thompson, R. F. *Foundations of physiological psychology.* New York: Harper & Row, 1967.

Thwin, H. Department of Psychology, University of Rangoon, Burma. *Psychologia*, 1962, **5**, 107-111.

Tsai, H. J., & Liu, S. Y. Lambda waves of human subjects of different age levels. (In Chinese) *Acta Psychologica Sinica*, 1965, **8**, 343-352.

Tsao, C. Y., & Shen, Y. Developmental studies on the recognition and generalization of Chinese characters in primary school children. III. Development of the discrimination of detail. (In Chinese) *Acta Psychologica Sinica*, 1965, **8**, 135-140.

Tsao, J. C. On the fundamental viewpoints of psychology. (In Chinese) *Acta Psychologica Sinica*, 1965, **9**, 101-105.

Tsao, J. C., Li, C. C., Ching, C. C., Chang, T. H., Yü, C. S., Feng, K. C., & Chu, T. H. Human factors in signal design of control room of an electric power station. (In Chinese) *Acta Psychologica Sinica*, 1966, **9**, 53-58.

Umemoto, T. Japanese studies in verbal learning and memory. *Psychologia*, 1959, **2**, 1-9.

Van Dusen, W. LSD and enlightenment of Zen. *Psychologia*, 1961, **4**, 11-16.

Yen, F., & Cheng, F. Y. Binocular disparity, stimulus intensity, and the way of light presentation have to do with necessary stimulus duration time to produce depth perception. *Acta Psychologica Taiwanica*, 1966, **8**, 85-91.

Yokose, Z. Theoretical formula of vector-field and its experimental proof. *Psychologia*, 1957, **1**, 17-21.

Yoshida, M. Studies of psychometric classification of odors (5). *Japanese Psychological Research*, 1964, **6**, 145-154.

Yuki, K. Experimental psychology. In A. H. Livermore (Ed.), *Science in Japan.* Washington, D.C.: American Association for the Advancement of Science, 1965. Pp. 335-373.

Zaidi, S. M. H. Pakistan: A society in transition. *Psychologia*, 1964, **7**, 15-21.

FURTHER READINGS

Akhilananda, S. *Hindu psychology.* London: Routledge, 1953.

Krishman, B. A review of contributions of Indian psychologists (1950-1960). In T. K. N. Menon (Ed.), *Recent trends in psychology.* Orient Longmans, 1961.

Suzuki, D. T. *Zen Buddhism.* Garden City, N.Y.: Anchor Books, 1956.

Tanaka, Y. Status of Japanese experimental psychology. *Annual Review of Psychology*, 1966, **17**, 233-272.

Yuki, K. Experimental psychology. In A. H. Livermore (Ed.) *Science in Japan.* Washington, D.C.: American Association for the Advancement of Science, 1965. Pp. 335-373.

PSYCHOLOGY IN THE EMERGING NATIONS: LATIN AMERICA, AFRICA, AND THE MIDDLE EAST*

Larry D. Reavis,
Southern Methodist University,
Dallas, Texas

Very few attempts have been made by psychologists in the nations of Latin America, Africa, and the Middle East to build formal theories or systems. What little research has been executed usually has been oriented toward solving practical problems, ranging from the licensing of motor-vehicle operators to the acculturation of traditional peoples into modern industrial societies. Isolated instances of research of more general interest do occur, however. Some of these are reviewed under Further Readings at the end of this appendix.

Rather than review the sparse theory-building efforts, which frequently have been published in readily available journals of the affluent nations, we feel that it may be more profitable to consider the factors affecting the development of psychology in the emerging nations. Special emphasis will be devoted to factors that affect the growth of a scientific psychology, such as the adequacy of communication, the growth of industrial technology, and domination from abroad. It is hoped that this approach will in turn promote insight into the reasons for the differential growth of scientific psychology in various parts of the world, to the mutual benefit of colleagues in both the rich and poor nations.

*The preparation of this chapter was facilitated by National Science Foundation Grant No. GY-5671.

GENERAL CONDITIONS THAT AFFECT PSYCHOLOGY

The per capita annual income in the wealthy countries of the world has been estimated to be about $1,700. In the poor nations it is only about $110 (Blackett, 1967). It is not surprising, then, that the most salient characteristic of psychology in the emerging nations is its lack of economic support. Although many of the countries discussed in this appendix have enjoyed a long history in scientific psychology, only Israel and the Republic of South Africa have provided psychology with the funds necessary for vigorous and autonomous growth.

In addition to the general lack of affluence characteristic of the emerging nations, psychology's poverty is also due to the lack of acceptance of the social sciences in these countries. The reasons vary greatly. Problems studied by social scientists compete for funds with more urgent problems, such as water purification, sanitation, and food production (Mahal, 1967). In totalitarian states, which abound among the emerging nations, the social sciences may be suppresssed because it is suspected that some findings may contradict prevailing ideologies (Horowitz, 1967; Sanford, 1952). Professors may be dismissed for political views (Hall, 1946) or imprisoned for their research (Chirinos, 1967). Military "committees of inquiry" continue to take their toll, and major universities recently have been destroyed by tnem (Nussenzveig, 1969). Countries with small, powerful elites may study social problems that result from the concentration of power, but classify the results to prevent their distribution (see Holleman, Mann, & Van den Berghe, 1962, for example). Even in relatively advanced countries psychological explanations of behavior compete with superstition (Hartocollis, 1966; Hes, 1964; Jahoda, 1968). Everywhere public and governmental apathy regarding science, especially social science, compounds the problem. For example, while many psychologists from the emerging nations publish papers showing how psychology might be used in nation building, Mundy-Castle (1968) has observed that a special issue of the Organization for Economic Cooperation and Development's *OECD Observer* (September, 1966), devoted to developmental aid, contains only fifteen lines on "social transformation." Some fifty pages are devoted to trade, foreign investment, and other topics outside the focus of the social sciences.

In many countries the newer disciplines, such as psychology and sociology, are actively opposed by better-established disciplines. Treatment of behavior disorders by psychologists, for example, is likely to be opposed by medical associations, as is the case in Argentina (Ardila, 1968). In a few countries, such as Lebanon, such treatment is even prohibited by law (Melikian, 1964). Opposition and lack of interest are also reflected in the absence of legal recognition in most countries. In only two of fifteen Latin-American countries covered in a recent report was any legal recognition accorded to psychologists (Ardila, 1968).

Understandably, then, psychologists in the emerging nations have not been able to establish a clear image for themselves in the public eye. Psychologists frequently are seen as poorly trained physicians (Ardila, 1968), and physicians with training in psychotherapy, or other nonpsychologists, may refer to themselves as psychologists (Abt, 1964). Part of the image problem emanates from the university, where psychology classes are often taught by M.D.'s, education specialists, etc. The failure of psychology to evoke a clear image of an independent discipline also hampers its search for support.

Whatever the causes, the consequences of underfunding and lack of recognition are severe and probably are related to the following characteristics of psychology in the nations under consideration.

LOW BUDGETS FOR TRAINING

Funds for education are generally quite limited, and the problem is greater for psychologists and other behavioral scientists than for those in the older disciplines. Reports of internationally known professors in the social sciences who earn as little as $80 or $100 per month continue (Janowitz, 1968: Nussenzveig, 1969). A more typical case might be that of an acquaintance of the author who fared only slightly better. His appointment received from one of the largest universities in Latin America paid about $2,000 (plus health and other benefits) for the nine-month term. It was considered a half-time appointment, but included duties of teaching twenty hours per week in classes or laboratories!

In many Latin-American universities, including those which are state-supported, the salary may be so small as to constitute a mere honorarium. In such cases, professional persons contribute a few hours of their time each week to teach a single course in the spirit of public service or for prestige. As might be expected, the adequacy of instruction in such a system is quite variable.

Most of the countries of Africa and the Middle East are just beginning to train their own psychologists. With the exception of Israel, the Republic of South Africa, the United Arab Republic, and a very few others, countries there are relying on expatriate Europeans or others for their training.

POOR COMMUNICATION

Publications. "Prestige" publications from the technologically advanced nations predominate in the emerging nations. Since much of this material must be translated into Arabic, Hebrew, Spanish, or other languages for maximum utilization, communication problems are even more dependent upon money for solution in the emerging nations than in the affluent nations.

Good texts for advanced courses in scientific psychology are still rare, and the communication value even for good translated texts is limited by the long translation lag. For material translated from English into Spanish, for example, the lag is about 8.5 years (Campos, 1964). This lag, added to the estimated six-year publication lag for most data that eventually will be so translated (Díaz-Guerrero,

1968), makes such information old indeed when it first appears in Spanish. Because of the infrequency of translation, it can become much older still before newer information appears, as the author learned from a Latin American who studied general psychology a few years ago in a large Mexican university. That course's text was a translation of Max Meyer's *Psychology of the other one,* first published in 1921.

Conventions and Associations. Poor written communication is paralleled by poor communication via conventions held by national or regional associations. Several Latin-American states have yet to found an association or hold a convention. In the Middle East and Africa, only Israel, the United Arab Republic, and the Republic of South Africa have national associations. Plans for national associations are nearing completion in Ghana, Nigeria, Iran, and Sierra Leone.

The only regional association of consequence is the Inter-American Society of Psychology, founded in 1951. Psychologists from virtually every country in both North and South America belong to this organization. It has sponsored an almost yearly congress since the first in 1953. In recent years, the proceedings of the congress have been published, and since 1967 the *Revista Inter-Americana de Psicologia* has been published quarterly by this organization. Both have greatly facilitated communication in the Americas.

No corresponding regional association is currently active in Africa or the Middle East, although a West African Psychological Association is being organized.

Other communication depends mainly upon the technologically advanced countries. The international Union of Psychological Science, for example, provides a variety of communication services for psychologists in any country, in addition to providing special recognition and aid to member associations. Five of its thirty-five member associations are found in Latin America. Only South Africa in Africa and Israel in the Middle East have member associations. Among its publications are the *International Journal of Psychology,* the *International Directory of Psychologists,* and, with the APA, *International Opportunities for Advanced Training and Research in Psychology.* It also sponsors meetings.

The United Nations Educational, Scientific, and Cultural Organization publishes bibliographies and other materials, including the *International Social Science Journal.* Other communication resources for the emerging nations include the *Latin American Research Review,* published by the University of Texas; the *Newsletter,* from the University of Illinois; and *FAR Horizons,* from the Foreign Area Research Coordination Group of the United States government.

A little-known service is provided by the Science Information Exchange of the National Science Foundation. Created to provide information concerning research in progress, its abstracts are provided on demand to scientists in any country without charge. Its coverage of United States government-sponsored projects is moderately complete, and it also includes some projects sponsored by private foundations. Projects sponsored by Canada or other foreign nations are occasionally included.

LACK OF RESEARCH

Psychology in the least developed countries may be described as predominantly academic—a classroom enterprise. In the more advanced of the emerging nations may be found at least some form of applied psychology, such as selection testing or psychological treatment of behavioral disorders, but seldom is there much emphasis upon research or training in research methodology.

The major impediment to research is, predictably, lack of funds. The funding problem is especially acute for cross-cultural and other research offering no obvious contribution to national development (Odbert, 1964; Santos, 1964).

Research in Latin America

Research-oriented movements, such as behaviorism, are just beginning to make themselves felt in Latin America. Despite very early recognition of the possibility of scientific psychology by early Spaniards such as Juan Huarte, who in 1575 suggested the use of tests for academic selection, the general absence of science in Spain and Portugal has hampered the scientific movement in Latin America (Basalla, 1967). This absence was due, at least in part, to an aversion for manual labor. In Latin America this aversion is manifested in avoidance of such tedious activities as data collection. It is exemplified by early Brazilian naturalists who assigned their Negroes the task of collecting and preparing specimens (Kidder, 1845). Even Latin-American psychologists trained abroad have traditionally preferred a nonquantitative approach (Abt, 1964). This distaste for the manual labor of data collection is probably the result of many class-conscious members of Latin America's educated elite viewing it as a lower-class activity.

Coupled with a disdain for data collection and analysis is a glorification of philosophical approaches (Chavez, Lozada, & Arestegui, 1966; Hall, 1946). One reviewer of ten Latin-American introductory psychology texts found that nine devoted whole chapters to philosophical psychology. Other common topics were philosophical treatments of instincts, association of ideas, character, consciousness, passion, will, etc. (Campos, 1964). A typical author (Celaya, 1961) has asserted that he reduced the physiological basis of his text to a minimum and instead emphasized the cultural and spiritual. The affirmation by the first Congreso Argentino de Psicologia of the goal of valuable action, the truth, the core of human knowledge, and God, the meaning of everything that is, is not unusual in its alliance with the philosophical approach rather than with the scientific (Ruiz, 1963).

Another source of resistance to behavioral research can be traced to the arrival of French philosophical thought. The French viewpoint achieved dominance among Latin Americans during the last century, largely because French intellectuals espoused political freedom and independence cherished by nations newly independent of Spain. It was also esteemed because it was a Latin movement of some prestige among the nations of the world.

French positivism of the Comte school became especially influential. Unfortunately for scientific psychology, its emphasis upon strict operationalism quickly drove difficult psychological problems out of the laboratories and into philosophy departments, thus strengthening the affinity between psychology and philosophy (Beebe-Center & McFarland, 1941). The early interpreters of positivism (such as Lèvy-Brühl, 1900) also urged the division of empirical psychology into sociology and physiology. Acceptance of this doctrine, together with the founding of two of the first active psychological laboratories in Latin America around the turn of the century by a physiologist (Horacio Pinero), further fractionated psychology.

One might not expect the fraction of psychology belonging to the philosophers to develop an empirical tradition. It would seem, however, that the physiologists and physicians might have established an empirical psychology within their own discipline. The failure of this expectation to be fully realized as the educational and technological capability of these nations grew can be traced largely to the introduction of Freudian thought. The association of psychoanalysis with medicine led to its early acceptance by prestigious university faculties of medicine. Freud's philosophical style of thinking and writing seems to have been more attractive to Latin-American academicians than to those in non-Latin countries.

Philosophical psychoanalytical psychology now dominates psychology in almost all Latin-American universities. In keeping with this domination, Latin-American students studying in the United States are heard to complain that their classes should be more philosophical and clinical (Campos, 1964). One may predict that the resulting skepticism regarding the value of scientific research into clinical or other problems (for example, see Nuñez, 1964) will continue to inhibit Latin-American empirical research on psychological topics.

Research in Africa and the Middle East

In Africa south of the Sahara, psychological research is well established only in South Africa. A beginning has been made in Zambia, Ghana, Senegal, Nigeria, Uganda, and a few other places. In most of these nations research is still guided by whites. It has been asserted that traditional African social values, while attractive for other reasons, modulate the tough-minded assertiveness that may be necessary for a rigorous science (Mundy-Castle, 1968). What research is performed seems to be found more frequently where the British academic tradition prevails than in the twenty French-speaking states, where psychology is often identified with philosophy (Prothro & Melikian, 1955). Accordingly, a reviewer of French-language psychological studies from Africa remarked that he found few relevant bibliographies (Wickert, 1967). It is tempting to speculate that the Latin turn of mind that seems to adore the philosophical approach when found among Latin Americans is also at work in French-speaking Africa. It should be noted, however, that other observers have reported a vigorous empirical psychology current in France itself (see Appendix A, for example), thus casting doubt on such a hypothesis.

In the Middle East, Israel clearly leads in research. Almost none seems to be executed in the Arab states outside of the United Arab Republic and, to a lesser degree, Lebanon. Competence in the latter nation is growing, but until recently only a few Lebanese publications appear to have had direct scientific value (Melikian, 1964).

In all the nations under consideration, the little research that is executed is focused on "applied" problems. "Basic" research is neglected. In Africa, this imbalance characterizes research executed in the French as well as the English tradition (Wickert, 1967). In many nations applied research has preceded by many years any type of basic or academic research.

The pressure from governmental or other social institutions to solve practical problems has deflected all types of research away from the universities and into special institutes. Usually these institutes are concerned with specific objectives, such as rehabilitating juvenile delinquents, reducing alcoholism, aiding governmental licensing bodies, etc. The APA's *International Opportunities for Advanced Training and Research in Psychology* lists several dozen such institutes in Latin America, and observers have commented on their importance (Beebe-Center & McFarland, 1941; Hall, 1946). Almost as many may be found in Africa and the Middle East.

The current growth of these institutions suggests that what resources are allotted to psychological research in the emerging nations will continue to be devoted to applied rather than basic problems. This trend is probably a healthy one in view of the current needs of these countries. One may hope, however, that eventually the emerging nations will elaborate their own viewpoints to complement the ethnocentric biases of the affluent nations—a problem to be treated at length in the following section.

FOREIGN DOMINATION

This domination assumes several forms. The dominating position of foreign literature in the emerging nations was mentioned earlier in this appendix. An equally influential force involves the exchange of people. In the early 1960s about 270,000 students were abroad. About half of them were from the developing nations and were studying in the affluent nations (Ajmal, 1967; Angell, 1967). Many of the students, as well as more mature scholars who seek research or other experience in the affluent nations, fail to return. Such loss stunts the growth of the donor and, because of acculturation and training in the affluent culture, seldom makes psychology in the latter more universal. If the scholar does return home, he may not be easily reintegrated into his home culture because of "culture shock" or because he is viewed as a threat by older but less well-trained scholars (Gollin, 1964; Price-Williams, 1968; Whyte, 1969). Nor does sending teaching personnel from the affluent nations to the emerging nations reduce feelings of domination, for this procedure perpetuates the dependent role of the latter. Such teaching personnel are also finding themselves subject to increasing political attacks in the emerging nations. Distrust for United States personnel is especially great, for their activities are frequently seen to differ only in method from the intervention of the United States military or the CIA, which is almost universally disapproved of in the countries under consideration (Whyte, 1969).

Neither the dominant position of foreign publications nor the migration of personnel, however, stirs international controversies among psychologists as much as research executed by the affluent nations in and on the emerging nations. One observer has noted that the resentment is understandable when one realizes that the intellectual harvests from such projects inevitably are reaped mainly in the United States or other affluent nations that can afford to sponsor projects executed abroad (Smith, 1968b). Elsewhere he observed that no special empathy is required to understand why members of a modernized elite resent having their less sophisticated compatriots studied as "natives," specimens in a human museum (Smith, 1968a).

Aside from the above implications of research executed abroad, much of it may be described as "tourist research," executed by investigators who are unfamiliar with the host culture and who may spend no more than a few weeks during the summer in the host country. Research conducted in this manner is usually of doubtful validity (Mundy-Castle, 1967). An increasing number of areas are also being viewed as "overresearched" or "saturated" (Hughes, 1966; Walsh, 1966). A member of the U.S. Department of State reviewed a number of government documents and found 191 foreign-area research centers in United States universities alone (Platig, 1968).

For several years, citizens of the emerging nations have held the suspicion that United States psychological research might be an instrument of Western imperialism (Prothro & Melikian, 1955). The fact that currently more than 50 percent of government-sponsored foreign-area research in the United States is supported by the Department of Defense (Platig, 1968) augments this suspicion.

The most startling evidence that psychology and other behavioral sciences could indeed serve Western imperialism is project Camelot (see Horowitz, 1965; Vallance, 1966; Walsh, 1966). This counterinsurgency project was expected to cost 4 to 6 million dollars over its anticipated life of three to four years. The American University in Washington, D.C., accustomed to executing research for the government, was chosen by the Army sponsors to administer the funds. It has been suggested that university identification was desired as camouflage for the militaristic implications of the project (Horowitz, 1965). That the project was hardly a disinterested search for understanding may be concluded from a recruiting letter sent to scholars throughout the world (but excluding the Communist nations, it is safe to assume). The goals, as stated in the letter, were to make it possible to predict and influence politically significant aspects of social change in the developing nations of the world. Needless to say, any increase in ability to influence politically significant aspects of social change would serve mainly the interests of the affluent nations and, perhaps, their wealthy friends in the developing nations.

Counter to the spirit of free inquiry, certain unquestioned assumptions seem to have been implicit in the project. Among them was the desirability of political stability. Studies of Paraguay, where repressive dictatorship prevailed, were recommended, apparently because of that country's stability. The desirability of successful revolution appears never to have been considered by Camelot personnel, a point criticized by Senator Fulbright, chairman of the Senate Foreign Relations Committee. Knowledge of these assumptions and purposes disseminated in Chile caused such a furor that the project was aborted in mid-1965, before any data were collected, by then Secretary of Defense McNamara, after consultation with the President.

The project has been defended. Some have argued that its successful completion would have increased the behavioral scientists' ability to modify some of the unattractive aspects of militarism in our foreign policy. The fact that the Army even considered such a mammoth project was offered as evidence that the behavioral sciences could play a guiding role in certain military activities. More likely, however, the military viewed the project as quite minor, having committed to it less than 1/30,000th of its total budget anticipated for the three- or four-year period under consideration.

Perhaps extensive changes in attitudes may be required before the problems of foreign domination of the behavioral sciences in the developing nations can be significantly reduced. The nature of those changes may be inferred from questions posed by a United States sociologist (Moskos, 1968). He asks: "Why should it be so difficult to conceive of a group of Latin American sociologists studying the American military-industrial complex? Or to conceive of African economists looking at patterns of American investments overseas? Or to conceive of Asian political scientists examining the decision-making process in the growth of U.S. military commitments overseas?" (p. 2).

STAGES OF DEVELOPMENT

The nations under consideration in this appendix might profitably be classified into three stages of development in regard to their achievements in scientific psychology. The following classification is made primarily on the basis of the education in psychology that is available within each country and the psychological research published by the country's scholars. Much of the information used for the classification (especially the information regarding education in psychology) comes from the APA's *International Opportunities for Advanced Training and Research in Psychology* (1966). Most of that information was submitted during 1964 and 1965 and therefore is somewhat dated. Newer information is available for some of the countries, but it was felt that mixing new with old information would reduce the comparability of the information upon which the classification rests. Table D-1 presents the resulting classification. (Case studies for stage 2 and stage 3 are given at the end of this appendix.)

Stage 1. Countries at this stage of development do not have degree-granting psychology departments. However, a few of the nations italicized in the table, such

Table D-1. Stages of development in scientific psychology of nations in Latin America, Africa, and the Middle East

Stage 1:	Aden, Afghanistan, Cameroon, Central African Republic, Chad, Congo (Brazzaville), Dahomey, Gabon, Federation of South Arabia, Ivory Coast, Jordan, Kuwait, Liberia, Libya, Morocco, Rhodesia, Saudi Arabia, Sierra Leone, Sudan, Syria, Tunisia *Costa Rica, Ghana, Malagasy, Nigeria, Senegal, Uganda, Zambia*
Stage 2:	Algeria, Chile, Colombia, Congo (Leopoldville), Ecuador, El Salvador, Guatemala, Iran, Iraq, Lebanon, Panama, Paraguay, Peru, Uruguay *Argentina, Brazil, Cuba, Mexico, United Arab Republic, Venezuela*
Stage 3:	Israel *Republic of South Africa*

NOTE: The italicized nations are considered to be somewhat advanced over others in the same stage of development.

as Senegal and Malagasy, offer certificates in psychological studies that are roughly equivalent to B.A. degrees in psychology. Little or no research is conducted by the nonitalicized countries. Most of the italicized nations have established at least one permanent center for psychological research that is relatively independent of the guidance of a foreign institution. These centers are usually staffed by expatriate psychologists from Europe or elsewhere.

Stage 2. Countries at this stage of development do have one or more universities that offer degrees in psychology. Frequently their universities are several centuries old and may have promoted psychological studies for as long as the average university in Europe or the United States. Generally they are wealthier than the countries in stage 1. For one reason or another, however, psychology—especially rigorous, scientific psychology—has not prospered in most of these countries, where high-quality psychological education is rare. The nonitalicized countries conduct only sporadic research, except in connection with student theses. The italicized countries usually support at least a handful of researchers in psychology, but have achieved excellence in only a few areas of research.

Stage 3. Only the Republic of South Africa and Israel have achieved the breadth and rigor in psychology required for classification at stage 3. They also differ in that they are relatively affluent, with perhaps only Kuwait, Venezuela, and Argentina comparable to them on this dimension. South Africa is remarkably wealthy if the poverty of that nation's blacks is ignored. It should also be noted that both nations, but especially Israel, devote a large proportion of their wealth to education and welfare rather than to consumer goods. The number of TV sets per 1,000 population, for example, was recorded by the UN's *Statistical yearbook* (1965) as only six for Israel. This compares with three for Zambia, five for Iran, twelve for Syria, eighteen for Peru, and forty-two for Mexico, all countries that are poorer than Israel. Argentina and Venezuela, which are comparable to Israel in wealth, are reported to have had seventy-two and seventy-five, respectively. Israel's support of welfare is evidenced by the fact that it has perhaps the best doctor-population ratio of any country in the world.

GROWTH AND PROSPECTS FOR THE FUTURE

It has been asserted that scientific research doubled in Africa during the period 1950 to 1964, when most nations there were enjoying their first years of independence (Adiseshiah, 1964). Psychological research there also exhibited some growth in quantity during that period. Greater advances were achieved in terms of the quality of psychological research. Research conducted prior to independence has frequently been charged with reflecting colonial bias (Doob, 1965; Wickert, 1967). Certainly the problems studied now are more relevant to the needs of the Africans than was the case during the colonial period.

Nevertheless, there are some factors operating on both continents that must lead one to modify the general prediction of continuing growth.

In Latin America, education definitely has lagged behind industrialization and other trends toward modernization. The literacy rate in some Latin-American nations actually may have fallen during the last two decades. In the mid 1960s, no major city in Latin America had classrooms for more than 70 percent of its school-age population. Opportunities for education were much poorer still in rural areas. The quality of education was also marginal, with teaching usually considered to be an underpaid, low-status profession. There is no indication that education in Latin America will greatly improve in the foreseeable future.

Profound commitment to formal education has been said to distinguish the new African nations from other emerging nations (Foster, 1964). Several years ago some African nations were already enrolling up to 80 percent of all primary-age children in school (Hunter, 1962). Unfortunately, fewer than 10 percent or so of primary school graduates can be accommodated into secondary schools (McQueen, 1968). It is also true that, in spite of government commitment to education, the African populace remains uninspired by education. University education is still very rare in Africa, but the gains being reported in this area of education permit some degree of optimism.

Education in the Middle East varies from good in Israel and in tiny, wealthy Kuwait to inadequate almost everywhere else. In most places only a minority of school-age children attend school. Even Egypt entered the second half of this century with about two-thirds of its population illiterate, and Egypt is generally considered to be more advanced than most other countries in the Middle East in regard to education. The illiteracy rate there is probably still about 50 percent.

Consideration of economic factors leads one to be no more optimistic regarding psychology's future than consideration of educational factors does. During the last decades of the colonial period, which ended in most places after World War II, the economies of the poor countries grew only about 1 percent per year. Since then the increase has been about 4 percent per year, but the population has increased at the rate of about 2.5 percent per year. The net gain of about 1.5 percent, although about 1 percent lower than that in the wealthy countries, nevertheless would permit a small rise in wealth (Blackett, 1967). Unfortunately, there is reason to fear that the growth rate of the emerging nations may actually decline from its present low level. Past growth in many of the emerging nations has been purchased, at least in part, at the expense of agricultural productivity and consumption. At least one analysis in fact shows a decline in animal-protein consumption in the emerging nations generally of about 10 percent from the late thirties to the late fifties. At the end of that period, the emerging nations were consuming, per person, only about one-fifth the animal protein being consumed in the rich nations (Keyfitz, 1967). Total per capita food availability is also decreasing (Hoelscher, 1969). Surely the emerging nations must increase, or at least hold constant, their food consumption, even if this means some slowing of advancement in the fields of education and science.

It also appears that much of the past growth in the emerging nations has resulted from the rich nations' foreign-aid programs. Because of the tremendous wealth of the affluent nations, their contribution of only 1 percent of their annual product would boost the income of the poor nations by about 6 percent (Blackett, 1967). At one time the United States, one of the biggest contributors of foreign aid, met the 1 percent figure. But in recent years actual dollars-and-cents figures have declined, despite a booming economy and inflation that alone would have reduced the percentage contributed even if the dollars contributed had remained constant.

The recurrent financial problems of some of the nations that continue to commit a larger percentage to foreign aid, such as France, lead one to fear that they, too, may reduce their contributions. These decreases come at a time when many exports of the emerging nations are being driven from the markets by synthetic goods produced in the affluent nations. All these problems, compounded by religious and other opposition to birth-control attempts, paint a forbidding picture of the economic future of the emerging nations. To the extent that psychology's future is tied to educational and economic growth in these nations, slow growth would appear to be the most that realistically can be hoped for.

CONCLUSION

In none of the emerging nations can one find a tradition of scientific psychology that is perceptibly autonomous from scientific psychology found in the industrialized nations. An autonomous psychology in Africa and in Israel is precluded by the dominating role of expatriates from the industrialized nations. Scientific psychology in the Arab Middle East is still too poorly supported to be able to elaborate its own viewpoints. The Moslem psychology found there clearly does offer alternative viewpoints. However, its tradition is much older than upstart scientific psychology's tradition, and it appears not yet to have felt the need to offer empirical data to support its hypotheses.

Latin-American psychologists generally remain skeptical regarding the value of scientific psychology. The few Latin Americans who have engaged in empirical psychological research usually have been those who have been most influenced by the viewpoints found in the industrialized nations. As might be expected, their contributions frequently reflect non-Latin thinking.

A strong case can be presented in support of the argument that the wealthy nations should help pay the costs of nurturing psychology's growth in the emerging nations. Apart from the moral issue involved in disregarding their perpetual poverty and dependency upon the industrialized nations, support for the emerging nations' intellectual as well as political independence could produce identifiable benefits for the rich nations too. The pinpointing of generalization failures in our theories would be only the most obvious benefit. In addition, wholly unforeseen avenues of research might be fostered by psychologists who come from cultures that, for one reason or another, have not grown industrially as the rich nations have. If this turned out to be the case, then the sum sophistication of scientific explanations for behavior probably would advance more than if the same amount of support were confined to research executed by the rich. And, to the extent that such explanations became integrated into the decision-making processes of the rich countries, perhaps even some of their socioeconomic problems might become more amenable to solution than hitherto has been the case.

An integrated psychology derived from the experiences of both the emerging and the developed nations appears difficult to achieve. Admittedly, the pattern of the fifties and the sixties that centered mostly upon counterinsurgency and the design and implementation of large-scale technical development projects has probably passed its zenith. But we need not mourn its decline. The counterinsurgency business probably was never wholesome for either the rich or the poor nations, and increasing evidence suggests that many of the development projects were not viable because of economic and technical factors that were overlooked by the experts (see Hoelscher, 1969, for recent examples of failures of expertise). Such projects did not warrant the social engineering that often was provided for them by scientific psychology. If scientific psychology has nothing more to offer, then perhaps it merits its infirmity in the emerging nations.

There is reason to hope, however, that a more salubrious role may be arising for social scientists. It was described well by George A. Miller (1969) in his presidential address to the APA. Miller claims that our responsibility is less to assume the role of experts than to give away scientific psychology to the people who really need it—everyone. Space limitations prohibit a delineation of his vision here, but it seems to the present author that it does not differ greatly from that which is forming in the United States "counterculture," with its distinctive life-style (see Roszak, 1969). Significantly, Miller draws some of his inspiration from a Latin American (Varela, 1970) and is echoed by an increasing number of scientists from the emerging nations who, despairing of political revolutions, are calling for profound social revolutions (e.g., see Chirinos, 1967; Nussenzveig, 1969). Feeble though this hope may be, it appears to be providing new vigor to many of our best minds and, if for no other reason, deserves further consideration.

Mexico, Stage 2. With a population of about 50 million, Mexico is the world's largest Spanish-speaking nation. Less wealthy than several other stage 2 nations, its per capita gross national product is only about one-tenth that of the United States, and it is not well distributed. Labor's portion of the income is less than half of labor's portion in the United States, and it has steadily decreased for several decades, while the profit portion has greatly increased. Nevertheless, the expanding economy plus adequate control of inflation has provided improved living conditions for most Mexicans in recent years. Urbanization is advancing at a fast pace, and a slight majority of Mexicans now live in cities with 5,000 or more inhabitants. Education has advanced much less rapidly than industrial growth or urbanization. Probably fewer than half the nation's children between the ages of six and twelve attend school. Illiteracy estimates range from 30 to about 50 percent.

Psychology courses in Mexico have been offered since 1918 (Nuñez, 1961), and degrees have been offered since 1936 (Ribes-Iñesta, 1968). Growth in psychology has accelerated in recent years. In 1964 only five universities offered degrees in psychology, whereas in 1968 more than twenty-five hundred psychology majors studied in ten universities (Ribes-Iñesta, 1968). As elsewhere in Latin America, most were women—a consequence of psychology's low status there. The National University was the first in Latin America to grant the Ph.D. in psychology (Abt, 1964), but its graduate program still is not well developed.

At most Mexican universities, as elsewhere in Latin America, courses last both semesters rather than one, and they tend to be organized in lock-step sequence. Until the 1960s, full-time teachers of psychology were almost nonexistent in Mexico (Abt, 1964). Most courses have been taught by part-time professors trained in medicine, education, engineering, law or philosophy.

No legal recognition has been achieved for psychologists except for occasional local laws regarding the use of the title *psychologist*. Several psychological journals have appeared in Mexico, but now are defunct. The Mexican Psychological Society, organized in 1967, plans to publish a journal of psychological research in the near future (Ribes-Iñesta, 1968).

Psychological research of sorts began in Mexico in 1925, when examination of juvenile delinquents prior to sentencing was instituted. The Psycho-pedagogical Institute, a branch of the Department of Public Education, then was founded for studying and resolving the problems of school-age children (Nuñez, 1961). Probably no more than a dozen or so Mexican psychologists currently are engaged in research as a regular part of their professional activities. What research is executed is funded by the universities or by occasional grants from the United States government or philanthropic organizations. There is no regular source of support for research outside the universities.

At least three scholars in Mexico may be said to have achieved international recognition for their work on topics of interest to psychologists. Raul Hernandez-Peón, who received his training in medicine at the National University in Mexico

City, was well known for his work in physiological psychology. A review of his and other investigators' studies of brain functions, especially those related to sleep, may be found in a paper in the *Annual Reivew of Psychology* (Hernandez-Peón & Sterman, 1966). A review of his work on the role of reticular mechanisms in sensory control may be found in an earlier paper (Hernandez-Peón, 1961).

Perhaps the most significant single study covered in the latter review is one that examines neural mechanisms involved in the direction of attention (Hernandez-Peón, Scherrer, & Jouvet 1956). In this study, it was shown that the neural activity in the auditory nerve of cats practically disappeared when a jar of mice was placed in front of the subject. Other attention-getting stimuli, such as fish odors or a shock to the forepaw, produced similar results. It would appear that the auditory response is suppressed or tuned out when attention is directed elsewhere. Other sensory modes, such as vision, presumably are affected similarly by shifting attention.

Recently Hernandez-Peón and his students undertook an extensive series of studies into the implications for brain functioning of Freud's speculations on dreams. For a review of the preliminary findings of this research, see Hernandez-Peón (1967). His untimely death in 1968 represents a costly loss not only to Mexico but also to physiological psychology generally.

Rogelio Díaz-Guerrero received his Ph.D. under the direction of Kenneth Spence at the State University of Iowa. He also holds an M.D. from the National University. As the third president of the Mexican Psychological Society, a past president of the Interamerican Society of Psychology, and a member of other organizations, he has been active in professional affairs as well as in research and teaching. Several of his cross-cultural comparisons and other social-psychological studies may be found in his book (Díaz-Guerrero, 1967). He has held several positions in the National University.

Erich Fromm is in charge of training in psychotherapy at the medical school of the National University. His speculations have furnished personality theorists with hypotheses during many years of work in Mexico and elsewhere.

A review of research in Mexico would not be complete without mention of the Instituto Interuniversitario para Investigaciones Fundamentales en Ciencias Sociales en Yucatan, A.C. More than five hundred scholars from psychology and at least fourteen other disciplines visited the institute during the first five years after its activation in 1964. Funded by grants obtained by Fred L. Strodtbeck, of the University of Chicago, and others, it has worked in close collaboration with Mexican scholars. Victor Castillo Vales, chairman of the University of Yucatan's psychology department, has provided especially valuable guidance for many non-Mexican social scientists who have conducted research there, including the present author.

Israel, Stage 3. Israel was created in 1948 by the United Nations. At that time it was a poor nation with a population of about 700,000. The total population in 1965 was about 2.6 million, of which about 300,000 were non-Jews. Much of the population growth since 1948 is attributable to the immigration of about 1.1 million Jews between 1948 and 1965, of which about 400,000 were from Europe or the United States (Weinberg, 1967).

Primary education is excellent and enrolls most of the children. However, only a minority attend secondary schools. As of 1965, psychology was offered as a major subject at three universities. The M.A. in psychology was offered at Bar-Ilan University, and the Ph.D. at the Hebrew University of Jerusalem. New advanced degree programs are being organized at other universities. The quality of instruction is excellent. Nevertheless, a substantial proportion of students still seek training abroad. Psychology in Israel continues to be dominated by those who have studied in the United States, Europe, and the U.S.S.R.

Until 1948, Israeli psychology was oriented toward the psychoanalytic approach. Then the only department was at the Hebrew University. When the head of the department was killed in an ambush, the department became inactive until 1956. In that year both Hebrew University and Bar-Ilan University opened new departments. In contrast to the previous emphasis upon psychoanalytical clinical psychology, these new departments both were experimentally oriented (Greenbaum, 1967).

Research is currently conducted in at least a dozen special institutes, hospitals, and governmental agencies, as well as in the universities. It is predominantly centered upon problems of social or national interest. Often it is experimental in method. Basic research is by no means neglected, and it is supported both by Israeli governmental and other Israeli organizations and by foreign groups. Research is frequently conducted in collaboration with investigators in the United States or another foreign country.

The influence of the United States is especially notable in Israeli research. This influence is attributable to the United States psychologists who have accepted permanent positions in Israel, and it is maintained by a steady stream of visiting psychologists from the United States and by research funds supplied by United States organizations.

One institute of special interest that is partly supported by United States organizations (The American Committee for Social Research in Israel, Inc., and others) is the Israel Institute of Applied Social Research. First formed as a volunteer research group by the underground defense army in 1947, the institute was officially established in 1949 by Louis Guttman (known in the United States for his work in the measurement of attitudes) and Uriel G. Foa with the aid of a grant by the Israeli government. After operating under the auspices of the Defense Ministry, and later under the Prime Minister's Office, the institute now functions as an independent, nonprofit organization. Its permanent professional staff of about twenty performs under the leadership of Guttman, who stayed on after the founding to become its scientific director. A part-time field staff working throughout the country facilitates large-scale studies in opinion polling, economics, mass communications, community planning, social problems of medicine and health, etc. To date, several hundred projects have been completed in the above fields, plus others in the general areas of social psychology, sociology, and psychology.

REFERENCES

Abt, L. E. Clinical psychology in Latin America. In L. E. Abt & B. F. Riess (Eds.), *Progress in clinical psychology.* Vol. 6. New York: Grune & Stratton, 1964. Pp. 235-241.

Adiseshiah, M. S. The planned development of scientific research. *Impact of Science on Society,* 1964, **14**(3), 137-144.

Ajmal, M. Academic freedom. *Psychological Quarterly,* 1967, **2**,14-18.

Angell, R. C. The growth of transnational participation. *Journal of Social Issues,* 1967, **23**, 108-129.

Ardila, R. La psicologia en Colombia. *Revista Inter-Americana de Psicologia,* 1967, **1**, 239-249.

Ardila, R. Psychology in Latin America. *American Psychologist,* 1968, **23**, 567-574.

Basalla, G. The spread of Western science. *Science,* 1967, **156**, 611-621.

Beebe-Center, J. G., & McFarland, R. Psychology in South America. *Psychological Bulletin,* 1941, **38**, 627-667.

Blackett, P. M. S. The ever widening gap. *Science,* 1967, **155**, 959-964.

Campos, L. P. Some problems in the teaching of psychology in Spanish at the Covell College, U.S.A. Paper presented at the Ninth Interamerican Congress of Psychology, Miami, December, 1964.

Celaya, M. *Psicologia.* (Primera edic.) Buenos Aires: Luis Lassere & Cia, S. A., Editores, 1961.

Chavez, E. U., Lozada, N. B., & Arestegui, A. A. Estudio comparativo de la formación académica del psicólogo. Paper presented at the Tenth Interamerican Congress of Psychology, Lima, April, 1966.

Chirinos, E. Limitaciones y perspectivas de la psicología y de las ciencias del comportamiento en los paises de subdesarrollo economico. *Proceedings of the Eleventh Interamerican Congress of Psychology,* Universidad Nacional Autonomo de Mexico, 1967.

Díaz-Guerrero, R. Estudios de psicología del Mexicano. Mexico: Editorial F. Trillas, S. A., 1967.

Díaz-Guerrero, R. Problems of scientific communication. *Journal of Social Issues,* 1968, **24**, 217-226.

Doob, L. Psychology. In R. A. Lystad (Ed.), *The African world: A survey of social research.* London: Pall Mall Press for African Studies Association, 1965.

Foster, P. J. Status, power, and education in a traditional community. *School Review,* 1964, **72**, 158-182.

Gollin, A. Acquiring development skills: Two decades of a United States aid program in Latin America. Paper presented at the Ninth Interamerican Congress of Psychology, Miami, December, 1964.

Greenbaum, C. V. Personal correspondence, 1967.

Hall, M. E. The present status of psychology in South America. *Psychological Bulletin*, 1946, **43**, 441-476.

Hartocollis, P. Psychiatry in contemporary Greece. *American Journal of Psychiatry*, 1966, **123**, 457-462.

Hernandez-Peón, R. Reticular mechanisms of sensory control. In W. A. Rosenblith (Ed.), *Sensory communication.* New York: Wiley, 1961.

Hernandez-Peón, R. Un modelo neorofisiologico de los ensueños. *Proceedings of the Eleventh Interamerican Congress of Psychology,* Universidad Nacional Autonomo de Mexico, 1967.

Hernandez-Peón, R., Scherrer, H., & Jouvet, M. Modification of electrical activity in the cochlear nucleus during "attention" in unanesthetized cats. *Science*, 1956, **123**, 331-332.

Hernandez-Peón, R., & Sterman, M. B. Brain functions. *Annual Review of Psychology*, 1966, **17**, 363-394.

Heron, A. Studies of perception and reasoning in Zambian children. *International Journal of Psychology,* 1968, **3**, 23-29.

Hes, J. P. From native healer to modern psychiatrist: Afro-Asian immigrants to Israel and their attitude towards psychiatric facilities. *Israel Annals of Psychiatry and Related Disciplines, International Studies Quarterly*, 1964, **2**, 192-208

Hoelscher, H. E. Technology and social change. *Science*, 1969, **166**, 68-72.

Holleman, J. F., Mann, J. W., & Van den Berghe, P. L. A Rhodesian white minority under threat. *Journal of Social Psychology*, 1962, **57**, 315-338.

Horowitz, I. The life and death of Project Camelot. *Trans-Action,* 1965, 3(1), 3-7, 44-47. (Republished: *American Psychologist,* 1966, **21**, 445-454.)

Horowitz, I. Social science and public policy: An examination of the political foundations of modern research. *International Studies Quarterly,* 1967, **2**, 32-62.

Huarte, J. The examination of the mind. 1575. Cited by G. Basalla, The spread of Western science. *Science,* 1967, **156**, 611-621.

Hughes, T. L. Scholars and foreign policy: Varieties of research experience. *American Psychologist,* 1966, **21**, 471-478.

Hunter, G. *The new societies of tropical Africa.* London: Oxford University Press, 1962.

Jahoda, G. Some research problems in African education. *Journal of Social Issues,* 1968, **24**, 161-175.

Janowitz, M. International perspectives on militarism. *American Sociologist,* 1968, **3**, 12-16.

Keyfitz, N. National populations and the technological watershed. *Journal of Social Issues,* 1967, **23**, 62-78.

Kidder, D. P. Sketches of residence and travels in Brazil. Vol. 1. Philadelphia, 1845. Cited in G. Basalla, The spread of Western science. *Science,* 1967, **156**, 611-621.

Lèvy-Brühl, L. La philosophie d'Auguste Comte. Paris: Felix Alcan, 1900.

Mahal, A. S. Mental illness in different nations. *International Journal of Psychiatry,* 1967, **4**, 455-458.

McQueen, A. Education and marginality of African youth. *Journal of Social Issues,* 1968, **24**, 179-194.

Melikian, L. Clinical psychology in the Arab Middle East. In L. E. Abt & B. F. Riess (Eds.), *Progress in clinical psychology.* Vol. 6. New York: Grune & Stratton, 1964. Pp. 242-249.

Miller, G. A. Psychology as a means of promoting human welfare. *American Psychologist,* 1969, **24**, 1063-1075.

Moskos, C. C., Jr. Research in the "third world." *Trans-Action,* 1968, **5**(7), 2-3.

Mundy-Castle, A. C. Psychology. In D. Brokensha & M. Crowder (Eds.), *Africa in the wider world.* London: Pergamon Press, 1967. Pp. 222-260.

Mundy-Castle, A. C. The development of nations: Some psychological considerations. *Journal of Social Issues,* 1968, **24**, 45-54.

Nuñez, R. Social-psychological problems of the profession of clinical psychology in Mexico. Mimeographed translation of a paper presented in Spanish at the Seventh Interamerican Congress of Psychology, Mexico, December, 1961.

Nuñez, R. Sobre el intercambio de estudiantes profesores de psicologia clinica entre los paises americanos. Paper presented at the Ninth Interamerican Congress of Psychology, Miami, December, 1964.

Nussenzveig, H. M. Migration of scientists from Latin America. *Science,* 1969, **165**, 1328-1332.

Odbert, H. S. Evaluation of needs for the development of psychology within the Americas. Paper presented at the Ninth Interamerican Congress of Psychology, Miami, December, 1964.

Platig, E. R. Research and analysis. *Annals of the American Academy of Political and Social Science,* 1968, **380**, 50-59.

Price-Williams, D. Problems of research training. *Journal of Social Issues,* 1968, **24**, 227-232.

Prothro, E. T., & Melikian, L. H. Psychology in the Arab Near East. *Psychological Bulletin,* 1955, **52**, 304-310.

Ribes-Iñesta, E. Psychology in Mexico. *American Psychologist,* 1968, **23**, 565-566.

Roszak, T. *The making of a counter culture.* Garden City, N.Y.: Anchor Books, 1969.

Ruiz, D. J. *Curso de psicologia.* (Decimaprimera edic.) Buenos Aires: Editorial Estrada, 1963.

Sanford, F. H. Toward a sociology of psychology. *American Psychologist,* 1952, **7**, 83-85.

Santos, J. F. The exchange of faculty and students in the Americas. Paper presented at the Ninth Interamerican Congress of Psychology, Miami, December, 1964.

Seers, D. *Report of the UN/ECA/FAO Economic Survey Mission: The economic development of Zambia.* Addis Ababa: United Nations Economic Commission for Africa, 1964.

Smith, M. B. Conference report: International conference on social-psychological research in developing countries. *Journal of Personality and Social Psychology,* 1968, **8**, 95-98. (a)

Smith, M. B. Some reflections on the Ibadan Conference. *Journal of Social Issues,* 1968, **24**, 41-61. (b)

U.N. Statistical Office, *Statistical yearbook* (1965). New York: United Nations, 1966.

Vallance, T. R. Project Camelot: An interim postlude. *American Psychologist,* 1966, **21**, 441-444.

Varela, J. A. *Introduction to social science technology.* New York: Academic Press, 1970.

Walsh, J. Foreign affairs research: Review process rises on ruins of Camelot. *American Psychologist,* 1966, **21**, 438-440.

Weinberg, A. A. Immigration from Western countries in Israel. *International Migration,* 1967, **5**, 22-37.

Whyte, W. F. The role of the U.S. professor in developing countries. *American Sociologist,* 1969, **4**, 19-28.

Wickert, F. R. *Readings in African psychology.* East Lansing: Michigan State University, African Studies Center, 1967.

FURTHER READINGS

Cravioto, J. Nutrition deprivation and psycho-biological development in children. Pan American Health Organization Report on Deprivation in Psychological Development, Regional Office of the World Health Organization, Washington. Ref.: Res 418, 16 June, 1965.

Crijus, A. G. African personality structure: A critical review of bibliographical sources and of principal findings. *Gawein,* 1966, **14**, 239-248.

Lystad, R. A. (Ed.) *The African world: A survey of social research.* London: Pall Mall Press for African Studies Association, 1965.

Mann, J. W. *Race attitudes today.* Johannesburg: The Institute for the Study of Man in Africa, 1967.

Nelson, G. K. The electroencephalogram in Kwashiorkor. *Electroencephalography and Clinical Neurophysiology,* 1959, **11**, 73-84.

GLOSSARY

abacus.   A manual computational device using beads that slide on rods; though of ancient origin, an abacus may be used for some operations by an expert at a speed as great as that of a desk calculator.

abreaction.   A process of emotional release that occurs with the reliving of past experiences (psychoanalytic); the basic mechanism in catharsis ("talking-out cure").

act psychology.   A school of psychology that stressed mental processes rather than the contents of consciousness (Brentano).

adaptive act.   Carr's primary unit of behavior, which involves three phases: (1) a motivating stimulus, (2) a sensory situation, and (3) a response that alters the situation to satisfy the motivating conditions.

adder.   A device for adding numbers; the adders in electronic digital computers are almost without exception designed to add binary numbers because the adding equipment is much simpler to build for base-two arithmetic.

afferent stimulus interaction.   Hull's postulate that stimuli interact in such a manner that the resulting behavior is more than a mere summation of the behavioral effects of the stimuli taken separately.

afterimage.   The lingering sensation following the removal of stimulation; usually noted in connection with visual stimulation.

anal stage.   The period in an individual's development which is marked by interest in the anal region and which has certain concomitant effects on personality that may be characteristic of the adult individual if fixation at this stage occurs (Freud).

analysis.   Separation into constituent parts; conceptually, as in science, as well as physically.

and.   A commonly used connective in Boolean algebra; $C = A \cdot B$ may be read "C is true if and only if A and B are both true."

anecdotal method.   The utilization of casually observed events as scientific data.

anima.   A well-developed archetype representing the feminine characteristics in man (Jung).

animus. A well-developed archetype representing the masculine characteristics in woman (Jung).

anthropomorphism. The attributing of human characteristics or capacities to other things, especially infrahuman species.

anthroponomy. A term advocated by Hunter as a name for the "science of human behavior."

antimosaic hypothesis. The theoretical view opposed to structuralist bundle hypothesis.

apperception. A clear and vivid perception.

approach-approach conflict. A conflict which occurs when an individual desires to achieve two goals, only one of which can be obtained (Lewin).

approach-avoidance conflict. A conflict which is characterized by one anticipated goal which is both desired and not desired (Lewin).

archetypes. Inherited predispositions to perceive or act in a certain way (Jung).

associationism. The view that mental complexity is produced via learned associations of simple sensations and ideas.

asthenic. The body type identified by Kretschmer as tall and thin.

attensity. Clearness of sensation which varies with attention rather than with the objective characteristics of the stimulus (Titchener).

avoidance-avoidance conflict. A conflict which is present when two anticipated consequences are both undesirable (Lewin).

axiom. A self-evident truth; a proposition not susceptible to proof or disproof.

bandwidth. The effective frequency range to which a particular instrument or channel responds; for example, a particular filter may have a bandwidth of 100 cycles per second.

basic anxiety. The feeling a child has of being isolated and helpless in a potentially hostile world (Horney).

behaviorism. Generally, the systematic position that all psychological functions can be explained in terms of muscular reactions and glandular secretions, and *nothing more;* therefore, the objective study of the stimulus and response aspects of behavior (Watson). Specifically, 1. *methodological* (empirical) behaviorism: the view that behavior is all that scientists can study and that strictly objective techniques are therefore required, as in all other natural science; 2. *metaphysical* (radical) behaviorism: the philosophical position that there is no mind—a kind of physical monism.

belief-value matrix. Hierarchies of learned expectations concerning environmental objects and their roles in relation to behavior (Tolman).

belongingness, principle of. The proposition that items are more easily associated if they are related in a recognizable way.

binary number. A number to the base two; in any place the value of the coefficient can be one of only two values, 0 or 1.

birth trauma. The emotional experience of the infant ending its prenatal life (emphasized by Rank as having subsequent effects on personality).

bonds. Connections of stimulus and response; hypothetical linkage used to account for the formation of associations.

Boolean algebra. The algebra of sets, developed by George Boole.

bundle hypothesis. The assumption that complex perceptions are a group of simple perceptions.

canalization. The development of a single preferred means of satisfying a need (Murphy).

catharsis. The psychoanalytic principle of releasing tension and anxiety by emotionally reliving experiences; originally described as the "talking-out cure" (Breuer and Freud).

cathexis. The investing of psychic energy in some object, person, or thing (Freud).

centralism. A viewpoint which stresses brain functions in the explanation of psychological phenomena.

centrifugal group factor. The tendency to make gestures away from the body; an expressive factor in Allport's theory of personality.

cerebrotonia. A pattern of temperament characteristic of a bookish, shy, and sensitive individual (Sheldon).

circular conditioned response. A conditioned response sequence in which each successive response serves as a stimulus for the ensuing response.

clinical validation. The demonstration of a theoretical principle through successive confirmations within the same clinical setting from which it was derived.

coded. Transformed into other than the original form; for example, the letters of the alphabet might be coded by transforming each into a unique decimal number, which in turn might be coded into binary numbers, which finally might be coded as holes in a punched card.

cognitive. Pertaining to the mental process involved in achieving awareness or knowledge of an object.

cohesive forces. The tendency of excitations in the cortex to attract one another (Gestalt).

collective unconscious. That part of a person's unconscious which is inherited phylogenetically and is common to all members of the species (Jung).

compensation. Development in those areas in which an individual feels inferior, and the attempt to overcome this inferiority.

compile. To translate a program written in a problem language into the language of machine instructions; the problem language is designed to be more natural for the programmer to use than the machine language.

computer. A device, usually electronic, which carries out a sequence of operations under the control of a stored program of operation.

condensation. The representation of more than one latent element by a single manifest dream element (psychoanalytic).

conditioning, classical. Relatively simple associative learning in which the reinforcement occurs contiguously with the learned response but independently of its performance.

conditioning, instrumental. Relatively simple associative learning in which the opportunity to engage in one behavior (e.g., eating, observing, or sexual activity) is made contingent upon the performance of the response to be learned (e.g., pressing a bar or passing a test).

conditioning, operant. Instrumental conditioning in which the subject "emits" the learned response in the absence of any particular eliciting stimulus (Skinner); the *free operant* is a response whose emission leaves the subject in a position to make further such responses (e.g., pressing a bar in a box, as contrasted with running down a runway).

conditioning, respondent. Classical conditioning, in which there is an eliciting stimulus and in which reinforcement occurs independently of the performance of the response.

confirming reaction. A cerebral function hypothesized by Thorndike as the physiological basis of reinforcement through reward.

conflict. The simultaneous operation of two or more contradictory tendencies; the condition resulting therefrom.

connectionism. The school of psychology which considers a stimulus-response connection or bond to be the basis of all or most behavior.

consensual validation. Validation of a symbol or word by agreement on its meaning by a number of people (Sullivan).

conservation of energy, principle of. The proposition that energy is neither created nor destroyed in physical systems; it is only transferred into other forms and hence "conserved."

construct. A concept that represents relationships between objects or events.

contemporaneity, principle of. The proposition that only present factors influence present behavior; the past influences behavior only as it is represented in the present (Lewin).

context theory of meaning. The view that the meaning of anything results from the context in which it occurs in consciousness (Titchener).

contiguity. Nearness in time and/or space.

continuum. A variable whose values are continuous, that is, such that another value can always be found between any two given values.

control. 1. The method by which extraneous variation is eliminated in science, permitting a less ambiguous assignment of cause-and-effect relationships. 2. The exerting of influence over some variable(s).

controlled variable. A condition whose differential influence on the dependent variable in an experiment is eliminated. This is sometimes achieved by eliminating all variations in the controlled variables (for example, by eliminating the influence of sex by using only one sex) and sometimes by equating the value of the controlled variable for each value of the independent variable (for example, by putting equal numbers of men and women in each group).

corollary. A proposition that follows directly from another which has been proved or postulated; a natural consequence which follows, without additional effort, from an action.

correlation. A relationship between two or more variables so that a change in one occurs whenever a change occurs in the other; the degree to which two or more variables are so related.

creative synthesis. The proposition that new characteristics emerge from the combination of elements into wholes (Wundt).

criterion analysis, method of. A method of factor analysis in which two groups known to differ in some hypothesized underlying factor are selected; test batteries are then administered, and only those tests which differentiate between the groups are submitted to factor analysis (Eysenck).

data processing. The manipulation of data, usually for the purpose of making them more comprehensible; most frequently used when the data are to be handled by a computer.

decoded. Converted back into a form which had been coded into some other form; for example, if letters of the alphabet were *coded* into numbers, the numbers would be *decoded* into letters of the alphabet.

deduction. A type of reasoning in which one proceeds from a set of given statements, via transformation rules, to generate further valid statements. The classic example goes from the premise "all men are mortal" and "Socrates is a man" to the conclusion "Socrates is mortal."

delayed response. A response whose performance is permitted only after some set duration of time following the original presentation of the relevant stimuli.

dependent variable. The variable in an experiment whose values are treated as potentially a function of the values of the independent variable; in psychology, the dependent variable measured is usually some feature of the subject's responses.

detection theory. The theory which treats problems in sensitivity to signals. It is a branch of statistical decision theory and is often called the *theory of signal detectability* (TSD). Using this theory, it is possible to separate criterion considerations from sensitivity considerations.

determining tendency. A predisposition to behave in a particular manner.

determinism. An assumption that all phenomena can be explained by natural law in a cause-and-effect manner; the view that all events are therefore explicable entirely in terms of relevant antecedent events.

diacritical design. The division of intertwined variables into subclasses in an attempt to separate the variables (Brunswik).

dimensional analysis. The structuring of a total situation into specific continua which are measurable.

discrimination. The process of differentiating between objects or actions; the ability to point to a difference.

displacement. The temporary substitution of a secondary goal for a primary one (psychoanalytic).

distal effects. Alterations of the environment which result from an organism's responses.

distal stimuli. Objects in the environment which produce stimuli at the receptor surfaces of the organism (the latter are *proximal stimuli*).

double-alternation task. An experimental design in which the responses must be AABB.

double-aspect view. The metaphysical position in which both mind and body are assumed to be a function of one underlying reality.

dramatization. Children's play activities which emulate adult behavior (Sullivan).

drive (*D*). A construct used by Hull to indicate a condition of the organism resulting from a deprivation which increases the organism's activity toward a particular class of stimuli.

drive discriminations. The demonstrated ability of organisms to behave differentially under different deprivation conditions.

dualism. The metaphysical position in which both mind and body are assumed to exist.

dynamism. A habitual way of responding toward others (Sullivan).

dysplasia. Disharmony or disproportioning between body parts (Sheldon).

eclecticism. The selection of what seems best from various systems, theories, or procedures.

ecological validity. The extent to which cues aid an organism's accomplishing a successful interaction with the environment (Brunswik).

ecology, psychological. The study of those parts of the environment which play an important role in an individual's life space (Lewin).

ectomorphy. A body type characterized as tall thin, and small-boned (Sheldon).

effect, law of. The proposition that strengthening of stimulus-response connections, as measured by the increased probability of the occurrence of a response in a particular stimulus situation, results from the action of reward following a response (satisfying aftereffects, as formulated by Thorndike); the original corollary proposition that punishing aftereffects produce a weakening of responses was subsequently discarded by Thorndike.

effect, spread of. The proposition that reinforcement by reward tends to strengthen erroneous responses in close temporal and/or spatial contiguity (Thorndike).

ego. 1. The self. 2. That part of mental activity which is conscious and in close contact with reality (psychoanalytic).

ego-defense mechanism. Any unconscious process which protects the individual from unpleasant reality; an irrational manner of dealing with anxiety (psychoanalytic).

element. The irreducible unit into which all conscious states can be broken down (Titchener).

elementarism. The methodological bias that mental and behavioral states and processes should be analyzed as far as possible into their constituent components; strongly attacked by Gestalt psychology (structuralism).

emergentism. The view that unique properties emerge in combinations of elements, properties not predictable from knowledge of the elements per se. Life and mind, according to this view, would not be completely reducible to physical principles.

empathy. The sympathetic awareness of an emotional state in another person.

empirical. Relating to facts and sensory experience; denotes reliance on observation.

empiricism. 1. The school of philosophical thought that believes all knowledge originates in experience. 2. A methodology that emphasizes data and minimizes theoretical inference.

endomorphy. A body type characterized as soft, fleshy, and round (Sheldon).

entropy. In physics, the energy of a physical system which is unavailable for work; in information theory, the average information content of a symbol emitted by a source.

epiphenomenalism. The metaphysical position in which mind is assumed to be a noncausal by-product of body.

epistemology. A branch of philosophy concerned with the acquisition and the validity of knowledge.

equipotentiality, principle of. The principle which states that within cerebral areas performing the same function, all parts are equally capable of carrying on that function (Lashley).

equivalence belief. A hypothesized state of an organism as a result of which it behaves as though a subgoal were the goal (Tolman).

erg. An underlying motivational trait having a hereditary origin (Cattell).

erogenous zones. Different zones or regions of the body which are especially sensitive to manipulation (psychoanalytic).

exercise, law of. The proposition that performance of a response improves subsequent performance through practice alone.

existential psychology. 1. The name often given to structuralism because it treated the elements of consciousness as existent. 2. The school of personality theorists who stress the individual's understanding of himself. It derives from existentialism in philosophy; the emphasis is on the concrete events in experience and man's free will in choosing how he wishes to live his life.

exploitative orientation. A means of escaping insecurity by obtaining objects valued by others (Fromm).

expressive behavior. That aspect of behavior which is related to an individual's own style of behaving rather than to the behavior's adaptive function (Allport).

exteroceptor. A sense organ or receptor directly stimulated by energy sources outside the body (e.g., eye).

extrasensory perception (psi phenomenon). Responsivity to external events that are not mediated by any known sense modality.

extraversion. The mode of responding to the world in which the person's attention is directed toward the external world (Jung).

fact. A verbal statement accepted by a certain group at a particular time.

factor analysis. A statistical technique utilizing sets of correlations; used to extract the underlying dimensions or factors which account for the observed relationships between scores.

factor theory. Personality theory which emphasizes the isolation of factors by the statistical analysis of test performances.

feedback. In an energy system, the part of the output energy that is returned to the system to regulate further output.

fictional future. A person's plans and aspirations for the future which are presently believed in (Adler).

field-cognition modes. A combination of thinking, perceiving, and remembering on the part of the organism which gives rise to a specific way of knowing some characteristic of the environment (Tolman).

field expectations. A set of the organism that a particular response to a certain cue or stimulus will produce a particular situation or consequence (Tolman).

field theory. Any psychological theory which attempts to utilize fields of force analogous to those in physics as an explanation for psychological data.

figure-ground. A general property of perception; the figure is that which stands out and is attended to, while the ground is that which surrounds the figure and is secondary to it.

film color. A transparent color which is not substantial and lacks definite localization.

fixation. 1. Perserveration of a particular response. 2. The persistence of immature behavior or thought processes accompanied by a lack of normal development (psychoanalytic).

fractional antedating goal response. A stimulus-trace concept utilized in the explanation of the acquisition of a response chain; an implicit goal response which occurs progressively earlier in the response chain, thus providing stimuli which may become conditioned to ensuing responses (Hull, Spence).

free association. An unrestrained sequence of ideas or thoughts; the technique of having a subject respond with unrestricted verbalizations for clinical purposes (psychoanalytic).

free operant. See conditioning, operant.

frequency, law of. The proposition that the rate of learning is a function of the frequency of occurrence of a response.

functional autonomy. The performance of a task for its own sake; the drive state is thus independent of the need which gave rise to it (Allport).

functionalism. The psychological system that stresses the function or utility of behavior in adapting to the environment (Angell, Carr, Woodworth).

genital stage. The final psychosexual stage in the individual's development, in which one desires sexual relations with members of the opposite sex (Freud).

Gestalt. A figure or configuration which is a whole greater than the sum of its parts and which, if analyzed into its parts, is destroyed.

Gestalt psychology. The psychological system that stresses the phenomenological study of molar stimulus and response units, with emphasis placed on the primacy of wholes and on the existence of brain fields and configurations (Wertheimer, Koffka, Köhler).

Gestaltqualität. Patterns of time and space that are presumed to inhere in the mind and so are independent of physical elements; emphasis thereon is often considered the immediate precursor of Gestalt psychology (von Ehrenfels).

goal gradient. The progressive increment in response strength that occurs as a function of closeness to the goal (Hull).

gynandromorphy. Refers to bisexuality as denoted by the physique (Sheldon).

hab. A unit of learning invented to qualify habit strength ($_SH_R$); equal to 1 percent of the physiological maximum (Hull).

habit family hierarchy. The ordering into a hierarchy of strength of the total set of habits which may occur in a given stimulus situation (Hull).

habit strength ($_SH_R$). An intervening variable representing learning; a function of (1) number of reinforcements, (2) amount of reinforcement, (3) time between stimulus and response, and (4) time between response and reinforcement (Hull, 1943); in the final Hullian system (1951, 1952) only (1) was retained as a determiner.

hallucination. A false perception for which appropriate external stimuli are absent.

hedonism. The philosophical belief that behavior is directed at the attainment of pleasure and the avoidance of pain.

Heisenberg principle. A mathematical proof that exact simultaneous measurement of the position and the momentum of a single electron is impossible.

hodological space. A qualitative geometry of spatial relations invented by Lewin to utilize vectors to represent dynamic psychological factors.

holistic. Referring to the theoretical position stressing that an organism must be studied as a whole since the whole is greater than its constituent parts.

hypochondria. A neurosis which is characterized by excessive concern for one's health.

hypothesis. 1. A proposition concerning the relationship between variables. 2. A tentative explanation.

hypothetical construct. A construct whose meaning goes beyond the relationship between the antecedent (stimulus) and consequent (response) conditions which it represents.

hypothetico-deductive method. A method of theory construction which starts with a few general postulates from which testable theorems and corollaries are derived by rigorous deduction.

hysteria. The manifestation of such bodily symptoms as anesthesia and paralysis as the result of psychic trauma or conflict.

id. A psychic structure or process which is the original reservoir of psychic energy and operates according to the pleasure principle (Freud).

ideal observer. An abstract mathematical ideal within detection theory; the behavior of this ideal defines the ideally achievable behavior within specified situations amenable to the necessary mathematical treatment.

ideomotor action. A term expressing the belief that an idea, unless inhibited by other ideas, will lead directly to motor action (James).

idiographic. Referring to an individual case or event and to that methodology which stresses intensive rather than extensive investigation of an individual.

image. The relatively faint reproduction in consciousness of a previous sensation (Titchener).

imageless thought. Mental processes or functions which elude introspective analysis into elements.

independent variable. The factor whose influence (on the dependent variable) is determined in an experiment.

induction. A mode of logic which proceeds from specific statements to general conclusions.

inferiority complex. The feeling an individual has as the result of real or imagined deficiencies (Adler).

information. Whatever reduces uncertainty (information theory); the receipt of an information-bearing message reduces uncertainty or ignorance by reducing the number of alternative possible messages or by biasing their probabilities so that the remaining uncertainty is reduced.

information theory. The mathematical theory which deals with the coding, decoding, and transmission of messages.

inhibition, conditioned. The hypothesized acquisition of inhibitory properties to a stimulus through its repeated association with reactive inhibition.

inhibition, reactive. The hypothesized explanation for the decrement of a learned response owing to the effortfulness of the activity (Hull).

insight. 1. A sudden understanding of a previously insoluble problem. 2. A sudden reorganization of the perceptual field (Gestalt).

instinct. 1. An innate, complex, stereotyped mode of behaving. 2. Need (Freud).

instinct, death. The wish of an organism to return to an inorganic state (Freud).

instinct, life. The desire of the organism to maintain a balance between the anabolistic and catabolistic forces of the body—to maintain life (Freud).

instructions. Specifications of computer operations to be performed; the typical computer has approximately sixty basic instructions to which it can respond, and all the more complex functions carried out by the computer are synthesized from these basic instructions.

interactionism. The metaphysical position in which mind and body are assumed to be two separate but interrelated entities.

interbehaviorism. Field theory with emphasis on the interaction between stimulus and response functions (Kantor).

interoceptor. A sense organ or receptor within the organism sensitive to stimuli within the body.

intervening variable. An intraorganismic construct which abstracts the relationship between antecedent (stimulus) and consequent (response) conditions, with no meaning beyond this relationship.

introspection. A generic term for any method which relies upon the subjective report of the subject.

introversion. The mode of responding to the world in which the person's attention is directed toward himself (Jung).

irradiation. The phenomenon of generalization, with the implication of excitatory brain functions (Pavlov).

isomorphism. The 1:1 relationship assumed to hold between brain fields and experience (Gestalt).

J curve. The graphic description of the distribution of responses when some social institution influences behavior in a particular direction so that scores pile up markedly at one end of the scale (F. Allport).

kinesthetic. Pertaining to the sense of body movement or position.

kymograph. A revolving drum which makes graphic records; often used in recording respiration and other metabolic processes.

Lamarckian evolution. The doctrine of the inheritance of acquired characteristics: The use or disuse of organic structures results in changes which are passed on to the organism's offspring.

latent learning. Learning in the absence of reinforcement (Tolman).

law. 1. A statement of a regular and predictable relationship between empirical variables. 2. A well-accepted theoretical proposition.

lens model. Conceptualization of the interaction of the functional variables affecting behavior (Brunswik).

level of aspiration. The performance level which an individual expects to reach in a given situation and by which he judges his performance as a success or failure (Lewin).

libido. Energy in the service of the life instincts (Freud).

life space. The totality of effective psychological factors for a given person at a particular moment in time (Lewin).

life-style. The particular manner which an individual develops in order to deal with reality (Adler).

likelihood ratio. The ratio of the probability that an observed event would occur given one hypothesis to the probability that it would occur given some second hypothesis; within detection theory, the hypotheses are most commonly that "a signal was presented" and that "noise alone was presented."

linear graph. A graph representing an equation of the first degree between two variables.

linear perspective. A monocular depth cue in which parallel lines tend to converge.

Lloyd Morgan's canon. Law of parsimony applied to comparative psychology: "In no case may we interpret an action as the outcome of the exercise of a higher psychical faculty, if it can be interpreted as the outcome of the exercise of one which stands lower on the psychological scale."

logical positivism. A philosophical movement headed by Schlick to rid philosophy of metaphysics and to establish a science of science.

mandala. The magic circle found in many religious cults which Jung believed to be symbolic of man's striving for unity.

manic-depressive insanity. A psychotic disorder characterized by marked emotional cycles from extreme elation to marked depression.

marketing orientation. A means of escaping insecurity by emulating the social stratum in which one lives (Fromm).

masculine protest. The desire of both males and females to overcome femininity (Adler).

mass action, principle of. The principle which states that brain tissues function as a whole in higher mental processes (Lashley).

materialism. The metaphysical position in which a single underlying physical reality is assumed.

means-end readiness. A state of selective readiness which endures independently of the present motivational state of the organism and which leads to the acquisition of certain expectancies more readily than others (Tolman).

mechanism. A purposive response or set of responses (Woodworth).

mental activity. The generic term for adaptive behavior according to Carr.

mental chemistry. The doctrine that simple ideas coalesce to form new, more complex ideas and lose their individual identity (John Stuart Mill).

mental mechanics. The doctrine which states that a complex idea is no more than the simple ideas from which it is formed and which maintain their individual identity (James Mill).

mesomorphy. A body type characterized as tough, muscular, and athletic (Sheldon).

metaerg. An underlying motivational trait acquired through environmental influence (Cattell).

metaphysics. A branch of philosophy concerned with the identification and understanding of ultimate reality.

metatheory. A set of general rules governing the construction of a theory; a theory about a theory.

method, scientific. The fundamental process by which all science proceeds; it is characterized by analysis and control.

modal need. The need to perfect some type of behavior (Murray).

model, deterministic. Any theoretical position which stresses the complete predictability of a response when the antecedent conditions are known.

model, mathematical learning. Any learning theory expressed in mathematical form.

model, stochastic. Any model in which one uses the stochastic assumption, i.e., that in a long series of trials, the probability of an outcome approaches the true probability of that outcome.

molar. Referring to large units of study.

molecular. Referring to small units of study.

monad. The element of all being, which is indestructible, uncreatable, immutable, and active (Leibniz).

monism. A metaphysical position in which only one basic reality is assumed, either mind or body.

morphogenotype. A hypothetical unchanging biological state of the organism which determines both body type and temperament (Sheldon).

morphology. The study of biological forms and structures.

motor patterns. Responses and combinations of responses.

movement-produced stimuli (mps). Stimuli originating in the movements of the organism (Guthrie).

nativism. The doctrine which emphasizes hereditary factors in the development of an organism rather than environmental ones.

neurosis. A class of personality disorders which are characterized by extreme anxiety and which are not usually severe enough to require hospitalization.

neurotic trends. The particular environmental approach an individual utilizes in an attempt to avoid conflict and find security (Horney).

noise. Anything (e.g., meaningless sounds) which interferes with the signal being transmitted.

nomothetic. Referring to the use of group data in an attempt to discover laws that apply to groups.

non-Euclidean geometry. A geometry using a different set of axioms from those of Euclidean geometry; the most famous example is the geometry used in relativity theory, which rejects the Euclidean postulate concerning parallel lines.

nonsense syllable. A "meaningless" item often composed of two consonants separated by a vowel; used by Ebbinghaus to reduce variations in learning rate which might otherwise result from differences in prior experience with the materials used for experimentation on human verbal learning and memory.

Occam's razor. See parsimony, principle of.

Oedipal conflict. The feeling of hostility of the child toward the parent of the same sex and love for the parent of the opposite sex (Freud).

operant behavior. Behavior which is characterized by its effect on the environment and for which there is usually no known or manipulated eliciting stimulus (Skinner).

operationism. A movement intended to clarify the language of science; an operational definition is any definition in which the term is synonymous with the corresponding set of operations (Bridgman).

or. A connective used in writing Boolean algebraic equations; typically the inclusive *or* is used, and $C = A + B$ would then mean "C is true if A is true or if B is true or if both A and B are true."

oral stage. The first period in an individual's psychosexual development; marked by interest in the oral region (Freud).

organ inferiority. See inferiority complex.

organismic. Pertaining to any point of view which stresses studying the behavior of the whole organism rather than its particular parts.

parameter. 1. A constant in an equation; the values of the constants determine which curve of a family will represent the relationship between the dependent variable and the independent variable or variables. Parameters in equations would be expected to correspond to the values at which controlled variables were set in an experiment. 2. Less precisely, a parameter is a particular value of a variable; for example, one might say that the value of the stimulus *parameter* was changed in order to produce novelty in the experiment.

parapsychology. A branch of psychology which studies extrasensory phenomena, or those which do not fall within the range of known sensory modalities (e.g., clairvoyance, telepathy).

parataxic. Cognitive or emotional systems which are not adequately related to other systems; they then constitute logic-tight compartments (Sullivan).

parsimony, principle of. The scientific principle that the simpler of two hypotheses should be accepted, other things being equal. It does not negate the acceptance of complex explanations if the data require them. (Also called *William of Occam's razor* and, in comparative psychology, *Lloyd Morgan's canon.*)

penis envy. The repressed female desire to possess a penis; the female form of castration anxiety (Freud).

peripheralism. The explanation of psychological phenomena emphasizing muscular action and other distal events rather than the functioning of the central nervous system.

permutations. All the possible arrangements of a certain number of different items; each arrangement is called a *permutation.*

persona. A well-developed archetype which represents man's social self (Jung).

personal unconscious. The part of a person's unconscious containing material originating in personal experience (Jung).

personification. The attribution of human characteristics to nonhuman entities.

personification, eidetic. A personification which persists and influences a person's opinion of others (Sullivan).

phallic stage. The period in an individual's development when the Oedipus complex develops; marked by interest in the penis (Freud).

phenomenalism. The metaphysical position in which neither mind nor body is considered real; only ideas resulting from sensory impressions exist.

phenomenology. A method of observation in which experimental data are accepted in a more or less naïve manner, without any attempt at analysis.

phenotype. 1. A bodily characteristic, as contrasted with the underlying hereditary factor (genotype). 2. The physique of an individual (Sullivan).

phi phenomenon. The name given by Wertheimer to the perception of apparent motion generated by stationary stimuli.

phrenology. The belief that mental characteristics can be determined by examining the contours of the skull (Gall).

physicalism. The philosophical position that all scientific propositions are ultimately reducible to the language of physical science.

physiologizing. Advancing physiological explanations and conjectures in the absence of definite physiological knowledge.

pleasure principle. The immediate satisfaction of instinctual desires; governs the development of the id (Freud).

positivism. A metatheoretical and general scientific position that emphasizes parsimony and operationism in data language and eschews theorizing and inferential commitment.

postremity, postulate of. The proposition that the last response made in a particular stimulus situation is the one most likely to occur on the next occasion of that stimulus situation; a primary postulate in one formalization of Guthrie's contiguity theory of learning (Voeks).

postulate. 1. A fundamental assumption not meant to be tested. 2. A theoretical proposition used within a given logical framework and tested indirectly by means of its empirical implications (theorems).

practitioner. One trained in a scientific or similar discipline; one who is engaged in some service function in a profession in which he has been more or less intensively trained to practice at a relatively high level of responsibility.

pragmatism. Validation of a principle through its utility; the philosophical position that that which is useful is true.

Prägnanz, law of. The Gestalt principle that a figure will be perceived in its best possible form.

preconscious. That part of mental activity which consists of materials not presently conscious but readily recallable (psychoanalytic).

press. The environmental forces acting upon the individual (Murray).

primary memory image. A lingering memory trace postulated to maintain a sensation for a relatively short duration of time, permitting an accurate introspective report (Titchener).

primary process. Direct and immediate instinctual satisfaction, mediated by the id (psychoanalytic).

primary qualities. Those qualities which are alleged to inhere within the object and to be independent of the perceiver, such as size and shape (Locke).

primitive term. A term which is not defined by any more basic term within a theory.

probabilistic functionalism. Egon Brunswik's position, which emphasizes that both the correctness of perception and the effectiveness of action are only probable. The adaptive, functional relating of distal stimuli to distal effects of responses on the environment is seen as the task of the organism.

proceeding. A person's interaction with an object or another person, of sufficient duration to have dynamic significance (Murray).

process need. A need for activity per se (Murray).

program. A sequence of instructions that can be carried out by a computer.

programmatic. Lacking in systematic specificity.

projection. A defense mechanism in which the individual attempts to externalize his own values, faults, and ideas (psychoanalytic).

proprioceptor. A sense organ or receptor sensitive to the position or the movement of the body (e.g., vestibular canal).

protensity. Temporal duration of a sensation or an image (Titchener).

prototaxic. Referring to a cognitive process in which the individual experiences directly without attaching meaning to his sensations; an infantile type of perception (Sullivan).

proximal reactions. The peripheral motor responses of the organism, without regard for the consequences on the environment (Brunswik).

proximal stimuli. Stimuli as they are when they impinge upon the organism (Brunswik).

psychical satiation. A reduction in performance of an activity as a function of the continued repetition of the activity.

psychoanalysis. 1. A school of psychology developed by Sigmund Freud which places a great deal of emphasis upon unconscious motivation, conflict, and symbolism. 2. A type of psychiatry stressing the free-association technique and long-term, deep psychotherapy.

psychogenesis. The origin and development of mind or behavior.

psychometrist. A person skilled in the administration and scoring of mental tests.

psychopathology. The scientific discipline which studies abnormal behavior.

psychophysical parallelism. The metaphysical position in which mind and body are independent and yet perfectly correlated entities.

psychophysics. The scientific study of the relationship between stimuli and sensations.

psychosis. A class of severe behavior disorders which are characterized by the patient's general lack of contact with reality and which usually require hospitalization.

purposivism. The doctrine that behavior is more than purely mechanical and that it is directed toward some goal.

puzzle box. An enclosure which prevents an organism from reaching a goal until a particular device is manipulated (Thorndike).

pyknic. Short and squatty body type (Kretschmer).

Q sort. A personality inventory, utilizing factor analysis, in which the subject evaluates his own personality by sorting into different piles statements which apply to him (Stephenson).

qualitative. That which can be distinguished or identified as different in kind.

quantification. The process of establishing relationships between empiricial objects of study and the mathematics of real numbers.

quantitative. That which can be distinguished or identified as different in number or amount.

rationalism. The philosophical position which maintains that truth can be found only through pure reason.

rationalization. A form of projection in which the individual attempts to find a justifiable cause for his actions (psychoanalytic).

reaction potential ($_SE_R$). An intervening variable that indicates the degree of strength of a particular response (Hull).

reaction time, motor. Latency of response made with attention to the response rather than to the stimulus onset.

reaction time, sensory. Latency of response made with attention to the stimulus onset rather than to the response.

readiness, law of. The principle which states that when a conduction unit is ready to conduct, conduction by it is satisfying, providing nothing is done to alter its action (Thorndike).

reality principle. The ego's realization of the demands of the environment leading to the eventual satisfaction of these demands in such a way that the organism continues to exist (Freud).

receiver operating characteristic curve. A curve relating the probability of a "hit" (correct report of detection) to the probability of a "false alarm" (incorrect report of detection).

recency, law of. The principle stating that other things being equal, that which is best remembered is that which is most recently learned.

receptive orientation. A means of escaping insecurity by strong identification with a group or its leader (Fromm).

reduction screen. An opaque screen with two small holes, used to view stimuli without the subject's knowledge of the surrounding illumination.

reductionism. The position holding that complex phenomena should be understood through analysis (reduction) of them into simpler components.

redundant. Repetitious of information; redundant transmission systems are systems carrying information which is less than the system could potentially carry.

reflex. An unlearned, involuntary, stereotyped response of a body part to a stimulus.

reflex arc. The simplest functional unit in the nervous system, composed of a receptor, synapse, and effector.

reflexology. The school of psychology which holds that reflexes and combinations of reflexes are the basis of all behavior (Bekhterev).

regression. The return to a former state or condition.

reinforcement. Any process by which a response is strengthened; generally assumed to involve more than mere contiguity of stimulus and response elements.

repetition compulsion. An irrepressible desire to repeat some act over and over (Freud).

representative design. An experimental approach allowing a large sample of variables to change together in a random fashion, thus better "representing" the effects of all the possible combinations of variables and values (Brunswik).

repression. The unconscious removal of unpleasant thoughts or events from consciousness (Freud).

resistance. Opposition by a patient to the recall of past events, presumably because of unconscious repression (psychoanalytic).

respondent behavior. Behavior which is characterized by its identification with a specific eliciting stimulus.

restraining forces. Brain excitations preventing attraction of cohesive forces; usually the result of present stimulation (Gestalt).

retinal disparity. A visual depth cue resulting from the slight difference between the two retinal images in binocular vision.

retroactive inhibition. The interference of a second task with the retention of a previously learned task.

retrospection. Introspection on a past event.

reward. An object or activity that satisfies some motivating condition; often assumed to be necessary for learning (as in Thorndike's law of effect or Hull's S-R behavior system).

routine. A computer program or part of a program, generally so named because it is designed to carry out a specific function (for example, finding square roots); the word *routine* is ordinarily used if the portion of the program is on the main line of the program, whereas the word *subroutine* is used for units which are called upon periodically from the main program.

scaling. The construction of any type of ordered measuring device used to represent any type of continuum.

schedule, fixed-interval (FI). A program of reinforcement in which reinforcement is given for the first response made after some fixed period of time.

schedule, fixed-ratio (FR). A program of reinforcement in which reinforcement is given for the first response made after some fixed number of responses.

schedule, reinforcement. A program indicating how the presentation of some reinforcing stimulus is arranged.

schedule, variable-interval (VI). A program of reinforcement in which reinforcement is given for the first response made after some variable period of time.

schedule, variable-ratio (VR). A program of reinforcement in which reinforcement is given for the first response made after some variable number of responses.

schizophrenia. A psychotic disorder characterized by disturbances of the thought processes and lack of contact with reality.

school. A collection of adherents to a particular systematic position, with varying degrees of temporal and spatial contiguity.

science. The enterprise by which men obtain ordered knowledge about natural phenomena, working with a particular methodology (controlled observation and analysis) and set of attitudes (skepticism, objectivity, etc.).

science, applied. That part of science which is concerned with investigations believed to have immediate practical utility.

science, pure. That part of science which is concerned only with the discovery of new facts and the development of theories without regard for the immediate utility of such knowledge.

secondary process. Conscious activity of the ego guided by external reality; it is thus distinguished from the primary-process activity of the id (psychoanalytic).

secondary qualities. Those qualities alleged to inhere not within the object but within the perceiver, such as color (Locke).

secondary reinforcement. The reinforcement of behavior by a previously neutral stimulus which has acquired its reinforcing properties through association with a primary reinforcer.

self. 1. An existing picture of an individual's past behavior and experiences as perceived by him. 2. A summary name for a set of psychological processes, usually including evaluative and attitudinal functions, involving an individual and his relationship to the world.

sensation. A conscious experience which cannot be further analyzed (Titchener).

separation anxiety. Anxiety resulting from birth trauma and basic to neurotic symptoms (Rank).

serial. A group of proceedings which follow one another in a coherent fashion, involving planning on the part of the organism and providing direction and meaning (Murray).

set. A predisposing disposition or determining tendency.

shadow. A well-developed archetype inherited from man's prehuman ancestors; the animal instincts (Jung).

shaping. A technique used to produce a desired behavioral pattern by selectively reinforcing responses that approximate or are a part of it.

sibling rivalry. Competition among offspring (Adler).

sign learning. Learning of the relationships between signs—what leads to what (Tolman).

sign significate (sign Gestalt). An object which gives rise to the expectation that a particular response will lead to a goal (Tolman).

Skinner box. An operant conditioning chamber; a box provided with a device which the organism can manipulate to produce some type of reinforcement.

solipsism. The philosophical view that one can be certain of nothing but one's own experience.

solution learning. Overt instrumental learning or problem solving (Mowrer).

somatotonia. An active, aggressive personality pattern supposed to be associated with the mesomorphic body type (Sheldon).

somatotype. A ratio of body measurements which represents an individual's body type (Sheldon).

state variable. A hypothesized enduring condition of the organism which is the result of a past interaction of the organism and the environment.

stereotypy. A condition in which the organism persistently manifests certain invariable responses.

stimulus error. The paying of attention to the properties of the stimulus rather than to the characteristics of the sensation (Titchener).

stimulus field. The totality of stimuli that act on the organism at any given moment (Gestalt).

stimulus-intensity dynamism. The principle that reaction potential or response amplitude increases monotonically with the intensity of the stimulus (Hull).

stimulus pool. The total population of stimuli from which different samples may be drawn (Estes).

stimulus trace. A presumed continuation of activity in the nervous system after brief stimulation has ceased (Hull).

structuralism. The system that stresses the analysis of consciousness into elements through the method of introspection (Wundt, Titchener).

subjective idealism. The metaphysical position in which a single underlying mental or spiritual reality is assumed.

subjectivism. The tendency to be biased in perception and thinking by preconceived ideas.

sublimation. The permanent substitution of a secondary goal for a primary one (Freud).

superego. The psychic structure or process which develops out of the ego; the internal representation of external values (Freud).

surface color. Color seen as lying on the surface of an object.

symbol. Anything that "stands for" or "means" something else.

synchronicity. The occurrence of events at the same time but without causal relation (Jung).

syntality. The dimensions or traits of a social institution, analogous to the traits of an individual (Cattell).

syntaxic. Referring to a cognitive process in which thoughts and ideas become connected in a logical fashion (Sullivan).

system. An organization and interpretation of the data and theories of a subject matter, with special assumptions (postulates), definitions, and methodological biases.

systematic design. Classic experimental methodology utilizing rigorous control of variables.

tabula rasa. Blank tablet; usually refers to the doctrine that the mind at birth is blank and is developed through sensory experience.

technician. One trained to provide technical services for the practitioner or scientist.

teleology. The explanation of behavior in terms of its ultimate utilities, in the absence of evidence that these are actually determining factors.

tension system. A motivational factor in which some particular act or set of acts acquires directive influence in behavior until dissipated (Lewin).

terminal focal event. The response of the organism which may be either perceptual or instrumental (Brunswik).

thema. A unit describing behavior in terms of the press and need which are involved (Murray).

theorem. A statement derived from postulates through the rules of deduction; to be directly tested empirically.

theory. 1. A group of laws deductively connected. 2. Generalizations beyond the data which are used to bridge gaps in knowledge and to generate research.

thing constancy. The tendency of an organism to view an object as having a stable size and shape irrespective of variations in the retinal image (Brunswik).

topology. A nonmetric and nondirectional geometry of spatial relationships in which boundaries are the critical factors and a variety of transformations may be achieved; utilized by Lewin as a model for representation of behavior functions (see also hodological space).

trait. A generalized and focalized neuropsychic system (peculiar to the individual) with the capacity to render many stimuli functionally equivalent and to initiate and guide consistent (equivalent) forms of adaptive and expressive behavior (Allport).

trait theory. Personality theory which emphasizes the isolation of factors accounting for consistency and integration of behavior.

traits, constitutional. Traits having an innate origin (Cattell).

traits, environmental-mold. Consistencies in behavior which are acquired through environmental influences, especially social institutions (Cattell).

traits, source. Underlying general predispositions which account for observed consistencies in behavior (Cattell).

traits, surface. Observed consistencies in behavior (Cattell).

transducer. A device that changes energy from one form to another; a radio receiver is a transducer that changes electromagnetic energy into acoustic energy; the human retina transduces light energy into the electrochemical energy of the nerve impulse.

transference. The shifting of emotion from an object or person to the psychoanalyst during therapy (Freud).

transposition experiment. An experiment in which a subject is trained to respond to one of two stimuli which stand in a particular relationship to each other (for example, the rewarded stimulus is *larger than* the nonrewarded stimulus). During later test trials, typically the stimulus previously rewarded is paired with a stimulus which has the relationship to it which it previously had to the other training stimulus (i.e., the other test stimulus is now *larger than* the previously rewarded stimulus). The question is whether the subject will respond to the relationship (demonstrate transposition) by choosing the new, larger stimulus or will respond to absolute stimulus properties by choosing the old, previously rewarded stimulus.

tropism. A forced movement of the whole organism which is a direct function of stimulation.

two-factor learning theory. Any theoretical position in which two separate learning processes are considered essential in the acquisition of behavior.

typology. A systematic personality classification according to types or kinds.

uncertainty. That property of a set of alternatives which determines its information content; the amount of uncertainty in a set of messages or alternatives is the same as the amount of information transmitted in reducing that uncertainty to zero (see information).

unconscious. The collective term for mental activities of which the person is not aware (psychoanalytic).

unconscious inference. The drawing of a conclusion, as in perception, in the absence of any reasoning process of which one is aware (Helmholtz).

variable. Usually, any property that may change and be assigned a number (see also controlled variable, dependent variable, independent variable, and intervening variable).

viscerotonia. A comfort-loving personality pattern associated with the endomorphic body type (Sheldon).

vitalism. The philosophical position that life cannot be explained entirely in terms of physicochemical principles.

volumic color. Color seen as occupying volume, as in the case of colored smoke.

Weber-Fechner law. In the more sophisticated form presented by Fechner, a law stating that the intensity of a sensation is proportional to the logarithm of stimulus intensity.

Weber's law. A psychophysical law which states that a noticeable change in a stimulus intensity is always a constant proportional part of the original stimulus.

Zeigarnik effect. The name for the finding that tasks which are not completed are better remembered than tasks which are completed (Lewin).

INDEX

Page numbers in boldface indicate bibliography references; page numbers in *italics* indicate glossary definitions.